Why Buy the 4th Edition of This Book?

Why buy the new edition of this text, the cost-conscious student may reasonably ask. Why not settle for an older, used edition? It's a fair question that deserves an honest answer. We've revised and updated this 4th edition because important developments in persuasion research and practice have taken place since the last edition. In point of fact, the material in every chapter has been updated to reflect current research findings and current practices.

1 **Addition of new and emerging media for persuasion:** How people go about persuading each other is constantly evolving and changing. As consumers grow more savvy about one form of persuasion, persuaders are busily trying out other forms of persuasion. In this edition, we include research findings on new and emerging media as outlets for persuasion.

2 **Discussion of cynicism with traditional media:** Younger consumers are cynical of traditional media. They respond to messages they believe to be genuine and authentic. And that is precisely why marketers are gearing their messages toward unpretentious branding, products that support causes, or goods that have a story to tell. Socially responsible marketing is now in vogue. We discuss many of these recent trends in this edition.

3 **Exploration of the increasingly visual nature of persuasion:** Visual persuasion is becoming more and more prominent. Would it surprise you to learn that 57 percent of Americans have not read a single book in the past year (Jackson, 2008)? Images have become a potent force on the Web, in movies, and on TV. Viral videos can push a brand past the tipping point. A "YouTube moment" can cost a politician an election. In this edition we emphasize the importance of visual persuasion.

4 **Inclusion of additional theories:** This edition includes a discussion of the *theory of planned behavior*, which is an extension of the *theory of reasoned action*. There is also a discussion of the *unimodel of persuasion*, an alternative to dual process models; as well as a discussion of *neurolinguistic programming* or NLP as its proponents refer to it. We've also added new material on the *goals-plans-action model* (GPA) of compliance gaining, *cultivation theory*, and the phenomenon known as *psychological reactance*.

5 **Discussion of additional strategies:** From the standpoint of persuasive practices, this edition includes a discussion of *segmentation analysis* and *micromarketing*, an examination of *message framing, negative social proof*, and additional sequential strategies such as *legitimizing paltry contributions, the fear-then-relief*, and the *happiness-then-disappointment tactics*. This edition also provides an expanded treatment of *viral marketing, tipping points*, and *buzz marketing*.

6 **Discussion of additional topics:** This edition features the addition of several traditional topics, including a discussion of the *types of evidence*. There is also an examination of the ways in which social ostracism influences behavior.

Persuasion is as vital as it has ever been. Much of persuasion functions as it did in Ancient Greece, more than 2,000 years ago when Aristotle wrote, *The Rhetoric*, one of the earliest treatises on persuasion. Yet much is new about persuasion, such as the role of product placement, the Internet, the blogosphere, texting, Twitter, YouTube, and social networking sites. In this 4th edition we keep the reader informed of both classic and modern approaches to persuasion. We do so by discussing the very latest research and by providing current, practical examples of persuasion in the real world.

FOURTH EDITION

PERSUASION, SOCIAL INFLUENCE, AND COMPLIANCE GAINING

ROBERT H. GASS
California State University, Fullerton

JOHN S. SEITER
Utah State University

Allyn & Bacon

Boston   Columbus   Indianapolis   New York   San Francisco   Upper Saddle River   Amsterdam
Cape Town   Dubai   London   Madrid   Milan   Munich   Paris   Montreal   Toronto   Delhi
Mexico City   São Paulo   Sydney   Hong Kong   Seoul   Singapore   Taipei   Tokyo

Editor-in-Chief: Karon Bowers
Acquisitions Editor: Jeanne Zalesky
Assistant Editor: Megan Lentz
Senior Managing Editor: Linda Mihatov Behrens
Associate Managing Editor: Bayani Mendoza de Leon
Development Manager: David B. Kear
Associate Developmental Editor: Patrick Barb
Marketing Manager: Blair Tuckman
Media Producer: Megan Higginbotham
Editorial Production Services: GGS Higher Education Resources, A division of PreMedia Global Inc.
Manufacturing Buyer: Mary Ann Gloriande
Cover Manager: Anne Bonanno Nieglos
Cover Image: Michael Blann/Digital Vision/Getty Images

Library of Congress Cataloging-in-Publication Data

Gass, Robert H.
   Persuasion, social influence, and compliance gaining / Robert H. Gass, John S. Seiter.—4th ed.
      p. cm.
   Includes bibliographical references and index.
   ISBN-13: 978-0-205-69818-9
   ISBN-10: 0-205-69818-2
   1. Persuasion (Psychology)   2. Influence (Psychology)   3. Manipulative behavior.   I. Seiter, John S.
II. Title.

BF637.P4G34 2010
303.3'42—dc22

2009040887

> *To my high school sweetheart and wife, Susan, thanks for all your*
> *love and support through the best and worst of times.*
> *—Robert Gass*

> *To Miss Gordon, my second-grade teacher, for knowing that*
> *self-concept is the proper starting place.*
> *—John Seiter*

> *To our families—Susan, Jordan, Graham, Debora, Dean, Andy, and*
> *Christian—for doing without us when we were writing and*
> *for putting up with us when we weren't.*
> *—Robert Gass and John Seiter*

Allyn & Bacon
is an imprint of

10 9 8 7 6 5   HPC   13 12

www.pearsonhighered.com   ISBN-13: 978-0-205-69818-9
                                 ISBN-10:   0-205-69818-2

CONTENTS

11 | Compliance Gaining   225

12 | Deception   248

13 | Motivational Appeals   270

16 | The Ethics of Persuasion   337

PREFACE

The field of persuasion is constantly changing and evolving. It is therefore difficult for any text to keep pace with all the developments in the field. Fascinating areas of influence that demand attention are always popping up. We view persuasion not only as a desirable form of activity but as an indispensable feature of human interaction. We hope students will catch our enthusiasm for this field of study and come away with a better understanding of how persuasion functions, an improved knowledge of ways to maximize their own persuasive efforts, and a greater ability to resist influence attempts, especially unscrupulous influence attempts by others.

NEW TO THIS EDITON

With each edition of this text, we have marveled at how much new research there is on the subject of persuasion. In addition to studies on persuasion using traditional media, there is a growing body of literature on new and emerging media. The blogosphere, Facebook, Flickr, MySpace, Twitter, and YouTube are all conduits for persuasion that didn't exist a decade ago. What's more, new media aren't simply a source of entertainment or a narcissistic pastime. New media played a key role in the 2008 U.S. presidential election. The Obama campaign leveraged social media to its benefit. For example, Barack Obama enjoyed a 6 to 1 advantage over John McCain in MySpace friends and a 5 to 1 advantage in Facebook friends (PEW Project for Excellence in Journalism, 2008). As another example, new media, especially cellphone images and Twitter, played an important role in disseminating persuasive messages about the controversial election in Iran in 2009. In this edition, we've included a good deal of research on new and emerging media and persuasion.

Since the last edition of this text, studies on compliance gaining and interpersonal influence have also flourished. Unlike past studies, which often relied on hypothetical scenarios, checklists of strategy preferences, and confusing taxonomies, recent studies have focused on actual behavioral compliance in real-world settings. A French scholar, Nicolas Guéguen, for example, has published several dozen studies on compliance gaining in the past few years alone (http://nicolas.gueguen.free.fr/). Recent studies measuring behavioral outcomes have covered a wide range of topics and settings, such as apparel and appearances, aromas and odors, background music, the classroom, courtship behavior, helping behavior, hitch-hiking, language factors, mimicry, patient compliance, philanthropy and fundraising, seduction, shoplifting, and tipping behavior. We examine the current state of compliance-gaining research in this edition.

As intriguing as research on new media and compliance gaining are, we remain fascinated with traditional forms of persuasion, too. Take infomercials as just one example. Admit it: If you don't already own a Snuggie or a Sham-Wow, wouldn't you like to have one? We would. Who could ignore the late Billy Mays as he shouted about Oxi-Clean,

Mighty MendIt, or the Awesome Auger on cable or satellite TV? What is remarkable is that as corny and low budget as the infomercials for these products are, they are effective. Against the backdrop of much more sophisticated commercial campaigns, costing hundreds of thousands of dollars more, these simplistic ads work. In this edition, we focus on traditional persuasion, too, by examining source credibility, message structure and organization, types of evidence, and language factors.

More than 50 years ago, Vance Packard published *The Hidden Persuaders*, a landmark work that examined the psychology of advertising (Nelson, 2008; Packard, 1957). Since then, dozens more texts aimed at informing consumers and increasing their awareness of persuasive strategies have been published. For example, studies have focused on the effects of product placements and viral marketing. One of our continuing goals in this edition, as in previous editions, is to improve ordinary people's ability to resist influence attempts. In this edition, we emphasize the defensive function in connection with viral, buzz, or word-of-mouth marketing.

The primary audience for this text is college students, although we've heard many other folks read our book, too. Gen Y, or Millenials, as they are sometimes called, represent a stubborn demographic group. They have been inundated with sophisticated marketing campaigns their entire lives (Maciejewski, 2004). For this reason, they are especially cynical of mainstream media, such as television commercials and print ads. And yet, youth culture exhibits as much brand fetishism as any other generation. Young adults are enamored with Abercrombie & Fitch clothing, Adidas footwear, BlackBerry cellphones, iPhones, iPods, Juicy Couture handbags, Mossimo clothing, Nike PlayStations, Red Bull, Scion cars, Starbucks, VitaminWater, and Xboxes. One explanation is that the very lifestyles of youth culture have become commodified. Gen Y is *never not* being marketed to. Hip-hop culture, for example, its music, its clothing, its bling, its branding (i.e., Busta Rhymes' "Pass the Courvoisier," Run DMC's "My Adidas") is a commercialized lifestyle. Social networking sites also are a vast landscape for persuasion. In this edition we explore persuasion as it relates to youth culture. Our aim is to increase young adults' awareness of the pervasiveness of persuasion.

ACKNOWLEDGMENTS

Both authors would like to offer their heartfelt thanks to everyone at Pearson/Allyn & Bacon for their support throughout all four editions of this text. They are a most talented, capable group. We are extremely grateful to Karon Bowers, who gave us our first shot at publishing a text. We applaud Jeanne Zalesky for taking over the reins for the 4th edition without a hitch. She was most patient with us while we dithered over the cover concept. We thank Patrick Barb, who kept us on schedule and on track and fielded our many questions. We are especially thankful to Megan Lentz, who was "in the trenches" so to speak and dealt with many of the nuts and bolts of the project. She was always helpful, obliging, and quick to answer our questions. Finally, we'd like to thank Chitra Ganesan for her team's exacting copyediting and proofreading. We swear we don't know how those typos got in there!

Robert Gass thanks his family for allowing him to occupy the kitchen table and dining room table for long stretches at a time while writing on his laptop. He apologizes to Clarissa and Banjo, two devoted English Setters, for not walking them *every* morning when he needed to write.

John Seiter wishes to thank Richard Seiter, Harold Kinzer, and Jennifer Peeples, all of whom supplied material and stories for the book. He thanks his wife, Debora, who provided assistance, ideas, chocolate, encouragement, and support, and, on occasion, served as his harshest—yet most appreciated—critic.

Both authors are extremely grateful to the graduate and undergraduate students who offered numerous illustrations of real-life examples of persuasion. Every time we think we have taught the brightest group of students ever, another sharp group comes along. Both authors also want to thank the many instructors using our book who have sent us comments and suggestions for this edition, as well as the many short course participants who have offered ideas and insights leading up to this edition.

The following supplementary materials are available for *Persuasion, Social Influence, and Compliance Gaining 4/e*: Prepared by the authors and Jennifer Acosta-Licea, each chapter of the Instructor's Manual/Test Bank contains Key Terms, a Chapter Summary, Exercises, Weblinks, Multiple Choice questions, and Essay questions. The MyTest Computerized Test Bank is a flexible, online test generating program containing all questions found in the Test Bank section of the Instructor's Manual/ Test Bank. The PowerPoint Presentation, also prepared by the authors, provides a basis for your lectures with PowerPoint slides to accompany each chapter of the book. All materials are available at www.pearsonhighered.com/irc. Contact your local Pearson representative to request access.

REFERENCES

Maciejewski, J. J. (2004). Is the use of sexual and fear appeals ethical? A moral evaluation by Generation Y college students. *Journal of Current Issues in Research in Advertising, 26*, 97–105.

Nelson, M. R. (2008). The hidden persuaders, then and now. *Journal of Advertising, 37*, 113–126.

Packard, V. (1957). *The hidden persuaders*. New York: David McKay.

PEW Project for Excellence in Journalism (September, 15, 2008). "JohnMcCain.com v. BarackObama.com." Retrieved on June 27, 2009, from http://pewresearch.org/pubs/951/mccain-obama-websites.

CHAPTER 1

Why Study Persuasion?

One of the authors was enjoying a day at the beach with his family. As he sat in a folding chair, lost in a good book, he could hear the cries of seagulls overhead and the pounding of the surf. Nothing was bothering him. He was oblivious to the world around him. Or so he thought. As he reflected more on the situation, however, he became aware that he was being bombarded by persuasive messages on all sides. A boom box was playing a few yards away. During commercial breaks, various ads tried to convince him to subscribe to a wireless phone service, switch auto insurance companies, and try a new bacon cheeseburger. A nearby sign warned that no alcohol, glass objects, or fires were permitted on the beach. A plastic bag in which a nearby family's children had brought their beach toys advertised Wal-Mart on its side. The family picnic cooler proudly displayed its manufacturer, Igloo, as well.

And that was only the beginning. A plane flew overhead, trailing a banner that advertised a collect calling service. A sailboat tacked up and down the coast, sporting an advertisement on its sail. The lifeguard's truck, a specially equipped Nissan, announced in bold lettering that it was the "official rescue vehicle" of "Surf City," Huntington Beach. Oh, the indignity of being rescued by an unofficial vehicle!

There were oral influence attempts too. His son tried to goad him into the water by saying, "Come on, the water's not that cold." But the author knew better. His son *always* said that, no matter how cold the water was. "Would you mind keeping an eye on our things?" the family next to the author's asked. I guess our family looks trustworthy, the author thought. His wife asked him, "Do you want to walk down to the pier in a while? They have frozen bananas." She knew he would be unable to resist the temptation.

And those were only the overt persuasive messages. A host of more subtle messages also competed for the author's attention. A few yards away a woman was applying sun block to her neck and shoulders. The author decided he'd better do the same. Had she nonverbally influenced him to do likewise? Nearby a young couple was soaking up the sun. Both were wearing hats with Nike's "swoosh" logo. Were they "advertising" that brand? A man about 10 yards away had a large, conspicuous tattoo of a spider on his back. Was he trying to convince the author and others that he was tough? A young man with a boogie board ran by, headed for the water. His head was shaved and he displayed enough body piercing to make the author wince. Did his appearance advocate a particular set of values or tastes? Was he a billboard for an "alternative" lifestyle? A trio of attractive young women in bikinis strolled down the beach. Every male head on the beach turned in unison as they walked by. Were the males "persuaded" to turn their heads, or was this simply an involuntary reflex? Two tan, muscular males were tossing a Frisbee back and forth. Both had six-pack abs. The author made a mental note to do more sit-ups. Some young teens were smoking. Were they negative role models for other children? There seemed to be as many persuasive messages, or potentially persuasive messages, as there were shells on the beach.

The preceding examples raise two important issues. First, persuasion is pervasive. We are surrounded by influence attempts, both explicit and implicit, no matter where we are. Second, it is difficult to say with any certainty what is and is not "persuasion." Where should we draw the line between persuasion and other forms of communication? How do we distinguish between influence attempts and ordinary behavior? We address the first of these issues in this chapter. Here we examine the pervasive nature of persuasion and offer a rationale for learning more about its workings. In the next chapter, we tackle the issue of what constitutes *persuasion* and related terms such as *social influence* and *compliance gaining*.

AIMS AND GOALS

This is a book about persuasion. Its aims are academic and practical. On the academic side, we examine how and why persuasion functions the way it does. In so doing, we identify some of the most recent theories and findings by persuasion researchers. On the practical side, we illustrate these theories and findings with a host of real-life examples of persuasion. We also offer useful advice on how to become a more effective persuader and how to resist influence attempts, especially unethical influence attempts, by others.

If learning how to persuade others and avoid being persuaded seems a bit manipulative, remember, we don't live in a society populated with unicorns and rainbows. The real world is brimming with persuaders. Even as you are reading this book, they are practicing their craft. You can avoid learning about persuasion, perhaps, but you can't avoid persuasion itself.

Besides, we can't tell you everything there is to know about persuasion. Nobody knows all there is to know about persuasion. One of the points we stress throughout this book is that people aren't that easy to persuade. Human beings are complex. They aren't that malleable. They can be stubborn, unpredictable, and intractable, despite the best efforts of persuaders.

Persuasion is still as much an "art" as it is a "science." Human nature is too complicated, and our understanding of persuasion too limited, to predict in advance which influence attempts will succeed and which will fail. Think how often you flip the channel when a commercial costing millions of dollars to produce and air appears on television. As one advertising executive put it, "half the money [spent] on advertising is wasted . . . but we don't know which half" (Berger, 2004, p. 1). Think how many candidates for public office have spent fortunes campaigning, only to lose their elections. Or think how difficult it is for the federal government to convince people to stop smoking, practice safe sex, or buckle up.

The science of persuasion is still in its infancy. Despite P. T. Barnum's axiom that "there's a sucker born every minute," people are uncannily perceptive at times. It is tempting to believe that if one only knew the right button to push, one could persuade anybody. More often than not, though, there are multiple buttons to push, in the right combination, and the sequence is constantly changing. What's more, the persuader has to guess what the buttons are.

Even so, persuasion is not entirely a matter of luck. Much is known about persuasion. Persuasion has been scientifically studied since the 1940s.[1] Written texts on persuasion date back to ancient Greece.[2] A number of strategies and techniques have been identified and their effectiveness or ineffectiveness documented. Persuaders are a long way from achieving an Orwellian nightmare of thought control, but a good deal is known about how to capture the hearts and minds of individuals. Before proceeding further, we want to address a common negative stereotype about persuasion.

PERSUASION IS NOT A DIRTY WORD

The study of persuasion has gotten some bad publicity over the years. Everyone seems to agree that the subject itself is fascinating, but some are reluctant to embrace a field of study that conjures up images of manipulation, deceit, or brainwashing. There is, after all, a sinister side to persuasion. Adolph Hitler, Charles Manson, Jim Jones, David Koresh, Marshall Applewhite, and Osama bin Laden, were/are all accomplished persuaders—much to the detriment of their followers.[3] We, however, do not think of persuasion as the ugly stepsister in the family of human communication. Rather, we find the study of persuasion to be enormously intriguing. Persuasion forms the backbone of many of our communicative endeavors. We can't resist the urge to learn more about how and why it works. Part of our fascination stems from the fact that persuasion is, on occasion, used for unsavory ends. It is therefore all the more important that researchers learn as much as they can about persuasion to expose the strategies and tactics of unethical persuaders.

PERSUASION IS OUR FRIEND

Persuasion isn't merely a tool used by con artists, chiselers, charlatans, cheats, connivers, and cult leaders. Nobel Peace Prize recipients and Pulitzer Prize–winning journalists are also persuaders. In fact, most "professional" persuaders are engaged in socially acceptable, if not downright respectable, careers. They include advertising executives, writers, celebrity endorsers, clergy, congresspersons, infomercial spokespersons, lawyers, lobbyists, media pundits, motivational speakers, political activists, political cartoonists, political campaign managers, public relations experts, radio talk show hosts, salespersons, senators, and syndicated columnists, to name just a few.

Let's focus on the good side of persuasion for a moment. Persuasion helps forge peace agreements between nations. Persuasion helps open up closed societies. Persuasion is crucial to the fund-raising efforts of charities and philanthropic organizations. Persuasion convinces motorists to buckle up when driving or to refrain from driving when they've had a few too many drinks. Persuasion is used to convince an alcoholic or drug-dependent family member to seek professional help. Persuasion is how the coach of an underdog team inspires the players to give it their all. Persuasion is a tool used by parents to urge children not to accept rides from strangers or to allow anyone to touch them in a way that feels uncomfortable. In short, persuasion is the cornerstone of a number of positive, prosocial endeavors. *Very little of the good that we see in the world could be accomplished without persuasion.*

Persuasion, then, is a powerful and often positive social force. Having highlighted the positive side of persuasion, we address the question of *why* the study of persuasion is so valuable. The next section, therefore, offers a justification for the study of social influence.

THE PERVASIVENESS OF PERSUASION: YOU CAN RUN BUT YOU CAN'T HIDE

We've already mentioned one of the primary reasons for learning about this subject: Persuasion is a central feature of every sphere of human communication. We can't avoid it. We can't make it go away. Like the smog hanging over Los Angeles, persuasion is all around us. Like Elvis impersonators in Las Vegas, persuasion is here to stay. Various estimates suggest that the average person is exposed to anywhere from 300 to 3,000 messages per day.[4]

It is fairly obvious that persuasion is an indispensable ingredient in a number of professions. In this regard, Simons (1986) observes, "The so-called people professions—politics, law, social work, counseling, business management, advertising, sales, public relations, the ministry—might as well be called persuasion professions" (p. 4). Walsh similarly states, "Psychologists, demographers, artists, writers, marketers, and business leaders collaborate to create messages expressly intended to shape opinions and change our behaviors" (1995, p. 33). Persuasion is part and parcel of such occupations.

What's That Buzz You're Wearing?

An illustration of the pervasiveness of persuasion can be found in *buzz marketing* (also known as *stealth marketing, guerrilla marketing, covert marketing*, and *social media marketing*). Once regarded as novel, buzz marketing is now so common that the word "buzz"

Persuasion is everywhere—even in the womb!

© Baby Blues Partnership. Reprinted with special permission of King Features Syndicate.

has become, well, a buzz term. Such marketing relies on word of mouth (WOM) to dissem-inate persuasive messages from person to person (Balter & Butman, 2005; Levinson, 2007; Martin & Smith, 2008; Rosen, 2009). So why all the buzz about this strategy? Consumers have grown cynical. They no longer trust traditional advertising. They are bored with media hype. They place more trust in friends than in Madison Avenue. According to one report, "67 percent of sales of U.S. consumer goods are now influenced by word of mouth" (Salzman, Matathia, & O'Reilly, 2003, p. 31). As a result, a message that is spread via social networks can be highly successful. Like tossing a rock into a pond, the ripples of influence spread among social circles.

Because buzz marketing relies on friendships to spread positive word of mouth, it is essential that it be perceived as genuine (Salzman et al., 2003). Buzz marketing succeeds when it seems authentic rather than manufactured, spontaneous rather than choreographed, and peer driven rather than corporate-sponsored. Buzz enjoys several advantages over tra-ditional advertising and marketing techniques. It operates largely through interpersonal channels (face to face, cellphone, email, IM, texting), lending it an air of authenticity. It is inexpensive compared to traditional media. And it is self-perpetuating. Buzz can multiply a message's impact exponentially. Moreover, buzz is more effective than mainstream media at reaching younger audiences.

Tipping Points

Key concepts and principles associated with buzz marketing have been laid out by Malcolm Gladwell (2000) in his bestseller *The Tipping Point*. Gladwell likens WOM to a virus. Consistent with the viral metaphor, a message is spread via social networks until the whole society is "infected." The message thus becomes self-perpetuating. And the public-ity is free. Under the right circumstances, he suggests, a small number of influential peo-ple, what he calls *"the law of the few,"* can generate a groundswell of support for an idea, a brand, or a phenomenon. Once a message gains a certain amount of momentum, it reaches a tipping point and becomes "contagious." In order to reach the tipping point, however, a number of things have to happen.

Uber Influencers

First, the right kinds of people must be involved in spreading the message. Gladwell iden-tifies three types of people who are essential to the process. *Mavens* possess specialized expertise. They are in the know. They may be celebrity chefs, eco-enthusiasts, fashion afi-cionados, fitness gurus, tech geeks, or wine snobs. Mavens needn't be rich or famous, but they must be ahead of the curve. They are the early adopters, or what some call alpha con-sumers, the ones who hear about ideas and try out gadgets first. Keller and Barry (2003) refer to such people as *influentials*; opinion leaders who shape others' opinions. "One American in ten," they maintain, "tells the other nine how to vote, where to eat, and what to buy" (p. 1).

In addition to mavens, Gladwell maintains that *connectors* are also essential. Based on the viral metaphor, they are carriers. They have larger social networks. They know everyone. When connectors learn from mavens what the "next big thing" is, they spread the word. They blog, chat, email, IM, text, and Twitter everyone in their social network.

Since social circles tend to be overlapping, forwarding messages spreads them increasingly outward from their epicenter.

The last type of person Gladwell identifies is *salespeople*. They receive the message from a connector and then sell it to their own smaller circle of friends. Salespeople tell their friends, "You must see this movie," "You have got to try this restaurant," or "You gotta to read this book." Unlike mavens, who can be somewhat aloof, salespeople are friendly and outgoing. They charm, cajole, and coax us. "Email and texting are so yesterday," a salesperson might say. "You need to Twitter, dude."

Orchestrating the Next Big Thing

In addition to having the right kinds of people, some additional conditions must be satisfied for an idea to go viral. *Context* is critical. The idea must come along at the right time and place. Social networking sites, for example, wouldn't have been possible before there was widespread access to the Internet. An idea also must possess *stickiness*, which means it is inherently attractive. Without some sort of natural appeal, people won't gravitate toward the idea or pass it along (Heath & Heath, 2008). The yellow Livestrong bracelets associated with the Lance Armstrong Foundation had stickiness. They offered a simple, convenient way for people to display their support for the fight against cancer. *Scalability* is another requirement: It must be easy to ramp up production of the idea, product, or message to meet demand. *Effortless transfer* is yet another ingredient in the recipe for an effective viral campaign. For a virus to spread, it must be communicable. A viral campaign has to leverage free media, hence the reliance on "word of mouse." Ideas that can be spread by forwarding an email, including an attachment, or embedding a link are easy to disseminate. The more time, effort, or money it takes to spread the word, the less likely the idea will go viral.

An example of a successful viral campaign was the group OK Go's music video "Here it Goes Again," which has been viewed more than 44 million times on YouTube. The video features band members performing a synchronized treadmill dance. The low-budget video, choreographed by the lead singer's sister, became an Internet sensation and eventually won a Grammy award. There are no guarantees, however. For every success story like OK Go's, there is a litany of failures. Viral marketing holds considerable potential, but it is a hit-or-miss strategy, with far more misses than hits.

Infectious or Inexplicable?

Despite the popularity of viral persuasion, the phenomenon itself isn't that predictable or easy to manufacture. Evidence for the effectiveness of tipping points is largely anecdotal. Many messages go viral, but few are planned, deliberate efforts to persuade. Duncan Watts, one of Gladwell's critics, says that influentials are overrated (Watts, 2007; Watts & Dodds, 2007). Orchestrating a viral campaign can be difficult. There is no guarantee an idea will gain traction. Trends come and go. Consistent with the viral metaphor, sometimes they mutate into something else. As an example, when Wal-Mart launched a Facebook page to promote its brand image, its "Wall" was riddled with negative comments about low pay and poor working conditions (Voight, 2007).

The very concept of viral marketing is something of an oxymoron. A viral campaign is planned to appear unplanned. It is contrived to seem genuine. The more prevalent the practice becomes, the more people will become sensitized to it and the less effective it will be. Despite these shortcomings, traditional persuasion is no more effective. Television commercials, print ads, and radio spots are also hit and miss. People aren't lemmings who'll jump off a cliff just because a friend texted them to do so. Okay, most people aren't.

Not only is traditional persuasion, such as advertising and marketing, becoming less obvious, persuasion also plays an important role in a variety of not-so-obvious contexts as well. We examine two such contexts in the following sections: the sciences and the arts.

Persuasion in the Sciences

You may not think of them this way, but scientists are persuaders. Even in fields such as chemistry, mathematics, or physics—the so-called hard sciences—persuasion plays a major role.[5] Scientists often have to convince others that their research possesses scientific merit and social value, that their experiments have been properly designed and carried out, and that their interpretations of their results are correct. They also have to argue for the superiority of their theories over competing theories (see, for example, Levy, 1994). In this respect, Thomas Kuhn (1970) argues that all scientists employ "techniques of persuasion in their efforts to establish the superiority of their own paradigms over those of their rivals" (p. 151). Similarly, Mitroff (1974) comments that "the notion of the purely objective, uncommitted scientist [is] naïve . . . . The best scientist . . . not only has points of view but also defends them with gusto" (p. 120).

There are controversial issues in every scientific field, including anthropology, astronomy, biology, epidemiology, genetics, paleontology, physics, seismology, and zoology. As just one example, theoretical physicists aren't sure how much matter there is in the universe or whether the universe will continue to expand or contract at some point (Bryson, 2003; Greene, 1999; Hawking, 1996; Rubin, 1998). Scientists must do more than take measurements and conduct experiments. They must also persuade other scientists, funding agencies, and the public at large. The controversy over global warming illustrates the persuasive nature of science.

Persuasion in the Arts

Another not-so-obvious context for persuasion is the arts. Not all art is created "for art's sake." Art serves more than an aesthetic or decorative function. Artists have strong opinions, and they don't always keep them to themselves. They lend expression to their opinions in and through their work. Consider film as an art form, for example. Movies such as *Dead Poets Society, Life Is Beautiful*, and *Schindler's List* demonstrate the power of the camera to increase awareness, change attitudes, alter beliefs, and shape opinions. Other art forms have the capability to persuade as well. Playwrights, painters, muralists, sculptors, photographers, and dancers give voice to their political and social views through their art.

Think about painting for a moment. Many of the famous works hanging in museums throughout the world were created out of a sense of social conscience. Using images, rather than words, artists comment on social conditions, criticize society, and attempt to transform the social order. We examine this issue in more detail in Chapter 14, but for now let's consider one particular work of art, Pablo Picasso's *Guernica*. Through this painting,

Picasso offered a moral indictment of war and man's inhumanity to man. The painting features people and animals, the victims of the indiscriminant bombing of a Basque town during the Spanish Civil War, in various states of agony, torment, and grief. As Von Blum (1976) notes, "the purpose of the painting is frankly propagandistic. The artist's intent was to point out the inhuman character of Franco's fascist rebellion" (p. 92). Picasso wasn't trying to paint a "pretty" picture. He was making a moral statement. The painting has been dubbed by one art historian "the highest achievement in modernist political painting" (Clark, 1997, p. 39). Not only Picasso but also many other artists express persuasive points of view in and through their art.

Other Not-So-Obvious Contexts for Persuasion

Persuasion operates in a variety of other contexts, some of which are not so obvious. We highlight a few here as illustrations. Several social scientists have studied bumper stickers as a form of political expression and as an unobtrusive means of measuring attitudes (Ehlert, Ehlert, & Merrens, 1973; Endersby & Towle, 1996; Sechrest & Belew, 1983). Scholars have examined the effects of intercessory prayer (offered for the benefit of another person) on recovery from illness (Frank & Frank, 1991; Hodge, 2007). Other researchers have focused on 12-step programs, such as Alcoholics Anonymous, and other support groups as forms of self-help and group influence (Johnson & Chappel, 1994; Jurik, 1987; Kassel & Wagner, 1993). One scholar has written about compliance-gaining tactics found in dramatic plays, such as Shakespeare's *Hamlet*, and Ibsen's *A Doll's House* (Kipnis, 2001). Another has written about architecture and how the size, shape, design, or layout of a building or other structure can shape people's perceptions and behavior in rather profound ways (Hattenhauer, 1984). One of the authors investigated various styles and strategies of panhandling to see which ones proved most effective (Robinson, Seiter, & Acharya, 1992).

Weird Persuasion

Sometimes persuasion is downright weird. A case in point is the town of Dish, Texas, formerly known as Clark, Texas. Its citizens agreed to rename their town as part of an endorsement deal with Dish Network. In exchange for the naming rights, Dish Network agreed to provide all 125 residents free satellite TV service for 10 years. The main opponent of the idea, not surprisingly, was one Mr. Clark, after whom the town was originally named.

Why would Dish Network and the town's citizens agree to such a deal? In a word, buzz. The strangeness of the transaction generated free publicity. The mayor of the town said he hoped the new name would attract more customers. One wonders where a small town should draw the line. Could there be a Viagra, Virginia, next? Will there be a Depends, Delaware, in the not-too-distant future?

Another kooky example of persuasion involved the sale of William Shatner's kidney stone on eBay. In an effort to boldly go where no other eBayer had gone before, the actor auctioned off his kidney stone to an online casino for $25,000. The happy ending is that all the proceeds were donated to a charity. Again, the zaniness of the stunt generated free publicity. The authors are thankful Mr. Shatner suffered from kidney stones and not hemorrhoids.

Yet another example of weird persuasion occurred in Mansfield, Nottinghamshire, U.K. The citizens wanted to stop rowdy teens from loitering at an underpass at night. Their solution was to install street lights with a bright pink hue. Why pink, you ask? Pink light highlights acne. Teens with blemishes didn't want to be seen with bright, glowing acne. The plan worked: The teens moved on (Spotty Teens, 2009).

Scholars sometimes investigate quirky aspects of persuasion, too. Did you know that participants in a study who consumed caffeine were more easily persuaded than participants who had no caffeine (Martin, Hamilton, McKimmie, Terry, & Martin, 2007)? Now you do. As long as the participants were motivated to pay attention to the message, caffeine consumption increased agreement. Other researchers found that mixed-handed people were more persuadable and more gullible than purely left- or right-handed people (Christman, Henning, Geers, Propper, & Niebauer, 2008). And Briñol & Petty (2003) discovered that asking people to nod their heads up and down (as if in agreement) made them more agreeable than nodding their heads back and forth (as if in disagreement). What is the point of such research, you ask? We would suggest the knowledge function identified earlier. From a practical standpoint, however, you now know that if you want to convince a friend to do you a favor, pick an ambidextrous friend, take him or her to Starbucks for a dose of caffeine, and ask the friend to nod his or her head up and down while you make the request.

Persuasion, then, can be found in obvious and not-so-obvious places. Before concluding this section, we examine one additional context in which persuasion occurs. This is the context in which most of the influence attempts we encounter on a daily basis occur: the interpersonal arena.

Persuasion in Interpersonal Settings

Interpersonal encounters, no matter where they take place, function as major arteries for persuasion. Try to think of a conversation you've had lately that *didn't* involve some persuasion. On a daily basis we are bombarded with persuasive requests in the interpersonal arena. Your brother wants you to hurry up and get out of the bathroom. A homeless person asks if you can spare some change. Your parents try to talk you out of getting a tongue stud. Or worse yet, your significant other uses the "F" word to redefine your relationship: that's right; she or he just wants to be "friends." Aaahhh! Naturally, we persuade back as well, targeting others with our own entreaties, pleadings, and requests for favors.

The extent of influence exerted in the interpersonal arena should not be underestimated. In fact, although we may think of Madison Avenue as manipulative, persuasion is most effective in face-to-face interaction. Why? Because influence attempts tend to operate less conspicuously in interpersonal encounters. Consider the following scenario:

The bait: Your friend calls up and says, "Hey, what are you doing Friday night?"

The nibble: Anticipating an invitation to go somewhere, you reply, "Nothing much, why?"

You're hooked and reeled in: "Well, I wonder if you could help me move into my new apartment then?"

At least when you watch a television commercial you *know* the sponsor is after something from the outset. In interpersonal encounters, others' motives may be less transparent. Most communication scholars agree that if one can choose the setting for an influence attempt, one "should definitely choose the interpersonal arena" (Wenburg & Wilmot, 1973, p. 28). Thus, persuasion tends to operate at maximum effectiveness in interpersonal settings, because we aren't always aware of what is going on. Our advice: Next time you want to turn in a paper late, talk to the professor in person!

From our discussion thus far, it should be apparent that persuasion functions as a pervasive force in virtually every facet of human communication. Kenneth Burke (1945, 1950, 1966), among others, has written that humans are, by their very nature, symbol-using beings. One vital aspect of human symbolicity involves the tendency to persuade others. We are symbol users, and one of the principal functions of symbol usage is persuasion.

The recognition that social influence is an essential, pervasive feature of human symbolic action provides the strongest possible justification for the study of persuasion. Persuasion is one of the major underlying impulses for human communication. By way of analogy, one can't understand how an automobile works without taking a look under the hood. Similarly, one can't understand how human communication functions without examining one of its primary motives—persuasion.

FOUR BENEFITS OF STUDYING PERSUASION

Given that persuasion is an inevitable fact of life, we offer four primary benefits of learning about persuasion. We refer to these as the instrumental function, the knowledge and awareness function, the defensive function, and the debunking function. We examine each of these in turn.

The Instrumental Function: Be All That You Can Be

One good reason for learning about persuasion is so that you can become a more effective persuader yourself. We refer to this as the *instrumental function* of persuasion, because persuasion serves as an instrument, or a means to an end. We view the ability to persuade others as an important aspect of communication competence. *Communication competence* involves acting in ways that are perceived as effective and appropriate by oneself and others (Kellermann, 1992; Spitzberg & Cupach, 1984). Competent communicators possess the skills needed to achieve their objectives in fitting ways for the particular situation.

A competent persuader needs to know how to analyze an audience in order to adapt the message to the audience's frame of reference. She or he needs to be able to identify which strategies are appropriate and which will enjoy the greatest likelihood of success. A competent persuader also must know how to organize and arrange a persuasive message for maximum benefit. These are only some of the abilities required for successful persuasion.

But achieving the desired outcome is only one facet of communication competence. How one goes about persuading also matters. A competent persuader needs to be viewed as persuading in acceptable, appropriate ways. This means a persuader must be aware of social and cultural norms governing the persuasive situation. For example, a parent who publicly berates his or her child during a soccer match may be seen by other parents as engaging in boorish behavior. A good deal of what is considered appropriate persuasion falls under the heading of ethical persuasion, a subject we touch on in other chapters and to which Chapter 16 is devoted.

We are confident that by learning more about persuasion you will become a more effective and appropriate persuader. Of course, not every influence attempt will succeed. By applying the principles and processes presented in this text, and by adhering to the ethical guidelines we offer, you should be able to improve your competence as a persuader.

The Knowledge and Awareness Function: Inquiring Minds Want to Know

Another good reason for learning about persuasion is because it will enhance your knowledge and awareness of a variety of persuasive processes. Knowledge is power, as the saying goes. There is value in learning more about how persuasion operates. You may not plan on going into advertising for a living, but simply knowing how image-based advertising operates is worthwhile in and of itself. You may not plan on joining a cult (who does?), but learning more about what makes persons susceptible to cult conversion is worthwhile nonetheless. Simply from the standpoint of an observer, learning about these topics can be fascinating.

An additional benefit of learning about how persuasion functions concerns overcoming *habitual persuasion*. Persuasion is second nature to us, like breathing. We've been doing it all our lives. However, many people rely on habitual forms of persuasion, regardless of whether they are effective. They get comfortable with a few strategies and tactics that they use over and over again. A good deal of our communication behavior is "mindless," as opposed to mindful, meaning we don't pay much attention to how we communicate (Langer, 1978, 1989a, 1989b). Sometimes persuasion operates this way. Just as runners, swimmers, and other athletes need to learn to adjust their breathing in response to different situations, persuaders—to maximize their effectiveness—need to learn to adapt their methods to different audiences and situations. Persuasion isn't a "one-size-fits-all" form of communication.

The Defensive Function: Duck and Cover

A third reason for learning about how persuasion operates is vital in our view: The study of persuasion serves a defensive function. This is one of the chief benefits of taking a class on this subject. By studying how and why influence attempts succeed or fail, you can become a more discerning consumer of persuasive messages, unlike the hapless fellow depicted in the accompanying cartoon. If you know how persuasion works, you are less likely to be taken in. It is worth noting that people tend to *underestimate* the influence of advertising on themselves and *overestimate* its effects on others, a phenomenon known as the *third-person effect* (Davidson, 1983; Jensen & Collins, 2008). Thus, you may be more defenseless than you realize.

Throughout this text we expose a number of persuasive tactics used in retail sales, advertising, and marketing campaigns. For example, we have found in our classes that

"That's it, Henry—you've dialed your last mattress!"

A little persuasive acumen just might save you from yourself.

after students are given a behind-the-scenes look at how car salespeople are taught to sell, several students usually acknowledge, "Oh yeah, they did that to me." Admittedly, a huckster could also take advantage of the advice we offer in this book. We think it is far more likely, however, that the typical student reader will use our advice and suggestions as weapons *against* unethical influence attempts. Box 1.1, for example, offers advice on how to recognize various propaganda ploys. In later chapters of this book we warn you about common ploys used by all manner of persuaders, from cult leaders, to panhandlers, to funeral home directors.

The Debunking Function: Puh-Shaw

A fourth reason for studying persuasion is that it serves a debunking function. The study of human influence can aid in dispelling various "commonsense" assumptions and "homespun" theories about persuasion. Traditional wisdom isn't always right, and it's worth knowing when it's wrong. Unfortunately, some individuals cling tenaciously to stereotypes and folk wisdom about persuasive practices that are known by researchers who study persuasion to be patently false. For example, many people believe that subliminal messages are highly effective and operate in a manner similar to that of post-hypnotic suggestion. This belief is pure poppycock, as we point out in Chapter 15.

Of considerable importance, then, are empirical findings that are *counterintuitive* in nature—that is, they go against the grain of common sense. By learning about research findings on persuasion, the reader can learn to ferret out the true from the false, the fact from the fiction.

We hope you'll agree, based on the foregoing discussion, that there are quite a few good reasons for studying persuasion. We hope we've persuaded you that the study of persuasion can be a prosocial endeavor. That brings us back to an earlier point, however: Not all persuaders are scrupulous. At this juncture, then, it seems appropriate that we address two common criticisms related to the study of persuasion.

Persuasion versus Propaganda and Indoctrination | BOX 1.1

What are propaganda and indoctrination and how do they differ from persuasion? To a large extent, whether an influence attempt is considered persuasion or propaganda is a matter of perspective. People tend to label their *own* messages as persuasion and the *other guy's* as propaganda. The same applies to indoctrination: We tend to think that our government educates its citizens, but foreign governments, especially governments we dislike, indoctrinate their citizens. Understood in this way, *propaganda* and *indoctrination* are largely pejorative terms used to describe persuasive messages or positions with which people disagree. Gun control advocates claim the NRA uses propaganda to thwart legislation that would place restrictions on gun sales. Opponents of school prayer think that requiring students to recite a prayer each day in class constitutes a form of religious indoctrination. When accused of propagandizing or indoctrinating, the common defense is to state that one was only engaged in an education or information campaign. Thus, whether a given attempt at influence, such as the D.A.R.E. campaign, is persuasion, propaganda, or indoctrination is largely in the eye of the beholder.

Definitions of propaganda are many and varied, but we happen to think Pratkanis and Aronson's (1991) definition does a good job of capturing the essence of the term:

> *Propaganda* was originally defined as the dissemination of biased ideas and opinions, often through the use of lies and deception . . . . The word *propaganda* has since evolved to mean mass "suggestion" or influence through the

manipulation of symbols and the psychology of the individual. Propaganda is the communication of a point of view with the ultimate goal of having the recipient come to "voluntarily" accept the position as if it were his or her own. (p. 9)

Different scholars have offered different views on the nature and characteristics of propaganda (see Ellul, 1973; Jowett & O'Donnell, 1986; Smith, 1989). However, there are some essential characteristics on which most scholars agree. These are as follows:

- Propaganda has a strong ideological bent. Most scholars agree that propaganda does not serve a purely informational function. Propaganda typically embodies a strong bias, such as that of a "left-wing" or "right-wing" agenda. The campaign of People for the Ethical Treatment of Animals (PETA) to promote animal rights would fall into this category, as would the Army of God's efforts to ban abortion. Propagandists aren't trying to be neutral or objective. They are working a specific agenda.
- Propaganda is institutional in nature. Most scholars agree that propaganda is practiced by organized groups, whether they happen to be government agencies, political lobbies, private corporations, religious groups, or social movements. When the AIDS epidemic first struck in the 1980s, the federal government, through agencies such as the Centers for Disease Control, mounted full-scale propaganda

(continued)

campaigns to convince people to practice safe sex. Although individuals might use propaganda too (a parent might tell a child "Santa only brings presents for good girls and boys"), the term usually is associated with institutional efforts to persuade.

- Propaganda involves mass persuasion. Most scholars agree that propaganda targets a mass audience and relies on mass media to persuade. Propaganda is aimed at large numbers of people and, as such, relies on mass communication (TV, radio, posters, billboards, email, mass mailings, etc.) to reach its audience. The audience may be global, it may be regional, or it may consist of specific demographic groups, such as senior citizens, Hispanics, or teens. Thus, gossip that was shared by one office worker with another at the water cooler wouldn't constitute propaganda, but a corporate rumor that was circulated via email would.

- Propaganda tends to rely on ethically suspect methods of influence. Propagandists tend to put results first and ethics second. This characteristic is probably the one that laypersons most closely associate with propaganda and the one that gives it its negative connotation.

What are some of the questionable tactics used by propagandists? The Institute for Propaganda Analysis, which was founded in 1937, identified seven basic propaganda techniques, which still exist today (Miller, 1937). These include the *plain folks appeal* ("I'm one of you"), *testimonials* ("I saw the aliens, sure as I'm standing here"), the *bandwagon effect* (everybody's doing it), *card-stacking* (presenting only one side of the story), *transfer* (positive or negative associations, such as guilt by association), *glittering generalities* (idealistic or loaded language, such as "freedom," "empowering," "family values"), and *name calling* ("racist," "tree hugger," "femi-Nazi").

TWO CRITICISMS OF PERSUASION

Does Learning about Persuasion Foster Manipulation?

We've already touched on one of the common criticisms of studying persuasion: the notion that it fosters a manipulative approach to communication. We address ethical concerns surrounding the study and practice of persuasion more specifically in Chapter 16. For the time being, however, a few general arguments can be offered in response to this concern. First, our principal focus in this text is on the *means* of persuasion (e.g., how persuasion functions). We view the means of persuasion not so much as moral or immoral, but rather as amoral, or ethically neutral. In this respect, persuasion can be likened to a tool, such as a hammer. Like any other tool, persuasion can be put to good or bad use. If this sounds like a cop-out, read what Aristotle had to say on this same point in his *Rhetoric*:

> If it is urged that an abuse of the rhetorical faculty can work great mischief, the same charge can be brought against all good things (save virtue itself), and especially against the most useful things such as strength, health, wealth, and military skill. Rightly employed, they work the greatest blessings; and wrongly employed, they work the greatest harm. (1355b)

Related to this idea is the fact that tools can be used in good or bad ways, depending on their user. We believe that first and foremost, a *persuader's motives* determine whether a given influence attempt is good or bad, right or wrong, ethical or unethical. We maintain that the moral quality of a persuasive act is derived primarily from the ends a persuader seeks, and only secondarily from the means the persuader employs. It isn't so much *what* strategies and tactics a persuader uses as *why* he or she uses them.

To illustrate this position, suppose you asked us whether the use of "fear appeals" is ethically justified. We would have to say, it depends. If a fear appeal were being used to inform a sexually active teen of the risks of HIV infection from unprotected sex, we would tend to say the fear appeal was justified. If a fear appeal were being used by a terrorist who threatened to kill a hostage every hour until his demands were met, we would say the fear appeal was unjustified. In each case, the motives of the persuader would "color" the use of the fear appeal. Consistent with our tool analogy, fear appeals, like other persuasive strategies, can be used for good or bad ends.

A second response to this criticism was highlighted earlier. The study of persuasion performs a *defensive function* insofar as it educates people to become more discriminating consumers of persuasive messages. For instance, we believe our "Tips on Buying a New or Used Car" (see Box 1.2) are useful to any potential car buyer who wants to avoid being manipulated at a car lot. By increasing your awareness of the ploys of would-be persuaders, this text performs a watchdog function. You can use the information contained herein to arm yourself against the tactics of unscrupulous persuaders.

Tips on Buying a New or Used Car | BOX 1.2

Given the current state of the economy and the economic fix in which car dealers find themselves, buying a car nowadays is easier than before. Car dealers are eager to sell cars. Nevertheless, car salespersons, especially *used* car salespersons, have a bad reputation. These bad reputations may be undeserved. We've met some honest, upstanding sellers. We've also met some shady operators. Because a car is a major purchase, one would be well advised to err on the side of caution when negotiating with a car salesperson. *Caveat emptor*, as the saying goes: Let the buyer beware.

1. Be wary. Remember, buying a car is a great American ritual in which the car dealer has the upper hand. This is the prototype for high-pressure sales. They are professionals. They sell cars every day. You are an amateur. Who do you think has more experience with persuasion in this setting?

2. Do your homework *before* you go visit a car dealer. Read up on the makes and models in which

you're interested. Find out about performance criteria, standard features, and options before setting foot on a car lot. *Consumer Reports* sells an excellent paperback that compares used cars on reliability, safety, and other criteria based on data from actual owners. Research shows that doing your homework may save you money (Seiter & Seiter, 2005).

3. Keep a poker face. If the salesperson knows you are eager or excited about the car purchase, he or she will smell blood. Once the salesperson knows you are emotionally attached to a particular car, you'll wind up paying more.

4. Take a calculator with you. Car salespersons like to pretend that the prices of things are entirely up to the calculator ("Hey, let's see how the numbers shake out"). The implication is that the numbers aren't negotiable or flexible. Everything is negotiable! Do your own figuring to see if the numbers "shake out" the same way. If not, ask why.

(continued)

5. Once you are on the car lot, dealers will try to keep you there. They may put you in a little cubicle, holding you "hostage" during the negotiations. Their psychological strategy is to wear you down. After hours of haggling, you'll become mentally drained and more likely to give in. They may ask for the keys to your trade-in, presumably to look it over and determine its value. Once they have your keys you can't leave.

6. The car salesperson will want to *avoid* talking about the total price of the car, opting instead to discuss the monthly payment you can afford. You, however, should focus on four things: (a) the total purchase price, (b) the finance period, (c) the interest rate, and (d) the monthly payment. Don't discuss the monthly payment unless you are clear on the finance period involved (a 3-year loan, 4-year loan, 5-year loan, etc.). If you admit you can afford $300 per month, the salesperson may simply switch to a longer finance period—say, 4 years, instead of 3, thereby adding thousands of dollars to the total purchase price.

7. During the negotiations, the salesperson may leave the room a number of times to talk with the "sales manager." This is all choreographed. The salesperson can't agree to anything without checking with this mysterious figure, so the person with whom you are negotiating really can't commit to anything. You, however, will be asked to commit to a lot of things. Don't!

8. The salesperson will act like he or she is your best friend, even though you just met. The salesperson will look for ways to identify with you or ingratiate himself or herself to you to establish camaraderie ("You like fly fishing? That makes two of us." "Whaddya-know, my granddaughter is named 'Fifi' too!"). During the negotiations the salesperson will pretend he or she is on your side and is willing to go out on a limb for you ("Well, my sales manager may kick my butt for even taking him this offer, but hey, I like you!"). Remember these two are working as a team, *against you*. Don't be confused for a moment about where the salesperson's loyalties reside.

9. The car salesperson will do all kinds of things to get you to make a commitment to buy ("What would it take to get you to buy this car? Just tell me, whudda-I-godda-do to get you in this car?"). Often the salesperson will ask you to write down any amount you're offering on a slip of paper or an offer sheet, even though it isn't legally binding (it does increase your psychological commitment, however). The car dealer *wants* you to sit in the car, take it for a test spin, smell the upholstery, because then you will become psychologically committed to owning the car.

10. If you get close to a deal, or alternatively, if a deal seems to be coming apart, don't be surprised if another salesperson comes in to take over the negotiations. Often a "closer" is sent in (sort of like a relief pitcher in baseball) to complete the sale.

11. Beware of "loss leaders" (advertised specials at absurdly low prices). These are come-ons designed to get you onto the lot. Once there, however, you'll be subjected to the "old switcheroo." You'll find there is/was only one car at that price. You will probably be told, "Sorry, it's already sold . . . but I can make you a honey of a deal on . . ."

12. The sale isn't over simply because you've agreed on a price! You still have to deal with the dreaded "finance person." You'll be given the impression that you're simply seeing the finance person to sign documents and process paperwork. Don't let down your guard. The finance person will try to add on thousands of dollars in the form of extended warranties, anti-theft systems, and protective coatings.

13. The interest rate is just as important as the price of the car. Shop around for a car loan from a bank or credit union *before* you shop for a car. The rates may be lower and you can find out exactly how much you qualify for in advance.

14. Shop around for prices on options such as stereos before you go to a car dealer. People often bargain well on the purchase price, then give up everything they've gained by failing to bargain on the price of extras. The price of everything is negotiable!

15. Don't let the salesperson know in advance that you have a trade-in. Any bargaining gains you make on the purchase price of the new car will just be deducted from the trade-in value of your used car. Sell the used car on your own if at all possible. If that's not possible, you can always mention your trade-in after you've negotiated the price of the new car.

16. Don't get a lemon. Buying a used car can be particularly risky. One of the authors bought a used sports car on EBay. How did he know from a mere picture and description whether the car was in good shape? He ran a CARFAX history on the car, easily available online (see www.carfax.com) for about $10, which revealed that the car had had only one previous owner; had never been stolen, totaled, or repossessed; had correct odometer readings; and had passed a smog check each year when the vehicle registration was renewed. Since the car was coming from another state, the author went one step further and hired an independent mechanic to perform a "prepurchase inspection" on the car, at a cost of about $150. We strongly suggest you do the same for any used car. After all, how much can the average consumer tell about a car from looking under the hood and kicking the tires?

A third response that bears mentioning is that in denouncing the study of persuasion, anti-manipulation types are also attempting to persuade. The message that persuasion is manipulative or exploitative is itself a persuasive appeal that seeks to engender certain attitudes, beliefs, and values about the "proper" study of communication. When one group claims to know best how human communication should be studied, they are, in fact, standing on the persuasion soapbox themselves.

Are Persuasion Findings Too Inconsistent or Confusing?

An additional complaint that has been leveled against the study of persuasion is that it has led to findings that are overly qualified, or contradictory in nature. Empirical investigations of persuasion, it is argued, have not yielded clear and consistent generalizations. There is no "$E = MC^2$," no "second law of thermodynamics," no universal when it comes to persuasion.

First, the complaint that persuasion isn't worth studying because the findings are often inconclusive or contradictory makes little sense. Quite the opposite: We believe that persuasion warrants study precisely because it *is* so elusive. Underlying this criticism seems to be the expectation that reality is, or should be, simple and uncomplicated. Like it or not, understanding reality is hard work. As we've already noted, human beings are complex creatures who rarely respond to messages for one and only one reason. Actually, we find this to be a redeeming feature of humanity. We rejoice in the fact that we aren't an altogether gullible, predictable, or controllable species.

A second response to this criticism is simply that research *has* revealed a number of significant, relevant generalizations about persuasion. You'll find many such generalizations throughout this book. Newer techniques of statistical analysis, such as *meta-analysis*,[6] have made it possible to reconcile some of the previous inconsistencies in the literature. In this text, we identify a number of noteworthy, albeit qualified, generalizations that are based on the most recent meta-analyses available.

You'll notice in this book that we've drawn on the people in the trenches themselves to learn how persuasion works in particular contexts and settings. We've talked to used car salespersons, funeral home operators, retail clothing clerks, advertising firms, former cult members, door-to-door salespersons, and telemarketers to find out—from the horse's mouth, so to speak—how persuasion operates.

ETHICAL CONCERNS ABOUT THE USE OF PERSUASION

We would be remiss if we concluded this chapter without emphasizing the importance of ethics in the persuasion process. We wish to underscore the point that the use of persuasion is fraught with ethical concerns. We raise a number of such concerns in Box 1.3 for you to ponder. Our position is that in learning how to become a more effective persuader, you should strive to be an ethical persuader as well. In the final chapter we address a number of ethical questions related to various strategies and techniques of persuasion discussed throughout the text. We wait until the final chapter to fully examine ethical concerns for

---

| **Ethical or Unethical Persuasion? You Decide** | **BOX 1.3** |

Instructions: For each of the following scenarios, indicate how ethical or unethical you perceive the persuader or the persuasive strategy to be, *based on a five-point scale* (with 1 being "highly ethical" and 5 being "highly unethical").

1. A student pretends to cry in a professor's office in an attempt to coax the professor into giving her a makeup exam. Is this ethical persuasion?

2. A persuader advances an argument he doesn't believe in, but that he thinks will be convincing to his listeners. The argument isn't untrue or invalid; it just happens to be one with which the persuader himself does not agree. Is this ethical persuasion?

3. A car salesperson emphasizes that the model of car a customer is considering has "more horse-power and better mileage than the competition." The salesperson fails to mention that the car has worse reliability, and a worse safety record than the competition. Is this ethical persuasion?

4. A skilled attorney successfully defends a client she knows to be guilty. Is this ethical persuasion?

5. A minister tells his congregation that a vote for a particular candidate is "a vote for the Devil incarnate" and that the scriptures demand that the

faithful cast their ballots for another candidate. Is this ethical persuasion?

6. A persuader sincerely believes in the arguments she is presenting, but the facts and information she cites are incorrect and outdated. Is this ethical persuasion?

7. Parents use a fear appeal to convince their child to clean her room. "Santa doesn't bring presents to children with dirty rooms," they warn. Is this ethical persuasion?

8. A children's cereal states on the box, "High in the vitamins kids need!" but doesn't mention that the cereal is high in sugar too. Is this ethical persuasion?

9. A newlywed husband is upset that his wife wants to go to a dance club with some of her single friends for drinks. "If you go," he warns, "I'm going to a strip club with some of my friends." Is this ethical persuasion?

10. A political campaign runs a series of negative attack ads against an opponent, not because the campaign manager prefers to, but because voter surveys show that negative ads will work, whereas ads that take the political "high road" won't. Is this ethical persuasion?

two reasons: First, until you've learned more about persuasion, you may not fully appreciate all of the ethical issues that are involved. Second, after you've studied the full scope of persuasion as we present it in this text, you'll be in a much better position to place these ethical questions in perspective.

SUMMARY

We hope that we've convinced you of the ubiquity of persuasion in human interaction. The capacity to persuade is one of the defining features of humankind. This fact provides the strongest possible reason for studying persuasion. Given that learning about persuasion serves an instrumental function, a knowledge and awareness function, a defensive function, and a debunking function, we believe there is ample justification for studying this topic. Finally, rejoinders to two current criticisms of the study of persuasion were offered. Hopefully, a persuasive case has been made for learning about persuasion.

One other thing: Did we mention that learning about persuasion can also be fun?

ENDNOTES

1. The scientific study of persuasion dates back to the 1940s and 1950s, when Carl Hovland founded the Yale Attitude Research Program as part of the war effort. The government wanted to know how to counter enemy propaganda that could affect the morale of troops and how susceptible POWs were to brainwashing.

2. Aristotle's work *Rhetoric* is one such text that has survived the test of time. Written in the fourth century B.C., Aristotle's work has had a lasting influence on our understanding of persuasion. Many of his insights and observations are considered valid even today.

3. Note that with the exception of Hitler, these charismatic leaders enjoyed a limited following. The rest of us weren't taken in by their claims, suggesting that people, in general, aren't that gullible after all.

4. Rosseli, Skelly, & Mackie (1995) state, "even by conservative estimates, the average person is exposed to 300–400 persuasive messages a day from the mass media alone" (p. 163). Kurtz (1997) claims that the average TV viewer watches more than

150 commercials a day, including promos for upcoming shows, and more than 1,000 in a typical week (cited in Berger, 2004, p. 7). Dupont (1999) states that we live "in a world where we are potentially exposed to 3,000 advertising messages per day" (p. 14). Jones (2004) pegs the number of advertising messages at 300 to 1,500 every day, but indicates that some estimates are as high as 3,000 per day—a number Jones labels fanciful (p. 12). Without saying who says so, Berger (2004) reports that "some estimate that we are exposed to 15,000 commercial messages each day" (p. 101).

We are suspicious of such estimates, however, because they may simply represent "unknowable" statistics. At the very least, estimates of the number of persuasive messages to which the average person is exposed involve extrapolations, and the criteria upon which the extrapolations are based aren't always provided. What's more, the estimates often contradict one another. By way of illustration, Berger (2004) maintains that "advertisers spend around $800 per person in the United

States on advertising" (p. 101), whereas Dupont (1999) claims, "In the U.S., close to $400 for every man, woman, and child are invested in advertising each year" (p. 8). Which, if either, estimate is correct?

5. We don't have sufficient space to devote to this topic here, but suffice it to say that the traditional notion of scientific realism is under siege from the anti-realism camp (see Kourany, 1998). The anti-realists argue that science is neither purely objective nor impartial but heavily value laden (see also Laudan, 1984; Longino, 1990).

6. *Meta-analysis* refers to a statistical technique that allows a researcher to combine the results of many separate investigations and examine them as if they were one big super study. A meta-analysis is capable of revealing trends across a number of studies and resolving apparent inconsistencies among studies.

REFERENCES

Aristotle. (1932). *Rhetoric* (L. Cooper, Trans.). Englewood Cliffs, NJ: Prentice Hall.

Balter, D., & Butman, J. (2005). *Grapevine: The new art of word-of-mouth marketing*. Penguin Books.

Berger, A. A. (2004). *Ads, fads, and consumer culture* (2nd ed.). Lanham, MD: Rowman & Littlefield.

Briñol, P., & Petty, R. E. (2003). Overt head movements and persuasion: A self-validation analysis. *Journal of Personality and Social Psychology, 84*(6), 1123–1139.

Bryson, B. (2003). *A short history of just about everything*. New York: Broadway Books.

Burke, K. (1945). *A grammar of motives*. Englewood Cliffs, NJ: Prentice Hall.

Burke K. (1950). *A rhetoric of motives*. Englewood Cliffs, NJ: Prentice Hall.

Burke, K. (1966). *Language as symbolic action*. Berkeley: University of California Press.

Christman, S. D., Henning, B. R., Geers, A. L., Propper, R. E., & Niebauer, C. (2008). Mixed-handed persons are more easily persuaded and are more gullible: Interhemispheric interaction and belief updating. *Laterality, 13*(5), 403–426.

Clark, T. (1997). *Art and propaganda in the twentieth century*. New York: Harry N. Abrams Inc.

Davidson, W. P. (1983). The third-person effect in communication. *Public Opinion Quarterly, 47*, 1–15.

Dupont, L. (1999). *Images that sell: 500 ways to create great ads*. Sainte-Foy, Quebec, Canada: White Rock Publishing.

Ehlert, H., Ehlert, N., & Merrens, M. (1973). The influence of ideological affiliation on helping behavior. *Journal of Social Psychology, 89*(2), 315–316.

Ellul, J. (1973). *Propaganda: The formation of men's attitudes*. New York: Knopf.

Endersby, J. W., & Towle, M. J. (1996). Political and social expression through bumper stickers. *Social Science Journal, 33*(3), 307–319.

Frank, J. D., & Frank, J. B. (1991). *Persuasion and healing: A comparative study of psychotherapy* (3rd ed.). Baltimore, MD: Johns Hopkins University Press.

Gladwell, M. (2000). *The tipping point*. Boston: Little, Brown, and Company.

Greene, B. (1999). *The elegant universe: Superstrings, hidden dimensions, and the quest for the ultimate theory*. New York: W. W. Norton.

Hattenhauer, D. (1984). The rhetoric of architecture: A semiotic approach. *Communication Quarterly, 32*, 71–77.

Hawking, S. (1996). *The illustrated brief history of time*. New York: Bantam Books.

Heath, C., & Heath, D. (2008). *Made to stick: Why some ideas survive and others die*. New York: Random House.

Hodge, D. R. (2007). A systematic review of the empirical literature on intercessory prayer. *Research on Social Work Practice, 17*(2), 174–187.

Jensen, K., & Collins, S. (2008). The third-person effect in controversial advertising. *American Behavioral Scientist, 52*, 225–242.

Johnson, N. P., & Chappel, J. N. (1994). Using AA and other 12-step programs more effectively. *Journal of Substance Abuse Treatment, 11*, 137–142.

Jones, J. P. (2004). *Fables, fashions, and facts about advertising*. Thousand Oaks, CA: Sage.

Jowett, G. S., & O'Donnell, V. (1986). *Propaganda and persuasion*. Newbury Park, CA: Sage.

Jurik, N. C. (1987). Persuasion in self-help groups: Processes and consequences. *Small Group Behavior, 18*, 368–397.

Kassel, J. D., & Wagner, E. F. (1993). Processes of change in Alcoholics Anonymous: A review of possible mechanisms. *Psychotherapy, 30*, 222–233.

Keller, E., & Barry, J. (2003). *The influentials*. New York: The Free Press.

Kellermann, K. (1992). Communication: Inherently strategic and primarily automatic. *Communication Monographs, 59,* 288–300.

Kipnis, D. (2001). Influence tactics in plays. *Journal of Applied and Social Psychology, 31*(3), 542–552.

Kourany, J. A. (1998). *Scientific knowledge: Basic issues in the philosophy of science.* Belmont, CA: Wadsworth.

Kuhn, T. S. (1970). *The structure of scientific revolutions* (2nd ed.). New York: Springer-Verlag.

Kurtz, B. (1997). *Spots: The popular art of American television.* New York: Arts Communications.

Langer, E. J. (1978). Rethinking the role of thought in social interaction. In J. H. Harvey, W. J. Ickes, & R. F. Kidd (Eds.), *New directions in attribution research* (Vol. 2, pp. 35–58). New York: John Wiley & Sons.

Langer, E. J. (1989a). *Mindfulness.* Reading, MA: Addison-Wesley.

Langer, E. J. (1989b). Minding matters. In L. Berkowitz (Ed.), *Advances in experimental social psychology* (Vol. 22, pp. 137–173). New York: Addison-Wesley.

Laudan, L. (1984). *Science and values.* Berkeley, CA: University of California Press.

Levinson, J. C. (2007). *Guerrilla marketing: Easy and inexpensive strategies for making big profits from your small business* (4th ed.). Boston: Houghton Mifflin.

Levy, S. (1994, May 2). "Dr. Edelman's brain." *The New Yorker,* pp. 62–73.

Longino, H. (1990). *Science as social knowledge: Values and objectivity in scientific inquiry.* Princeton, NJ: Princeton University Press.

Martin, K. D., & Smith, N. C. (2008). Commercializing social interaction: The ethics of stealth advertising. *American Marketing Association, 27*(1), 45–56.

Martin, P. E., Hamilton, V. E. , McKimmie, B. M., Terry, D. J., & Martin, R. (2007). Effects of caffeine consumption on persuasion and attitude change: The role of secondary tasks in manipulating systematic message processing. *European Journal of Social Psychology, 37,* 320–338.

Miller, C. P. (1937). How to detect propaganda. *Propaganda analysis.* New York: Institute for Propaganda Analysis.

Mitroff, I. I. (1974, November 2). Studying the lunar rock scientist. *Saturday Review World,* pp. 64–65.

Pratkanis, A. R., & Aronson, E. (1991). *Age of propaganda: The everyday use and abuse of persuasion.* New York: W. H. Freeman.

Robinson, J. D., Seiter, J. S., & Acharya, L. (1992, February). *I just put my head down and society does the rest: An examination of influence strategies among beggars.* Paper presented at the annual meeting of the Western Communication Association, Boise, ID.

Rosen, E. (2009). *The anatomy of buzz revisited.* New York: Random House.

Rosseli, F., Skelly, J. J., & Mackie, D. M. (1995). Processing rational and emotional messages: The cognitive and affective mediation of persuasion. *Journal of Experimental Social Psychology, 31,* 163–190.

Rubin, V. C. (1998). Dark matter in the universe. *Scientific American,* Special Quarterly Issue of Scientific America Presents, *9*(1), 106–110.

Salzman, M., Matathia, I., & O'Reilly, A. (2003). *Buzz: Harness the power of influence and create demand.* New York: John Wiley & Sons.

Sechrest, L., & Belew, J. (1983). Nonreactive measures of social attitudes. *Applied Social Psychology Annual, 4,* 26–63.

Seiter, J. S., & Seiter, D. L. (2005). Consumer persuasion: The use of evidence when negotiating the price of a new automobile. *Journal of Applied Social Psychology, 35*(4), 1197–1205.

Simons, H. W. (1986). *Persuasion: Understanding, practice, analysis* (2nd ed.). New York: McGraw-Hill.

Smith, T. J. (Ed.). (1989). *Propaganda: A pluralistic perspective.* New York: Praeger.

Spitzberg, B. H., & Cupach, W. R. (1984). *Interpersonal communication competence.* Beverly Hills, CA: Sage.

"Spotty teens deterred from underpasses by acne light" (2009, March 25). *The Telegraph.* Retrieved on March 29, 2009, from www.telegraph.co.uk/news/newstopics/politics/lawandorder/5049757/Spotty-teens-detered-from-underpasses-by-acne-light.html.

Voight, J. (2007, October 8). "Social marketing do's and don'ts." *Adweek.* Retrieved on February 16, from the Lexis-Nexis academic database.

Von Blum, P. (1976). *The art of social conscience.* New York: Universe Books.

Walsh, D. (1995). *Selling out America's children: How America puts profits before values and what parents can do.* Minneapolis, MN: Fairview Press.

Watts, D. J. (2007). Challenging the influentials hypothesis. *WOMMA Word of Mouth Marketing Association, 3,* 201–211.

Watts, D.J., & Dodds, P.S. (2007). Influentials, networks, and public opinion formation. *Journal of Consumer Research, 34,* 441–458.

Wenburg, J. R., & Wilmot, W. W. (1973). *The personal communication process.* New York: John Wiley & Sons.

What Constitutes Persuasion?

What is persuasion? How broad or narrow is the concept? Is persuasion a subset of human communication in general, much like baseball is a subset of sports? Or is persuasion an element found in all human communication in the same way that coordination plays a role in every sport? Not surprisingly, different authors view the concept of persuasion in different ways and have, therefore, adopted different definitions of the term. In this chapter we explore some of the ways persuasion has been defined. We offer our own rather broad-based, far-reaching conceptualization of persuasion based on five limiting criteria. We also offer our own model of what persuasion is (Gass & Seiter, 1997, 2000, 2004) and examine two additional models (Chaiken, 1979, 1980, 1987; Eagly & Chaiken, 1993; Petty & Cacioppo, 1986a, 1986b) of how persuasion functions.

You may have encountered some unusual uses of the term *persuasion.* For example, we have a friend in the construction industry who refers to his sledgehammer as his "persuader." He tends to err on the side of cutting a 2 × 4 board too long, rather than too short, and then "persuading" it into place. As another example, you may recall seeing one of those old gangster movies in which a mob boss orders his henchman to take somebody out back "for a little gentle persuasion," meaning a beating. Although we don't normally associate persuasion with pounding lumber or pummeling people, even in ordinary usage the term does have a wide variety of meanings. Consider each of the hypothetical situations in Box 2.1, "What Constitutes Persuasion?" Which of these scenarios do *you* consider to be persuasion?

Adding to the difficulty of defining persuasion is the fact that persuasion also goes by a variety of other names. Some of its aliases include terms such as *advising, brainwashing, coercion, compliance gaining, convincing, education, indoctrination, influence, manipulation,* and *propaganda.* Of course, whether these terms are considered pseudonyms for persuasion, or simply related terms, depends on one's definition of persuasion.

Defining a concept is analogous to building a fence. A fence is designed to keep some things in and other things out. In the same way, a definition encompasses some elements or aspects of a concept within its domain while excluding others. Which "species" of human communication is to be found inside the "barnyard" of persuasion depends on the size and shape of the fence a particular author builds. Fortunately, the differences in various definitions can be clarified, if not resolved, by focusing on two key considerations. We turn to these next.

What Constitutes Persuasion?	BOX 2.1

1. Muffin notices a grubby-looking weirdo in one of the front seats of the bus she is boarding. She opts for a seat toward the rear of the bus. Did the man "persuade" her to sit elsewhere?

2. Benny Bigot is the principal speaker at a park rally to recruit more members to the American Nazi party. Many of the people who hear Benny are so turned off by his speech that they are more anti-Nazi than they were before they attended the rally. Did Benny "persuade" them?

3. During a dramatic pause in his lecture for his 3-hour night class, Professor Hohum hears a student's stomach growling. The professor then decides it would be a good time for the class to take a break. Did the student "persuade" Professor Hohum?

4. Babbs is standing at a street corner, watching passersby. The first three people she sees are wearing sweatshirts with political and/or social slogans emblazoned across the front. The fourth person to pass by is wearing a plain white T-shirt. Are the first three people "persuading" Babbs? Is the fourth?

5. Fifi is contemplating going on a major diet. She realizes she is overweight because she tips the scales at just under 250 pounds, and her obesity affects her self-esteem. However, she has read that obese people who lose lots of weight typically gain the weight back within a short period of time and that people are genetically predisposed to be a certain weight. She convinces herself that there is no point in dieting. Did Fifi "persuade" herself?

6. Bubba is at the supermarket, pondering which of two brands of beer to purchase, a cold-filtered brew or a fire-brewed brew. After studying both brands attentively, he opts for the cold-filtered variety. Unbeknownst to him, another shopper observed his deliberations. That shopper then walks over to the display and selects the same brand. Did "persuasion" take place?

7. Trudy is an impressionable freshperson who is in a jam. She has just realized a term paper is due in her philosophy class. Desperate, she asks Rex, who is the captain of the debate squad, if he will help her. Rex offers to give her an "A" paper he submitted when he had the same class two years prior *if* Trudy will sleep with him. Is Rex using "persuasion"?

PURE VERSUS BORDERLINE CASES OF PERSUASION

The first consideration is whether one is interested in pure persuasion, or borderline cases of persuasion. By *pure persuasion*, we mean clear-cut cases of persuasion, on which most people would agree. Everyone would agree that a presidential debate, or a television commercial, or an attorney's closing remarks to a jury are instances of persuasion. Such examples represent "paradigm cases" (O'Keefe, 1990; Simons, 1986) of persuasion because they are at the core of what we think of when we envision persuasion at work. Other instances, though, lie closer to the boundary or periphery of what we normally think of as persuasion. These instances we refer to as *borderline cases* of persuasion. Not everyone would agree that a derelict's mere appearance "persuades" passersby to keep their distance. Nor would everyone agree that involuntary reflexes such as burps, blinking, and pupil dilation constitute "persuasive" phenomena. These cases are less clear-cut, more "iffy." Much of the disparity in definitions is rooted in the fact that some authors are concerned with pure persuasion, whereas other authors are concerned with borderline cases as well. It isn't so much

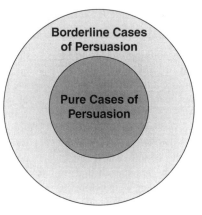

FIGURE 2.1   Preliminary Model of Persuasion.

a matter of being right or wrong as it is a matter of how wide a net each author wishes to cast. The preliminary model of the scope of persuasion (Figure 2.1) illustrates this distinction in approaches.[1] As the shading in the model suggests, the dividing line between pure and borderline persuasion is fuzzy, rather than distinct.

Although we don't think there is a single, correct definition of persuasion, we do think there are some things that a functional, contemporary definition of persuasion ought to do. A contemporary definition should take into account the rich complex of verbal, nonverbal, and contextual cues found in interpersonal encounters, which, as we noted in Chapter 1, is the arena in which most influence attempts occur. A contemporary definition also should acknowledge the many subtle, implicit cues that accompany face-to-face influence attempts. By implicit cues, we mean communication that occurs at a very low level of awareness, or even unconsciously. As an example, cultural factors might influence a person's choice of compliance-gaining strategies, without the person even realizing it (Wiseman et al., 1995). Such implicit communication is, in fact, quite common (Langer, 1978, 1989a, 1989b; Roloff, 1980) and an important ingredient in persuasion. The definition and model of persuasion that we offer later in this chapter take these features into account.

LIMITING CRITERIA FOR DEFINING PERSUASION

A second consideration in defining persuasion involves the limiting criteria that form the basis for a given definition. Different scholars apply different litmus tests when defining persuasion. Five basic criteria can be gleaned from the various definitions offered in the literature (Gass & Seiter, 2004). We examine each of these criteria in turn.

Intentionality

Is persuasion necessarily conscious or purposeful? Is there such a thing as "accidental" persuasion? Many who write about persuasion adopt a source-centered view by focusing on the sender's intent as a defining feature of persuasion. Bettinghaus and Cody (1994) adopt this view, stressing that "persuasion involves a conscious effort at influencing the thoughts or actions of a receiver" (p. 5). For some authors, intentionality is the litmus test that distinguishes persuasion from *social influence* (Gass & Seiter, 2000, 2004).

Certainly, pure persuasion would seem to be intentional. When we think of obvious cases of persuasion we tend to think of situations in which one person purposefully tries to influence another. But what about borderline cases of persuasion? We believe that many influence attempts take place without any conscious awareness on the part of the persuader.

As just one instance, parents quite commonly instill beliefs, impart values, and model behavior for their children, a phenomenon known as *social modeling* (Bandura, 1977). Yet they may not realize how much of what they say and do is absorbed by their young-uns. As any parent will attest, many of the lessons parents "teach" their children are completely unintended. Another form of unintentional influence involves *socialization* processes. From the moment children are born, they are socialized into their respective gender roles, cultural customs, religious practices, and socio-economic habits. Some socialization processes are mindful, but many are not. A second way in which an intent criterion is problematic is that people do not always know what specific outcome they are seeking. Face-to-face encounters, in particular, are laden with spontaneity. Social influence may arise in and through our interaction with others, rather than as a result of planning and forethought. Sometimes persuasion just happens.

A third problem with relying on an intent criterion involves situations in which there are unintended receivers. Imagine a scenario in which two people are discussing which bets to place on a horse race. One tells the other about an inside tip on a horse that's a "sure thing." A third party overhears the conversation and places a wager on the horse. In such situations, persuaders don't intend for third parties to be influenced, yet they often are. Two studies (Greenberg & Pyszczynski, 1985; Kirkland, Greenberg, & Pyszczynski, 1987) clearly demonstrate the operation of the *unintended receiver effect*. In these studies, the researchers created a situation in which third parties overheard an ethnic slur directed against an African American. The results of both studies revealed that the overheard ethnic slur led to lower evaluations by the third parties of the individual at whom the slur was directed. Notice that a reliance on an intent standard for defining persuasion tends to make senders less accountable for the consequences of their unintended communication. If a message has harmful effects, the source can disavow any responsibility by claiming "that's not what I intended."

A fourth limitation lies in the difficulty of ascertaining another's intent. There can be a difference between a persuader's *stated* intent versus his or her *actual* intent. Who makes the determination in such cases? The sender? The receiver? A third party? There are many vagaries involved in determining whose perception counts. An athlete whose conduct on or off the field is questioned may proclaim, "I'm not a role model," but fans and the media may reply, "Oh yes you are."

Finally, resolving the issue of intent is particularly difficult in interpersonal contexts, in which both parties may be simultaneously engaged in attempts at influence. When there are two interactants, whose intent counts? Intent-based definitions, we believe, are ill-suited to modern conceptualizations of human interaction as a two-way venture. The linear view of persuasion that such definitions imply, from sender to receiver, ignores opportunities for mutual influence.

Effects

The effects criterion poses the question: Has persuasion taken place if no one is actually persuaded? Some authors adopt a receiver-oriented definition of persuasion by restricting its use to situations in which receivers are somehow changed, altered, or affected. Daniel O'Keefe (1990) underscores this perspective when he writes:

> The notion of *success* is embedded in the concept of persuasion. Notice for instance, that it doesn't make sense to say, "I persuaded him, but failed." One can say, "I *tried* to persuade him, but failed," but to say simply, "I persuaded him" is to imply a successful attempt to influence. (p. 15)

The stronger version of this perspective views persuasion as successful if it achieves the specific outcome sought by the persuader. The weaker version of this perspective settles for outcomes falling short of what the persuader ideally had in mind. Although we recognize the attraction of this point of view, we believe there are problems with limiting the definition of persuasion in this way. We take the position that even if a person is communicating badly, he or she is *still* communicating. Similarly, we believe that a person can be engaged in persuasion even if it is *ineffective* persuasion. The same can be said for most other activities. A salesperson might fail to close a deal but would still be engaged in selling. A dancer might dance badly, stepping on his or her partner's toes, but would still be engaged in dancing. In short, a person can be engaged in an activity whether the person is doing it well or not.

An effects criterion emphasizes persuasion as a *product*. But such an orientation bears little fidelity to current conceptualizations of human communication as a *process*. If we think of persuasion only as an outcome or a thing, then an effects orientation makes perfectly good sense. We maintain that persuasion is better understood as an activity in which people engage. This is more than semantic quibbling. By approaching persuasion as a process, scholars and researchers are more likely to gain insights into how it functions, or what makes it tick, because they are focusing on *what's going on*, not simply on how things turn out.

A second weakness is the same as that already associated with an intent criterion: An effects criterion embodies a linear view of persuasion, from source to receiver. In face-to-face encounters, however, there isn't simply *a* source and *a* receiver. Both parties may be simultaneously engaged in persuasion.

A third problem with relying on an effects criterion is that it is often difficult, if not impossible, to measure persuasive effects. Rotzoll and Haefner (1996), for example, concluded that only 20 to 40 percent of advertising is effective. The other 60 to 80 percent is also persuasion; it's just ineffective persuasion. In fact, the ability to measure persuasive outcomes may hinge entirely on the sensitivity of one's measuring instruments (scales, surveys, sales figures, etc.). Furthermore, what constitutes the threshold for a successful versus unsuccessful attempt at persuasion? How much attitude or behavior change must take place to say persuasion has occurred? And what about the occasional odd circumstance in which persuasion "boomerangs"—that is, a persuader achieves an effect that is *contrary* to his or her intended purpose? Such questions, we believe, point out the many vagaries inherent in relying on an effects criterion.

We do agree that, as with an intent criterion, pure cases of persuasion can usually be evaluated by their overall effectiveness. Even then, persuasion is rarely an all or nothing venture. If one also wishes to focus on borderline cases of persuasion, one must accept the fact that partial persuasion is more the rule than the exception. Notice, too, that there is some tension between relying on intent and effects as limiting criteria: What is achieved isn't always what is intended, and what is intended isn't always what is achieved. We happen to think some of the most interesting persuasive campaigns are those that are unsuccessful, or only partially successful, or that in fact, achieve the opposite of the effect being sought.

Free Will and Conscious Awareness

Many authors endorse the view that there is a distinction between persuasion and coercion. This view is also receiver based, but it focuses on whether a person is aware that she or he is being persuaded and how much freedom the person has to accept or reject the message. Persuasion, these authors suggest, is noncoercive. As Herbert Simons (1986) puts it, "persuasion is a form of influence that predisposes, but does not impose" (p. 22). Richard Perloff (1993) also makes this point when he states that a "defining characteristic of persuasion is free choice. At some level the individual must be capable of accepting or rejecting the position that has been urged of him or her" (p. 16).

It naturally follows that if a person is unaware that an influence attempt is taking place, she or he can't consciously resist it. Thus, mindfulness is a prerequisite for free choice. Nevertheless, we believe persuasion can and does occur without the conscious awareness of receivers. In fact, many influence attempts succeed precisely because they operate at a low level of awareness. Clandestine persuasion may be unethical, but it does exist, and it can be effective. For example, consumers generally may be aware that product planting (placing products in movies and TV shows) is common, but they may not know how prevalent the practice is, let alone recognize each and every instance of product planting that occurs. Persuasion that relies on social networking, such word of mouth (WOM), is designed to seem spontaneous rather than planned. A person might receive a link to a funny Website from a friend, not realizing that the site was developed as a marketing tool by a commercial entity.

Coercive strategies aren't necessarily limited to negative sanctions. Coercion also can take place in the form of rewards, incentives, inducements, flattery, ingratiation, or bribery. Seen in this way, persuasion and coercion aren't so much polar opposites as they are close relatives. A message or message strategy can easily cross the line from one to the other. Moreover, many communication encounters contain both voluntary and involuntary elements. A simple request by a superior to a subordinate, "Boswell, can you give me a lift to pick up my car?" may carry with it an implicit threat for noncompliance. A parent may give a child three good reasons to eat broccoli but may issue a negative sanction as well, "or no dessert for you, young lady."

"I insist."

"Persuasion" and "coercion" often coexist side by side.

In fact, we would suggest that most influence attempts we encounter in daily life include both persuasive and coercive elements. Rarely in life is one free to make a completely unfettered choice. There are almost always strings attached. This is particularly true of face-to-face encounters. If a friend asks to borrow 20 bucks, we can say "no," but there may be relational consequences for declining.

Rarely, too, are influence attempts completely coercive. For example, holding a gun to another person's head would seem to be an obvious example of coercion. We readily admit that this situation is *primarily* coercive. But what if the victim doesn't believe the gun is loaded? Or what if the victim thinks the threatener is bluffing? To be successful, a threat—even a threat of violence—must be perceived as credible. Thus, even in what might seem like a clear-cut case of coercion there are persuasive elements at work. And conversely, even in what appear to be cut-and-dried cases of persuasion, there may be coercive features operating. In our view, the issue isn't so much *whether* a situation is persuasive or coercive as *how* persuasive or coercive the situation is.

Symbolic Action

A number of authors maintain that persuasion begins and ends with symbolic expression, which includes language as well as other meaning-laden acts, such as civil disobedience and protest marches. This approach focuses on the means, or channel, of persuasion as a limiting criterion. Gerald Miller (1980) evinces this view, writing, "persuasion relies upon symbolic transactions . . . the scholarly endeavors of persuasion researchers—and for that matter, the ordinary language usages of the term 'persuasion'—have consistently centered on the manipulation of symbols" (pp. 14–15).

Authors who limit the scope of persuasion to symbolic action fear that without such a limitation all human behavior could be construed as persuasion. Their point is well taken. However, restricting the medium for persuasion to words or symbols leads to a rather disjointed view of persuasion. We believe that a definition that limits persuasion to words and clearly codified symbols leaves out too much. Most magazine ads emphasize pictures rather than words. In fact, one study suggests that the text of a typical ad is read by fewer than 10 percent of the readers (Starch, cited in Dupont, 1999). The same is true of television commercials. It seems arbitrary to limit persuasion to the words contained in an ad or a commercial, without considering the role of the images as well. We think that the *whole* ad or the *whole* commercial persuades.

We also believe that some of the most intriguing aspects of persuasion can be found in nonverbal behavior, which lies on the periphery of symbolic action. For example, research on the physiological correlates of deception demonstrates that a variety of involuntary nonverbal cues (such as blinking, smiling, and pupil dilation) are positive indicators of lying (DePaulo, Stone, & Lassiter, 1985). We focus on deception as a form of persuasion in Chapter 12. Research on source credibility reveals that physical attributes, such as height or attractiveness, influence judgments of source credibility (Chaiken, 1979). We examine such factors in Chapter 4. We see little justification for excluding such forms of influence from beneath the umbrella of persuasion. We also can think of situations in which pure behavior, for example, nonsymbolic actions, are nevertheless persuasive. When a basketball player makes a head fake to fool a defender, we would maintain that the player is *persuading* the defender to go the wrong way. The fake is all behavior, but the player has to *sell* the fake to get the defender to "bite" on it.

We believe that restricting the study of persuasion exclusively to symbolic expression leads to a fragmented understanding of the subject. Persuasion involves more than language usage or symbol usage. A whole host of factors are at work. Interestingly, many authors who profess an adherence to symbolic action nevertheless treat a variety of nonsymbolic aspects of behavior, such as those just mentioned, in their texts.

Interpersonal versus Intrapersonal

How many actors are required for persuasion to take place? A last limiting criterion that deserves mention is whether persuasion can involve only one person or whether persuasion requires the participation of two or more distinct persons. Some scholars adopt the view that engaging in persuasion is like dancing the tango; it takes two (Bettinghaus & Cody, 1994; Johnston, 1994; Perloff, 1993). We agree in the case of the tango, but not in the case of persuasion. In fact, we maintain that attempts at self-persuasion are quite common. A person who is on a diet might stick a picture of a lean, "chiseled" model on the refrigerator door to reinforce his or her motivation to lose weight. A person might search for a rationalization to do something he or she wants, such as blowing the rent money on front-row concert tickets. In such cases, people engage in self-persuasion by talking themselves into whatever they wish to do.

We are sympathetic to the "two or more" perspective but suggest that, once again, the issue comes down to whether one wishes to focus exclusively on pure cases of persuasion or borderline cases as well. We heartily agree that when we think of pure cases of persuasion, we conjure up an image of one person persuading another. When we include borderline cases, we imagine instances in which individuals sometimes try to convince themselves.

A MODEL OF THE SCOPE OF PERSUASION

In light of the five limiting criteria just discussed, we can now offer an enhanced model (see Figure 2.2) that encompasses both pure and borderline cases of persuasion (Gass & Seiter, 1997, 2000, 2004). Note that, as with the preliminary model, the inner circle represents pure persuasion—that is, what we think of as the core of persuasion. The outer circle represents borderline persuasion. Superimposed on top of these two circles are five wedges, each representing one of the five limiting criteria previously discussed. The inner portion of each wedge represents the pure case for that criterion. The outer portion represents the borderline case. Once again, the shading between the inner and outer circles reflects the fuzzy dividing line that exists between pure and borderline persuasion.

Based on this enhanced model, you can appreciate the fact that different definitions feature different wedges of the inner and outer circles. Source-oriented definitions restrict persuasion to the inner circle of the "intentional-unintentional" wedge. Receiver-based definitions limit persuasion to the inner circle of the "effects-no effects" wedge. Other receiver-based definitions favor the inner circle with respect to the "free choice-coercion" criterion, and so on.

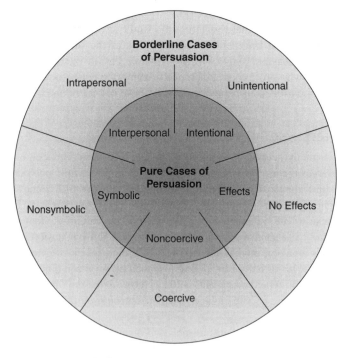

FIGURE 2.2   Enhanced Model of Persuasion.

As you can also see from the enhanced model, some definitions concern themselves with several wedges at the same time, whereas other definitions are based on a single limiting criterion. It's worth noting that all definitions of persuasion—including our own, which we present shortly—are linguistic constructs. They exist in the world of words. Whether a given situation involves persuasion is not a matter of fact, but of judgment.

Our own preference is for an expanded view of persuasion that includes borderline cases as well as pure persuasion. We tend to side with the view that persuasion is sometimes unintentional; that it sometimes has no discernable effects; that people aren't always aware of when it is occurring; that it often includes at least some coercive features; that it needn't be conveyed exclusively via symbols; and that humans do, on occasion, engage in self-persuasion. Many of the topics discussed in later chapters reside in the outer ring of our model. As we've already indicated, we believe that some of the most intriguing aspects of persuasion can be found there. We firmly believe we must look at both the inner and outer rings to fully understand the phenomenon of persuasion.

THE CONTEXT FOR PERSUASION

Consistent with current conceptualizations of persuasion, we view social influence as a process. Thus far, however, our model has remained relatively static. A final feature must be incorporated into our model to reflect the nature of persuasion as a process. That feature is the *context* for persuasion. The context in which persuasion occurs, for example, within a small group, via mass media, in an organizational setting, and so forth, is crucial because it is the context that determines the nature of the communication process. In a face-to-face setting, for example, influence is a mutual, two-way process. In an advertising setting, influence tends to be more linear, from the advertiser to the consumer (there may be feedback from consumers, but it is delayed). Each context imposes its own unique set of constraints on the options available to persuaders.

By context, we don't simply mean the number of communicators present, although that is certainly one key factor. The context for communication also includes how synchronous or asynchronous communication is. Synchronous communication refers to the simultaneous sending and receiving of messages. Such is the case in face-to-face interaction. Asynchronous communication refers to a back-and-forth process that involves some delay, such as email or texting.

Another contextual factor is the ratio of verbal to nonverbal cues that are present. A print ad consisting entirely of text would rely exclusively on verbal cues (words) to persuade. A poster featuring only an image would rely exclusively on nonverbal cues to persuade. Most persuasive messages involve both verbal and nonverbal cues. The ratio of verbal to nonverbal cues available in any persuasive situation imposes particular constraints on the persuasion process.

An additional contextual factor is the nature and type of media used in the persuasion process. Television commercials, radio ads, magazine ads, and telemarketing are traditional media for persuasion. New media include MySpace, Facebook, the Blogosphere, YouTube, and Twitter, among many others. Face-to-face encounters, such as door-to-door sales and panhandling, are unmediated. As with the other contextual factors, each medium imposes its own constraints on the persuasion process.

Yet another contextual factor involves the goals of the participants. Often, but not always, participants enter into communication encounters with specific objectives in mind (Dillard, 1990, 1993, 2004; Dillard, Segrin, & Harden, 1989). Canary and Cody (1994) break down these goals into three types—*self-presentational goals, relational goals,* and *instrumental goals.* Self-presentational goals have to do with identity management. People want to project a favorable image of themselves to others. Relational goals have to do with what people want out of their relationships—how to develop them, improve them, change them, and so forth. Instrumental goals involve attempts at compliance gaining. People's goals may be thwarted or may change during a persuasive encounter.

A final contextual variable involves sociocultural factors that affect the persuasion process. People from different cultures or subcultures may persuade in different ways (Ma & Chuang, 2001). They may respond to persuasive messages differently as well. For example, research suggests that some cultures prefer more indirect approaches to compliance gaining (hinting, guilt, reliance on group norms), whereas other cultures prefer more direct approaches to compliance gaining (direct requests, demanding) (Wiseman et al., 1995). Different cultural traditions can dramatically affect what is expected or accepted in the way of influence attempts.

Note that all of these contextual factors are operating at once in a given persuasive situation. Each of the contextual factors constrains the process of persuasion in one way or another. The context involves the totality of the relationships among all these factors. The final version of our model, depicted in Figure 2.3, illustrates how persuasion is shaped by context (Gass & Seiter, 1997, 2000). Context, then, is what determines the nature of the process involved in a given persuasive situation.

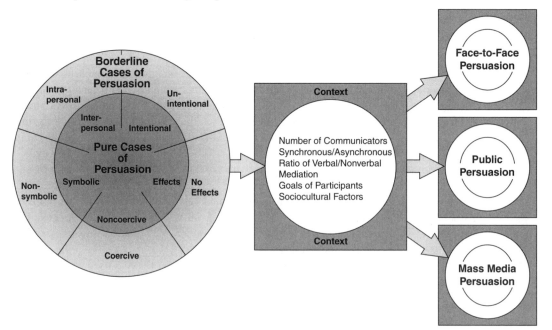

FIGURE 2.3   Completed Model of Persuasion. This figure illustrates three of many possible persuasive situations.

A WORKING DEFINITION OF PERSUASION

At last we arrive at our own definition of persuasion. Our view is that *persuasion involves one or more persons who are engaged in the activity of creating, reinforcing, modifying, or extinguishing beliefs, attitudes, intentions, motivations, and/or behaviors within the constraints of a given communication context.* The advantage of our definition is that it encompasses the full scope of persuasion, both pure *and* borderline cases. Our definition also emphasizes persuasion as an activity or a process; it is something people do. Our definition encompasses the notion that in face-to-face encounters persuasion is a two-way street. Each party has an opportunity to influence the other. This explains our reluctance to label only one party the sender, as an intent criterion seems to suggest, or only one party as the receiver, as an effects criterion tends to imply. With respect to our definition, we also wish to stress that persuasion doesn't involve simply changing one's own or another's mind, though that is the most typical connotation (Miller, 1980). Persuasion also can involve creating new beliefs or attitudes, where none existed before. It also can involve reinforcing, strengthening, or solidifying attitudes already held by receivers. And persuasion also can involve attempts to extinguish or eliminate beliefs and attitudes. The latter approach is exemplified by Alcoholics Anonymous' position that alcoholics must abandon the belief that other people are responsible, or circumstances are to blame, for their dependency.

If our definition seems expansive, it is because we believe the topic of persuasion itself is rather far-ranging. We wish to examine not only the core of persuasion in this text but its periphery as well. The majority of our examples focus on pure cases of persuasion. However, from time to time we dabble on the fuzzy outer edges. We find some of the borderline cases of persuasion quite interesting, and we believe you will too.

SO WHAT ISN'T PERSUASION?

Given the breadth of our definition, you're probably wondering, "What *isn't* persuasion?" We address this concern now. Our position is that the ingredients for persuasion can be found in most, if not all, communication transactions. The degree to which these persuasive ingredients are present, not their mere presence or absence, is what matters. We think most human communication involves at least the *potential* to influence. Of course, one may choose not to focus on the persuasive, or potentially persuasive, elements in a communication situation. One can concentrate on some other aspect of communication instead. The potential for persuasion remains nonetheless. What matters, then, is how persuasive a given communication situation is, not whether a communication situation is persuasive.

Many other features of communication besides persuasion can command one's attention. For example, one can examine the role of self-disclosure and relationship satisfaction without discussing persuasion. One can study effective listening skills, whether the message listened to is persuasive or not. One can study nonverbal cues and liking without focusing on persuasion. One can look at how people try to save face during conflicts without involving persuasion. Persuasive elements needn't comprise the focus of attention even if they are present. One can focus on other relevant features of human communication to the exclusion of persuasive processes.

Although we believe that nearly all human communication is potentially persuasive, we don't believe the same about all human behavior. The mere act of breathing, in and of itself, doesn't seem like persuasion to us—although under the right circumstances it could be (such as pretending to be out of breath). Tripping over a rock, by itself, doesn't seem like a persuasive act to us, although, again, under certain conditions it could be (such as feigning clumsiness). We don't think torture is a form of persuasion, although former vice president Dick Cheney might disagree. A good deal of human behavior, then, we don't consider to be persuasion, unless and until some additional conditions are met. We don't think everything humans do is persuasive.

There are also some forms of communication that we've excluded from consideration in this text for purely practical reasons. For example, we don't address the possibility of human-to-animal persuasion, or vice versa, though such a case probably could be made. We don't examine the power of hypnotic suggestion as a form of influence. We don't examine attempts to persuade via paranormal or psychic activity either. We've heard that some people with cancerous tumors try to "talk to" their cancer and "persuade" it to go away. We don't deal with that topic here, except insofar as it may constitute a form of self-persuasion. We don't consider terrorism to be a form of persuasion, though a case could be made that it is an intentional effort to change attitudes. We also don't address a host of other intriguing topics, such as the role of genetics and neuropsychology in persuasion. We simply don't have the space to devote to those topics here. Thus, as big as the fence that we've built is, there is a lot of human communication we've left out.

DUAL PROCESSES OF PERSUASION

Now that we've clarified what we think persuasion is, we want to take a look at how it functions. To this end, we present a brief explanation of two prevailing models of persuasion. Both are known as *dual process* models (Chaiken & Trope, 1999) because they postulate that persuasion operates via two basic paths. The two models share many similarities and, in our opinion, both do an excellent job of explaining how persuasive messages are perceived and processed.

The Elaboration Likelihood Model of Persuasion

Richard Petty and John Cacioppo's (1986a, 1986b) *elaboration likelihood model of persuasion (ELM)*, is one of the most widely cited models in the persuasion literature.[2] Their model proposes two basic routes to persuasion that operate in tandem. The first of these they call the *central route*. The central route, or *central processing*, as they sometimes refer to it, involves *cognitive elaboration*. That means thinking about the content of a message, reflecting on the ideas and information contained in it, and scrutinizing the evidence and reasoning presented. The second route to persuasion is known as the *peripheral route*. The peripheral route, or *peripheral processing*, as it is sometimes called, involves focusing on cues that aren't directly related to the substance of a message. For example, focusing on a source's physical attractiveness, or the sheer quantity of arguments presented, or a catchy jingle as a basis for decision making would entail peripheral processing. According to the ELM, the two routes represent the ends, or anchor points, of an elaboration continuum (Petty, Rucker, Bizer, & Cacioppo, 2004). At one end of the continuum, a person engages in no or low elaboration. At the other end, a person engages in high elaboration.

To illustrate the two basic routes, imagine that Rex and Trudy are on a date at a restaurant. Trudy is very health conscious, so she studies the menu carefully. She looks to see whether certain dishes are fatty or high in calories. When the food server arrives to take their order, she asks, "What kind of oil is used to prepare the pasta?" She might sound picky, but Trudy is engaging in central processing. She is actively thinking about what the menu says. Rex, however, is smitten with Trudy's good looks. He hardly looks at the menu, and when the food server asks for his order, he says, "I'll have what she's having." Rex is engaging in peripheral processing. He's basing his decision on cues that are unrelated to the items on the menu.

Petty and Cacioppo acknowledge the possibility of *parallel processing*—that is, using both routes at once (Petty, Kasmer, Haugtvedt, & Cacioppo, 2004). However, they suggest that there is usually a trade-off between central and peripheral processing, such that a person tends to favor one route over the other. Whether a person emphasizes the central or the peripheral route hinges on two basic factors. The first of these is the individual's *motivation* to engage in central processing. Because central processing requires more mental effort, a person with greater motivation is more likely to rely on central processing. Typically, this means the person has *high involvement* with the topic or issue. That is, the topic or issue matters to him or her or affects him or her personally. If a person has *low involvement* with a topic or issue, he or she will be less inclined to engage in central processing, and more likely to resort to peripheral processing.

The second factor that determines whether a person will rely on central or peripheral processing is his or her *ability* to process information. A person must not only be willing but also able to engage in central processing. Some people are more adept at grasping ideas, understanding concepts, and making sense of things. Some people also have more knowledge of or expertise in certain topics or issues than others. Thus, receivers are more likely to process a persuasive message via the central route if they have the motivation and ability to do so. If they lack the motivation or the ability, they will tend to rely on peripheral processing instead.

Aside from ability and motivation, a variety of other factors can tilt the balance in favor of central or peripheral processing. These include distractions, such as background noise, time constraints, a person's mood, or a personality trait called *need for cognition.* Need for cognition has to do with how much a person enjoys thinking about things. We discuss this trait in more detail in Chapter 5.

The type of processing affects the persistence of persuasion. Researchers have found that persuasion via the central route tends to be more long-lasting, whereas persuasion via the peripheral route tends to be more short-lived (Petty, Haugtvedt, & Smith, 1995). This seems sensible: When we think about ideas, they are more likely to be absorbed. Similarly, persuasion that takes place via central processing also tends to be more resistant to counterinfluence attempts than persuasion via peripheral processing. This also makes sense: If you've thought through your position, you're less likely to "waffle." Researchers have also found that if receivers disagree with the content of a message, using central processing causes them to generate more counterarguments. That is, they mentally rehearse their

Peripheral processing in action.

objections to the message. If receivers disagree with a message and rely on peripheral processing, however, they will generate fewer counterarguments or other unfavorable thoughts about the message. A useful generalization when persuading, then, is that to make persuasion last, you've got to make people think.

The Heuristic Systematic Model of Persuasion

Another model of persuasion that bears many similarities to the ELM is Shelley Chaiken and Alice Eagly's *heuristic systematic model*, or *HSM* (Chaiken, 1980, 1987; Chaiken, Liberman, & Eagly, 1989; Chaiken & Trope, 1999; Eagly & Chaiken, 1993). As with the ELM, the HSM operates on the assumption that individuals rely on two different modes of information processing. One mode, called *systematic processing*, is more thoughtful and deliberate. Systematic processing in the HSM is roughly analogous to central processing in the ELM. The other mode, called *heuristic processing*, relies on mental shortcuts. Heuristic processing is based on the application of *decision rules* or *heuristic cues* that help simplify the thought process. An example of a decision rule would be buying a TV based on its brand name ("Sony televisions are reliable"). An example of a heuristic cue would be choosing one wine over another because the bottle is prettier. Heuristic processing in the HSM is roughly equivalent to peripheral processing in the ELM.

Chaiken and Eagly's model also maintains that *simultaneous processing* of messages is commonplace. That is, messages travel the heuristic and systematic routes concurrently. As with the ELM, the HSM states that *motivation* and *ability* are two primary determinants of the extent to which heuristic or systematic processing will be used. A problem for both models is that, to date, there is limited empirical evidence of simultaneous processing, at least in laboratory studies of persuasion (Booth-Butterfield et al., 1994; Chaiken et al., 1989).

Another feature of the HSM is the *sufficiency principle*, which states that people strive to know as much as they need to when making a decision but no more or less. On the one hand, people want to devote the time and attention to issues that they deserve. On the other hand, people can't afford to spend all their time and mental energy worrying about every little thing. Therefore, people balance their heuristic and systematic processing to create the best "fit" for the issue at hand.

By way of illustration, suppose Irwin is thinking of buying a digital camera. If Irwin didn't know much about such devices, he could take one of two approaches. He could rely on systematic processing by reading up on digital cameras in electronics magazines. He would likely adopt this route if he thought he really needed a digital camera (motivation) and he lacked the necessary knowledge about them (sufficiency principle). But he would also need to have time to gather information and be able to understand it (ability). Alternatively, he could opt for heuristic processing. He could base his decision on a friend's advice using a simple decision rule ("Lance knows his cameras"). Or he could base his decision on a heuristic cue, such as the brand ("Canon is the best brand"). He would be more likely to resort to heuristic processing if he didn't really need a digital camera—it was only an electronic toy (low motivation)—or if he didn't think he could make sense of the information about cameras anyway (lack of ability).

Both the ELM and HSM are useful for explaining and predicting people's reactions to persuasive messages. Literally dozens of studies devoted to testing the explanatory and predictive power of these two models have been conducted. These studies have generally upheld the models' utility. Although both models have their critics (see Kruglanski & Thompson, 1999a, 1999b; Mongeau & Stiff, 1993; Stiff & Boster, 1987), it is safe to say that they enjoy considerable support in the literature. We develop and amplify principles related to the ELM and HSM throughout this text. Because we refer to both models repeatedly, it would be worth your while to familiarize yourself with their basic concepts for later reference.

The Unimodel of Persuasion

An alternative to dual process models of persuasion is the *unimodel* developed by Arie Kruglanski and Erik Thompson (Kruglanski & Thompson, 1999a, 1999b). Kruglanski and Thompson posit that, rather than two distinct modes of information processing, there is a single route to persuasion. Central processing isn't qualitatively different from peripheral processing, according to the *unimodel*; there is simply more or less of it. Kruglankski maintains that the alleged differences in processing based on the ELM and HSM merely reflect differences in the messages themselves. Longer, more complex messages require more thought, while shorter, simpler messages require less thought (Erb, Pierro, Mannetti,

Spiegel, Kruglanski, 2007; Kruglanski et al., 2006; Pierro, Mannetti, Erb, Spiegel, & Kruglanski, 2005).

Despite the simplicity of the *unimodel*, we believe there are cases in which persuasive messages are processed in fundamentally different ways (Petty, Wheeler, & Bizer, 1999). For example, a consumer who responded to a fear appeal emotionally or reflexively would be quite different from a consumer who responded to a fear appeal rationally or reflectively. Even so, the *unimodel* raises important questions about whether and how dual processing occurs. Some scholars have questioned whether dual-processing has ever been empirically documented (Booth-Butterfield et al., 1994).

SUMMARY

We began this chapter by presenting a preliminary model of persuasion that distinguishes pure from borderline cases of persuasion. We identified five limiting criteria for defining persuasion that are reflected in our own model of persuasion. We followed our model with our own broad-based, far-reaching definition of persuasion. Finally, we provided a brief explanation of Petty and Cacioppo's *elaboration likelihood model* (ELM) of persuasion and Chaiken and Eagly's *heuristic systematic model* (HSM) of persuasion. An alternative to dual-process models, the *unimodel*, also was presented.

ENDNOTES

1. More than two decades ago, Simons (1986, p. 116) introduced a model of persuasion having concentric circles, representing pure persuasion, peripheral persuasion, and non-persuasion. Our preliminary model (Figure 2.1) draws on his work.

2. Not all scholars are enamored with Petty and Cacioppo's model. Among others, Mongeau and Stiff (1993) and Stiff and Boster (1987) have criticized the ELM for its theoretical and empirical limitations. Petty, Wegener, Fabrigar, Priester, and Cacioppo (1993) and Petty, Kasmer, Haugtvedt, and Cacioppo (2004) have responded to many of the criticisms directed against their model.

REFERENCES

Bandura, A. (1977). *Social learning theory.* Englewood Cliffs, NJ: Prentice Hall.

Bettinghaus, E. P., & Cody, M. J. (1994). *Persuasive communication* (6th ed.). Forth Worth, TX: Harcourt Brace.

Booth-Butterfield, S., Cooke, P., Andrighetti, A., Casteel, B., Lang, T., Pearson, D., & Rodriguez, B. (1994). Simultaneous versus exclusive processing of persuasive arguments and cues. *Communication Quarterly, 42,* 21–35.

Canary, D. J., & Cody, M. J. (1994). *Interpersonal communication: A goals–based approach.* New York: St. Martin's Press.

Chaiken, S. (1979). Communicator physical attractiveness and persuasion. *Journal of Personality and Social Psychology, 37,* 1387–1397.

Chaiken, S. (1980). Heuristic versus systematic information processing and the use of source versus message cues in persuasion. *Journal of Personality and Social Psychology, 39,* 752–766.

Chaiken, S. (1987). The heuristic model of persuasion. In M. P. Zanna, J. M. Olson, & C. P. Herman (Eds.), *Social influence: The Ontario Symposium* (Vol. 5, pp. 3–39). Hillsdale, NJ: Erlbaum.

Chaiken, S., Liberman, A., & Eagly, A. H. (1989). Heuristic and systematic information processing within and beyond the persuasion context. In J. S. Uleman & J. A. Bargh (Eds.), *Unintended thought* (pp. 212–252). New York: Guilford Press.

Chaiken, S., & Trope, Y. (Eds.). (1999). *Dual-process theories in social psychology*. New York: Guilford Press.

DePaulo, B. M., Stone, J. I., & Lassiter. G. D. (1985). Deceiving and detecting deceit. In B. R. Schlenker (Ed.), *The self and social life* (pp. 323–370). New York: McGraw-Hill.

Dillard, J. P. (1990). Primary and secondary goals in interpersonal influence. In M. J. Cody & M. L. McLaughlin (Eds.), *Psychology of tactical communication* (pp. 70–90). Clavendon, U.K.: Multilingual Matters.

Dillard, J. P. (1993). A goal-driven model of interpersonal influence. In J. P. Dillard (Ed.), *Seeking compliance: The production of interpersonal influence messages* (pp. 41–56). Scottsdale, AZ: Gorsuch, Scarisbrick.

Dillard, J. P. (2004). The goals-plans-action model of interpersonal influence. In J. S. Seiter & R. H. Gass (Eds.), *Perspectives on persuasion, social influence, and compliance gaining* (pp. 185–206). Boston: Allyn & Bacon.

Dillard, J. P., Segrin, C., & Harden, J. M. (1989). Primary and secondary goals in the interpersonal influence process. *Communication Monographs, 56,* 19–39.

Dupont, L. (1999). *Images that sell: 500 ways to create great ads*. Sainte-Foy, Quebec, Canada: White Rock Publishing.

Eagly, A. H., & Chaiken, S. (1993). *The psychology of attitudes*. New York: Harcourt, Brace, Jovanovich.

Erb, H. P., Pierro, A., Mannetti, L., Spiegel, S., & Kruglanski, A. W. (2007). Biased processing of persuasive evidence: On the functional equivalence of cues and message arguments. *European Journal of Social Psychology, 37,* 1057–1075.

Gass, R. H., & Seiter, J. S. (1997, November). On defining persuasion: Toward a contemporary perspective. Paper presented at the annual convention of the Western Communication Association, Monterey, CA.

Gass, R. H., & Seiter, J. S. (2000, November). *Embracing divergence: A reexamination of traditional and nontraditional conceptualizations of persuasion*. Paper presented at the annual convention of the National Communication Association, Seattle, WA.

Gass, R. H., & Seiter, J. S. (2004). Embracing divergence: A definitional analysis of pure and borderline cases of persuasion. In J. S. Seiter & R. H. Gass (Eds.), *Perspectives on persuasion, social influence, and compliance gaining* (pp. 13–29). Boston: Allyn & Bacon.

Greenberg, J., & Pyszczynski, T. (1985). The effect of an overheard ethnic slur on evaluations of the target: How to spread a social disease. *Journal of Experimental Social Psychology, 21,* 61–72.

Johnston, D. D. (1994). *The art and science of persuasion*. Madison, WI: William C. Brown.

Kirkland, S. L., Greenberg, J., & Pyszczynski, T. (1987). Further evidence of the deleterious effects of overheard derogatory ethnic labels: Derogation beyond the target. *Personality and Social Psychology Bulletin, 13*(2), 216–227.

Kruglanski, A. W., Chen, X., Pierro, A., Manneti, L., Erb, H.-P., & Spiegel, S. (2006). Persuasion according to the Unimodel: Implications for cancer communication. *Journal of Communication, 56,* S105–S122.

Kruglanski, A. W., & Thompson, E. P. (1999a). Persuasion by a single route: A view from the Unimodel. *Psychological Inquiry, 10,* 83–109.

Kruglanski, A. W., & Thompson, E. P. (1999b). The illusory second mode or, the cue is the message. *Psychological Inquiry, 10*(2), 182–193.

Langer, E. J. (1978). Rethinking the role of thought in social interaction. In J. H. Harvey, W. J. Ickes, & R. F. Kidd (Eds.), *New directions in attribution research* (Vol. 2, pp. 35–58). New York: John Wiley & Sons.

Langer, E. J. (1989a). *Mindfulness*. Reading, MA: Addison-Wesley.

Langer, E. J. (1989b). Minding matters. In L. Berkowitz (Ed.), *Advances in experimental social psychology* (Vol. 22, pp. 137–173). New York: Addison-Wesley.

Ma, R., & Chuang, R. (2001). Persuasion strategies of Chinese college students in interpersonal contexts. *Southern Communication Journal, 66*(4), 267–278.

Miller, G. R. (1980). On being persuaded: Some basic distinctions. In M. E. Roloff & G. R. Miller (Eds.), *Persuasion: New directions in theory and research* (pp. 11–28). Beverly Hills, CA: Sage.

Mongeau, P. A., & Stiff, J. B. (1993). Specifying causal relationships in the Elaboration Likelihood Model. *Communication Theory, 3,* 65–72.

O'Keefe, D. (1990). *Persuasion: Theory and research*. Newbury Park, CA: Sage.

Perloff, R. M. (1993). *The dynamics of persuasion*. Hillsdale, NJ: Erlbaum.

Petty, R. E., Kasmer, J. E., Haugtvedt, C. P., & Cacioppo, J. T. (2004). Source and message factors in persuasion: A reply to Stiff's critique of the Elaboration Likelihood Model. *Communication Monographs, 54,* 233–249.

Petty, R. E., & Cacioppo, J. T. (1986a). The Elaboration Likelihood Model of persuasion. In L. Berkowitz (Ed.), *Advances in experimental social psychology* (Vol. 19, pp. 123–205). New York: Academic Press.

Petty, R. E., & Cacioppo, J. T. (1986b). *Communication and persuasion: Central and peripheral routes to attitude change.* New York: Springer-Verlag.

Petty, R. E., Haugtvedt, C., & Smith, S. M. (1995). Elaboration as a determinant of attitude strength: Creating attitudes that are persistent, resistant, and predictive of behavior. In R. E. Petty & J. Krosnick (Eds.), *Attitude strength: Antecedents and consequences* (pp. 93–130). Mahwah, NJ: Erlbaum.

Petty, R. E., Rucker, D., Bizer, G., & Cacioppo, J. T. (2004). The Elaboration Likelihood Model of persuasion. In J. S. Seiter & R. H. Gass (Eds.), *Readings in persuasion, social influence, and compliance gaining* (pp. 65–89). Boston: Allyn & Bacon.

Petty, R. E., Wegener, D. T., Fabrigar, L. R., Priester, J. R., & Cacioppo, J. T. (1993). Conceptual and methodological issues in the Elaboration Likelihood Model of persuasion: A reply to the Michigan State critics. *Communication Theory, 3*(4), 336–362.

Petty, R. E., Wheeler, S. C., & Bizer, G. Y. (1999). Is there one persuasion process or more? Lumping versus splitting in attitude change theories. *Psychological Inquiry, 10,* 156–163.

Pierro, A., Mannetti, L., Erb, H. P., Spiegel, S., & Kruglanski, A. W. (2005). Informational length and order of presentation as determinants of persuasion. *Journal of Experimental Social Psychology, 41,* 458–469.

Roloff, M. E. (1980). Self-awareness and the persuasion process: Do we really *know* what we're doing? In M. E. Roloff & G. R. Miller (Eds.), *Persuasion: New directions in theory and research* (pp. 29–66). Beverly Hills, CA: Sage.

Rotzoll K. B., & Haefner, J. E., with Hall, S. R. (1996). *Advertising in contemporary society: Perspectives toward understanding.* Urbana, IL: University of Illinois Press.

Simons, H. W. (1986). *Persuasion: Understanding, practice, and analysis* (2nd ed.). New York: McGraw-Hill.

Stiff, J. B., & Boster, F. J. (1987). Cognitive processing: Additional thoughts and a reply to Petty, Kasmer, Haugtvedt, and Cacioppo. *Communication Monographs, 54,* 250–256.

Wiseman, R. L., Sanders, J. A., Congalton, K. J., Gass, R. H., Sueda, K., & Ruiqing, D. (1995). A cross-cultural analysis of compliance-gaining: China, Japan, and the United States. *Intercultural Communication Studies, 5*(1), 1–17.

CHAPTER 3

Attitudes and Consistency

The word *attitude* doesn't mean the same thing to social scientists that it does to rappers. When social scientists say someone "has an attitude," they don't mean the person is being defensive or petulant. Social scientists have long been fascinated with the study of attitudes. They continue to occupy the center stage of persuasion research even today. The recent emphasis on compliance gaining, with its focus on behavioral conformity, has meant that attitudes have had to share the limelight with behavioral measures of persuasion's effectiveness. Nevertheless, attitudes remain a vital element in understanding how persuasion works.

Just why are attitudes so important to understanding persuasion? The reason is that attitudes help to predict, explain, and modify behavior. Just as a baker uses yeast as a catalyst in baking bread, persuaders rely on attitudes as a means of bringing about changes in receivers. An understanding of attitudes is, therefore, a key ingredient in any recipe for persuasion. For this reason, this chapter is devoted to a discussion of attitudes. We begin by considering what an attitude is.

WHAT IS AN "ATTITUDE" IN 15 WORDS OR LESS?

Although once hotly debated, there is now general agreement among social scientists that an attitude is a learned predisposition to respond favorably or unfavorably toward some attitude object (Fishbein & Ajzen, 1975). Let's examine more closely some of the assumptions contained in this definition. First, attitudes are *learned,* not innate. A person isn't born with his or her attitudes already in place. Attitudes are developed by interacting with others, through personal experience, from the media, and so forth.

Second, attitudes are *predispositions to respond,* which means they precede and, to some extent, direct people's actions. Researchers call attitudes "precursors of behavior" for this reason. We don't have time to reflect on each and every action we take in life, so attitudes provide us with mental shortcuts that guide our behavior. This is not to say there is a one-to-one correspondence between attitudes and behaviors. A person may have a favorable attitude toward losing weight, but may not stay on a diet. To a large extent, though, our attitudes do correspond with our behaviors. For example, people who favor gun control laws are less likely to own guns than people who oppose such laws.

A third feature of attitudes is that they represent favorable or unfavorable evaluations of things.[1] In other words, they reflect likes or dislikes, agreement or disagreement, positive or negative feelings. This *evaluative dimension* is, perhaps, the most central feature of attitudes (Dillard, 1993; Fabrigar, Krosnick, & MacDougall, 2005). If a person says, "I can't stand Miley Cyrus" or "I adore Zac Efron," the person is expressing his or her attitudes toward the two celebrities.

A fourth and final aspect of attitudes is that they are always directed toward an *attitude object*. People hold attitudes *about* things or *toward* things. The attitude object can be another person, an idea, a policy, an event, or a situation. Attitudes toward a complex issue, such as elective abortion, may be comprised of multiple attitudes toward a variety of sub-issues, such as elective abortions after the second trimester, elective abortions in cases of rape or incest, and so on.

SO HOW DO YOU MEASURE THE DURN THINGS?

If you want to know how much you weigh, you can stand on a scale. If you want to know how tall you are, you can use a tape measure. But what if you want to measure someone's attitudes? Attitudes can't be observed directly. They are inside people's heads and must therefore be measured indirectly.[2] Social scientists have developed a variety of scales for measuring people's attitudes toward almost everything. Let's now take a closer look at a few of these scales.

Standardized Self-Report Scales

One means of measuring attitudes is via standardized scales based on self-reports. These are informally referred to as *paper–pencil* measures of attitude. Two widely used rating scales are *Likert* scales and *semantic differential* scales.

Likert Scales

Rensus Likert (1932) developed a method that allowed for measuring gradations in attitudes. His "equal appearing interval" scales remain the gold standard for measuring attitudes today.[3] Likert scales are easy to construct and administer and enjoy widespread acceptance in academia, government, and industry. You've probably already completed a number of them yourself. A Likert scale consists of a series of statements about some attitude object, followed by a continuum of choices ranging from "strongly agree" to "strongly disagree" (see Figure 3.1). A respondent's attitude is represented by the average of his or her responses to all the statements in the scale.

Semantic Differential Scales

In 1957, Charles Osgood, Percy Tannenbaum, and George Suci developed the *semantic differential* scale as a means for measuring attitudes. Although the scale's name may be unfamiliar, you are probably already acquainted with this approach to measuring attitudes as well (see Figure 3.1). A *semantic differential* scale is based on the *connotative* meanings words have for people. The scale consists of a series of bipolar adjective pairs or, stated more simply, opposites, such as light–dark, fast–slow, happy–sad, and so on.[4] In completing the scale, a respondent checks the "semantic" space between each adjective pair that best reflects his or her overall attitude toward the concept in question. The respondent's overall attitude is represented by the average of the spaces checked on all of the items. An example of one of the better-known *semantic differential* scales is McCroskey's "ethos scale," which

Sample Likert-type scale items from Infante and Wigleyís (1986) Verbal Aggressiveness scale.

1 = almost never true
2 = rarely true
3 = occasionally true
4 = often true
5 = almost always true

_____ I am extremely careful to avoid attacking individuals' intelligence when I attack their ideas.
_____ When individuals are very stubborn, I use insults to soften the stubbornness.
_____ I try to make people feel good about themselves even if their ideas are stupid.
_____ When individuals insult me, I get a lot of pleasure out of really telling them off.

Sample Semantic Differential scale, featuring some of the adjective pairs used by McCroskey (1966) to measure source credibility or ethos.

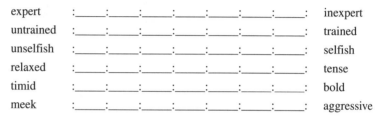

Dr. Laura Schlesinger

FIGURE 3.1   Likert-Type Scale and Semantic Differential Scale Samples.

Likert-type scale from Infante, D. A., & Wigley, C. J. (1986). Verbal aggressiveness: An interpersonal model and measure. *Communication Monographs, 53*, 61–69. Copyright by the National Communication Association, 1986. Semantic Differential scale from McCroskey, J. C. (1966). Scales for the measurement of ethos. *Speech Monographs, 33*, 65–72. Copyright by the National Communication Association, 1966.

is used to measure source credibility (McCroskey, 1966; McCroskey & Young, 1981). A few of the bipolar adjectives used in this scale are displayed in Figure 3.1.

Visually Oriented Self-Report Scales

Other more visually oriented methods of measuring attitudes via self-reports have been developed. Ostrum, Bond, Krosnick, and Sedikides (1994) discuss several of these, including simple drawings of facial expressions. The expressions represent different degrees of favorability or unfavorability toward the attitude object, ranging from smiling to frowning (see Figure 3.2). Visually oriented approaches make it easier for respondents to conceptualize their attitudes, because they can "see" where their attitudes fit on a scale or continuum.

Pitfalls in Measuring Attitudes

Although our discussion thus far might suggest that measuring attitudes is easy, there are pitfalls to watch out for. Four such difficulties are noted here. The first is known as *social desirability bias*. When people know their words or actions are on display, they may

1. _____   2. _____   3. _____   4. _____

5. _____   6. _____   7. _____

FIGURE 3.2 Example of a Visually Oriented Attitude Scale.

From Shavitt, S., & Brock, T. C. (1994). *Persuasion: Psychological Insights and Perspectives*. Published by Allyn & Bacon, Boston. Reprinted by permission from the author.

exhibit what they perceive to be socially acceptable norms of conduct (Fisher, 1993). During a job interview, for example, a person might express "politically correct" attitudes in order to appear to be a good job prospect.

A second pitfall involves the problem of *non-attitudes*. People don't want to appear uninformed or unintelligent. So quite often, when they are asked for their attitude on a particular issue, they simply make one up—on the spot! They fear that saying "I don't know" or "I don't care" will make them look uninformed.

A third pitfall is *acquiescence bias* (Ostrum et al., 1994). Some respondents are inclined to agree with any statement contained in a survey or questionnaire. This tendency is especially pronounced in oral, in-person interviews. One reason may be that some respondents feel inclined to agree with the position they think the researcher supports.

The fourth pitfall relates to the issue of *mindfulness*. In order for a person to mark the space on any self-report measure, the person must first know or be aware of what his or her attitude is. Unfortunately, respondents often, quite literally, don't know their own minds (see Box 3.1). For example, a person could harbor racist, sexist, or homophobic attitudes,

| When Do Attitudes Coincide with Behavior? | BOX 3.1 |

Just because a moviegoer tends to prefer action-adventure movies over comedies doesn't mean he or she will *always* insist on seeing the former instead of the latter. So when can we expect attitudes to coincide with behavior? There tends to be greater *attitude–behavior consistency* (ABC) when:

1. Multiple attitudes aren't confused with single attitudes. A person doesn't have only *one* attitude toward "immigrants," for example. A person's attitudes toward legal versus illegal immigrants, first-generation versus second-generation immigrants, or immigrants from one country versus another, may vary. ABC is greater when a single attitude is measured within a specific situation, place, and time.

2. "Multiple act criteria" are employed. Giving people different opportunities to manifest their attitudes through their behavior improves the "fit" between attitudes and behavior. If you want to assess a person's attitudes toward homeless people, for example, you should examine her or his behavior toward more than one homeless person. If you want to assess a person's attitudes toward "honesty" you should provide him or her with multiple opportunities to perform honest acts (e.g., returning a lost wallet, refusing to cheat on a test, admitting to breaking something).

3. The attitudes are based on personal experience. Attitudes that have been formed as a result of direct personal experience tend to correspond more closely with actual behavior (Fazio, 1986; Fazio & Zanna, 1981). Secondhand attitudes, shaped by the media or based on what others have told us, do not predict behavior as well. For example, a person's attitudes toward alcoholics will more closely coincide with her or his behavior toward alcoholics if she or he has had firsthand experiences with alcoholics, as opposed to simply reading about them.

4. Attitudes that are central to the belief system are involved. Attitudes that are central to an individual's core beliefs and values tend to be more reliable predictors of behavior than attitudes that are tangential to an individual's belief system. A person's attitudes about "marital fidelity" would tend to reveal more about his or her behavior in relationships than his or her preferences regarding pineapple on pizza.

5. Self-monitoring behavior is taken into account. Self-monitoring is a trait-like quality found in people. High self-monitors (HSMs) are more likely to adapt their behavior to fit the situation. They take cues from other people and the situation to determine how they should behave. Low self-monitors (LSMs) tend to "do their own thing" and respond based on their own internal states. Research suggests that greater ABC is found among LSMs than HSMs, because the former are less inclined to tailor their behavior to fit perceived situational expectations. We discuss self-monitoring in more detail in Chapter 5.

6. The attitude is accessible or can be activated. How accessible an attitude is—that is, how easily it comes to mind—bears on the ABC relationship. Attitudes that immediately spring to mind are better predictors of behavior than attitudes one must ponder. Let's say we're playing a word association game: If we say the word "cats," what's the first word that comes to mind? If you immediately thought "allergies," then that attitude was highly accessible to you. If it took you time to think of a word that went with "cats," then your attitude toward the concept was not as accessible. Similarly, attitudes that have been activated are more likely to correspond with behavior than unactivated attitudes. Sometimes a persuader must remind receivers what their attitudes are to bring them to conscious awareness. A parent, for example, might remind a child, "Your new bicycle helmet looks cool" to activate a positive attitude toward bicycle safety in the child.

without consciously realizing it. To the extent that persons aren't mindful of their own attitudes, the use of such scales is problematic (Hample, 1984; Nisbett & Wilson, 1977).

Can You Trust What You Can't See?

Because attitudes exist "inside" people, the most basic way to measure them is by asking people. Until someone "invents a better mousetrap" for measuring attitudes, standardized scales will continue to enjoy widespread use. A myriad of mental phenomena, such as beliefs, opinions, emotions, and intentions, cannot be observed directly. Social scientists can't see attitudes "in the flesh," as it were, but can infer their existence through their influence on behavior, communication, and decision making.

Roundabout Methods of Measuring Attitudes

In addition to self-reports, a variety of other means are used to assess people's attitudes. These include inferring attitudes from appearances, from associations, and from behavior.

Judging a Book by Its Cover—Appearances

Attitudes may be inferred from appearances. This process is less scientific than using standardized scales, but we all do it from time to time. A person wearing a sweatshirt with David Beckham's name on it, for instance, would likely have a favorable attitude toward the soccer superstar. A person with a swastika tattoo may well hold anti-Semitic attitudes. In support of this assumption, an experiment conducted by Mathes and Kemper (1976) revealed that observers were able to make reliable determinations about another person's sexual behavior based on the other's clothing.

The danger of relying on such appearance-based cues, however, is that the person may be making a "sweeping generalization." For example, not everyone sporting a bandana or baggy pants is a gang member.

Birds of a Feather—Associations

"You can tell a person," so the saying goes, "by the company he or she keeps." A person who enjoys hunting, for example, may well belong to the NRA. A cancer survivor might participate in a bike ride for the Lance Armstrong Livestrong Foundation. It makes sense that people enter careers, join organizations, and establish affiliations with groups of like-minded people. Politicians rely on the fact that people who share similar attitudes tend to form memberships. This enables politicians to curry favor with "voting blocs."

How does all of this relate to persuasion? Obviously, by knowing that members of unions, professional associations, churches, and other organizations tend to share similar attitudes, politicians are able to tailor their messages to each group's frame of reference. Marketers use a technique called *segmentation analysis* to target their advertising campaigns to specific groups of consumers, such as soccer moms, NASCAR dads, or Gen Y consumers. We focus more on this topic in Chapter 5.

Note that the approach of inferring attitudes based on associations is not without limitations. If you rely on this approach, exercise caution. People may join organizations for all kinds of reasons, some of which have little or nothing to do with the group's avowed purpose.

You Are What You Do—Behavior

A person's overt actions, mannerisms, habits, and nonverbal cues can be used to infer attitudes. If a person marches in a gay rights parade, it's a pretty good indication he or she holds pro-gay marriage attitudes. If a person buys season tickets to the philharmonic orchestra, it's a fairly safe bet that he or she likes classical music. Indeed, concealing one's attitudes can be difficult, precisely because one's actions tend to give one away. Actions speak louder than words, as the saying goes.

Inferring attitudes from behavior, however, can also be fraught with difficulties. A meta-analysis (Kim & Hunter, 1993) of more than 100 attitude-behavior studies sheds some light on the extent to which attitudes reflect behavior and vice versa. Kim and Hunter found that in many cases, researchers made poor choices about which attitudes to examine in relation to particular behaviors. They found that when the attitude measures employed were *truly relevant to the behaviors in question,* attitude–behavior consistency (ABC) was quite high. Past studies that found weaker ABC may thus have been looking at the wrong attitudes. The bottom line is that behavior can be extremely revealing of attitudes, but care must be exercised in determining which attitudes are germane to which behaviors.

Physiological Measures of Attitude

Attitudes are often accompanied by physiological reactions. To date, however, efforts to identify biological and neurological indicators of attitude change have produced "iffy" results (Fabrigar, Krosnick, & MacDougall, 2005; Ito & Cacioppo, 2007; Petty & Cacioppo, 1983). Researchers have studied pupil dilation, which can signify arousal; galvanic skin response (GSR), which refers to changes in the electrical conductivity of the skin; facial electromyography (EMG), which is based on micromomentary facial movements; and even event-related brain proposals (ERP), which measure momentary electrical activity near the surface of the brain.

The problem is that these measures aren't all that reliable. Some of these methods are *bi-directional* indicators of attitude, meaning they can signal positive or negative reactions. For example, a person's heart rate might increase upon seeing someone she or he loves, or upon seeing something frightening. So far, none of these approaches offers a practical means of gauging people's attitudes.

More recent interest has centered on functional magnetic resonance imaging (fMRI) as a means of measuring attitudes (Aron et al., 2007; Cacioppo & Petty, 1986; Crites & Cacioppo, 1996; Crites, Cacioppo, Gardner, & Berntson, 1995; Ito & Cacioppo, 2007). To wit, during the 2008 presidential campaign a group of neuroscientists conducted brain scans using fMRI, on a group of swing voters while the voters looked at pictures of the candidates (Iacoboni et al., 2007).

The results, however, were dubious: The neuroscientists concluded that "Mitt Romney shows potential" and "John Edwards has promise," whereas Barack Obama and John McCain "indicated a notable lack of any powerful reactions, positive or negative" (p. 14). At a cost of $1,000 per brain scan, one would hope for more accurate results.

Bear in mind that the more complex the attitudes are, the more difficult the task of reducing them to purely physiological terms. At present, physiological measures appear to be less reliable, and more difficult to administer, than "paper–pencil" measures of attitude.

THE THEORY OF REASONED ACTION

Martin Fishbein and Isaac Ajzen developed the *theory of reasoned action* (TRA). Their theory does a good job of accounting for the role of attitudes and intentions on behavior (Ajzen & Fishbein, 1980; Fishbein & Ajzen, 1975). The TRA offers a rational model of the persuasion process. That is, the TRA assumes that people are rational decision makers who make use of all the information available to them.

We think the easiest way to understand the theory is to start at the end and work backward (see Figure 3.3). The endpoint of the theory is a person's overt behavior, what she or he actually does. But what shapes a person's behavior? The theory presumes that *intentions* are the best guide to behavior. If you know a person intends to get a haircut, it's a pretty good bet that she or he will actually do so. Of course, intentions don't always predict behavior. Nevertheless, a number of empirical studies have validated this assumption of the TRA (Ajzen & Fishbein, 1973; Kim & Hunter, 1993; Sheppard, Hartwick, & Warshaw, 1988).

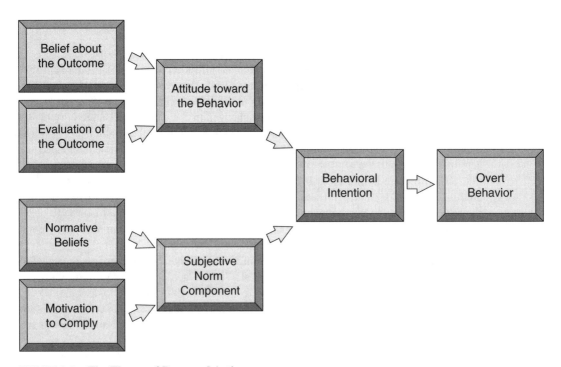

FIGURE 3.3   The Theory of Reasoned Action.

Adapted from Ajzen, I., & Fishbein, M. (1980). *Understanding attitudes and predicting social behavior*. Englewood Cliffs, NJ: Prentice Hall.

Attitude toward the Behavior

Working backward again, the TRA posits that intentions are, themselves, the result of two additional components. The first of these is the person's *attitude toward the behavior* in question (see Figure 3.3). For example, let's say we are trying to guess whether Bjorn will wear a helmet when riding a skateboard. The best guide to whether Bjorn will or will not wear a helmet is his intention to do so. If he intends to wear a helmet, then in all likelihood he will wear one. Bjorn's intention, in turn, will be influenced by his attitude toward helmets. If he has a favorable attitude toward helmets (they look cool, they provide safety), then his intention to wear one will be stronger. If he has an unfavorable attitude toward helmets (they are hot, they mess up my hair), then his intention to wear one will be lower.

The theory also states that Bjorn's attitude toward the behavior (wearing a helmet) will be based on his *beliefs about the outcome* of performing the behavior and his *evaluation of the outcome.* To illustrate, Bjorn might believe that his friends will make fun of him if he wears a helmet. That would be a negative outcome. But Bjorn also might believe that if he wears a helmet his parents will think he is responsible and allow him to go to a skateboard park. That would be a positive outcome. According to the TRA, Bjorn's beliefs about these outcomes and his evaluation of them will shape his attitude toward wearing a helmet.

Subjective Norm

Finally, the TRA states that intentions are also guided by a second component, the *subjective norm* (see Figure 3.3). The subjective norm is a person's perception of what others, especially relevant others, think about the behavior in question. Thus, Bjorn's assessment of what relevant others—his friends, parents, other skateboarders—think of wearing a helmet would constitute his subjective norm toward the behavior. According to the TRA, the subjective norm is, itself, based on two factors; a person's *normative beliefs,* and a person's *motivation to comply.* Normative beliefs are based on perceived social pressure by relevant others to engage in the behavior in question. In Bjorn's case, this could be peer pressure or parental pressure to wear or not wear a helmet. Motivation to comply is based on how willing a person is to conform to social pressure by relevant others. In Bjorn's case, this would constitute his motivation to comply with his friends' or parents' expectations. Bjorn's normative belief, then, would be based on his perceptions of what relevant others think about wearing a helmet and his desire to live up to their expectations.

Figure 3.3 illustrates the basic elements of the TRA as just described. The TRA has been tested on a wide variety of topics and issues, including AIDS risk reduction (Cochran, Mays, Ciaretta, Caruso, & Mallon, 1992), belief in extraterrestrials (Patry & Pelletier, 2001), condom use (Albarracín, Johnson, Fishbein, & Muellerleile, 2001; Greene, Hale, & Rubin, 1997), drinking and driving (Gastil, 2000), exposure to the sun (Steen, Peay, & Owen, 2000), low-fat milk consumption (Booth-Butterfield & Reger, 2004), organ donation (Weber, Martin, & Corrigan, 2007), recycling (Park, Levine, & Sharkey, 1998), and voting behavior (Granberg & Holmberg, 1990). The TRA has been especially useful in predicting the role of intentions on health-related behavior.

Gals, Guys, Culture, and the TRA

Individuals differ in the importance they attach to the components of the TRA. Take the example of tanning: One person might care much more about the risk of skin cancer (attitude component), whereas another might care more about what peers think of a deep tan (subjective norm). In general, intention is driven more by the attitude component than by the subjective norm component (Eagly & Chaiken, 1993). This is not always the case, however. Gender differences are also at work (Greene, Hale, & Rubin, 1997). And, not surprisingly, studies have shown that a person's culture affects the relative importance or weight of the attitudinal and normative components (Lee & Green, 1991; Godin et al., 1996).

THE THEORY OF PLANNED BEHAVIOR

The *theory of planned behavior* (TpB) represents an extension of the *theory of reasoned action* (Ajzen, 1985, 1991). What is added is a third prong; *perceived behavioral control* (Ajzen, Albarracin, & Hornick, 2007). Whereas the TRA presumes that behavior is generally under a person's control, the TpB acknowledges that behavior is not always volitional.

Several factors may impinge on a person's perceived behavioral control. First, *internal factors,* such as a lack of knowledge or skills, could prevent someone from performing an intended action. Second, *external factors,* such as limited resources or extenuating circumstances, also might inhibit someone from carrying out an intended action.

To be successful, persuaders need to bolster receivers' perceived behavioral control—that is, their confidence that they can perform the recommended action (Ajzen, 2002). One approach is to address ways of overcoming obstacles. Suppose a physician advises a patient to exercise more. "Try jogging," the doctor says. "I can't," the patient complains, "my knees ache when I jog." "In that case, try walking at a brisk pace, or using an elliptical trainer, or swimming. All three are easier on the knees." The physician is demonstrating that regular exercise is within the patient's control.

The TpB has been validated by a number of real-world studies on issues such as condom use (Albarracín, Johnson, Fishbein, & Muellerleile, 2001), college drinking (Johnston & White, 2003), marijuana use (Lac, Alvaro, Crano, & Siegel, 2009), road safety (Rosenbloom, Levi, Peleg, & Nemrodov, 2009) and nutrition (Wu, Snider, Floyd, Florence, Stoots, & Makamey, 2009). A meta-analysis of the TpB conducted by Armitage and Connor (2001) revealed that adding perceived behavioral control to the equation did a much better job of explaining behavioral intent than the TRA alone (Armitage & Conner, 2001; Godin & Kok, 1996; Madden, Ellen, & Ajzen, 1992).

THE PERSISTENCE OF ATTITUDES

A final feature of attitudes we wish to address is their persistence. Attitudes change over time. They aren't as fleeting as moods or emotions, but neither are they etched in stone. Sometimes a person's attitude will change in response to a single, brief exposure to a persuasive message. Sometimes a person's attitude will endure for years. What makes some attitudes so durable and others so transitory?

Petty and Cacioppo's (1986a, 1986b) *elaboration likelihood model* (ELM), discussed in the previous chapter, provides a useful answer to this question. Recall from Chapter 2 that the ELM posits that there are two basic routes to persuasion: a *central route,* which is based on thought and reflection, and a *peripheral route,* which is based on mental shortcuts. Petty and Cacioppo argue that attitudes formed via the central route are more persistent and resistant to change than attitudes formed via the peripheral route (Haugtvedt & Petty, 1992; Petty, Cacioppo, Strathman, & Priester, 2005; Petty, Haugtvedt, & Smith, 1995). The reason is because actively thinking about an issue seems to internalize the content of the message more. Peripheral processing, however, requires little mental effort. Attitudes formed as a result of peripheral processing thus tend to be more short-lived.[5]

What does this mean for you as a persuader? If you want a message to have a lasting effect on receivers' attitudes, you should design it and deliver it in such a way as to actively promote central processing (i.e., thought, analysis, and reflection). How can you encourage central processing? In the previous chapter we noted that increasing receivers' involvement is one way of promoting central processing. Explaining why a topic or an issue is relevant to receivers and how it affects them personally will increase their *motivation* to use central processing. Adapting your message to the receivers' levels of understanding will increase their *ability* to engage in central processing. In short, if you can get your listeners to actively think about your message, you are more likely to change their attitudes for the long term, not just the short term.

ATTITUDES AS ASSOCIATIVE NETWORKS: YOUR MIND IS A WEB

Our attitudes are interrelated. In some ways our attitudes, beliefs, and values can be likened to a spider's web. Like the fine silky threads of a spider's web, they are connected to one another in a delicate balance. Attitudes, therefore, exist in elaborate *associative networks* (Tesser & Shaffer, 1990). An individual may or may not be consciously aware of all these connections. To a large extent, these associative networks operate implicitly—that is, without the individual's conscious awareness. A change in one attitude affects other attitudes, beliefs, opinions, and values. Like jiggling a spider's web, a vibration in one attitude can trigger reverberations in other cognitive structures. These mental reverberations may be quite minor, or they can be of major consequence to the individual.

MANUFACTURING FAVORABLE ASSOCIATIONS: JIGGLING THE WEB

Why would anyone buy automobile insurance from a company whose spokesperson is a cute, computer generated Gecko with an Aussie accent? Or, for that matter, why would anyone buy a laundry detergent because its logo is emblazoned on a race car? The associative networks in which attitudes exist are critical to such influence attempts. In a nutshell, here is why: Persuaders try to create connections among these networks. They want to link their messages with favorable attitudes and avoid associations with unfavorable attitudes.

Image-Oriented Advertising: That's the Life!

A clear case of manufacturing favorable associations can be found in *image-oriented advertising.* The whole point of image-oriented advertising is to link products with favorable attitudes, values, and lifestyles. As Schudson (1984) emphasizes, advertising "does not claim to picture reality as it is but reality as it should be—life and lives worth imitating" (p. 215). To illustrate, let's examine advertisements and commercials for beer. The ads almost always depict people in pairs or groups (never drinking alone!) socializing and having a good time. What is the image or association the ads are projecting? *Beer = fun.* It's a simple formula. Drinking beer is equated with good times and camaraderie.

Even nonalcoholic beers play on this theme. It matters not if one is the designated driver. One can still be popular if one throws back a tall, cool, nonalcoholic brew. But wait. Why does the designated driver need to drink a beer facsimile *at all*? Because the image being portrayed is that *if you aren't drinking beer, you aren't having fun.* No suds, no buds.

Who Are You Wearing? Brand Personality

Some brands have their own personality. They are imbued with human characteristics and qualities with which consumers identify (Aaker, 1997). Some consumers may regard a brand as they would a best friend (Fournier, 1998), while others may view brands, such as iPod or Blackberry, as extensions of themselves (Belk, 1998). Such brands thereby serve as vehicles for self-expression (Swaminathan, Stilley, Ahluwalia, 2009). An automobile brand, for example, might portray a sophisticated image (Jaguar), a rugged image (Ford Trucks), or a fun image (Mini Cooper). A particular brand might be seen as young or old, liberal or conservative, feminine or masculine. Aaker (1997) developed the *Brand Personality Scale* to measure brand traits based on the dimensions sincerity, excitement, competence, sophistication, and ruggedness.

Branding occurs in other ways. *Aspirational brands* are those that consumers admire and aspire to one day own. They represent the ideal. Luxury brands such as Rolex watches, Viking stoves, and Gucci handbags fall into this category. The Martha Stewart brand is aspirational. Few women will actually make the complicated recipes featured in her magazine, but they like to think that they could.

Another approach is brand *authenticity,* which emphasizes genuineness and integrity. Authentic brands may be handmade or eco-friendly. They are often cause related or have a story to tell. They have a heart. Dell's Livestrong laptop computer is an example. Toyota's Prius is another example. Its cachet is not based on luxury, but rather fuel efficiency. Gap's (Product) Red line of clothing promotes efforts to combat AIDS in Africa. Half of all the profits are donated to women and children affected by AIDS.

A product's image or personality is created through advertising, and its construction is key to its success. A brand's personality must leverage associations that add value to the product itself. A person who buys "fair trade" coffee isn't just buying coffee. She or he is buying a pat on the back for being a conscientious consumer.

Sloganeering

Another means of fostering favorable associations is through *sloganeering.* Consider the following products and their advertising slogans. Notice the positive associations the slogans are designed to instill with respect to each product.

> "When you're here, you're family." (Olive Garden)
> "Breakfast of champions." (Wheaties)
> "I'm lovin' it." (McDonald's)
> "We'll leave the light on for you." (Motel 6)

The slogans imbue the products with positive qualities that, over time, become embedded in receivers' minds. If you feel like "eatin' good in the neighborhood," where would you go for dinner?

Sponsorship

Another way of linking products and services with favorable attitudes is through *sponsorship.* If you watch any automobile race, you'll see corporate logos and insignia plastered all over the cars. In fact, most major sporting events now have corporate sponsors who provide funding in return for the right to associate their products with the event. Almost every stadium and ballpark in America now has a corporate sponsor.

Naturally, advertisers aren't the only ones who try to tie themselves to favorable associations. When candidates for political office kiss babies, eat home cooking, and stand next to the flag, they are trying to link themselves to positive, patriotic values. Negative political campaigning, or "mudslinging," serves the same purpose in reverse: A candidate seeks to link his or her opponent with negative associations.

A major tenet of persuasion thus involves establishing favorable connections between attitudes and attitude objects. Persuaders try to establish these connections by selling an image or a lifestyle. When you buy a product, you are buying into the image as well (Fournier, 1998). But do you really need to have a relationship with your credit card ("My card, my city" [American Express])? Do you really want brands to define you ("Do you speak Prada?")? Sometimes it is important to break the connections that advertisers are trying to create.

PSYCHOLOGICAL CONSISTENCY

We now turn our attention to another important aspect of attitudes and persuasion: psychological consistency. People like to be consistent. They like to avoid the appearance of being inconsistent. These simple principles form the basis for a whole host of theories, variously known as "attitude change" or "cognitive consistency" theories (Festinger, 1957; Heider, 1958; Newcomb, 1953; Osgood & Tannenbaum, 1955). Consistency was originally conceived of as a "drive-reduction" theory. More current thinking suggests that consistency is also socially motivated, and is as much an attempt to manage face and project a favorable self-image as it is an internal drive (Greenwald & Ronis, 1978; Matz & Wood, 2005; Scher & Cooper, 1989). Individuals, therefore, differ in their need for consistency and their tolerance for inconsistency. Recent research demonstrates that there may be a cultural component involved as well (Cialdini, Wosinska, Barrett, Butner, & Gornik-Durose, 1999; Kitayama, Snibbe, Markus, & Suzuki, 2004). Although the individual theories differ somewhat in their approaches, we've integrated the tenets of several theories here in order to present a more coherent perspective. Though this principle is fairly basic, the recognition that most people strive to remain consistent in their thoughts, words, and deeds reveals a good deal about processes of social influence.

The Inner Peace of Consistency

When harmony exists among our attitudes, beliefs, values, and behavior, life is ducky. When there are inconsistencies in what we think, say, or do, however, we tend to experience psychological discomfort. A classic example is that, for smokers, the knowledge that they smoke and that smoking causes cancer is psychologically uncomfortable. Another example involves children whose parents are undergoing a divorce or separation. The children often experience psychological conflict because they can't understand why two people, whom they love, don't want to remain married.

The amount of psychological discomfort that results from holding incompatible attitudes is not the same in all situations. The degree of discomfort depends on the centrality of the attitudes involved. If the issue is relatively minor (for example, a person prefers plastic grocery bags but knows paper bags are better for the environment), the amount of psychological discomfort will be small. If the issue is major, as when attitudes involve core beliefs or values, then the psychological consequences can be enormous (for example, the mother of a teenage girl is fervently pro-life but learns that her daughter has just obtained an abortion).

To understand the nature and effects of psychological consistency, attitude theorists have developed a means of graphically depicting compatible and incompatible attitude states. For example, suppose that Muffin thinks of herself as a firm believer in animal rights. However, while out shopping, she finds a leather jacket that looks "totally cool." Her attitudes toward animal rights and owning the jacket are in conflict. Her psychological dilemma is depicted in Figure 3.4.

According to consistency theory, Muffin will experience psychological stress no matter what decision she makes. If she buys the jacket she'll sacrifice her principles; if she doesn't buy the jacket she'll forgo an opportunity to look cool. Muffin's case is not unique.

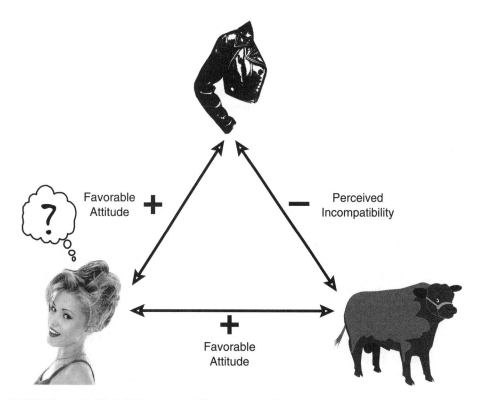

FIGURE 3.4   Muffin's Dilemma: An Illustration of Consistency Theory.

We are all confronted with dilemmas involving our attitudes, beliefs, and behaviors on a daily basis. Because psychological inconsistency is unpleasant we are motivated to avoid it, deny it, reduce it, or eliminate it when it occurs.

Methods of Maintaining Consistency

How do people go about reconciling incompatible attitudes when they occur? People don't necessarily preserve or restore psychological consistency in logical ways. They do so in psycho-logical ways, that is, ways they find psychologically satisfying or comfortable but that may or may not be strictly logical. Using the example of Muffin, scholars suggest a number of possible routes for resolving inconsistency:

1. Denial: Denying or ignoring any inconsistency. "I really don't like that jacket after all" or "I don't really need a jacket now."

2. Bolstering: Rationalizing or making excuses. "That cow is already dead, so what difference can it make?" or "Sooner or later someone will come along and buy that jacket anyway."

3. Differentiation: Separating or distinguishing the attitudes that are in conflict. "The jacket is cowhide. Cows aren't an endangered species. It's not as if I'm buying a jacket made from a baby harp seal or a spotted owl."

4. Transcendence: Focusing on a larger or higher level. "No one is perfect. We all give in to temptation every once in a while."

5. Modifying one or both attitudes: Altering the attitudes themselves to become more consistent. "I need to be more practical and keep my concern for animals' rights in perspective."

6. Communicating: Trying to convince others to change or convince others one did the right thing. "I'll just have to convince my friends that I'm not a hypocrite when they see me in my new jacket."

Of course, these are only some of the ways people go about reducing cognitive dissonance. In trying to gauge which approach a person will use, a good rule of thumb is that a person tends to reduce dissonance in the most efficient way possible. That is, he or she tends to follow the path of least resistance in finding a way to restore consistency. Changing an inconsequential attitude to restore consistency, for example, is much more likely than changing a core attitude.

Marketing Strategies: How to Have Your Cake and Eat It Too!

Now that you understand the basic nature of consistency theories, let's look at how neatly consistency theories apply to persuasion. Imagine that you are at the supermarket. You have a craving for ice cream, but you're on a diet. No problem! You can buy a "low carb" brand with reduced fat and fewer calories. In fact, thanks to modern technology you can

"Remember, the enemy of your enemy is your friend."

choose from a veritable array of frozen desserts including ice milk, frozen yogurt, diabetic ice cream, fruit sorbet, or a non-fat, non-dairy product. Think how many other products at the grocery store rely on the principle of "having your cake and eating it too." There are "light," "fat free," "cholesterol free," "high fiber," "low sodium," "calcium enriched," and "natural" food products on every shelf. The marketing strategy behind such products is to allow consumers to make food purchases that are consistent with their beliefs regarding health and nutrition.

Brand Loyalty: Accept No Substitute

The concept of *brand loyalty* offers another useful illustration of psychological consistency. Advertisers want us to experience psychological discomfort if we change brands. By instilling brand loyalty in us, advertisers hope to discourage product switching. We are trained by Madison Avenue to remain faithful to one motor oil, be true to one long-distance provider, stay devoted to one pain reliever, or cherish a particular make of car. Consider the following slogans:

> "Don't leave home without it." (American Express)
> "Like nothing else." (Hummer)
> "Only in a Jeep." (Jeep)
> "When you care enough to send the very best." (Hallmark cards)

All of these slogans are designed to foster brand loyalty on the part of the consumer and feelings of psychological inconsistency if consumers betray their usual brands.

Write and Tell Us Why You Love This Book in 24 Words or Less

Yet another means of reinforcing brand loyalty is through active participation on the part of the consumer. Viewers can text in their vote on *American Idol*. Sometimes a prize is offered for calling a radio station or writing an essay about a product. Win or lose, the mere act of calling, writing, or texting is bound to increase one's allegiance. Active participation increases commitment.

Brand loyalty can also be encouraged through merchandising. People who wear branded clothing (an L.A. Lakers jersey, a Porsche sport cap, a Fender guitar T-shirt) are paying for the right to serve as walking billboards—and engaging in self-persuasion to boot.

An example of how consumers succumb to merchandising pressure involves one of this book's ever-gullible authors. He liked the Indian maiden logo on Land O' Lakes butter. So when he learned he could order two Land O' Lakes mugs for only $7.95, plus three proof-of-purchase seals from any Land O' Lakes product, he couldn't resist. He switched from margarine to butter. He bought only Land O' Lakes butter for the next three months (the amount of time it took to accumulate three proof-of-purchase seals). When he found he'd lost one of the proof-of-purchase seals he was despondent. Did he give up? Of course not. He went out and bought another package of Land O' Lakes butter *he didn't even need,* just to complete the trio of proof-of-purchase seals! The author is now the proud owner of

Merchandising can increase consumer commitment.

Photo by Robert Gass.

a pair of Land O' Lakes mugs, complete with Indian maiden logo, but let's examine what can be learned from this lesson:

- The merchandising offer got the author actively involved in the process of reinforcing his own brand loyalty. Because the mugs themselves cost little to manufacture, the author was paying Land O' Lakes for the privilege of becoming a loyal consumer.
- The merchandising offer secured the author's brand loyalty for a period of 3 to 4 months. Although the author has subsequently switched back to margarine, he still buys the Land O' Lakes brand whenever he purchases butter (after all, he has the mugs to remind him where his loyalty lies).
- The author bought and used far more butter than he otherwise would have without the mug offer. In fact, as he was closing in on that elusive third proof-of-purchase seal, he was searching high and low for ways to use butter!

Admittedly, the author got a little carried away, but that's the beauty of brand loyalty. We don't necessarily think or act rationally when our allegiance to a particular brand takes over.

Marketing Inconsistency

Of course, other advertising campaigns, typically those for newer products or products with a smaller market share, use just the opposite strategy. These ads encourage us to switch brands. They realize consumers can be set in their ways. These advertisers try to create psychological imbalance. They want us to have second thoughts about the products and services on which we've been relying unquestioningly year after year. Consider the following advertising slogans:

"Think different." (Macintosh computers)
"Think outside the bun." (Taco Bell)
"It's waaay better than fast food" (Wendy's)
"I could have had a V8!" (V8 vegetable juice)

Such slogans are based on the recognition that consumers can be set in their ways and seek to overcome this inertia by encouraging brand switching. Many other types of advertising campaigns are based on creating a state of psychological inconsistency.

Capitalizing on Inconsistency

The use of consistency theory isn't only for advertisers, marketers, and other "professional" persuaders. You, too, can incorporate the principles of consistency theory in your own persuasive messages. One way you can accomplish this is to align your message with your audience's frame of reference. It is much easier to tailor a suit to fit a person than it is to change a person's figure to fit a suit. Similarly, successful persuasion isn't so much a matter of shifting receivers' attitudes over to your position as it is a matter of adapting your message to the attitudes of your audience. A child who suggests to her mother, "Let's play hooky and go to the Zoo today. Zoos are very educational!" is adapting her message to the mother's value system. Such adaptation is key to persuasion, which is why we discuss this strategy in more detail in Chapter 5.

Another way you can apply principles of consistency theory is to highlight potential inconsistencies in receivers' attitudes. If you can demonstrate that some of the attitudes held by your receivers are incompatible, you may motivate them to change their attitudes in the direction you are advocating. Be cautious, however, when employing this strategy. If you attempt to drive too big a psychological wedge between your receivers' attitudes, they may simply change their attitudes and come to dislike you.

COGNITIVE DISSONANCE THEORY

In January, 2007, Hillary Clinton announced her candidacy for the presidency of the United States. At the time, most media pundits considered her a shoe-in for her party's nomination. Flash forward to June 2008, when she conceded to Barack Obama after a bitter primary battle. Many Clinton loyalists could not accept her defeat. They blamed the sexist media. They fumed about shenanigans in counting delegates. They were, according to some commentators, "sore losers" (Merida, 2008).

One might think that once Obama had clinched the nomination, Hillary supporters would have fallen in line behind their party's nominee. Not so. Many Clinton loyalists were so committed to her candidacy that they ignored her own calls for party unity. The name the die-hards gave themselves was "PUMAS," an acronym for "party unity, my ass." Some vowed to keep campaigning. Others declared they would sit out the election. Some announced they would cast their votes for John McCain. Why were Clinton's supporters so begrudging? We think *cognitive dissonance theory* does a good job of explaining why (Cooper, 2007; Festinger, 1957, 1964; Festinger & Carlsmith, 1959; Festinger & Carlsmith, 2007; Harmon-Jones & Harmon-Jones, 2008; Mills, 1999).

Originated by Leon Festinger (1957), *cognitive dissonance theory* (CDT) focuses on decisions people make or behaviors in which they engage and how they rationalize those decisions and behaviors. The basic idea is that after making a decision or performing a behavior, a person worries about whether she or he made the right decision or did the right thing. The person is therefore motivated to reduce the resulting dissonance. For this reason, CDT is often referred to as a "post-decision theory." According to the theory, Clinton supporters backed a losing candidate, so they were motivated to reduce their angst. What is intriguing is *how* they went about doing this: They didn't give in nicely, but threw a political tantrum.

CDT is quite useful. It has been used to explain willingness to exercise (Chatzisarantis, Hagger, & Wang, 2008), the timing of marriage decisions (Balestrino & Ciardi, 2008), willingness to eat fried grasshoppers (Zimbardo, Weisenberg, Firestone, & Levy, 1965), and high-altitude climbers' rationalizations for turning back (Burke, Sparkes, & Allen-Collinson, 2008).

Cognitive Dissonance and Buyer's Remorse

The theory of cognitive dissonance is closely connected to the phenomenon known as *buyer's remorse.* Imagine that a consumer shelled out a lot of money for a big-screen

Can you find a source of cognitive dissonance in this picture?

Photo by Robert Gass.

plasma TV, only to find out a few weeks later that a newer, better model was available for less money. To assuage their lingering doubts, buyers engage in dissonance-reduction strategies. One method, known as *selective exposure,* involves seeking out consonant information and avoiding dissonant information. The TV buyer might reread ads and articles recommending the brand he or she purchased and avoid ads and articles for other brands. Cognitive dissonance isn't an all-or-nothing phenomenon. It occurs in varying degrees. The amount of dissonance one experiences is known as the *magnitude of dissonance.* Spending $8,000 on a plasma TV that wasn't very reliable would produce more dissonance than spending $8 on a movie that wasn't very good.

Polarization of Alternatives

When a person has to make a tough decision, he or she tends to polarize the attractiveness of the alternatives once the decision is made. Suppose Lola has to decide between an iPhone and a Blackberry. It is a close call: Each model has its pros and cons. Once Lola makes her choice she will tend to disparage the unchosen brand and value the chosen brand even more. What was formerly a tough choice becomes a "no brainer." The tendency to spread the alternatives is a form of self-justification (Tavris & Aronson, 2007). It is easier to see choices in terms of "black and white," rather than shades of gray. This explains why voters who were initially torn between Clinton and Obama might adore one and disdain the other, once they cast their ballot in a primary election.

Cognitive Dissonance, Self-Image, and Culture

Cognitive dissonance can be largely internal in nature, such as when a person is confronted with a moral dilemma. Dissonance can also arise when one's self-image is inconsistent with one's beliefs, attitudes, or behaviors. For instance, a person who thinks of himself or herself as unprejudiced but who laughs at a racist, sexist, or homophobic joke might experience cognitive dissonance. There is a cultural component to dissonance as well. For Americans and others from individualistic cultures, dissonance tends to be more internally motivated, while for Asians and others from more collectivistic cultures, dissonance tends to be more socially motivated (Hoshino-Browne, Zanna, Spencer, Zanna, Kitayama, & Lackenbauer, 2005; Kitayama et al., 2004). While some studies suggest that Asians have a greater tolerance for inconsistency (Aaker & Sengupta, 2000; Nisbett, 2003), others suggest just the opposite (Xie, Jang, & Cai, 2007). There is also evidence that dissonance is a culturally universal phenomenon (Egan, Santos, & Bloom, 2007).

Factors That Affect the Magnitude of Dissonance

Four paradigms that moderate cognitive dissonance have been studied by researchers (Beauvois & Joule, 1999; Harmon-Jones & Mills, 1999). One of these, known as the *free choice paradigm,* states that the more free choice one has in making a decision, the more dissonance one will suffer. Cooper (2007) emphasizes that dissonance occurs *only* if the negative outcome of a freely chosen decision was foreseeable at the time the person made his or her choice. Otherwise the person can say "How was I to know?" A second paradigm, known as *belief disconfirmation,* argues that dissonance is aroused when a person encounters information contrary to his or her beliefs. A person will tend to engage in selective exposure or distort information that contradicts his or her belief system. A third paradigm for dissonance research is called *induced compliance.* When a person is forced to do something, little dissonance is aroused because the person can rationalize the action by saying "I had no choice." The fourth paradigm, called the *effort justification paradigm,* centers on the amount of effort or sacrifice required: the greater the effort, the greater the dissonance.

Dissonance and Persuasion: Putting It All Together

Persuasive messages can be tailored to either increase or decrease dissonance in receivers. A persuader might want to arouse dissonance in a target audience to get them to rethink their position on an issue. Or, conversely, a persuader might seek to allay an audience's doubts by reassuring them that their decision or action was justified. In this case, the persuader would want to convince receivers that they did the right thing and they had no other realistic alternative. Recent research shows that attitude change brought about by CDT can have lasting effects (Sénémeaud & Somat, 2009).

FORBIDDEN FRUIT: PSYCHOLOGICAL REACTANCE

In 2003, Barbra Streisand filed a lawsuit against a photographer for taking aerial photos along California's coastline, including her Malibu home, and posting them on the Web. Prior to the lawsuit, few people had bothered to look at the photos. After the publicity surrounding the lawsuit, however, people flocked to the Website in droves (Arthur,

2009). Half a million viewers logged on to see what the fuss was about. A judge subsequently dismissed the suit. Similarly, when the MPAA filed a lawsuit against The Pirate Bay for facilitating illegal downloading of movies, the Website became more popular than ever (Sullivan, 2009). Attempts to muzzle information on the Web often backfire, a phenomenon Mike Masnick termed "the Streisand effect" (2005).

When people believe that their freedom is being threatened, they tend to rebel. Tell a little kid not to play with a particular toy and the kid won't be able to keep his grubby little hands off it. Tell your teenage daughter that you disapprove of her new boyfriend and she'll like him even more. The tendency to react defensively to perceived encroachments on our freedom is called *psychological reactance* (Brehm, 1966; Brehm & Brehm, 1981). You may also know of it as "reverse psychology."

Psychological reactance can help or hinder persuasion. Suppose a mother wants to get her picky 3-year-old to eat her broccoli. The mother could use a controlling message such as, "You are going to sit there until you finish your broccoli." This approach might backfire, however, if the daughter is willing to sit and pout for an hour. Instead, the mother could use psychological reactance to her advantage by saying, "Mabel, there is no way you can eat that broccoli in less than a minute. No way." Now the daughter may want to prove she's up to the challenge.

A wealth of studies on littering behavior reveal that a negative or punitive message ("No littering!" or "Don't you dare litter.") actually *increases* littering compared to a polite message ("Please pitch in.") (Hansmann & Sholz, 2003; Horsley, 1988; Huffman, Grossnickle, Cope, & Huffman, 1995). Stated simply, asking is a more effective strategy than ordering. Psychological reactance also has been examined on a variety of other topics, including alcohol consumption (Dillard & Shen, 2005), condom use (Quick & Stephenson, 2007), drug use (Burgoon et al., 2002), promotional health messages (Miller, Lane, Deatrick, Young, & Potts, 2007), and smoking (Miller, Burgoon, Grandpre, & Alvaro, 2006). The tendency to react negatively to perceived threats varies from person to person. These individual differences can be measured with the *Psychological Reactance Scale* (Hong, 1992; Hong & Faedda, 1996).

To avoid a boomerang effect, a persuader should be cautious about using controlling language. A politician who says "You must vote for this proposition. It is the only way" is practically daring voters to reject the measure. To use psychological reactance to his or her advantage, a persuader should acknowledge listeners' personal autonomy. A politician who says "I personally favor this measure, but you are free to vote anyway you want on it" is less likely to invoke resistance. A persuader also can use psychological reactance against an opponent. For example, a candidate might argue "My opponent wants to limit your health care options, but I want you to be able to choose your own health care provider." We return to the subject of psychological reactance in Chapter 8 when we discuss the *scarcity principle*.

COUNTERATTITUDINAL ADVOCACY: PLAYING DEVIL'S ADVOCATE

An even better approach to changing another's attitudes is to get the person to persuade himself or herself. This can be accomplished by having the person engage in what is called *counterattitudinal advocacy* (CAA). CAA involves having a person create and present (orally or in writing) a message that is at odds with his or her existing attitudes, for example, claiming you favor capital punishment when, in fact, you oppose it. Research demonstrates that after engaging in CAA, the person's attitudes will tend to shift in the direction of the position advocated (Festinger, 1957; Kelman, 1953; Preiss & Allen, 1998; Sénémeaud & Somat, 2009). Mind you, the person's attitudes don't undergo a complete reversal. Some degree of attitude change takes place, such that the initially counterattitudinal position becomes somewhat more favorable in the person's mind.

The explanation offered by *cognitive dissonance theory* for this phenomenon is that CAA causes psychological conflict within the individual. He or she is aware of the inconsistency between his or her privately held beliefs and attitudes and his or her public behavior. One means of resolving the conflict is to make one's private beliefs and attitudes more consistent with one's public behavior, hence, the resultant shift in attitudes. This suggests an effective way of getting another person to persuade himself or herself. Simply try to get the person to speak or act in a manner that is contrary to his or her attitudes. This can be accomplished by asking the other to role-play for a few minutes, or to play devil's advocate for a while. The research demonstrates that attitude change should follow in the direction of the counterattitudinal position. When using this technique, however, it is important that the other person *choose* to engage in CAA, as opposed to being forced to do so. A meta-analysis by Preiss and Allen (1998) revealed that voluntarily engaging in CAA was the key to this strategy's effectiveness.

I'M ALL IN: INCREASING COMMITMENT

Commitment goes hand in hand with persuasion. When people become committed to ideas, groups, causes, or decisions they find it difficult to change their minds. By way of example, did you know that once horse racing fans have bet on a horse, they become even more convinced their horse will win (Knox & Inkster, 1968)? Individuals who volunteer their time to work for political campaigns tend to overestimate the prospects of their candidate winning. The more public the nature of the commitment, the more psychologically entrenched people become.

Many social customs and rituals are designed to increase a person's sense of psychological commitment to an idea, group, cause, or decision. Wedding engagements do so. Fraternity initiation rituals do so as well. Boot camp in the military serves this purpose. Baptism achieves this goal. This also explains why people often announce their New Year's resolutions publicly. Doing so binds them all the more to their commitments. Political rallies, protest marches, and demonstrations accomplish this function for the participants. Whenever we make public statements or engage in public actions, we tend to become bound by our words or deeds. Yes, we can renege on what we've said or done, but we will pay a psychological price for doing so. The greater the public commitment, the greater the toll paid.

Commitments Can "Grow Legs"

Robert Cialdini (1993) makes the interesting point that commitments sometimes "grow legs." By this he means that once we become committed to a given course of action, we tend to remain steadfast in our determination, even if the original reason for selecting that course of action is diminished, altered, or eliminated. A story involving one of the authors illustrates this phenomenon. The author wanted to build a retaining wall in his backyard. He was planning to spend $1,000 for a wall. Once he got several bids for the job, he discovered it would cost $3,000 to $4,000 for a stone wall, rather than a block wall. He considered "fake" rock (cast cement in a pattern), a cheaper option, but by then he had his heart set on the real thing. He signed a contract with the lowest bidder for a $3,000 retaining wall made of genuine river rock. A few days before the contractor was to begin work, the author had another idea. As long as he was going to all the trouble and expense, why not build in a recessed bench for reading? And, his wife added, why not add some steps, so it would be easy to get up and down the wall? The $3,000 wall soon became a $4,000 wall. But it didn't end there. Once the wall was completed, the author sprang for sprinklers and landscaping. After all, the wall looked so good, it was worth a little extra to make it a focal point of the backyard. In the end, the $1,000 wall became a $4,500 wall. Once the author got started, his commitment to build the rock wall of his dreams grew legs. He loves the wall, of course. He has to. It cost him a bundle.

We all engage in similar behavior from time to time. The owner of an unreliable car keeps spending money on repairs, hoping this brake job or that muffler repair will finally be the last. The repair bills keep mounting, until they may eventually exceed the car's resale value. Does the owner throw in the towel? Nope. The owner becomes even more resolute the next time something breaks. "I've already poured two grand into that car. I can't give up now." A gambler bets on a football team that loses. The next week, he doubles the bet, feeling confident that he will win the next time around. He loses again. Does he wise up and cut his losses? No way. He becomes more determined than ever that the team will win. His commitment actually increases with each loss.

Once we've invested our time and energy or poured our hearts and souls into a cause, a person, an idea, a project, or a group we find it difficult to let go. We may have second thoughts, but we repress them. We build up layers of rationalizations for remaining true to our original convictions.

Keep in mind that a large initial commitment isn't required in order for persuaders to take advantage of us. Even relatively simple acts, such as raising your hand, signing a petition, or filling out a form, can be enough. The fact that commitments can grow legs means that we are vulnerable to self-persuasion as well. Remember, we manufacture the additional reasons for bolstering our commitment ourselves. Once we become committed, we may become blind to alternative ways of seeing, thinking, or acting. Thus, we need to remain on guard, not only from others seeking to extract commitments from us but also from ourselves.

Before concluding this section, we wish to note that several worthwhile lessons can be learned from our discussion of commitment and consistency. First, don't allow persuaders to "box you in" by getting you to commit to something when you really don't want to. Feel free to say, "I want to think it over" or "I want to consider some other options first" or "You're not trying to rush me into a hasty decision are you?" Second, don't paint yourself into a corner by making public commitments you really don't want, or intend, to keep. Be willing to say, "Sorry, I'd rather not" or "I have to say 'No' this time." Third, if you do happen to make an ill-advised commitment, admit it and see what you can do to correct it.

Don't be so preoccupied with saving face that you follow through on a really dumb decision. When buying anything, ask about a return or refund policy in advance.

SUMMARY

The concept of *attitude* is central to the study of persuasion. Attitudes can't be directly observed. They can, however, be inferred and measured through a variety of indirect means, most commonly via standardized scales, such as Likert or semantic differential scales. The theory of reasoned action, and its companion theory of planned behavior, provide useful, rational models of how attitudes and intentions guide behavior. People's attitudes tend to correlate with their behavior, but only if and when a number of important conditions are satisfied. Attitudes formed via central processing are more predictive of behavior than attitudes formed via peripheral processing. Attitudes formed via central processing are also more persistent and resistant to change. We discussed the fact that attitudes exist in associative networks, and that advertisers use these connections to foster favorable images and associations with their products and services. People have a tendency to strive for consistency among their attitudes, beliefs, and behaviors. Persuaders can adapt their messages either to reinforce consistency or to attempt to create inconsistency. Cognitive dissonance, a specialized form of consistency theory, explains how people go about rationalizing decisions after they have made them. The phenomenon of psychological reactance can be used to a persuader's advantage. Engaging in counterattitudinal advocacy or making commitments, especially public commitments, are two important means of facilitating influence, based on the theory of cognitive dissonance.

ENDNOTES

1. At one time, attitudes were conceptualized as having three dimensions: cognitive (thought), affective (feeling), and conative (behavior). This tripartite characterization of attitudes no longer enjoys widespread support. Rather, these three elements now tend to be viewed not as dimensions of attitudes themselves but as ways in which attitudes are manifested (Tesser & Shaffer, 1990).

2. Standardized scales, such as Likert scales, are sometimes referred to as "direct" measures of attitude, meaning that they are taken directly from an individual, or from "the horse's mouth," so to speak. Such measures are still, strictly speaking, indirect, because the researcher cannot observe, measure, or

quantify the attitude as an entity in itself, apart from the respondent's self-report about his or her attitude.

3. They are called "equal appearing interval" scales because each space on the continuum represents the same increment or degree of attitude change as the other spaces. This is an important feature of Likert scales because it allows for mathematical comparisons among attitudes to be made. An attitude of "+2" on a 7-point Likert scale would be considered twice as strong as an attitude of "+1" on the same scale. A problem with Likert scales, however, and most other attitude scales, involves the middle or neutral point. When a respondent checks the middle space on a

Likert scale, it doesn't mean she or he has no attitude at all. It could mean he or she doesn't understand the item, doesn't care about the issue, or is torn between the two extremes.

4. As with Likert scales, semantic differential scales presume that the spaces on the scale are "equidistant" from one another, making mathematical comparisons of attitudes possible.

5. This explanation is highly consistent with findings based on *inoculation theory*, which we discuss in Chapter 9. Inoculating receivers against opposing arguments (e.g., giving them a small dose of the arguments they are likely to hear along with answers to those arguments) requires that they actively think about message content. This increased mental effort makes them more resilient to opposing arguments presented at a later date.

REFERENCES

Aaker, J. L. (1997). Dimensions of brand personality. *Journal of Marketing Research, 34*(3), 347–356.

Aaker, J. L., & Sengupta, J. (2000). Additivity versus attenuation: The role of culture in the resolution of information incongruity. *Journal of Consumer Psychology, 9*, 67–82.

Ajzen, I. (1985). From intentions to actions: A theory of planned behavior. In J. Kuhl & J. Beckmann (Eds.), *Action control: From cognition to behavior* (pp. 11–39). New York: Springer-Verlag.

Ajzen, I. (1991). The theory of planned behavior. *Organizational Behavior and Human Decision Processes, 50*, 179–211.

Ajzen, I. (2002). Perceived behavioral control, self-efficacy, locus of control, and the theory of planned behavior. *Journal of Applied Social Psychology, 32*, 665–683.

Ajzen, I., Albarracín, D., & Hornik, R. (Eds.)(2007). *Prediction and change of health behavior: Applying the reasoned action approach.* Mahwah, NJ: Lawrence Erlbaum Associates.

Ajzen, I., & Fishbein, M. (1973). Attitudinal and normative variables as predictors of specific behaviors. *Journal of Personality and Psychology, 27,* 41–57.

Ajzen, I., & Fishbein, M. (1980). *Understanding attitudes and predicting social behavior: Attitudes, intentions and perceived behavioral control.* Englewood Cliffs, NJ: Prentice Hall.

Albarracín, D., Johnson, B. T., Fishbein, M., & Muellerleile, P. A. (2001). Theories of reasoned action and condom usage: A meta-analysis. *Psychological Bulletin, 127*(1), 142–161.

Armitage, C. J., & Conner, M. (2001). Efficacy of the theory of planned behaviour: A meta-analytic review. *British Journal of Social Psychology, 40,* 471–499.

Aron, A., et al. (2007, November 14). "Politics and the brain." *New York Times.* Retrieved on March 30, 2009, from www.mytimes.com/2007/11/14/opinion/iweb14brain.html.

Arthur, C. (2009, March 19). The Streisand effect: Secrecy in the digital age. *The Guardian, U.K.,* p. 6.

Balestrino, A., & Ciardi, C. (2008). Social norms, cognitive dissonance, and the timing of marriage, *The Journal of Socio-Economics, 37*, 2399–2410.

Beauvois, J. L., & Joule, R. V. (1999). A radical point of view on dissonance theory. In E. Harmon-Jones & J. Mills (Eds.), *Cognitive dissonance: Progress on a pivotal theory in social psychology* (pp. 43–70). Washington, DC: American Psychological Association.

Belk, R. W. (1988). Possessions and the extended self. *Journal of Consumer Research, 2* (2), 139–68.

Booth-Butterfield, S., & Reger, B. (2004). The message changes belief and the rest is theory: The "1% or less" milk campaign and reasoned action. *Preventive Medicine, 39*, 581–588.

Brehm, J. W. (1966). *A theory of psychological reactance.* San Diego, CA: Academic Press.

Brehm, J. W., & Brehm, S. S. (1981). *Psychological reactance: A theory of freedom and control.* San Diego, CA: Academic Press.

Burgoon, M., Alvaro, E. M., Broneck, K., Miller, C., Grandpre, J. R., Hall, J. R., & Franck, C. (2002).Using interactive media tools to test substance abuse prevention messages. In W. D. Crano & M. Burgoon (Eds.), *Mass media and drug prevention: Classic and contemporary theories and research* (pp. 67–87). Mahwah, NJ: Lawrence Erlbaum.

Burke, S. M., Sparkes, A. C., & Allen-Collinson, J. (2008). High altitude climbers as ethnomethodologists making sense of cognitive dissonance: Ethnographic insights from an attempt to scale Mt. Everest. *The Sport Psychologist, 22,* 336–355.

Cacioppo, J. T., & Petty, R. E. (1986). In M. G. H. Cole, E. Donchin, & S. W. Porges (Eds.), *Social processes in psychophysiology: Systems, processes, and applications* (pp. 646–679). New York: Guilford Press.

Chatzisarantis, N. L. D., Hagger, M. S., & Wang, J. C. K. (2008). An experimental test of cognitive dissonance theory in the domain of physical exercise. *Journal of Applied Sport Psychology, 20,* 97–115.

Cialdini, R. B. (1993). *Influence: Science and practice* (3rd ed.). LaPorte, IN: HarperCollins.

Cialdini, R. B., Wosinska, W., Barrett, D. W., Butner, J., & Gornik-Durose, M. (1999). Compliance with a request in two cultures: The differential influence of social proof, commitment/consistency on collectivists and individualists. *Personality and Social Psychology Bulletin, 25*(10), 1242–1253.

Cochran, S. D., Mays, V. M., Ciaretta, J., Caruso, C., & Mallon, D. (1992). Efficacy of the theory of reasoned action in predicting AIDS related risk reduction among gay men. *Journal of Applied Social Psychology, 22,* 1481–1501.

Cooper, J. (2007). *Cognitive dissonance: Fifty years of a classic theory.* Los Angeles, CA: Sage.

Crites, S. L., & Cacioppo, J. T. (1996). Electrocortical differentiation of evaluative and nonevaluative categorizations. *Psychological Science 7,* 318–321.

Crites, S. L., Cacioppo, J. T., Gardner, W. L., & Berntson, G. G. (1995). Bioelectrical echoes from evaluative categorization: II. A late positive brain potential that varies as a function of attitude registration rather than attitude report. *Journal of Personality and Social Psychology 68,* 997–1013.

Dillard, P. (1993). Persuasion past and present: Attitudes aren't what they used to be. *Communication Monographs, 60*(1), 90–97.

Dillard, J. P., & Shen, L. (2005). On the nature of reactance and its role in persuasive health communication. *Communication Monographs, 72,* 144–168.

Eagly, A. H., & Chaiken, S. (1993). *The psychology of attitudes.* New York: Harcourt, Brace, Jovanovich.

Egan, L. C., Santos, L. R., & Bloom, P. (2007). The origins of cognitive dissonance: Evidence from children and monkeys. *Psychological Science, 18*(11), 978–983.

Fabrigar, L. R., Krosnick, J. A., & MacDougall, B. L. (2005). Attitude measurement: Techniques for measuring the unobservable. In T. C. Brock & M. C. Green (Eds.), *Persuasion: Psychological insights and perspectives* (pp. 17–40). Thousand Oaks, CA: Sage.

Fazio, R. H. (1986). How do attitudes guide behavior? In R. M. Sorrentino & E. T. Higgins (Eds.), *The handbook of motivation and cognition: Foundations of social behavior* (pp. 204–243). New York: Guilford Press.

Fazio, R. H., & Zanna, M. P. (1981). Direct experience and attitude-behavior consistency. In L. Berkowitz (Ed.), *Advances in experimental social psychology* (Vol. 14, pp. 161–202). New York: Academic Press.

Festinger, L. (1957). *A theory of cognitive dissonance.* Stanford, CA: Stanford University Press.

Festinger, L. (1964). *Conflict, decision and dissonance.* Stanford, CA: Stanford University Press.

Festinger, L., & Carlsmith, J. M. (1959). Cognitive consequences of forced compliance. *Journal of Abnormal and Social Psychology, 58,* 203–210.

Festinger, L., & Carlsmith, J. M. (2007). Does cognitive dissonance explain why behavior can change attitudes? In J. A. Nier (Ed.) *Taking sides: Clashing views in social psychology* (2nd ed., pp. 74–91). Dubuque, IA: McGraw-Hill.

Fishbein, M., & Ajzen, I. (1975). *Belief, attitude, intention, and behavior: An introduction to theory and research.* Reading, MA: Addison-Wesley.

Fisher, R. J. (1993). Social desirability bias and the validity of indirect questioning. *Journal of Consumer Research, 20,* 303–315.

Fournier, S. (1998). Consumers and their brands: Developing relationship theory in consumer research. *Journal of Consumer Research, 24,* 343–373.

Gastil, J. (2000). Thinking, drinking, and driving: An application of the theory of reasoned action to DWI prevention. *Journal of Applied Social Psychology, 30*(11), 2217–2232.

Godin, G., & Kok, G. (1996). The theory of planned behavior: A review of its applications to health-related behaviors. *American Journal of Health Promotion, 11,* 87–98.

Godin, G., Maticka-Tynadale, E., Adrien, A., Manson-Singer, S., Williams, D., & Cappon, P. (1996). Cross-cultural testing of three social cognitive theories: An application to condom use. *Journal of Applied Social Psychology, 26,* 1556–1586.

Granberg, D., & Holmberg, S. (1990). Intention–behavior relationship among U.S. and Swedish voters. *Social Psychology Quarterly, 53,* 44–54.

Greene, K., Hale, J. L., & Rubin, D. L. (1997). A test of the theory of reasoned action in the context of condom use and AIDS. *Communication Reports, 10*(1), 21–33.

Greenwald, A. G., & Ronis, D. L. (1978). Twenty years of cognitive dissonance: Case study of the evolution of a theory. *Psychological Review, 85*(1), 53–57.

Hample, D. (1984). On the use of self-reports. *Argumentation and Advocacy, 20,* 140–153.

Hansmann, R., & Scholz, R.W. (2003). A two-step informational strategy for reducing littering behavior in a cinema. *Environment and Behavior, 35* (6), 752–762.

Harmon-Jones, E., & Harmon-Jones, C. (2008). Cognitive dissonance theory: An update with a focus on the action-based model. In J. Shaw & W. Gardner (Eds.) *Handbook of motivation* (pp. 71–83), New York: Guilford Press.

Harmon-Jones, E., & Mills, J. (Eds.). (1999). *Cognitive dissonance: Progress on a pivotal theory in social psychology.* Washington, DC: American Psychological Association.

Haugtvedt, C., & Petty, R. E. (1992). Personality and persuasion: Need for cognition moderates the persistence and resistance of attitude changes. *Journal of Personality and Social Psychology, 63,* 308–319.

Heider, F. (1958). *The psychology of interpersonal relations.* New York: John Wiley & Sons.

Hong, S. M. (1992). Hong's Psychological Reactance Scale: A further factor analytic validation. *Psychological Reports, 70,* 512–514.

Hong, S. M., & Faedda, S. (1996). Refinement of the Hong psychological reactance scale. *Educational and Psychological Measurement, 56,* 173–182.

Horsley, A. D. (1988). The unintended effects of a posted sign on littering attitudes and stated intentions. *Journal of Environmental Education, 19*(3), 10–14.

Hoshino-Browne, E., Zanna, A. S., Spencer, S. J, Zanna, M. P., Kitayama, S., & Lackenbauer, S. (2005). On the cultural guises of cognitive dissonance: The case of easterners and westerners. *Journal of Personality and Social Psychology, 89,* 294–310.

Huffman, K. T., Grossnickle, W. F., Cope, J. G., & Huffman, K. (1995). Litter reduction: A review and integration of the literature. *Environment and Behavior, 27,* 153–183.

Iacoboni, M., Freedman, J., Kaplan J., Jamieson, K. H., Freedman, T., Knapp, B., and Fitzgerald, K. (2007, November 11). "This is your brain on politics." *New York Times,* Sec. 4, p. 14. Retrieved on March 30, 2009, from www.nytimes.com/2007/11/11/opinion/11freedman.html?_r=1

Infante, D. A., & Wigley, C. J. (1986). Verbal aggressiveness: An interpersonal model and measure. *Communication Monographs, 53,* 61–69

Ito, T. A., & Cacioppo, J. T. (2007). Attitudes as mental and neural states of readiness. In B. Wittenbrink & N. Schwartz (Eds.), *Implicit measures of attitude* (pp. 125–158). New York: Guilford Press.

Johnston, K. L., & White, K. M. (2003). Binge-drinking: A test of the role of group norms in the theory of planned behavior. *Psychology and Health, 18,* 63–77.

Kelman, H. C. (1953). Attitude change as a function of response restriction. *Human Relations, 6,* 185–214.

Kim, M., & Hunter, J. E. (1993). Attitude–behavior relations: A meta-analysis of attitude relevance and topic. *Journal of Communication, 43*(1), 101–142.

Kitayama, S., Snibbe, A. C., Markus, H. Z., & Suzuki, T. (2004). Is there any "free choice"? Self and dissonance in two cultures. *Psychological Science, 15*(8), 527–533.

Knox, R. E., & Inkster, J. A. (1968). Postdecision dissonance at post time. *Journal of Personality and Social Psychology, 3,* 319–323.

Lac, A., Alvaro, E. M., Crano, W. D., & Siegel, J. T. (2009). Pathways from parental knowledge and warmth to adolescent marijuana use: An extension of the theory of planned behavior. *Prevention Science, 10*(1), 22–32.

Lee, C., & Green, R. T. (1991). Cross-cultural examination of the Fishbein behavioral intention model. *Journal of International Business Studies, second quarter,* 289–305.

Likert, R. (1932). A technique for the measurement of attitudes (special issue). *Archives of Psychology, 22,* 1–55.

Madden, T. J., Ellen, P.S., & Ajzen, I. (1992). A comparison of the Theory of Planned Behavior and the Theory of Reasoned Action. *Personality and Social Psychology Bulletin, 18*(3), 3–9.

Masnick, M. (2005, January). Since when is it illegal to just mention a trademark online? *Techdirt.* Retrieved on March 10, 2009, from www.techdirt.com/articles/20050105/0132239.shtml

Mathes, E. W., & Kemper, S. B. (1976). Clothing as a nonverbal communicator of sexual attitudes and behavior. *Perceptual and Motor Skills, 43,* 495–498.

Matz, D. C., & Wood, W. (2005). Cognitive dissonance in groups: The consequences of disagreement. *Journal of Personality and Social Psychology, 88*(1), 22–37.

McCroskey, J. C. (1966). Scales for the measurement of ethos. *Speech Monographs, 33,* 65–72.

McCroskey, J. C., & Young, T. J. (1981). Ethos and credibility: The construct and its measurement after three decades. *Central States Speech Journal, 32,* 24–34.

Merida, K. (2008, June 27). "Hill, Yes! O., No! The battle isn't over for many women who fought for Clinton. *The Washington Post*, p. C1.

Miller, C. H., Burgoon, M., Grandpre, J., & Alvaro, E. (2006). Identifying principal risk factors for the initiation of adolescent smoking behaviors: The significance of psychological reactance. *Health Communication, 19,* 241–252.

Miller, C. H., Lane, L. T., Deatrick, L. M., Young, A. M., & Potts, K. A. (2007). Health messages: The effects of controlling language, lexical concreteness, and the restoration of freedom. *Human Communication Research, 33,* 219–240.

Mills, J. (1999). Improving the 1957 version of dissonance theory. In E. Harmon-Jones & J. Mills (Eds.), *Cognitive dissonance: Progress on a pivotal theory in social psychology* (pp. 25–42). Washington, DC: American Psychological Association.

Newcomb, T. M. (1953). An approach to the study of communicative acts. *Psychological Review, 60,* 393–404.

Nisbett, R. E. (2003). *The geography of thought.* New York: The Free Press.

Nisbett, R. E., & Wilson, T. D. (1977). Telling more than we know: Verbal reports on mental processes. *Psychological Review, 84,* 231–259.

Osgood, C. E., & Tannenbaum, P. H. (1955). The principle of congruity in the prediction of attitude change. *Psychological Review, 62,* 42–55.

Osgood, C. E., Tannenbaum, P. H., & Suci, G. J. (1957). *The measurement of meaning.* Urbana: University of Illinois Press.

Ostrum, T. M., Bond, C. F., Krosnick, J. A., & Sedikides, C. (1994). Attitude scales: How we measure the unmeasurable. In S. Shavitt & T. C. Brock (Eds.), *Persuasion: Psychological insights and perspectives* (pp. 15–42). Boston: Allyn & Bacon.

Park, H. S., Levine, T. R., & Sharkey, W. F. (1998). The theory of reasoned action and self-construals: Understanding recycling in Hawaii. *Communication Studies, 49*(3), 196–208.

Patry, A. L., & Pelletier, L. G. (2001). Extraterrestrial beliefs and experiences: An application of the theory of reasoned action. *The Journal of Social Psychology, 141*(2), 199–217.

Petty, R. E., & Cacioppo, J. T. (1983). The role of bodily responses in attitude measurement and change. In J. T. Cacioppo & R. E. Petty (Eds.), *Social psychophysiology: A sourcebook* (pp. 51–101). New York: Guilford Press.

Petty, R. E., & Cacioppo, J. T. (1986a). The Elaboration Likelihood Model of persuasion. In L. Berkowitz (Ed.), *Advances in experimental social psychology* (Vol. 19, pp. 123–205). New York: Academic Press.

Petty, R. E., & Cacioppo, J. T. (1986b). *Communication and persuasion: Central and peripheral routes to attitude change.* New York: Springer-Verlag.

Petty, R. E., Cacioppo, J. T., Strathman, A. J., & Priester, J. R. (2005). To think or not to think: Exploring two routes to persuasion. In T. Brock & M. C. Green (Eds.), *Persuasion: Psychological insights and perspectives* (pp. 81–116). Thousand Oaks, CA: Sage.

Petty, R. E., Haugtvedt, C., & Smith, S. M. (1995). Elaboration as a determinant of attitude strength: Creating attitudes that are persistent, resistant, and predictive of behavior. In R. E. Petty & J. A. Krosnick (Eds.), *Attitude strength: Antecedents and consequences* (pp. 93–130). Mahwah, NJ: Erlbaum.

Preiss, R. W., & Allen, M. (1998). Performing counterattitudinal advocacy: The persuasive impact of incentives. In M. Allen & R. Preiss (Eds.), *Persuasion: Advances through meta-analysis* (pp. 231–239). Cresskill, NJ: Hampton Press.

Quick, B. L., & Stephenson, M. T. (2007). Further evidence that psychological reactance can be modeled as a combination of anger and negative cognition. *Communication Research, 34*(3), 255–276.

Rosenbloom, T., Levi, S., Peleg, A., & Nemrodov, D. (2009). Effectiveness of road safety workshop for young adults. *Safety Science, 47*(5), 608–613.

Scher, S. J., & Cooper, J. (1989). The motivational basis of dissonance: The singular role of behavioral consequences. *Journal of Personality and Social Psychology, 56,* 899–906.

Schudson, M. (1984). *Advertising: The uneasy persuasion.* New York: Basic Books.

Sénémeaud, C., & Somat, A. (2009). Dissonance arousal and persistence in attitude change. *Swiss Journal of Psychology, 68*(1), 25–31.

Sheppard, B. H., Hartwick, J., & Warshaw, P. R. (1988). The theory of reasoned action: A meta-analysis of past research with recommendations for modifications and future research. *Journal of Consumer Research, 15,* 325–343.

Steen, D. M., Peay, M. Y., & Owen, N. (2000). Predicting Australian adolescents' intentions to minimize sun exposure. *Psychology and Health, 13*(1), 111–119.

Sullivan, T. (2009, April 22). "The Pirate Bay case: Not necessarily a victory for Hollywood." *Christian Science Monitor*, p. 6.

Swaminathan, V., Stilley, K. M., & Ahluwalia, R. (2009). When brand personality matters: The moderating role of attachment styles. *Journal of Consumer Research, 35*(6), 985–1002.

Tavris, C., & Aronson, E. (2007). *Mistakes were made (but not by me).* New York: Harcourt.

Tesser, A., & Shaffer, D. R. (1990). Attitudes and attitude change. In M. W. Rosenzweig & L. W. Porter (Eds.), *Annual review of psychology* (pp. 479–573). Palo Alto, CA: Annual Reviews.

Weber, K., Martin, M. M., & Corrigan, M. (2007). Real donors, real consent: Testing the theory of reasoned action and organ donor consent. *Journal of Applied Social Psychology, 37*(10), 2435–2450.

Wu, T., Snider, J. B., Floyd, M. R., Florence, J. E., Stoots, J. M., & Makamey, M. I. (2009). Intention for healthy eating among southern Appalachian teens. *American Journal of Health Behavior, 33*, 115–124.

Xie, X., Jang, A., & Cai, D. A. (2007, November 15). *Are Asians really okay with contradictions? Using dissonance to explain cultural differences in responding to contradictions.* Paper presented at the annual meeting of the National Communication Association, Chicago, IL.

Zimbardo, P. G., Weisenberg, M., Firestone, I., & Levy, B. (1965). Communicator effectiveness in producing public conformity and private attitude change. *Journal of Personality, 33,* 233–255.

CHAPTER 4

Credibility

Barack Obama has it. So did John F. Kennedy. Adolf Hitler had it, unfortunately. Dr. Martin Luther King, Jr. had it, as did both Princess Grace and Lady Di. Depending on whom you ask, Oprah Winfrey, Steve Jobs, and Emeril Lagasse may have it. What all these people have, or had, is *charisma*.[1] Charisma is a lay term used to describe someone who possesses a certain indefinable charm or allure. Such a person may be said to have a magnetic personality.

There is a problem with describing people as charismatic, however. The term has no clear, precise meaning. It isn't the same as popularity. Nor is it synonymous with leadership. It can't be equated with assertiveness either. Indeed, part of the attraction of charismatic persons may be that their appeal is somewhat magical or elusive.

Because charisma is a fuzzy concept, persuasion researchers tend to rely instead on a different but related concept called *ethos,* or *credibility.* Ethos bears some similarity to charisma. However, whereas charisma represents an elusive, ineffable quality, ethos can be defined and measured with much greater precision. In this chapter, we examine the concept of ethos, or credibility, and its relationship to persuasion. First we examine credibility as it relates to celebrity endorsers and spokespersons. Next we offer a definition, discuss the basic features, and explore the underlying dimensions that make up credibility. Then we consider how credibility functions according to Petty and Cacioppo's *elaboration likelihood model* of persuasion (1986), and we examine a phenomenon known as the *sleeper effect.* Finally, we discuss credibility as it applies to both institutions and interpersonal settings.

CELEBRITY SELLING POWER: THE ANSWER IS IN THE STARS

Did you know that roughly one in five commercials features a famous person (Solomon, 2009)? Were you aware that approximately 10 percent of all advertising expenditures go to pay celebrity endorsers (Agrawal & Kamakura, 1995)? That translates into almost $1 billion per year. No wonder Berger (2004) claims we now live in a *celebritocracy.* Celebrities and athletes with a high "Q" (their selling quotient) can command salaries in millions of dollars. Whereas men once dominated celebrity endorsements, there are now nearly as many women endorsers as men. One reason is that women have more purchasing power than ever before. Another reason is that female consumers are less willing than they used to be to defer to the say-so of male spokespersons. Hence, the success of Beyoncé, Martha Stewart, and Oprah Winfrey at hawking their own and others' wares.

"Which celebrities do this type of yoga?"

Because commercials cost so much to produce (about $400,000 for a 30-second spot) and because big-name stars and athletes command high salaries, some commercials feature celebrities in niche roles. For example, John Krasinski, who plays the part of Jim Halpert on the TV show *The Office*, does the voice-over for some BlackBerry commercials. In some cases, fictional characters, such as secret agent Austin Powers, have been used to sell products.

Considering all the money that is spent on celebrity endorsements, you might be wondering whether they actually work. When asked this same question in a public opinion poll, only 3 percent of respondents said they would try a new product based on the recommendation of a celebrity endorser ("Study finds . . . ," 2000). The evidence suggests otherwise. Celebrities do help the "bottom line" (Erdogan, Baker, & Tagg, 2001; Farrell, Karels, Monfort, & McClatchey, 2000). If celebrities didn't reap profits, advertisers wouldn't use them.

The Match-Up Hypothesis: Why Seth Rogen Should Not Be Revlon's Spokesperson

The *match-up hypothesis* suggests that a celebrity endorser must be a good "fit" for the brand being endorsed (Kahle & Homer, 1985; Kamins & Gupta, 1994; Koernig & Boyd, 2009; Till & Busler, 2000). Sean Connery's seasoned elegance makes him a good match for Louis Vuitton luggage, a brand that appeals to an older demographic. Rapper 50 Cent and NBA star LeBron James are the faces of Vitaminwater, which appeals to a younger demographic. There is a good reason why Tiger Woods, not Amy Winehouse, is Nike's top endorser. While some endorsers have universal appeal, such as NBA legend Michael Jordan, others, like skateboarding great Tony Hawk, have niche appeal.

One explanation for why celebrities should fit the brands they endorse comes from the *meaning transfer perspective*. According to this view, an endorser's public persona is projected onto a brand. The brand's image is then incorporated into the consumer's self-concept (McCracken, 1986, 1989). By way of illustration, Ellen DeGeneres danced her way through one of American Express's "My Life, My Card" commercials. Independent-minded consumers who see themselves as "dancing to their own tune" can identify with DeGeneres, whom they see as successful while doing her own thing.

Catch a Falling Star

There can be a downside to relying on well-known celebrities, athletes, or other famous figures. What happens if a famous person becomes embroiled in a scandal or a legal proceeding? When Olympic gold medalist Michael Phelps was photographed smoking pot from a bong, his endorsement deal with Kellogg went up in smoke. Visine, are you interested? Nike and Coca-Cola sacked NFL star Michael Vick after he was convicted of animal cruelty for operating a dog fighting ring. After singer Chris Brown was charged with assault against his girlfriend, Rihanna, his endorsement deal with Doublemint gum took a beating too.

As these examples clearly show, if a celebrity, an athlete, a journalist, or a politician is tainted by a scandal, it can rub off on the sponsor's credibility (Till & Shimp, 1998). Hence, almost all endorsement deals include a "moral turpitude" clause that allows the sponsor to void the contract for any serious infraction.

To avoid the risk and expense of actual endorsers, many companies rely on fictional spokespersons. Aunt Jemima would never engage in insider trading, the Geico gecko will never be arrested for sexual assault, Mr. Clean won't ever test positive for steroid use, and the Keebler elves won't be charged with child pornography in an FBI sting operation. Having examined the downside of relying too heavily on credibility as a tool of persuasion, let's consider more carefully what it actually is and how it actually works.

WHAT IS CREDIBILITY?

O'Keefe (1990) defines credibility as "judgments made by a perceiver (e.g., a message recipient) concerning the believability of a communicator" (pp. 130–131). We would extend this definition to include not only persons as communicators but institutions as well. Private companies and governmental agencies also have images and reputations to protect. They want to be viewed favorably, too. In addition, it should be recognized that in face-to-face encounters there are really *two* sources whose credibility is at stake, because each party to the interaction is simultaneously a sender and a receiver of messages.

Credibility Is a Receiver-Based Construct

An important feature of O'Keefe's definition is the recognition that credibility is a *receiver-based construct.* In other words, credibility exists in the eye of the beholder. For example, Hillary Clinton may be credible to one person, while Sarah Palin may be credible to another. Rappers need "street cred," or the perception of being dangerous (scars from bullets or knife wounds help). In short, if these folks are credible, it is because we bestow credibility on them. Modifying a time-worn philosophical question, one might ask, "If a source stood in the middle of a forest and there were no one around to perceive him or her, would there be any credibility?" Our answer is no. Different sources possess different abilities and attributes, but the value assigned to these abilities and attributes resides in the receiver, not in the source. Credibility is a perceptual phenomenon.

Credibility Is a Multidimensional Construct

A second important feature of credibility is that it is not a one-dimensional construct, that is, made up of only one element. Credibility represents a composite of several characteristics that receivers perceive in a source. Thus, credibility is a *multidimensional construct.* An analogy may serve to clarify this point. Imagine that you were trying to define *athleticism.* It would be difficult to single out only one thing that makes an individual athletic. Athleticism requires strength, coordination, stamina, and quick reflexes, among other things. In the same way, credibility isn't a single quality but a combination of qualities a source is believed to possess. We discuss these qualities shortly.

Credibility Is a Situational/Contextual Phenomenon

A third feature of credibility is that it is a *situational* or *contextual phenomenon.* The very qualities that are revered in a communicator in one situation or context may be reviled in another setting. Thus, a persuader's credibility is subject to change as he or she moves from one audience to another, or one setting to another. The president of the National Rifle Association might be well received when speaking before an audience of hunting and fishing enthusiasts. The same source might encounter a hostile reception, however, if he spoke before a group of animal rights advocates, such as People for the Ethical Treatment of Animals. Your own credibility is subject to such situational changes too. You may enjoy more credibility in one context—for example, work, family, friends, school—than in another.

Credibility Is Dynamic

Credibility can change over time. George W. Bush's credibility soared after the invasion of Afghanistan, yet he left office with the lowest public approval ratings of any U.S. president. Indeed, Bush has the dubious distinction of notching the highest and the lowest presidential approval ratings on record (Gass & Seiter, 2009; Thee-Brenan, 2009). It is important to recognize, then, that credibility is *dynamic:* It fluctuates from audience to audience, from situation to situation, and from time to time. A source's credibility can change even during the course of a single speech, sales pitch, or boardroom presentation.

THE FACTOR ANALYTIC APPROACH TO CREDIBILITY

Just as chefs are interested in what ingredients go into award-winning recipes, persuasion researchers have tried to determine the "ingredients," or underlying dimensions, of credibility. In fact, as long ago as 380 B.C., Aristotle proclaimed in th*e Rhetoric* that the ingredients "which inspire confidence in the orator's character . . . that induce us to believe a thing apart from any proof of it . . . [are] good sense, good moral character, and good will" (1378). Aristotle wasn't far off the mark.

In the 1960s and 1970s researchers began to use a statistical technique known as *factor analysis* to uncover the underlying dimensions or ingredients of credibility. Controversy emerged during this period over how many credibility dimensions there were and what they should be called (see Berlo, Lemert, & Mertz, 1969; Cronkhite & Liska, 1976; McCroskey, 1966; Pornpitakpan, 2004). Subsequent investigations, though, have clarified the situation considerably, if not completely.

There is now fairly solid evidence that there are three primary dimensions of credibility, which are almost always relevant to the evaluation of sources, and several secondary dimensions that are more situation-specific. If you are trying to enhance your own credibility, you should focus on the primary dimensions. The secondary dimensions may or may not matter depending on your particular situation. We discuss both sets of dimensions next and provide the scale items commonly used to measure these dimensions in Box 4.1.

Bipolar Adjectives Used to Measure Credibility with a Semantic Differential Scale	BOX 4.1

Primary Dimensions

  Expertise (also called competence or qualification)

    experienced/inexperienced

    informed/uninformed

    trained/untrained

    qualified/unqualified

    skilled/unskilled

    intelligent/unintelligent

    expert/inexpert

    competent/incompetent

    bright/stupid

  Trustworthiness (also called character, safety, or personal integrity)

    honest/dishonest

    trustworthy/untrustworthy

    open-minded/close-minded

    just/unjust

    fair/unfair

    unselfish/selfish

    moral/immoral

    ethical/unethical

    genuine/phony

  Goodwill

    cares about me/doesn't care about me

    has my interests at heart/doesn't have my interests at heart

    not self-centered/self-centered

    concerned with me/not concerned with me

    sensitive/insensitive

    understanding/not understanding

Secondary Dimensions	calm/anxious
Extroversion	excitable/composed
timid/bold	**Sociability**
verbal/quiet	honest/dishonest
meek/aggressive	selfish/unselfish
talkative/silent	high character/low character
Composure	
poised/nervous	
relaxed/tense	

Adapted from McCroskey, J. C., & Young, T. J. (1981). Ethos and credibility: The construct and its measurement after three decades. *Central States Speech Journal, 32,* 24–34; and McCroskey, J. C., & Teven, J. J. (1999). Goodwill: A reexamination of the construct and its measurement. *Communication Monographs, 66,* 90–103.

Primary Dimensions of Credibility

The first primary dimension of credibility is *expertise* (Berlo et al., 1969; Hovland, Janis, & Kelly, 1953; McCroskey, 1966; Pornpitakpan, 2004). To be credible, a persuader must know his or her stuff or, at least, *appear* to know his or her stuff. Sometimes a title alone, such as M.D., Ph.D., or CPA, can confer credibility on a source. You have to be careful, though; not all titles mean what they say. For instance, Dr. Laura (Laura Schlessinger), the radio talk show host, is neither a medical doctor nor a psychiatrist. Her Ph.D. is in physiology, even though she sometimes calls herself a "shrink." When tradespersons place ads in the Yellow Pages of the telephone directory, they often state that they are licensed or certified and have been in business for many years. They, too, want to bolster their credibility.

To be regarded as an expert, a source needn't possess advanced degrees, specialized training, licenses, or credentials, however. Joe "the plumber" Wurzelbacher became a poster boy for Republicans during the 2008 presidential campaign, even though it was reported that he had no plumber's license and owed back taxes (Cauchon & Eisler, 2008). As another example, at an Alcoholics Anonymous meeting, a member who had been an alcoholic for 20 years, and who had been sober for the past 10 years, would likely be perceived as having expertise. Such a member would know what he or she was talking about, because he or she had "been there" (Denzen, 1987; Robertson, 1988). Even astrologers, fortune-tellers, and psychics make attempts to establish their expertise. "Don't pay for advice from phony psychics," a psychic hotline or Website proclaims, "We have *genuine, certified psychics* waiting to take your call."

Interestingly, a source's expertise doesn't always have to be in the field in which he or she is attempting to persuade. Catherine Zeta-Jones, for example, isn't an expert on telecommunications. Yet she is an effective endorser for T-Mobile. Endorsements by famous persons enjoy a *halo-effect* that allows them to carry their credibility to new, unrelated fields. An interesting study by Bruce Rind (1992) shows that this phenomenon isn't limited to famous people either.

In Rind's study, a confederate working with the experimenter approached shoppers in the food court of a mall and asked them to buy raffle tickets. In one of the experimental conditions, the confederate amazed the shoppers with his calculating ability (the confederate was actually wired with a hidden transmitter, through which he received the correct answers). In another condition, the confederate made a fool of himself by exhibiting poor calculating skills. In a third control condition, the confederate didn't profess to have any amazing skills. Shoppers bought significantly more raffle tickets when the confederate demonstrated astonishing calculating skills than in either of the other two conditions. It mattered not that the purpose of the raffle was unrelated to the confederate's amazing talent. Expertise, even unrelated expertise, then, can be an asset in persuasion. Bear in mind, however, that purchasing a raffle ticket is a fairly trivial act. We suspect that on a more involving issue, relevant expertise would be valued more highly by receivers.

The second primary dimension of credibility is *trustworthiness* (Applbaum & Anatol, 1972; Berlo et al., 1969; Hovland et al., 1953; McCroskey, 1966; Pornpitakpan, 2004). A source may appear knowledgeable, but what if you don't think he or she is being truthful or can be trusted? If your car needs a brake job, you not only want a qualified mechanic, you want an *honest,* qualified mechanic. To be successful, persuaders must, therefore, convey an impression of honesty and integrity.

Perhaps you've noticed that some advertisements in magazines or newspapers carry the logo "As Seen On TV." The purpose in displaying this logo is to instill trust. Many consumers unthinkingly presume that only reputable companies can afford television commercials. The same applies to Yellow Pages ads that feature the *ichthys* logo, the Christian sign of the fish. The idea behind displaying this symbol is that the electrician, plumber, or carpenter is a Christian and is, therefore, unlikely to rip off his or her customers. Such "sign reasoning" may have merit. But then again, couldn't an unscrupulous tradesperson simply use the *ichthys* logo to dupe customers into believing he or she was trustworthy? Perhaps you remember Richard Hatch, the winner of the first *Survivor* show on CBS. Although he came across as cunning and strategic, he didn't seem like someone who could be trusted. For this reason, even though he won the million-dollar prize, he had trouble translating his fame into commercial endorsements. A grim reminder of why one should exercise caution before placing one's trust in a stranger is provided in Box 4.2.

The third primary dimension of credibility is *goodwill.* Until recently, it was generally accepted that there were only two primary dimensions of credibility. However, McCroskey and Teven (McCroskey & Teven, 1999; Teven & McCroskey, 1997) have provided solid research support for a third primary dimension. In fact, McCroskey and Teven refer to goodwill as the "lost dimension" of credibility, because it was one of the three dimensions of ethos identified by Aristotle. McCroskey and Teven (1999) point out that the opposite of goodwill isn't ill-will, or malicious intent, but simply indifference.

McCroskey and Teven (1999) suggest that goodwill is synonymous with *perceived caring.* That is, a source who seems to care about and take a genuine interest in the receiver is displaying goodwill. Goodwill can be demonstrated by displaying understanding for another person's ideas, feelings, or needs. Goodwill can also be demonstrated by displaying empathy—that is, identifying with another person's feelings or situation. Goodwill can be displayed by responsiveness as well, by acknowledging and responding to another's

| Are There Horns Beneath That Halo? | BOX 4.2 |

On April 7, 1978, the body of 12-year-old Kimberly Leach was found near Suwannee River State Park in Florida. She was the last of Ted Bundy's victims. The infamous serial killer was executed for the murder of Kimberly Leach and two other women on January 24, 1989. He confessed to killing at least 35 others. Many had been lured to Bundy's car with a seemingly innocent ploy: He feigned an injury and asked his victims to help him carry things to his car. How was it possible that Ted Bundy was able to deceive so many women? According to author Ann Rule (1989), who knew Bundy:

> Ted has been described as the perfect son, the perfect student, the Boy Scout grown to adulthood, a genius, as handsome as a movie idol, a bright light in the future of the Republican party, a sensitive social worker, a budding lawyer, a trusted friend, a young man for whom the future could surely hold only success.

From this description, or from any glance at a picture of Ted Bundy, it is clear that he did not fit the stereotypical image of a serial killer. And that's why he was so dangerous. We often trust people because they appear credible. Good looks and an articulate manner act as a halo that can blind us to the possible horns underneath. Attractiveness and a "way with words" are not the only halos that can fool us. Sometimes we trust people because of the way they talk, how they dress, or who they know.

How can you avoid the problems associated with the "halo effect"? Perhaps the best advice we can offer is to heed two pieces of childhood advice: "Don't judge a book by its cover" and "Never talk to strangers."

communication attempts. A source who said, "I hear where you are coming from" or "I can relate to that" or "I sympathize with how you feel" would be displaying this quality.

Of the three primary dimensions just discussed, expertise seems to have the greatest effect on persuasion. Although they did not examine the goodwill construct specifically, Wilson and Sherrell (1993) revealed in a meta-analysis that the effect of expertise was greater than that of trustworthiness, attraction, or similarity on persuasion. The importance of the dimensions on persuasive outcomes, however, may depend on the particulars of the topic or context for persuasion.

Secondary Dimensions of Credibility

Researchers have uncovered several other dimensions of credibility that tend to be more situation specific. One of these, termed *dynamism* by some (Berlo et al., 1969) and *extroversion* by others (Burgoon, 1976; McCroskey & Young, 1981), has to do with how energetic, animated, or enthusiastic the source appears. The late TV spokesperson Billy Mays, who shouted his way through infomercials, personified this dimension. Former actor-turned-politician Arnold Schwarzenegger also embodies this dimension. Obviously, it wouldn't do for a fitness trainer, like the *Biggest Loser's* Jillian Michaels, to appear sluggish or lethargic. Certain situations call for the source to be "peppy" and full of energy. However, a person who is too bubbly and effervescent, especially at the wrong times, may lose credibility (Burgoon, 1973). The trick is for a source to match his or her level of dynamism to the demands of the situation.

Perceived expertise is a prerequisite for credibility.

Another secondary dimension of credibility is *composure* (Miller & Hewgill, 1964). In some situations, we expect a source to remain calm, cool, and collected. The character of James Bond, secret agent 007, exudes this quality. Captain Chesley "Sully" Sullenberger, who safely landed US Airways flight 1549 on the Hudson River, retained his composure during the entire ordeal. The flight recordings released by the FAA revealed that Sully was "the epitome of composure under life-threatening pressure" (McShane, 2009, p. 12). On the flip side of the coin, a source who loses composure, or who seems nervous or ill at ease, may lose credibility. When Tom Cruise jumped up and down on Oprah's couch, while proclaiming his love for Katie Holmes, viewers felt he had lost it. Similarly, at the Laugh Factory, Michael Richards (a.k.a. Kramer on the *Seinfeld* show) hurled a sting of racial epithets at some hecklers in the audience. His career took a nosedive.

An additional secondary dimension of credibility has been dubbed *sociability*. This dimension refers to a source's friendliness or likableness. To us, Reese Witherspoon, Ken Griffey, Jr., Rachael Ray, and Will Smith possess this quality, as do others who relate to people easily. Sanders (2006) emphasizes that friendliness, empathy, and authenticity go a long way in trying to persuade people. Sociability is particularly important in the "people professions," such as sales, law, education, social work, and the like.

THE FACTOR ANALYTIC APPROACH AND THE REAL WORLD

Given the extraordinary amount of attention devoted to the study of credibility, how do these dimensions hold up in the real world? The answer is, quite well. A study by Kouzes and Posner (1993) examined employees' perceptions of their managers' credibility in actual organizational settings. The results revealed a striking chemistry between managers and employees. Employees who rated their manager favorably in expertise and trustworthiness (honesty) exhibited much higher morale than employees who rated their manager unfavorably in these categories. As Kouzes and Posner (1993) observe, "Respondents who felt their manager was honest, competent, and inspiring were significantly more likely to feel a strong sense of teamwork, organizational values alignment, and organizational commitment than were those who found their managers less honest, competent, and inspiring" (pp. 282–283). Thus, a manager's credibility tends to "rub off" on his or her employees.

CREDIBILITY AS A PERIPHERAL CUE

Now that we've explained what credibility is, we turn our attention to how and why it facilitates persuasion. To do so, we return to Petty and Cacioppo's (1986) *elaboration likelihood model* of persuasion (ELM), which was introduced in Chapter 2. Petty and Cacioppo conceptualize credibility as a peripheral cue to persuasion. According to the ELM, there are two distinct routes to persuasion, which operate in tandem. One route, which they label the *central route,* involves a focus on the substance or the content of a message. Receivers who process a persuasive message via the central route engage in "cognitive elaboration," which simply means that they think about, and reflect on, the ideas and information contained in the message.

The ELM acknowledges that in most persuasive situations receivers tend to favor one route over another. Which route they favor depends, among other things, on their involvement in the issue. When receivers have a stake in the outcome, their motivation to pay attention to a message is higher. They, thus, tend to favor the central route. When receivers have little at stake their motivation to pay attention to a message is lower. They, therefore, tend to favor the peripheral route.

This is where credibility enters the picture. As a general rule, source credibility exerts more influence on receivers who aren't highly involved in an issue. Credibility matters much less if receiver involvement is already high. Instead, credibility tends to work its magic when receiver involvement is low (Benoit, 1987). Receivers with low involvement are more likely to defer to sources, because doing so requires less mental effort than concentrating on the substance of a message. To put it bluntly, low-involved receivers are cognitively lazy. This limitation notwithstanding, we mustn't underestimate the importance of credibility. Credibility may be conceptualized as a peripheral cue, but it is still a big peripheral cue.

You can use this information to your advantage if you are trying to persuade receivers who perceive you as having low credibility. You should do everything you can to increase their involvement in the topic or issue. Explain why the issue is relevant to them.

Emphasize how the topic or issue affects them directly. If you can increase your target audience's involvement in the topic or issue, they'll pay more attention to the message and less attention to your credibility.

IT'S WHAT'S UP FRONT THAT COUNTS

When should a source's expertise be identified; at the beginning or end of a persuasive message? Research findings strongly suggest that credibility tends to work only if the source is identified *prior* to the actual presentation of a persuasive message (Benoit & Strathman, 2004; Nan, 2009; O'Keefe, 1987). If the source is identified after the fact, credibility has little or no effect. Several studies, for example, found no differences in the persuasiveness of high versus low-credibility sources when the sources were identified after the messages were presented (Greenberg & Tannenbaum, 1961; O'Keefe, 1987; Sternthal, Dholakia, & Leavitt, 1978; Ward & McGinnies, 1974). Benoit and Strathman (2004) suggest that this is because credibility affects the way receivers process a message. For credibility to do any good, therefore, receivers must consider the source's credibility as they process a persuasive message.

THE SLEEPER EFFECT

The traditional view is that the impact of a persuasive message diminishes over time (Hovland, Lumsdaine, & Sheffield, 1949; Stiff, 1994). Receivers forget what was said or who said it. Persuasion wears off. The sleeper effect, however, suggests that under the right circumstances, the delayed impact of a message may be more effective than its initial impact (Kumkale & Albarracin, 2004). That is, the message might grow on receivers. Specifically, the sleeper effect posits that a message from a low-credibility source may increase in persuasiveness as time passes, compared to a message from a high-credibility source. Sound unlikely? It is, to some extent. Yet the sleeper effect has been documented by researchers, dating back more than 50 years (Hovland et al., 1949). How the sleeper effect works requires some explanation.

Imagine that one audience is exposed to a persuasive message from a source with high credibility. A second audience is exposed to the same persuasive message, but from a source with low credibility, by means of a *discounting cue*. A discounting cue consists of a disclaimer containing negative information about the source, the message, or both. For example, let's say the first group heard a message in favor of irradiating fruits and vegetables to kill bacteria before they are shipped to market. The second group would hear the same message, plus a disclaimer saying the message was drafted by a lobbyist for the agricultural industry whose real concern was agricultural profits, not consumer safety. The discounting cue would thus serve as an impediment to the effectiveness of the second message, a "ball and chain," so to speak. Afterward, each group's attitudes toward irradiated produce would be measured.

Initially, the first group's attitudes should be much more favorable toward the topic than the second group's. After all, the first group heard the message from the high-credibility source. With the passage of time, however, things might change. The first group's attitudes

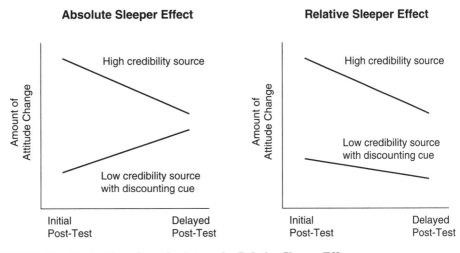

FIGURE 4.1   **Illustration of an Absolute and a Relative Sleeper Effect.**

would gradually decay over time, according to the traditional view. The second group's attitudes, however, might undergo a process known as *disassociation,* whereby the message is separated from its source in the minds of receivers. That is, the second group might remember the message, but forget the discounting cue. If you've ever heard someone say, "I heard somewhere that . . ." or "I read somewhere that . . ." you've observed disassociation in action. Once the second group disassociated the message from its source, the ball and chain would be removed. The result would be that as the first group's attitudes diminished, the second group's attitudes would become more positive. Voilà! The sleeper effect.

Although the sleeper effect has been demonstrated in a number of laboratory studies (Appel & Richter, 2007; Kumkale & Albarracin, 2004), it is difficult to produce on a consistent, reliable basis. Only a few studies have demonstrated an *absolute* sleeper effect (see Figure 4.1) of the type we've been discussing (Gruder et al., 1978; Watts & Holt, 1979; Watts & McGuire, 1964). An absolute sleeper effect occurs when a message from a high-credibility source loses favor over time, whereas a message from a low-credibility source gains favor over time. Other studies have demonstrated a *relative* sleeper effect (see Figure 4.1), meaning that both messages lose favor over time, but the high-credibility message loses more favor than the low-credibility message (see reviews by Allen & Stiff, 1989, 1998). Some studies have failed to find a sleeper effect at all (see reviews by Allen & Stiff, 1989, 1998). One study employed exactly the same methodology, using two different topics to produce the sleeper effect. It worked for one topic (opposing a four-day work week) but not for the other (allowing right turns on red lights) (Gruder et al., 1978). The sleeper effect, then, can be pretty fickle.

What implications does this hold for you as a persuader? In practice, it would be very difficult for an ordinary persuader, as opposed to a laboratory researcher, to satisfy all of the requirements for obtaining a sleeper effect. We believe there are far too many "ifs" associated with this strategy to recommend it to an ordinary persuader. The dubious nature of the sleeper effect prompted Petty and Cacioppo (1986) to warn that "although the sleeper effect is of considerable conceptual significance, obtaining it may require conditions that are infrequently present in the 'real world' or in persuasion research" (p. 183). Our advice is that you would be much better off trying to enhance your credibility as much as possible in the first place.

CREDIBILITY AND IMAGE MANAGEMENT

Thus far, we've discussed credibility strictly in connection with people or persons. We believe the concept of credibility can be extended to corporations, organizations, governmental agencies, social movements, and other institutions as well. Such group entities care about how they are perceived by the public and other constituencies. They want to project positive images. And to a large extent, their power and ability to influence are linked to their images and their reputations. For these reasons, we maintain that the credibility construct applies equally well to institutional entities and individuals. In fact, one recent study examined the role of perceived credibility for sources of information in a virtual institution: the Internet (Flanagin & Metzger, 2000).

By way of illustration, think about the charitable and philanthropic activities of major corporations. McDonald's established Ronald McDonald House to provide assistance to hospital-bound children and their families. The National Football League donates generously to the United Way. A number of companies contribute to the Make-A-Wish Foundation. In so doing, these corporations are demonstrating that they are good citizens in their communities. Doing good deeds enhances public perceptions of goodwill. We aren't suggesting that corporations are disingenuous when they make charitable contributions or that corporate altruism is based entirely on the profit motive. We do wish to point out, however, that philanthropic acts make for good public relations.

So important is image management for corporations, institutions, government agencies, and the like that entire departments, divisions, and staffs exist for just this purpose. Major corporations have large public relations (PR) departments whose primary purpose is to feature the corporation in a positive light. Political campaigns employ political consultants, to offer positive "spin" on events that unfold during a campaign. Industries and organizations employ lobbyists on Capitol Hill to help ensure that their interests are perceived favorably by legislators and regulators. Even the military employs public relations officers, because good PR is part of good military strategy. Whatever the title of these types of positions, one of their primary missions is to maintain the credibility of the host institution.

On occasion, corporations, institutions, and government agencies commit blunders that damage their credibility. They must then act quickly to restore their image and regain the public's trust. William Benoit (1995) refers to this process as *image restoration* and notes that such efforts are highly persuasive in nature (p. 6). Examples in which circumstances have forced corporations and other institutions to engage in image restoration abound. AIG was faulted for its role in the banking meltdown. The CIA's image was tarnished by its reliance on faulty intelligence about Iraq's weapons of mass destruction. Major League Baseball got a black eye after revelations of widespread steroid use surfaced.

Benoit (1995) notes that such defensive campaigns are commonplace. They are undertaken out of a necessity to restore the credibility of the corporation, institution, or agency whose image has been tarnished. Benoit highlights a number of strategies associated with image restoration. The specific strategies employed, of course, depend on the nature of the difficulty in which the institution finds itself and the range of available defenses.

We can see, then, that corporations and other institutions, not only individuals, possess credibility in varying amounts. We suspect that the same primary dimensions of credibility that apply to individuals apply equally well to corporations. We suspect that the secondary dimensions of credibility discussed previously, however, might differ. After all, the secondary dimensions don't always appear in studies of individuals' credibility. This would appear to be a fruitful topic for future scholarly inquiry.

INTERPERSONAL CREDIBILITY, IMPRESSION MANAGEMENT, FACEWORK, AND ACCOUNTS

Ordinary folks can't hire their own public relations firm, like corporations do, or employ a publicist, as the rich and famous do, to maintain a positive public image. They do engage in public relations campaigns, nonetheless. Ordinary persons tend to function as their own PR departments through impression management and facework.

Impression management theory (Tedeschi & Reiss, 1981) seeks to explain how persons go about trying to project a positive self-image.[2] Individuals want others to form favorable impressions of them. In short, individuals want to be perceived as credible. Individuals attempt to manage others' impressions of themselves by trying to say and do the right things. Engaging in "politically correct" behavior is an example of impression management at work.

Our position is that when an individual is engaging in impression management, he or she is engaging in persuasion. He or she is attempting to influence others' impressions of him or her. At the same time, he or she is vulnerable to influence attempts by others. This is because persons are highly susceptible to persuasive appeals aimed at enhancing their own self-image. By way of illustration, a common preoccupation of teenagers, especially younger teens, is "looking cool." If one teen can convince another that dressing a certain way, or acting a certain way, will make him or her "look cool," the other teen is likely to conform to that style of dress or behavior. Most of us need look no further than our high school yearbooks to realize that we, too, were susceptible to the fads, trends, and fashions of our day.

Impression management also requires that people engage in *facework,* a term coined by Erving Goffman (1967, 1974). A person's "face" refers to his or her social standing in the eyes of others. Facework involves negotiating one's social standing and social worth with others (Ting-Toomey, 1988, 1994; Ting-Toomey & Kurogi, 1998). For example, committing a social faux pas could result in the loss of one's own face. Facework would be required to restore one's face. Threatening or challenging another person could cause the other to lose face. Facework would again be required for the other to regain face.

As with identity management, we suggest that facework is inherently persuasive in nature. Facework involves goal-oriented communication that seeks particular outcomes or ends, namely, "satisfying one's own face wants and the face wants of one's interlocutor" (Cupach & Imahori, 1993, p. 117). For example, consider the related social rituals of asking someone out on a date and declining someone's invitation for a date. Both rituals, asking and declining, are persuasive in nature, and both are laden with face-saving implications. Although not synonymous with credibility, we see the concepts of face and facework as being closely related to the credibility construct. Maintaining one's face, we believe, is akin to maintaining one's credibility in the eyes of others.

STRATEGIES FOR ENHANCING ONE'S CREDIBILITY

Having gained a better understanding of what credibility is and how it works, what can you do to enhance your credibility when persuading? A number of general guidelines are offered for improving your credibility. Keep in mind that because credibility is a receiver-based construct, what works on one listener or audience may not work on the next.

1. Heed the Boy Scout motto: "Be prepared." Before making your case, be as well prepared and well organized as possible. Think through your position beforehand and anticipate likely objections to your position. If you don't seem to know what you are talking about, your credibility will suffer. Research shows that unorganized messages are far less convincing than organized ones (McCroskey & Mehrley, 1969; Sharp & McClung, 1966).

2. Cite evidence for your position and identify the sources of your evidence. In a review of the effects of evidence usage, Reinard (1988) concluded that in almost all cases, citing evidence and sources significantly enhanced speaker credibility. This advice applies especially to low-credibility sources.

3. Cite your own or your sources' qualifications and expertise on the topic or issue up front. Remember, expertise is one of the primary dimensions of credibility. For credibility to enhance persuasion, however, the source's credentials must be identified prior to presenting the message. If you have expertise on a topic or an issue, let your listener(s) know. If you lack expertise on an issue, don't dwell on your deficiencies. Instead, explain how you came to develop an interest in the subject. Also, consider this: If, in fact, you know little or nothing about a topic, then you have no business trying to persuade others about that topic in the first place!

4. Attempt to build trust by demonstrating to your listener that you are honest and sincere. One approach is to demonstrate that you possess good moral character. Another is to acknowledge that although compliance would benefit you, it would benefit the other person as well; compliance would be in both parties' mutual interest.

5. Display goodwill toward your audience. Don't seem aloof or indifferent. Show that you care about others, that you understand their ideas and their situation, that you empathize with their feelings and views, and that you are attentive and responsive to their communication attempts. For example, if a listener asks you a question, begin your answer by saying, "If I heard you correctly, you want to know . . . " and end by asking, "Does that address what you were asking?"

6. Improve your likeability, or L-factor. Likeability or sociability is one of the secondary dimensions of credibility that affects how you and your message are received. Some view likeability as a form of emotional intelligence (Sanders, 2006). You can improve your L-factor by conveying warmth and immediacy. Smile. Often. Remember people's names. Listen. Thank people and accept compliments sincerely. Being genuine and authentic goes a long way.

7. Adopt a language and delivery style appropriate to the listener(s), topic, and setting. Your style of speech should be tailored to your particular receiver(s). Different receivers have different needs. In general, nonfluencies, pauses or gaps, and a choppy style of delivery hinder credibility (Berger, 1985, 1994; Miller & Hewgill, 1964). A reliance on "uhms," "ahs," and other fillers impairs credibility as well. An overreliance on slang, colloquialisms, or trite expressions can also compromise credibility.

8. Avoid a powerless style of communication. Use an assertive style of communication instead. A powerless communication style involves using tag questions ("That was a good movie, don't you think?"), hesitations ("uhm," "uh"), qualifiers ("kind of," "sort of," "perhaps," "maybe"), and negative preambles ("This will probably sound really dumb, but . . ."). A reliance on powerless language signals to the other party that you perceive yourself as occupying a lower status position in the relationship. For more about this topic, refer to Chapter 7, where we examine the role of language in persuasion.

9. Emphasizing your similarity to another may indirectly enhance your credibility. Listeners find it easier to identify with sources they perceive as similar to themselves. O'Keefe (1990) points out two important caveats regarding similarity and influence. First, he emphasizes, the similarities must be relevant to the topic or issue. Commenting, "Hey, I'm a Libra, too!" will probably get you nowhere unless the topic happens to center on astrology, horoscopes, and other similar topics. Second, O'Keefe notes that the perceived similarities must involve positive, rather than negative, qualities. Stressing, "I was arrested for shoplifting once, too" may not enamor you to a new acquaintance, even though he or she may have confessed to a similar mistake.

10. If you think you are perceived as having low credibility, try to increase receiver involvement and emphasize the central route to persuasion. Remember, receivers who are highly involved in a topic place less emphasis on source credibility and more emphasis on the substance of a message. If you suspect your target audience is skeptical of your credibility, explain how the topic or issue is directly relevant to them and then focus on the substance of the message. That will tend to encourage central processing on the part of your audience.

11. Have another source who is already perceived as highly credible introduce or endorse you. This is a common strategy used in election campaigns. Salespersons also use this strategy when they rely on referrals. The technique allows a source to piggyback on the established credibility of the person making the introduction or endorsement. Acquiring credibility via endorsements and introductions emphasizes the peripheral route to persuasion.

SUMMARY

As we've seen, credibility is a complex construct. Yet there is one overriding generalization about credibility that persuaders can "take to the bank": *Credibility is a good thing to have if you are a persuader.* As long as we keep in mind that credibility is a perceptual phenomenon, the generalization that high-credibility sources are more influential than low-credibility sources is as close as one can come to a universal "law" of persuasion.

In advancing this generalization, however, we believe it is important to underscore the point that credibility is a complex, multidimensional, situational communication phenomenon. Credibility can't be bought in a bottle or purchased out of a vending machine. In many persuasive settings, a source who has low or no initial credibility can do little or nothing about it. Low-credibility sources tend to be dismissed out of hand; receivers simply fail to attend to their messages. There is an old joke about how to become a multimillionaire: "It's simple: First, get a million dollars, then . . . " Much the same advice can be offered for using credibility to enhance persuasion: "It's simple: First, get a lot of credibility, then . . . "

ENDNOTES

1. The term was first coined by German sociologist Max Weber (1968), who defined *charisma* as "a certain quality of the individual personality by virtue of which he is set apart from ordinary men and women and treated as endowed with supernatural, superhuman, or at least exceptional powers and qualities" (p. 240).

2. Impression management theory also has been referred to as identity management theory (IMT for short) by William Cupach and Todd Imahori (1993).

REFERENCES

Agrawal, J., & Kamakura, W. A. (1995). The economic worth of celebrity endorsers: An event study analysis. *Journal of Marketing, 59*(3), 56–62.

Allen, M., & Stiff, J. B. (1989). Testing three models for the sleeper effect. *Western Journal of Speech Communication, 53*(4), 411–426.

Allen, M., & Stiff, J. B. (1998). An analysis of the sleeper effect. In M. Allen & R. W. Preiss (Eds.), *Persuasion: Advances through meta-analysis* (pp. 175–188). Cresskill, NJ: Hampton Press.

Appel, M., & Richter, T. (2007). Persuasive effects of fictional narratives increase over time. *Media Psychology, 10*, 113–134.

Applbaum, R. L., & Anatol, K. W. E. (1972). The factor structure of source credibility as a function of the speaking situation. *Speech Monographs, 39*, 216–222.

Aristotle. (1954). *Rhetoric* (W. R. Roberts, Trans.) New York: Random House.

Benoit, W. L. (1987). Argumentation appeals and credibility appeals in persuasion. *Southern Speech Communication Journal, 52,* 181–187.

Benoit, W. L. (1995). *Accounts, excuses, and apologies: A theory of image restoration strategies.* Albany: State University of New York Press.

Benoit, W. L., & Strathman, A. (2004). Source credibility and the elaboration likelihood model. In J. S. Seiter & R. H. Gass (Eds.), *Readings in persuasion, social influence, and compliance gaining* (pp. 95–111). Boston: Allyn & Bacon.

Berger, A. A. (2004). *Ads, fads, and consumer culture.* Lanham, MD: Rowman & Littlefield Publishers, Inc.

Berger, C. R. (1985). Social power and interpersonal communication. In M. L. Knapp & G. R. Miller (Eds.), *Handbook of interpersonal communication* (pp. 439–499). Newbury Park, CA: Sage Publications.

Berger, C. R. (1994). Power, dominance, and social interaction. In M. L. Knapp & G. R. Miller (Eds.), *Handbook of interpersonal communication* (2nd ed., pp. 450–507). Newbury Park, CA: Sage Publications.

Berlo, D. K., Lemert, J. B., & Mertz, R. J. (1969). Dimensions for evaluating the acceptability of message sources. *Public Opinion Quarterly, 33,* 563–576.

Burgoon (Heston), J. K. (1973, April). *Ideal source credibility: A reexamination of the semantic differential.* Paper presented at the International Communication Association Convention, Montreal, Quebec.

Burgoon, J. K. (1976). The ideal source: A reexamination of source credibility measurement. *Central States Speech Journal, 27,* 200–206.

Cauchon, D., & Eisler, P. (2008, October 17). " 'Joe the plumber' caught in post-debate glare; Obama tax plan would likely help Ohioan." *USA Today*, p. 2-A.

Cronkhite, G., & Liska, J. (1976). A critique of factor analytic approaches to the study of credibility. *Communication Monographs, 43,* 91–107.

Cupach, W. R., & Imahori, T. T. (1993). Identity management theory: Communication competence in intercultural episodes and relationships. In R. L. Wiseman & J. Koester (Eds.), *Intercultural communication competence* (pp. 112–131). Newbury Park, CA: Sage.

Denzen, N. K. (1987). *The recovering alcoholic.* Newbury Park, CA: Sage.

Erdogan, B. Z., Baker, M. J. & Tagg, S. (2001). Selecting celebrity endorsers: The practitioner's perspective. *Journal of Advertising Research, 41*(3), 39–49.

Farrell, K. A., Karels, G. V., Monfort, K. W. & McClatchey, C. A. (2000) Celebrity performance and endorsement value: the case of Tiger Woods. *Managerial Finance*, 26(7), 1–15.

Flanagin, A. J., & Metzger, M. J. (2000). Perceptions of Internet information credibility. *Journalism & Mass Communication Quarterly, 77*(3), 515–540.

Gass, R. H., & Seiter, J. S. (2009). Credibility and public diplomacy. In N. Snow & P. M. Taylor (Eds.), *The public diplomacy handbook* (pp. 154–165). New York: Routledge.

Goffman, E. (1967). *Interaction ritual essays on face-to-face behavior.* Garden City, NY: Anchor Books, Doubleday.

Goffman, E. (1974). *Frame analysis: An essay on the organization of experience.* Cambridge, MA: Harvard University Press.

Greenberg, B. S., & Tannenbaum, P. H. (1961). The effects of bylines on attitude change. *Journalism Quarterly, 38,* 535–537.

Gruder, C. L., Cook, T. D., Hennigan, K. M., Flay, B. R., Alessi, C., & Halamaj, J. (1978). Empirical tests of the absolute sleeper effect predicted from the discounting cue hypothesis. *Journal of Personality and Social Psychology, 36,* 1061–1074.

Hovland, C. I., Janis, I. L., & Kelly, H. H. (1953). *Communication and persuasion.* New Haven, CT: Yale University Press.

Hovland, C. I., Lumsdaine, A., & Sheffield, F. (1949). *Experiments on mass communication.* Princeton, NJ: Princeton University Press.

Kahle, L. R., & Homer, P. (1985). Physical attractiveness of the celebrity endorser: A social adaptation perspective. *Journal of Consumer Research, 11*(4), 954–961.

Kamins, M. A., & Gupta, K. (1994). Congruence between spokesperson and product types: A match-up hypothesis perspective. *Psychology & Marketing, 11*(6), 569–586.

Koernig, S. K., & Boyd, T. C. (2009). To catch a tiger or let him go: The match-up effect and athlete endorsers for sport and non-sport brands. *Sport Marketing Quarterly, 18,* 25–37.

Kouzes, J. M., & Posner, B. Z. (1993). *Credibility.* San Francisco, CA: Jossey-Bass.

Kumkale, G. T., & Albarracin, D. (2004). The sleeper effect in persuasion: A meta-analytic review. *Psychological Bulletin, 130*(l), 143–172.

McCracken, G. (1986). Culture and consumption: A theoretical account of the structure and movement of the cultural meaning of consumer goods. *Journal of Consumer Research*, 13, 71–84.

McCracken, G. (1989). Who is the celebrity endorser? *Journal of Consumer Research, 16,* 310–321.

McCroskey, J. C. (1966). Scales for the measurement of ethos. *Speech Monographs, 33,* 65–72.

McCroskey, J. C., & Mehrley, R. S. (1969). The effects of disorganization and nonfluency on attitude change and source credibility. *Speech Monographs, 36,* 13–21.

McCroskey, J. C., & Teven, J. J. (1999). Goodwill: A reexamination of the construct and its measurement. *Communication Monographs, 66*(1), 90–103.

McCroskey, J. C., & Young, T. J. (1981). Ethos and credibility: The construct and its measurement after three decades. *Central States Speech Journal, 32,* 24–34.

McShane, L. (2009, February 6). "Caught on tape! Supercool Sully." *Daily News*, p. 12.

Miller, G. R., & Hewgill, M. A. (1964). The effect of variations in nonfluency on audience ratings of source credibility. *Quarterly Journal of Speech, 50,* 36–44.

Nan, X. (2009). The influence of source credibility on attitude certainty: Exploring the moderating effects of source identification and individual need for cognition. *Psychology and Marketing, 26*(4), 321–332.

O'Keefe, D. J. (1987). The persuasive effects of delaying identification of high- and low-credibility communicators: A meta-analytic review. *Central States Speech Journal, 38,* 63–72.

O'Keefe, D. J. (1990). *Persuasion: Theory and research.* Newbury Park, CA: Sage.

Petty, R. E., & Cacioppo, J. T. (1986). *Communication and persuasion: Central and peripheral routes to attitude change.* New York: Springer-Verlag.

Pornpitakpan, C. (2004). The persuasiveness of source credibility: A critical review of five decades' evidence. *Journal of Applied Social Psychology, 34*(2), 243–281.

Reinard, J. C. (1988). The empirical study of the persuasive effects of evidence: The status after fifty years of research. *Human Communication Research, 15,* 3–59.

Rind, B. (1992). Effects of impressions of amazement and foolishness on compliance. *Journal of Applied Social Psychology, 22*(21), 1656–1665.

Robertson, N. (1988). *Getting better: Inside Alcoholics Anonymous.* New York: Morrow.

Rule, A. (1989). *The stranger beside me.* New York: Signet.

Sanders, T. (2006). *The likeability factor: How to boost your L-factor and achieve your life's dreams.* New York: Three Rivers Press.

Sharp, H., & McClung, T. (1966). Effects of organization on the speaker's ethos. *Speech Monographs, 33,* 182–183.

Solomon, M. R. (2009). *Consumer behavior: Buying, having, and being.* Upper Saddle River, NJ: Pearson Education/Prentice Hall.

Sternthal, B., Dholakia, R., & Leavitt, C. (1978). The persuasive effect of source credibility: A situational analysis. *Public Opinion Quarterly, 42,* 285–314.

Stiff, J. B. (1994). *Persuasive communication.* New York: Guilford Press.

"Study finds ads induce few people to buy." (2000, October 17). *Wall Street Journal,* p. B10.

Tedeschi, J. T., & Reiss, M. (1981). Identities, the phenomenal self, and laboratory research. In J. Tedeschi (Ed.), *Impression management theory and social psychological research* (pp. 3–22). New York: Academic Press.

Teven, J. J., & McCroskey, J. C. (1997). The relationship of perceived teacher caring with student learning and teacher evaluation. *Communication Education, 46,* 1–9.

Thee-Brenan, M. (2009, January 17). "Poll finds disapproval of Bush unwavering." *The New York Times,* p. A–11.

Till, B. D., & Busler, M. (2000). The match-up hypothesis: Physical attractiveness, expertise, and the role of fit on brand attitude, purchase intent, and brand beliefs. *Journal of Advertising, 29*(3), 1–13.

Till, B. D., & Shimp, T. A. (1998). Endorsers in advertising: The case of negative celebrity information. *Journal of Advertising, 27*(1), 67–82.

Ting-Toomey, S. (1988). Intercultural conflict styles: A face-negotiation theory. In Y. Y. Kim & W. Gudykunst (Eds.), *Theories in intercultural communication* (pp. 213–235). Newbury Park, CA: Sage.

Ting-Toomey, S. (1994). *The challenge of facework: Cross-cultural and interpersonal issues.* Ithaca, NY: SUNY Press.

Ting-Toomey, S., & Kurogi, A. (1998). Facework competence in intercultural conflict: An updated face negotiation theory. *International Journal of Intercultural Relations, 22,* 187–225.

Ward, C. D., & McGinnies, E. (1974). Persuasive effect of early and late mention of credible and noncredible sources. *Journal of Psychology, 86,* 17–23.

Watts, W. A., & Holt, L. E. (1979). Persistence of opinion change induced under conditions of forewarning and distraction. *Journal of Personality and Social Psychology, 37,* 778–789.

Watts, W. A., & McGuire, W. J. (1964). Persistence of induced opinion change and retention of inducing message content. *Journal of Abnormal and Social Psychology, 68,* 223–241.

Weber, M. (1968). *On charisma and institution building.* Chicago: University of Chicago Press.

Wilson, E. J., & Sherrell, D. L. (1993). Source effects in communication and persuasion research: A meta-analysis of effect size. *Journal of the Academy of Marketing Science, 21,* 101–112.

Communicator Characteristics and Persuadability

Several years ago, not far from where one of the authors lives, a strange story involving a man named Bruce Jensen unfolded. When Jensen's "wife" of more than 3 years was arrested on suspicion of unlawful use of credit cards, authorities discovered that she was really a he (Groutage, 1995). Not surprisingly, on learning this, Jensen was confused. Officers had to convince him it was true, which, we imagine, was not much fun. Said Grant Hodgson, the detective who broke the news to Jensen, "I've done a lot of death notifications that were easier."

Here's Jensen's description of what happened: After he met Felix Urioste, who was then posing as a female doctor named Leasa, they dated for a month. When Urioste claimed to be pregnant with twins, they were married, but later Urioste maintained that the twins were stillborn. Jensen claimed he didn't know Urioste was a man because he had never seen Urioste naked, Urioste took hormones to look like a female, and Urioste claimed that normal sex was impossible because of a previous rape (Groutage, 1995).

Sounds unbelievable? If you are at all like we were after hearing this story, you're probably dubious. But authorities claimed, after considerable investigation, that they believed Jensen was simply a nice guy who was incredibly naïve (Groutage, 1995). And we suppose when you consider all possible people, it's likely that someone would be gullible enough to fall for such a scheme.

However, although it seems that some people are more persuadable than others, the search for a single underlying trait or characteristic that makes people persuadable has not been successful.[1] Persuasion is more complicated than that. And so are people. Even so, the characteristics of the people in a persuasive interaction cannot be ignored. All communicators are unique in terms of gender, age, personality, and background, and such characteristics are important to understanding the nature of social influence.

In this chapter, we explore the role communicator characteristics play in the process of persuasion. Although we don't have room to cover all the characteristics that have been studied, we discuss several that past research have identified as being important to social influence. Then we discuss ways in which a communicator might analyze and adapt to an audience when trying to be persuasive.

Before we begin, however, we note, as we have in earlier chapters, that persuasion is a two-way street. Thus, when we use the term *communicator characteristics,* we are not limiting our discussion to one person. The characteristics of all the interactants in a persuasive encounter are part of the equation.

DEMOGRAPHIC VARIABLES AND PERSUASION

If someone asked you to use 10 words to describe yourself, there is a good chance you would use demographic information to do so. Demographics include characteristics such as age, gender, ethnicity, and intelligence. In the following sections we discuss how each of these is related to persuasion.

Age and Persuasion: Pretty Please with Sugar on Top

The expression "It's like taking candy from a baby" suggests that children are easy targets for persuasion, and research indicates that this is generally true: Children tend to be especially vulnerable to persuasive trickery because they lack the ability to understand the nature and intent of persuasive attempts. The implications of such research can be frightening. Indeed, we've all heard stories of children who have been tricked or lured away by criminals (for more on this issue, see Box 5.1).

"Never Take Candy from Strangers"   **BOX 5.1**

I was certain it could never happen. After all, I'm a very street-savvy, New York City parent. I write articles advising moms and dads on child safety. Needless to say, I've been so conscientious in teaching my own children that my husband insists I'm paranoid, and my daughter has more than once rolled her eyes heavenward at my often repeated warnings. Which is why I can hardly describe the sick feeling in my stomach as I watched my red-headed little boy and his friend Tahlor march right out of the park one spring afternoon with a total stranger. (Rosen, 1994, p. 108)

Fortunately for Margery Rosen, this scene was only part of an informal experiment. To test how well she had trained her children, she had gotten Kenneth Wooden, an expert on the ways in which sex offenders lure children, to see if he could persuade her children to leave the playground with him. He didn't have much trouble. He told the boys he had lost a puppy and would give them money if they would help him find it. They went right with him, and so did several other children involved in the experiment (Rosen, 1994).

Many children aren't as fortunate as those involved in Rosen's experiment. Indeed, it's been estimated that one in four girls and one in eight boys are sexually abused by age 18 (Wooden, 1988). Clearly, children are especially susceptible to persuasion, and sometimes the results are tragic. For

that reason, Kenneth Wooden (1988) argued, "Teaching your kids about the tricks that molesters use could save them from grievous harm—even death" (p. 149).

In an effort to prevent children from being molested, Wooden interviewed convicted molesters, pimps, and murderers and discovered 11 lures that are commonly used on children. Of the lures he said, "Knowledge of them is so basic to a child's safety that they should be taught—indeed must be taught—by every parent" (Wooden, 1988, p. 149). With this in mind, if you know, are, or plan to be a parent, here is a brief list of the lures and prevention strategies that Wooden (1988; see also Rosen, 1994; Dickinson, 2002) identified:

1. The assistance lure. The lost puppy example described previously is an example of this lure. In it, the molester asks kids for directions, for help carrying packages, or for some other type of assistance. Children should be advised to keep their distance from strangers in cars. Children should tell the assistance seeker to ask another adult for help.

2. The authority lure. Some molesters lure children by posing as a police officer or some other authority figure. If told to "Come with me" by such a person, children should ask an adult to inspect the person's credentials.

3. The affection/love lure. Some molesters lure children by promising them love and affection. Parents should know that 75 to 80 percent of sex crimes are committed by someone a child knows and trusts. Children should beware of anyone who wants excessive time alone with them and be encouraged to tell their parents about improper advances. Parents should trust their instincts.

4. The bribery lure. Children are often offered gifts from molesters. Parents should be suspicious of any new toys their children have. The age old saying "Never take candy from strangers" is still true today.

5. The ego/fame lure. Youngsters are sometimes lured by modeling jobs or beauty contests that should be kept secret from mom and dad. For that reason, parents should accompany kids to such events, encourage openness, and check the credentials of "would-be" modeling agencies.

6. The emergency lure. To catch children off guard and lure them into a car, molesters might trick them by claiming "a house is on fire" or "mommy had to go to the hospital." To prevent falling for this, parents and children should prearrange an emergency plan. Under no circumstance should a child ride with a stranger.

7. The fun and games lure. Molesters sometimes turn tickling, wrestling, and other games into intimate contact. Children need to be taught that there are good and bad touches. Bad touches (e.g., anywhere under a bathing suit) should be reported.

8. The magic and rituals lure. Sometimes, abuse is disguised as magic, sorcery, or satanism in order to fascinate children. Parents, therefore, should discuss with their kids the concepts of good and evil and beware if their kids begin to reject family values.

9. The pornography lure. Molesters have been known to use pornography to destroy their victims' inhibitions. Wooden, therefore, advises parents to keep pornography out of the home so it does not seem legitimate.

10. The hero lure. Because children admire heroes, molesters might pose as Santa, Big Bird, or other characters to obtain children's trust. Children should be taught that bad people can play tricks on children and that real heroes won't do certain things.

11. The jobs lure. Molesters sometimes lure children by promising high-paying jobs. When suspicious, parents should accompany children to interviews, especially if the interview is in a secluded or unusual place, and ask to see a business license.

Finally, though not discussed by Wooden, parents and children need to be aware that the Internet has become a vehicle for strangers who prey on children. Officials with the Children's Internet Crimes Task Force suggest that children who spend large amounts of time online may be in danger. Parents should watch for warning signs, including pornography on a child's computer (often sent by sexual predators to desensitize victims) and telephone calls or mail from strangers ("Beware 'Net predators," 2001).

Although some psychologists have argued that teaching children about a potential molester only serves to terrify them and prevent the formation of friendships (for a discussion, see "Teaching fear," 1986), Rosen (1994) and others have argued that teaching children to be cautious about potential molesters is little different from teaching them to be safe around stoves or electrical sockets. Education should start at a young age, with the goal of making children cautious, not paranoid. As Wooden (1988) noted, children should be taught that most people are good and won't hurt them but should also realize that some people are bad and sick. Finally, research suggests that behavioral (e.g., role playing) approaches are more effective at preventing abuse than are cognitive-only approaches (Bromberg & Johnson, 1997).

What we may be less aware of, however, are other types of persuasive messages that may be influencing our children. For instance, did you know that in the United States, typical kids are exposed to 360,000 commercials by the time they graduate from high school (Berger, 2004)? This number becomes especially meaningful when you realize that, until age eight, children do not understand the persuasive nature of advertising. Instead, kids think that ads are just there to inform them (Oates, Blades, & Gunter, 2002). With that in mind, what might be done to protect children?

At least two variables seem to decrease children's vulnerability to advertising: adult influence and getting older. First, research shows that if you interact with children during ads, you can increase their ability to critically examine the ads and provide them with a better understanding of the nature and purpose of advertising. One study, for example, found that when adults made factual (e.g., "Those ads aren't telling the truth. Those toys look different in real life.") or evaluative ("These ads are dumb. These toys aren't fun.") comments during advertisements for toys, children who heard the comments were less persuaded by the ads (Buijzen, 2007). Second, as children become older, they become more susceptible to peer pressure but less susceptible to the persuasive appeal of ads. Notice, however, we say *less* susceptible, not immune. For example, Atkin, Hocking, and Block (1984) found that teenagers who were exposed to a greater number of alcohol advertisements consumed larger amounts of alcohol.

From our discussion so far, we've made it clear that young people tend to be highly susceptible to persuasion. But what about older people? When you think about people who are retired, you might picture the gullible granny being swindled by someone selling swamp land.

However, some research indicates that stereotypes about the "gullible and elderly" are unwarranted. Indeed, Alwin and Krosnick (1991; Krosnick & Alwin, 1989) noted that older Americans, compared to their younger counterparts, may be less persuadable because their attitudes and beliefs are formed and tend to remain stable. Moreover, a study by Brown, Asher, and Cialdini (2005) found that as people grow older, their preference for being consistent with their attitudes increases. Of course, knowing this along with the information on consistency we presented in Chapter 3 could be helpful to you when trying to persuade people in this demographic group. For example, if you focus on how your request is consistent with their attitudes, elderly people might be especially likely to be persuaded by you.

Gender Differences and Persuasion: The Times, They Aren't a Changin'

Do men and women differ in their ability to influence others? Before you answer, we should warn you: This is a trick question. Although the lion's share of research reveals that men are more successful than women in their attempts to persuade others (see Carli, 2004), their success has little to do with ability but rather has to do with audiences' perceptions. This conclusion is supported by the work of Carli (2004), who demonstrated that gender stereotypes cause audiences to perceive males as more competent than females and to expect females to be warmer and more nurturing than males. As a result, women experience a double bind: They must perform better than men to be considered equally competent, and they are perceived negatively when they try to be direct, assertive, and forceful.

Consistent with this argument is Klingle's (2004) *reinforcement expectancy theory,* which applies to persuasive encounters between doctors and patients. According to the theory, once a doctor has tried to persuade a patient to do something (e.g., take medication), the patient judges the appropriateness of the doctor's message. If the message is viewed as inappropriate, the patient rejects it. If it is viewed as appropriate, it guides the patient's future behavior. How does this relate to gender? According to Klingle (2004), because of certain norms, female doctors can't get away with using aversive strategies the same way that male doctors can. When female doctors use such strategies, they violate patients' expectations about what is appropriate, and, as a result, patients are less likely to comply. According to the theory, then, male doctors can increase compliance by using either positive (e.g., "Regular eating will make you feel so much better") or negative ("You have two choices—change your diet or spend the rest of your life wishing you had") influence strategies, but female doctors can increase compliance by using only positive strategies (Klingle, 2004).

Up to this point, we've seen that men and women differ regarding how successful they are when trying to persuade other people. But how do men and women compare when it comes to being persuaded? Early research suggested that women were more easily persuaded than men (e.g., Chaiken, 1979; Janis & Field, 1959; Scheidel, 1963). Later, however, researchers who examined and summarized large numbers of studies on the topic questioned the notion of whether women were any different from men when it came to being persuaded (e.g., Becker, 1986; Eagly, 1978; Eagly & Carli, 1981). As a result, many researchers abandoned the idea of general gender effects and instead tried to explain *when* gender differences could be expected. For instance, in Eagly's 1978 study, 32 percent of the studies published before 1970 (generally regarded as the onset of the women's move- ment) found that women were more easily influenced than men, but only 8 percent of the studies published after 1970 found the same result. Thus, evaporating gender differences might be the result of changing times and the attitudes of and toward women. However, considering the research we have discussed on how gender stereotypes affect males' versus females' ability to persuade, we doubt that this explanation is correct.

Even so, there is another possible explanation for the change in research findings before and after 1970. Specifically, earlier studies used male rather than female sources (Ward, Seccombe, Bendel, & Carter, 1985), which means that male receivers were being persuaded by members of the same sex, whereas females were being persuaded by mem- bers of the opposite sex. That is, in the earlier studies, there may have been a *cross-sex effect*, by which people were more easily influenced by members of the opposite sex than by members of the same sex. This effect, however, may be stronger for males persuading females than for females persuading males (Ward et al., 1985).

From our review so far, it is clear that generalizations about gender and persuasion are hard to come by. As Cody, Seiter, and Montagne-Miller (1995) argue, "There is no sim- ple model that links 'gender' or 'sex' to influenceability" (p. 312). Instead, following Miller and Read (1991), these researchers argue that persuadability is not so much related to one's gender as it is to one's goals, plans, resources, and beliefs (Cody et al., 1995). For instance, imagine that you are in a shopping mall, looking at clothing. If you don't intend to buy anything (goal), have decided you will look now and buy later (plan), have very lit- tle money (resources), and think that all salespersons are dishonest (beliefs), you will prob- ably be more difficult to influence than if you intend to buy now, have lots of money, and believe salespersons are honest. In other words, it may not matter so much whether you are male or female; how easy you are to influence depends on your goals, plans, resources, and beliefs. Gender matters only to the extent that males and females have different goals, plans, resources, and beliefs. For instance, Cody et al. (1995) found that when shopping for clothes, men and women tend to have different goals and that such goal differences were related to influenceability and the effectiveness of certain sales tactics.

Ethnicity, Culture, and Persuasion: "Me" and "We" Perspectives

Cultural differences play a major role, both in terms of how people fashion influence attempts and how they respond to them. Perhaps the most commonly discussed dimension of cultural variability is known as *individualism–collectivism* (Hofstede, 1983). Whereas collectivist cultures (e.g., China) tend to value harmony, concern for others, and the goals of the group over the goals of the individual, individualistic cultures (e.g., the United States) tend to value independence and the goals of the individual over the goals of a collective.

With that in mind, consider the following list of slogans that were used in magazine advertisements (see Han & Shavitt, 1994) and imagine which you would use to appeal to a collectivistic culture and which you would use to appeal to an individualistic culture:

> "The art of being unique."
> "She's got a style all her own."
> "We have a way of bringing people closer together."
> "The dream of prosperity for all of us."
> "A leader among leaders."
> "Sharing is beautiful."

A study by Han and Shavitt (1994) found that advertisements, such as the first, second, and fifth in the previous list, that appealed to individual benefits, personal success, and independence were used more in the United States (an individualistic culture) than in Korea (a collectivistic culture) and were more persuasive in the United States than in Korea. Ads, such as the third, fourth, and sixth, that appealed to group benefits, harmony, and family were used more often and were more persuasive in Korea than in the United States.

Another difference between people from individualistic and collectivistic cultures is that those from individualistic cultures tend to view themselves consistently across situations, while those in collectivistic cultures view the self as more malleable. Not surprisingly, then, Petrova, Cialdini, and Sills (2007) found that once people from individualistic cultures had complied with a request, they were more likely than people from collectivistic cultures to be consistent and comply with a second, similar request.

Also consistent with the notion that people from collectivistic cultures focus on groups and relationships, Fu and Yukl (2000) found that Chinese managers rated "emphasizing coalitions" and "gift-giving" among the most effective influence tactics, whereas managers from the United States preferred rational persuasion. Similarly, a study by Wiseman et al. (2009) found differences between the persuasive strategies used by people from the United States, China, and Japan. For example, when trying to persuade roommates to be more quiet, people from the United States, who tend to be more individualistic and less concerned with saving face, preferred more direct strategies (e.g., "You are making too much noise. Please be quiet") and strategies with individually controlled sanctions ("If you don't quiet down, I'll be as noisy as possible when you are trying to study"). People from

China, who tend to be more collectivistic, preferred indirect strategies (e.g., commenting on how they like quiet moments) and strategies with group-controlled sanctions (e.g., "Your noisiness shows a lack of consideration for others"). However, people from Japan hinted less than people from both the United States and China, leading Wiseman and colleagues (2009) to conclude that collectivism and individualism may not be opposite orientations. In other words, the fact that people from Japan sometimes behave consistently with individu- alistic behavior and sometimes behave consistently with collectivistic behavior "suggests that individualism and collectivism are actually two separate continua that may ebb and flow in their significance in influencing communication practices" (Wiseman et al., 2009 p. 12). Thus, depending on the situation, cultures such as Japan may demonstrate either collectivistic or individualistic behaviors.

Although individualism and collectivism are important values affecting the cross- cultural differences in persuasion, they are not the only ones. For example, after conduct- ing interviews with people from the People's Republic of China and Taiwan, Ma and Chuang (2001) identified three influence tactics reflecting additional values of importance. First, *anshi,* or "hinting" (e.g., telling a friend who loaned you money that you'd like to buy something if you weren't broke), compared to more direct strategies (e.g., demanding the money a friend borrowed), not only preserves harmony in a relationship, it is more respect- ful and seeks to save another person's face. Second, *yi shen zuo ze,* or "setting an example by one's own action" (e.g., a manager works exceptionally hard hoping her subordinates will do likewise), reflects the Chinese culture's mistrust of words. Third, *tou qi suo hao,* or "feeding people what they relish" (e.g., agreeing to do something another person loves before asking a favor), reflects a preference for indirectness, other-orientedness, and grant- ing people "face" (Ma & Chuang, 2001).

Similarly, a study by Fitch (1994) found that distinctive cultural systems of beliefs, values, and symbols underlie differences in the influence messages used by people in the United States and Colombia. A recurring theme in the influence strategies used in the United States was "empowerment." For instance, a manager observed in Fitch's study argued:

> A stumbling block to empowerment is the low self-esteem of people who have been told what to do. If we want them to make their own decisions, we have to build up their self- esteem. And that starts with asking, not telling people what to do. (p. 194)

In contrast, Colombians' influence attempts centered around the concept of *confianza* (having trust or closeness in a relationship). Fitch argued that, in some instances, *confianza* is an important prerequisite for trying to influence people, whereas in others, it can be a hindrance. For example, Colombians commonly ask intermediaries who have closer rela- tionships with persuadees to deliver influence messages for them (e.g., "You know Dioselina better than I do. Will you ask her to put up the signs?"). However, Colombians believe that too much *confianza* is bad in superior and subordinate relationships. In such relationships, superiors must learn to balance *confianza* with authority (Fitch, 1994).

Intelligence and Persuasion: Dumb and Dumber

Imagine you were offered a million dollars to persuade either Forrest Gump (if you haven't seen the movie, Forrest isn't known for his brains) or Albert Einstein to believe or do something. Who would you choose? Earlier work (e.g., McGuire, 1968) suggested that neither Forrest nor Albert—but rather someone with moderate intelligence—should be chosen. The idea was that Forrest should be difficult to persuade because he would be unable to comprehend a message, while Albert should be difficult because he would be better at scrutinizing a message. Later work, however, indicated that Forrest should be your choice. Indeed, a review of research by Rhodes and Wood (1992) indicated that less intelligent people are easier to persuade than people with a lot of smarts. Even so, we imagine that other variables may be important too. When persuasive messages are extremely complex, for example, we suspect that intelligence plays a larger role than when persuasive messages are simple.

PSYCHOLOGICAL AND COMMUNICATION STATES AND TRAITS

Someone once said there are two types of people in the world: those who put everything into categories and those who don't. People who study communicator characteristics and persuasion belong in the first group. As you've probably gathered from our discussion so far, often the goal of these researchers is to classify people based on differences (e.g., age, gender) and then to use those group differences to explain why some people are easier to persuade than others or why some people use one strategy to persuade and others use a different strategy.

Two common explanations for why people differ from one another centers around the notion of traits and states. A *trait* is a characteristic of a person presumed to be relatively stable across situations. A *state* varies from situation to situation. For instance, if we conceptualize anxiety as a trait, we would predict that a person possessing the trait would be anxious in practically all situations. On the other hand, if we conceptualize anxiety as a state, we would predict that there are certain situations in which a person becomes anxious. For instance, some people become very anxious when talking with authorities or when meeting members of the opposite sex. With these definitions in mind, we now turn to a discussion of some specific traits and states that have been the focus of research in the area of persuasion.

Self-Esteem and Persuasion: Feelin' Kinda Low

Are individuals with low self-esteem more susceptible to influence attempts than individuals with high self-esteem? Although this notion seems reasonable, it is not supported by research (Perloff, 1994; Rhodes & Wood, 1992). This is because to be persuaded, a person must both receive and yield to a message. However, although people with low self-esteem may feel less confident in themselves and their opinions and be more likely to yield to a message, they may also be too concerned about their appearance and behavior to be receptive to a persuasive message. On the other hand, although people with high self-esteem are more likely to receive a message, they are more confident in themselves and are less likely to change their attitudes and behaviors. Thus, research indicates that people with moderately high self-esteem are easier to persuade than people with either high or low self-esteem (Rhodes & Wood, 1992).

Anxiety and Persuasion: Living in Fear

Unless you've grown up in a closet, you've undoubtedly been exposed to messag[es] dangers of global warming, secondhand cigarette smoke, gang violence, and so do you react to such messages? Do they make you overly nervous or tense? If so, y[ou] chronically anxious. Research suggests that anxiety, whether chronic or acute, may be related to persuadability, although the relationship is not clear. For instance, Nunnally and Bobren (1959) found that anxious people were more persuadable than nonanxious people, whereas Janis and Feshbach (1965) found just the opposite. Moreover, research by Lehmann (1970) indicated that anxiety is related to persuasion as much as self-esteem is. Specifically, anxious people, compared to the nonanxious, may be more likely to yield to a message. However, because they may be distracted or overly worried, they may be less likely to receive a message. On the other hand, nonanxious people, compared to the anxious, may be more likely to receive a message but less likely to want to do something about it (Lehmann, 1970).

Whatever the relationship between anxiety and persuasion, one thing is clear: When trying to persuade anxious people, be sure to include specific recommendations for avoiding the harms, along with reassurances that if they follow the recommendations, everything will be okay. As you'll see in more detail in Chapter 13, without such reassurances, people who are anxious may not respond well to fear appeals.

Self-Monitoring and Persuasion: Periscope Up

In high school, a sister of one of the authors dated a guy who was a maniac on the dance floor. Out of context, you'd never have guessed he was dancing. He used to stomp his feet and flap his hands wildly and out of rhythm. Some said he looked badly wounded. Others simply stared. But whatever went on around him, he seemed oblivious, not caring what others thought of him.

The account you've just read is related to a personality trait called *self-monitoring* (Snyder, 1974, 1979). The wild dancer in the story is what people who study personality would call a *low self-monitor*. If you are a low self-monitor, you tend to be less sensitive than others to social cues. In addition, you are not that concerned about what others think of your behavior. You are individualistic and may not always act in ways that are considered socially appropriate. You honestly express your thoughts and feelings, even though you may not be conforming to other people's expectations.

However, if you are a *high self-monitor*, you tend to be very sensitive to social cues. You pay close attention to what's considered appropriate in a given situation and act accordingly. You watch other people's behavior and are good at adapting to different audiences because you have a large repertoire of social skills. You are concerned with appearances and try to "fit in" with others, even when such behavior may contradict what you believe.

As you might expect, high and low self-monitors are persuaded differently. For instance, Becherer, Morgan, and Richard (1982) reported that high self-monitors, because they try to fit in, are more influenced by reference groups than are low self-monitors. In addition, White and Gerstein (1987) conducted a study to investigate how high and low self-monitors might be persuaded to offer help to people with disabilities. Because they knew that high self-monitors want to "look good," these researchers suspected that high self-monitors could be persuaded to help if they thought a social reward would result. To test this, high and low self-monitors heard lectures about Kitty Genovese, a woman who was murdered in New York City while many people watched but did not help. In one version of the lecture, subjects learned that people who help receive social rewards. In another version, subjects were told that helping others usually does not result in social rewards. Later, the subjects were phoned and asked to volunteer to help visually impaired people. Of those who'd been told that helping results in social rewards, 80 percent of the high self-monitors volunteered, but only 48 percent of the low self-monitors did. When subjects did not expect social rewards, 68 percent of the low self-monitors volunteered, and only 40 percent of the high self-monitors did. In other words, high self-monitors are influenced by situations that yield social benefits or enhance their images. Low self-monitors are less susceptible to such appeals.

Similarly, research in advertising suggests that high self-monitors are more influenced by "image-based" advertising. In contrast, low self-monitors are more interested in "product-quality" advertising. For example, Snyder and DeBono (1989) found that high self-monitors were willing to pay more money for a product that promised to improve their image (e.g., an ad shows a bottle of Canadian Club resting on a set of house blueprints and reads, "You're not just moving in, you're moving up"), whereas low self-monitors would pay more for a product that suggests high quality (e.g., an ad for Canadian Club that reads, "When it comes to great taste, everyone draws the same conclusion"). According to DeBono (2006), high self-monitors are also more responsive to strong arguments when the arguments accompany image-based ads, while low self-monitors are more responsive to strong arguments when the arguments accompany product-quality ads.

High self-monitors: Daffodil Queen contestants eavesdropping on contestant interviews.

Reprinted by permission of Steven G. Smith.

Ego Involvement: Not Budging an Inch

One of the most important explanations of the process by which people are persuaded, presented by Muzafer Sherif, Carolyn Sherif, and Robert Nebergall (Sherif & Sherif, 1967; Sherif, Sherif, & Nebergall, 1965), is known as *social judgment theory.* We present the theory here because it focuses on receivers and is particularly relevant to a psychological characteristic known as *ego involvement.*

According to the theory, on any topic, whether it be abortion, an advertised product, or a favorite movie, there are a range of possible opinions that a person can hold. For example, one topic is what should be done with people who have been found guilty of first-degree murder. Here are several positions, some extreme, some moderate, that you might embrace on this topic. Murderers should:

1. Be rewarded for decreasing the population.
2. Be slapped on the hand and sent away.
3. Be given a $500 fine.
4. Receive a 5-year prison term.
5. Receive a 20-year prison term.
6. Receive a life sentence with a chance for parole.
7. Receive a life sentence with no chance for parole.
8. Be put to death.
9. Be tortured to death, along with all other lawbreakers, jaywalkers included.

Social judgment theory argues that on this continuum of positions, we each have a most preferred position, called an *anchor.* For instance, imagine that two people, Muffy and Mort, both agree most with position 7, that murderers should spend their lives in prison with no chance for parole. In Figure 5.1, this anchor point is represented by an "X." Of course, the anchor position is not the only position a person might find acceptable. You can see in Figure 5.1, for example, that Muffy also would accept the death penalty as a fitting punishment. Together, with Muffy's anchor, these positions represent Muffy's *latitude of acceptance.* In other words, these are positions she finds tolerable. She would not, however, agree with all positions, for in addition to the latitude of acceptance, social judgment theory describes two other latitudes. The first, called the *latitude of noncommitment,* contains positions about which a person feels neutral or ambivalent. Muffy is neither for nor against murderers receiving life sentences with the possibility of parole; she is neutral. The second, called the *latitude of rejection,* contains positions that a person would reject. For example, Muffy rejects the idea that murderers be rewarded, slapped, fined, spend 5 to 20 years in prison, or be tortured.

Notice in Figure 5.1 that the span of these latitudes is different for different people. Compared to Mort, Muffy has a larger latitude of rejection and narrower latitudes of non-commitment and acceptance. For this reason, Muffy is a good example of an ego-involved person. People are ego-involved when an issue has personal significance to them and their sense of self. Thus, they become strongly committed to their stand on the issue and are more likely to reject other positions. A person might also be ego-involved about one issue and not another. For instance, Muffy might have strong feelings about what happens to murderers, but care less about abortion, gun control, or gasoline prices.

What should be done with murderers?

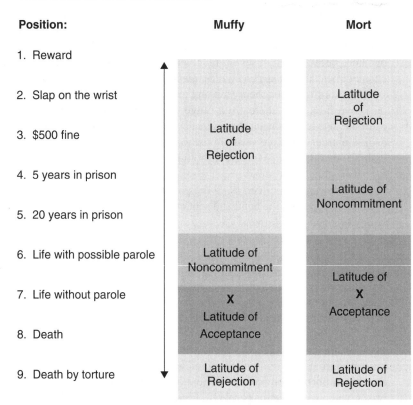

FIGURE 5.1   Illustration of Social Judgment Theory.

Social judgment theory makes several important predictions about the process of persuasion. First, because people judge everything according to their anchor position, it is difficult, if not impossible, to persuade them to accept a position too far away from that anchor. For instance, if you tried to convince Mort that murderers should be rewarded, you'd be wasting your time (see Figure 5.1); messages falling inside a person's latitude of rejection are bound to fail. In fact, the theory argues that when a message falls too far away from a person's anchor position, the person perceives the message to be farther away from the anchor than it really is. This is known as the *contrast effect.* However, the *assimilation effect* occurs when a message that falls within a person's latitude of acceptance is perceived to be closer to the anchor position than it really is. For example, although Mort would prefer that murderers be severely punished, if you told Mort that murderers should be moderately punished, he might decide that you basically agree and accept your position. Thus, whereas contrast leads to the rejection of a message, assimilation leads to successful persuasion.

You might have guessed by now that the contrast effect is more likely in ego-involved people than in people who are not ego-involved. Indeed, it's difficult to persuade someone who is ego involved (e.g., Sherif, Kelly, Rodgers, Sarup, & Tittler, 1973). Because their latitude of rejection is so large (and their latitude of acceptance is so narrow), obviously, they will reject most persuasive messages.

One of the things we like best about *social judgment theory* is how it suggests that persuasion is not a "one-shot deal." We think the theory does a good job of illustrating that persuasion may have to occur over time. For example, imagine trying to persuade Muffy that murderers should merely be slapped (see Figure 5.1). We've already seen that trying to convince her of that will lead to rejection. But aiming messages nearer the anchor point might meet with more success. You might try to persuade Muffy that life in prison with a chance for parole is a good position. Then, if she agrees to that, later you could try to convince her that 20 years in prison is justified. Get the idea? Anchor positions need to be moved gradually.

Issue Involvement: What's This Have to Do with Me?

Although we just stated that involvement inhibits persuasion, in reality, things are more complicated than that. Indeed, the effect of involvement on persuasion depends on the type of involvement we're considering. Specifically, Johnson and Eagly (1990) argued that two types of involvement are ego-involvement (a.k.a. *value-relevant involvement),* which is linked to enduring values embedded in a person's self-concept, and *outcome-relevant involvement* (a.k.a. *issue involvement*), which has to do with a person's current goals or outcomes (e.g., a cancer patient with the goal of using marijuana to minimize physical pain). Based on this notion, Johnson and Eagly analyzed a large number of studies and found that, consistent with social judgment theory, value-relevant involvement inhibited persuasion. Meanwhile, consistent with the *elaboration likelihood model* (see Chapter 2), issue involvement caused people to pay closer attention to arguments in persuasive messages. Issue involvement facilitated persuasion when arguments were strong but inhibited persuasion when arguments were weak.

Dogmatism and Authoritarianism: You Can't Teach an Old Dog New Tricks

In the classic movie *A Few Good Men,* Tom Cruise and Demi Moore defend two Marines, who, while following orders from their superior officers, accidentally killed a fellow soldier. Their defense? "We were simply following orders."

History is replete with examples of this excuse. It was used by Nazi defendants at Nuremberg. It was repeated again during the Vietnam War by soldiers involved in the My Lai massacre, by Ollie North in the Iran-Contragate scandal, and by U.S. soldiers in charge of Iraqi detainees at Abu Ghraib. "We were following orders" is a timeworn excuse and a reflection of a personality trait known as *authoritarianism.*

Authoritarian people respect authoritative leadership and tend to follow authorities blindly (Adorno, Frenkel-Brunswik, Levenson, & Sanford, 1950; Allport, 1954). They condemn those who question and deviate from conventional norms, exhibit hostility toward out-group members, and help cause and inflame intergroup conflict (Altemeyer, 1999). They raise children who are unaccepting of out-groups and who tend to associate with bullies (Knafo, 2003). They believe that power and rigid control are acceptable, and are likely to use physical punishment. Finally, if you are authoritarian, you may not have the self-insight to recognize it. According to Altemeyer (1999):

> If you tell people about authoritarianism, including the part about authoritarians being aggressive when backed by authority, and then ask them how willing they would be to help the federal government eliminate authoritarians, then—you guessed it—High [authoritarians] will be more willing to volunteer than others, to hunt themselves down. . . . And yet, compared with most people, they think their minds are models of rationality and self-understanding. (p. 159)

A personality trait that is very much related to authoritarianism is *dogmatism* (Rokeach, 1960). In fact, according to Christie (1991), dogmatism was introduced as a more general type of authoritarianism; although some argue that authoritarianism and dogmatism scales measure the same thing, others claim that the authoritarianism scale tends to identify close-minded conservatives, whereas the dogmatism scale identifies close-minded liberals and conservatives. Whatever the case, dogmatic people, like authoritarians, tend to be deferential to authorities. In addition, dogmatics are close-minded, have difficulty being objective, and tend to believe there is only one right way to do things (i.e., their way).

With this in mind, you might think that such close-mindedness makes authoritarian and dogmatic people difficult to persuade. Interestingly, however, a meta-analysis by Preiss and Gayle (1999) found just the opposite. That is, compared to their counterparts, dogmatic and authoritarian people were *easier* to persuade. The authors suggested that the rigid beliefs of people with such traits might interfere with the way they scrutinize messages, thereby resulting in greater agreement with a message.

Note, however, that although Preiss and Gayle's (1999) analysis is useful in some respects, we think it's too soon to conclude that dogmatic and authoritarian people are easy to persuade. Indeed, we suggest that more research needs to be conducted to determine *when* dogmatism/authoritarianism is positively related to persuasion and when it is not. By way of example, successfully persuading such people might depend on the nature of the source. Harvey and Beverly (1961), for instance, reported that high authoritarians, compared to low authoritarians, are more likely to be influenced by a person who is a high-status authority. Similarly, a study by DeBono and Klein (1993) found that when dogmatic people received persuasive messages from experts, they did not think much about the messages and, regardless of the quality of the messages, were more persuaded than people who were not dogmatic. However, when they received persuasive messages from nonexperts, dogmatics were more persuaded by strong arguments than by weak ones. Thus, it may be that authoritarians and "high dogs," as people who are highly dogmatic are called by researchers, are especially vulnerable to messages from authority figures.

Finally, it may be that the *type* of persuasive message influences the degree to which authoritarians are persuaded. For example, because authoritarians are predisposed to see the world as dangerous and "stand about ten steps closer to the panic button than the rest of the population" (Altemeyer, 1996, p. 100), Lavine and his colleagues (1999) suspected that authoritarian people would be especially vulnerable to being influenced by threats. To test this idea, about a week before a presidential election, these researchers had high and low authoritarians read "pro-voting" messages that were either threatening (e.g., "voting ensures that freedom won't be taken away by the wrong people getting into power") or rewarding (e.g., "voting allows one to be heard"). Results of their study confirmed their suspicions. Specifically, threatening messages were the most persuasive with high authoritarians, and rewarding messages were most persuasive with low authoritarians (Lavine et al., 1999).

Cognitive Complexity and Need for Cognition

How would you describe your best friend? Fun or boring? Intelligent or stupid? Superficial or disclosive? Even-tempered or moody?

According to a theory known as *constructivism* (Clark & Delia, 1976; Delia & Crockett, 1973; Delia, O'Keefe, & O'Keefe, 1982), people attempt to make sense of their world by using constructs like the ones just mentioned. *Constructs* are perceptual categories (e.g., fat/thin, popular/unpopular, strong/weak) that we use when evaluating everything from professors, to textbooks, to music, to arguments. Constructs can be compared to eyeglasses: Just as you see things differently depending on whether you're wearing thick or thin lenses, the constructs you use affect the manner in which you perceive the world. For instance, someone who evaluates you on the sole basis of whether you are Christian or non-Christian will see you much differently than someone who uses more constructs (such as kind or cruel, shy or extroverted, happy or sad, playful or serious, emotional or stoic) to evaluate you. Obviously, everyone has a unique system of constructs, and some people clearly use more constructs than others. People who use a large number of different and abstract constructs that are well integrated are known as *cognitively complex,* whereas those who use fewer and less abstract constructs are *cognitively simple.*

People who are more cognitively complex, compared to those who are not, are better at seeing the world from their listeners' perspective. As a general rule, they are better at adapting their messages to their listeners and are much more persuasive (Waldron & Applegate, 1998).

When it comes to *being* persuaded, cognitively complex people may also differ from those who are cognitively simple. For instance, cognitively complex people may be more willing than people low in cognitive complexity to tolerate messages that are inconsistent with their cognitions (McGill, Johnson, & Bantel, 1994).

In addition to being different in the degree to which they are cognitively complex, research shows that people differ in their *need for cognition* (Cacioppo & Petty, 1982). People who are high in the need for cognition enjoy effortful thinking more than those low in the need. We also bet they like playing chess and torturing themselves with logic puzzles! According to some researchers, need for cognition is one facet of cognitive complexity (McGill et al., 1994). Whatever the case, compared to people who are low in the need for cognition, those high in the need for cognition are viewed by discussion partners as more effective persuaders who generate more valid arguments for their views (Shestowsky & Horowitz, 2004).

Research also shows that people high in the need for cognition are persuaded differently than their brain-relaxing counterparts. Although people high in the need for cognition pay close attention to messages, evaluating and scrutinizing all the time, people low in the need for cognition are less motivated to attend to messages and are persuaded by peripheral cues instead (Cacioppo & Petty, 1982).[2] Thus, if you're high in the need for cognition, you are persuaded by quality arguments. If you're low in the need for cognition, you may be persuaded by an attractive speaker (see Perlini & Hansen, 2001), a celebrity spokesperson (Williams-Piehota, Schneider, Pizarro, Mowad, & Salovey, 2003), a lot of examples, or a snappy-sounding sales pitch, even if the arguments used are weak. For example, Bakker (1999) found that high school students who were high in the need for cognition were persuaded to practice safer sex (e.g., develop favorable attitudes about using condoms to prevent AIDS) by reading a brochure with well-written and informative arguments about AIDS prevention. In contrast, students low in the need for cognition were most persuaded by brochures that contained a cartoon and presented information in a fun or humorous way (Bakker, 1999). Similarly, Kaufman, Stasson, and Hart (1999) found that when reading an article on evolution theory, the evaluations of people high in the need for cognition were not affected by the source of the article. In contrast, people low in the need for cognition rated the article favorably, but only if they thought it came from the *Washington Post* (a highly credible source). If they thought the article was from the *National Enquirer,* they did not rate it favorably. At least one implication is clear: If the ghost of Elvis Presley *really* wants a following, it should seek coverage in a more reputable publication.

Persuasion and Aggression: Sticks and Stones

Persuasion is not always pretty. Spouse abuse is rampant. Parents beating children as a way to get them to behave is all too common. And who hasn't been called "chicken," "wimp," "bitch," or "brat" by someone wanting to see a change in behavior? Clearly, aggression is the dark side of persuasion. On the other hand, Dominic Infante (1987) argues that aggression is not always bad; aggressive acts can be either constructive or destructive (or both), depending on the type of aggression and how it affects an interpersonal relationship (Infante, 1987; Infante & Rancer, 1982; Infante, Rancer, & Womack, 1997; Rancer, 2004). According to Infante, there are several forms of aggressive communication. We discuss two of them here.

First, *verbal aggressiveness,* a destructive form of aggression, involves the tendency to attack someone by using threats, profanity, insults, and teasing, and by insulting their character, competence, background, appearance, and so forth (Infante et al., 1997; Rancer, 2004). In short, verbal aggression is aimed at damaging another person's self-concept. As might be expected, compared to nonviolent marriages, violent ones are characterized by higher verbal aggressiveness (Infante, Chandler, & Rudd, 1989).

In contrast, *argumentativeness,* a constructive form of assertiveness, involves the tendency to defend and refute positions on controversial issues. Argumentative people approach arguments while nonargumentative people avoid them (Rancer, 2004). Although we sometimes have negative connotations about the word "argument," research shows that argumentativeness is associated with employee satisfaction (Infante & Gordon, 1991) and success in college (Infante, 1982). Moreover, while students perceive verbally aggressive instructors as having low credibility, they perceive argumentative instructors as having high credibility (Edwards & Myers, 2007).

To us, perhaps the most interesting line of research on traits and influence examines the ways in which people "edit" their persuasive messages before they present them. Perhaps you've caught yourself doing this—you want to use a particular strategy, but something keeps you from doing it. A study by Hample and Dallinger (1987) explored the reasons people keep themselves from using certain influence strategies and found that verbal aggressiveness is associated with these reasons. For example, compared to verbally aggressive people, those who are not verbally aggressive tend to suppress arguments because the arguments violate their principles (e.g., threats may be seen as unethical) or for person-centered reasons (e.g., using certain strategies may harm a person's image or a personal relationship). (For more detail on this topic, see Rancer, 2004.)

Finally, although we've painted a rather grim picture of verbal aggression, some of our own work (Seiter & Gass, in press) argues that such aggression may be acceptable in certain situations. Take political contests as an example. Unlike many people we've heard grumbling about how negative and nasty political campaigns have become, we welcome political attacks. Don't get us wrong; we are not condoning all comments. Foes who labeled John Quincy Adams a tyrant and pimp and Abraham Lincoln an ape and butcher were clearly out of line. On the other hand, we do not mind attacks, even those aimed at a politician's character, as long as the attacks are truthful, relevant, and appropriate. Voters should have the information they need to make tough choices, even if that information comes at a cost to potentially ineffective or unethical folks who are running for public office.

ANALYZING AND ADAPTING TO AUDIENCES

To us, the most entertaining part of Super Bowl Sunday is its television advertisements. This, of course, is not surprising when you consider that businesses spend billions of dollars every year analyzing their audiences, trying to determine what will pique interests and sell products. Despite the big bucks, however, when attempting to market products to different cultural groups, businesses have made some pretty big blunders. Copeland and Griggs (1985) list some classic examples:

- Pan Am had to spend a great deal of money redoing and replacing billboards that showed a reclining Japanese woman. The problem? In Japan, only prostitutes recline.
- Latin Americans confused Parker Pen's slogan "Prevent embarrassment—use Parker Ink" for a birth control ad. Why? "Embarazo," the Spanish word Parker used for *embarrassment,* actually means "pregnancy."
- In the United States, the Japanese tried to market a baby soap called "Skinababe."
- Imagine how those in the auto industry felt when they learned that, in Spanish, Nova means "It doesn't go"; in Portuguese, Pinto is slang for "a small male organ"; and Esso, pronounced phonetically in Japanese, means "stalled car."

The lesson here is simple: If you want to be influential, know whom you are talking to and adapt accordingly. Remember what we said earlier about cognitively complex people? Research shows that such people are more persuasive because they are able to see the world from other people's points of view. As a result, they tend to use person-centered influence tactics (i.e., tactics tailored specifically to the person they are trying to persuade; Waldron & Applegate, 1998). This, to us, seems to be what persuasion is all about: adapting a message so it coincides with the receiver's frame of reference. To be sure, a persuader doesn't move the receiver to the message, the persuader moves the message to the receiver. It's what's called being "market-driven" in business, "audience-centered" in public speaking, and "listener-oriented" in interpersonal communication. It may also be the most important lesson you can learn about how to be a successful persuader. To influence other people, you should know as much as possible about them so you can appeal to their needs and wants, while, at the same time, avoid offending them. Of course, attempting to be too diplomatic can go too far. For example, we once heard a story of some people who asked a politician where he stood on a particular issue. So as not to alienate anyone, the politician replied, "Some of my friends are for it, some of my friends are against it, and I'm for my friends." If we'd been in the audience, we would not have been impressed. Thus, it's important to adapt to an audience without coming across as insincere, "smooth," or deceptive.

Entire books have been written on audience analysis (McQuail, 1997), and we cannot give full treatment to the topic here. However, to help you understand the types of issues involved, we discuss segmentation analysis, a special type of audience analysis, in Box 5.2. In addition, we list a few guidelines that might be useful if you're ever faced with an audience that needs to be analyzed.

"Most of these pelts were suicides."

Adapting the message to the audience's frame of reference.

Bull's-Eye! An Examination of Targeted Micromarketing | BOX 5.2

When you consider the billions of dollars advertisers spend each year, it shouldn't surprise you to find out how much time they devote to learning "things" about their audience. But we have to admit—we were surprised, even scared a little, by some of the things these folks know, or at least claim to know. Did you realize, for example, that based on your zip code, market researchers claim to know what you eat for breakfast, what kind of car you drive, what you watch on television, and a whole lot more? They base these predictions on research showing that people who have the same zip codes tend to be remarkably similar. Not only that, based on your zip code, marketers have dubbed you with funny-sounding nicknames like "Blue-Blood Estates," "Money and Brains," and "Single City Blues." So, for example, if your zip code is 94117 or 15232, you are a "Bohemian Mix," you're probably 18 to 34 years old, you enjoy liberal politics and classical records, read *The New Yorker*, and eat frozen waffles (Berger, 2004). See? Spooky!

Using zip codes to categorize consumers is just one example of what is known as *micromarketing* or *market segmentation*, which involves "breaking a market down to definable, manageable segments and then tailoring your efforts to just one or two (Ogden, 2000, p. 29; Schewe & Meredith, 2004). It sounds complicated, but nowadays, it's necessary. Clearly, advertising, campaigning, and marketing are not as easy as they used to be. For example, Penn (2007) argued that a once-universal audience has fragmented into hundreds of small groups or niches. Examples include "Tech Fatales" (women prone to buying technological equipment), "30 Winkers" (people getting less than seven hours of sleep a night), and "Late-breaking gays" (gay people who have come out of the closet later in life due to more social acceptance of homosexuality). These small groups, if understood correctly, can be adapted and appealed to, thus starting "microtrends" that can affect business and society in profound ways.

Of course, it's not only zip codes that help marketers segment audiences. They have a large list of ways to categorize their consumers. Knowing

your age, for instance, may help them design ads that appeal to you. But wait! It gets more complicated! For example, it is not enough to know that your main audience is composed of children. One marketing firm has argued that there are "six species of kids," each requiring a different approach (Gertner, 2004, p. 102). According to Debra Phillips (1999), it may sound funny, but there's a big difference between being 10 years old and being 14, and advertisements aimed at teens are different than those aimed at "the legions of 9- to 12-year-olds whimsically referred to as ''tweens'''(p. 126). Whereas 'tweens may scoff at the likes of Mickey Mouse and his pals (Phillips, 1999), younger children are still attracted to such characters.

If your head isn't spinning yet, just wait. We all know, for instance, that kids like candy, but different groups of kids (and adults) may have different tastes. If you're a marketer, here's when knowing the ethnicity of your target audience can come in handy. For example, market research suggests that while African Americans enjoy very sweet, hard candies in nonchocolate flavors like mint and coconut, Hispanic Americans like "aggressive" flavors like lollipops coated with chili powder and mixed with tamarind. Asian Americans, on the other hand, like the texture of chocolate ("Serving ethnic markets," 1999). When you consider this, along with the fact that African Americans, Hispanic Americans, and Asian Americans make up a large portion of the U.S. population, it is clear why marketers are targeting these groups with all sorts of appeals, including ethnic "aisles" in grocery stores, specialty items such as piñatas, and packaging that attracts certain ethnic groups (e.g., for many Asian Americans, candy packaged in tins connotes quality) ("Serving ethnic markets," 1999).

Of course, by now, we're sure you see that the number of ways marketers can segment consumers is almost limitless. Indeed, in addition to using age, zip codes, and ethnicity, marketers design messages on the basis of gender, education, economic status, and career choice, just to name a few. As time goes by, consumer markets only promise to get smaller. This is especially true on the

(continued)

Internet, which, according to Bianco, Lowry, Berner, Arndt, and Grover (2004), is an interactive medium that enables marketers to personalize messages and products for each consumer. One of the authors, for example, is a member of Netflix, a company that lets you order movies online. After viewing a movie, you can rate it and, based on your ratings, the company provides you with personalized recommendations for other movies you might like. If you have ever purchased a product from Amazon.com, you might have noticed the same feature: Every time you make a purchase, you may be giving information that can be used to persuade you in the future!

Pay Attention to the Situation

Remember what we discussed earlier in the chapter: Communicator characteristics *and* situations affect how audiences respond to persuasive messages. Knowing details about some aspects of a situation can be useful when preparing to persuade someone. For instance, will you be talking to one person or to a large audience? Will the setting be noisy, hot, colorful? Will the persuasion occur in the morning or evening? Will you be inside or out, in a church, or on a football field? Might there be hecklers? Are you expected to talk for five minutes, or can you blab for hours?

Obviously, the number of possible situations is endless. Even so, knowing something about the situation can help you adapt. It's important to try to put yourself in the shoes of your audience. Try to figure out what would persuade and appeal to you if you were in their situation and then adapt your message accordingly. Of course, remember to be an ethical persuader. In our opinion, analyzing the situation can help you do this. We'll have more to say about this topic in Chapter 16.

Keep Your Audience's Mind in Mind

In the movie *What Women Want,* Mel Gibson plays a male chauvinist advertiser who, after a freak accident, is able to read women's minds. Not surprisingly, Mel not only becomes an expert at attracting the opposite sex but can also design advertisements that women can't resist. The movie illustrates how much easier persuasion might be if you had ESP. Indeed, if you could look into people's minds and know their attitudes, values, and needs, we imagine that adapting your persuasive messages would be a piece of cake.

Although we can't teach you to be a psychic, we can give you a few tips about "reading" people's attitudes, values, and needs. First, as you already know from reading Chapter 3, there are a number of ways to measure or make guesses about people's attitudes (e.g., using scales, simply asking them, and so on). Once you know a person's attitudes, it is easier to show him or her how that attitude may be inconsistent with other attitudes, shifted to be stronger, and so forth.

Second, it may be possible to make guesses about a person's values based on other information. For example, values are often culturally determined. By learning the values of a culture, there's a reasonable chance you've learned the values held by an individual within the culture. For instance, earlier in this chapter, we saw that people from the United States tend to value individuals over collectives and that people from China tend toward the opposite. With that in mind, persuasive messages that highlight and promote these values in their respective cultures should be more influential than those that do not. Remember, though, that stereotypes are not always accurate. Keep in mind that cultural values serve as guidelines for developing persuasive messages. Even so, such messages might backfire on some individuals.

Finally, though different individuals' needs may vary drastically, some needs may be universal. Knowing about such needs could prove useful for designing messages that are more persuasive. For example, do you think people who design and advertise smoke alarms know about basic security needs? You bet they do! If you've ever seen one of those advertisements with a family standing at the curb in their pajamas while their house burns down in the background, you know what we're talking about. Advertisers know how to appeal to people's needs.

To help you get a better handle on the types of needs that may be used to motivate people, consider the now-classic typology presented by the humanistic psychologist Abraham Maslow (1962, 1970). According to Maslow, human needs are hierarchical, with the most basic biological needs at the lowest level of the hierarchy and more complex needs at the top. Specifically, Maslow argued that human needs were arranged in the following order, from most basic to most complex: physiological (e.g., the need for food and water), safety (e.g., the need for stability and security), belonging (e.g., the need for acceptance and love), esteem (e.g., the need to feel important and unique), and self-actualization (e.g., the need to grow, create, and understand). According to Maslow, before people are motivated to satisfy higher-level needs, their lower-level needs must be met. Thus, a person who is starving to death will be more interested in obtaining food than in boosting his or her self-esteem.

Remember the Importance of Audience States and Traits

You know by now that communicator traits and states play a large role in persuasion. It's something to keep in mind if you're ever confronted by someone with traits or in the states we've discussed. For example, we noted that anxious people require specific recommendations and reassurances when using fear appeals and that high self-monitors respond well to messages that promise to help them "fit in." People with certain traits may be more difficult to persuade, but if you keep in mind that ego-involved people have narrow latitudes of acceptance and that dogmatics and authoritarians respond better to people in powerful positions, you'll be better equipped as a persuader.

Don't Forget About Audience Demographics

As you've learned from reading this chapter, demographics are important in the process of persuasion. And a person who can adapt to people of different ages, genders, cultures, and so forth obviously will be more successful than a person who can't. For example, when speaking to small children, using lots of statistics would probably lead to lots of "ants in the pants." By the same token, a group of senior citizens would probably squirm or snooze if forced to listen to a speech about planning for pregnancy.[3] Moreover, although we noted that there do not appear to be gender differences in persuadability, it doesn't mean a speaker can ignore the gender of her audience. Notice, for example, by using the word *her* in the previous sentence, we failed to address males who might be reading this book. In short, we're sure you get the point: Whenever possible, know about your audience's age, gender, socioeconomic status, and so forth. Then adapt.

SUMMARY

In this chapter we discussed several communicator characteristics that affect the process of persuasion. First, we examined demographic variables, noting that some (e.g., age, ethnicity) influence the sending and receiving of persuasive messages, whereas others (e.g., gender) do not appear to be related to influenceability. Second, we showed how several psychological and communication states and traits (i.e., self-esteem, anxiety, self-monitoring, ego-involvement, dogmatism, authoritarianism, cognitive complexity, need for cognition, and aggression) influence persuasive communication. Finally, we examined the notion of audience analysis, indicating that persuaders, when possible, should attempt to adapt to the needs, wants, backgrounds, and so forth of their audiences.

ENDNOTES

1. Brinol, Rucker, Tormala, and Petty (2004) reported that people's beliefs about their own persuadibility predicts how easy they are to persuade, but only in some situations. Specifically, in conditions involving little cognitive elaboration, people who believe they are easy to persuade tend to be more persuadable than those who do not hold such beliefs.

2. A person who is very involved in an issue will act similarly to a person who is high in the need for cognition. However, need for cognition is a trait and will, therefore, affect attention to a variety of messages. However, a person with a lot of involvement will have a high need for cognition only on topics relevant to the issue in which he or she is involved.

3. A study by Hummert and Shaner (1994) found that when people held negative stereotypes toward someone elderly, they tended to use a more patronizing speech style. Thus, attempting to adapt to an audience might backfire if done inappropriately.

REFERENCES

Adorno, T., Frenkel-Brunswik, E., Levenson, D., & Sanford, N. (1950). *The authoritarian personality.* New York: Harper.

Allport, G. W. (1954). *The nature of prejudice.* Reading, MA: Addison-Wesley.

Altemeyer, B. (1996). *The authoritarian specter.* Cambridge, MA: Harvard University Press.

Altemeyer, B. (1999). To thine own self be untrue: Self-awareness and authoritarians. *North American Journal of Psychology, 1*(2), 157–164.

Alwin, D. F., & Krosnick, J. A. (1991). Aging, cohorts, and the stability of sociopolitical orientations over the lifespan. *American Journal of Sociology, 97,* 169–195.

Atkin, C., Hocking, J., & Block, M. (1984). Teenage drinking: Does advertising make a difference? *Journal of Communication, 34,* 157–169.

Bakker, A. B. (1999). Persuasive communication about AIDS prevention: Need for cognition determines the impact of message format. *AIDS Education and Prevention, 11*(2), 150–162.

Becherer, R. G., Morgan, F., & Richard, L. M. (1982). Informal group influence among situationally/dispositionally-oriented consumers. *Journal of the Academy of Marketing Science, 10,* 269–281.

Becker, B. J. (1986). Influence again: An examination of reviews and studies of gender differences in social influence. In J. S. Hyde & M. C. Linn (Eds.), *The psychology of gender: Advances through meta-analysis* (pp. 178–209). Baltimore: Johns Hopkins University Press.

Berger, A. A. (2004). *Ads, fads, and consumer culture: Advertising's impact on American character.* Lanham, MD: Rowman & Littlefield.

Beware 'Net predators. (2001, March 7). *The Herald Journal, 92*(66), 1, 12.

Bianco, A., Lowry, T., Berner, R., Arndt, M., & Grover, R. (2004, July). The vanishing mass market. *BusinessWeek, 3891,* 60.

Brinol, P., Rucker, D. D., Tormala, Z. L., & Petty, R. E. (2004). Individual differences in resistance to persuasion: The role of beliefs and meta-beliefs. In E. S. Knowles & J. A. Linn (Eds.), *Resistance and persuasion* (pp. 83–104).Mahwah, NJ: Erlbaum.

Bromberg, D. S., & Johnson, B. T. (1997). Behavioral versus traditional approaches to prevention of child abduction. *School Psychology Review, 26,* 622–633.

Brown, S. L., Asher, T., & Cialdini, R. B. (2005). Evidence of a positive relationship between age and preference for consistency. *Journal of Research in Personality, 39,* 517–533.

Buijzen, M. (2007). Reducing children's susceptibility to commercials: Mechanisms of factual and evaluative advertising interventions. *Media Psychology, 9,* 411–430.

Cacioppo, J. T., & Petty, R. E. (1982). The need for cognition. *Journal of Personality and Social Psychology, 42,* 116–131.

Carli, L. L. (2004). Gender effects on social influence. In J. S. Seiter & R. H. Gass (Eds.), *Readings in persuasion, social influence and compliance gaining* (pp. 133–148). Boston: Allyn & Bacon.

Chaiken, S. (1979). Communicator physical attractiveness and persuasion. *Journal of Personality and Social Psychology, 37,* 1387–1397.

Christie, R. (1991). Authoritarianism and related constructs. In J. P. Robinson, P. R. Shaver, & L. S. Wrightsman (Eds.), *Measures of personality and social psychological attitudes* (pp. 501–571). San Diego, CA: Academic Press.

Clark, R. A., & Delia, J. G. (1976). The development of functional persuasive skills in childhood and early adolescence. *Child Development, 47,* 1008–1014.

Cody, M. J., Seiter, J. S., & Montagne-Miller, Y. (1995). Men and women in the marketplace. In P. J. Kalbfleisch & M. J. Cody (Eds.), *Gender, power, and communication in human relationships* (pp. 305–330). Hillsdale, NJ: Erlbaum.

Copeland, L., & Griggs, L. (1985). *Going international: How to make friends and deal effectively in the global marketplace.* New York: Random House.

DeBono, K. G. (2006). Self-monitoring and consumer psychology. *Journal of Personality, 73,* 715–737.

DeBono, K. G., & Klein, C. (1993). Source expertise and persuasion: The moderating role of recipient dogmatism. *Personality and Social Psychology Bulletin, 19,* 167–173.

Delia, J. G., & Crockett, W. H. (1973). Social schemas, cognitive complexity, and the learning of social structures. *Journal of Personality, 41,* 413–429.

Delia, J. G., O'Keefe, B. J., & O'Keefe, D. J. (1982). The constructivist approach to communication. In F. E. X. Dance (Ed.), *Human communication theory* (pp. 147–191). New York: Harper & Row.

Dickinson, A. (2002, April). What to say to your kids. *Time, 159*(17), 48.

Eagly, A. H. (1978). Sex differences in influenceability. *Psychological Bulletin, 85,* 86–116.

Eagly, A. H., & Carli, L. L. (1981). Sex of researchers and sex-typed communications as determinants of sex differences in influenceability: A meta-analysis of social influence studies. *Psychological Bulletin, 90,* 1–20.

Edwards, C., & Myers, S. A. (2007). Perceived instructor credibility as a function of instructor aggressive communication. *Communication Research Reports, 24,* 47–53.

Fitch, K. L. (1994). A cross-cultural study of directive sequences and some implications for compliance-gaining research. *Communication Monographs, 61,* 185–209.

Fu, P., & Yukl, G. (2000). Perceived effectiveness of influence tactics in the United States and China. *Leadership Quarterly, 11*(2), 251–266.

Gertner, J. (2004, November 28). Hey Mom, is it OK if these guys market stuff to us? *New York Times Magazine, 154*(53047), 100–107.

Groutage, H. (1995, July 14). "Missing 'wife' is a wife not at all." *Deseret News Archives,* p. 2.

Hample, D., & Dallinger, J. M. (1987). Individual differences in cognitive editing standards. *Human Communication Research, 14,* 123–144.

Han, S., & Shavitt, S. (1994). Persuasion and culture: Advertising appeals in individualistic and collectivistic societies. *Journal of Experimental Social Psychology, 30,* 326–350.

Harvey, O. J., & Beverly, G. D. (1961). Some personality correlates of concept change through role playing. *Journal of Abnormal and Social Psychology, 63,* 125–130.

Hofstede, G. (1983). Dimensions of national cultures in fifty countries and three regions. In J. Deregowski, S. Dzuirawiec, & R. Annis (Eds.), *Explications in cross-cultural psychology* (pp. 335–355). Lisse, The Netherlands: Swets and Zeitlinger.

Hummert, M. L., & Shaner, J. L. (1994). Patronizing speech to the elderly as a function of stereotyping. *Communication Studies, 45,* 145–158.

Infante, D. A. (1982). The argumentative student in the speech communication classroom: An investigation and implications. *Communication Education, 3,* 141–148.

Infante, D. A. (1987). Aggressiveness. In J. C. McCroskey & J. A. Daly (Eds.), *Personality and interpersonal communication* (pp. 157–192). Newbury Park, CA: Sage.

Infante, D. A., Chandler, T. A., & Rudd, J. E. (1989). Test of an argumentative skill deficiency model of interspousal violence. *Communication Monographs, 56,* 163–177.

Infante, D. A., & Gordon, W. I. (1991). How employees see the boss: Test of an argumentative and affirming model of supervisors' communicative behavior. *Western Journal of Speech Communication, 55,* 294–304.

Infante, D. A., & Rancer, A. S. (1982). A conceptualization and measure of argumentativeness. *Journal of Personality Assessment, 46,* 60–69.

Infante, D. A., Rancer, A. S., & Womack, D. F. (1997). *Building communication theory* (3rd ed.). Prospect Heights, IL: Waveland Press.

Janis, I. L., & Feshbach, S. (1965). Effects of fear-arousing communications. *Journal of Personality and Social Psychology, 1,* 17–27.

Janis, I. L., & Field, P. B. (1959). A behavioral assessment of persuadability. In C. I. Hovland & I. L. Janis (Eds.), *Personality and persuadability* (pp. 29–54). New Haven, CT: Yale University Press.

Johnson, B. T., & Eagly, A. H. (1990). Effects of involvement on persuasion: a metaanalysis. *Psychological Bulletin, 106,* 290–314.

Kaufman, D. O., Stasson, M. F., & Hart, J. W. (1999). Are the tabloids always wrong or is that just what we think? *Journal of Applied Social Psychology, 29,* 1984–1997.

Klingle, R. S. (2004). Compliance in medical contexts. In J. S. Seiter & R. H. Gass (Eds.), *Readings in persuasion, social influence and compliance gaining* (pp. 289–315). Boston: Allyn & Bacon.

Knafo, A. (2003). Authoritarians, the next generation: Values and bullying among adolescent children of authoritarian fathers. *Analysis of Social Issues and Public Policy, 3*(1), 199–204.

Krosnick, J. A., & Alwin, D. F. (1989). Aging and susceptibility to attitude change. *Journal of Personality and Social Psychology, 57,* 23–30.

Lavine, H., Burgess, D., Snyder, M., Transue, J., Sullivan, J. L., Haney, B., & Wagner, S. H. (1999). Threat, authoritarianism, and voting: An investigation of personality and persuasion. *Personality and Social Psychology Bulletin, 25*(3), 337–347.

Lehmann, S. (1970). Personality and compliance: A study of anxiety and self-esteem in opinion and behavior change. *Journal of Personality and Social Psychology, 15,* 76–86.

Ma, R., & Chuang, R. (2001). Persuasion strategies of Chinese college students in interpersonal contexts. *Southern Journal of Communication, 66*(4), 267–278.

Maslow, A. (1962). *Toward a psychology of being.* New York: Van Nostrand.

Maslow, A. (1970). *Motivation and personality.* New York: Harper & Row.

McGill, A. R., Johnson, M. D., & Bantel, K. A. (1994). Cognitive complexity and conformity: Effects on performance in a turbulent environment. *Psychological Reports, 75,* 1451–1472.

McGuire, W. J. (1968). Personality and attitude change: An information-processing theory. In A. G. Greenwald, T. C. Brock, & T. M. Ostrom (Eds.), *Psychological foundations of attitudes* (pp. 171–196). San Diego, CA: Academic Press.

McQuail, D. (1997) *Audience analysis.* Thousand Oaks, CA: Sage.

Miller, L. C., & Read, S. J. (1991). Inter-personalism: Understanding persons in relationships. *Advances in Personal Relationships, 2,* 233–267.

Nunnally, J. C., & Bobren, H. M. (1959). Variables concerning the willingness to receive communications on mental health. *Journal of Personality, 27,* 275–290.

Oates, C., Blades, M., & Gunter, B. (2002). Children and television advertising: When do they understand persuasive intent? *Journal of Consumer Behavior, 1*(3), 238–245.

Ogden, M. (2000, February 4). To succeed globally, think small in marketing efforts. *Kansas City Business Journal, 18*(22), 29.

Penn, M. J.; with Zalesne, E. K. (2007). *Microtrends: The small forces behind tomorrow's big changes.* New York: Twelve.

Perlini, A. H., & Hansen, S. D. (2001). Moderating effects of need for cognition or attractiveness stereotyping. *Social Behavior and Personality, 29*(4), 313–322.

Perloff, R. M. (1994). Attributions, self-esteem, and cognitive responses to persuasion. *Psychological Reports, 75,* 1291–1295.

Petrova, P. K., Cialdini, R. B., & Sills, S. J. (2007). Consistency-based compliance across cultures. *Journal of Experimental Social Psychology, 43,* 104–111.

Phillips, D. (1999, September). 'Tween beat: Targeting pre-teenage consumers. *Entrepreneur, 27*(9), 126.

Preiss, R. W., & Gayle, B. M. (1999, February). *Authoritarianism, dogmatism, and persuasion: A meta-analytic review.* Paper presented at the Annual Meeting of the Western States Communication Association, Vancouver, BC.

Rancer, A. S. (2004). Argumentativeness, verbal aggressiveness and persuasion. In J. S. Seiter & R. H. Gass (Eds.), *Readings in persuasion, social influence and compliance gaining* (pp. 113–131). Boston: Allyn & Bacon.

Rhodes, N., & Wood, W. (1992). Self-esteem and intelligence affect influenceability: The mediating role of message reception. *Psychological Bulletin, 111,* 156–171.

Rokeach, M. (1960). *The open and closed mind.* New York: Basic Books.

Rosen, M. D. (1994, August). Don't talk to strangers. *Ladies Home Journal, 111,* 108, 109, 153, 154.

Scheidel, T. M. (1963). Sex and persuadability. *Speech Monographs, 30,* 353–358.

Schewe, C. D., & Meredith, G. (2004). Segmenting global markets by generational cohorts: Determining motivations by age. *Journal of Consumer Behavior, 4*(1), 51–63.

Seiter, J. S., & Gass, R. H. (in press). Aggressive communication in political contexts. In T. A. Avtgis & A. S. Rancer (Eds.), *Arguments, aggression, and conflict: New directions in theory and research.* New York: Routledge.

Serving ethnic markets. (1999, May–June). *Professional Candy Buyer, 7*(3), 76.

Sherif, C. W., Kelly, M., Rodgers, H. L., Jr., Sarup, G., & Tittler, B. I. (1973). Personal involvement, social judgment and action. *Journal of Personality and Social Psychology, 27,* 311–328.

Sherif, C. W., Sherif, M., & Nebergall, R. E. (1965). *Attitude and attitude change: The social judgment-involvement approach.* Philadelphia: W. B. Saunders.

Sherif, M., & Sherif, C. W. (1967). Attitudes as the individual's own categories: The social-judgment approach to attitude and attitude change. In C. W. Sherif & M. Sherif (Eds.), *Attitude, ego-involvement, and change* (pp. 105–139). New York: John Wiley & Sons.

Shestowsky, D., & Horowitz, L. M. (2004). How the need for cognition scale predicts behavior in mock jury deliberations. *Law and Human Behavior, 28*(3), 305–337.

Snyder, M. (1974). Self-monitoring of expressive behavior. *Journal of Personality and Social Psychology, 30,* 526–537.

Snyder, M. (1979). Self-monitoring processes. In L. Berkowitz (Ed.), *Advances in experimental and social psychology* (Vol. 12, pp. 85–128). New York: Academic Press.

Snyder, M., & DeBono, K. G. (1989). Understanding the functions of attitudes: Lessons from personality and social behavior. In A. R. Pratkanis, S. J. Brecklet, & A. G. Greenwald (Eds.), *Attitude structure and function* (pp. 339–359). Hillsdale, NJ: Erlbaum.

"Teaching fear." (1986, March 10). *Newsweek,* p. 62.

Waldron, V. R., & Applegate, J. L. (1998). Person-centered tactics during verbal disagreements: Effects on student perceptions of persuasiveness and social attraction. *Communication Education, 47,* 53–66.

Ward, D. A., Seccombe, K., Bendel, R., & Carter, L. F. (1985). Cross-sex context as a factor in persuadability sex differences. *Social Psychology Quarterly, 48,* 269–276.

White, M. J., & Gerstein, L. H. (1987). Helping: The influence of anticipated social sanctions and self-monitoring. *Journal of Personality, 55,* 41–54.

Williams-Piehota, P., Schneider, T. R., Pizarro, L. M., Mowad, L., & Salovey, P. (2003). Matching health messages to information processing styles: Need for cognition and mammography utilization. *Health Communication, 15*(4), 375–392.

Wiseman, R. L., Sanders, J. A., Congalton, K. J., Gass, R. H., Sueda, K., & Du, R. (2009). A cross-cultural analysis of compliance gaining: China, Japan, and the United States In B. Hoffer and N. Honna (Eds.), *Intercultural communication: Beyond the canon* (pp. 186–212). San Antonio, TX: International Association for Intercultural Communication Studies.

Wooden, K. (1988, June). How sex offenders lure our children. *Reader's Digest,* pp. 149–154.

6

Conformity and Influence in Groups

Bo, Peep, sheep, and the Hale-Bopp comet may sound like the makings of a good fairy tale, but, as the saying goes, truth is stranger than fiction, and, unfortunately, the story of Bo and Peep's sheep is a true one. We refer to the people of the Heaven's Gate cult as sheep because who else but sheep would believe what these people were told—that they should commit mass suicide so they might shed their bodies and be whisked away by an alien spaceship that was flying around in the tail of the Hale-Bopp comet. Whether they believed it or not, they did what their leaders, Bo and Peep, told them to do. In late March of 1997, sheriff's deputies found the corpses of 21 women and 18 men decomposing in a home in Rancho Santa Fe, California. All of the members of the cult had apparently ingested a fatal mixture of pheno-barbital, applesauce, pudding, and vodka (Chua-Eoan, 1997; Gleick, 1997b).

As authors who are interested in the process of social influence, we can't help but wonder how and why people like those in the Heaven's Gate cult can be persuaded to such extremes. Clearly, several factors must have contributed to the largest mass suicide in U.S. history. The cult members—though reportedly bright and happy—must have been highly persuadable. Moreover, the leaders of the cult, Marshall Herff Applewhite and Bonnie Lu Nettles (known as Bo and Peep), were highly charismatic and trusted by their followers, who believed that Bo and Peep were extraterrestrial representatives of the "Kingdom Level Above Humans." But beyond the characteristics of the cult leaders and members, we believe that a strong group dynamic may have contributed to the suicide. Indeed, although from society's perspective the members of the cult were deviants, there seemed to be pressure within the cult to "fit in." For instance, the members of the cult reportedly looked the same, so much so that when the corpses were first discovered, they were believed to be men only. The cult members were described as having androgynous appearances; the women wore cropped hair, and many of the men, including the cult's leader, had been castrated. Finally, the cult members were known to dress the same, wearing what one person described as black pajamas. When the 39 corpses were found, each was dressed in black: black pants, black shirt, and brand-new black Nike shoes (Gleick, 1997b).

We imagine that, if nothing else, being a member of a cult satisfies a need to belong. Cults often attract new members by providing seemingly loving environments for their new recruits. Along with this, however, comes pressure to fit in. Cults often enforce strict rules and regimens for their members.

With such pressure to fit in, it's easier to see how a cult member might have been sucked into the suicide. When you identify so strongly with people who are carrying out some action, the action not only seems more "right," it becomes necessary for you to participate if you want to be part of the group. This is true not only in cults, a topic we revisit later in this chapter, but in other social collectives as well. Families, peer groups, workplaces, even classrooms, exert strong pressure on their members to behave in certain ways. Groups are a powerful persuasive force. For that reason, this chapter examines the role of groups in the process of social influence. We begin by discussing the topic of conformity.

CONFORMITY AS PERSUASION: IN WITH THE CROWD

During a lecture by a sociology professor, in a classroom that held more than 100 people, an undergraduate student, known by both of your authors, removed his shirt, pants, shoes, and socks. Then, almost naked, he stood in the aisle of the classroom, waiting to be noticed. The professor, who had been looking down at his notes, did not notice our friend until other people in the classroom began gasping and laughing. When the professor finally did look up, he was stunned. Undaunted, the nearly naked student looked down at himself and asked, "Does this count?"

Apparently, just before the student had disrobed, the professor had been lecturing on the topic of norms and conformity. *Norms* are expectations held by a group of people about what behaviors or opinions are right or wrong, good or bad, acceptable or unacceptable, appropriate or inappropriate (Andrews, 1996). Once norms are understood, we feel pressure to conform to them. Of course, the professor had probably explained to our friend and his other students that some norms are explicit. *Explicit norms* are written or spoken openly. For example, road signs indicate how fast you are permitted to drive, employee manuals may tell you how to dress, and game rules may send you to jail without collecting $200. Some norms, however, are *implicit* and not so openly stated. For example, we imagine that when you're a guest in someone's home, you don't put your feet on the dinner table even though you've never read a rule saying you shouldn't. Likewise—and this is what the sociology professor told his class—because we all conform to social norms, no one would take his or her clothes off in the middle of a classroom lecture. Of course, our friend, who prides himself on being a nonconformist, couldn't resist this challenge. The rest is history, and the professor now has a good story to tell whenever he lectures about norms and conformity.

In the Beginning: Early Research on Conformity Effects

Not everyone is like our friend, the student-stripper in the sociology class. As we've noted, in most cases, people know the norms and try to go along with the crowd. One of the first researchers to examine this conformity effect was Muzafer Sherif (1935). Sherif used an optical illusion called the *autokinetic effect* to show how groups can influence an individual's behavior. Here's how the autokinetic effect works: If you are sitting in a dark room and look at a pinpoint of light, the light appears to move even when it is stationary. Try it with your friends sometime. Each will say the light moved, but they may differ in their judgments, some thinking the light moved an inch, others thinking it moved even farther.

This is exactly what Sherif found until he brought all of his subjects together and tried the experiment again. This time he allowed his subjects to report out loud how far they thought the light moved. Interestingly, Sherif found that after a while the individuals' judgments began to converge. The individuals began to conform, agreeing on a midpoint of light movement.

Perhaps the most compelling experiment on the effects of conformity was conducted by Solomon Asch (1956). Here's how his experiment worked: Asch gathered several (seven to nine) college students into a classroom and told them that they would be participating in an experiment in visual judgment. The students were asked to look at two large, white cards. As can be seen in Figure 6.1, a single vertical line appeared on the first card, and three vertical lines, each of different length, appeared on the second card. The students' task was simple: After observing both cards, they were asked to match lines. That is, each student was asked to report out loud, to the rest of the group, which of the three lines on the second card was the same length as the line on the other card.

According to Asch (1966), the experiment began uneventfully but changed rapidly:

> The subjects announce their answers in the order in which they have been seated in the room, and on the first round every person chooses the same matching line. Then a second set of cards is exposed: Again the group is unanimous. The members appear ready to endure politely another boring experiment. On the third trial there is an unexpected disturbance. One person near the end of the group disagrees with all the others in his selection of the matching line. He looks surprised, indeed incredulous, about the disagreement. On the following trial he disagrees again, while the others remain unanimous in their choice. The dissenter becomes more and more worried and hesitant as the disagreement continues in succeeding trials; he may pause before announcing his answer and speak in a low voice, or he may smile in an embarrassed way. (p. 320)

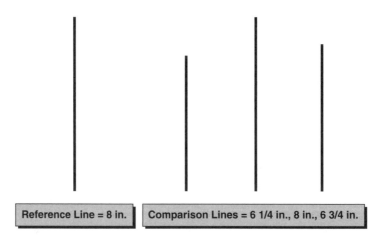

Reference Line = 8 in. | Comparison Lines = 6 1/4 in., 8 in., 6 3/4 in.

FIGURE 6.1   Example of Visuals Used in Asch's Experiment. Subjects are asked which of the three lines on the comparison card (right) match the line on the reference card (left).

What the dissenting student in Asch's study did not know was that all of the other students in the group were planted by Asch and told beforehand to give the wrong answers. In other words, Asch was really interested in what a person would do when he or she was giving correct answers that are contrary to the answers of a near-unanimous group decision. What he found was that conformity was common; under group pressure, 75 percent of the subjects gave the wrong answer in at least one of the trials.

In short, then, Asch's experiment illustrates the tremendous power of groups to exert influence. Even so, not all of Asch's subjects behaved in the same way. For instance, about 25 percent remained fairly independent, rarely conforming to the group's answers. Moreover, about 10 percent of the subjects agreed with the group on almost every trial. Thus, it is probably true that some individuals are more prone to conformity than others. In addition, some situations may produce more conformity than others, a topic we discuss next.

Variables Related to Conformity

Does Group Size Affect Conformity? The More the Scarier?

On the television show *Who Wants to be a Millionaire?* contestants can make a bundle of money if they can answer a series of questions that become progressively more difficult. Of course, if they get stumped, the rules allow them to "poll the audience," asking those in the studio for advice on one, and only one, question. With that in mind, if you were a contestant on the show and had the choice of an audience with 5 people or 500 people, which audience would you want? What if your choice were between an audience of 499 and 500 people? Would the extra person make a very big difference and, if not, at what point does adding people to the audience become less relevant?

Regardless of whether they watch *Who Wants to be a Millionaire?* for some time researchers have been interested in the role that group size plays in persuasion. Two of many theories that make different predictions about the relationship between group size and persuasion are *social impact theory (SIT)* (Latané, 1981; Latané & Wolf, 1981) and the *social influence model (SIM)* (Tanford & Penrod, 1984). The first, SIT, argues that the first person you add to a group has the most influence. Each additional member has some impact, but each has less than the person added before him or her. In contrast, SIM argues that the third and fourth people added to a group have the most impact because no minority is possible with only two people. In other words, it is easier to disagree with one person than it is to disagree with two or three people. After three or four people are added, however, the pressure to conform levels off.

Empirical results and meta-analyses on which is the better of these two perspectives are mixed (see Bond, 2005; Bond & Smith, 1996; Latané & Wolf, 1981; Tanford & Penrod, 1984); some studies support one perspective, some the other, and some neither. After reviewing the literature, we suspect that both models have found support because both may be accurate when you consider an additional variable. Specifically, Campbell and Fairey (1989) argued that when you are making a decision in a group, you are motivated by two things: You want to be right and you want to be liked. According to these authors, sometimes we conform to a group because the group has *informational influence*. That is, we have a desire to be right and we conform to the group because we think the group may be correct. However, sometimes we conform to a group because it has *normative influence*. This means that we conform in order to gain rewards (e.g., be liked) and avoid punishments (e.g., scorn) that are associated with agreement and disagreement.

What does this have to do with group size? According to Campbell and Fairey (1989), increasing the number of people in a group affects informational and normative processes differently. Specifically, when you want to be right, as in the millionaire example, the first person added has the most impact because each additional person's judgment is more likely to be redundant with others in the group. On the other hand, imagine you are just playing an "at home" version of *Who Wants to be a Millionaire?* with some new neighbors. Your goal is not to win money, but just to fit in, be liked, and make some new friends. In this case, agreeing with the neighbors, especially when the number of them reaches two or three, is more likely, even if you think they are wrong. According to Bond (2005), normative influence is stronger when people respond in front of the group, while informational influence is stronger when people respond in private. (For more about group size and conformity, see Box 6.1)

Security in Numbers: The Effect of More Than One Dissenter
Research indicates that having an ally helps a person resist conforming to a group. For example, Allen and Levine (1971) found that a single subject is likely to conform when he or she is faced with four other people who disagree, but if one of those four sides with the subject, the subject continues to dissent. Interestingly, this seems to be the case even when the supporting partner's judgments are questionable. For example, Allen and Levine (1971) found that when trying to make judgments about visual stimuli, even a supporting partner who seemed visually impaired (e.g., wore thick glasses and seemed to have a hard time seeing) prevented subjects from conforming.

Indoctrination: Intense Initiations and Mindless Membership
The only time one of your authors was formally initiated into a group, his high school's Varsity Club, he had to wear a dress and sing Christmas carols in a shopping mall (and it

Majority Rules: How to Influence When You're Alone in a Group | BOX 6.1

This chapter discusses the ways in which a majority of people can influence a minority. As many minority groups have illustrated throughout history, however, influence is not always so simple. Sometimes, the minority can influence the majority. This is especially true when the person in the minority is believed to have experience and expertise in whatever topic the group is discussing (Hart, Stasson, & Karau, 1999).

Even when the person in the minority is not an expert, however, it may be possible for him or her to influence the majority. According to a review of research by Tanford and Penrod (1984), two strategies that a minority can try are (1) conforming with the group and then deviating and (2) consistently disagreeing with the group. The first tactic involves accumulating what might popularly be known as brownie points. Specifically, by going along with the group on most issues, you are more favorable in the group's eyes when you disagree. As a result, you may actually convince the group to go along with your point of view. In contrast, the second tactic involves disagreeing with the group consistently and competently. By doing this, whoever holds the minority point of view looks more confident and may get the group's attention (Moscovici & Faucheux, 1972; Moscovici, Lage, & Naffrechoux, 1969). Of course, these two tactics involve opposite behaviors, so if you're in the minority, don't try both; pick one tactic and stick to it. If you're able to convince even one member of the majority to join you, research suggests that others may follow suit (see Clark, 1999).

wasn't even Christmas time). Of course, there are more severe initiations than this. In 2003, for instance, a group of Chicago high school girls viciously hazed some younger girls by kicking, strangling, and pelting them with feces, urine, fish entrails, and blood. The same year, three young football players in Bellmore, New York, were sodomized with broomsticks, golf balls, and pinecones during a hazing incident. And although Hansen's (2004) sources indicate that nearly 80 percent of college athletes and fraternity and sorority members have been involved in hazing, students are not the only ones participating. A story on CNN, for example, discussed "blood pinning," a sadistic ritual in which marines "take turns punching, pounding and grinding gold pins into the bloody chests of the new initiates, who scream and writhe in pain" (Gleick, 1997a, p. 30).

As brutal as these rituals sound, some argue that such practices build cohesiveness by encouraging bonding among new recruits (see Hansen, 2004). Interestingly enough, this may be true. Research suggests that we value a group more if our indoctrination into the group is severe and intense (e.g., Aronson & Mills, 1959). Not only that, once we value a group, we are likely to conform to it. Unfortunately, a number of groups have figured this out and have ruined a lot of lives as a result. As the introduction to this chapter illustrated, religious cults provide a frightening example of the high level of compliance that may result from intense levels of indoctrination. Indeed, a disturbing number of cult members have died in mass suicides that were encouraged by their leaders (Freckelton, 1998) (see Box 6.2).

Apparently, cults are effective persuaders. Whitsett and Kent's (2003) sources, for example, estimate that as many as 5 million Americans are or have been involved with cultic groups. Surprisingly, the majority of these members are of above-average intelligence, oftentimes recruited from college campuses (Shaw, 2003). How do cults lure such people into their trap? After conducting numerous interviews with former cult members,

Modern-Day Cults: A Sad Chronology	BOX 6.2

1978: Reverend Jim Jones and 900 followers, including children, commit suicide in Jonestown, Guyana, by drinking cyanide-laced punch.

1991: A Mexican minister and 29 followers suffocate after he instructs them to keep praying and ignore toxic fumes filling the church.

1993: At least 80 Branch Davidians, followers of David Koresh, perish in a fire and shoot-out with the BATF at their compound in Waco, Texas.

1993: Using primitive weapons, 53 Vietnamese tribal villagers commit suicide in the belief that they will go straight to heaven.

1994: Sixty-seven members of the "Order of the Solar Temple" cult are found burned to death in the French Alps in Switzerland and in Quebec, Canada.

1997: Thirty-nine members of the "Heaven's Gate" cult, led by Marshall Applewhite, commit suicide in California. They die so they can join the Mother Ship following the Hale-Bopp comet.

2000: More than 900 members of a reclusive Christian doomsday cult in Africa are murdered by their leaders. Many are burned to death, many are buried in mass graves.

2003: Members of the Raelians (a cult founded by Claude Vorilhon), now known as "Rael," claim that with the assistance of Clonaid, a human cloning company, they have cloned two or more human infants. The claims have never been substantiated.

Baron (2000) noted that indoctrination into cults occurs in four stages. First, in the *softening-up stage,* recruits, often targeted when vulnerable (e.g., following a divorce or death of a loved one) (Lifton, 1986), are befriended by a member and invited to meetings. There, recruits are showered with attention and praise from cult members, a technique referred to as "love bombing" (Richmond, 2004). Often, recruits are "squired" by enthusiastic group members or "messianic" leaders, deprived of sleep, and then confused. The idea here is to lure, then stress, the recruits. In the second stage, *compliance,* the recruits, feeling important and loved, tentatively experiment with some of the behaviors requested by the cult, which may include changes in diet, sleep, and appearance. Though in this stage, recruits may simply be paying lip service to the demands of the cult, by the third stage, *internalization,* the recruits begin to consider some of the demands and beliefs of the cult (e.g., all nonmembers are evil) to be more acceptable. Finally, in the *consolidation stage,* recruits become loyal to the cult and demonstrate their allegiance with costly behaviors such as abandoning their careers or academic goals, donating all their personal possessions to the cult, and recruiting new members (Baron, 2000; Richmond, 2004).

Previous literature suggests that a number of influence principles may contribute to such conformity by recruits. One perspective argues that cults create climates that are difficult and painful to leave. Members become so emotionally dependent on the group that they can't bear to be shunned (Zablocki, 1999). Regardless of which of these explanations is best, the lesson is clear: The harder it is to get into a group, the more likely we are to comply once we're in it.

Identification and Conformity: You're My Kind of People

The notion of *identification* is central to Kenneth Burke's (1950) conceptualization of rhetoric. According to Burke, identification occurs when people are united in substance (i.e., when they share attitudes, activities, ideas, possessions, and so forth). Burke argued that although

Cartoon by John Seiter.

humans are fundamentally divided, they are motivated to communicate with one another to create identification. The notion of identification is important here because the more a person identifies with a group, the more power the group has to influence that person.

A group that has the power to influence us through the process of identification is known as a *reference group*. Of course not all groups are reference groups. For example, you might get together with several other students to study for a test. It's unlikely that such a group would exert much influence on the way you think and behave on a daily basis. However, a group of people you admire and want to be like might have a strong impact on you, often without your even knowing it. Because we identify with reference groups, we tend to dress the way they dress, think the way they think, and act the way they act. With this in mind, it's not surprising that a considerable amount of research indicates that we tend to conform more to a group of people who are similar to us than to a group of people who are not (Abrams, Wetherell, Cochrane, Hogg, & Turner, 1990; Bond & Smith, 1996). One study, for example, found that university students were likely to consume more alcohol when they identified strongly with friends, peers, and fraternity/sorority members who looked favorably upon heavy drinking (Reed, Lange, Ketchie, & Clapp, 2007).

Although fitting in and getting along with others can be a good thing, Seiter (1998) argued that too much identification can have negative consequences in a variety of contexts. For example, in intercultural contexts, *ethnocentrism,* or the belief that one's culture is the standard by which all others should be evaluated, occurs when members of a culture identify too strongly with their own culture. In small group contexts, *groupthink* (Janis, 1972) occurs when the members in a group are so concerned with achieving consensus and getting along with each other that they don't disagree when they should. In organizational communication contexts, too much identification can lead to what Tompkins and his colleagues (Bullis & Tompkins, 1989; Tompkins & Cheney, 1985) call *strong culture.* Strong cultures exist when employees identify so much with their organization that they conform to the organization's values and actions.

As you might imagine, ethnocentrism, groupthink, and strong culture can result in some seriously negative consequences. For instance, ethnocentrism can lead to intolerance, hatred, discrimination, and violence toward members of another culture (Gudykunst & Kim,

1997; Parrillo, 1985). Moreover, groups and organizations characterized by groupthink and strong culture are notorious for bad decision making, because they involve collectives of people are all thinking in the same way. Seiter (1995), for example, showed how a lumber company with a strong culture had difficulty communicating with people outside the organization. That's because inside the company, everyone thought things were rosy, and, as a result, the organization found itself threatened in the face of environmentalist attacks. Clearly, organizations and groups need members who will occasionally "rock the boat" and "blow whistles" (Locke et al., 2001; Redding, 1985). In short, then, it is clear that identification, by enabling us to communicate, organize, and decrease division, can be a worthwhile goal. However, we must be moderate in promoting it because too much identification can be "too much of a good thing" (Seiter, 1998).

Communicator Characteristics and Conformity

In Chapter 5, we discussed in some detail the ways in which communicator characteristics are related to persuasion. Many of the same characteristics examined there have also been studied by researchers interested in the topic of conformity.

Gender. In an analysis of a large number of studies examining the relationship between gender and conformity, Bond and Smith (1996) concluded that females are more likely to conform than males. This seems to be the case regardless of when the studies were conducted (i.e., gender differences have not narrowed over time) or whether the participants in the studies were in the presence of the other group members. A study consistent with these findings examined 115 men and 111 women in a cafeteria line (Guarino, Fridrich, & Sitton, 1994). The research question was this: If the person you are dining with selects a dessert before you do, are you more likely to select a dessert yourself? The study revealed that 77 percent of the women conformed to the dessert-selecting behavior of the person ahead of them in line but only 43 percent of the men did. In addition, the gender of the person who selected the dessert first made a difference. Specifically, if the first person to select a dessert was a female, 75 percent of the women also selected a dessert but only 27 percent of the men did. Men were more likely to conform when following a male dessert eater than when following a female dessert eater. Whatever the case, here's our suggestion after reading this study: If you're on a diet, make sure you're the first person in line!

Peer-suasion. Peer pressure exerts strong pressures on teens to comply. Indeed, according to McCoy (1991), one study conducted on more than 3,000 teenagers found that more than two-thirds of them felt substantial peer pressure to have sex, drink, and take drugs. Gordon (1986) found that peer pressure is the most important factor in determining whether teens begin smoking. Moreover, because teens so desperately want to be accepted by their peers, for those who do not believe that they fit in with groups that pressure them, the consequences can be severe. For instance, not fitting in can lead to depression, the number-one risk factor for teen suicide (Royte, 1994). That being said, we must keep in mind that peer pressure is not always a bad thing. Although parents must communicate openly with their children about what is right and wrong and be cautious of negative peer pressure, they shouldn't forget that peers also can praise, encourage, teach compromise, and help a child develop a sense of morality (Hoyt, 1995).

"Gee, Tommy, I'd be lost without your constant peer pressure"

Personality

Several studies have identified various aspects of personality that are related to conformity. First, McGill, Johnson, and Bantel (1994) found that managers with high cognitive complexity (i.e., those who have a large number of diverse and integrated mental constructs for interpreting the world) tend to perform best in turbulent environments largely because they conform less than managers with low cognitive complexity. Second, Burger (1987) found that people high in the desire to control events in their lives react negatively to group pressure and are, therefore, less likely to conform than people with a low desire for control. Third, high self-monitors, who pay close attention to social cues on appropriate behavior, are more likely to conform than low self-monitors (Snyder, 1987). Finally, Rose, Shoham, Kahle, and Batra (1994) found that people who are high in the need for affiliation and group identification conform more than people without such needs. Interestingly, those with needs for affiliation and group identification prefer clothing with popular brand names and styles, whereas those without such needs prefer clothing that is comfortable and durable.

Culture

After surveying more than 100,000 people in 40 different cultures, Hofstede (1984) identified four different dimensions of values along which any culture can be placed. He labeled these dimensions *power distance, uncertainty avoidance, masculinity-femininity,* and *individualism-collectivism.* Recently, Lustig and Cassotta (1996) argued that each of Hofstede's value dimensions can be applied to the study of persuasion to determine which cultures are more likely to conform than others.

First, people from cultures that score high on power distance value hierarchy and obedience to authority, whereas those who score low on power distance prefer equality and participative decision making. For that reason, Lustig and Cassotta (1996) argued that people from cultures with low power distance scores (e.g., Israel, Australia, western European countries) are less likely to conform than those from cultures with high power distance scores (e.g., the Philippines, Mexico, Venezuela, India, Singapore).

Second, people from some cultures avoid uncertainty and have little tolerance for ambiguity, whereas people from other cultures are more at ease with the unknown. Because ambiguous stimuli foster conformity more than unambiguous stimuli, Lustig and Cassotta (1996) argued that cultures that are uncomfortable with ambiguous situations (e.g., Greece, Portugal, Japan, Peru, Chile, Spain) should conform more than cultures that are comfortable with ambiguity (e.g., the United States, Singapore, India, England, Sweden).

Third, some cultures can be characterized as "masculine" because they value competition, strength, assertiveness, and achievement, whereas others can be characterized as "feminine" because they value cooperation, affection, intuition, and nurturance. As such, members from masculine cultures (e.g., Japan, Italy, Austria, Mexico, England, Venezuela) should conform less than members from feminine cultures (e.g., Scandinavian countries, Portugal, the Netherlands).

Finally, while individualistic cultures value personal goals and self-autonomy, collectivistic cultures emphasize the importance of group goals and harmony. For that reason, Lustig and Cassotta (1996) argued that individualistic cultures (e.g., the United States, England, Australia, Canada, Italy, Denmark) are less conforming than collectivistic cultures (e.g., Colombia, Korea, Peru, Taiwan, Pakistan, Chile). A meta-analysis by Bond and Smith (1996) supports this conclusion, finding conformity to be much higher in collectivistic cultures than in individualistic cultures.

The "Whys" of Conformity

Up to this point, we've discussed the "whats," "wheres," and "whens" of conformity, but perhaps a more important question concerns the "whys" of conformity. That is, why are people motivated to conform to the majority's behavior or point of view? According to Insko and Schopler (1972), past scholars have suggested at least five different reasons conformity occurs. These include the following:

- **The group locomotion hypothesis:** This view suggests that members of a group are motivated to achieve the group's goals. When a member of the group believes that going along with the group will help achieve those goals, he or she is motivated to conform.
- **Social comparison theory:** How do you decide if you are attractive, tall, weird, or good at something? This theory suggests that you determine such things by comparing yourself to others (usually others who are similar to you). Clearly, doing so can lead to conformity. For instance, if, as a parent, you spank your children but learn that none of your friends spank their children, you may stop spanking your children.
- **Consistency (or balance) theory:** This theory suggests that it is uncomfortable to disagree with a group that you like and find attractive. Thus to restore balance you are motivated to go along with the group and perhaps even convince yourself that the group was correct all along.
- **Epistemological weighting hypothesis:** This view suggests that we gain knowledge in two ways: personally, through trial and error and perceptual observation; and socially, through observations and communication with others. When our view

differs from a group's view, these two modes of knowledge compete with one another. For instance, in Asch's experiment (discussed earlier), subjects thought they were seeing one thing (personal knowledge) but the group convinced them that they were seeing something else (social knowledge). The epistemological weighting hypothesis suggests that the degree to which a person conforms depends on how much weight is given to personal and social knowledge. Clearly, this weighting differs for different people, which is why some people conform more than others.

- **The hedonistic hypothesis:** This view argues that we conform to avoid pain (e.g., rejection, censure, scorn) and gain pleasure (e.g., acceptance, love, approval).

Social Proof: Using the Sheep Factor to Persuade Others

"But, Mom, *everybody's* doing it," is a familiar childhood refrain. Even so, children are not the only ones who pattern their behavior after others. Much of adult behavior is based on what Cialdini (1993) has termed *social proof*:

> The tendency to see an action as more appropriate when others are doing it normally works quite well. As a rule, we will make fewer mistakes by acting in accord with social evidence than contrary to it. Usually when a lot of people are doing something, it is the right thing to do. This feature of the principle of social proof is simultaneously its major strength and its major weakness. Like the other weapons of influence, it provides a convenient shortcut for determining how to behave, but, at the same time, makes one who uses the shortcut vulnerable to the attacks of profiteers who lie in wait along its path. (p. 116)

One of the authors once met a person who makes money by playing a guitar and singing in subways and on street corners. The person explained that, even before she starts singing, she throws some of her own money into the open guitar case. Why? When people pass by, they think others have contributed and are more likely to do the same. Not surprisingly, this subway minstrel is not the only one who uses the principle of social proof to persuade others. In fact, the success of "viral marketing" (also discussed in Chapter 1) is largely based on this principle. In his bestselling book *The Tipping Point*, for example, Malcolm Gladwell (2002) argued that in the same way a sick person can start an epidemic of the flu, so too can a small group of influential people cause a fashion trend or the popularity of a new product. The idea is that consumers will see products being used or talked about by others and follow suit. This strategy of relying on social proof or word of mouth has become known as *viral marketing* and is catching on. Did you know, for example, that companies are hiring "real people" to use their products? These "undercover" consumers are meant to provide proof that the product is effective or worthwhile. For example, Ford gave a handful of Focus cars to "key influencers" who presumably drove around influencing others to follow suit, and Hebrew National hired "mom squads" to host hotdog barbeques (Goodman, 2001). Other marketers have hired bar "leaners" to talk up the merits of certain liquors and moms to talk about new laundry detergents at their kids' little league games (Eisenberg, 2002). Marketers for the energy drink Red Bull decided they didn't even need people to spread the word. Instead, they filled sidewalk trash cans and bar tables with empty cans of the stuff (Eisenberg, 2002).

Once again, the idea is the same; if people see or hear about others using a product, they're more likely to try the product themselves. Research supports this notion as well. For example, a study by Cody, Seiter, and Montagne-Miller (1995) found that when people are buying gifts for others, social proof is one of the most effective tactics that a salesperson can use. In fact, when salespersons told their customers that a particular product was "the most popular," "the best selling," or "selling faster than we can bring them in," customers spent more money than when the salespersons used other tactics, such as praising the customer, doing favors for the customer, and trying to demonstrate expertise and trustworthiness (Cody et al., 1995). Why? It may be that people are less certain about purchases when buying for others than when buying for themselves.

Though social proof is probably a universally effective persuasion tactic, it may be more effective when used in some cultures than others. Recall, for example, our earlier discussion about the distinction between individualistic and collectivistic cultures. According to Cody and Seiter (2001), because social proof is rooted in people's tendency to conform, it should be especially effective in collectivistic cultures where conformity is prevalent. This seems to be the case. For instance, Cialdini, Wosinska, Barrett, Butner, and Gornik-Durose (2001) conducted a study to see how well social proof worked in the United States (an individualistic culture) and Poland (a collectivistic culture). In the study, people from both cultures were asked to indicate how willing they would be to comply with three requests: once while considering that all their peers had complied with the request (high social proof), once while considering that half their peers had complied with the request (moderate social proof), and once while considering that none of their peers had complied (no social proof). Results of the study indicated that, in both cultures, as the level of social proof increased, so did compliance. This was especially true in Poland (Cialdini et al., 2001).

Before concluding this section, we should mention that social proof might be counterproductive to persuasion as well. For example, Cialdini and his colleagues (2006) suspected that when people try to condemn particular behaviors by pointing out the large number of people who engage in them, a type of "negative social proof" might occur. Specifically, the researchers wondered if messages like those from the FDA announcing that "more than 3 million youths in the U.S. smoke cigarettes" or like those from the U.S. Forest Service mascot, Woodsy Owl, proclaiming that "American will produce more litter this year than ever before" might cause people to smoke and litter more. To test this idea, the researchers posted two types of signs in Arizona's Petrified Forest National Park. One said, "Please don't remove petrified wood from the park." The other said, "Many past visitors have removed the petrified wood from the park, changing the state of the Petrified Forest." The researchers then placed marked pieces of petrified wood in designated locations along visitor pathways and checked periodically to see how much had been stolen. As suspected, the sign mentioning that other people had stolen wood resulted in significantly more theft!

OSTRACISM: SHUNS AND GUNS

In 1976, on the campus where one of the authors teaches, a disturbed man shot and killed six students and one communication professor. Similarly, in 1999, at Columbine High School in Colorado, two students, Eric Harris and Dylan Klebold, shot and killed 12 students and a teacher before committing suicide. And more recently, in 2007, Seung-Hui Cho killed 32 people on the Virginia Tech campus before committing suicide. Sadly, such school shootings are all too prevalent. They leave us shaking our heads and asking,

"Why?" What would lead people to do such horrible things? One explanation is *ostracism*, the act of excluding and ignoring others (Carter-Sowell, Chen, & Williams, 2008). Indeed, according to Zadro and Williams' (2006) sources, the Columbine killers acted out as a form of retaliation after being shunned by their peers.

Up to this point, we have seen how people's desire to belong to a group can lead them to conform to that group, even if they think the group is wrong. The study of ostracism underlines just how important this need can be and how desperate for attention ostracized people can become. By way of example, Carter-Sowell et al. (2008) noted that the "Bind, Torture, Kill" serial killer was so desperate for recognition that he wrote about it to the press: "How many do I have to kill, before I get my name in the paper or some national attention?" (p. 144).

Although the act of ostracism does not always lead to such violent incidents, research suggests that it can affect behavior in other ways. For instance, in order to get the attention they desire, ostracized people may behave in more socially acceptable ways (Williams & Sommer, 1997). As Carter-Sowell et al. (2008) argued, however, the need to fit in may render ostracized people easy prey for persuaders and con artists. To test this notion, they conducted a study. In it students played "Cyberball," a computer ball-tossing game with two other players, who, unbeknownst to the students, are actually computer generated and programmed to ostracize the students by hardly ever tossing the ball to them. After taking about five minutes of such shunning, the students were excused from the game, but, shortly after, were approached by another student, who was collecting donations and who was secretly part of the study. As suspected, the students who had been ostracized were significantly more likely to be persuaded by the solicitor.

DEINDIVIDUATION AND SOCIAL LOAFING: GETTING LOST IN THE CROWD

In previous sections we saw how people can be pressured to conform to a group. This, however, is not the only way that groups can influence an individual. In this section we examine how groups can affect a person's behavior by causing the person to lose his or her sense of self or by making the person feel less responsible for his or her actions.

What a Riot: An Examination of Deindividuation

Crowds influence people's behavior; once we get lost in them, we tend to do things that we would never do alone. If you don't believe us, ask our friend who was one of the 500,000 people at the Woodstock concert in 1969. She won't say whether she was one of the people running around naked, but she admits to doing things she wouldn't have done if she had not been lost in the crowd.

This tendency "to get lost in the crowd" was first labeled *deindividuation* by Festinger, Pepitone, and Newcomb (1952). Deindividuation is said to occur when being in a group causes people to become less aware of themselves and less concerned with how others will evaluate them (Diener, 1980). Because being in a large group makes a person both more aroused and anonymous, the person focuses less on himself or herself and behaves less rationally and more impulsively.

Although running around naked at concerts may sound harmless enough, it is clear that deindividuation can have much more severe consequences. For example, one of the authors was a student at the University of Southern California when the Los Angeles riots broke out in 1992. Seeing firsthand the trashed storefronts and burnt buildings of the riot's aftermath made the potentially cruel nature of deindividuation all too real. The riots made it clear to everyone how powerful the effects of a crowd can be: When one person starts wreaking havoc, others may be likely to follow. Consider, for example, the comments of a U.S. soldier trying to explain what caused him to kill innocent children and civilians during the My Lai massacre:

> I just went. My mind just went. And I wasn't the only one that did it . . . a lot of people were doing it, so I just followed suit. I just lost all sense of direction, of purpose. I just started killing. I just started killing any kinda way I could kill. It just came. I didn't know I had it in me. (Biton & Sim, cited in Epley & Gilovich, 1999, p. 578)

A classic study by Diener, Fraser, Beaman, and Kelem (1976) illustrates how deindividuation can lead to such antisocial behavior. The researchers suspected that if any night of the year would lead to deindividuation, it was Halloween. To be sure, children usually trick-or-treat in groups and, because they wear costumes, are more anonymous than usual. To see if deindividuation would affect children's behavior, these researchers gave 1,352 trick-or-treaters, who were either trick-or-treating alone or in groups, the opportunity to steal candy or money from 27 homes in Seattle. How did the experiment work? When trick-or-treaters came to the door, an experimenter greeted them, commenting on their costumes. The experimenter asked some of the children their names, and other children were allowed to remain anonymous. The experimenter then left the room after telling the trick-or-treaters they could take one of the candies that was in a bowl near the door (there was also a bowl full of nickels and pennies). Unbeknownst to the children, a hidden observer watched how much candy (and money) the children really took, and here's what the observer saw: When children were trick-or-treating alone, 7.5 percent of them took more candy than they were supposed to. When they were in groups, however, the thievery increased substantially; 20.8 percent stole candy. Moreover, when the children remained anonymous, they stole more candy and money than they did when the experimenter asked their names. In short, deindividuation led the trick-or-treaters to a night of petty crime.

Unfortunately, the negative effects of deindividuation do not stop with vandalism, killing, and stealing, as illustrated by a number of laboratory studies which demonstrate that people who think they are delivering electric shocks to other people tend to be much more aggressive (i.e., administer more shocks) when in a deindividuated state than when they are not. Such aggressiveness is true of both deindividuated males and females, although males tend to be more aggressive than females when deindividuation is not present (Lightdale & Prentice, 1994).

Perhaps the most disturbing research on the relationship between deindividuation and aggression focused on violent behaviors perpetrated outside the laboratory. First, in one study, Mann (1981) examined more than 150 newspaper accounts of what happened when people threatened to kill themselves by jumping from buildings. Mann found that in some cases people who had gathered on the streets below actually baited the potential jumpers, encouraging them to leap to their deaths. Can you guess what was one of the factors determining whether the crowd engaged in such behavior? According to Mann, when the crowds contained more than 300 people, baiting was more common than it was in smaller crowds. This, of course, is consistent with the notion that larger crowds produce more deindividuation.

Second, in an even more disturbing study, Mullen (1986) examined the relationship between the size of lynch mobs and the severity of atrocities committed by such mobs. To do so, he analyzed more than 300 newspaper reports to determine the following: (1) the number of people in each lynch mob; (2) whether the lynchings included violent acts, such as hanging, shooting, burning, lacerating, and dismembering the victims; and (3) whether the lynchings happened quickly or were prolonged and torturous. Results of the study indicated that victims suffered more when the lynch mobs were larger. Mullen (1986) concluded that "these results support the contention that lynchers become less self-attentive, and thereby more likely to engage in acts of atrocity, as the lynchers become more numerous relative to the number of victims" (p. 191).

Considering these studies, an important question concerns how deindividuation might be attenuated. Because deindividuation results from low self-awareness, the answer may lie in making people more aware of themselves. According to Prentice-Dunn and Rogers (1982), however, there are two types of self-awareness and only one is related to deindividuation. First, *public self-awareness* refers to how we view ourselves as social objects and our concerns about such things as our appearance and the impression we are making on others. *Private self-awareness* refers to our focus on hidden aspects of ourselves such as our thoughts, feelings, and perceptions (see Buss, 1980). Prentice-Dunn and Rogers (1982) have found that deindividuation is decreased only when a person's private self-awareness is increased. This suggests, then, that to attenuate deindividuation, the object is to get people to focus on their own thoughts and feelings. Thus, rather than state that people will get in trouble for their actions or look bad for doing something, it may be better to have them reflect on their personal views on what is right and wrong in a given situation. (For more on deindividuation in a specific context, see Box 6.3.)

Social Loafing: Not Pulling Your Own Weight

Have you ever had to push a stalled car or move a heavy piece of furniture with several other people? If so—be honest for a moment—did you give it your all? Did you work your hardest, exerting all of your energy? Or, because there were others to share the burden, did you slack off a bit? If you're at all like the average research participant, you probably did not work as hard as you could have. Indeed, research suggests that when working in groups, people may not try as hard as they do when working alone (e.g., Harkins, Latané, & Williams, 1980; Karau & Williams, 1993; Latané & Darley, 1970). In short, like a lot of other people, you may be a social loafer.

According to Karau and Williams (1993), "social loafing is the reduction in motivation and effort when individuals work collectively compared with when they work individually or coactively" (p. 681). What causes such loafing? There are several explanations, though we only have room to discuss the most prominent perspectives (for a review of others, see Guerin, 1999; Karau & Williams, 2001; Locke et al., 2001).

| Computer-Mediated Conformity: When Group Members Flame the Same | **BOX 6.3** |

From what you've read in this chapter so far, you can see that being in the presence of a group can seriously affect your behavior. With that in mind, what do you suppose might happen if you were still able to communicate with a group but were removed physically from the group's presence? Liberation from social pressure? Freedom to do as you please without worrying about fitting in?

If that's what you were thinking, think again. Optimists once figured that email and the Internet might provide emancipation from group pressure, but empirical research suggests otherwise. For instance, a study by Williams, Cheung, and Choi (2000) found that people using Internet chat rooms are likely to conform to the unanimous incorrect judgments of a group of strangers, especially after being ostracized by a previous group. Moreover, Postmes, Spears, and Lea (2000) found that the same types of norms and conformity that occur in face-to-face groups evolve in computer-mediated groups as well.

With that said, you probably won't be surprised to learn that communicating over the computer does not make you immune to negative behaviors often evidenced in groups. In fact, some studies (e.g., Jessup, Connolly, & Tansik, 1990) suggest that the anonymity afforded to people who communicate via computers makes uninhibited and inappropriate behavior (e.g., insulting others, using profanity) more likely than it is in face-to-face conversations. Such "flaming," as it is called in the world of computer users, has been blamed on deindividuation, which, as you already know, is fostered by anonymity.

The good news is that computer-mediated group communication does not necessarily lead to negative behavior, but rather positive or negative behavior depending on the norms of the group with which one is communicating (Spears, Lea, & Lee, 1990). Specifically, the *social identity of deindividuation model effects* (SIDE; Postmes, Spears, & Lea, 1998, 2000) argues that the anonymity associated with computer-mediated communication fosters a decrease in your sense of self (i.e., personal identity) and an increase in the degree to which you identify with a group (social identity). However, unlike deindividuation theory, which suggests that a lost sense of self leads to anti-normative behavior, SIDE argues that immersion in a group prompts greater conformity to the group's norms. Thus, if the group's norms are positive, you are more likely to engage in prosocial behaviors. If the group's norms are negative, you are more likely to "flame." Moreover, anything that decreases your anonymity also tends to decrease your level of conformity. For instance, in a study by Spears and colleagues (1990), students discussed a range of topics via computers. Half the students communicated without being able to see each other. The other students were able to see each other while communicating on their computers. The results of the study showed that only those students who were isolated and anonymous shifted their behavior toward the norms of the group. In short, it's not computers, but rather a decreased sense of self (which may be more likely when communicating via computers) that promotes conformity.

First, the *collective effort model* (Karau & Williams, 2001) argues that we tend to get lazy if we don't expect our efforts to lead to personally valued outcomes or if we don't think our effort will be instrumental in obtaining those outcomes. Thus, social loafing occurs because we don't think we will get the credit we are due or achieve the results we desire. Moreover, when working in groups, our efforts do not always determine outcomes, and, even if they did, valued outcomes are often divided among all group members rather than given to one person (Karau & Williams, 2001).

Second, the *free ride effect* suggests that when they can get away with it, people try to benefit from the efforts of others. That is, they slack off when others are working, when they are anonymous, and when they don't think their own efforts will be evaluated. Working in groups not only allows them to "hide in the crowd" without getting blamed for poor work but also enables them to reduce their own effort and still enjoy an equal share of the rewards (see Karau & Williams, 2001; Locke et al., 2001).

Finally, the *sucker effect* occurs when people suspect that others may be taking a free ride. Rather than be a "sucker" who does all the work, people slack off in order to match the level of work done by others (see Locke et al., 2001).

Whatever the reason for social loafing, one thing is clear: It, like deindividuation, can have disastrous effects. For example, in a well-known case in the 1960s, a woman named Kitty Genovese was beaten and stabbed for more than 30 minutes outside her New York apartment. While this happened, more than 30 people watched from their windows without helping or without even calling the police. Finally, this same type of behavior has been repeated again and again in the laboratory. For instance, in a study by Latané and Darley (1970), subjects were led into a room, given earphones and a microphone, and told that they would be having a conversation over an intercom with other subjects in the study. Some were told they would be talking with one other person; others were told they would be talking with either two or five other people. In reality, there were no other subjects. The only true subject was listening to tape-recorded messages. At some point during the conversation, one of the phony subjects (i.e., the tape recorder), who had previously claimed to have epilepsy, began choking and gasping as if having a seizure. Did the supposed victim receive help? The answer is "it depends." When subjects thought they were in groups with five other people, only 30 percent of them went to help the supposed victim. With two other people, 62 percent went to help. It was only when the subjects thought they were alone with the victim that 85 percent went to help. In short, the larger the group, the less likely people are to get involved.

Considering our discussion so far, you might be wondering how social loafing can be decreased. According to Karau and Williams (1993), social loafing can be reduced or overcome by:

> providing individuals with feedback about their own performance or the performance of their work group, monitoring individual performance or making such performance identifiable, assigning meaningful tasks, making tasks unique such that individuals feel more responsibility for their work, enhancing the cohesiveness of work groups, and making individuals feel that their contributions to the task are necessary and not irrelevant. (p. 700)

Furthermore, it may be easier to attenuate social loafing if you know the conditions under which it occurs. For instance, earlier in this chapter we talked about how we are more likely to conform to groups with which we identify. Knowing this, it's not surprising to find that people who identify with a group are not as likely to loaf as those who do not identify (Barreto & Ellemers, 2000). For those who do not identify, another approach is to make them accountable for their work. According to some, if people think they will be held responsible for their efforts and then evaluated, they'll work just as hard as high identifiers (Barreto & Ellemers, 2000). In fact, some research suggests that under such conditions, a *social facilitation effect* may be observed. That is, if people in the group think their performance will be evaluated by the group, they may even work harder than they would when alone (see Gagne & Zuckerman, 1999). On the other hand, some evidence suggests that monitoring and reporting on a person's performance does little to discourage loafers. Dommeyer (2007), for example, suspected that university students working in groups would be less likely to loaf if everyone in the group kept a diary about each other's performance that would ultimately be turned in to the instructor. Contrary to predictions, however, loafers kept loafing. Even so, the diaries seemed to make nonloafers more aware and less tolerant of loafers. Indeed, compared to people who did not keep diaries, those who did were much more likely to "fire" loafers from their groups.

Another variable that influences the potential for loafing is the nature of the people involved in the task, suggesting that before you join a group, you should know whom you're joining up with. First, research indicates that people who are open to new experiences, conscientious, agreeable, and high in the need for cognition (see Chapter 5) are less likely to loaf than their counterparts (Klehe & Anderson, 2007; Smith, Kerr, Markus, & Stasson, 2001; Tan & Tan, 2008). Second, the way in which people perceive themselves might influence the degree to which they loaf. Specifically, a study by Huguet, Charbonnier, and Monteil (1999) found that people who see themselves as uniquely superior to others are most likely to loaf when working collectively on an easy task (i.e., imagining different uses for a knife). This is because they perceive their contribution to such a task as redundant, dispensable, and unlikely to make others aware of their superior talents. However, these types of people tend to work extra hard on difficult tasks (i.e., imagining different uses for a doorknob) (Huguet et al., 1999) or when they perceive their teammates as being unequipped for handling the task (Plaks & Higgins, 2000). And why not? Such *social compensation,* as it is called in the literature, helps them maintain the belief that they are unique and reap possible rewards if their group does well (Huguet et al., 1999). What can we learn from such research? Consider this: If you ever ask a group to perform an easy task, watch out for people who think they're the cat's meow. If that sounds simple, consider one more thing: Most people see themselves as superior to the average person (see Goethals, Messick, & Allison, 1991). Unfortunately, this probably means that when tasks are easy, there are a lot of loafers out there.

HOW GROUPS AFFECT DECISION MAKING: TO RISK OR NOT TO RISK

In the previous sections, we've seen that it is easy to get lost in groups and that groups can cause us to do things that we would never do by ourselves. The same is true when making decisions. To illustrate this, consider the following example: Imagine that you're the parent of a small child, a daughter, with a terrible heart condition. Because of the condition, your daughter has to refrain from any activity that might put too much strain on her. Your child's doctor, however, presents you with some interesting news: There's a new surgery your child can have that will make her completely healthy. There's a catch, however: The doctor tells you that there is a 1 percent chance your child will die from the surgery. What would you do? Would you allow the doctor to perform the surgery? If you thought "yes," imagine that the odds are different; instead of a 1 percent chance, what if there were a 50 percent chance your child would die? Or worse, yet, what if the chances of death were 80 or 90 percent?

Interestingly, research has shown that when selecting between alternatives like the preceding ones, groups and individuals make different decisions. The first study on this subject was conducted by Stoner (1961, cited in Brauer, Judd, & Gliner, 1995), who found that individuals made riskier decisions when they were in groups than they did when alone. In other words, while an individual might decide to allow the surgery when there was a 1 percent chance of death, a group might allow it when there was a 50 percent chance. Following Stoner's study, several other researchers confirmed these results, and soon this effect became known as the *risky shift phenomenon.* Not all studies, however, confirmed this phenomenon. In fact, some later studies found just the opposite effect. Sometimes groups made decisions that were *less* risky than decisions made by individuals (e.g., Knox & Safford, 1976; Myers & Arenson, 1972). How might such results be explained? According to Myers and Arenson (1972), instead of a risky shift phenomenon, what actually occurs is a *group polarization phenomenon.* In short, groups cause people to become more extreme in their decisions. Thus, if you are predisposed to making a slightly risky decision, being in a group may cause you to make a riskier decision; if you are predisposed to make a conservative decision, being in a group may cause you to make an even more conservative decision. As you might suspect, as decisions become more extreme, they might also become less accurate. Indeed, in one study (Palmer & Loveland, 2008), poor, good, and average lecturers were evaluated by individuals or by people who engaged in group discussions about the lecturers' performances. Results showed that group discussion led to less accurate ratings of the lectures.

Ever since the group polarization phenomenon was identified, at least 200 studies have been conducted to examine it (Brauer et al., 1995). Many of these have been devoted to identifying why group polarization occurs. Although there are many explanations, two are most prominent (see Boster, 1990; Brauer et al., 1995; Pavitt, 1994). The first, *social comparison theory*, was mentioned earlier in this chapter. Recall that according to this theory, we learn about ourselves by comparing ourselves to others. Because most people are average, when they compare their view to the views of others, they don't find much difference. Interestingly, however, because most people want to see themselves in a positive light, they don't want to be average; they want to be "better than average." Thus, according to this theory, when people learn that their position is the same as that of everyone else in the group, they shift their position so that it is more extreme. Because everyone tends to do this, group polarization occurs.

A second perspective, *persuasive arguments theory*, asserts that, before entering a group discussion, each member has one or more arguments that support his or her own position. If you consider all these arguments together, there will be more supporting one position than another (e.g., there may be more support for a risky decision than there is for a conservative one). Persuasive arguments theory asserts that the position that has the best and largest number of arguments supporting it is the position toward which members shift.

Several authors have argued that these theories are not contradictory (Boster, 1990; Isenberg, 1986; Pavitt, 1994). In other words, *both* social comparison and persuasive arguments might contribute to group polarization. In addition, Brauer and colleagues (1995) have argued that a third process might contribute to the extreme decisions made by groups.

GREGORY

"Sure, I follow the herd—not out of brainless obedience, mind you, but out of a deep and abiding respect for the concept of community."

They noted that although social comparison and persuasive arguments explanations both focus on interpersonal processes (e.g., what we hear from other group members), *intra*personal processes also may affect polarization. Specifically, they argued that when making decisions in groups, we not only hear from other group members, we state our own opinion and defend it several times. Such repetition, they argued, also moves us toward polarization. To test this notion, they conducted a study in which group members repeated their own positions on a topic often or very little. Moreover, members also heard arguments from other group members. Results indicated that all three processes (i.e., social comparison, persuasive arguments, and repeated expressions) may contribute to group polarization.

Before concluding this section, we wish to point out that, like the other topics we've discussed in this chapter, group polarization can have disastrous effects. For instance, imagine being on the frontlines in a hopeless battle. Who would you want deciding whether you should take a hill: one military leader or a group of them? How about if a decision were being made to start a war or send a missile? Or imagine an innocent person accused of a crime. Would he or she be better off with or without a jury deciding on a verdict? You get the idea. As frequent members of groups, it is important to remember the effects groups can have on us. Only then might we hope to be less vulnerable to their influence.

SUMMARY

In this chapter we examined several topics related to influence in groups. First, we discussed early research on conformity and saw that several perspectives explain why people tend to conform. In addition, several factors (i.e., group size, having an ally, the intensity of indoctrination, the degree to which we identify with a group, communicator characteristics, and culture) influence how likely we are to conform. We also saw that social proof can be a powerful persuasive tactic because it relies on people's tendency to conform. We then saw that because people are less aware of themselves in groups or because people feel less responsible in groups, deindividuation and social loafing can result. Finally, for various reasons, groups tend to make more extreme decisions than do individuals (group polarization).

Before concluding, we wish to note that although this chapter has often discussed group influence in a negative light, without some degree of conformity, we could not communicate. If everyone did whatever he or she wanted, whenever, chaos would reign. Imagine a classroom or business meeting in which everyone talked at the same time or a freeway on which cars went in all directions and never yielded to one another. Clearly, without norms and some conformity, we could never get anything done. However, this chapter underlines the potentially dire consequences of group influence and illustrates the importance of balancing conformity and independence. As Asch (1966) stated:

> Life in society requires consensus as an indispensable condition. But consensus, to be productive, requires that each individual contribute independently out of his experience and insight. When consensus comes under the dominance of conformity, the social process is polluted and the individual at the same time surrenders the powers on which his functioning and feeling and thinking being depends. That we have found the tendency to conformity in our society so strong that reasonably intelligent and well-meaning young people are willing to call white black is a matter of concern. It raises questions about our ways of education and about the values that guide our conduct. (p. 324)

REFERENCES

Abrams, D., Wetherell, M., Cochrane, S., Hogg, M. A., & Turner, J. C. (1990). Knowing what to think by knowing who you are: Self-categorisation and the nature of norm formation, conformity and group polarisation. *British Journal of Social Psychology, 29,* 97–119.

Allen, V. L., & Levine, J. M. (1971). Social support and conformity: The role of independent assessment of reality. *Journal of Experimental Social Psychology, 4,* 48–58.

Andrews, P. H. (1996). Group conformity. In R. S. Calthcart, L. A. Samovar, & L. D. Henman (Eds.), *Small group communication* (7th ed., pp. 184–192). Madison, WI: Brown & Benchmark.

Aronson, E., & Mills, T. (1959). Effects of severity of initiation on liking for a group. *Journal of Abnormal and Social Psychology, 59,* 177–181.

Asch, S. E. (1956). Studies of independence and conformity: A minority of one against a unanimous majority. *Psychological Monographs, 70,* entire volume.

Asch, S. E. (1966). Opinions and social pressure. In A. P. Hare, E. F. Borgatta, & R. F. Bales (Eds.), *Small groups: Studies in social interaction* (pp. 318–324). New York: Alfred A. Knopf.

Baron, R. S. (2000). Arousal, capacity, and intense indoctrination. *Personality and Social Psychology Review, 4*(3), 238–254.

Barreto, M., & Ellemers, N. (2000). You can't always do what you want: Social identity and self-presentational determinants of the choice to work for a low-status group. *Personality and Social Psychology Bulletin, 26*(8), 891–906.

Bond, R. (2005). Group size and conformity. *Intergroup Relations, 8,* 331–354.

Bond, R., & Smith, P. B. (1996). Culture and conformity: A meta-analysis of studies using Asch's (1952b, 1956) line judgment task. *Psychological Bulletin, 119*(1), 111–137.

Boster, F. J. (1990). Group argument, social pressure, and the making of group decisions. In J. A. Anderson (Ed.), *Communication yearbook 13* (pp. 303–312). Newbury Park, CA: Sage.

Brauer, M., Judd, C. M., & Gliner, M. D. (1995). The effects of repeated expressions on attitude polarizations during group discussions. *Journal of Personality and Social Psychology, 68*(6), 1014–1029.

Bullis, C. A., & Tompkins, P. K. (1989). The forest ranger revisited: A study of control practices and identification. *Communication Monographs, 56,* 287–306.

Burger, J. M. (1987). Desire for control and conformity to a perceived norm. *Journal of Personality and Social Psychology, 35*(2), 355–360.

Burke, K. (1950). *A rhetoric of motives.* New York: Prentice Hall.

Buss, A. H. (1980). *Self-consciousness and social anxiety.* San Francisco: W. H. Freeman.

Campbell, J. D., & Fairey, P. J. (1989). Informational and normative routes to conformity: The effect of faction size as a function of norm extremity and attention to the stimulus. *Journal of Personality and Social Psychology, 57*(3), 457–468.

Carter-Sowell, A. R., Chen, Z., & Williams, K. D. (2008). Ostracism increases social susceptibility. *Social Influence, 3*, 143–143.

Chua-Eoan, H. (1997, April 7). Imprisoned by his own passions. *Time, 149*(14), 40–41.

Cialdini, R. B. (1993). *Influence: The psychology of persuasion* (Rev. Ed.). New York: Morrow.

Cialdini, R. B., Demaine, L. J., Sagarin, B. J., Barrett, D. W., Rhoads, K., & Winter, P. L. (2006). Managing social norms for persuasive impact. *Social Influence, 1*, 3–15.

Cialdini, R. B., Wosinska, W., Barrett, D. W., Butner, J., & Gornik-Durose, M. (2001). The differential impact of two social influence principles on individualists and collectivists in Poland and the United States. In W. Wosinska, R. B. Cialdini, D. W. Barrett, & J. Reykowski (Eds.), *The practice of social influence in multiple cultures* (pp. 33–50). Mahwah, NJ: Erlbaum.

Clark, R. D. (1999). Effect of number of majority defectors on minority influence. *Group Dynamics: Theory, Research, and Practice, 3*(4), 303–312.

Cody, M. J., & Seiter, J. S. (2001). Compliance principles in retail sales in the United States. In W. Wosinska, R. B. Cialdini, D. W. Barrett, & J. Reykowski (Eds.), *The practice of social influence in multiple cultures* (pp. 325–341). Mahwah, NJ: Erlbaum.

Cody, M. J., Seiter, J. S., & Montagne-Miller, Y. (1995). Men and women in the marketplace. In P. Kalbfleisch & M. Cody (Eds.), *Gender, power and communication in human relationships* (pp. 305–329). Hillsdale, NJ: Erlbaum.

Diener, E. (1980). Deindividuation: The absence of self-awareness and self-regulation in group members. In P. B. Paulus (Ed.), *The psychology of group influence* (pp. 209–242). Hillsdale, NJ: Erlbaum.

Diener, E., Fraser, S. C., Beaman, A. L., & Kelem, R. T. (1976). Effects of deindividuation variables on stealing among Halloween trick-or-treaters. *Journal of Personality and Social Psychology, 33*(2), 178–183.

Dommeyer, C. J. (2007). Using the diary method to deal with social loafers on the group project: Its effects on peer evaluations, group behavior, and attitudes. *Journal of Marketing Education. 29*, 175–188.

Eisenberg, D. (2002, September 2). It's an ad, ad, ad, ad world. *Time, 160*(10), 38–41.

Epley, N., & Gilovich, T. (1999). Just going along: Nonconscious priming and conformity to social pressure. *Journal of Experimental Social Psychology, 35*, 578–589.

Festinger, L., Pepitone, A., & Newcomb, T. (1952). Some consequences of deindividuation in a group. *Journal of Abnormal Social Psychology, 47*, 382–389.

Freckelton, I. (1998). "Cults," calamities and psychological consequences. *Psychiatry, Psychology and Law, 5*(1), 1–46.

Gagne, M., & Zuckerman, M. (1999). Performance and learning goal orientations as moderators of social loafing and social facilitation. *Small Group Research, 30*(5), 524–544.

Gladwell, M. (2002). *The tipping point.* New York: Little, Brown and Company.

Gleick, E. (1997a, February 10). Marine blood sports. *Time, 149*(6), 30.

Gleick, E. (1997b, April 7). The marker we've been waiting for. *Time, 149*(14), 28–36.

Goethals, G. R., Messick, D. M., & Allison, S. T. (1991). The uniqueness bias: Studies of constructive social comparison. In J. Suls & T. A. Wills (Eds.), *Social comparison: Theory and research* (pp. 149–176). Hillsdale, NJ: Erlbaum.

Goodman, E. (2001, August 11). Advertising hits zany levels. *The Herald Journal, 92*(223), A4.

Gordon, N. P. (1986). Never smokers, triers and current smokers: Three distinct target groups for school-based antismoking programs. *Health Education Quarterly, 13*, 163–179.

Guarino, M., Fridrich, P., & Sitton, S. (1994). Male and female conformity in eating behavior. *Psychological Reports, 75*, 603–609.

Gudykunst, W. B., & Kim, Y. Y. (1997). *Communicating with strangers: An approach to intercultural communication* (3rd ed.). Reading, MA: Addison-Wesley.

Guerin, B. (1999). Social behaviors as determined by different arrangements of social consequences: Social loafing, social facilitation, deindividuation, and a modified social loafing. *The Psychological Record, 49*, 565–578.

Hansen, B. (2004, January 9). Hazing: Should more be done to stop it? *The CQ Researcher, 14*(1), 1–24.

Harkins, S. G., Latané, B., & Williams, K. (1980). Social loafing: Allocating effort or taking it easy? *Journal of Experimental Social Psychology, 16*, 457–465.

Hart, J. W., Stasson, M. F., & Karau, S. J. (1999). Effects of source expertise and physical distance on minority influence. *Group Dynamics: Theory, Research, and Practice, 3*(1), 81–92.

Hofstede, G. (1984). *Culture's consequences: International differences in work-related values.* Beverly Hills, CA: Sage.

Hoyt, C. (1995, October). When peer pressure is good for your child. *Good Housekeeping, 221,* 233–235.

Huguet, P., Charbonnier, E., & Monteil, J. (1999). Productivity loss in performance groups: People who see themselves as average do not engage in social loafing. *Group Dynamics: Theory, Research, and Practice, 3*(2), 118–131.

Insko, C. A., & Schopler, J. (1972). *Experimental social psychology.* New York: Academic Press.

Isenberg, D. J. (1986). Group polarization: A critical review and metaanalysis. *Journal of Personality and Social Psychology, 50,* 1141–1151.

Janis, I. L. (1972). *Victims of groupthink.* Boston: Houghton Mifflin.

Jessup, L. M., Connolly, T., & Tansik, D. A. (1990). Toward a theory of automated group work: The deindividuating effects of anonymity. *Small Group Research, 21*(3), 333–348.

Karau, S. J., & Williams, K. D. (1993). Social loafing: A meta-analytic review and theoretical integration. *Journal of Personality and Social Psychology, 65*(4), 681–706.

Karau, S. J., & Williams, K. D. (2001). Understanding individual motivation in groups: The collective effort model. In M. E. Turner (Ed.), *Groups at work: Theory and research. Applied social research* (pp. 113–141). Mahwah, NJ: Erlbaum.

Klehe, U., & Anderson, N. (2007). The moderating influence of personality and culture on social loafing in typical versus maximum performance situations. *International Journal of Selection and Assessment, 15,* 250–262.

Knox, R. E., & Safford, R. K. (1976). Group caution at the racetrack. *Journal of Experimental Social Psychology, 12,* 317–324.

Latané, B. (1981). The psychology of social impact. *American Psychologist, 36,* 343–356.

Latané, B., & Darley, J. M. (1970). *The unresponsive bystander: Why doesn't he help!* New York: Appleton-Century-Crofts.

Latané, B., & Wolf, S. (1981). The social impact of majorities and minorities. *Psychological Review, 88,* 438–453.

Lifton, R. J. (1986). *Thought reform and the psychology of totalism.* New York: W. W. Norton.

Lightdale, J. R., & Prentice, D. A. (1994). Rethinking sex differences in aggression: Aggressive behavior in the absence of social roles. *Personality and Social Psychology Bulletin, 20*(1), 31–44.

Locke, E. A., Tirnauer, D., Roberson, Q., Goldman, B., Latham, M. E., & Weldon, E. (2001). The importance of the individual in an age of groupism. In M. E. Turner (Ed.), *Groups at work: Theory and research* (pp. 501–528). Mahwah, NJ: Erlbaum.

Lustig, M. W., & Cassotta, L. L. (1996). Comparing group communication across cultures: Leadership, conformity, and discussion processes. In R. S. Calthcart, L. A. Samovar, & L. D. Henman (Eds.), *Small group communication* (7th ed., pp. 316–326). Madison, WI: Brown & Benchmark.

Mann, L. (1981). The baiting crowd in episodes of threatened suicide. *Journal of Personality and Social Psychology, 30,* 729–735.

McCoy, K. (1991, May). Help your child beat peer pressure. *Reader's Digest,* pp. 67–70.

McGill, A. A., Johnson, M. D., & Bantel, K. A. (1994). Cognitive complexity and conformity: Effects on performance in a turbulent environment. *Psychological Reports, 75*(2), 1451–1472.

Moscovici, S., & Faucheux, C. (1972). Social influence, conforming bias, and the study of active minorities. In L. Berkowitz (Ed.), *Advances in experimental social psychology* (Vol. 6, pp. 149–202). New York: Academic Press.

Moscovici, S., Lage, E., & Naffrechoux, M. (1969). Influence of a consistent minority on the responses of a majority in a color perception task. *Sociometry, 32,* 365–379.

Mullen, B. (1986). Atrocity as a function of lynch mob composition: A self-attention perspective. *Personality and Social Psychology Bulletin, 12*(2), 187–197.

Myers, D. G., & Arenson, S. J. (1972). Enhancement of dominant risk tendencies in group discussion. *Psychological Reports, 30,* 615–623.

Parrillo, V. N. (1985). *Strangers to these shores* (2nd ed.). New York: John Wiley & Sons.

Palmer, J. K., & Loveland, J. M. (2008). The influence of group discussion on performance judgments: Rating accuracy, contrast effects, and halo. *The Journal of Psychology, 142,* 117–130.

Pavitt, C. (1994). Another view of group polarizing: The "reasons for" one-sided oral argumentation. *Communication Research, 21*(5), 625–642.

Plaks, J. E., & Higgins, E. T. (2000). Pragmatic use of stereotyping in teamwork: Social loafing and compensation as a function of inferred partner–situation fit. *Journal of Personality and Social Psychology, 79,* 962–974.

Postmes, T., Spears, R., & Lea, M. (1998). Breaching or building social boundaries? Side-effects of computer-mediated communication. *Communication Research, 25*(6), 689–715.

Postmes, T., Spears, R., & Lea, M. (2000). The formation of group norms in computer-mediated communication. *Human Communication Research, 26*(3), 341–371.

Prentice-Dunn, S., & Rogers, R. W. (1982). Effects of public and private self-awareness on deindividuation and aggression. *Journal of Personality and Social Psychology, 43*(3), 503–513.

Redding, W. C. (1985). Rocking boats, blowing whistles, and teaching speech communication. *Communication Education, 34,* 247–276.

Reed, M. B., Lange, J. E., Ketchie, J. M., & Clapp, J. D. (2007). The relationship between social identity, normative information, and college student drinking. *Social Influence, 2,* 269–294.

Richmond, L. J. (2004). When spirituality goes awry: Students in cults. *Professional School Counseling, 7*(5), 367–375.

Rose, G. M., Shoham, A., Kahle, L. R., & Batra, R. (1994). Social values, conformity, and dress. *Journal of Applied Social Psychology, 24*(17), 1501–1519.

Royte, E. (1994, November–December). They seemed so normal. *Health, 8,* 76–80.

Seiter, J. S. (1995). Surviving turbulent organizational environments: A case study of a lumber company's internal and external influence attempts. *Journal of Business Communication, 32*(4), 363–382.

Seiter, J. S. (1998). When identification is too much of a good thing: An examination of Kenneth Burke's concept in organizational, intercultural, and small group communication contexts. *Journal of the Northwestern Communication Association, 26*(1), 39–46.

Shaw, D. (2003). Traumatic abuse in cults: A psychoanalytic perspective. *Cultic Studies Review, 2*(2), 101–127.

Sherif, M. (1935). A study of some social factors in perception. *Archives of Psychology, 27,* 187.

Smith, B. N., Kerr, N. A., Markus, M. J., & Stasson, M. F. (2001). Individual differences in social loafing: Need for cognition as a motivator in collective performance. *Group Dynamics, 5*(2), 150–158.

Snyder, M. (1987). *Public appearances, private realities: The psychology of self-monitoring.* New York: W. H. Freeman.

Spears, R., Lea, M., & Lee, S. (1990). De-individuation and group polarization in computer-mediated communication. *British Journal of Social Psychology, 29,* 121–134.

Tan, H. H., & Tan, M. L. (2008). Organizational citizenship behavior and social loafing: The role of personality, motives, and contextual factors. *The Journal of Psychology, 142,* 89–108.

Tanford, S., & Penrod, S. (1984). Social Influence Model: A formal integration of research on majority and minority influence processes. *Psychological Bulletin, 95*(2), 189–225.

Tompkins, P. K., & Cheney, G. E. (1985). Communication and unobtrusive control. In R. McPhee & P. Tompkins (Eds.), *Organizational communication: Traditional themes and new directions* (pp. 179–210). Beverly Hills, CA: Sage.

Whitsett, D., & Kent, S. A. (2003). Cults and families. *Families in Society, 84*(4), 491–502.

Williams, K. D., & Sommer, K. L. (1997). Social ostracism by one's coworkers: Does rejection lead to loafing or compensation? *Personality and Social Psychology Bulletin, 23,* 693–706.

Willams, K. D., Cheung, C. K. T., & Choi, W. (2000). Cyberostracism: Effects of being ignored over the Internet. *Journal of Personality and Social Psychology, 79,* 748–762.

Zablocki, B. D. (1999). Hyper compliance in charismatic groups. In F. David (Ed.), *Mind, brain, and society: Toward a neurosociology of emotion* (pp. 287–310). Stanford, CA: JAI Press.

Zadro, L., & Williams, K. D. (2006). How do you teach the power of ostracism? Evaluating the train ride demonstration. *Social Influence, 1,* 81–104.

CHAPTER 7

Language and Persuasion

W hen William Shakespeare wrote, "A rose by any other name would smell as sweet," he found an eloquent way to note that words and the things they represent have no necessary connection. Indeed, you can't change a flower's scent just by renaming it "armpit" or "manure." That being said, sometimes the names we give things affect how we react to those things. For example, because we attach meanings to words and names, we might react differently to a woman named "Rose" than we would to a man with the same name. As another illustration, consider the story of Adolf Hitler Campbell, a 3-year-old from Hunterdon County, New Jersey, whose parents were unable to get a supermarket to write the child's name on his birthday cake, presumably because of the connotations associated with such an infamous name. After meeting with resistance, the family, including Adolf's little sister, JoyceLynn Aryan Nation Campbell, hightailed it to Pennsylvania, where a Wal-Mart employee was willing to produce their cake ("Three-year-old Hitler," 2009).

These examples illustrate an interesting property of language that is one of the main themes of this chapter. Specifically, because we associate meanings with words, words have the power to influence us. Indeed, the maxim, "The pen is mightier than the sword," is correct. Words are the primary means of persuasion. They not only affect our perceptions, attitudes, beliefs, and emotions but they also create reality.

Because words are so important in the process of persuasion, the purpose of this chapter is to examine words and their effects on social influence. We begin by discussing the nature of symbols and of meaning, which are integral to understanding the relationship between language and persuasion.

SYMBOLS, MEANING, AND PERSUASION: THE POWER OF BABBLE

What is a *symbol?* A very basic definition is that a symbol is something that represents something else. Names are a good example. Your name represents who you are, just as the word "pig" represents an animal with a curly tail and slimy snout.

As noted above, one important characteristic of symbols is that they are arbitrary. In other words, symbols have no necessary connection to what they represent, although we sometimes seem to forget this. For example, S. I. Hayakawa (cited in Adler, Rosenfeld, & Towne, 1995) told the story of a little boy who thought that pigs were called pigs because they are so dirty. The word "pig," however, has no direct connection to the curly-tailed animal, just as your name, although it may seem to fit, has no necessary connection to you. That is, when your parents were trying to decide what to call you, there was nothing written in stone that said you had to be given a certain name. You could just as easily have been called Binky or Unga Bunga. Don't laugh—the singer Frank Zappa named his children Moon Unit and Dweezil, and when tax authorities told a Swedish couple that they had to give their 5-year-old son a name or pay a fine, the couple named the child "Brfxxccxxmnpcccclllmmnprxvclnmckssqlbb11116" ("The best and worst," 1996). As wrong as such names might seem, however, they're not. When it comes to finding representations of things, there's not one "right" word or symbol.

Because they are arbitrarily connected to what they represent, a second characteristic of symbols is that they are conventionalized, which means that if we want to use a symbol to communicate to someone else, we have to agree on the symbol's meaning. Without some measure of agreement on the meanings of words, communication and persuasion would be difficult, if not impossible. If you've ever tried to communicate with someone who speaks a different language, you know this is true.

Connotative and Denotative Meaning: That's Not How I See It

Up to this point, we've noted how important it is for communicators to agree on the meaning of the symbols they use. With that said, however, we are certain that, without telepathy, total agreement on the meaning of symbols is impossible. Of course, the degree to which people agree may depend on the type of meaning with which we're concerned. There are at least two meanings for every word. The first, the *denotative* meaning, is a word's direct, explicit dictionary definition.

The second type of meaning, *connotative*, refers to the thoughts and emotions associated with a word. As you might expect, the connotations associated with words vary widely from person to person. To illustrate, let's return to pigs. Although all of us might agree on the denotative meaning of the word "pig" (i.e., curly-tailed animal with snout, etc.), our attitudes associated with the word may be quite different. For instance, compared to a farmer's child who grew up sloppin' hogs, a person who grew up reading books or watching movies about cuddly, talking pigs, such as Wilbur from *Charlotte's Web* or Babe from the movie *Babe,* would probably have a different view of pigs. In contrast, the members of some religious groups, Jews and Muslims are forbidden to eat pork, which is perceived as unclean. Not long ago, in fact, a woman in Israel was sentenced to 50 years for depicting Allah as a pig.

As persuaders, it is important to recognize that the meanings of words are subjective. As scholars in the field of communication are fond of saying, "Meanings are in people, not in words." Effective persuaders are aware of this and attempt to adapt their messages accordingly.

Ultimate Terms: Speak of the Devil

Although connotative meanings tend to be more subjective than denotative meanings, sometimes the connotations associated with certain words are shared by large groups of people (i.e., societies and cultures). As a result, such words can be powerfully persuasive tools for motivating people. This is especially true of what Richard Weaver (1953) labeled *ultimate terms,* which are words or phrases that are highly revered, widely accepted, and carry special power in a culture. According to Weaver, there are three types of ultimate terms. The first, *god terms,* carry the greatest blessing in a culture and demand sacrifice or obedience (see Foss, Foss, & Trapp, 1985; Hart, 1997). When Weaver wrote, he used terms such as "fact" and "progress" as examples of god terms. Modern-day god terms include "family values," "critical thinking," and "balanced budget."

In contrast to god terms, Weaver argued that some terms, which he labeled *devil terms,* are perceived by a culture as associated with the absolutely abhorrent and disgusting. Examples of past devil terms include "Communism," "Nazi," and "Fascist" (Foss et al., 1985). Today, terms such as "dead-beat dad," "racist," "terrorist," "gang member," "sweat shop," and "sexual harassment" might be considered devil terms. Because such terms represent what is evil or detestable to a culture, they can also be extremely persuasive (Hart, 1997).

Finally, Weaver labeled a third type, *charismatic terms.* Unlike god and devil terms, which are associated with something observable, charismatic terms, much like a charismatic person, have a power that in some ways is mysteriously given (Foss et al., 1985):

> "Freedom" and "democracy" are charismatic terms in our culture. We demand sacrifice in the name of these terms, yet the referents most of us attach to them are obscure and often contradictory. In fact, Weaver says, we may resist the attempt to define such terms, perhaps fearing that a term defined explicitly will have its charisma taken away. (p. 66)

What becomes clear, then, is that although god, devil, and charismatic terms have power, their ability to persuade is not stable; the connotations associated with such terms may change over time. For instance, calling someone a communist today would not have the same impact as it did in the days of Senator Joseph McCarthy.

Considering the power of ultimate terms, it is not surprising that politicians spend considerable amounts of money discovering the "right" terms to use in their ads and speeches. By way of example, Lemann (2000) noted that politicians use focus groups in order to discover specific words that should and should not be used in campaigns. The people in such groups watch ads and speeches while moving dials from right to left, indicating when they like or dislike what they are hearing and seeing. As a result, politicians learn an entirely new vocabulary of god and devil terms. For example, based on his research with focus groups, Frank Luntz, a political consultant, advises his candidates to say

> "Department of Defense" instead of "Pentagon," "opportunity scholarships" instead of "vouchers," "tax relief" instead of "tax cuts," and "climate change" instead of "global warming." The terms "Washington" and "I.R.S.," Luntz says, always play as super-negative and should be attached to a policy you want to turn people against. "Prosperity" is super-positive. In general, words starting with an "r" or ending with an "-ity" are good—hence "reform" and "accountability" work and "responsibility" really works. (Lemann, 2000, p. 100)

Politicians might also use language to create other images. For instance, following the September 11 attacks on the World Trade Center and Pentagon, George W. Bush used words such as "evil," "those people," and "demons" to characterize people of Arab/Middle

Eastern descent. Merskin (2004) argued that Bush's speeches were carefully constructed and that the use of such words creates an enemy image by dehumanizing the "other."

In addition to politicians, people in the business world are fond of using ultimate terms as persuasion devices. For instance, the word "empowerment" is a modern-day charismatic term on which marketers and advertisers have capitalized. Products and services that promise to *empower* people have become unavoidable. For instance, as a former suit salesman, one of the authors was regularly asked by customers where the "power ties" could be found or what was the "power color" for ties this year. The Hotel del Coronado in Southern California offers its guests "power walks" in the morning, and one of our colleagues told us about a seminar his sister attended that teaches its clients how to take "power naps." Finally, one of the authors was recently notified that he is a *Time* magazine "Power Subscriber." He can now read the news with gusto!

Other terms that seem to have appeal these days are "extreme," "alternative," and "indie." Indeed, these words are popular now as "rebel" labels for things. There are, of course, alternative music and alternative clothes (e.g., baggy pants, visible boxer shorts, tattoos, piercings). There are also extreme sports, such as snowboarding, bungee jumping, skateboarding, and mountain biking. But does placing words in front of something necessarily make it cooler, or more "edgy"? Is "alternative golf" really alternative simply because the people playing it have goatees and wear tennis shoes (instead of golf shoes)? Does throwing some bacon and Monterey cheese on a Whopper really make it an "Xtreme burger," as Burger King claims?

What is clear from this discussion is that words, when widely accepted as representing what is good or evil in a culture, have incredible persuasive potential. As we've noted, being labeled a communist in the 1950s was hazardous. In the late 1600s, being labeled a witch in Salem, Massachusetts, was deadly. A little later, we explore more thoroughly the power of such labeling. But first, we examine a topic related to ultimate terms.

Familiar Phrases and Persuasion: Have I Heard You Somewhere Before?

Similar to Weaver's idea that ultimate terms are shared by large groups of people, Daniel Howard (1997) argued that certain phrases (e.g., "Rome wasn't built in a day," "Money doesn't grow on trees") are familiar, widely accepted in a culture, and persuasive. Not only that, Howard conducted a study to find out when such phrases are influential. Using the elaboration likelihood model (see Chapter 2) as a theoretical base, Howard suspected that familiar phrases would be persuasive only when people weren't able or motivated to scrutinize a message. That is, familiar phrases, Howard thought, would act as peripheral cues to persuasion. To test this idea, he had groups of students listen to radio commercials trying to persuade them to plan for retirement. The commercials contained either familiar phrases (e.g., "Don't put all your eggs in one basket") or literal phrases (e.g., "Don't risk everything on a single venture"). Half the students were able to carefully attend to the commercials, but the rest were distracted (i.e., they were asked to watch and record the nonverbal behavior of another person in the room). Results of the study indicated that the students who had seen commercials with familiar phrases were more persuaded than those who had not, but only when they were distracted. Those who were not distracted were persuaded (by strong arguments), regardless of whether familiar or literal phrases were used (Howard, 1997).

The Power of Labeling

Earlier, we stated that names such as Dweezil and Brfxxccxxmnpccccllllmmnprxvclnmckssqlbb11116 are not wrong, but we might have lied to you. As arbitrary symbols, they work just fine, but pragmatically, how would you like to be saddled with such a name? Perhaps you wouldn't mind, but, whatever the case, one thing is clear: The name you use affects the way people respond to you. In fact, we know a person who changes his name every decade because he says that people respond differently to him depending on whether he's a Richard, a Jay, or a Hank. And research supports the idea that our friend is not simply a kook. For instance, according to the sources of Adler and colleagues (1995), compared to names like Percival, Elmer, Isadore, and Alfreda, common names such as John, Michael, Karen, and Wendy are rated as more likable, active, and stronger. Moreover, when such names were placed on essays and evaluated by teachers, the more common names tended to receive higher grades than the less common ones. Finally, in a small study, a graduate student at MIT put 24 photos on the website www.hotornot. com. Interestingly, with different first names attached, the same photos were judged as more "hot" or more "not" (Strasser, 2005, p. E22).

As it turns out, your name doesn't just affect how others behave; it affects how you behave as well. Did you know, for example, that your name might influence where you live or the profession you choose? According to Pelham, Mirenberg, and Jones (2002), because of our need for self-enhancement (a.k.a., *implicit egotism*), we tend to favor things that we associate with ourselves. Thus, they suspected, people might be more likely to choose professions and places to live that sounded like themselves. Based on a wide-ranging analysis of census data and other records, the researchers confirmed their suspicions. For instance, even though there are roughly equal numbers of men named Walter, Jerry, and Dennis in the world, people named Dennis were over 40 percent more likely to become dentists. Similarly, Lawrences were more likely to be lawyers and Georges more likely to be geoscientists. Not only that, the researchers found a disproportionate number of Florences living in Florida, Georgias living in Georgia, Louisas living in Louisiana, and Virginias living in Virginia. We suggest that you keep this in mind, alongside real-life locations like Nothing, Arizona; Hooker, Oklahoma; and Pee Pee, Ohio, before naming a child.

The power of such labels extends far beyond the names that people are given (see Box 7.1). To be sure, the labels we use to describe people or things reflect our attitudes about them and affect others' reactions to the people and things labeled. For example, many years ago, children with divorced parents came from "broken homes." Talk about stigmatization! Nowadays, we say children belong to "single-parent" or "blended" families.

The notion that the labels we use affect our attitudes about what we label lies at the heart of criticisms aimed at sexist language. For example, if a professor refers to all of his male students as "men" or "sirs" and to all of his female students as "girls," "broads," or "dears," it not only says something about the professor's attitudes toward men and women but it also has the power to shape attitudes. According to what is commonly known as the *Sapir-Whorf hypothesis,* the language we use determines the way we understand the world

Just a Spoonful of Sugar (and a Well-Chosen Name) Makes the Medicine Go Down	BOX 7.1

In this chapter, we've shown that names affect how we react to people. As you might have suspected, they also influence our reaction to products. For example, did you know that people react more favorably to sweaters and jellybeans that are given ambiguous color names (e.g., Moody Blue, Alpine Snow, and Monster Green) than less ambiguous color names (e.g., blueberry blue) (Miller & Kahn, 2005)? Considering this, it's not surprising that a lot of attention goes into naming products. This may be especially true when naming prescription drugs.

Most of us refer to prescription drugs by their brand names. For example, we say "Prozac" rather than "fluoxetine" and "Valium" rather than "diazepam." We do this because we've been trained to by pharmaceutical manufacturers. Drug companies engage in "branding" when they air commercials and print ads urging us to "ask our doctor about _____." Is the Purple Pill right for you? Ask your doctor, but first go to the company's Website for more online propaganda to offer your doctor.

Naming a drug is extremely important to how the drug is perceived by consumers/patients and, in turn, to the drug maker's bottom line (Kirkwood, 2003). The name has to be short (no more than three syllables), unique, easy to pronounce, easy to remember, and, importantly, it must convey the essence of what the drug does. But the name cannot be false or misleading, according to the FDA. Viagra, a pill for erectile dysfunction sufferers, is a classic case of the power of naming as it applies to drugs. The name Viagra was conjured up to convey two themes: vigor, virility, or vitality and power or force, such as the raw power of Niagara Falls. Yes, the Freudian association with a torrent of powerful water is intentional. Viagra sounds more manly than sildenafil citrate, its generic name, don't you think? Celebrex, an arthritis medicine, was so named because it suggests celebrating—celebrating one's freedom to move without pain.

Companies such as the Brand Institute and Name Base/Medibrand are paid $250,0000 or more to come up with names for drugs that conjure up idealized associations. See if you can guess the positive associations pharmaceutical manufacturers are trying to create for the following drugs.

- **Alleve:** hint—it <u>allev</u>iates something, right? (and that something happens to be minor arthritis pain).
- **Ambien:** hint—it creates a soothing <u>ambien</u>ce (to help you sleep better).
- **Claritin:** hint—it <u>clari</u>fies things, like watery eyes and a runny nose due to allergies.
- **Levitra:** hint—it <u>levi</u>tates something (need we say more?).
- **Prevacid:** hint—it <u>prev</u>ents something (and that something has to do with the last four letters of its name. (Sounds better than its generic name, lansoprazole, doesn't it?)
- **Propecia:** hint—it <u>propag</u>ates something (like hair restoration).

The letters X and Z are popular in drug names because people think they sound scientific, hence names like Nexium, Paxil, Vioxx, Zanex, Zocor, and Zoloft. Now that you know how drugs are named, see if you can come up with effective names for hypothetical new drugs that would help Alzheimer's sufferers, diabetics, or kids with attention-deficit/hyperactivity disorder (ADHD).

(Sapir, 1949; Whorf, 1956). Thus, when women are wrongly described in ways that make them seem inferior to men, people begin to believe that women truly are inferior.

The same dynamics are at work when people use racist language, which perpetuates the illusion that one racial group is superior to another. Ethnic/cultural references carry vastly different meanings. For example, Americans with an African heritage have been identified by terms such as *African American, black, Negro, colored,* and more derogatory terms as well. Such derogatory terms, whether racist or sexist, have the power to shape perceptions.

Euphemisms and Doublespeak: Making the Worse Appear the Better and Vice Versa

In the fifth century B.C., a group of teachers known as Sophists created private schools in Athens, Greece. Students who wanted to learn from the Sophists were charged fees and were taught, among other subjects, oratory and persuasion. Soon, however, being a Sophist was so profitable that the occupation attracted a number of charlatans, who gave the Sophists a bad reputation (today, "sophistry" connotes deceitful or fallacious reasoning). In fact, Plato argued that the Sophists were more interested in lies than truths and more interested in dazzling audiences than in instructing them. Sophists, Plato argued, were skilled at making the "worse cause appear the better" (Corbett, 1971).

The practice of using words to make the worse appear the better (and vice versa) is still alive and well. Modern-day Sophists commonly use *doublespeak* (ambiguous or evasive language) and *euphemisms* (inoffensive terms substituted for offensive ones) to create messages with less sting. For example, in the business world, no one gets fired or laid off anymore. Instead, companies engage in "downsizing," "right-sizing," or even "bright-sizing." Mercedes doesn't sell used cars anymore; it sells "pre-owned automobiles" (try asking the Mercedes dealer, "Was this car previously used, or simply owned?"). To appear more "healthy," Kentucky Fried Chicken has taken the "fried" right out of its name; now it's Kitchen Fresh Chicken. Other companies give their employees job titles that sound more important or grandiose than they really are. A garbage collector is now a "sanitation engineer." And, in Great Britain, legislation was introduced to substitute the stigmatized word "prostitute" with the phrase "person who sells sex persistently" (Stinchfield, 2007).

The use of doublespeak and euphemisms is rampant in other places as well. For example, the military refers to civilian casualties, killing enemy soldiers, and combat operations as "collateral damage," "servicing the target," and "peacekeeping missions," respectively. Flight attendants don't talk about crashing in the ocean, only "water landings" (Murphy, 2001). In the medical field, terms such as assisted suicide, transsexual surgery, and cancer might instead be labeled "hastening death" (or "death with dignity"), "gender reassignment," and "a growth," respectively. Politicians don't raise taxes or lie, they adopt "revenue enhancing measures" and "misremember." And one of our friends is not allowed to have parties in her high school classes so, instead, has "reinforcement for desirable behavior days." In the world of undertakers and funeral directors, people "pass away" rather than die, are "interred" rather than buried, and are called "cases" or "patients" rather than corpses. Instead of saying "No," parents are fond of saying "We'll see" or "Maybe later." And finally, in the abortion controversy, the words you use probably depend on the side you take. For example, "pro-life" is more value-laden than "anti-abortion" or "anti-choice." "Pro-choice" avoids the term "abortion" altogether and sounds much nicer than "anti-life" or "anti-anti-abortion."

In the midst of all this word spinning, researchers (McGlone & Batchelor, 2003) have identified two possible motives people might have for using euphemisms. First, people might use euphemisms because such words are less threatening and more respectful, therefore saving the "face" of audience members. Second, people might use euphemisms in order to be regarded as tasteful and sensitive, thereby saving their own "face." To test these competing explanations, McGlone and Batchelor (2003) asked students communicating

If You Can't Say Something Nice, Spin It	BOX 7.2

If you've ever been asked to serve as a reference for someone, you know that it can be complex business. Because what you say may no longer be confidential, saying something negative can lead to all kinds of personal and legal tangles. With that in mind, Robert Thornton (2006) has created the Lexicon of Inconspicuously Ambiguous Recommendations (LIAR). Here are some examples of what to say about people, depending on their flaws:

If the person is woefully inept: "I enthusiastically recommend this candidate with no qualifications whatsoever."

If the person is extremely lazy: "You would be very fortunate to get this person to work for you."

If the person is chronically absent: "A person like this is hard to find."

If the person is dishonest: "She's an unbelievable worker."

If the person is a drunk: "Every hour with her was a happy hour."

Although we don't actually recommend using this lexicon, we think it is an entertaining way to illustrate how tricky language can be.

with someone via computer to describe various photographs, including two that depicted the aftermath of a urinating dog and a defecating parrot. Some students were led to believe that their identity would later be revealed to the person they were communicating with, while others were not. Results showed that the first group of students was more prone to using euphemisms, suggesting that saving their own face seemed to be their priority. It turns out, however, that when trying to create favorable impressions by spinning words, not just any euphemism will do. Indeed, a study by McGlone, Beck, and Pfeister (2006) found that because euphemisms with longer "careers" (e.g., "use the restroom," " go number two") are more familiar and draw less attention, people who use them are perceived more favorably than those who use newer, less familiar euphemisms (e.g., "make room for tea," "cast a pellet") (for more on doublespeak, see Box 7.2).

LANGUAGE INTENSITY, VIVIDNESS, AND OFFENSIVENESS

So far, we've examined the nature of symbols and how they relate to the notion of meaning and the process of persuasion. We now turn to a discussion of specific variables related to language and persuasion. Three of these include language intensity, vividness, and offensiveness. These three variables are closely related. For example, when studying intense language, some authors include reviews of research on profanity, which, of course, have the potential to be quite offensive. However, it is possible to use intense language without being offensive. Moreover, although some definitions imply that vividness is a component or outcome of intense language (e.g., see Hamilton & Stewart, 1993), others do not (e.g., see Bowers, 1964). Because these three topics are so closely related, we examine them together in this section. We then turn to a discussion of several theories that have been used to explain the relationship between intense language and persuasion.

DILBERT: © Scott Adams/Dist. by United Feature Syndicate, Inc.

##@**!!!!##: Profanity and Persuasion

When Bono, of U2 fame, appeared on the Golden Globe Awards show in 2003, he inadvertently dropped an "F-bomb." The word, as it turns out, is part of his everyday vocabulary—so much so that he can't seem to speak without resorting to it. As a result of the utterance, NBC was fined by the FCC and, after the case was appealed to the U.S. Supreme Court, Justice Antonin Scalia wrote for the majority that it was high time the FCC cracked down on "the foul-mouthed glitterati from Hollywood." While he and others were clearly offended, others were left wondering why hearing the "F" word once during an awards show was any worse than having the family sit through three erectile dysfunction commercials during the same broadcast. If nothing else, this incident illustrates one of the themes running throughout this chapter: Symbols are arbitrary, yet people react to them as if they were real.

Even though profanity, like any symbol, is arbitrary, it clearly plays a role in the process of persuasion, mostly because such strong connotations are associated with swearing. Perhaps this is why ancient rhetoricians like Quintilian advised against using profanity (Rothwell, 1971). Because profanity is so common (Cameron, 1969), some authors have asserted that it merits more attention as a form of persuasion. For instance, J. Dan Rothwell (1971) argued

> Despite centuries of negative criticism, verbal obscenity has become a more frequent rhetorical device. It is successful in creating attention, in discrediting an enemy, in provoking

violence, in fostering identification, and in providing catharsis. Its effects are governed by a variety of circumstances which need to be understood more fully. It has precipitated a police riot, brutal beatings, and even death. Hoping it will go away will not make it so. It is time to accept verbal obscenity as a significant rhetorical device and help discover appropriate responses to its use. (p. 242)

To explore more thoroughly people's perceptions of profanity, E. Scott Baudhuin (1973) gave students "swear word" booklets and asked the students to evaluate several words according to how offensive they were. Based on the students' perceptions, he found that the words could be categorized into one of three categories: religious, excretory, and sexual. Which type of profanity did students find most offensive? The results of the study indicated that sexual words received the most negative responses. Religious profanities were perceived to be the least offensive.

If profanity is perceived to be offensive, are people who use it perceived negatively and are they less persuasive? Several studies have been conducted to test this question and most, but not all (e.g., see Rassin & Van Der Heijden, 2005), indicate that if you want to be perceived as attractive, credible, and persuasive, you should clean up your language. For example, a study by Powell and his colleagues asked students to evaluate applicants who either did or did not cuss during a job interview. The researchers found that applicants with filthy mouths, regardless of their gender, were perceived as significantly less attractive than their counterparts (Powell et al., 1984). Similarly, Bostrom, Baseheart, and Rossiter (1973) found that, in general, using profanity damages a speaker's credibility. On the other hand, Scherer and Sagarin (2006) noted that society's stance about swearing has become more relaxed since many of these earlier studies were conducted. As such, they revisited the relationship between obscenity, credibility, and persuasion by having students listen to speeches in which a male speaker either did or did not use the word "damn." Results showed that cussing had no effect on perceptions of the speaker's credibility, but when the speaker cussed, he was more persuasive than when he did not. Before you decide to become potty-mouthed the next time you're speaking, however, consider this: the students in this study were listening to speeches in favor of lowering tuition, a topic they presumably would be in favor of. In contrast, most of the classic studies on this topic asked participants to listen to topics they did not favor. In short, it may be that profanity is persuasive, but only under very specific conditions.

Political Correctness

Obviously, using profanity is not the only way to be verbally offensive. Earlier we discussed the notion of political correctness, which, in many ways, is all about being nonoffensive. Indeed, political correctness refers to issues of inclusive speech and advocacy of nonracist, nonageist, and nonsexist terminology (Hoover & Howard, 1995).

Although political correctness is relevant to a wide range of contexts and topics, including issues of gender, race, ethnicity, age, socioeconomic status, and so forth, a study by Seiter, Larsen, and Skinner (1998) focused on political correctness as it related to speaking about people with disabilities. In the study, college students read one of four hypothetical scenarios, each involving a person seeking donations who portrayed people with disabilities as "normal" (e.g., "uses a wheelchair"), "heroic" (e.g., "handicapable"), "disabled" (e.g.,

DILBERT: © Scott Adams/Dist. by United Feature Syndicate, Inc.

"confined to a wheelchair"), or "pathetic" (e.g., "abnormal"). After reading the scenarios, participants rated the speakers on scales measuring credibility and persuasiveness. Results of the study showed that, compared to communicators who portrayed people with disabilities as "pathetic," communicators who portrayed such people as "normal," "heroic," and "disabled" were perceived as significantly more trustworthy and competent (Seiter et al., 1998). However, only communicators portraying people with disabilities as "heroic" and "disabled" were perceived as more persuasive than the communicator portraying such people as "pathetic." How did the authors interpret these results? Perhaps by trying *not* to portray people with disabilities as victims, the communicator using "normal" language also did not demonstrate as urgent a need to help people with disabilities as the communicators using "disabled" and "heroic" language did (e.g., a child described as "being confined to a wheelchair," or one who is pandered to may be perceived as requiring more help than a child described as "using a wheelchair"). Whatever the case, the results of this study suggest that individuals seeking donations for people with disabilities face a dilemma: How can a person raise money to help people with disabilities while at the same time describe people with disabilities in a politically correct and dignified manner?

The Effects of Vividness: A Picture's Worth a Thousand Words

According to Nisbett and Ross (1980), vivid information captures and holds our attention and excites our imagination because it is "emotionally interesting, concrete and imagery-provoking, and proximate in a sensory, temporal, or spatial way" (p. 45). By way of

"Love it! 'People of smoke' instead of 'Smokers.'"

example, it's more vivid to say "the glass crashed and shattered into pieces" than it is to say "the glass broke." It's more vivid to display the name of every person killed in the Vietnam War than it is to give us statistics.

Although vivid words may be more effective than pallid information (bland, plain descriptors) at holding our attention (Childers & Houston, 1984; Reyes, Thompson, & Bower, 1980), evidence that vivid information is more persuasive than pallid information is questionable (see Frey & Eagly, 1993; Ralston & Thameling,1988; Taylor & Thompson, 1982). Although some research suggests that vivid messages are persuasive, some suggest just the opposite.

How can these apparent inconsistencies be reconciled? According to Smith and Shaffer (2000), vividness may either help or hinder the persuasiveness of a message; it all depends on how congruent the vivid image is with the message. Specifically, these researchers suspected that when vividness is congruent with a message (i.e., when the imagery in the message is relevant to its content), it helps us process the message. This is because vividness grabs our attention and brings to mind relevant information that is stored in our memories. However, they suspected that vivid imagery that is incongruent keeps us from processing a message by priming irrelevant thoughts and undermining our motivation to think about the message.

To test this notion, Smith and Shaffer had students read strong and weak arguments on a variety of topics (e.g., drinking alcohol is dangerous to your health). Some of the students read vivid messages that were congruent (e.g., alcohol consumption could result in bloody, bone-crushing accidents), some read vivid and incongruent messages (e.g., when drinking alcohol, reaction time is slowed to a snail's pace—note, this has nothing to do with the main argument on health dangers), and others read pallid messages. Results of the study confirmed the researchers' suspicions. Specifically, compared to participants who read the incongruent and pallid messages, those who read the congruent messages recalled more of the message's arguments and were better at differentiating strong and weak arguments (Smith & Shaffer, 2000). In short, vividness can be an effective persuasive tool; you simply need to know when to use it.

Language Intensity

"You are shockingly stupid" versus "You are not real smart."

"The lumber industry is raping our forests" versus "The lumber industry is cutting down a lot of trees."

In the preceding pairs of phrases, which phrase has the strongest connotative meaning? Obviously, the first phrase in each pair. The terms *shockingly* and *raping* are more intense than terms found in the other phrases. Language that is intense is emotional, metaphorical, opinionated, specific, forceful, and evaluative. For that reason, perhaps, Bowers (1964) defined *language intensity* as "the quality of language which indicates the degree to which the speaker's attitude deviates from neutrality" (p. 215). Clearly, someone who compares "cutting down trees" to "rape" is far from neutral in his or her attitudes about the lumber industry. But is a person who uses such language persuasive? The best answer to that question may be "it depends." To be sure, several variables have been found that affect the persuasiveness of intense language. With that said, let's examine four different theories that attempt to explain when and why intense language does or does not persuade.

First, *reinforcement theory* assumes that people are motivated to avoid pain and seek pleasure. Bradac, Bowers, and Courtright (1979, 1980) assumed that the same is true when people are being persuaded. If a person generally agrees with the position advocated by a source, the person will find it rewarding and evaluate the source positively. The reverse is true if the person generally disagrees with the position advocated by the source. Language intensity is believed to enhance this effect. Specifically, if the listener generally agrees with the speaker, when the speaker throws some forceful language at the listener, the listener is even more motivated to agree. However, a listener who generally disagrees will react even more negatively than he or she normally would when the speaker uses intense language (Bradac et al., 1980).

A second perspective on language intensity is found in *language expectancy theory* (see Burgoon & Siegel, 2004). This theory assumes that we have expectations about what types of language are normal to use when trying to persuade other people. For example, we may not think it is normal for a speaker to use intense words such as "rape" and "shockingly." According to language expectancy theory, when persuaders violate our expectations concerning normal language, those violations can either help or hurt the effectiveness of the persuasive message, depending on whether the violations are perceived in a positive or negative way. How violations are perceived depends on who is using the language. For instance, Burgoon and Siegel (2004) noted that highly credible sources are granted a "wider bandwidth" of acceptable communication than those with low credibility. As such, sources with low credibility are likely to be perceived in a negative way when they use language that is aggressive and intense. This, in turn, leads them to be less persuasive. The reverse is true for highly credible sources.[1]

Third, Hamilton and Stewart (1993) have extended *information processing theory* (McGuire, 1968, 1989) to explain the effects of intensity on persuasion. The theory argues that to be persuaded, you must first attend to and comprehend a persuasive message. If you attend to and comprehend the message, you then compare your own position on the message to the position that's being argued by the source. Ultimately, you may either accept or reject the source's position. According to Hamilton and Stewart (1993), language intensity affects this process by making a source's position on an issue seem more extreme compared to your own position. This can be good, up to a point. In general, some discrepancy between a persuader and a receiver's positions leads to increased attention and, therefore, more attitude change. However, as we noted in our discussion of social judgment theory in Chapter 5, too much discrepancy may lead a receiver to reject a message or to scrutinize a message so much that he or she fails to attend to all of the message's content. In addition, intense language tends to be more specific and vivid.

Finally, *communication accommodation theory* (Giles & Wiemann, 1987; Street & Giles, 1982) argues that when we communicate with others we adjust our style of speaking to their style in order to gain approval and increase communication efficiency. For example, we may try to talk the same way others talk so that they will like us better. Aune and Kikuchi (1993) conducted a study to see if this theory would predict the effectiveness of messages that either were or were not intense. Specifically, speakers delivered intense and nonintense messages to people whose language style could be categorized as either intense or nonintense. Results of the study supported communication accommodation theory. Specifically, speakers using intense language were most persuasive with people who use intense language, whereas speakers using nonintense language were most persuasive with people who use nonintense language. Speakers who "matched" the style of their audience also were perceived as more credible.

POWERLESS LANGUAGE AND PERSUASION: "UMS" THE WORD

As a student, one of the authors had two speech professors who did not like the utterance "um" too much. One called "ums" social burps. The other, when listening to speeches, smacked her pencil on a desk whenever the author said "um." It was not fun, but it beat electrical shocks. In retrospect, the author supposes he should be grateful to these professors, because "ums," as well as a number of other utterances, prevent people who use them from being persuasive. Why? Because such utterances create the perception of *powerlessness.* In case you want to avoid using them when you talk, here is a list of such speech mannerisms with some examples in italics (also see Bradley, 1981; Erickson, Lind,

Johnson, & O'Barr, 1978; Lakoff, 1973, 1975; Lowenberg, 1982; Newcombe & Arnkoff, 1979; O'Barr, 1982):

- **Hesitations** (signal uncertainty or anxiety): "*Well,* I, *uh, you know, um,* would like to borrow a dollar."
- **Hedges** (qualify the utterance in which they occur): "I *guess I sort of* like you and *kind of* want to know you."
- **Intensifiers** (fortify the utterance): "I *really* believe that and agree with you *very* much."
- **Polite forms** (indicate deference and subordination): "*Excuse me, if you wouldn't mind too much, I'd appreciate it* if you'd *please* shut the door. *Thank you.*"
- **Tag questions** (lessens the force of a declarative sentence): "This is fun, *don't you think?* Much more fun than yesterday, *isn't it?*"
- **Disclaimers** (utterances offered before a statement that anticipate doubts, signal a problem, or ask for understanding): "I know this is a *really dumb question,* but...?"
- **Deictic phrases** (phrases indicating something outside the speaker's vicinity): "That man *over there* is the one who stole my wallet."

As noted previously, a considerable amount of research indicates that using these powerless forms of speech can prevent you from being persuasive (Erickson et al., 1978; Newcombe & Arnkoff, 1979). However, the relationship between power and speech may depend on additional factors. Two are noteworthy.

First, the type of powerless language a person uses may influence how he or she is perceived. Specifically, one problem with some research on powerless language is that it has lumped together all of the powerless forms previously discussed. However, some research indicates that this may not be the best idea, because not all of the forms may be detrimental to a speaker. For instance, in one study, Bradac and Mulac (1984) found that using polite forms actually enhanced speakers' credibility. Similarly, Hosman (1989) found that intensifiers, when used together with hesitations and hedges, are perceived as powerless. When used alone, however, intensifiers are perceived as powerful.

Second, the type of language that is most effective may depend on who is using it. For example, Blankenship and Craig (2007) found that when low credible sources used tag questions, the sources were less persuasive regardless of whether their messages contained strong or weak argument. In contrast, when high-credible sources used tag questions, the sources were more persuasive, but only when their messages contained strong arguments. Why? Presumably, if you already assume that a source is credible, tag questions get you to think more carefully about the message being presented. If the message is strong, you will be more persuaded by it (Blankenship & Craig, 2007).

In addition to sources' credibility, Carli (1990) found that sources' and receivers' sex affects the persuasiveness of language. Specifically, females were persuasive with men when they used powerless forms of speech but persuasive with females when using powerful speech. For male speakers, it did not matter what form of speech was used.[2] This may mean that women, compared to men, need to be more sensitive about the style of speech they use when trying to be persuasive. Clearly, along with the topics we discussed earlier, the results of this study suggest that men have negative stereotypes about women who use powerful speaking styles.

SUMMARY

In this chapter, we examined the role of language in the process of persuasion. We began with an examination and definition of the term *symbol*. Symbols are arbitrary but have the power to shape perceptions and construct social reality. Symbols also have connotative and denotative meanings, both of which affect persuasion. For example, we examined ultimate terms, which, because of their strong connotations, have incredible persuasive power in a culture. We also examined the power of labels and how, oftentimes, through the use of euphemisms and doublespeak, persuaders attempt to lessen (or strengthen) the connotative impact of a word. Finally, we discussed several language variables that affect persuasion. By making their words more vivid, intense, offensive, and powerless/powerful, persuaders affect the way audiences respond to their messages.

ENDNOTES

1. Language expectancy theory argues that we not only have expectations about how intense language should or should not be, we also have expectations concerning the use of fear appeals, verbal aggression, and other types of persuasive language.

2. Erickson and colleagues (1978) found that males rate males who use powerless speech low in credibility.

REFERENCES

Adler, R. B., Rosenfeld, L. B., & Towne, N. (1995). *Interplay: The process of interpersonal communication* (6th ed.). Fort Worth, TX: Harcourt, Brace.

Aune, R. K., & Kikuchi, T. (1993). Effects of language intensity similarity on perceptions of credibility, relational attributions, and persuasion. *Journal of Language and Social Psychology, 12*(3), 224–237.

Baudhuin, E. S. (1973). Obscene language and evaluative response: An empirical study. *Psychological Reports, 32*, 399–402.

The best and worst of everything. (1996, December 29). *Parade Magazine*, pp. 6, 7, 10.

Blankenship, K. L., & Craig, T. Y. (2007). Language and persuasion: Tag questions as powerless speech or as interpreted in context. *Journal of Experimental Psychology, 43*, 112–118.

Bostrom, R. N., Baseheart, J. R., & Rossiter, C. M. (1973). The effects of three types of profane language in persuasive messages. *Journal of Communication, 23*, 461–475.

Bowers, J. W. (1964). Some correlates of language intensity. *Quarterly Journal of Speech, 50*, 415–420.

Bradac, J., Bowers, J., & Courtright, J. (1979). Three language variables in communication research:

Intensity, immediacy, and diversity. *Human Communication Research, 5*, 257–269.

Bradac, J., Bowers, J., & Courtright, J. (1980). Lexical variations in intensity, immediacy, and diversity: An axiomatic theory and causal model. In R. W. St. Clair & H. Giles (Eds.), *The social psychological contexts of language* (pp. 193-223). Hillsdale, NJ: Erlbaum.

Bradac, J. J., & Mulac, A. (1984). A molecular view of powerful and powerless speech styles: Attributional consequences of specific language features and communicator intentions. *Communication Monographs, 51*, 307–319.

Bradley, P. H. (1981). The folk-linguistics of women's speech: An empirical evaluation. *Communication Monographs, 48*, 73–90.

Burgoon, M., & Siegel, J. T. (2004). Language expectancy theory: Insight to application. In J. S. Seiter & R. H. Gass (Eds.), *Readings in persuasion, social influence, and compliance gaining* (pp. 149–164). Boston: Allyn & Bacon.

Cameron, P. (1969). Frequency and kinds of words in various social settings, or what in the hell's going on? *Pacific Sociological Review, 12*, 101–104.

Carli, L. L. (1990). Gender, language, and influence. *Journal of Personality and Social Psychology, 59,* 941–951.

Childers, T. L., & Houston, M. J. (1984). Conditions for a picture-superiority effect on consumer memory. *Journal of Consumer Research, 11,* 643–654.

Corbett, E. P. J. (1971). *Classical rhetoric for the modern student* (2nd ed.). New York: Oxford University Press.

Erickson, B., Lind, E., Johnson, A., & O'Barr, W. M. (1978). Speech style and impression formation in a court setting: The effects of "powerful" and "powerless" speech. *Journal of Experimental Social Psychology, 14,* 266–279.

Foss, S. K., Foss, K. A., & Trapp, R. (1985). *Contemporary perspectives on rhetoric.* Prospect Heights, IL: Waveland Press.

Frey, K. P., & Eagly, A. H. (1993). Vividness can undermine the persuasiveness of messages. *Journal of Personality and Social Psychology, 65,* 32–44.

Giles, H., & Wiemann, J. M. (1987). Language, social comparison, and power. In C. R. Berger & S. H. Chaffee (Eds.), *The handbook of communication science* (pp. 350-384). Newbury Park, CA: Sage.

Hamilton, M. A., & Stewart, B. L. (1993). Extending an information processing model of language intensity effects. *Communication Quarterly, 41*(2), 231–246.

Hart, R. P. (1997). *Modern rhetorical criticism* (2nd ed.). Boston: Allyn & Bacon.

Hoover, J. D., & Howard, L. A. (1995). The political correctness controversy revisited. *American Behavioral Scientist, 38*(7), 963–975.

Hosman, L. A. (1989). The evaluative consequences of hedges, hesitations, and intensifiers. *Human Communication Research, 15*(3), 383–406.

Howard, D. J. (1997). Familiar phrases as peripheral persuasion cues. *Journal of Experimental Social Psychology, 33,* 231–243.

Kirkwood, J. (2003, September 1). "What's in a name?" *The Eagle Tribune.* Retrieved on June 5, 2005, from www.igorinternational.com/press/eagletrib-drug-names.php.

Lakoff, G. (1973). Language and woman's place. *Language Society, 2,* 45–79.

Lakoff, G. (1975). *Language and woman's place.* New York: Harper & Row.

Lemann, N. (2000, October 16, 23). The word lab: The mad science behind what the candidates say. *The New Yorker,* pp. 100–112.

Lowenberg, I. (1982). Labels and hedges: The metalinguistic turn. *Language and Style, 15,* 193–207.

McGlone, M. S., & Batchelor, J. A. (2003). Looking out for number one: Euphemism and face. *Journal of Communication, 53,* 251–264.

McGlone, M. S., Beck, G., & Pfiester, A. (2006). Contamination and camouflage in euphemisms. *Communication Monographs, 73,* 261–282.

McGuire, W. J. (1968). Personality and susceptibility to social influence. In E. F. Borgotta & W. W. Lambert (Eds.), *Handbook of personality theory and research* (pp. 1130–1187). Chicago: Rand McNally.

McGuire, W. J. (1989). Theoretical foundations of campaigns. In R. E. Rice & C. K. Atkin (Eds.), *Public communication campaigns* (2nd ed., pp. 43–65). Newbury Park, CA: Sage.

Merskin, D. (2004). The construction of Arabs as enemies: Post September 11 discourse of George W. Bush. *MASS Communication and Society, 7*(2), 157–175.

Miller, E. G., & Kahn, B. E. (2005). Shades of meaning: The effect of color and flavor names on consumer choice. *Journal of Consumer Research, 32,* 86–92.

Murphy, A. G. (2001). The flight attendant dilemma: An analysis of communication and sensemaking during in-flight emergencies. *Journal of Applied Communication Research, 29*(1), 30–53.

Newcombe, N., & Arnkoff, D. B. (1979). Effects of speech style and sex of speaker on person perception. *Journal of Personality and Social Psychology, 37,* 1293–1303.

Nisbett, R., & Ross, L. (1980). *Human inference: Strategies and shortcomings in social judgment.* Englewood Cliffs, NJ: Prentice Hall.

O'Barr, W. M. (1982). *Linguistic evidence: Language, power, and strategy in the courtroom.* New York: Academic Press.

Pelham, B. W., Mirenberg, M. C., & Jones, J. T. (2002). Why Susie sells seashells by the seashore: Implicit Egotism and major life decisions. *Journal of Personality and Social Psychology, 82,* 469–487.

Powell, L., Callahan, K., Comans, C., McDonald, L., Mansell, J., Trotter, M. D., & Williams, V. (1984). Offensive language and impressions during an interview. *Psychological Reports, 55,* 617–618.

Ralston, S. M., & Thameling, C. A. (1988). Effect of vividness of language on the information value of reference letters and job applicants' recommendations. *Psychological Reports, 62,* 867–870.

Rassin, E., & Van Der Heijden, S. (2005). Appearing credible? Swearing helps! *Psychology, Crime & Law, 11*(2), 177–182.

Reyes, R. M., Thompson, W. C., & Bower, G. H. (1980). Judgmental biases resulting from differing availabilities of arguments. *Journal of Personality and Social Psychology, 39,* 2–12.

Rothwell, J. D. (1971). Verbal obscenity: Time for second thoughts. *Western Speech, 35,* 231–242.

Sapir, E. (1949). *Culture, language and personality.* Berkeley: University of California Press.

Scherer, C. R., & Sagarin, B. J. (2006). Indecent influence: The positive effects of obscenity on persuasion. *Social Influence, 1,* 138–146.

Seiter, J. S., Larsen, J., & Skinner, J. (1998). "Handicapped" or "Handi-capable"?: The effects of language describing people with disabilities on perceptions of source credibility and persuasiveness. *Communication Reports, 11*(1), 1–11.

Smith, S. M., & Shaffer, D. R. (2000). Vividness can undermine or enhance message processing: The moderating role of vividness congruency. *Personality and Social Psychology Bulletin, 26*(7), 769–779.

Stinchfield, K. (2007). *A synonym for streetwalker.* Retrieved on September 30, 2008, from www.time.com/time/specials/2007/top10/article/0,30583,1686204_1690170_1690508,00.html.

Strasser, T. (2005, June 2). "A big flop in the name of love." *Los Angeles Times,* p. E22.

Street, R. L., Jr., & Giles, H. (1982). Speech accommodation theory: A social cognitive approach to language and speech behavior. In M. Roloff & C. R. Berger (Eds.), *Social cognition and communication* (pp. 193–226). Beverly Hills, CA: Sage.

Taylor, S. E., & Thompson, S. C. (1982). Stalking the elusive "vividness" effect. *Psychological Review, 89,* 155–181.

Thornton, R. J. (2006). *Lexicon of inconspicuously ambiguous recommendations.* Retrieved on March 26, 2009, from www.curezone.com/blogs/fm.asp?i=984027.

Three-year-old Hitler can't get name on cake (2008, Dec. 17). *MSNBC.com.* Retrieved on April 8, 2009, from www.msnbc.msn/id/28269290/.

Weaver, R. M. (1953). *The ethics of rhetoric.* Chicago: Henry Regnery.

Whorf, B. L. (1956). *Language, thought, and reality.* New York: John Wiley & Sons.

CHAPTER 8

Nonverbal Influence

Shelley's boyfriend was probably frowning as he watched one of this book's authors reach out and take Shelley's hand. At the time, the author was not thinking about Shelley's boyfriend, though; he was thinking about how pretty Shelley was. He remembers leaning toward her and gazing into her eyes. Her lips tightened into a grin as she squeezed the author's hand. He'd never talked to her before this and was nervous, but even so, he had no trouble finding words. They came out smooth and suggestive. "Pass the salt," he whispered. And, after swallowing hard and leaning even closer, he repeated those words—"Pass the salt, pass the salt"—again and again.

Don't get the wrong idea. Even after writing a book about persuasion, neither author is even close to Don Juan status. When one of us met Shelley years ago, he was a sophomore in college, where he, Shelley, and Shelley's boyfriend were taking an acting class. As part of an exercise, the instructor paired each of us students up with a stranger and asked us to convince the rest of the class that we were deeply and passionately in love. "Pass the salt," however, was the only phrase we were allowed to use.

In retrospect, the author is not sure how persuasive an actor he was, but he did learn something that day: The words "I love you" are not all they are cracked up to be. Sure, it's nice to hear those words, but if you can convey the same meaning with "pass the salt," who needs them? The point here is that, when we are trying to interpret meaning, there is a lot more involved than simply words. As the old saying goes, "it's not what a person says, it's *how* the person says it that's important," which is why it is crucial that we understand something about nonverbal communication—how we say things through the use of gestures, body movements, touch, spatial behavior, appearance, eye contact, and so forth. In this chapter, we are interested in focusing on one particular question about nonverbal communication. That is, in what way does nonverbal communication influence the process of persuasion?

According to Burgoon (1994), nonverbal communication plays an important role in the process of social influence for several reasons. First, we can use nonverbal behavior to create certain impressions of ourselves. If we are successful in making ourselves appear powerful, authoritative, credible, or attractive, we may also be more persuasive. (For a different twist on nonverbal behavior and impression management, see Box 8.1.) Second, through the use of nonverbal behaviors, people can establish intimate relationships. In other words, nonverbal cues, such as touch, can be influential in developing rapport. Third, nonverbal behaviors can heighten or distract attention from persuasive messages that are likely to reinforce learning. For example, a teacher can use nonverbal cues to get his or her students to pay more attention to a message, and a heckler can use such tactics to distract

<table>
<tr><td>

Smirks and Sneers behind Your Back: Influencing
Impressions of Others

</td><td>

BOX 8.1

</td></tr>
</table>

Impression management theory (see Goffman, 1959; Schlenker, 1980; Tedeschi & Reiss, 1981) suggests that people control their behaviors—particularly nonverbal behaviors—in order to create desired impressions of themselves (Leathers, 1997). If you want to be liked, for instance, you might smile. If you want to be intimidating, you might frown. Clearly, however, our nonverbal behavior can affect impressions other than those made about us. Seiter (2001), for example, argued that impression management theory should be expanded to include the ways in which we strategically attempt to control impressions made of others. Although such attempts might be aimed at making others appear better, Seiter maintained that sometimes our attempts to appear honest and desirable are undermined by others. That is, sometimes other people may attempt to make us appear undesirable and dishonest.

One context in which such attempts might occur is a political debate. Indeed, because candidates' versions of a story often differ, they may look for opportunities to make their opponents appear deceptive. For instance, in the last several presidential debates, where split screens allowed viewers to see both the speaker and nonspeaking debater simultaneously, candidates were criticized for their silent, yet derogatory, background behavior.

To see if such background behavior is effective in undermining an opponent, Seiter and his colleagues (Seiter, 1999, 2001; Seiter, Abraham, & Nakagama, 1998; Seiter & Weger, 2005; Seiter, Weger, Kinzer, & Jensen, 2009) conducted studies that asked students to watch one of four versions of a televised debate. One version used a single-screen presentation, showing only the speaker, while the other three versions used a split-screen presentation in which the speaker's opponent displayed constant, occasional, or no nonverbal disbelief regarding the content of the speaker's message. In other words, in some versions of the tape, the nonspeaking debater was shown shaking his head, rolling his eyes, and frowning while his opponent was speaking. After watching the videos, students rated the debaters. Results indicated that, in general, when any background disbelief was communicated by the nonspeaking debater, the speaker's credibility improved (Seiter et al., 1998). However, when the audience was led to be suspicious of the debaters' truthfulness, moderate background behavior on the part of the nonspeaking debater made his speaking opponent appear more deceptive (Seiter, 2001). Be warned, however. If you're ever in a debate and are thinking about silently deriding your opponent, you'll probably hurt your own image in the process. To be sure, the studies also found that any derogatory background behavior led the nonspeaking debater to be perceived as more deceptive, less credible, less likable, and inappropriate (Seiter, 1999, 2001; Seiter et al., 2009; Seiter & Weger, 2005).

listeners. Fourth, through nonverbal cues, a person can be reinforced to imitate a model's behavior. Fifth, nonverbal cues can be used to signal a person's expectations and elicit behavior that conforms to those expectations. For example, a simple frown can inform a child that he or she is not behaving appropriately. And finally, nonverbal behaviors can be used to violate people's expectations so as to distract them. Later in the chapter, for instance, we'll see that standing too close to another person can, under some circumstances, make that person more compliant.

Of course, we do not have the space needed in one chapter to discuss every aspect of nonverbal communication. We have, therefore, chosen to focus on those areas that we find the most important and intriguing. We begin by discussing a model that suggests the relationship between nonverbal behavior and persuasion is quite simple.

THE DIRECT EFFECTS MODEL OF IMMEDIACY

People who study nonverbal behavior use the term *immediacy* to describe actions that communicate warmth, closeness, friendliness, and involvement with other people (Andersen, 2004). If, for instance, you smile, make a lot of eye contact, nod, and lean forward when talking to someone else, you are demonstrating some common immediacy cues. According to the *direct effects model of immediacy* (see Andersen, 2004; Segrin, 1993), there is a simple relationship between nonverbal behavior and social influence. That is, warm, involving, immediate behaviors lead to increased persuasion (Andersen, 2004). As you'll see in the remainder of this chapter, a considerable amount of research supports this model and the effectiveness of immediacy behaviors in a number of different contexts, including intercultural (Booth-Butterfield & Noguchi, 2000), educational (Comadena, Hunt, & Simonds, 2007), organizational (Teven, 2007), athletic (Turman, 2008), and interpersonal settings (e.g., Hinkle, 1999). However, some research presents a more complicated picture. As we turn now to a discussion of the different types of nonverbal behavior, you will see that demonstrating immediacy may generally be a good rule of thumb, but an awareness of other factors may be necessary to sort out the sometimes complex relationship between nonverbal behaviors and persuasion.

TYPES OF NONVERBAL COMMUNICATION

Before discussing specific forms of nonverbal behavior, we think it's important to point out that such behaviors are interdependent. By way of illustration, we should probably tell you that the "Shelley story" is not yet over. There's still the part about Shelley's boyfriend, Louis, who responded to the "pass the salt" line by attacking the author after class. With eyes wide and fists clinched, Louis called the author a "lousy something-or-other" and then slugged him. In response, the author merely chuckled, because he could see that Louis was only having fun; Louis was smiling, and the punch was only a playful "tap."

As it turns out, Louis's behavior was probably not all that uncommon. Indeed, like us, you may have seen people (probably men) play-fighting as a means of greeting one another. But how do we know that they are only playing? We know because we don't see *only* their punches or *only* their eyes; we see other cues that help us interpret their messages. In other words, although there are many types of nonverbal communication, they do not occur in isolation. Nonverbal behaviors occur simultaneously, and how we interpret one behavior can affect our interpretations of other behaviors. Thus, although we discuss each of the following codes separately, it is important to realize that each code rarely operates alone.

With that said, we now examine seven types of nonverbal communication that are important in the process of persuasion; kinesics, haptics, proxemics, chronemics, artifacts, physical appearance, and paralinguistics.

Kinesics: Head, Shoulders, Knees and Toes, Knees and Toes

The word *kinesics* was derived from the Greek term *kinein*, which means "to move" and refers to the study of eye contact, facial expressions, gestures, and body movements and posture. We start by taking a look at eye contact.

The Eyes Have It

Ralph Waldo Emerson once claimed that "The eyes of men converse as much as their tongues." And when you think of all the expressions we have regarding the communication potential of eyeballs (e.g., "evil eyes," "bedroom eyes," "shifty eyes," "laughing eyes," "lying eyes"), Emerson's claim does not seem so far-fetched. Besides being an important means of expressing interest, attraction, and intimacy, eye contact has been found to convey dominance, persuasiveness, aggressiveness, and credibility (Burgoon & Dillman, 1995).

As potential targets of persuasion, we need to keep in mind that everyday persuaders are well aware of the power of eye contact and use it to their advantage. One of the authors, for instance, was involved in a study that investigated the influence strategies used by beggars when attempting to get money from strangers (Robinson, Seiter, & Acharya, 1992). As part of the study, 36 beggars were interviewed, and several claimed that, before even asking for money, the first thing they tried to do was establish eye contact with whomever was passing by. Without eye contact, the beggars argued, it was easier for their "targets" to ignore them and walk on by.

If eye contact helps beggars get more money, does it also help communicators to be more persuasive? Some evidence seems to support this notion. For example, Murphy (2007) found that people who looked more at their interaction partners while speaking and listening were perceived as more intelligent than those who did not. Moreover, in a meta-analysis of several studies on eye contact, Segrin (1993) found that in all but one study, gazing at listeners produced more compliance than averting gaze.

Speakers who do not use eye contact to their advantage may have problems gaining trust. During speeches, for instance, Ronald Reagan and Bill Clinton, who had/have reputations for being effective communicators, were also well known for their direct and sincere eye contact. However, Richard Nixon, who had to be tutored in order to minimize his problems with making eye contact, was advised to place his speeches right on top of the camera so that he would be forced to establish eye contact with it (Webbink, 1986). In his debates with Kennedy, Nixon also had problems with being perceived as "shifty eyed." Likewise, research by Guéguen and Jacob (2002) found that people, especially females, were less likely to comply when persuaders quickly averted their glance than when they maintained eye contact.

Before concluding this section, we should note that using more eye contact does not always mean that you will be more persuasive. A study by Kleinke (1980), for instance, illustrates that the effectiveness of eye contact may depend on other factors, such as the legitimacy of the request you make. In Kleinke's study, persuaders were instructed to approach people in an airport and ask them for money. Some of the targets were told that the money would be used to make an important phone call (a legitimate request), whereas others were told that the money would be used to pay for a candy bar or gum (an illegitimate

Illustration of Kleinke's (1980) Results		**TABLE 8.1**
	Legitimate Request	**Illegitimate Request**
Eye contact	Persuadee complies with request	Persuadee does not comply with request
No eye contact	Persuadee does not comply with request	Persuadee complies with request

Adapted from Kleinke, C. L. (1980). Interaction between gaze and legitimacy of request on compliance in a field setting. *Journal of Nonverbal Behavior, 5,* 3–12.

request). It turned out that people who thought the persuader needed to make a phone call gave more money, but only when the persuader looked at them. Interestingly, however, eye contact actually decreased compliance when the persuader made an illegitimate request (see Table 8.1). Perhaps, as the researcher suggested, looking away while making an illegitimate request makes a person seem more humble or embarrassed, thereby increasing his or her persuasiveness by winning the sympathy of others (Kleinke, 1980).

About Face. Of all possible facial expressions, smiling has probably been studied the most. To be sure, research has shown that by smiling, waitresses earn more tips (Tidd & Lockard, cited in Guéguen & Fischer-Lokou, 2004), therapists are judged to be warmer and more competent (Leathers, 1997), job interviewees create positive impressions of themselves (Washburn & Hakel, 1973) and are more likely to get jobs (Forbes & Jackson, 1980), female hitchhikers get more rides (Guéguen & Fischer-Lokou, 2004), students accused of cheating are treated with greater leniency (LaFrance & Hecht, 1995), and teachers inspire students to pay more attention (Saigh, 1981). One study found that right after being smiled at, people were more willing to help a third person who dropped some computer disks on the ground (Guéguen & De Gail, 2003).

We do not, however, want to give you the impression that influence is always as easy as a smile. As noted in Chapter 4, persuaders need to come across as trustworthy and sincere. Not all smiles accomplish this goal, however. A study by Krumhuber, Manstead, and Kappas (2007), for instance, found that when smiles appear quickly, the smiling person is perceived as less trustworthy and attractive than when smiles have a slower onset. In addition, people who smile too much may not always be perceived as authentic. Similarly, in situations where a dominant demeanor would be most persuasive, positive and likable facial expressions could be counterproductive. For instance, a study by Mehrabian and Williams (1969) found that, although smiling and nodding were more persuasive when used by people of equal status, dominant behaviors are more effective in established hierarchies. Moreover, Kaplan, Greenfield, and Ware (cited in Buller & Street, 1992) found that patients were healthier in follow-up visits when their doctors expressed negative emotions (e.g., disapproval) in prior visits. The expression of positive emotions did not have this effect.

The situational nature of facial expressions and other nonverbal behaviors is even more apparent if you consider research that has been done on the topic of *mirroring* or *mimicry*. Such research indicates that, rather than using any one type of nonverbal behavior, a persuader should try to build rapport with others by mimicking their nonverbal cues. In other words, smile when people smile and frown when people frown. For example, in one study (Chartrand & Bargh, 1999), research participants interacted with a person who had been told beforehand either to mimic or not mimic the research participants' behavior (e.g., the mimickers crossed or did not cross their arms when the research participants did). Results indicated that people who mirrored the research participants' behavior were liked much more than those who did not. Another study found that negotiators who mirrored others' behavior were more likely to reach a deal than those who did not (Maddux, Mullen, & Galinsky, 2008), and yet another found that when people were interviewed about products they were tasting (e.g., snacks and sports drinks), the people had the most favorable attitudes toward the products when the interviewer mimicked their behavior (Tanner, Ferraro, Chartrand, Bettman, & Van Baaren, 2007). Of course, if you choose to be unpopular, you can always forget such chameleon-like behavior. For instance, research suggests that when people want to be disliked, they compensate others' behaviors, meeting smiles with frowns, and eye contact with disinterest (Floyd & Burgoon, 1999). Interestingly, research also suggests that we may engage in such behaviors unconsciously as a way of maintaining relationships. For example, one study (Karremans & Verwijmeren, 2008) found that people who were in romantic relationships mimicked the behavior of attractive, opposite-sex strangers less than people who were not in romantic relationships.

From the Neck Down: Persuasion and Body Language

Some of the principles of persuasion that we discussed in relation to the eyes and the face also apply to communication with the body. For example, just as you can mirror a person's facial expressions, you can mirror his or her gestures and body movements. Moreover, consistent with the direct effects model of immediacy (discussed previously), people who lean forward when communicating tend to be more persuasive than those who do not. In addition to these findings, research shows that people are more persuasive when they are pictured using open body positions (i.e., when their arms and legs are positioned away from their bodies) rather than neutral or closed positions (McGinley, LeFevre, & McGinley, 1975). (Did you know that body position may also make you more persuadable? See Box 8.2.)

Perhaps most of the research on body movement and persuasion, however, has focused on the use of gestures. Although various researchers have discussed a number of different gestures, Argyle (1988) argued that it is most useful to focus on three: emblems, illustrators, and self-touching.

Emblems. According to Ekman and Friesen (1969), *emblems* are nonverbal behaviors, usually hand movements, that have precise verbal meaning. Thus, emblems can substitute for words. Traffic cops, referees, baseball catchers, and scuba divers are well-known emblem users, but we all use them. Think of all the words for which we have gestures: hello, good-bye, come here, crazy, quiet or shush, peace, I don't know, good luck, think, and shame on you, not to mention the ever-popular middle finger gesture used by motorists.

Emblems are an important part of communication and serve many functions, persuasion included. But what part do emblems play in social influence? Several scholars have argued that a prerequisite for persuasion is attention to and retention of a message (e.g., McGuire, 1968; Petty & Cacioppo, 1986), and it seems that by providing more visual

Did you know that the nonverbal behavior of people receiving messages can affect how likely they are to be persuaded? Over the years, researchers have found that when people are highly involved with a topic, it affects how persuaded they are by messages about that topic (Petty & Cacioppo, 1986; Roser, 1990; Roser & Thompson, 1995). People who are highly involved tend to be less persuaded by opposing arguments than are uninvolved people. But Petty, Wells, Heesacker, Brock, and Cacioppo (1983) found that, even when people are not involved with a topic, their nonverbal behavior can fool them into thinking so. The researchers hypothesized that, when people are standing, they are more prone to agitation and attack than when they are relaxing. Thus, the researchers suspected that standing might predispose

people to respond more negatively to a message with which they already disagreed. To test this notion, the researchers had people listen to counterattitudinal messages while either standing or lying comfortably. Results confirmed the hypothesis. Standing participants were less persuaded than relaxing ones. In similar studies, researchers found that people who listened to messages while nodding their heads (a sign of agreement) were more persuaded than those who moved their heads back and forth horizontally (Tom, Ramil, Zapanta, Demir, & Lopez, 2006; Wells & Petty, 1980).

The moral of the story, then, is that when someone is trying to persuade you, you need not only monitor the persuader's behavior, you need to keep an eye on your own as well!

DILBERT: © Scott Adams, Reprinted with permission, United Media. All Rights Reserved.

information, emblems play a large role in fostering attention and retention in persuadees. Woodall and Folger (1981), for example, found that people recalled 34 percent of a verbal message when it was accompanied by an emblem compared to only 11 percent when other types of gestures were used.

Illustrators. Although emblems have meaning independent of verbal communication, *illustrators,* a second type of gesture, accompany speech (Ekman & Friesen, 1969). Like their name implies, illustrators illustrate, emphasize, or repeat what is being said. A child saying she loves you "this much" while spreading her arms wide is using an illustrator. Likewise, we can use illustrators to give directions, show our excitement, follow a rhythm, demonstrate a shape, and so forth.

Several studies indicate that the use of illustrators increases a speaker's persuasiveness. In one study, for instance, actors who used more forceful and rhythmic gestures were more persuasive than those who did not (Maslow, Yoselson, & London, 1971). Moreover, Mehrabian and Williams (1969) found that speakers were rated as more persuasive when they used more illustrators. In addition, some illustrators make speakers appear more effective and composed (Maricchiolo, Gnisci, Bonaiuto, & Ficca, 2009), which doesn't hurt when you are trying to be persuasive.

Self-Touching Behaviors (Adaptors). Although emblems and illustrators seem to increase people's persuasiveness, the jury is not yet out on the effect of *self-touching behaviors* (e.g., scratching your arm, rubbing your cheek, picking your nose, stroking your hair), also known as *adaptors* (Ekman & Friesen, 1969). For example, while some research suggests that the use of adaptors was associated with less persuasion (Maslow et al., 1971; Mehrabian & Williams, 1969), other research shows the opposite (Maricchiolo et al., 2009). Even so, most research agrees that self-touching behaviors are often seen as a sign of anxiety and lack of composure (unless, perhaps, you are Britney Spears or Madonna). With that in mind, our best advice at this point is to avoid using adaptors if you want to be persuasive.

Haptics: Reach Out, Reach Out and Touch Someone

If touching yourself makes you less persuasive, does touching other people have the same effect? Many years ago, three researchers interested in the topic of *haptics* (or touch) conducted a simple yet classic study to explore this question. In the study, library clerks did one of two things when they handed library cards back to university students who were checking out books: Either they did not touch the students or they made light physical contact by placing a hand over the students' palms. After their cards were returned, students were asked to rate the quality of the library, and, interestingly, those who were touched evaluated the library much more favorably than those who were not (Fisher, Rytting, & Heslin, 1976).

The persuasive impact of touch has been demonstrated in other contexts as well. For example, touch has been found to increase the number of people who volunteered to score papers (Patterson, Powell, & Lenihan, 1986), sign petitions (Willis & Hamm, 1980), complete questionnaires (Vaidis & Halimi-Falkowicz, 2008), return money that had been left in a telephone booth (Kleinke, 1977), accept invitations to dance in nightclubs (Guéguen, 2007), provide phone numbers to prospective dating partners (Guéguen, 2007), and help someone pick up items that had been dropped (Guéguen & Fischer-Lokou, 2003). Similarly, when food servers touch diners appropriately, the servers earn higher tips (Hornick, 1992), and the diners are more likely to take servers' recommendations about what to order (Guéguen, Jacob, & Boulbry, 2007). Hornick (1992) found that touching bookstore customers on the arm caused them to shop longer (22.11 minutes versus 13.56 minutes), purchase more ($15.03 versus $12.23), and evaluate the store more positively than customers who had not been touched. Hornick (1992) also found that supermarket customers who had been touched were more likely to taste and purchase food samples than untouched customers. Kaufman and Mahoney (1999) found that customers in bars drank significantly more alcohol when they were touched by cocktail waitresses than when they were not touched. Finally, Nannberg and Hansen (1994) found that people who had already agreed to participate in a lengthy and difficult survey completed more survey items if they had been touched.

Considering this research, it seems, then, that all the stuff we learned as kids about "the Midas touch" may not be such a fairy tale. Touching people seems to be persuasive. Touch may put people in a good mood, making them more likely to comply with requests (Hornick, 1992; Nannberg & Hansen, 1994). Another explanation is that people who touch create more favorable impressions of themselves and, therefore, are more persuasive (Hornick, 1992; Nannberg & Hansen, 1994). Finally, people who touch may be more persuasive because, through touch, they augment their image of power (Nannberg & Hansen 1994; Patterson et al., 1986).

Whatever the reason for the persuasive impact of touch, one thing is clear: The use of touch for persuasive purposes is tricky because touch is so ambiguous. What one person may interpret as "friendly," for example, another may see as "flirtatious." Can the "brushing" of one employee against another be interpreted as accidental or as a form of sexual harassment? Clearly, interpretations of touch depend on a vast array of factors, including context, gender, and culture. In most of the studies we've just discussed, touching generally occurred on the hands or arms. We suspect that too much touching or touching other parts of a person might actually backfire, making persuasion less likely. As potential persuadees, it is important to realize that even touches, such as those enacted in most of the studies we discussed, wield tremendous persuasive power. Such touches may be so subtle that we might not even be aware that they are being used for persuasive purposes. But do not be fooled. Touch is persuasive, as is the use of space—our next topic. (For more on the persuasive effects of touch, see Box 8.3.)

Keep Your Distance?: Proxemics and Persuasion

The study of *proxemics,* or how we use space to communicate, covers a variety of topics, such as territoriality and dominance. In this chapter, however, we are less concerned with

---

If It Feels Good, Buy It: The Role of Touching Merchandise on Persuasion	BOX 8.3

When you are shopping, do you find yourself picking things up, feeling the texture of fabrics, and running your fingers over merchandise? If so, you may be what researchers have called *high in the need for touch* (NFT) (Peck & Childers, 2003a, 2003b; Peck & Wiggins, 2005). High NFTs get frustrated while shopping if they cannot touch things. Not all NFTs are the same, however. Some, called *instrumental NFTs*, use touch to evaluate products, while others, called *autotelic NFTs*, touch things because it is fun and pleasurable for them. With that in mind, autotelic NFTs are persuaded when there are pleasurable things to touch, even when those things are not relevant to what is being marketed (e.g., soft swatches of fabric on a pamphlet seeking donations for a nature center). Instrumental NFTs, however, are persuaded only when what is being touched is relevant to what is being marketed (e.g., feathers and tree bark samples on a pamphlet seeking donations for a nature center) (Peck & Wiggins, 2005).

those topics and, instead, focus our discussion on the topic of distance. Two lines of research suggest that being at close distances to people affects how persuasive you are. First, some studies show that being geographically close to another person facilitates attraction, which, in turn, fosters persuasion. Others suggest that such geographical proximity leads to persuasion because those who live or work closer to us seem more accessible, familiar, and likely to be encountered in the future (for a review of these perspectives, see Moon, 1999). Findings from other research studies (Brucks, Reips, & Ryf, 2007; Moon) however, call these explanations into question. In these studies, research participants received persuasive messages while communicating with others via computer. Some of the participants were told that the other people were in close proximity, while some were told the other people were farther away. Results of the studies indicated that when participants thought the other people were geographically closer, they were more persuaded by the other people and perceived the people as more credible than when they thought the people were far away. Why are these findings significant? Presumably, a computer makes people living 2,000 miles away just as accessible and familiar as those living 2 miles away, indicating that something else must explain the relationship between geographical proximity and persuasion. Moon (1999) suggests that perhaps people assume that those who live in closer geographical proximity are similar to them, and similarity leads to persuasiveness.

Closely related to the topic of geographical distance is the concept of *personal space,* which refers to what might be considered an invisible bubble that surrounds us. An obvious case in point is that a door-to-door salesperson should not stick his or her nose in a potential customer's face. However, there is some evidence that indicates that the opposite is the case: That is, violating a person's space may be more persuasive.

In a study by Baron and Bell (1976), for instance, diners in a cafeteria were approached by an experimenter and asked to volunteer for a survey for a period of 30 minutes to 2 hours and 30 minutes. The experimenter stood close to some diners (12 to 18 in.) and farther away from others (3 to 4 ft.). Results of the study showed that diners volunteered to participate for longer periods of time when they were approached at closer distances.

How can we explain this finding? First, because people tend to stand closer to people they like (Argyle, 1988), persuadees may simply be reciprocating the liking by complying with the violator's requests (Baron & Bell, 1976). In addition, because people find spatial invasion uncomfortable, those invaded may perceive persuaders as more demanding, desperate, and needful (Baron & Bell, 1976).

As with other forms of nonverbal communication, some caution is advised when making generalizations about the role of proxemics in persuasion. Indeed, at least two studies indicate that closer distances may not encourage compliance. For instance, Smith and Knowles (1979) found that pedestrians who had their space invaded without justification were less likely to return a lost object than those who had not had their space invaded. Moreover, a study by Albert and Dabbs (1970) found that speakers were more persuasive the farther they were from other people (i.e., speakers were more persuasive when standing 4 to 5 or 14 to 15 ft. from their audiences than they were when standing 1 to 2 ft. from their audiences).[1]

If the conflicting results of these studies seem confusing, you might be interested in a theory presented by Judee Burgoon (1978, 1992, 1994).[2] It is called *expectancy violations theory,* and we think it provides a strong and elegant explanation for the ways in which space violations affect the process of social influence.

According to the theory, we all have expectations about how close other people should stand to us. When people violate those expectations and get either too close or too far away, we experience arousal and may become distracted. How we react to the violation, however, depends on several factors, perhaps the most important being the "reward value" of the violator. If he or she is attractive, has the power to reward or punish us, or is just plain likable, the violation is perceived as a pleasant surprise, and we are more likely to be persuaded. However, if the violator has low reward value, the violation will be perceived as negative, and compliance will be less likely. In addition, the theory states that if violations are so extreme that they are perceived as threatening, they also will decrease compliance.

The theory has received a considerable amount of support and implies several practical suggestions for those interested in persuading others. First, if you think the person you are trying to persuade sees you as attractive, powerful, or credible, it is best to stand a little farther or a little closer to that person than would be expected. Second, if you think you are perceived by someone as powerless and icky, you should maintain appropriate distances. Finally, never overdo it. If you stand too close or too far away, you will probably not be persuasive.

Chronemics: All Good Things to Those Who Wait?

In science, the concepts of space and time are often discussed together. However, in the study of persuasion, although considerable research has examined the topic of proxemics, little attention has been paid to *chronemics,* or the study of how time is used to communicate. Even so, we know that time can be an important commodity, especially in a culture like the United States.

A common expression in the military, especially among soldiers with lower ranks, is "hurry up and wait." Oftentimes, it seems that such soldiers are expected to be on time although their superiors can show up whenever they want to. The point is, the higher your status, the more power you have over other people's time.

This is true in other contexts as well. For instance, how much time have you spent waiting in doctors' offices? Do you have to make appointments to see some professors or to get interviewed for a job? And don't be fooled: If you are a subordinate and show up more than a few minutes late to a business meeting, do you think you'll be very persuasive? We suspect not.

Practically speaking, then, you might be wondering whether it is okay to be late if you have a lot of status. Our suggestion is "be careful." Indeed, a study mentioned in the work of Burgoon and colleagues (1989) found that people who arrive 15 minutes late are considered dynamic, but much less competent, composed, and sociable than people who arrive on time. Plus, we think making people wait is rude.

Time not only affects perceptions of people but it can also be used as a persuasive ploy. For instance, for people in a hurry, drive-through banking or fast-food restaurants may have appeal, as may establishments such as Jiffy Lube, Lenscrafters, and 1-Hour Photo. When such services save you time, it's terrific. But beware! Just because an exercise video promises to transform your buns into steel in only 3 minutes a day, or a flyer claims you can earn $60,000 a year working at home in your spare time, or an audiotape claims it will teach you how to play guitar in 2 weeks doesn't mean that will really happen. Too often, people seek quick solutions to complicated problems. We want to buy a product, take a pill, or push a button, and make a problem go away. Persuaders prey on this quick-fix mentality.

In addition to ploys offering to save time, sometimes strategies are based on what Cialdini (1993) calls the principle of *scarcity*. According to Cialdini and others (e.g., Brehm, 1966; Brehm & Brehm, 1981), people love freedom, and when that freedom is threatened or limited, people experience something called *psychological reactance*, a concept we introduced in Chapter 3. For example, a person in a store may decide she likes a certain dress. If a salesperson explains to the customer that there is only one more dress like that in her size (i.e., the dress is *scarce*), the woman, who might have thought that she was free to buy the dress at any time, may now *react psychologically* by wanting the dress more than she did in the first place (Cialdini, 1993). As you well know, persuaders also attempt to use psychological reactance in their favor by making time scarce. For instance, by telling us that we must "act now" or that there is a "limited time offer," advertisers are relying on the principle of scarcity. By limiting our time, they hope to make us more likely to purchase their product or service. Assuming that the frequency with which a tactic is used indicates how effective advertisers believe a tactic is, then "limited time" offers are believed to be extremely effective. Indeed, in an analysis of 13,594 retail ads in several major newspapers, Howard, Shu, and Kerin (2007) found that scarcity appeals appeared in one in five ads and that limited time scarcity appeals accounted for an estimated $5.1 billion of newspaper display ads in the United States per year.

Interestingly, perhaps because psychological reactance is so uncomfortable, some persuaders have found that a "nonurgency" tactic is more successful. In other words, because people don't want to be rushed and pressured, sometimes coming across as if time is *not* an issue can be very persuasive. "No, no, no" sales use this approach: A consumer buys a mattress, a big-screen TV, or an appliance and pays no money down, no interest, and no monthly payments until anywhere from 90 days to a year later. Products or services that advertise a "free 30-day trial offer" also facilitate sales by removing time pressures. Some mega bookstores encourage customers to browse, have a cup of coffee or a muffin, and sit and read a book in the store. You might think this would be bad for business, but in fact customers often purchase additional books they otherwise wouldn't have if they rushed in and out.

Artifacts and Physical Features of the Environment: Dress for Success

While talking about the notion of time, did we mention that an expensive watch with a gold wristband couldn't hurt your image much? Obviously, the clothes and makeup we wear, the cars we drive, the furniture we own, and other physical objects, also known as *artifacts,* can communicate a great deal about our credibility and status. In our society, material goods are viewed as an extension of oneself. Why else would color analysts be getting rich by telling people whether to wear summer, autumn, winter, or spring colored makeup? And why else would someone pay thousands of dollars for an Armani suit?

Speaking of suits, we know a good story about how artifacts can affect people's perceptions. Many years ago, one of the authors sold men's suits for commission. Because he obviously did not earn anything unless he sold merchandise, when given a choice, the author tried to help customers who appeared as if they would spend a lot of money. One day a customer entered the store wearing a greasy T shirt, jeans, no socks, and filthy tennis shoes. Because at the time, there were plenty of other people shopping, the author decided to pick a more "profitable-looking" customer on whom to wait. One of the new employees, however, decided to help the greaseball. Much to the author's surprise, however, that "greaseball" ended up buying six very expensive suits. It seems that he was not a greaseball at all; he was a high-paid executive who had just lost all of his suits in a fire. He was restocking his wardrobe. Of course, the old saying "you can't judge a book by its cover" took on a whole new meaning that day!

Apparently, when it comes to making quick judgments like this, the author is not alone. Indeed, previous literature suggests that first impressions are not only powerful and enduring, they are often based on seemingly trivial appearance cues (see Burgoon, Buller, & Woodall, 1996). Research indicates, for example, that cues such as clothing (e.g., Gorham, Cohen, & Morris, 1999; Seiter & Dunn, 2000), grooming (e.g., Atkins & Kent, 1988),

"You're right. It does send a powerful message."

cosmetics (Johnson & Workman, 1991), hair length (Atkins & Kent, 1988), tattooing (Seiter & Hatch, 2005; Swami & Furnham, 2007), and body piercing (Seiter & Sandry, 2003) influence judgments about credibility, attractiveness, and whether or not to hire someone. In other words, if anything, such research indicates that such cues are not trivial at all and, in some contexts (e.g., when interviewing), may be more important than verbal cues (Goldberg & Cohen, 2004).

In addition to those discussed, other artifacts and features of the environment can be influential. For instance, power and status might be communicated through the size and location of a person's office. Large offices in corner spaces, for example, are often considered prestigious (Andersen, 1999). Not only that, one of our favorite studies (Teven & Comadena, 1996) illustrates that an office's appearance may be important as well. In the study, 97 students went one at a time to meet a professor in his office. On arriving for the meeting, however, they found no professor and were asked to wait 5 minutes for him. Some of the students waited in a disorganized and untidy office, whereas others waited in a clean and neatly arranged office. After the 5 minutes were up, the students were told that the professor could not make the meeting. Later, however, they saw the professor lecture and rated him on several scales. The results of the study showed that the professor's office had a significant influence on students' perceptions. Specifically, compared to students who visited the tidy office, those who visited the untidy one perceived the professor as less authoritative, less trustworthy, less open, less relaxed, less concerned about making a good impression, less animated, and less friendly. Interestingly, however, the "untidy" professor was seen as the most dynamic, perhaps because the disheveled office created the impression of a busy and energetic person (Teven & Comadena, 1996). Whatever the case, after reading this study, we'll be cleaning and rearranging.

And apparently, we're not the only ones. Other people know about the importance of structuring the environment. For example, if you're thinking of buying a house, before you do, remember that those dandy model homes may not look the same once you're living in them. Why not? The furniture is downsized to make the rooms look larger (Martin, 2000). Plus, empty closets, refrigerators without kiddie art, and the absence of other household necessities make such homes look tidy and ever so inviting.

Supermarkets are another example of how environments are arranged strategically (e.g., see Field, 1996; Meyer, 1997; Tandingan, 2001). Next time you're shopping, for instance, take a look around. You might notice that staples such as dairy, meat, and produce are in the back or on opposite sides of the store. Why? It forces shoppers to meander through the aisles where they'll be tempted to buy all kinds of other goodies. You'll also notice that chips, dips, and other products that "go together" are intentionally placed side by side, encouraging additional purchases. And it's no accident that children's products (e.g., Cap'n Crunch) are often placed on middle shelves so that they are at eye level to little precious who is seated in the shopping cart, whereas adult products (e.g., Grape Nuts) are at higher elevations. What's more, snack foods, which appeal to impulsive shoppers, are often located in check-out areas and at the ends of aisles where they're more likely to be snatched up. Clearly, such placement is adapted to particular audiences and aimed at making products noticeable to consumers.

In addition to the studies and tactics we've mentioned so far, considerable evidence shows that artifacts and physical features of the environment can not only make products more noticeable and people appear more (or less) credible but they can also lead to persuasion. Most of this research has focused on the impact of clothing. Lawrence and Watson (1991), for example, found that individuals asking for contributions to law enforcement and health-care campaigns earned more money when wearing sheriffs' and nurses' uniforms than when they did not. In another study, Bickman (1974) had young men, dressed as either civilians (i.e., wearing coats and ties), milkmen, or uniformed guards (with badges and no guns), approach pedestrians on the streets of New York and ask them to do one of three things. In one situation, pedestrians were shown a bag lying on the ground and were told, "Pick up this bag for me!" In another condition, the experimenter pointed at a man standing near a parked car and said, "This fellow is over-parked at the meter but doesn't have any change. Give him a dime!" In the final condition, a person standing at a bus stop was told, "Don't you know you have to stand on the other side of the pole? The sign says, 'No Standing.'" Results of the study showed that, in all three conditions, people complied more with the guard than they did with the milkman or civilian. In other words, something about a uniform tends to make us obedient.

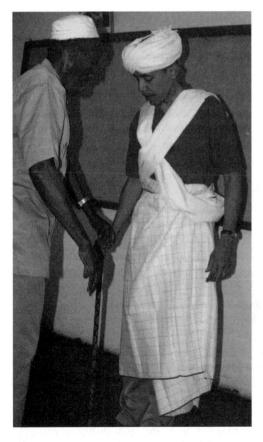

Dressing like your audience may make them identify with you more.

© AP Wide World Photos.

Although meta-analyses indicate that fancy suits, uniforms, and high-status clothing are related to higher rates of compliance (Segrin, 1993), such apparel might not always be necessary for persuasion. In some cases, it may also be possible to influence people by wearing clothing that makes them identify with a persuader. When visiting local factories or appearing on MTV, for instance, politicians are often seen without their usual suits and neckties. Moreover, Hensley (1981) found that well-dressed people were more persuasive in airports but casually dressed people were more persuasive at bus stops, and Rucker, Anderson, and Kangas (1999) found that, compared to Hispanics, Anglo-Americans thought that clothing was less important for making powerful impressions and fitting in with others.

In short, it appears that artifacts, particularly clothing, make a difference when trying to seek compliance. Of course, artifacts can also affect your appearance or attractiveness, which, in turn, can affect your persuasiveness. We now turn our discussion to this topic.

Physical Appearance: Of Beauties and Beasts

Beauty may only be skin deep, but it is persuasive. And the people out there trying to influence us know this. Beauty sells. For example, if Tyra Banks had a big nose and warts with hair growing out of them, do

Hot by Association: How Facebook Friends Affect Your Attractiveness   BOX 8.4

If you are one of the millions of people who use the social networking Website Facebook, you might be interested to know that people may be judging you by the company you keep. It has been known for some time that judgments of attractiveness are relative. For example, when photos of average-looking people are shown beside photos of attractive and unattractive people, a contrast effect occurs: Average people are seen as more attractive when seen alongside unattractive people and less attractive when seen alongside attractive people. If, however, the people judging attractiveness are told that a relationship exists between the people in the photos, the opposite effect (assimilation) occurs: Average people are now seen as less attractive when paired with unattractive people and more attractive when paired with attractive people (Melamed & Moss, 1975). Knowing this, Joseph Walther and his colleagues (Walther, Van Der Heide, Kim, Westerman, & Tong, 2008) suspected that the perceived attractiveness of Facebook users would be influenced by how attractive their friends were. To test this, the researchers set up mock Facebook profiles for average-looking college-aged males and females. Half the profiles featured photos of attractive friends and half featured photos of unattractive friends. Research participants viewed the profiles and then rated the profile owners' attractiveness. Results of the study confirmed the researchers' suspicions: In short, if you want to appear more "hot," it helps to have attractive friends on Facebook.

you think you'd have seen her face spread across the pages of makeup and lingerie ads? It seems, in fact, that the products being endorsed by attractive spokespersons do not even have to be connected with making us more attractive. Indeed, beautiful people are trying to sell us everything from milk, to law firms, to dog food.

Not surprisingly, plenty of research indicates that physical attractiveness is persuasive in contexts other than advertising (see Box 8.4). For instance, compared to their less-attractive counterparts, attractive people are judged to be happier, more intelligent, friendlier, stronger, and kinder and are thought to have better personalities, better jobs, and greater marital competence (Knapp, 1992). Attractive women get more dates, higher grades, and lighter court sentences than unattractive people. Seiter and Dunn (2000) found that it did not matter whether a woman was made to appear attractive in a pristine way (e.g., conservative clothing, makeup, and jewelry) or attractive in a sexy way (e.g., revealing clothes, heavy makeup). In both cases, she was believed more when claiming to have been sexually harassed than when she was made to appear unattractive (e.g., blotchy skin, greasy hair, no makeup). Messner, Reinhard, and Sporer (2008) found that although informing persuadees of one's intent to persuade them typically lowers compliance, if persuaders are attractive, this effect is reversed. Finally, a meta-analysis found that, compared to unattractive people, attractive ones fare better in a number of job-related outcomes including hiring, promotion, and evaluation (Hosoda, Stone-Romero, & Coats, 2003).

According to Cialdini (1993), these results may be due to a "halo effect," in which one positive characteristic of a person causes us to see everything about the person in a positive light. In other words, if the person is attractive, he or she must also be trustworthy, competent, and so forth. Whatever the case, given the preceding findings, perhaps you are wondering what physical characteristics are related to attractiveness. Although we know that standards for beauty change over time (e.g., did you know that, in medieval times, pale and plump people were perceived as the most attractive?) and that beauty is supposedly in the eye of the beholder, research tells us that some of the following characteristics are related to perceptions and/or persuasiveness:

1. Body shape: Dwayne "The Rock" Johnson, Celine Dion, and Kevin James represent the three basic body shapes. The first, a *mesomorph,* is athletic and muscular; the second, an *ectomorph* is thin and frail; and the third, an *endomorph,* is fat and round. Findings summarized by Argyle (1988) show that whereas mesomorphs are rated as, among other things, strong and adventurous; ectomorphs are seen as tense, pessimistic, and quiet; and endomorphs are seen as warm, sympathetic, agreeable, and dependent. Because of negative stereotypes, endomorphs tend to be perceived as less powerful, successful, attractive, and enthusiastic than those with different body shapes (Breseman, Lennon, & Schulz, 1999; Wade, Fuller, Bresnan, Schaefer, & Mlynarski, 2007). Moreover, endomorphs are less likely to get jobs, less likely to earn high salaries, and less likely to be accepted into colleges than thinner people with the same IQs (Argyle, 1988).

Even so, one study (Martins, Pliner, & Lee, 2004) indicated that perceptions based on body shape depend on other factors, specifically meal size. In the study, Canadian students reported their impressions of normal or overweight males and females who were portrayed as eating small or large meals. Overweight males eating large meals were perceived by all students as the least socially attractive, perhaps because they are thought to lack self-control (Martins et al., 2004). Interestingly, however, while female students perceived normal-weight females who ate small meals as the most socially attractive, male students rated normal-weight females who ate large meals as the most socially attractive. Why? The researchers suggested that males may perceive normal-weight females who eat heartily as more comfortable with themselves, more confident, and more honest (Martins et al.).

2. Facial appearance: According to Argyle (1988), faces are perceived as more attractive when they have wide cheekbones, narrow cheeks, high eyebrows, wide pupils, large smiles, noses that are not too long or too short, and eyes not too far apart or too close together. Baby-faced women are perceived as more attractive but immature by men (Berry & McArthur, 1986) and, whereas baby-faced people are cast into commercials that want to portray trustworthiness, mature-faced people are cast into commercials that want to emphasize expertise (Brownlow & Zebrowitz, 1990). Interestingly, because baby-faced speakers may look more honest (Masip, Garrido, & Herrero, 2004), they are more persuasive when their trustworthiness is questioned, while mature-faced speakers are more persuasive when their expertise is questioned (Brownlow, 1992).

3. Hair: Perceptions associated with body hair obviously change over time. Although the hippies of the 1960s rebelled by growing their hair long, today's skinheads do the same by befriending their razors. The same may be true of facial hair. For example, Disneyland, still striving for the clean-cut image, does not allow its employees to wear beards, even though some research indicates that men with beards are regarded as more masculine and mature than others (Argyle, 1988). And finally, although men supposedly prefer blondes, research shows that any color hair may be better than none. For instance, a study comparing hair loss among governors and members of Congress to the general public found that elected politicians are more likely to have a full head of hair than would be expected of men their age (Sigelman, Dawson, Nitz, & Whicker, 1990).

4. Height: Although little research has examined how height affects perceptions of women, we know that tall men seem to have an advantage. According to Argyle's (1988) sources, the taller candidate usually becomes president, taller men are more likely to get jobs, and men over 6 feet 2 inches receive higher salaries.

Paralinguistics and Persuasion: Pump Up the Volume?

Paralinguistics, or *vocalics,* is the study of vocal stimuli aside from spoken words. It includes such elements as pitch, rate, pauses, volume, tone of voice, silences, laughs, screams, sighs, and so forth. We know from prior research that the *way* in which persons speak affects not only their credibility and how much they are liked, but also their ability to persuade. Hinkle (2001), for instance, found that when managers spoke clearly and varied their tone, employees tended to like them better. Mehrabian and Williams (1969) found that people who spoke faster, louder, and more fluently and who varied their vocal frequency and intensity were perceived as more persuasive than those who did not. Similarly, Miller, Maruyama, Beaber, and Valone (1976) found that speeches delivered at fast speeds were more persuasive than those at slow or moderate speeds, perhaps because persuaders who speak faster appear more competent and knowledgeable. Finally, Simonds, Meyer, Quinlan, & Hunt (2006) found that instructors who spoke at slow speeds were rated by their students as less credible and less nonverbally immediate than instructors who spoke at faster speeds.

Although such research indicates a rather straightforward relationship between vocal cues and persuasion, several studies suggest that to fully understand the relationship between vocalics and influence, we must consider the effect of additional variables. For example, Chebat and Chebat (1999) found that when audiences heard advertisements on topics that were not personally relevant to them, they identified with sources who were not monotone and who spoke louder. When the topic was relevant, however, speaking louder distracted audiences and resulted in less persuasion (Chebat & Chebat, 1999). Similarly, Hall (1980) and Buller and Aune (1988) found that for persuasion to occur, the optimal rate of speech may depend on both the encoding ability of the sender and the decoding ability of the receiver. Specifically, although good decoders were more likely to comply with speeches delivered at fast rates, poor decoders preferred slower rates. In a related study, Smith and Shaffer (1995) found that speeches delivered at faster rates hinder people's ability to scrutinize messages. Thus, consistent with the elaboration likelihood model (see Chapter 2), people who heard a speech delivered at a normal speed were persuaded when the speech contained strong arguments, whereas those who heard accelerated speeches were persuaded equally by strong and weak messages.

Finally, you might be interested to know that not all studies on vocalics focus exclusively on human speech. Indeed, for those of you who've been unfortunate enough to answer your telephone and find one of those eerie computer-synthesized voices selling some product on the other end, here's an interesting study. The study asked people to listen to persuasive messages spoken by either a natural human voice or a synthetic computerized voice and then measured how persuaded the people were. Surprisingly, the results indicated that the synthetic voice was just as persuasive as the human voice (Stern, Mullennix, Dyson, & Wilson, 1999). Even so, in real life we bet those computers are easier to hang up on.

SUMMARY

In this chapter we learned that persuasion is not as simple as what you say. How you say something may be just as, if not more, important. We also learned that there are many categories of nonverbal communication that affect the process of persuasion. In our examination of kinesics, for instance, we saw that people are generally more persuasive when they (1) make eye contact, (2) use facial expressions and body movements that signal relaxation and sociability, and (3) use more emblems and illustrators but fewer adaptors. Similarly, we noted that people tend to be more compliant when they are touched or approached at distances that violate their expectations, as long as the touch and distances are not perceived as being too inappropriate. Moreover, people can make themselves appear more credible, dominant, or powerful, and, in turn, affect their persuasiveness through the use of time, artifacts, or physical appearance. Those who control others' time, wear the right clothing at the right time, and are attractive tend to be more persuasive than their counterparts. Finally, various features of the voice, particularly its rate, influence how persuasive one tends to be.

ENDNOTES

1. Interestingly, people sitting 4 to 5 feet from the speaker paid more attention to the contents of the speech, whereas those sitting 1 to 2 or 14 to 15 feet away paid more attention to the appearance of the speaker.

2. Recently, expectancy violations theory has also been applied to other areas of nonverbal communication, such as touch and gaze (e.g., Burgoon, Coker, & Coker, 1986; Burgoon et al., 1992).

REFERENCES

Albert, S., & Dabbs, J. M., Jr. (1970). Physical distance and persuasion. *Journal of Personality and Social Psychology, 15,* 265–270.

Andersen, P. A. (1999). *Nonverbal communication: Forms and functions.* Mountain View, CA: Mayfield.

Andersen, P. A. (2004). Influential actions: Nonverbal communication and persuasion. In J. S. Seiter & R. H. Gass (Eds.), *Readings in persuasion, social influence, and compliance gaining* (pp. 165–180). Boston: Allyn & Bacon.

Argyle, M. (1988). *Bodily communication* (2nd ed.). Madison, CT: International Universities Press.

Atkins, C. P., & Kent, R. L. (1988). What do recruits consider important during the employment interview? *Journal of Employment Counseling, 25,* 98–103.

Baron, R. A., & Bell, P. A. (1976). Physical distance and helping: Some unexpected benefits of "crowding in" on others. *Journal of Applied Social Psychology, 6,* 95–104.

Berry, D. S., & McArthur, L. Z. (1986). Perceiving character in faces: The impact of age-related craniofacial changes on social perception. *Psychological Bulletin, 100,* 3–18.

Bickman, L. (1974). The social power of a uniform. *Journal of Applied Social Psychology, 4,* 47–61.

Booth-Butterfield, M., & Noguchi, T. (2000). Students' perceptions of teachers' nonverbal behavior: Comparisons of American and international students' classroom response. *Communication Research Reports, 17*(3), 288–298.

Brehm, J. W. (1966). *A theory of psychological reactance.* New York: Academic Press.

Brehm, S. S., & Brehm, J. W. (1981). *Psychological reactance: A theory of freedom and control.* New York: Academic Press.

Breseman, B.C., Lennon, S. J., & Schulz, T. L. (1999). Obesity and powerlessness. In K. K. P. Johnson & S. J. Lennon (Eds.), *Appearance and power* (pp. 173–197). New York: Berg.

Brownlow, S. (1992). Seeing is believing: Facial appearance, credibility and attitude change. *Journal of Nonverbal Behavior, 16,* 101–115.

Brownlow, S., & Zebrowitz, L. A. (1990). Facial appearance, gender, and credibility in television commercials. *Journal of Nonverbal Behavior, 14,* 51–60.

Brucks, W. W., Reips, U., & Ryf, B. (2007). Group norms, physical distance, and ecological efficiency in common pool resource management. *Social Influence, 2,* 112–135.

Buller, D. B., & Aune, R. K. (1988). The effects of vocalics and nonverbal sensitivity on compliance: A speech accommodation theory explanation. *Human Communication Research, 14,* 301–332.

Buller, D. B., & Street, R. L., Jr. (1992). Physician–patient relationships. In R. S. Feldman (Ed.), *Applications of nonverbal behavioral theories and research* (pp. 119–142). Hillsdale, NJ: Erlbaum.

Burgoon, J. K. (1978). A communication model of personal space violations: Explications and an initial test. *Human Communication Research, 4,* 129–142.

Burgoon, J. K. (1992). Applying a comparative approach to nonverbal expectancy violation theory. In J. Blumler, K. E. Rosengren, & J. M. McLeod (Eds.), *Comparatively speaking: Communication and culture across space and time* (pp. 53–69). Newbury Park, CA: Sage.

Burgoon, J. K. (1994). Nonverbal signals. In M. L. Knapp & G. R. Miller (Eds.), *Handbook of interpersonal communication* (2nd ed., pp. 229–285). Thousand Oaks, CA: Sage.

Burgoon, J. K., Buller, D. B., & Woodall, W. G. (1996). *Nonverbal communication: The unspoken dialogue* (3rd ed.). New York: McGraw-Hill.

Burgoon, J. K., Coker, D. A., & Coker, R. A. (1986). Communicative effects of gaze behavior: A test of two contrasting explanations. *Human Communication Research, 12,* 495–524.

Burgoon, J. K., & Dillman, L. (1995). Gender, immediacy, and nonverbal communication. In P. J. Kalbfleisch & M. J. Cody (Eds.), *Gender, power, and communication in human relationships* (pp. 63–82). Hillsdale, NJ: Erlbaum.

Chartrand, T. K., & Bargh, J. A. (1999). The chameleon effect: The perception-behavior link and social interaction. *Journal of Personality and Social Psychology, 76,* 893–910.

Chebat, C. G., & Chebat, J. C. (1999). Impact of voice on source credibility in advertising: A self-monitoring approach. *North American Journal of Psychology, 1*(2), 323–342.

Cialdini, R. B. (1993). *Influence: Science and practice* (3rd ed.). New York: HarperCollins.

Comadena, M. E., Hunt, S. K., & Simonds, C. J. (2007). The effects of teacher clarity, nonverbal immediacy, and caring on student motivation, affective and cognitive learning. *Communication Research Reports, 24,* 241–248.

Ekman, P., & Friesen, W. V. (1969). The repertoire of nonverbal behavior: Categories, origins, usage, and coding. *Semiotica, 1,* 49–98.

Field, A. (1996, February). Outsmart your supermarket. *McCall's, 123,* 114–115.

Fisher, J. D., Rytting, M., & Heslin, R. (1976). Hands touching hands: Affective and evaluative effects of an interpersonal touch. *Sociometry, 39,* 416–421.

Floyd, K., & Burgoon, J. K. (1999). Reacting to nonverbal expressions of liking: A test of interaction adaption theory. *Communication Monographs, 66,* 219–239.

Forbes, R. J., & Jackson, P. R. (1980). Non-verbal behaviour and the outcome of selection interviews. *Journal of Occupational Psychology, 53,* 65–72.

Goffman, E. (1959). *The presentation of self in everyday life.* Garden City, NY: Anchor/Doubleday.

Goldberg, C., & Cohen, D. J. (2004). Walking the walk and talking the talk: Gender differences in the impact of interviewing skills on applicant assessments. *Group & Organization Management, 29*(3), 369–384.

Gorham, J., Cohen, S. H., & Morris, T. L. (1999). Fashion in the classroom III: Effects of instructor attire and immediacy in natural classroom interactions. *Communication Quarterly, 47*(3), 281–299.

Guéguen, N. (2007). Courtship compliance: The effect of touch on women's behavior. *Social Influence, 2,* 81–97.

Guéguen, N., & De Gail, M. (2003). The effect of smiling on helping behavior: Smiling and good Samaritan behavior. *Communication Reports, 16*(2), 133–140.

Guéguen, N., & Fischer-Lokou, J. (2003). Tactile contact and spontaneous help: An evaluation in a natural setting. *Journal of Social Psychology, 143,* 785–787.

Guéguen, N., & Fischer-Lokou, J. (2004). Hitchhikers' smiles and receipt of help. *Psychology Reports, 94,* 756–760.

Guéguen, N., & Jacob, C. (2002). Direct look versus evasive glance and compliance with a request. *Journal of Social Psychology, 142,* 393–396.

Guéguen, N., Jacob, C., & Boulbry, G. (2007). The effect of touch on compliance with a restaurant's employee suggestion. *Hospitality Management, 26,* 1019–1023.

Hall, J. A. (1980). Voice tone and persuasion. *Journal of Personality and Social Psychology, 38,* 924–934.

Hensley, W. E. (1981). The effects of attire, location, and sex on aiding behavior: A similarity explanation. *Journal of Nonverbal Behavior, 6,* 3–11.

Hinkle, L. L. (1999). Nonverbal immediacy communication behaviors and liking in marital relationships. *Communication Research Reports, 16,* 16–26.

Hinkle, L. L. (2001). Perceptions of supervisor nonverbal immediacy, vocalics, and subordinate liking. *Communication Research Reports, 18,* 128–136.

Hornick, J. (1992). Tactile stimulation and consumer response. *Journal of Consumer Research, 19,* 449–458.

Hosoda, M., Stone-Romero, E. F., & Coats, G. (2003). The effects of physical attractiveness on job-related outcomes: A meta-analysis of experimental studies. *Personnel Psychology, 56,* 431–462.

Howard, D. J., Shu, S. B., & Kerin, R. A. (2007). Reference price and scarcity appeals and the use of multiple influence strategies in retail newspaper advertising. *Social Influence, 2,* 18–28.

Johnson, K. K. P., & Workman, J. E. (1991). The role of cosmetics in impression formation. *Clothing and Textiles Research Journal, 10*(1), 630–667.

Karremans, J. C., & Verwijmeren, T. (2008). Mimicking attractive opposite-sex others: The role of romantic relationship status. *Personality and Social Psychology Bulletin, 34,* 939–950.

Kaufman, D., & Mahoney, J. M. (1999). The effect of waitress touch on alcohol consumption in dyads. *Journal of Social Psychology, 139,* 261–267.

Kleinke, C. L. (1977). Compliance to requests made by gazing and touching experimenters in field settings. *Journal of Experimental Social Psychology, 13,* 218–223.

Kleinke, C. L. (1980). Interaction between gaze and legitimacy of request on compliance in a field setting. *Journal of Nonverbal Behavior, 5,* 3–12.

Knapp, M. L. (1992). *Nonverbal communication in human interaction* (3rd ed.). New York: Holt, Rinehart Winston.

Krumhuber, E., Manstead, A. S. R., & Kappas, A. (2007). Temporal aspects of facial displays in person and expression perception: The effects of smile dynamics, head-tilt, and gender. *Journal of Nonverbal Behavior, 31,* 39–56.

LaFrance, M., & Hecht, M. A. (1995). Why smiles generate leniency. *Personality and Social Psychology Bulletin, 21*(3), 297–314.

Lawrence, S., & Watson, M. (1991). Getting others to help: The effectiveness of professional uniforms in charitable fund raising. *Journal of Applied Communication Research, 19,* 170–185.

Leathers, D. G. (1997). *Successful nonverbal communication* (3rd ed.). Boston: Allyn & Bacon.

Maddux, W. W., Mullen, E. & Galinsky, A. D. (2008). Chameleons bake bigger pies and take bigger pieces: Strategic behavioral mimicry facilitates negotiation outcomes. *Journal of Experimental Social Psychology, 44,* 461–468.

Maricchiolo, F., Gnisci, A., Bonaiuto, M. & Ficca, G. (2009). Effects of different types of hand gestures in persuasive speech on receivers' evaluations. *Language and Cognitive Processes, 24,* 239–266.

Martin, E. J. (2000, December 3). "Home's looks-both good and bad-can be deceiving." *Los Angeles Times,* p. K4.

Martins, Y., Pliner, P., & Lee, C. (2004). The effects of meal size and body size on individuals' impressions of males and females. *Eating Behaviors, 5*(2), 117–132.

Masip, J., Garrido, E., & Herrero, C. (2004). Facial appearance and impressions of credibility: The effects of facial babyishness and age on person perception. *International Journal of Psychology, 39*(4), 276–289.

Maslow, C., Yoselson, K., & London, H. (1971). Persuasiveness of confidence expressed via language and body language. *British Journal of Social and Clinical Psychology, 10,* 234–240.

McGinley, H., LeFevre, R., & McGinley, P. (1975). The influence of a communicator's body position on opinion change in others. *Journal of Personality and Social Psychology, 31,* 686–690.

McGuire, W. J. (1968). Personality and susceptibility to social influence. In E. G. Borgatta & W. W. Lambert (Eds.), *Handbook of personality theory and research* (pp. 1130–1187). Chicago: Rand McNally.

Mehrabian, A., & Williams, M. (1969). Nonverbal concomitants of perceived and intended persuasiveness. *Journal of Personality and Social Psychology, 13,* 37–58.

Melamed, L., & Moss, M. K. (1975). The effect of context on ratings of attractiveness of photographs. *Journal of Psychology, 90,* 129–136.

Messner, M., Reinhard, M., & Sporer, S. L. (2008). Compliance through direct persuasive appeals: The moderating role of communicator's attractiveness in interpersonal persuasion. *Social Influence, 3,* 67–83.

Meyer, M. (1997, August). Outsmart your supermarket and save. *Good Housekeeping, 225,* 147.

Miller, N., Maruyama, G., Beaber, R. J., & Valone, K. (1976). Speed of speech and persuasion. *Journal of Personality and Social Psychology, 34,* 615–624.

Moon, Y. (1999). The effects of physical distance and response latency on persuasion in computer-mediated communication and human–computer communication. *Journal of Experimental Psychology: Applied, 5*(4), 379–392.

Murphy, N. A. (2007). Appearing smart: The impression management of intelligence, person perception accuracy, and behavior in social interaction. *Personality and Social Psychology Bulletin, 33,* 325–339.

Nannberg, J. C., & Hansen, C. (1994). Post-compliance touch: An incentive for task performance. *Journal of Social Psychology, 134,* 301–307.

Patterson, M. L., Powell, J. L., & Lenihan, M. G. (1986). Touch, compliance and interpersonal affect. *Journal of Nonverbal Behavior, 10,* 41–50.

Peck, J., & Childers, T. L. (2003a). To have and to hold: The influence of haptic information on product judgments. *Journal of Marketing, 67,* 35–48.

Peck, J., & Childers, T. L. (2003b). Individual differences in haptic information processing: The "Need for Touch" Scale. *Journal of Consumer Research, 30,* 430–442.

Peck, J., & Wiggins, J. (2005). It just feels good: Customers' affective response to touch and its influence on persuasion. *Journal of Marketing, 70,* 56–69.

Petty, R. E., & Cacioppo, J. T. (1986). *Communication and persuasion: Central and peripheral routes to attitude change.* New York: Springer-Verlag.

Petty, R. E., Wells, G. L., Heesacker, M., Brock, T., & Cacioppo, J. T. (1983). The effects of recipient posture on persuasion: A cognitive response analysis. *Personality and Social Psychology Bulletin, 9,* 209–222.

Robinson, J. D., Seiter, J. S., & Acharya, L. (1992, February). *"I just put my head down and society does the rest." An examination of influence strategies among beggars.* Paper presented at the annual meeting of the Western Speech Communication Association, Boise, ID.

Roser, C. (1990). Involvement, attention and perceptions of message relevance in the response to persuasive appeals. *Communication Research, 17,* 571–600.

Roser, C., & Thompson, M. (1995). Fear appeals and the formation of active publics. *Journal of Communication, 45,* 103–121.

Rucker, M., Anderson, E., & Kangas, A. (1999). Clothing, power, and the workplace. In K. K. P. Johnson & S. J. Lennon (Eds.), *Appearance and power* (pp. 59–78). New York: Berg.

Saigh, P. A. (1981). Effects of nonverbal examiner praise on selected WAIS subtest performance of Lebanese undergraduate. *Journal of Nonverbal Behavior, 6,* 84–86.

Schlenker, B. R. (1980). *Impression management.* Monterey, CA: Brooks/Cole.

Segrin, C. (1993). The effects of nonverbal behavior on outcomes of compliance gaining attempts. *Communication Studies, 44,* 169–187.

Seiter, J. S. (1999). Does communicating nonverbal disagreement during an opponent's speech affect the credibility of the debater in the background? *Psychological Reports, 84,* 855–861.

Seiter, J. S. (2001). Silent derogation and perceptions of deceptiveness: Does communicating nonverbal disbelief during an opponent's speech affect perceptions of debaters' veracity? *Communication Research Reports, 18*(4), 334–344.

Seiter, J. S., Abraham, J. A., & Nakagama, B. T. (1998). Split-screen versus single-screen formats in televised debates: Does access to an opponent's nonverbal behaviors affect viewers' perceptions of a speaker's credibility? *Perceptual and Motor Skills, 86,* 491–497.

Seiter, J. S., & Dunn, D. (2000). Beauty and believability in sexual harassment cases: Does physical attractiveness affect perceptions of veracity and the likelihood of being harassed? *Communication Research Reports, 17*(2), 203–209.

Seiter, J. S., & Hatch, S. (2005). Effects of tattoos on perceptions of credibility and attractiveness. *Psychological Reports, 96,* 1113–1120.

Seiter, J. S., & Sandry, A. (2003). Pierced for success?: The effects of ear and nose piercing on perceptions of job candidates' credibility, attractiveness, and hirability. *Communication Research Reports, 20*(4), 287–298.

Seiter, J. S., & Weger, H. (2005). Audience perceptions of candidates' appropriateness as a function of nonverbal behaviors displayed during televised political debates. *Journal of Social Psychology, 145*(2), 225–235.

Seiter, J. S., Weger, H., Kinzer, H. J., & Jensen, A. S. (2009). Impression management in televised debates: The effect of background nonverbal behavior on audience perceptions of debaters' likeability. *Communication Research Reports, 26,* 1–11.

Sigelman, L., Dawson, E., Nitz, M., & Whicker, M. L. (1990). Hair loss and electability: The bald truth. *Journal of Nonverbal Behavior, 14,* 269–283.

Simonds, B. K., Meyer, K. R., Quinlan, M. M., & Hunt, S. (2006). Effects of instructor speech rate on student affective learning, recall, and perceptions of nonverbal immediacy, credibility, and clarity. *Communication Research Reports, 23*, 187–197.

Smith, R. J., & Knowles, E. S. (1979). Affective and cognitive mediators of reactions to spatial invasions. *Journal of Experimental Social Psychology, 15*, 437–452.

Smith, S. M., & Shaffer, D. R. (1995). Speed of speech and persuasion: Evidence for multiple effects. *Personality and Social Psychology Bulletin, 21*(10), 1051–1060.

Stern, S. E., Mullennix, J. W., Dyson, C., & Wilson, S. J. (1999). The persuasiveness of synthetic speech versus human speech. *Human Factors, 41*(4), 588–595.

Swami, V., & Furnham, A. (2007) Unattractive, promiscuous and heavy drinkers: Perceptions of women with tattoos. *Body Image, 4,* 343–352.

Tandingan, R. (2001, October 5). *Persuasion at the supermarket.* Retrieved from www.uoregon.edu/~bfmalle/sp/romila3.html.

Tanner, R. J., Ferraro, R., Chartrand, T. L., Bettman, J. R., & Van Baaren, R. (2007). Of chameleons and consumption: The impact of mimicry on choice and preferences. *Journal of Consumer Research, 34*, 754–766.

Tedeschi, J. T., & Reiss, M. (1981). Identities, the phenomenal self, and laboratory research. In Tedeschi, J. T. (Ed.), *Impression management theory and social psychological research* (pp. 3–22). New York: Academic Press.

Teven, J. J. (2007). Effects of supervisor social influence, nonverbal immediacy, and biological sex on subordinates' perceptions of job satisfaction, liking, and supervisor credibility. *Communication Quarterly, 55*, 155–177.

Teven, J. J., & Comadena, M. E. (1996). The effects of office aesthetic quality on students' perceptions of teacher credibility and communicator style. *Communication Research Reports, 13*(1), 101–108.

Tom, G. Ramil, E. Zapanta, I., Demir, K., & Lopez, S. (2006). The role of overt head movement and attention in persuasion. *The Journal of Psychology, 140*, 247–253.

Turman, P. D. (2008). Coaches' immediacy behaviors as predictors of athletes' perceptions of satisfaction and team cohesion. *Western Journal of Communication, 72*, 162–179.

Vaidis, D. C. F., & Halimi-Falkowicz, S. G. M. (2008). Increasing compliance with a request: Two touches are more effective than one. *Psychological Reports, 103*, 88–92.

Wade, T. J., Fuller, L., Bresnan, J., Schaefer, S., & Mlynarski, L. (2007). Weight halo effects: Individual differences in personality evaluations and perceived life success of men as a function of weight. *Personality and Individual Differences, 42*, 317–324.

Walther, J. B., Van Der Heide, B., Kim, S., Westerman, D., & Tong, S. T. (2008). The role of friends' appearance and behavior on evaluations of individuals on Facebook: Are we known by the company we keep? *Human Communication Research, 34*, 28–49.

Washburn, P. V., & Hakel, M. D. (1973). Visual cues and verbal content as influences on impressions formed after simulated employment interviews. *Journal of Applied Psychology, 58,* 137–141.

Webbink, P. (1986). *The power of the eyes.* New York: Springer-Verlag.

Wells, G. L., & Petty, R. E. (1980). The effects of overt head movements on persuasion: Compatibility and incompatibility of response. *Basic and Applied Social Psychology, 1*, 210–230.

Willis, F. N., & Hamm, H. K. (1980). The use of interpersonal touch in securing compliance. *Journal of Nonverbal Behavior, 5,* 49–55.

Woodall, W. G., & Folger, J. P. (1981). Encoding specificity and nonverbal cue context: An expansion of episodic memory research. *Communication Monographs, 48,* 39–53.

CHAPTER 9

Structuring and Ordering Persuasive Messages

The study of persuasion and the study of rhetoric, if not one and the same, are closely related. Aristotle, for instance, defined *rhetoric* as "the faculty of discovering all the available means of persuasion." Although, today the term "rhetoric" is often used in conjunction with words such as "empty" or "meaningless," the connotations surrounding the term were not always so negative. The ancient Greeks and Romans, for example, considered rhetoric an essential ingredient in a good education. By the time the great Roman orator Cicero wrote about rhetoric, its study was divided into five parts. Four were called *inventio, elocutio, memoria,* and *pronuntiatio,* which focused on finding and inventing arguments, speaking with style, remembering arguments, and delivering speeches effectively. The last part, *dispositio,* focused on selecting the most important arguments and ideas and on the effective and orderly arrangements of those ideas and arguments (Corbett, 1971). Quintilian, another Roman rhetorician, noted the significance of strategically planning and organizing a persuasive message. As Corbett (1971) wrote:

> Quintilian hints at the more important concern of disposition when he says that it is to oratory what generalship is to war. It would be folly to hold a general to a fixed, predetermined disposition of his forces. He must be left free to distribute his troops in the order and proportion best suited to cope with the situation in which he may find himself at any particular moment. So he will mass some of his troops at one point on the battle line, thin them out at other points, keep other troops in reserve, and perhaps concentrate his crack troops at the most crucial area. Guided by judgment and imagination, the general stands ready to make whatever adjustments in strategy eventualities may dictate. (pp. 299–300)

Clearly, when planning a persuasive message, we are often confronted with questions of strategy such as "What should I leave in, and what should I leave out?" "How should I arrange my arguments?" and "Should my strongest arguments come first or last?" However, in addition to questions concerning the order of arguments within persuasive messages, there is the issue of the sequencing of messages when more than one persuader is involved. For example, imagine that you are about to speak to a large audience and want to convince that audience to lower tuition at your school. You know that after you've spoken, another person will argue just the opposite: Tuition should be raised. Is there anything you can do to make your opponent's arguments less powerful? In this chapter we examine these issues.

IMPLICIT AND EXPLICIT CONCLUSIONS: LET ME SPELL IT OUT FOR YOU

According to Kardes, Kim, and Lim (1994), one of the key decisions facing advertisers is whether a hard-sell or a soft-sell strategy is best. One type of hard-sell strategy is to draw *explicit conclusions* for your audience. In other words, when employing an explicit conclusions approach, any claim that is made in a message is directly stated by the person sending the message (e.g., you should buy our product, our product is simply the best). In contrast, one type of soft-sell strategy involves the use of implicit conclusions. Here the persuader is more subtle, allowing persuadees to reach their own conclusions without being told what to do or believe (Kardes et al., 1994). For example, consider the following ad discussed by Sawyer (1988):

> A commercial ... begins when a perky young woman comes on the screen and says, "I've got a question. Pay attention, there will be a quiz later. People prefer their hamburgers at home and flame-broiled. Now, if McDonald's and Wendy's *fry* their hamburgers and Burger King *flame-broils* theirs ... where do you think people should go for a hamburger? (p. 159)

In this advertisement, an implicit conclusions approach is used because customers are allowed to make their own inferences (in this case, "People should go to Burger King!"). Had the spokesperson said, "People should go to Burger King!" the ad would have been an example of one using an explicit conclusion approach.

An obvious question facing persuasion researchers concerns whether there is an advantage to using one approach over the other (i.e., do implicit conclusions work best or vice versa?). According to Kardes and colleagues (1994), both approaches have potential risks and benefits. For instance, although explicit conclusions involve the use of very simple and straightforward claims, receivers could resent being told what to believe and might distrust the message. However, although people may perceive implicit conclusions as more valid because they came up with the conclusions themselves, they might fail to draw the desired conclusions or might draw the wrong conclusions altogether (Kardes et al., 1994).

Until recently, persuasion scholars have argued that explicit conclusions are more effective than implicit ones. For example, at least two studies (Fine, 1957; Hovland & Mandell, 1952) revealed that messages with explicit conclusions were more persuasive than those that led subjects to draw their own conclusions. Even so, sometimes implicit conclusions may be more effective. For instance, consistent with Petty and Cacioppo's (1986) elaboration likelihood model (ELM), Sawyer and Howard (1991) argued that when a message is personally relevant to a person, that person should be more motivated to draw his or her own conclusions. Thus, compared to people who are not personally involved with a topic, those who are should be more persuaded by an implicit conclusions approach. To test this hypothesis, Sawyer and Howard asked subjects to look at advertisements that used either implicit or explicit claims about disposable razors and toothbrushes. To make the ads more personally relevant, some of the subjects viewing the toothbrush ads were told that as a free gift for their participation, they would be allowed to choose from several brands of toothbrushes, including the one shown in the ad. However, to make the ads less personally relevant, other subjects viewing the toothbrush ads were told that they would get to choose a free razor. (Similarly, subjects watching razor ads were told they'd be choosing either razors or toothbrushes, depending on whether they were in the "relevant" or "nonrelevant" conditions.) The results of the study confirmed the researchers' hypothesis. Specifically, when subjects viewed ads that were personally relevant, they were more persuaded by implicit conclusions. For those watching ads that were not relevant, it did not matter whether implicit or explicit conclusions were used.

In a similar study, Kardes and colleagues (1994) found that it is better to let receivers draw their own conclusions about a product when the receivers have a lot of knowledge about that type of product (i.e., CD players). However, for people with little knowledge about the product type, it is more persuasive to include explicit conclusions in a message. Finally, Martin, Lang, and Wong (2003/2004) found that people high in the need for cognition (see Chapter 6) prefer implicit to explicit conclusions. In short, when trying to decide whether to draw conclusions for an audience, it is most important to know what type of person is in the audience.

GAIN-FRAMED VERSUS LOSS-FRAMED MESSAGES: KEEP ON THE SUNNY SIDE?

Imagine for a moment that one of those deadly swine or avian flu viruses has swept into your neighborhood and is predicted to kill 600 people if something is not done quickly. If you were in charge and given the following choices, which action would you choose?

> Action 1: guarantees that 200 of the 600 people will be saved.
>
> Action 2: gives a 33.3 percent chance that all 600 people will be saved and a 66.6 percent chance that no one will be saved.

> Got your answer?

If you are like the majority of people in a classic study conducted by Amos Tversky and Daniel Kahneman (1981), you picked Action 1. Interestingly, however, another group of people were presented with exactly the same scenario, with the options worded in a slightly different way:

> Action 1: guarantees that 400 of the 600 people will die.
>
> Action 2: gives a 33.3 percent chance that no one will die and a 66.6 percent chance that everyone will die.

Notice the difference? The first pair of actions look on the brighter side by focusing on how many lives will be saved, while the second pair of actions portray the glass half empty by focusing on how many will die. Persuasion scholars refer to messages like the first pair as *gain-framed* and messages like the second pair as *loss-framed*. And it turns out that such framing of messages can make a big difference. Indeed, the majority of people in the second group chose Action 2. In other words, simply reframing the message to focus on losses rather than gains reversed the choices people made!

How might these results be explained? Apparently, people fear losses much more than they prefer gains. As such, they are willing to take greater risks in order to avoid or recoup their losses (Tversky & Kahneman, 1981). Indeed, one of the authors, who enjoys playing poker, has noticed this effect many times at the tables; inexperienced players who are losing will often "loosen up," playing weaker cards and taking more chances in an effort to get lucky and get even before it's time to go home.

Previous research suggests that this tendency to take more risks in order to avoid losses has important implications for the use of loss- and gain-framed messages in health-related contexts (see Salovey, Schneider, & Apanovitch, 2002; Schneider, 2006). For example, because people may perceive disease-detecting behaviors (e.g., mammography, HIV screening) as risky in the sense that such behaviors might reveal something that is feared, using loss-framed messages may be a more effective way to motivate people to follow through on preventive medical check-ups. A doctor, for instance, might tell a patient, "If you don't detect cancer early, you narrow your options for treatment." In contrast, because people may perceive disease-preventing behaviors (e.g., wearing sunscreen, exercising) as less risky, using gain-framed messages may be more effective. For instance, a doctor might offer a health affirming message such as, "Eating a lot of veggies will help you maintain your good health."

Recent research (O'Keefe & Jensen, 2007) using meta-analysis suggests that, while gain-framed appeals are indeed more effective than loss-framed appeals when trying to promote dental hygiene, there were no differences between the effectiveness of loss- and gain-framed appeals for other preventive actions (e.g., safer sex behaviors, diet behaviors). With this in mind, Latimer, Salovey, and Rothman (2007) suggested that more research is necessary to identify the conditions under which gain-framed appeals are most effective. For example, because gain-framed appeals lead people to process and scrutinize messages more than do loss-framed messages (O'Keefe & Jensen, 2008), perhaps they are only effective under certain conditions (e.g., when arguments are strong).

QUANTITY VERSUS QUALITY OF ARGUMENTS: THE MORE THE MERRIER?

What are you going to have for your next dinner? If given the choice between an all-you–can-eat buffet and a fancy French restaurant, which would you pick? We imagine your answer depends on whether you like to treat your taste buds or fill your belly. Indeed, buffets usually offer lots of mediocre food, while a good French restaurant typically promises small portions of really tasty food. What appeals to you more than likely depends on your priorities.

The same is probably true of persuasive messages. For some people, it is the *quantity* of arguments presented that counts. For them, a "kitchen sink" approach in which an advocate throws in every available argument works best. For other people, it is the *quality* of arguments that counts. For such people, the number of arguments is inconsequential. They require "gourmet" arguments. To illustrate this notion, we return briefly to Petty and Cacioppo's (1986) elaboration likelihood model (ELM), which we discussed in more detail in Chapter 2.

Recall that, according to the ELM, there are two routes to persuasion: the peripheral route and the central route. First, when people are persuaded by a message that they have carefully scrutinized, they are being persuaded via the central route (of course, after scrutinizing a message, they may also remain unpersuaded). Sometimes, however, people do not scrutinize the persuasive messages they receive. For example, they may not have the ability or the motivation to think about the message. Even if that happens, however, they may still be persuaded via the peripheral route. For example, if there is some easy way for them to decide to be persuaded, they may very well change their attitude or behavior. If there is no "easy" cue, however, they will not be persuaded (Petty & Cacioppo, 1986).

According to Petty and Cacioppo (1984), one type of peripheral cue may be the number of arguments that a persuader uses. These researchers reasoned that some people might decide that a persuasive message containing a lot of arguments must be a lot better than one that does not ("It must be a good argument! Look at all those reasons!"). Of course, not all people would be persuaded by a lot of weak arguments. People who carefully scrutinized the arguments, they hypothesized, would not be fooled. Results of one study (Petty & Cacioppo, 1984) supported this hypothesis. Specifically, when people were not involved in a topic, the quality of the arguments they heard did not matter. Quantity did though. They tended to be persuaded by a lot of arguments, even if the arguments were weak. In contrast, when people were involved in the topic they were not taken in by a lot of weak arguments. They were persuaded only when strong arguments were used, especially when there were a lot of strong arguments (Petty & Cacioppo, 1984) (see Figure 9.1). The moral of this line of research, then, is the following: If you think your audience will

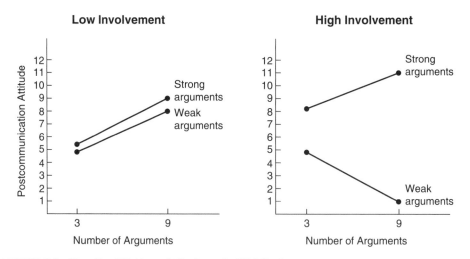

FIGURE 9.1   Results of Petty and Cacioppo's 1994 Study.

From Petty, R. E., & Cacioppo, J. T. (1984). The effects of involvement on responses to argument quantity and quality: Central and peripheral routes to persuasion. *Journal of Personality and Social Psychology, 46,* 69–81. Copyright © 1984 by the American Psychological Association. Reprinted with permission.

scrutinize your message, use strong arguments, but if your audience does not seem involved in the topic, a smorgasbord of arguments may be quite effective.

THE USE OF EVIDENCE: THE PROOF'S NOT IN THE PUDDING

Different persuasive claims require different types of proof. One common form of proof is evidence. Evidence comes in many forms including narratives, personal anecdotes, statistics, quotations, testimonials, graphs and charts, and more. Physical evidence may be offered as well (e.g., lipstick on a collar, a "smoking gun" memo). As a general rule, evidence facilitates persuasion. A meta-analysis by Reinard (1988) demonstrates that as long as the evidence is relevant to the claim being made, evidence is almost always persuasive. As is the case with the quantity versus quality of arguments discussed above, the quantity of evidence matters more when receivers have low involvement, whereas the quality of evidence matters more when receivers have high involvement.

Evidence sometimes functions as a peripheral cue. For example, a prosecutor might pile up a "mountain" of evidence against a defendant. The sheer quantity of evidence may seem so great that jurors infer that the defendant must be guilty. However, evidence is put to best use when receivers rely on central processing (Reynolds & Reynolds, 2002). A meta-analysis by Stiff (1986) revealed a significant positive correlation between evidence use and attitude change, especially when receivers were involved in the topic or issue.

Another benefit of using evidence is that it tends to increase a source's perceived credibility (O'Keefe, 1998). Reinard (1988) found a "ceiling effect" for the persuasiveness of evidence. If a source already has very high credibility, evidence won't help. Most everyday persuaders, however, need all the help they can get. Unless you are the foremost expert in the world on an issue, go ahead and include high-quality evidence, and lots of it, in your persuasive message.

One question that has been raised regarding evidence is whether narrative evidence is superior to statistics or quantitative evidence. At first glance, it would appear that the research findings are inconsistent. Some studies have found narratives to be more effective than statistics (Brosius & Bathelt, 1994), while other studies found the reverse to be the case (Dickson, 1982; Hoeken & Hustinx, 2003). A comprehensive meta-analysis by Allen and Preiss (1997) concluded that there was an overall advantage in using statistical proof rather than anecdotal proof.

There is, however, a twist. In most controlled laboratory studies, the participants are instructed to concentrate on the arguments and evidence contained in a persuasive message. Thus, their involvement tends to be high. Braverman (2008) wondered whether the comparative effectiveness of narrative versus statistical evidence might hinge on the amount of receiver involvement. Her hunch was correct. She found that when receiver involvement is low, narratives are more persuasive. When receiver involvement is high, statistics are more persuasive. This finding is consistent with the ELM.

Finally, and importantly, a persuader can have it both ways. Reinard (1988) suggests that an advocate combine narrative and statistical evidence for maximum effect. For example, a persuader might begin with a narrative example. The persuader would then go on to cite statistics demonstrating that the narrative example was not an isolated case. A compelling narrative might hit listeners in the heart or gut. Compelling statistics might hit them in their noggin.

REPETITION AND MERE EXPOSURE: YOU CAN SAY THAT AGAIN

Although earlier we saw that using a lot of arguments in a message can sometimes make you more persuasive, what happens if you use the *same* argument or message a lot of times? Stated differently, can repeating your message make you more persuasive? Several researchers have argued that repetition can be an effective tactic, although there is some disagreement concerning why. One perspective that has received considerable attention by persuasion scholars is known as the *mere exposure effect* (Zajonc, 1968). According to Sawyer (1981), "This theory hypothesizes that familiar objects are more liked than less familiar ones, and that by merely being repetitively exposed, something initially unfamiliar will be looked upon more favorably" (p. 238). In other words, mere exposure theory suggests that we really do "*acquire* tastes," that things can "grow on us," and that "familiarity does *not* breed contempt." By way of example, previous research has found that people's faces are rated as more likable (Rhodes, Halberstadt, & Brajkovich, 2001) and attractive (Peskin & Newell, 2004) after repeated viewing, suggesting that the old saying "love at first sight" should be reconsidered. Research also suggests that the effect might generalize to other, similar faces. For instance, one study found that, compared to White participants who had not been exposed to images of Black and Asian people's faces, those who had been exposed reported greater liking for a different set of Black and Asian faces (Zebrowitz, White, & Wieneke, 2008).

In one of our favorite classic studies, Zajonc (1968) found that repeated exposure even made the Chinese language more likable to people who didn't know how to read or speak it. In the study, subjects saw pictures of Chinese characters anywhere from 1 to 25 times. Afterward, the subjects were asked to guess the meanings of the characters. Interestingly, the characters that were seen most often were "defined" in much more positive ways than were the characters that were seen less often. With this in mind, it's not surprising to us that politicians pepper front yards, telephone poles, bumpers, and just about anything they can get their hands on with their names and faces.

Although research has shown that mere and repeated exposure to songs, people, languages, and posters may increase likability, there has been some disagreement about whether repeating longer or more complex messages is persuasive. For example, although Petty and Cacioppo (1979) found that strong messages were more persuasive after being heard three times than after being heard one time, Garcia-Marques and Mackie (2001) found that strong arguments were most persuasive after being heard just once.

How might this inconsistency be explained? According to a study by Claypool and her colleagues (Claypool, Mackie, Garcia-Marques, McIntosh, & Udall, 2004), the impact of repetition depends on how personally relevant the message is to the audience. Earlier, for example, we discussed a study involving messages about comprehensive exams. For students who thought they might have to take the exams, the messages were personally relevant. The opposite was true of those who thought they would never take the exams.

Claypool and her colleagues found that when people were presented with a familiar message that was not personally relevant to them, they were likely to respond to the message nonanalytically (analogous to peripheral processing in the ELM). In other words, rather than actively think about the message, the people responded to it merely on the basis of previously stored information. As a result, repetition did not increase the persuasiveness of strong over weak arguments.

On the other hand, when the people were presented with a familiar message that was personally relevant to them, they were likely to process the message analytically (this is analogous to ELM's central route to persuasion). Because repetition provided them with more opportunities to scrutinize the message, strong messages were more persuasive than weak ones when they were repeated (Claypool et al., 2004). In short, like other studies we have seen so far, the research on repetition illustrates the importance of knowing your audience before trying to persuade it.

ORDER EFFECTS AND PERSUASION: FIRST THINGS FIRST

In the preceding sections, we've seen that strong arguments are not always the most persuasive and that people are generally more willing to hear a strong argument repeated rather than a weak one. Sometimes, however, it is not so easy to separate strong from weak arguments. In other words, persuasive messages often contain many arguments, some stronger than others. When that happens, whoever is delivering the persuasive message must decide how he or she should arrange the arguments. For example, imagine you're planning to give a persuasive speech. Should you begin with your strongest argument to create a favorable first impression? Or would it be better to dazzle your audience at the end of your speech so that the audience leaves feeling motivated? Of course, there's always a third option: You could compromise and put your strongest argument in the middle of your speech.

When strong arguments come first, a message is said to have an *anticlimax order.* When they come last, a message has a *climax order.* A message with a *pyramidal order* has strong arguments in the middle. But which order works best? Most research on this subject suggests that putting your strongest argument either first *or* last is the best strategy (Gilkenson, Paulson, & Sikkink, 1954; Gulley & Berlo, 1956; Sikkink, 1956). Both seem to work better than sandwiching strong arguments in the middle of a speech, but beyond that, strong arguments seem effective at either the beginning or end of a message.

Of course, other variables may determine whether strong or weak arguments should go first or last. For example, Unnaba, Burnkrant, and Erevelles (1994) argued that the means, or channel, by which a message is transmitted should determine whether strong arguments go first or last. Their study found that when groups were visually exposed to information about the characteristics of a book bag, their attitudes about the bag were the same whether they were exposed first to strong or weak arguments about the bag's quality. However, if they received auditory messages about the bag, they had more favorable attitudes when strong arguments came before weak arguments. Thus, when information is presented for people to hear, order is important.

PRIMACY AND RECENCY EFFECTS: THE FIRST SHALL BE LAST, AND THE LAST SHALL BE FIRST

Up to this point, we've been looking at how arguments should be selected and organized within a single speech. The issue of what goes first and what goes last extends beyond single speeches, however. It is also possible to consider whether *who* goes first and *who* goes last affects the process of persuasion. Nowadays, it is quite common for political candidates to be involved in debates that are not very interactive. A coin is flipped, one candidate speaks, and then the other takes a turn. When that happens, is there any advantage to speaking first, or do all good things come to those who wait? As with research on climax and anticlimax, results in this area are mixed; some studies support a *primacy effect* (i.e., the first arguments presented have an advantage) but others support a *recency effect* (i.e., the later arguments presented have an advantage). However, several studies have investigated whether some circumstances favor primacy whereas others favor recency. We consider two such circumstances now.

First, a classic study by Miller and Campbell (1959) demonstrated that the passage of time determines whether primacy or recency prevails. Primacy, they found, works best when you hear two opposing messages, back to back, and then have to wait a while before deciding what to do about the messages. For instance, a primacy effect is likely when you hear one candidate speak right after another and then wait a week before voting for one of the candidates. Why should this scenario work to the advantage of the candidate who speaks first? According to Miller and Campbell (1959), with time we tend to remember information we receive first. In other words, first impressions may be lasting impressions.

However, Miller and Campbell (1959) found that the recency effect is more likely when you hear one message, wait some time before hearing the opposing message, and then decide immediately after the second message what you are going to do. For instance, a recency effect is likely if you hear one candidate give a speech and then, just before voting, hear the opposing candidate give a speech. Why, in this situation, should the second candidate prevail? The researchers argued that because we tend to forget information rapidly, we'll have forgotten most of the first message by the time we vote. However, voting immediately after hearing the second message should enable us to remember most of the candidate's message, giving him or her an advantage (see Figure 9.2).[1]

In addition to time delay, the content of a message may determine whether first messages are more persuasive than second messages or vice versa. For instance, some research indicates that material that is relatively unsalient, noncontroversial, uninteresting, and unfamiliar to the audience tends to produce a recency effect. However, salient, interesting, controversial, and familiar material tends to produce a primacy effect, perhaps because an audience starts with a high level of interest that decreases over time (Furnham, 1986; Rosnow, 1966; Rosnow & Robinson, 1967). Thus, if given the choice to speak first or last, you may want to base your decision on the nature of your material.[2]

Finally, it may be that both the manner in which arguments are presented and the nature of the audience work in combination to influence whether a primacy or recency effect occurs. An interesting study by Petty, Tormala, Hawkins, and Wegener (2001) investigated this possibility. These researchers noted that competing arguments can be presented in two different ways: "chunked," with clearly defined pro and con segments, or "unchunked," with pros and cons coming in an uninterrupted and uncategorized stream of

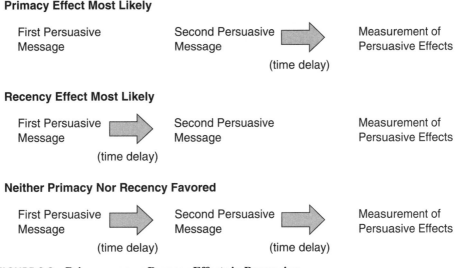

Primacy Effect Most Likely

First Persuasive Message   Second Persuasive Message ⟹   Measurement of Persuasive Effects

(time delay)

Recency Effect Most Likely

First Persuasive Message ⟹   Second Persuasive Message   Measurement of Persuasive Effects

(time delay)

Neither Primacy Nor Recency Favored

First Persuasive Message ⟹   Second Persuasive Message ⟹   Measurement of Persuasive Effects

(time delay)   (time delay)

FIGURE 9.2   **Primacy versus Recency Effects in Persuasion.**

information. To make this clearer, imagine a commercial for a new drug. If information is chunked in the ad, one speaker would present benefits of the drug, and a subsequent speaker would present nasty side effects. In contrast, if information is unchunked, a speaker might say a drug has many effects and then discuss benefits followed by side effects, without any interruption between (Petty et al., 2001).

Petty and his colleagues (2001) suspected that chunked and unchunked arguments might have different effects on people who are motivated to think carefully about arguments and people who are not so motivated. Why? Because chunking signals that there is a change in the nature of the information being presented (i.e., a change from pro to con), the break between segments might cause motivated people to consolidate the information they've heard, form an attitude, and stick with it (primacy effect). For unmotivated people who might normally ignore later information, however, the break might act as a "wake-up call," increasing the amount of attention they pay to later information (recency effect). In unchunked conditions, Petty and his colleagues (2001) suspected that the effects might be just the opposite. Specifically, motivated people might consolidate information after hearing all arguments, yet be most influenced by later arguments (recency effect), whereas unmotivated people, without an attention-grabbing interruption, might focus on early information (primacy effect).

To test these ideas, Petty and his colleagues presented arguments that were chunked (i.e., pros were presented on one sheet of paper and cons on another sheet of paper) or unchunked (i.e., pros and cons were presented on the same sheet of paper, with no break in between) to people who were motivated to think about the arguments and people who were not motivated. Results of the study confirmed the researchers' suspicions. In chunked conditions, motivated people were more vulnerable to primacy effects and unmotivated people were more vulnerable to recency effects. In unchunked conditions, motivated people were more susceptible to recency effects and unmotivated people were more susceptible to primacy effects (Petty et al., 2001).

INOCULATION, MESSAGE-SIDEDNESS, AND FOREWARNING: PREVENTING AND REFUTING THE PERSUASIVE ATTEMPTS OF OTHERS

When parents make clichés out of phrases such as "and if your friends told you to jump off a cliff, would you do that, too?" they may succeed in making their children feel stupid for succumbing to peer pressure but, truth be told, the act has already been done. Indeed, we're sure that parents would much rather prevent their children from being persuaded to engage in dangerous or unethical behaviors than deal with the problem after the fact. Likewise, governments have and still wish to prevent their citizens from adopting certain political viewpoints. For instance, did you know that citizens of the former Soviet Union were not supposed to play Monopoly, a clearly capitalistic game? Moreover, after World War II, there was widespread paranoia in the United States that Americans would be brainwashed by Communist propaganda. In short, although most of this book has been devoted to examining how people persuade other people, oftentimes a more immediate concern centers on how to *prevent* people from being persuaded. This section discusses research and theory on such preventive attempts. Because the term "prevention" often implies something happening *before* something else, we hope it's clear why we've included this topic in a chapter on order effects in persuasion. We begin by examining inoculation theory, a classic perspective developed by William McGuire (1964).

Inoculation Theory: Of Needles and Arguments

Inoculation theory might best be understood by using a biological analogy. Specifically, if you want to keep your body healthy, what should you do? One strategy is to eat your Wheaties and Flintstones vitamins, avoid fats and sugars, stay rested, and exercise. This is what is known as a *supportive strategy* or treatment. The rationale here is that a stronger body will be more effective at fending off diseases and viruses. A second way to stay healthy is through *inoculation*. Perhaps your rear end has forgotten all of those needles it encountered in your youth (e.g., DPT immunizations), but if you've ever had a flu shot or treated your dog or cat to a rabies booster, you're familiar with the reasoning behind such injections. The idea is that if you or Fido are exposed to a small dose of a disease virus, your bodies are better able to defend themselves against the virus later. This is because a dose that is too small to give you the disease often stimulates your body's defenses. Thus, if exposed to a stronger dose of the virus later, your body can overpower it.

According to McGuire (1964), this metaphor can also be applied to situations involving persuasion. For example, imagine you are a lawyer hired to defend someone who is accused of murder but who is innocent. You realize that after you have a chance to present your case, another lawyer will argue against you, presenting evidence that he or she hopes will help convict your client. With that in mind, what might you do? First, you could use a supportive strategy, making the jury's belief in your client's innocence as "healthy" as possible by spending a lot of time discussing reasons why the client is not guilty. On the other hand, you could inoculate the members of the jury by exposing them to weak doses of the other lawyer's arguments and by showing how such arguments might be refuted. The hope is that jurists exposed to weak doses of the opposition's argument will be less persuaded.

In a classic test of inoculation theory, McGuire and Papageorgis (1961) focused on the support and refutation of *cultural truisms*. A cultural truism is a belief whose truth is taken for granted. For example, the idea that "it is good to brush your teeth after every meal, if possible" is a cultural truism because it is generally accepted in our culture. According to McGuire and Papageorgis, however, cultural truisms should also be especially vulnerable when attacked. This is most likely because they have never been questioned. Returning to the biological metaphor for a moment, imagine that you were raised in a plastic bubble all your life, breathing only pure, germ-free air. What would happen if you stepped out of the bubble? Your body, having never been exposed to germs, would be especially vulnerable to them. Indeed, huge numbers of Native Americans died because of this when missionaries brought with them unfamiliar European viruses. According to McGuire and Papageorgis, the same thing can happen with cultural truisms. Unlike beliefs on such topics as capital punishment and the legalization of drugs, which may be challenged frequently, cultural truisms exist in what amounts to hermetically sealed bubbles; they've never been questioned, they've never required defense, and, therefore, they are sitting ducks when attacked. Even so, McGuire and Papageorgis (1961) argued that inoculation could help defend such beliefs.

To test this notion, these researchers exposed participants in their study to several messages that attacked cultural truisms (e.g., brushing your teeth too much damages the teeth's protective enamel). Two days before hearing the attacking messages, however, the participants were provided with one of two defenses against the attacks. One group of participants was equipped with a *supportive defense;* that is, they were presented with several arguments that supported the cultural truisms. A second group of participants received an *inoculation defense* against the attacking message; they heard weak messages attacking a cultural truism in addition to arguments that refuted the attacks. A third group of participants was not provided with any defense. After hearing the attacking messages, the participants rated the degree to which they believed the cultural truisms were true or false. Results of the study supported the researchers' expectations. Specifically, both the supportive and inoculation defenses were better than no defense at all at making participants more resistant to persuasion. Moreover, the group that had been inoculated was the most resistant to the attacking messages.

Although research exploring messages that attack cultural truisms shows that inoculation may be more effective than supportive strategies at inducing resistance, research exploring beliefs that are less generally accepted does not. To be sure, considerable research suggests that when messages are not attacking cultural truisms, supportive strategies are just as effective as inoculation strategies at inducing resistance to persuasion (e.g., Adams & Beatty, 1977; Pryor & Steinfatt, 1978).

Research also suggests that inoculating people against one particular argument may make them resistant to other, different arguments (Papageorgis & McGuire, 1961). This might be analogous to a flu shot that also protects you from polio or smallpox. For example, imagine you hold the belief that a person should drink eight glasses of water a day. A counterargument might be that too much water neutralizes acids that you need for proper digestion. To get you to resist such a counterargument, we might inoculate you by providing weak doses and refutations of the "neutralize acid" argument. In doing so, the research shows that you will become more resistant to other, new arguments to which you weren't originally exposed. For instance, you will be more resistant to a message that says drinking too much water now can wear out your bladder and lead to incontinence in old age.

Why would such generalized immunization work? According to Papageorgis and McGuire (1961), inoculation causes people to think of more arguments that support their beliefs, thereby making subsequent attacking arguments less credible. Thus, once a cultural truism has been defended, it is easier to defend again later, even if the arguments attacking it are different from the initial arguments (for more on inoculation, see Box 9.1).

When Smoke Gets in Your Eyes: Inoculation Theory Applied   BOX 9.1

It's clear from our discussion of inoculation theory that inoculation works effectively with messages that attack cultural truisms in laboratory settings. But how does the theory pan out when tested in "real-life" settings? First, Pfau, Van Bockern, and Kang (1992) argued that inoculation might be a good strategy to use if you want to prevent young adolescents from smoking cigarettes. According to these researchers' sources, more than 3,000 teenagers become smokers each day and, as a result, millions die of smoke-related diseases later in life. Because more than half of all smokers become "regulars" before high school, Pfau and colleagues (1992) conducted their study using seventh graders. The students were shown videos that (1) warned them that peer pressure might cause them to change their minds about smoking and (2) presented and refuted arguments that challenged the students' attitudes about smoking (e.g., smoking is cool). Results showed that inoculation helped students resist smoking, but only if the students had low self-esteem. Interestingly, however, a follow-up study 2 years later found just the opposite: Inoculation worked for students with high self-esteem but not for those with low self-esteem (Pfau & Van Bockern, 1994). Thus, inoculation may wear off for those with low self-esteem, but there may be a sleeper effect for those with high self-esteem. Whatever the case, the authors argue that inoculating children against smoking must occur between elementary school and high

school. After that, resistance strategies do not seem to work (Pfau & Van Bockern).

Second, Pfau, Kenski, Nitz, and Sorenson (1990) examined inoculation in political campaigns. These researchers noted that negative advertisements, in which one politician attacks another, are becoming more common and that one-third to one-half of all political ads may be negative. With that in mind, what should politicians do? One possibility is to inoculate voters, another is to wait until they are attacked and then refute the attacks. To test which strategy works best, Pfau and colleagues sent messages to voters during the 1988 presidential campaign. Voters received messages attacking their preferred candidate. Some of the voters were inoculated before being exposed to the attack message. Other voters, after being exposed to the attack message, received a message that refuted it. Results of the study found that an inoculation strategy worked the best. Those voters who had been inoculated were the least affected by the attack message.

In short, research has shown inoculation theory to be robust in applied contexts. Of course, given our space, we have only been able to scratch the surface here, but we hope you can imagine the wide array of contexts where an inoculation approach shows promise. For instance, Breen and Matusitz (2009) have detailed the ways in which inoculation theory might be used to prevent youths from joining gangs.

One-Sided versus Two-Sided Messages: Both Sides Now

In the previous section, we saw that either supportive or inoculation treatments can be effective at making people resistant to persuasion. With that in mind, you might be wondering if a *combination* of supportive and inoculation treatments might work even better. A considerable amount of past research has examined this issue by trying to determine whether a *one-sided message,* presenting arguments in favor of a single proposition, is more or less persuasive than a *two-sided message,* which presents arguments in favor of one proposition and considers opposing arguments as well. In other words, when trying to persuade an audience to accept your arguments and reject your opponent's arguments, is it best to address your opposition or ignore them?

The first empirical study to investigate this issue was conducted by Hovland, Lumsdaine, and Sheffield (1949), at the request of the War Department during World War II. The study's purpose was to determine the best way to convince U.S. soldiers that the war in Japan would last a considerable amount of time. The researchers asked their subjects to listen to one of two messages. One presented arguments that supported the war with Japan and argued that the war would be a long one. The other message included the same arguments as the first, in addition to a brief description of opposing arguments. Results of the study found that the effectiveness of one- or two-sided arguments depended on two factors: education level and initial attitude. First, the one-sided message was more effective for persuading subjects with little education, whereas the two-sided message was more effective for persuading subjects who had at least a high school education.[3] Second, when the subjects initially agreed with the argument presented, they were more persuaded by the one-sided argument. Just the opposite was true of subjects who initially disagreed with the argument presented.

Although the large number of studies examining the effects of one- and two-sided messages has produced some contradictory findings, recent work by Daniel O'Keefe (1999) and Mike Allen (1998) has demonstrated that such findings are not contradictory when you consider the type of two-sided messages that have been used in past studies. Specifically, they argue that some studies have used two-sided messages that are *nonrefutational.* In these messages, opposing arguments are mentioned but not argued against. However, some studies have used two-sided messages that are *refutational,* such as those used in the inoculation studies discussed earlier. In these messages, opposing arguments are not only mentioned but also shown to be inferior to the position advocated by the speaker.

These researchers suspected that two-sided messages that are refutational would be much more persuasive than those that merely mention opposing arguments. In fact, they suspected that two-sided arguments that did not refute opposing arguments might make a speaker less persuasive than would one-sided arguments. Hence, the contradictions of past research.

To test their idea, these researchers (Allen, 1998; Allen et al., 1990; O'Keefe, 1999) examined a large number of previous studies on message-sidedness, this time taking into account both types of two-sided messages. What they found confirmed their hypothesis: Two-sided messages were more persuasive than one-sided messages, as long as the two-sided messages were refutational. When they were not refutational, they were

Hierarchy of Effectiveness for Message Sidedness	**TABLE 9.1**

Type of Message	Effectiveness
Two-sided refutational message	Most effective (20% more effective than a one-sided message)
One-sided message	Second most effective (20% more effective than a two-sided nonrefutational message)
Two-sided nonrefutational message	Least effective

less persuasive than one-sided messages. Moreover, speakers who used two-sided refutational messages were more credible than those who used one-sided messages (O'Keefe) (see Table 9.1).

A study by Hale, Mongeau, and Thomas (1991) provides some insight into why two-sided refutational messages may be so effective. Results of these researchers' study found that although both types of two-sided messages cause an audience to have more favorable thoughts, this is especially so if the message is refutational. However, this does not explain why one-sided arguments are more persuasive than two-sided nonrefutational messages. Whatever the case, the practical implications of this research are clear: When delivering a message, present the opponent's perspective but make sure you "go all the way" by refuting your opponent's position.

Forewarning: You'd Better Watch Out

In the Oscar-nominated film *A Few Good Men,* Kevin Bacon and Tom Cruise play lawyers who are prosecuting and defending two marines accused of murder. At the beginning of the trial, Bacon's character, the prosecutor, tells the jury to beware; the defense, he warns, "will try a little misdirection, astonish you with stories of rituals, and dazzle you with official sounding terms like 'code red.'" A similar tactic was used in the 2000 presidential campaign, when Al Gore warned voters that George W. Bush would try to scare them about issues such as Medicare. In each of these cases, the warnings were not effective (both Bacon and Gore lost), but considerable research indicates that *forewarning* an audience of a persuasive message can be an effective way of making the audience resistant to that message. Of course, this line of research is related to inoculation, although the two tactics are distinct; whereas inoculation refutes and exposes people to a weakened dose of the attacking message, forewarning only makes people aware of a possible counterattitudinal attack.

According to Papageorgis (1968), there are two types of forewarning messages. First, you can simply warn people that they will hear a message intended to persuade them. Second, you can warn people by telling them about the topic and position taken in the persuasive message. Research indicates that both tactics are moderately effective at inducing resistance to persuasion (see Benoit, 1998). Even so, the process by which each tactic works may be different. For instance, when people are warned about a topic and position, it permits them to arm themselves with counterarguments before the attack. If forewarning about a persuasive topic and position works by making people counterargue, Freedman and Sears (1965) thought that the amount of time between the warning and the persuasive speech might be an important variable moderating the effect of forewarning. They hypothesized that people who were given more time between the warning and the persuasive message would be able to think of more counterarguments and should, therefore, be more resistant to persuasion than those who were given little time. To test this hypothesis, the researchers told high school students that they would hear a message arguing that teenagers were a menace on the road and should not be allowed to drive. After being warned, some of the students were exposed to the message immediately, although others did not hear the message for 2 or 10 minutes. Results of the study confirmed the hypothesis; the high schoolers who waited 10 minutes were most resistant to the message. Those who were exposed to the message immediately were least resistant. Similar studies (e.g., Petty & Cacioppo, 1977) have found that when warned and given time before hearing a message, people can think of and list more counterarguments and are more resistant to persuasion.

Despite these findings, some scholars have questioned the notion that forewarning leads to counterarguing and then resistance. Meta-analyses by Benoit (1998), Quinn and Wood (2004), and Wood and Quinn (2003), for instance, found that the presence of a delay between a warning and a message did not matter. Thus, there is some question as to whether counterarguing is really necessary for developing resistance.

To examine this issue further, Romero, Agnew, and Insko (1996) conducted a study. These researchers argued that if forewarning leads people to counterargue, then we should notice two things. First, people who are more motivated to counterargue should be more affected by forewarning than those who are not. Second, people who have the ability to counterargue should be more affected by forewarning than those who do not have the ability.

To test this notion, Romero and colleagues (1996) forewarned college students who either did or did not have the motivation or ability to counterargue with a persuasive message. The researchers motivated some of the students to counterargue by making the topic of the message more personally relevant to them. Specifically, they told some of the students that the message they were about to be exposed to argued that they all should be required to take comprehensive exams before graduation. The remaining students were told that the comprehensive exams would not be required for 10 years, long after they had left the university. Thus, this second group of students was not that motivated to counterargue. In addition, the researchers hindered some students' ability to counterargue by distracting them. Specifically, after they were warned, some students simply waited 3 minutes before being exposed to the message about comprehensive exams. Other students, however, were distracted during the 3 minutes with difficult letter and number puzzles. Thus, their ability to counterargue was hampered. Results of the study confirmed the researchers' suspicions; compared to students without the motivation and ability to counterargue, the students who found the topic personally relevant and who were not distracted by puzzles were more resistant to the persuasive message (for more on distraction and persuasion, see Box 9.2). In short, it seems that forewarning of topic and position makes people more resistant by encouraging counterarguing.

| Distraction and Persuasion | BOX 9.2 |

Did you know that it is not unheard of for people working on political campaigns to send hecklers to their opponents' speeches? The practice is known as *bracketing* ("Pinocchio index," 1996). It almost certainly is designed to fluster the heckled candidate. What bracketers may not be aware of, however, is that heckling may actually benefit the heckled speaker. Indeed, a study by Beatty and Kruger (1978) found that when an audience identifies with a heckled speaker, the speaker is more persuasive and is perceived as more credible. But how is it possible that the effects of heckling can be exactly opposite of those intended? According to one perspective, distraction, whether caused by hecklers, flashing lights, eating, static, loud noises, or other things, prevents people from scrutinizing a counterattitudinal message. And if they cannot scrutinize the message, people are more likely to be persuaded by it.

Although considerable research supports this explanation (e.g., Festinger & Maccoby, 1964; Keating & Brock, 1974; Osterhouse & Brock, 1970), Buller (1986) and Buller and Hall (1998) examined several studies and found more support for a different perspective. Specifically, learning theory (McGuire, 1969) argues that to be persuaded, people must first comprehend a message. Because distraction hinders comprehension, distraction also should decrease the persuasiveness of a message. Buller and Hall's work supports this notion by indicating that distraction generally reduces the effectiveness of a persuasive message. This may depend, however, on the type of distraction being examined. For instance, in addition to distraction that is external to a communicator (such as hecklers and loud noises), a second type of distraction can be initiated by the communicator. For example, you might be distracted by someone who stands too close or who uses intense language. According to Buller and Hall, when a distraction is initiated by a communicator, our reaction depends not so much on comprehension or counterarguments as on the communicator's credibility. Specifically, when distracted by a highly credible source, we tend to be more persuaded; when distracted by a less-credible source, we tend to be less persuaded. Thus, if you are a highly credible source and want to be persuasive, feel free to distract your audience.

It may be the case, however, that counterarguing is not the only factor mediating the effectiveness of forewarning. To be sure, a study by Jacks and Devine (2000) found that, for some people, forewarning heightened not only counterarguing but also irritation. That is, some people, when warned that specific attitudes they held would be attacked, became more agitated and angry. This, in turn, led them to be more resistant to attacks (Jacks & Devine, 2000).

Although warning people about a topic and position provides them an opportunity to think of and rehearse counterarguments, it is clear that the other type of warning—a warning about persuasive intent—does not. Indeed, if people don't know what the topic will be, how can they think of counterarguments? But if counterarguing is not responsible for the effectiveness of this type of warning, what is? As noted in Chapter 8, Brehm (1966) and Brehm and Brehm (1981) argued that when people feel that their freedom to behave or think in a certain way is restricted, they experience *psychological reactance* and attempt to restore their freedom. If you've ever tried reverse psychology on a child, you are familiar with how psychological reactance works. For instance, some time ago, one of the authors was having trouble getting his preschooler to pack up his toys, leave his pals, and get in the car to go home. The child, of course, thought he had the freedom to choose: stay with his pals or get in the car. However, when dad pretended he was leaving without his son, the child gathered his toys and hurried into the car. Why? His freedom to choose the ride home was being taken away. He was reacting to the loss of freedom.

According to some writers (see Fukada, 1986; Hass & Grady, 1975), this phenomenon occurs when you are warned that someone intends to persuade you. It's like a comedian who tells you he or she will make you laugh before telling a joke. We like to feel free to laugh or to be persuaded, and if we feel that freedom is in jeopardy, we experience *psychological reactance*; we don't laugh or we resist persuasion. To illustrate this principle, Fukada told one group of people that they would be exposed to a message intended to make them afraid and to change their attitude. Another group did not receive the warning. Later, both groups received a message that tried to persuade them to be tested for syphilis. Results indicated that the warned group not only experienced more psychological reactance, it was also less persuaded than the unwarned group.

Before concluding this section, we should note that not all research indicates that forewarning increases resistance to persuasion. Indeed, a meta-analysis by Wood and Quinn (2003; see also Quinn & Wood, 2004) found that, in some cases, forewarning shifts attitudes toward the impending message. It all depends on the motives of the audience. Specifically, as we have seen, when people want to defend their existing attitudes, forewarning is effective at increasing resistance. On the other hand, sometimes warnings threaten people's self-concepts by suggesting that they may be gullible or vulnerable to influence. Rather than resist, people may shift their attitude toward the future appeal in order to reduce its impact. In other cases, people may be concerned about the impressions they are leaving on others. For instance, they may not want to appear pig-headed to their peers. In these cases, warnings may move them to a more neutral, easily defensible position that helps them leave a good impression (Quinn & Wood, 2004).

Whatever the case, because forewarning has the potential to make people more resistant to persuasion, you might be wondering what you should do if you ever want to persuade an audience that has been warned or is aware of your intent to persuade them. With that question in mind, Benoit (1998) offered the following advice:

> In these cases, the persuader may wish to attempt to compensate for the inhibiting effects of forewarning. The persuader could stress a lack of bias, emphasize that the audience's best interests were considered (and not just the persuader's own selfish interests), explain that both sides of the issue were carefully considered before a position was taken, or simply ask the audience to keep an open mind. At the very least, persuaders should moderate their expectations for success, keeping in mind that their persuasive task is more difficult when the audience is forewarned. (pp. 147–148)

SUMMARY

In this chapter, we examined the topic of message selection and organization. First, we saw that, depending on the characteristics of the audience, it's sometimes better for a persuader to tell the audience what to believe, but at other times it's best to let the audience members draw their own conclusions. Second, we saw that the ways in which messages are framed affect how they are reacted to. Third, we saw that when selecting arguments to use for persuasion, quality arguments matter with audiences that will scrutinize the message, but quantity works for less-discerning audiences. Fourth, we discussed the role of evidence in the process of persuasion. Fifth, we examined message repetition and noted the conditions under which it increases and decreases persuasion. Sixth, we looked at the ways in which arguments might be ordered or arranged in a speech and indicated that the most effective order depends on several variables. Similarly, our examination of primacy and recency effects showed that when two people are giving opposing speeches, under some circumstances the first speaker may have the advantage, while under others the last speaker may have the advantage. Finally, we explored the ways in which people may be more resistant to persuasion, either by being inoculated with a weak dose of an opposing argument, by presenting two-sided refutational messages, or by being warned about the possibility of an attacking argument.

ENDNOTES

1. Miller and Campbell (1959) also found that if there is a time delay between both messages and between the second message and the measurement of attitude, neither primacy nor recency works better. Moreover, if there are no time delays between messages and the measurement of attitudes, neither primacy nor recency works better.

2. Of course, an additional advantage to speaking first is that you have the opportunity to inoculate your audience against your opponent's messages or at least warn your audience that opposing messages are forthcoming. The topics of inoculation and forewarning are discussed later in this chapter.

3. Subsequent studies have not always supported the notion that educational level interacts with message sidedness (see O'Keefe, 1999).

REFERENCES

Adams, W. C., & Beatty, M. J. (1977). Dogmatism, need for social approval, and the resistance to persuasion. *Communication Monographs, 44*, 321–325.

Allen, M. (1998). Comparing the persuasive effectiveness of one- and two-sided messages. In M. Allen & R. W. Preiss (Eds.), *Persuasion: Advances through meta-analysis* (pp. 87–98). Cresskill, NJ: Hampton Press.

Allen, M., Hale, J., Mongeau, P., Berkowitz-Stafford, S., Stafford, S., Shanahan, W., Agee, P., Dillon, K., Jackson, R., & Ray, C. (1990). Testing a model of message sidedness: Three replications. *Communication Monographs, 57*, 275–291.

Allen, M., & Preiss, R. W. (1997). Comparing the persuasiveness of narrative and statistical evidence using meta-analysis. *Communication Research Reports, 14*, 125–131.

Beatty, M. J., & Kruger, M. W. (1978). The effects of heckling on speaker credibility and attitude change. *Communication Quarterly, 26*(2), 46–50.

Benoit, W. L. (1998). Forewarning and persuasion. In M. Allen & R. Preiss (Eds.), *Persuasion: Advances through meta-analysis* (pp. 139–154). Cresskill, NJ: Hampton Press.

Braverman, J. (2008). Testimonials versus informational persuasive messages: Moderating effect of delivery mode and personal involvement. *Communication Research, 35*, 666–694.

Breen, G., & Matusitz, J. (2009). Preventing youths from joining gangs: How to apply inoculation theory. *Journal of Applied Security Research, 4*, 109–128.

Brehm, J. W. (1966). *A theory of psychological reactance.* New York: Academic Press.

Brehm, S. S., & Brehm, J. W. (1981). *Psychological reactance: A theory of freedom and control.* New York: Academic Press.

Brosius, H. B., & Bathelt, A. (1994). The utility of exemplars in persuasive communications. *Communication Research, 21*, 48–78.

Buller, D. B. (1986). Distraction during persuasive communication: A meta-analytic review. *Communication Monographs, 53,* 91–114.

Buller, D. B., & Hall, J. R. (1998). The effects of distraction during persuasion. In M. Allen & R. W. Preiss (Eds.), *Persuasion: Advances through meta-analysis* (pp. 155–173). Cresskill, NJ: Hampton Press.

Claypool, H. M., Mackie, D. M., Garcia-Marques, T., McIntosh, A., & Udall, A. (2004). The effects of personal relevance and repetition on persuasive processing. *Social Cognition, 22,* 310–335.

Corbett, E. P. J. (1971). *Classical rhetoric for the modern student* (2nd ed.). New York: Oxford University Press.

Dickson, P. R. (1982). The impact of enriching case and statistical information on consumer judgments. *Journal of Consumer Research, 8,* 398–406.

Festinger, L., & Maccoby, N. (1964). On resistance to persuasive communications. *Journal of Abnormal and Social Psychology, 68,* 359–366.

Fine, B. J. (1957). Conclusion-drawing, communicator credibility, and anxiety as factors in opinion change. *Journal of Abnormal and Social Psychology, 54,* 369–374.

Freedman, J. L., & Sears, D. O. (1965). Warning, distraction, and resistance to influence. *Journal of Personality and Social Psychology, 1,* 262–266.

Fukada, H. (1986). Psychological processes mediating the persuasion inhibiting effect of forewarning in fear arousing communication. *Psychological Reports, 58,* 87–90.

Furnham, A. (1986). The robustness of the recency effect: Studies using legal evidence. *The Journal of General Psychology, 113*(4), 351–357.

Garcia-Marques, T., & Mackie, D. M. (2001). The feeling of familiarity as a regulator of persuasive processing. *Social Cognition, 19,* 9–34.

Gilkenson, H., Paulson, S. F., & Sikkink, D. E. (1954). Effects of order and authority in an argumentative speech. *Quarterly Journal of Speech, 40,* 183–192.

Gulley, H. E., & Berlo, D. K. (1956). Effect of intercellular and intracellular speech structure on attitude change and learning. *Speech Monographs, 23,* 288–297.

Hale, J., Mongeau, P. A., & Thomas, R. M. (1991). Cognitive processing of one- and two-sided persuasive messages. *Western Journal of Speech Communication, 55,* 380–389.

Hass, R. G., & Grady, K. (1975). Temporal delay, type of forewarning, and resistance to influence. *Journal of Experimental Social Psychology, 11,* 459–469.

Hoeken, H., & Hustinx, L. (2003). The relative persuasiveness of different types of evidence. In F. H. van Eemeren, J. A. Blair, C. A. Willard, & A. F. Snoeck Henkemans (Eds.), *Proceedings of the fifth conference of the International Society for the Study of Argumentation* (pp. 497–501). Amsterdam: Sic Sat.

Hovland, C. I., Lumsdaine, A., & Sheffield, F. (1949). *Experiments on mass communication.* Princeton, NJ: Princeton University Press.

Hovland, C. I., & Mandell, W. (1952). An experimental comparison of conclusion-drawing by the communicator and by the audience. *Journal of Abnormal and Social Psychology, 47,* 581–588.

Jacks, J. Z., & Devine, P. G. (2000). Attitude importance, forewarning of message content, and resistance to persuasion. *Basic and Applied Social Psychology, 22*(1), 19–29.

Kardes, F. R., Kim, J., & Lim, J. S. (1994). Moderating effects of prior knowledge on the perceived diagnosticity of beliefs derived from implicit versus explicit product claims. *Journal of Business Research, 29,* 219–224.

Keating, J. P., & Brock, T. C. (1974). Acceptance of persuasion and the inhibition of counterargumentation under various distraction tasks. *Journal of Experimental Social Psychology, 10,* 301–309.

Latimer, A. E., Salovey, P., & Rothman, A. (2007). The effectiveness of gain-framed messages for encouraging disease prevention behavior: Is all hope lost? *Journal of Health Communication, 12,* 645–649.

Martin, B. A. S., Lang, B., & Wong, S. (2003/2004). Conclusion explicitness in advertising: The moderating role of Need for Cognition (NFC) and Argument Quality (AQ) on Persuasion. *Journal of Advertising, 32*(4), 57–65.

McGuire, W. J. (1964). Inducing resistance to persuasion: Some contemporary approaches. In L. Berkowitz (Ed.), *Advances in experimental social psychology* (pp. 191–229). New York: Academic Press.

McGuire, W. J. (1969). The nature of attitudes and attitude change. In G. Lindzey & E. Aronson (Eds.), *The handbook of social psychology* (2nd ed., pp. 136–314). Reading, MA: Addison-Wesley.

McGuire, W. J., & Papageorgis, D. (1961). The relative efficacy of various types of prior belief-defense in producing resistance to persuasion. *Journal of Abnormal and Social Psychology, 62,* 327–337.

Miller, N., & Campbell, D. T. (1959). Recency and primacy in persuasion as a function of the timing of speeches and measurements. *Journal of Abnormal and Social Psychology, 59,* 1–9.

O'Keefe, D. J. (1998). Justification explicitness and persuasive effects: A meta-analytic review of the effects of varying supportive articulation in persuasive messages. *Argumentation and Advocacy, 35,* 61–75.

O'Keefe, D. J. (1999). How to handle opposing arguments in persuasive messages: A meta-analytic review of the effects of one-sided and two-sided messages. In M. E. Roloff (Ed.), *Communication yearbook 22* (pp. 209–249). Thousand Oaks, CA: Sage.

O'Keefe, D. J., & Jensen, J. D. (2007). The relative persuasiveness of gain-framed loss-framed messages for encouraging disease prevention behaviors: A meta-analytic review. *Journal of Health Communication, 12,* 623–644.

O'Keefe, D. J., & Jensen, J. D. (2008). Do loss-framed persuasive messages engender greater message processing than do gain-framed messages? A meta-analytic review. *Communication Studies, 59,* 51–67.

Osterhouse, R. A., & Brock, T. C. (1970). Distraction increases yielding to propaganda by inhibiting counterarguing. *Journal of Personality and Social Psychology, 15,* 344–358.

Papageorgis, D. (1968). Warning and persuasion. *Psychological Bulletin, 70,* 271–282.

Papageorgis, D., & McGuire, W. J. (1961). The generality of immunity to persuasion produced by pre-exposure to weakened counterarguments. *Journal of Abnormal and Social Psychology, 62,* 475–481.

Peskin, M., & Newell, F. N. (2004). Familiarity breeds attraction. Effects of exposure on attractiveness of typical and distinctive faces. *Perception, 33,* 147–157.

Petty, R. E., & Cacioppo, J. T. (1977). Forewarning, cognitive responding, and resistance to persuasion. *Journal of Personality and Social Psychology, 35,* 645–655.

Petty, R. E., & Cacioppo, J. T. (1979). Effects of forewarning of persuasive intent and involvement on cognitive responses and persuasion. *Personality and Social Psychology Bulletin, 5,* 173–176.

Petty, R. E., & Cacioppo, J. T. (1984). The effects of involvement on responses to argument quantity and quality: Central and peripheral routes to persuasion. *Journal of Personality and Social Psychology, 46,* 69–81.

Petty, R. E., & Cacioppo, J. T. (1986). *Communication and persuasion: Central and peripheral routes to attitude change.* New York: Springer-Verlag.

Petty, R. E., Tormala, Z. L., Hawkins, C., & Wegener, D. T. (2001). Motivation to think and order effects in persuasion: The moderating role of chunking. *Personality and Social Psychology Bulletin, 27*(3), 332–344.

Pfau, M., Kenski, H. C., Nitz, M., & Sorenson, J. (1990). Efficacy of inoculation strategies in promoting resistance to political attack messages: Application to direct mail. *Communication Monographs, 57,* 1–12.

Pfau, M., & Van Bockern, S. (1994). The persistence of inoculation in conferring resistance to smoking initiation among adolescents: The second year. *Human Communication Research, 20,* 413–430.

Pfau, M., Van Bockern, S., & Kang, J. G. (1992). Use of inoculation to promote resistance to smoking initiation among adolescents. *Communication Monographs, 59,* 213–230.

Pinocchio index (1996, September 3). *Time,* p. 22.

Pryor, B., & Steinfatt, T. M. (1978). The effects of initial belief level on inoculation theory and its proposed mechanisms. *Human Communication Research, 4,* 217–230.

Quinn, J., & Wood, W. (2004). Forewarnings of influence appeals: Inducing resistance and acceptance. In S. Eric (Ed.), *Resistance and persuasion* (pp. 193–213). Mahwah, NJ: Erlbaum.

Reinard, J. C. (1988). The empirical study of the persuasive effects of evidence: The status after fifty years of research. *Human Communication Research, 15,* 3–59.

Reynolds, R. A., & Reynolds, J. L. (2002). Evidence. In J. P. Dillard & M. Pfau (Eds.), *The persuasion handbook: Developments in theory and practice* (pp. 427–444). Thousand Oaks, CA: Sage.

Rhodes, G., Halberstadt, J., & Brajkovich, G. (2001). Generalization of mere exposure effects to averaged and composite faces. *Social Cognition, 19,* 57–70.

Romero, A. A., Agnew, C. A., & Insko, C. A. (1996). The cognitive mediation hypothesis revisited: An empirical response to methodological and theoretical criticism. *Personality and Social Psychology Bulletin, 22,* 651–665.

Rosnow, R. (1966). Whatever happened to the "Law of Primacy." *Journal of Communication, 16,* 10–31.

Rosnow, R., & Robinson, E. (1967). *Experiments in persuasion.* New York: Academic Press.

Salovey, P., Schneider, T. R., & Apanovitch, A. M. (2002). Message framing in the prevention and early detection of illness. In J. P. Dillard & M. Pfau (Eds.), *The persuasion handbook: Developments in theory and practice* (pp. 391–406). Thousand Oaks, CA: Sage.

Sawyer, A. G. (1981). Repetition, cognitive responses, and persuasion. In R. E. Petty, T. M. Ostrom, & T. C. Brock (Eds.), *Cognitive responses in persuasion* (pp. 237–261). Hillsdale, NJ: Erlbaum

Sawyer, A. G. (1988). Can there be effective advertising without explicit conclusions? Decide for yourself.

In S. Hecker & D. W. Stewart (Eds.), *Nonverbal communication in advertising* (pp. 159–184). Lexington, MA: Lexington Books.

Sawyer, A. G., & Howard, D. J. (1991). Effects of omitting conclusions in advertisements to involved and uninvolved audiences. *Journal of Marketing Research, 28,* 467–474.

Schneider, T. R. (2006). Getting the biggest bang for your health education buck: Message framing and reducing health disparities. *American Behavioral Scientist, 49,* 812–822.

Sikkink, D. (1956). An experimental study of the effects on the listener of anticlimax order and authority in an argumentative speech. *Southern Speech Journal, 22,* 73–78.

Stiff, J.B. (1986). Cognitive processing of message cues: A meta-analytic review of the effects of supporting information on attitudes. *Communication Monographs, 53,* 75–89

Tversky, A., & Kahneman, D. (1981). The framing of decisions and the psychology of choice. *Science, 211,* 453–458.

Unnaba, H. R, Burnkrant, R. E., & Erevelles, S. (1994). Effects of presentation order and communication modality on recall and attitude. *Journal of Consumer Research, 21,* 481–495.

Wood, W., & Quinn, J. (2003). Forewarned or forearmed? Two meta-analytic syntheses of forewarning of influence appeals. *Psychological Bulletin, 129,* 119–138.

Zajonc, R. B. (1968). Attitudinal effects of mere exposure. *Journal of Personality and Social Psychology Monographs, 9*(2, part 2), 1–27.

Zebrowitz, L. A., White, B., & Wieneke, K. (2008). Mere exposure and racial prejudice: Exposure to other-race faces increases liking for strangers of that race. *Social Cognition, 26,* 259–275.

CHAPTER 10

Sequential Persuasion

"If you're a door-to-door salesperson," we're told by a friend of ours who once made his living selling encyclopedias, "half your job is getting into people's houses. Once you're inside," he informed us, "they're yours, all yours."

According to our friend, most door-to-door salespeople have sneaky ways of getting their feet into your doorway. Some mention your neighbors by name. Some ask for a glass of water. Our pal had a whole spiel based largely on deception. He's not proud of it now, he admitted, but when he greeted prospective customers, he was trained to look like anything but a salesperson.

"After introducing myself to the customers," he told us, "I promised I was not going to try to sell them anything. I was just in the neighborhood conducting surveys. I asked them if they would give me their opinions about their family's educational needs and told them that, if they did, I would repay them with 'educational materials.' That usually got me inside."

Once our friend was in the door, he asked his customers to respond to a phony "opinion survey" (e.g., "Do your kids use the library?" "Do your kids go to the library after dark?") and then showed them a set of encyclopedias that he was "willing to give them, for promotional reasons, if they promised to keep the set up to date." How could they do that? Simply by purchasing one yearbook per year for the next 10 years.

Many of the customers agreed to this seemingly unbelievable offer. What they did not realize was that the amount of money they paid for the yearbooks actually covered the cost of the encyclopedias and then some. They'd been "schmoozed" into buying something they thought they were getting for free.

This example, together with the previous chapter, shows that oftentimes persuasion is not as simple as making a single request or giving one speech. Persuasion, quite frequently, is a process that requires that a number of steps be enacted in the right order. Indeed, before making his pitch, our friend had to get himself into the customer's house. And for reasons we discuss later in this chapter, by getting customers to agree to the survey, our friend probably increased his chances of making a sale.

In this chapter we extend concepts discussed in Chapter 9 by examining the topic of "sequential persuasion," which encompasses a number of tactics aimed at getting people to behave in a particular way. We explore research that shows how people increase their persuasiveness, often at the expense of others, by saying or doing something before actually making their request. We begin with a strategy known as *pregiving*.

PREGIVING: THE OLD "I'LL-SCRATCH-YOUR-BACK-IF-YOU'LL-SCRATCH-MINE" APPROACH

Many years ago, when most cameras still used film, one of the authors received a package in the mail. The package contained two unused rolls of film and a letter explaining that the film was a gift. The letter went on to explain how, after using the film, the author could mail it to the company to be processed. And the funny thing is, the author did, even though the cost of the processing was more expensive than taking the film to a local developer. Why was the author persuaded to spend more money? Because the ploy used by the processing company is a well-known and effective tactic of persuasion known as pregiving. Pregiving entails trying to get someone to comply by acting nice or doing favors for him or her in advance. When supermarkets offer free samples of foods to taste, they are employing this strategy.

A classic study done by Dennis Regan (1971) showed how effective the pregiving strategy can be. In the study, first-year students at Stanford University who had been asked to participate in an experiment on "aesthetics" were seated in a room with another student. What the students had not been told was that the other student was a confederate who had been planted there by the researcher. After a few minutes, the confederate left the room. When he returned, he was either empty-handed or was carrying two Coca-Colas. If he was empty-handed, he simply sat back down. But if he had sodas, he offered one to the research subject and said, "I bought one for you too."

Seems nice enough, but there's a catch; later, the plant informed the subject that he was selling raffle tickets for a new high school gym and would appreciate it if the subject would do him a favor and buy some tickets. Not surprisingly, the results of the study revealed that subjects who had been given a soda ahead of time bought almost twice as many raffle tickets as those who had been given nothing.

Real-world persuaders are also known to put the pregiving tactic to use. For example, in touristy areas of big cities (the Louvre in Paris, the Dome of the Rock in Jerusalem, the Alamo in San Antonio, the Parthenon in Athens), panhandlers have figured out a tricky way to get donations from unsuspecting tourists. The panhandlers wait a block or two from a well-known tourist attraction. When tourists walk by, clearly headed for the attraction, the panhandlers catch up with them, walk in stride, and proceed to "guide" the tourists to their destination. Once there, the panhandlers ask for a donation for the unrequested and unneeded service rendered.

The pregiving tactic works in other contexts as well. For instance, as a suit salesperson, one of the authors was trained to ask customers if they would like to have their jackets pressed while they were shopping. Very few refused the favor, and even those who did were cheerfully surprised at the offer. What they did not understand was that there was a hidden rationale behind the gesture; not only was it an effective means of getting customers to spend more time shopping, but when it came to purchasing a suit, who better to buy from than the nice salesperson who had already done them a favor?

Our final example of the pregiving strategy is, to us, perhaps the most disturbing. Specifically, the next time a man asks if he can buy you a drink, women beware; a study by George, Gournic, and McAfee (1988) found that if women allow men to buy them drinks, both men and women perceive the women to be more sexually available than if the drinks are refused.[1] Once again, there seems to be an assumption that pregiving makes one obligated to return favors.

Finally, we should note that if you decide to try the pregiving strategy yourself, you should be careful. It does not always succeed. Groves, Cialdini, and Couper (1992) argue that people do not feel obligated to reciprocate positive behaviors "when the earlier behavior received is not viewed as a gift or a favor but as a bribe or an undue pressure to comply" (p. 480). In fact, when pregiving is perceived as a bribe or a pressure tactic, it actually decreases compliance (Groves et al., 1992). Hence, the pregiving must be perceived by the target as an altruistic act, not as a self-serving act.

Why Is the Pregiving Tactic Persuasive?

Common explanations for why pregiving works include liking, gratitude, impression management, and internalized social norms (see Burger, Sanchez, Imberi, & Grande, 2009; Goei, Roberto, Meyer, & Carlyle, 2007). The *liking explanation* suggests that people who give something to others are perceived as kind and good. As a result, they are well liked, and, in turn, more persuasive. The *gratitude explanation* suggests that receiving a favor leads to positive emotional states (i.e., feelings of gratitude) that motivate benevolent behavior. In other words, people comply because the favor creates a spirit of thankfulness and benevolence. The last two explanations, *impression management* and *internalized social norm*, are based on *the norm of reciprocity (or indebtedness), which* says it is desirable to repay what another person has provided us (Cialdini & Goldstein, 2004). The impression management explanation suggests that repaying favors is desirable because it keeps you from looking like an ungrateful freeloader. The internalized social norm explanation suggests that repaying favors is desirable because it makes people feel good about themselves when they do the right thing.

Although all of these explanations have received support, the studies that test them side-by-side favor some explanations over others. For example, in a study by Burger et al. (2009), after receiving or not receiving a favor (an unexpected bottled water), research participants were asked to complete and return a survey. Half the participants were told that the person who had done them the favor would be collecting the surveys personally, while the other half were told that they could leave the surveys in a clearly labeled drop-off box. Results indicated that participants who had received the favor were more likely to complete the surveys regardless of how they returned the surveys. This, of course, supported the internalized social norm explanation over the impression management explanation. To be sure, who cares about impressing a drop-off box?

A second study conducted by Goei and his colleagues (Goei et al., 2007) tested the liking, gratitude, and indebtedness explanations. Support was found for each of the explanations but depended on whether the person seeking compliance benefited from gaining compliance. Specifically, when the person doing a favor was seeking compliance for something that would personally benefit him or her (e.g., the person could win $50 by selling a lot of raffle tickets), the gratitude explanation was superior. If, however, the person doing the favor did not personally benefit from compliance (e.g., he or she was selling raffle tickets for a good cause), the liking explanation was superior. Although the study found no support for the indebtedness explanation, the authors did not rule out that it might be important under some circumstances. For example, they suggested that indebtedness might increase compliance when the favor being done is especially costly to the person seeking compliance or beneficial to the person receiving the favor. Regardless of which explanation holds true in a given situation, pregiving is a robust strategy that works well across cultures and persuasive contexts.

FOOT IN THE DOOR: THE "GIVE-ME-AN-INCH-AND-I'LL-TAKE-A-MILE" TACTIC

Not too long ago, one of the authors and a friend were leaving a shopping mall when they were approached by a woman. She was about 30 years old, nicely dressed, and had a small child with her.

"Excuse me," she said to the author, "would you please tell me what time it is?"

The author was nice enough to oblige.

"I was wondering if you could also spare a few dollars?" the woman added. She claimed that her car had run out of gas, she had forgotten her purse, and, if the author would give her his address, she would be happy to return the money to him.

Once again, the author obliged, giving her three or four dollars. He never heard from the woman again. The author's friend, however, saw the same woman several weeks later, using the same scam but at a different mall.

In retrospect, there were probably several things that made the woman successful in her attempt to gain compliance. The fact that she was well dressed made her story seem more believable. She gave a plausible reason for needing the money. And having a small child with her probably created more sympathy. Interestingly, however, having nice clothes, good reasons, and a small child may not have been the only keys to her success. A considerable amount of research shows that the woman might have increased her chances of compliance by asking for the time *before* she asked for money (hmm, maybe there is a good reason then for not giving a stranger "the time of day").

The tactic we have just described is often referred to as the *foot-in-the-door strategy,* hereafter called FITD. The tactic involves making a small request first and then making a second, larger request. Of course, it is the second, larger request that most interests the persuader. The first, small request is merely a setup. For instance, the encyclopedia salesperson we talked about earlier used this tactic when he asked people if they would answer a short survey before he asked for a sale. He didn't really care about their responses to the survey; he simply wanted to soften them up. For reasons we discuss later, when people comply with a smaller request, it often makes them more likely to comply with a second, larger request.

The first study to demonstrate the effectiveness of the FITD strategy was conducted by Jonathan Freedman and Scott Fraser (1966) at Stanford University. These researchers were interested in finding out if they could get housewives to agree to a very large request. Specifically, they asked housewives to allow a team of five or six men into their homes for 2 hours. The men, they were told, would have complete freedom in the house to go through the cupboards and storage spaces in order to classify all of the household products that were there. Before being approached with this request, however, some of the women were set up with a smaller initial request. That is, 3 days before making the large request, the researchers called some of the housewives and asked if they would participate in a survey about household products (e.g., "What brand of soap do you use?"). Surprisingly, about 50 percent of the housewives who agreed to answer the survey also agreed to let complete strangers rifle through their houses. However, when the researchers had not approached housewives with a smaller request first, only about 25 percent of the housewives agreed to the subsequent larger request (Freedman & Fraser, 1966).

According to Dillard (1991) more than 43 articles have been published on the FITD strategy. Recent reviews of these studies suggest that, given the right conditions, the strategy is effective (Burger, 1999; Dillard, Hunter, & Burgoon, 1984; Fern, Monroe, & Avila, 1986)[2] and has increased compliance for a variety of requests, such as those asking people (1) to put large signs on their front lawns (Freedman & Fraser, 1966), (2) to make contributions to charities (Pliner, Hart, Kohl, & Saari, 1974), and (3) to participate in research (Snyder & Cunningham, 1975; Wagener & Laird, 1980). The tactic is also effective across a variety of channels, including face-to-face, over the telephone, and when requests are made via computer (Guéguen, 2002).

Why Is a Foot in the Door So Persuasive?

The most common explanation for the effectiveness of the FITD tactic is based on Bem's (1972) *self-perception theory* (see DeJong, 1979; Freedman & Fraser, 1966). According to this theory, people come to know about their attitudes, emotions, and other internal states by inferring them from their own behavior (Bem, 1972). For example, if you notice yourself eating a lot of Nutrageous candy bars, you are likely to come to the conclusion that you have a favorable attitude toward chocolate. In other words, you use your behavior to infer your attitude.

As an explanation for the FITD effect, self-perception theory says this: When you agree to comply with a small request, you see yourself as an altruistic person who is likely to help. Once you form that impression, you are motivated to behave in a manner consistent with that impression. Thus, when a larger request is made, you are more easily persuaded.

Although some research points to the viability of self-perception theory as an explanation for the effectiveness of the FITD tactic, other evidence is not so optimistic. For example, Gorassini and Olson (1995) conducted a study that measured how helpful people perceived themselves to be after complying with a first, small request. They found that although people's self-ratings of helpfulness were affected by compliance with the small request, those changes did not always predict people's compliance with a second, larger request. Moreover, compliance with a second, larger request often occurred without people perceiving themselves as being more helpful. Dillard (1990) argued that results of studies such as these show that more theorizing about the FITD tactic is necessary.

A meta-analysis by Burger (1999), however, suggests that self-perception *does* affect how much people comply with FITD requests. All research may not indicate this, however, because self-perception is probably not the only process involved. Specifically, Burger noted that other psychological processes operating in an FITD situation may overwhelm whatever impact self-perception has. As a result, not all studies will support a self-perception account of the FITD's effectiveness. By way of example, people may be less willing to comply with a request if they think most other people would reject the request. Thus, as Burger (1999) notes, "it appears that whatever push self-perception gives toward agreement with the target request can be overwhelmed by telling the individual that few people go along with such requests" (p. 323). In short, self-perception probably plays a role in the FITD's effectiveness, but the tactic's success depends on a lot of other factors (see Cialdini & Goldstein, 2004). We discuss some of these next.

When Does a Foot in the Door Work?

Research tells us that some of the following conditions play an important role in determining the effectiveness of the FITD tactic:

1. Size of the initial request. Is getting a person to comply with any request enough to get the person to comply with later requests? Research shows that the initial request should be neither too large nor too small. Seligman, Bush, and Kirsch (1976) argued that "the first request must be of sufficient size for the foot in the door technique to work" (p. 519). However, the initial request cannot be so large that it is rejected. Thus, the persuader must strike a balance between making a large enough initial request to trigger the FITD effect but not so large that it is declined. For instance, asking for a penny so you might later get a larger donation probably would not work because the penny might be perceived as inconsequential. However, asking the average person for $1,000 to begin with might be a bit much. In short, the persuader wants to use the largest possible request that will be accepted.

2. Prosocialness of the request. In a review of several studies, Dillard and colleagues (1984) found that the FITD tactic is more effective when used for prosocial causes than it is when used for self-serving reasons. With this in mind, the FITD tactic would probably be more useful to social workers trying to raise money to help the homeless than it would be for commissioned salespeople.

3. External incentives to comply. Meta-analyses by Burger (1999) and Dillard and colleagues (1984) indicated that people are less susceptible to the FITD tactic if they are offered external incentives for complying with the first request. Most researchers use self-perception theory to explain these effects. Specifically, if you are receiving a gift for agreeing to listen to a sales pitch, you do not form an impression of yourself as someone who is willing to comply readily with requests. You are only complying because you have a material reason for doing so. Thus, because the pregiving strategy (discussed earlier) uses external incentives, it may not be a good idea to use it and the FITD strategies together (see Bell, Cholerton, Fraczek, Rohlfs, & Smith, 1994; Weyant, 1996).

4. Who makes the requests. For the FITD strategy to work, the same person needn't make both the initial and the follow-up requests. Indeed, it is often the case that a person who complies with a request by one person will also comply with a second request, even when the second request is made by a different person. In fact, research by Chartrand, Pinckert, and Burger (1999) found that when a different person made the second request, compliance was more likely than when the same person made both requests. This was especially true when there was no time delay between the first and second requests (Chartrand et al., 1999).

5. Labeling. Imagine that just after you donated blood to the Red Cross, a nurse tells you how generous you are and thanks you. Or better yet, imagine that the nurse gives you a pin or bumper sticker that says, "I Care Enough to Donate Blood." A review of studies by Burger (1999) reported that this type of labeling increases the odds that you will comply with larger follow-up requests (e.g., to donate blood every month for a year). This finding, of course, is consistent with self-perception theory. That is, if someone labels you as someone who is helpful, you may begin to see yourself that way and, as a result, act in accordance with your self-perception. (For a different spin on social labeling, see Box 10.1.)

6. Preference for consistency. You may remember from Chapter 3 that most people want their behaviors and attitudes to be consistent. How does this relate to the FITD tactic? If you agree to an initial request, you should be motivated to behave consistently by also agree-ing to a second request. This is especially true if the two requests are similar (see Burger, 1999). According to Cialdini, Trost, and Newsom (1995), some people have a greater need for such consistency than others. As might be expected, those with a higher need for consis-tency are more influenced by the FITD tactic than are those who are not (Cialdini et al., 1995). This is especially true when people with a higher need for consistency are reminded of how important consistency is (Guadagno, Asher, Demaine, & Cialdini, 2001).

7. Self-concept clarity. Did you know that some people have a clearer picture of their self-concepts than others? These folks are said to have "high self-concept clarity." Interestingly, research shows that these folks are more susceptible to the FITD tactic than are people with a fuzzier idea of self (Burger & Guadagno, 2003). Why? It turns out that people with high self-concept clarity are more likely to change their self-concepts. As such, after complying with an initial request, they are more likely than people with low self-concept clarity to see themselves as helpful and, in turn, comply with a second request (Burger & Guadagno, 2003).

THE-FOOT-IN-THE-MOUTH EFFECT: "HOW ARE YOU TODAY?"

The next time someone greets you by asking, "How are you?" you might want to grumble and tell the person you're feeling terrible. If you don't, you might be setting yourself up for what Howard (1990) calls the *foot-in-the-mouth effect*. That is, by telling someone that you're feeling wonderful, you may make yourself feel committed to behave in a way that is consistent with that declaration. Thus, you may be more likely to comply. Persuaders know this and use it to their advantage. For example, Howard (1990) points to the follow-ing excerpt from a lecture offered on fund-raising:

> Before you ask anyone for a donation, you first ask them how they're feeling. After they tell you they're feeling good, and you tell them you're glad they're feeling good, they'll be more likely to contribute to helping someone who isn't. (p. 1185)

| I'm So Hungry I Could Eat a Horse: The Darker Side of Labeling | BOX 10.1 |

Up to now, we've seen that labeling people in a positive way ("you're so helpful!") may lead them to perceive themselves in a positive way, which, in turn, may make them more likely to comply with requests for help. But what do you suppose would happen if people were labeled in a negative way? Is it possible that they would be more likely to comply with requests for help in order to restore their damaged self-esteem? A study by Nicolas Guéguen (2001) tested this possibility in a devilish way. More than 100 pedestrians on a busy street in France were approached individually by three women who were part of the study. The first woman asked each unsuspecting target, "Excuse me . . . , my bag is heavy and I would like to buy a magazine. . . . Would you mind keeping an eye on my bag while I go and get it?" If the pedestrians agreed, they were left with a bag, which contained a package on top labeled "Horse meat." Twenty seconds later, half of the pedestrians were approached

by the second woman, who looked at the bag and said, "It is really appalling to eat horse meat. When I think that it is thanks to the horse that we have evolved so much. You should be ashamed." Without waiting, the second woman left, the first woman returned with her magazine, thanked the pedestrians, and left with her bag of meat. Finally, the third woman approached the pedestrians and asked one of two things. Half of the pedestrians were asked to sign a petition favoring the proper treatment by the government of abandoned animals. The other half were asked to sign a petition favoring the limitation of traffic in the city center. Results of the study showed that pedestrians who received the negative label were significantly more likely to sign the petition, *but only if asked to sign the petition about the treatment of animals*. This, of course, makes sense: Once labeled as a horse eater, the second petition provided a way to disavow the negative label and prove their love for horses.

Research by Howard (1990) and Aune and Basil (1994) supports this conclusion. When asking for charitable donations, callers were more successful if they asked people how they were feeling, acknowledged the response, and then requested compliance than when they simply requested compliance.

THE DOOR-IN-THE-FACE TACTIC: "ASK FOR THE STARS"

One of our students used to work selling jewelry in a large department store. She tells us that her approach to sales was very different from that of the other salespeople with whom she worked. Most of them, she tells us, started by showing their customers the "bottom of the line" merchandise. To increase their sales, they then moved to more expensive merchandise, demonstrating that "more money" meant "more quality." However, our student started by showing her customers the most expensive merchandise first. Typically, they did not purchase what they were first shown but, even so, our student claims that while she worked at that store, her sales were always higher than anyone else's.

Actually, we are not surprised by our student's success as a salesperson. Whether she knew it or not, she was using a tactic of persuasion that researchers have known to be effective for many years. Often called the *door-in-the–face technique,* or DITF, this tactic is just the opposite of the FITD strategy. It works by first making a request so large that it is turned down, then following it up with a second, smaller request. Of course, just as with the FITD tactic, compliance with the second request is what the persuader has been aiming for all along.

The first empirical study of the DITF tactic was conducted by Robert Cialdini and his colleagues at Arizona State University (Cialdini et al., 1975). Cialdini (1993) explains what happened:

> Posing as representatives of the "County Youth Counseling Program," we approached college students walking on campus and asked if they would be willing to chaperone a group of juvenile delinquents on a day trip to the zoo. . . . As we expected, the great majority (83 percent) refused. Yet we obtained very different results from a similar sample of college students who were asked the very same question with one difference. Before we invited them to serve as unpaid chaperons on the zoo trip, we asked them for an even larger favor—to spend two hours per week as a counselor to a juvenile delinquent for a minimum of two years. . . . By presenting the zoo trip as a retreat from our initial request, our success rate increased dramatically. Three times as many of the students approached in this manner volunteered to serve as zoo chaperons. (p. 37)

Since the 1975 study of Cialdini and colleagues, the effectiveness of the DITF tactic has been demonstrated again and again (see reviews by Cialdini & Guadagno, 2004; Dillard et al., 1984; Fern et al., 1986; O'Keefe & Hale, 1998; O'Keefe & Hale, 2001). But rather than examining those studies, we turn now to a discussion of *why* the DITF tactic is thought to be so effective.

Why Is a Door in the Face So Persuasive?

During our years of teaching public speaking courses, we've heard the expression "That's a tough act to follow" more than once. We imagine that this phrase is especially meaningful to students who have speeches of questionable quality. Indeed, no one wants to present a mediocre speech *after* a student who has dazzled the professor and the rest of the class with his or her eloquence. The speech would undoubtedly look worse than it really was. This is known as the *perceptual contrast effect*.

The door in the face tactic gone awry.

As an explanation for the effectiveness of the DITF tactic, the contrast effect says this: People are likely to comply with a second, smaller request because, compared to the initial, larger request, the second request seems much smaller than it normally would have (Cialdini, 1993). In other words, a $500 diamond ring seems inexpensive compared to the $3,000 rings. Compared to the $100 rings, however, it seems expensive.

A second explanation for the effectiveness of the DITF tactic is known as *reciprocal concessions* (Cialdini et al., 1975; Cialdini & Goldstein, 2004). This explanation is related to the norm of reciprocity we discussed earlier; that is, when someone does us a favor, we feel obligated to return that favor. A similar thing happens when someone makes a concession. When that happens, we are motivated to make a concession in return. If the other person gives up something, we should, too.

So how does this relate to the DITF strategy? Quite simply, when a persuader follows up with a smaller request, it is often perceived as a concession. The persuader has made a more reasonable offer so we too should be reasonable. Thus, to "return the favor," people frequently comply with the second request. In the real world, negotiations often operate according to this process of reciprocal concessions. That is, negotiators often try to appear more reasonable by starting with a large request so they can make concessions later.

A third explanation for the effectiveness of the DITF tactic is the *self-presentation explanation* (Pendleton & Batson, 1979). According to this account, when people reject an initial request, they become concerned that they will be perceived negatively. Thus, they are more likely to comply with a second request in order to make themselves look better.

A fourth explanation for the effectiveness of the DITF tactic is the *social responsibility position* (Tusing & Dillard, 2000). Unlike the self-presentation position, which argues that we comply with a second request because of external concerns (i.e., we are worried about what *others* will think of us), the social responsibility perspective suggests that we comply because of internal standards. That is, if we think it is socially responsible to help people who deserve it, we're more likely to comply when follow-up messages ask for our help (Tusing & Dillard, 2000).

A final explanation for the effectiveness of the DITF tactic is the *guilt-based account* (O'Keefe & Figgé, 1997, 1999; Millar, 2002). This perspective argues that refusing an initial, prosocial request leads persuadees to experience guilt, which they attempt to reduce by agreeing to a second request. Interestingly, however, research indicates that agreeing to the second request may not make persuadees feel less guilty. Even so, the *expectation* that guilt will be reduced may be enough to make the DITF effective (O'Keefe & Figgé, 1999).

Although there are a large number of explanations for the DITF's effectiveness, we do not necessarily see all of these explanations as incompatible. For example, it might be the case that people experience *guilt* because they believe they did not behave in a *socially responsible* manner. It may also be the case that different explanations operate under different circumstances. For example, a study by Turner and her colleagues (Turner, Tamborini, Limon, & Zuckerman-Hyman, 2007) found that DITF requests are perceived as helping situations by friends but not by strangers. As such, friends and strangers may experience different degrees of guilt and responsibility when rejecting the initial DITF request.

When Does a Door in the Face Work?

Research tells us that some of the following conditions play an important role in determining the effectiveness of the DITF tactic:

1. Size of the initial request. For the FITD strategy to work, the first request must be large enough to guarantee rejection by the persuadee but not so large as to appear incredulous (Cialdini et al., 1975). But is there a right size for the initial request? A study by Even-Chen, Yinon, and Bizman (1978) addressed this question and concluded that the initial request must be large for the door in the face to work. However, they noted that the request must not be so large that it evokes anger, resentment, or incredulity in the persuadee (Even-Chen et al., 1978).

2. Prosocialness of the request. A meta-analysis by Dillard and colleagues (1984) found that the DITF tactic is not effective when used for self-serving reasons but can increase compliance as much as 17 percent when used for altruistic purposes.

3. Elapsed time between first and second requests. In their reviews of studies on the DITF, Dillard and colleagues (1984) and Fern and colleagues (1986) argued that the timing between the initial and follow-up requests influenced the successfulness of the tactic. Specifically, in order to increase compliance, the delay between the two requests must be brief, perhaps to capitalize on the perceptual contrast effect. If there is too much of a delay between the requests, compliance may actually decrease.[3]

4. Can a different person make the second request? Researchers who support the reciprocal concessions explanation (discussed earlier) like to point out that the DITF strategy does not work if the first and second requests are made by different people.[4] Indeed, if a door-to-door salesperson offers you a vacuum cleaner for $500, and a different salesperson offers you the appliance for $300, you might perceive a contrast but not a concession. However, if the same salesperson made both offers, you might be more likely to reciprocate the concession and comply with the second offer.[5]

5. Who answers the door. Research by Bell, Abrahams, Clark, and Schlatter (1996) indicated that some people are more susceptible to the DITF tactic than others. Specifically, to ensure that equity is maintained, exchange-oriented people tend to keep track of what they owe others and of what others owe them (Murstein, Wadlin, & Bond, cited in Bell et al., 1994). An exchange-oriented person, for instance, would not tend to forget if he or she borrowed money or owed you a favor. For that reason, perhaps, the DITF tactic is more effective on exchange-oriented people than it is on nonexchange-oriented people (Bell et al., 1996).

THE THAT'S-NOT-ALL TACTIC: SEEKING COMPLIANCE BY SWEETENING THE DEAL

Remember our friend who sold encyclopedias? We began the chapter by telling you how he used to weasel his way into houses with the foot-in-the-door tactic. But that's not all he did to sell his books. According to him, he also used what he calls the "but wait, that's-not-all" strategy. Here's how it worked: After presenting the books and before asking for the sale, he showed his customers several other items they could receive for free (an atlas, a dictionary, a thesaurus) *if* they agreed to buy the encyclopedias. Perhaps you've observed this strategy used in other contexts. For instance, haven't we all seen those commercials for food and vegetable slicers and dicers? Typically, after a demonstration, you're asked, "How much would you pay for this?" Then you're presented with an add-on knife. How much would you pay now? How about if a carrot cleaner was added? Well, you get the idea, so "call now!"

To see whether this tactic was effective, Jerry Burger (1986) conducted several studies. In one, the tactic was used on customers at a bake sale. When customers asked about the price of a cupcake, they were told one of two things. Some customers were told that a cupcake and two cookies sold for 75 cents. Other customers, however, were not told about the cookies right away—a few seconds after they'd been told that the cupcakes sold for 75 cents each, it was explained that the price included the cost of two cookies. Results of the study showed that the "that's-not-all" tactic sold more cupcakes. Specifically, although only 40 percent of the customers who had been presented cookies and cupcakes at the same time made a purchase, 73 percent of the "that's-not-all" customers made a purchase.

Why does this tactic work so well? According to Burger (1986), the "that's-not-all" tactic's effectiveness may be because of the norm of reciprocity and contrast effect (discussed earlier in this chapter). First, because the seller has sweetened the deal by adding on items, the customer may feel obligated to buy the product, thereby *reciprocating* the seller's action. Second, in *contrast* to the original deal, the revised deal may seem much better than it would have without the comparison.

But wait, there's more: Before concluding this discussion, we should note that the "that's-not-all" tactic can include more than adding on items to make a deal look better; it can also involve lowering the price of an item. For example, Burger (1986) found that more people bought cupcakes when the price was dropped from $1 to 75 cents than when the price was simply stated as 75 cents. You might have noticed that, in this form, the "that's-not-all" tactic is a lot like the door in the face approach. The difference is that, when using the door in the face approach, the persuader waits for the initial request to be rejected before following up with a lesser request. Persuaders using the "that's-not-all" tactic do not wait for the initial request to be rejected before sweetening the deal. Some evidence indicates that of the two techniques, the "that's-not-all" tactic is the more persuasive (Burger, 1986). (For a look at how these two tactics and others might be used together see Box 10.2.) Even so, salespeople or others wishing to use this tactic need to be careful. Some evidence suggests that it might backfire if the salesperson's initial request is too large (Burger, Reed, DeCesare, Rauner, & Rozolis, 1999). It's not difficult to imagine why. For example, if a salesperson asked you to buy a chocolate chip cookie for $5 and then lowered the price to 75 cents, you'd probably be suspicious that the initial price was purposely inflated and that the salesperson was trying to pull a fast one. (For more drawbacks on a related influence approach, see Box 10.3.)

THE LOWBALL TACTIC: CHANGING THE DEAL

If you've ever bought a car from a dealership, there's a chance that you've seen the *lowball tactic* in action. Here's how it works. First, the salesperson makes you a deal that looks too good to refuse. Perhaps the car you want is offered for several hundred dollars

---

Faces, Doors, and Feet: An Extension and Combination of Tactics | **BOX 10.2**

Although the other sections in this chapter discuss compliance-gaining tactics that require two steps, it is clear that sequential persuasion can be far more complex. For example, research by Fointiat (2000) found that although using the foot-in-the-mouth technique may be an effective way to persuade people, it's even more successful when combined with the door-in-the-face tactic. How does this work? If you're trying to get someone to do something, first ask him or her how he or she is feeling, wait for an answer, ask for something BIG, and when it is refused, follow up with a smaller request.

Similarly, research by Goldman and his colleagues (Goldman & Creason, 1981; Goldman, Creason, & McCall, 1981; Goldman, Gier, & Smith, 1981) indicated that combinations of other sequential tactics can be effective as well. For example, two doors in the face or two feet in the door made people more compliant than a single door or foot. Further research by Goldman (1986)

found that the door-in-the-face and foot-in-the-door techniques can also be combined. Here's how it works: First, people are presented with a very large request that they are almost sure to reject (e.g., "Would you call 150 people and ask them questions about the zoo?"). Second, people are presented with a moderate request that serves as a foot in the door. Because this request follows the very large request, however, it can be more difficult than the initial request that is typically used in the foot-in-the-door approach (e.g., "Would you participate in a 25-minute survey about the zoo?" versus "Would you answer three or four questions about the zoo?"). Finally, people are asked to comply with the request that the persuaders wanted them to comply with all along (e.g., "Would you stuff and address 75 envelopes with information about the zoo?"). Results of Goldman's (1986) study found that this combination approach was more persuasive than either tactic alone.

Cheapening Your Product by Sweetening the Deal: The Drawbacks of Including Free Gifts with Purchases | **BOX 10.3**

Not long ago, one of the authors, intending to buy a Valentine's Day gift for his wife, ended up at a cosmetics counter in a local department store. After sniffing at a dozen samples he'd dabbed on his arms, he settled on some perfumed lotions. It wasn't until he'd paid and was leaving the counter that the salesperson called after him, explaining she'd forgotten that those particular lotions came with a free gift—a little handbag with an orange ribbon. The author didn't think much of the handbag—after all, it was just a freebie, probably something that was out of style or didn't sell—but he didn't mention that when he presented it, alongside the lotions, as a gift to his wife. To his surprise, she was thrilled. In fact, she made a bigger fuss over that bag than those darned expensive lotions! At the time, the author chalked up the differences between his and his wife's perceptions to his lack of appreciation for handbags. But then he came across a study

suggesting that he was not alone; apparently, other people react the same way to free gifts. Indeed, in one study (Raghubir, 2004), research participants were asked to evaluate the desirability of a pearl bracelet. Half were told that the bracelet was a free gift accompanying the purchase of another item, while the other half were presented the bracelet as a stand-alone product. Results showed that the second group was willing to pay more for the bracelet than the first group. Similarly, another study showed that, compared to bundling items and selling them together, marketing them in "buy-one, get-one-free" offers led to a *value-discounting effect*—the free, add-on item was perceived as less valuable than when it was bundled with something else (Raghubir, 2005).

This research, of course, has implications for businesses that include their regular merchandise or services as free promotional items from time to

(continued)

time. By doing so, such businesses may cause their customers to perceive those items or services as less desirable. With that in mind, Raghubir (2004) suggests that customers should be informed of how valuable the gift is. For example, rather than say that a handbag is a "free gift," a salesperson should say something like, "You'll also receive this $50 handbag, with our compliments."

less than anyplace else you've shopped. Excited, you accept the offer. But then, a number of things might happen. For instance, the salesperson might inform you that the quoted price did not include an expensive option (e.g., air conditioning) that you thought was included. Or, the salesperson might check with his or her manager for approval and later report that the deal was rejected. Why? The dealership would lose money if the car were sold so cheap. In short, the original offer is taken back, and you are asked to pay a much higher price for the car.

Slimy? You bet. But also very effective. Indeed, in several studies conducted by Cialdini and his colleagues (Cialdini, Cacioppo, Bassett, & Miller, 1978), the lowball tactic was found to increase compliance significantly. In one of the studies, Cialdini and colleagues wanted to see if they could get undergraduate students to wake up early. Here's what happened: Some students were simply asked to participate in a "thinking" experiment at seven in the morning. Others, however, were asked to participate but were not told when the experiment would take place. If they agreed to participate, they were told the time of the experiment and asked if they were still willing to participate. In other words, the second group of students was lowballed. Results of the study showed that although only 31 percent of the nonlowballed students agreed to participate, 56 percent of the lowballed students agreed. Results of two other studies produced similar results (Cialdini et al., 1978).

As unethical as the lowball tactic seems, it is used far more often than might be expected. Credit card issuers, for instance, are known for tempting customers with low introductory "teaser" rates. The problem is that these rates may double or even triple in a few months. Rates on some adjustable mortgages do this too; a few years at a very reasonable rate, then—BAM!—a balloon payment is due. Even colleges and universities are not above suspicion. To be sure, most schools want to recruit new students, and who knows what they will resort to? An article in *Financial World* (Williams, 1995) sounds the following warning:

> When it comes to spelling out the true cost of schooling, all colleges—even the haughtiest Ivy League schools—lie through their teeth. If you think that makes colleges sound like car dealers, you've got it right, says Raymond Loewe, a financial planner in Marlton, N. J., whose firm, called College Money, specializes in helping parents pay school bills. "The dealer pulls you in by telling you the car costs $20,000 when it really costs $23,000 or $24,000 with options," says Loewe. "That's what colleges do. They lowball you on their estimates of what you will be paying and you only find out what it's really going to cost after you sign up." (p. 69)

Why Lowballing Works

According to Cialdini and colleagues (1978), commitment may be the reason for the lowball tactic's effectiveness. Let's use the automobile customer as an example. Cialdini and his colleagues would argue that when the customer agrees to the initial offer, he or she becomes psychologically committed to the idea of owning the car. Thus, even when the reasons for buying the car change, the customer has a hard time altering his or her decision and commitment.

A second reason for the lowball tactic's effectiveness was proposed by Burger and Petty (1981). These researchers thought that people fall victim to the tactic because agreeing with the initial request creates an unfulfilled obligation. In other words, people agree to a second, more costly request because they feel obligated to make good on their promises. In support of this hypothesis, Burger and Petty (1981) found that the lowball tactic works only when the same person who made the first request also makes the less attractive request. It does not work when a different person makes the less attractive request.

"SORRY, WE DON'T HAVE ANY MORE OF THOSE IN YOUR SIZE, BUT . . .": THE BAIT-AND-SWITCH TACTIC

The next time you see a big sale advertised, be careful. If you aren't, you may fall victim to a persuasion tactic that some authors (Joule, Gouilloux, & Weber, 1989) call "the lure":

> This tactic . . . is frequently used when goods are put on sale. For example, a beautiful pair of shoes marked 40% off is displayed quite conspicuously in a store window. The enticed consumer enters the store with the intention of taking advantage of this exceptional offer, but the salesperson informs him that they are out of the shoe in his size. Just when the disappointed customer is ready to leave the store, he is shown a new pair that resembles the shoes on sale but that is being sold at the regular price. (p. 742)

The travel industry uses the same ploy, which is more commonly known as the *bait-and-switch tactic*. For instance, a company might advertise an inexpensive vacation package as part of a promotion. However, as many prospective travelers discover, very few of these seats or packages are available, and they are often sold out by the time people have committed themselves to the idea of a vacation. The only solution is to go home and mope or buy a more expensive option.

Research by Joule and colleagues (1989) indicates that the bait and switch is an effective strategy for gaining compliance. In one study, these researchers got several students to sign up to participate in a rather interesting and well-paying experiment. When the students showed up for the experiment, however, they were told that it had been canceled. Even so, these students, compared to those who were not lured, were more willing to participate in another experiment that was less interesting and unpaid.

According to Joule and colleagues (1989) the bait and switch is similar to the lowball and foot in the door tactics but is also distinct. Like the lowball tactic, the bait and switch requires that the persuadee make two decisions, one before and one after the real cost of compliance is known. However, although the lowball situation concerns the same behavior (e.g., buying red shoes for $30 or buying the same shoes for $40), the bait and switch situation concerns different behaviors (e.g., buying one pair of red shoes for $30 or buying a different pair of red shoes for $40). Likewise, both tactics involve a less costly act followed by a more costly one. However, although the foot in the door requires a person to comply with a smaller request, in the bait and switch, a person is unable to comply with the smaller request (Joule et al., 1989).

THE DISRUPT-THEN-REFRAME TECHNIQUE: I'M SO CONFUSED

If we offered to sell you five Nutrageous candy bars for 400 pennies, would you buy them? It would be a bargain!

But before you decide to buy anything after being presented an offer like this, be careful! You might be falling for a sequential compliance tactic known as the *disrupt-then-reframe technique* (DTR). According to Davis and Knowles (1999) and Knowles and Linn (2003), the DTR rests on the assumption that certain requests (e.g., asking for charitable donations) create a conflict within persuadees. Specifically, persuadees want to help but are also resistant to the expense or effort required to do so. The DTR overcomes this problem by disrupting the persuadees' resistance. How? According to Davis and Knowles, certain confusion techniques (e.g., non sequiturs, requests stated in a peculiar way) can be used to divert people's minds from maintaining resistance. Once that is accomplished, reframing the request with a positive spin (e.g., "It's a bargain!") works to engage the persuadees' underlying desire to help.

To test the effectiveness of this technique, Davis and Knowles (1999) examined door-to-door salespeople who were trying to sell note cards in order to earn money for a worthy charity. The salespeople presented different messages to potential buyers. Some customers received a straightforward sales pitch—"The cards are $3. It's a bargain"—whereas others were presented with a slightly peculiar pitch (i.e., the DTR technique)—"The cards are 300 pennies . . . that's $3. It's a bargain." Results of the study indicated that when salespersons used the DTR technique, they sold significantly more cards than when they used the more straightforward approach (Davis & Knowles, 1999). A follow-up study by Fennis, Das, and Pruyn (2004) confirmed that the DTR technique was effective, specifically because it decreased counterarguing. Additional research suggests that the technique is not only effective when seeking donations in nonprofit contexts but also when seeking sales in for-profit settings and when trying to change attitudes (Fennis, Das, & Pruyn, 2004, 2006; Kardes, Fennis, Hirt, Tormala, & Bullington, 2007).

LEGITIMIZING PALTRY CONTRIBUTIONS: EVEN A PENNY WILL HELP

If you've ever sought donations for a charity, you've probably had people tell you things like "I can't afford that right now" or "I don't have the money for that." It's a common excuse but also one that might be diffused with a simple approach called *legitimizing paltry contributions*. Specifically, Cialdini and Schroeder (1976) found that while seeking donations for the American Cancer Society, adding the phrase "even a penny will help" to the persuasive message increased the percentage of donations. The approach is thought to be effective not only because it diffuses excuses, but it also makes the request seem like less of an imposition and might make people who refuse the request worry that they'll be perceived as heartless cheapskates (Cialdini & Schroeder, 1976; Pratkanis, 2007; Reeves, Macolini, & Martin, 1987; Takada & Levine, 2007). A good amount of previous research suggests that this approach and its variations (e.g., "Even a few minutes would help.") are an effective way of garnering donations and may be even more effective when combined with other influence techniques (e.g., social proof) and when used face-to-face (Andrews, Carpenter, Shaw, & Boster, 2008; Brockner, Guzzi, Kane, Levine, & Shaplen, 1984; Dejong & Oopik, 1992; Fraser & Hite, 1989; Fraser, Hite, & Sauer, 1988; Reeves et al., 1987; Shearman & Yoo, 2007; Takada & Levine, 2007). One potential downside of the approach is that it is counterproductive when used on people who have little ability to understand other's viewpoint, perhaps because they resent any additional pressure to comply (Takada & Levine, 2007). In addition, some, but not all, research suggests that the approach lowers the amount of the donation a person makes (see Fraser & Hite, 1989 and Shearman & Yoo, 2007, for a discussion). Even so, the larger number of donations may more than compensate.

FEAR-THEN-RELIEF AND HAPPINESS-THEN-DISAPPOINTMENT PROCEDURES: THE EMOTIONAL ROLLER COASTERS OF SOCIAL INFLUENCE

If you are a fan of detective novels and movies, you're undoubtedly familiar with the way the "good cop/bad cop" interrogation operates. First, the "bad cop" mistreats the suspect, humiliating, yelling at, and threatening to do harm to the suspect. Next, the "good cop" enters the interrogation room, asks the bad cop to chill out, and then woos the suspect into confessing with little more than a cup of coffee and a load of kindness. Based on this scenario, Dolinski and Nawrat (Dolinski, 2007; Dolinski & Nawrat, 1998) identified the *fear-then-relief procedure*. The assumption underlying the procedure is that fear causes people to react in a certain way. Specifically, the emotion launches an "action program" that typically stops all other activities while at the same time increasing cautiousness and behaviors such as freezing, fleeing, and so forth. When the fear is suddenly relieved, a "break between programs" occurs that, for a short time, leaves a person disoriented and prone to acting rather mindlessly. It is in that moment, that the person is most prone to influence attempts. Previous research indicates that the procedure is effective. For example, studies that have scared people (e.g., by blowing police whistles at jaywalkers or leaving "tickets" on illegally parked vehicles) and then relieved them (by having the people see that police weren't the ones blowing the whistles or that the tickets were really just leaflets), have found that those people are typically more compliant (e.g., willing to complete surveys) than people who have not undergone the procedure (see Dolinski, 2007). Research also suggests that the persuasive effect of seesawing emotions is not just confined to fear-then-relief. Indeed, one study found that a *happiness-then-disappointment procedure* (e.g., finding a note that had originally looked like money) also led people to comply more with later requests (Nawrat & Dolinski, 2007).

Before concluding this section, we think it's important to reiterate that a number of ethical concerns surround the use of influence tactics, perhaps even more so when persuasion involves unpleasant emotions such as fear. Remember, just because a tactic is effective does not mean it is ethical. Given the importance of these topics, we will have more to say about emotions and ethics in Chapters 13 and 16.

SUMMARY

In this chapter we examined the effectiveness of several sequential tactics of persuasion. Pregiving involves making a persuadee feel indebted so that he or she will be more compliant. The foot-in-the-door tactic involves making a small request and following up with a large one. The foot-in-the-mouth tactic works by getting people to admit to feeling terrific and then trying to get them to behave in a way consistent with their declaration. The door-in-the-face tactic involves making a large request and following up with a smaller one. The that's-not-all tactic seeks compliance by making deals more attractive before persuadees agree to them. When using the lowball tactic, persuadees are asked to agree with an attractive request but are expected to agree with a less attractive request later. Similarly, the bait-and-switch technique lures people with merchandise that is attractive in order to get them to buy substitute merchandise that is less attractive. The disrupt-then-reframe tactic diverts people from resisting requests and then persuades them by putting a positive spin on the request. The legitimization-of-paltry-favors approach minimizes excuses for making a donation. Finally, the fear-then-relief procedure uses changes in emotion to disorient and then persuade people. One thing all these strategies have in common is a home in the real world. They also share a view of persuasion as ongoing or dynamic rather than as a one-shot affair.

ENDNOTES

1. Although we don't think it's common, we don't rule out the possibility of women using this same approach on men.

2. Initially, the three meta-analyses on the foot in the door indicated that the effectiveness of the tactic was small (Beaman, Steblay, Preston, & Klentz, 1983; Dillard et al., 1984; Fern et al., 1986). However, analysis of studies that showed that at least 80 percent of research subjects complied with the first request indicated that the strategy was much more effective. Thus, for the foot in the door tactic to work, the initial request needs to be small enough to achieve a sufficient level of compliance.

3. In contrast, a delay between the first and second request does not seem to hinder the effectiveness of the foot in the door strategy as long as the second request reminds the persuadee of his or her earlier compliance (see DeJong, 1979).

4. Cialdini and Goldstein (2004) argue that this finding also weakens the social responsibility and guilt reduction explanation of the DITF effect.

5. Some prior research suggests that the foot in the door strategy works even when the first and second requests are made by different people.

REFERENCES

Andrews, K. R., Carpenter, C. J., Shaw, A. S., & Boster, F. J. (2008). The legitimization of paltry favors effect: A review and meta-analysis. *Communication Reports, 21,* 59–69.

Aune, R. K., & Basil, M. D. (1994). A relational obligations approach to the foot-in-the mouth technique. *Journal of Applied Social Psychology, 24,* 546–556.

Beaman, A. L., Steblay, N. M., Preston, M., & Klentz, B. (1983). Compliance as a function of elapsed time between first and second requests. *Journal of Social Psychology, 128,* 233–243.

Bell, R. A., Abrahams, M. F., Clark, C. L., & Schlatter, C. (1996). The door-in-the-face compliance strategy: An individual differences analysis of two models in an AIDS fundraising context. *Communication Quarterly, 44*(1), 107–124.

Bell, R. A., Cholerton, M., Fraczek, K. E., Rohlfs, G. S., & Smith, B. A. (1994). Encouraging donations to charity: A field study of competing and complementary factors in tactic sequencing. *Western Journal of Communication, 58,* 98–115.

Bem, D. J. (1972). Self-perception theory. In L. Berkowitz (Ed.), *Advances in experimental social psychology* (Vol. 6, pp. 2–62). New York: Academic Press.

Brockner, J., Guzzi, B., Kane, J., Levine, E., & Shaplan, K. (1984). Organizational fundraising: Further evidence on the effects of legitimizing small donations. *Journal of Consumer Research, 11,* 611–614.

Burger, J. M. (1986). Increasing compliance by improving the deal: The that's-not-all technique. *Journal of Personality and Social Psychology, 31,* 277–283.

Burger, J. M. (1999). The foot-in-the-door compliance procedure: A multiple-process analysis and review. *Personality and Social Psychology Review, 3*(4), 303–325.

Burger, J. M., & Guadagno, R. E. (2003). Self-concept clarity and the foot-in-the-door procedure. *Basic and Applied Social Psychology, 25*(1), 79–86.

Burger, J. M., & Petty, R. E. (1981). The low-ball compliance technique: Task or person commitment? *Journal of Personality and Social Psychology, 40,* 492–500.

Burger, J. M., Reed, M., DeCesare, K., Rauner, S., & Rozolis, J. (1999). The effects of initial request size on compliance: More about the that's-not-all technique. *Basic and Applied Social Psychology, 21*(3), 243–249.

Burger, J. M., Sanchez, J. Imberi, J. E. & Grande, L. R. (2009). The norm of reciprocity as an internalized social norm: Returning favors even when no one finds out. *Social Influence, 4,* 11–17.

Chartrand, T., Pinckert, S., & Burger, J. M. (1999). When manipulation backfires: The effects of time delay and requester on the foot-in-the-door technique. *Journal of Applied Social Psychology, 29*(1), 211–221.

Cialdini, R. B. (1993). *Influence: The psychology of persuasion* (Rev. Ed.). New York: Morrow.

Cialdini, R. B., Caciopppo, J. T., Bassett, R., & Miller, J. A. (1978). Low-ball procedure for producing compliance: Commitment then cost. *Journal of Personality and Social Psychology, 36,* 463–476.

Cialdini, R. B., & Goldstein, N. J. (2004). Social influence: Compliance and conformity. *Annual Review of Psychology, 55,* 591–621.

Cialdini, R. B., & Guadagno, R. E. (2004). Sequential request compliance tactics. In J. S. Seiter & R. H. Gass (Eds.), *Readings in persuasion, social influence, and compliance gaining* (pp. 207–222). Boston: Allyn & Bacon.

Cialdini, R. B., & Schroeder, D. A. (1976). Increasing compliance by legitimizing paltry contributions: When even a penny helps. *Journal of Personality and Social Psychology, 34,* 599–604.

Cialdini, R. B., Trost, M. R., & Newsom, J. T. (1995). Preference for consistency: The development of a valid measure and the discovery of surprising behavioral implications. *Journal of Personality and Social Psychology, 69,* 206–215.

Cialdini, R. B., Vincent, J. E., Lewis, S. K., Catalan, J., Wheeler, D., & Darby, B. L. (1975). Reciprocal concessions procedure for inducing compliance: The door in-the-face technique. *Journal of Personality and Social Psychology, 31,* 206–215.

Davis, B. P., & Knowles, E. S. (1999). A disrupt-then-reframe technique of social influence. *Journal of Personality and Social Psychology, 76*(2), 192–199.

DeJong, W. (1979). An examination of self-perception mediation of the foot-in-the-door effect. *Journal of Personality and Social Psychology, 37,* 2221–2239.

DeJong, W., & Oopik, A. J. (1992). Effect of legitimizing small contributions and labeling potential donors as "helpers" on responses to a direct mail solicitation for charity. *Psychological Reports, 71,* 923–928.

Dillard, J. P. (1990). Self-inference and the foot-in-the-door technique: Quantity of behavior and attitudinal mediation. *Human Communication Research, 16,* 422–447.

Dillard, J. P. (1991). The current status of research on the sequential-request compliance techniques. *Personality and Social Psychology Bulletin, 17,* 283–288.

Dillard, J. P., Hunter, J. E., & Burgoon, M. (1984). Sequential-request persuasive strategies: Meta-analysis of foot-in-the-door and door-in-the-face. *Human Communication Research, 10,* 461–488.

Dolinski, D. (2007). Emotional see-saw. In A. R. Pratkanis (Ed.), *The science of social influence: Advances and future progress* (pp. 137–153). New York: Psychology Press

Dolinski, D., & Nawrat, R. (1998). "Fear-then-relief" procedure for inducing compliance: Beware when the danger is over. *Journal of Experimental Social Psychology, 34,* 27–50.

Even-Chen, M., Yinon, Y., & Bizman, A. (1978). The door in the face technique: Effects of the size of the initial request. *European Journal of Social Psychology, 8,* 135–140.

Fennis, B. M., Das, E. H. H. J., & Pruyn, A. T. H. (2004). "If you can't dazzle them with brilliance baffle them with nonsense": Extending the impact of the disrupt-then-reframe technique of social influence. *Journal of Consumer Psychology, 14,* 280–290.

Fennis, B. M., Das, E. H. H. J., & Pruyn, A. T. H. (2006). Interpersonal communication and compliance: The disrupt-then-reframe technique in dyadic influence settings. *Communication Research, 33,* 136–151.

Fern, E. F., Monroe, K. B., & Avila, R. A. (1986). Effectiveness of multiple request strategies: A synthesis of research results. *Journal of Marketing Research, 23,* 144–152.

Fointiat, V. (2000). "Foot-in-the-mouth" versus "door-in-the-face" requests. *Journal of Social Psychology, 140*(2), 264–266.

Fraser, C., & Hite, R. E. (1989). The effect of matching contribution offers and legitimization of paltry contributions on compliance. *Journal of Applied Social Psychology, 19,* 1010–1018.

Fraser, C., Hite, R. E., & Sauer, P. (1988). Increasing contributions in solicitation campaigns: The use of large and small anchor points. *Journal of Consumer Research, 15,* 284–287.

Freedman, J. L., & Fraser, S. C. (1966). Compliance without pressure. *Journal of Personality and Social Psychology, 4,* 195–202.

George, W. H., Gournic, S. J., & McAfee, M. P. (1988). Perceptions of postdrinking female sexuality. *Journal of Applied Social Psychology, 18,* 1295–1317.

Goei, R., Roberto, A., Meyer, G., & Carlyle, K. (2007). The effects of a favor and apology on compliance. *Communication Research, 34,* 575–595.

Goldman, M. (1986). Compliance employing a combined foot-in-the-door and door-in-the-face procedure. *Journal of Social Psychology, 126,* 111–116.

Goldman, M., & Creason, C. R. (1981). Inducing compliance by a two-door-in-the-face procedure and a self-determination request. *Journal of Social Psychology, 114,* 229–235.

Goldman, M., Creason, C. R., & McCall, C. G. (1981). Compliance employing a two feet-in-the-door procedure. *Journal of Social Psychology, 114,* 259–265.

Goldman, M., Gier, J. A., & Smith, D. E. (1981). Compliance as affected by task difficulty and order of tasks. *Journal of Social Psychology, 114,* 75–83.

Gorassini, D. R., & Olson, J. M. (1995). Does self-perception change explain the foot-in-the-door effect? *Journal of Personality and Social Psychology, 69,* 91–105.

Groves, R. M., Cialdini, R. B., & Couper, M. P. (1992). Understanding the decision to participate in a survey. *Public Opinion Quarterly, 56,* 475–495.

Guadagno, R. E., Asher, T., Demaine, L., & Cialdini, R. B. (2001). When saying yes leads to saying no: Preference for consistency and the reverse foot-in-the-door effect. *Personality and Social Psychology Bulletin, 27,* 859–867.

Guéguen, N. (2001). Social labeling and compliance: An evaluation of the link between the label and the request. *Social Behavior and Personality, 29,* 743–748.

Guéguen, N. (2002). Foot-in-the-door technique and computer-mediated communication. *Computers in Human Behavior, 18,* 11–15.

Howard, D. (1990). The influence of verbal responses to common greetings on compliance behavior: The foot-in-the-mouth effect. *Journal of Applied Social Psychology, 20,* 1185–1196.

Joule, R. V., Gouilloux, F., & Weber, F. (1989). The lure: A new compliance procedure. *Journal of Social Psychology, 129,* 741–749.

Kardes, F. R., Fennis, B. M., Hirt, E. R., Tormala, Z. L., & Bullington, B. (2007). The role of the need for cognitive closure in the effectiveness of the disrupt-then-reframe influence technique. *Journal of Consumer Research, 34,* 377–385.

Knowles, E. S., & Linn, J. A. (2003). Approach–avoidance model of persuasion: Alpha and omega strategies for change. In E. S. Knowles & J. A. Linn (Eds.), *Resistance and persuasion* (pp. 117–148). Mahwah, NJ: Erlbaum.

Millar, M. (2002). Effects of a guilt induction and guilt reduction on door in the face. *Communication Research, 29*(6), 666–680.

Nawrat, R., & Dolinski, D. (2007). "See-saw of emotions" and compliance. Beyond the fear-then-relief rule. *Journal of Social Psychology, 147,* 556–571.

O'Keefe, D. J., & Figgé, M. (1997). A guilt-based explanation of the door-in-the-face influence strategy. *Human Communication Research, 24,* 64–81.

O'Keefe, D. J., & Figgé, M. (1999). Guilt and expected guilt in the door-in-the-face technique. *Communication Monographs, 66,* 312–324.

O'Keefe, D. J., & Hale, S. L. (1998). The door-in-the-face influence strategy: A random-effects meta-analytic review. In M. E. Roloff (Ed.), *Communication yearbook 21*(1–33). Thousand Oaks, CA: Sage.

O'Keefe, D. J., & Hale, S. L. (2001). An odds-ratio-based meta-analysis of research on the door-in-the-face influence strategy. *Communication Reports, 14*(1), 31–38.

Pendleton, M. G., & Batson, C. D. (1979). Self-presentation and the door-in-the face technique for inducing compliance. *Personality and Social Psychology Bulletin, 5,* 77–81.

Pliner, P., Hart, H., Kohl, J., & Saari, D. (1974). Compliance without pressure: Some further data on the foot-in-the-door technique. *Journal of Experimental Social Psychology, 10,* 17–22.

Pratkanis, A. R. (2007). Social influence analysis: An index of tactics. In A. R. Pratkanis (Ed.), *The science of social influence: Advances and future progress* (pp. 17–82). New York: Psychology Press.

Raghubir, P. (2004). Free gift with purchase: Promoting or discounting the brand? *Journal of Consumer Psychology, 14,* 181–186.

Raghubir, P. (2005). Framing a price bundle: The case of "buy/get" offers. *Journal of Product and Brand Management, 14,* 123–128.

Regan, D. T. (1971). Effects of a favor and liking on compliance. *Journal of Experimental Social Psychology, 7,* 627–639.

Reeves, R. A., Macolini, R. M., & Marin, R. C. (1987). Legitimizing paltry contributions: On-the-spot vs. Mail-in requests. *Journal of Applied Social Psychology, 17,* 731–738.

Seligman, C., Bush, M., & Kirsch, K. (1976). Relationship between compliance in the foot-in-the-door paradigm and size of first request. *Journal of Personality and Social Psychology, 33,* 517–520.

Shearman, S. M., & Yoo, J. H. (2007). "Even a penny will help!": Legitimization of paltry donation and social proof in soliciting donation to a charitable organization. *Communication Research Reports, 24,* 271–282.

Snyder, M., & Cunningham, M. R. (1975). To comply or not to comply: Testing the self-perception explanation of the "foot-in-the-door" phenomenon. *Journal of Personality and Social Psychology, 31,* 64–67.

Takada, J., & Levine, T. R. (2007). The effects of the even-a-few-minutes-would-help strategy, perspective taking, and empathetic concern on the successful recruiting of volunteers on campus. *Communication Research Reports, 24,* 177–184.

Turner, M. M., Tamborini, R., Limon, M. S., & Zuckerman-Hyman, C. (2007). The moderators of mediators of door-in-the-face requests: Is it a negotiation or a helping experience? *Communication Monographs, 74,* 333–356.

Tusing, K. J., & Dillard, J. P. (2000). The psychological reality of the door-in-the-face: It's helping, not bargaining. *Journal of Language and Social Psychology, 19*(1), 5–25.

Wagener, J. J., & Laird, J. D. (1980). The experimenter's foot-in-the-door: Self perception, body weight, and volunteering. *Personality and Social Psychology Bulletin, 6,* 441–446.

Weyant, J. M. (1996). Application of compliance techniques to direct-mail requests for charitable donations. *Psychology & Marketing, 13*(2), 157–170.

Williams, G. (1995, September 26). Tuition financing 101. *Financial World,* p. 69.

11

Compliance Gaining

Do you remember Felix, the cartoon cat with the bag of tricks, a veritable warehouse of gizmos and gadgets? It seems that whenever he had that polka-dotted bag, Felix could get himself out of any jam. The funny thing is, sometimes our students remind us of that cat. Take any exam week, for example. Some of the stories we hear are astounding. The only thing is, our students don't need a bag of tricks; they do a fine job of coming up with reasons for missing tests on their own. A popular favorite is a sick or dying grandparent. We don't want to sound unsympathetic here, but if our students are to be believed, mortality and morbidity among grandparents runs extraordinarily high during midterms and finals. We've heard of other tactics as well. One student tried to avoid an exam because he thought his house might be robbed if he came to school. Another one of our students explained that she was reluctant to take exams because of a foreboding horoscope. Who knows what we might hear next term?

Whatever reasons our students might muster, one point is clear: When faced with a situation requiring persuasion, people can come up with any number of strategies or tactics. But what types of strategies are available to people who are seeking compliance? What specific kinds of strategies are people most likely to use? Do the strategies that people use vary across situations?

All of these issues have been explored by researchers who are interested in a very broad topic area that is often labeled *compliance gaining* and that is considered by many to be one of the most important subjects in the study of interpersonal influence. Indeed, Boster (1995) argued that ". . . the study of compliance-gaining message behavior has held the attention of communication scholars as much as, if not more than, any other single topic in the discipline" (p. 91).

Because of the significance and prominence of compliance gaining in our field, we devote this chapter to an examination of compliance-gaining issues and research. Before proceeding, though, a few definitions are in order.

ACTIONS SPEAK THE LOUDEST: A DEFINITION OF COMPLIANCE GAINING

We used to know a guy who liked to say, "I don't care if you hate me, as long as you're nice to me." We think that this maxim is a fine illustration of the distinction between thoughts and actions that undergirds the primary difference between compliance and other forms of persuasion. As we mentioned in Chapter 2, it is useful to distinguish between the terms *persuasion* and *compliance*. Persuasion, an umbrella term, is concerned with changing beliefs, attitudes, intentions, motivations, and behaviors. Compliance is more restrictive, typically referring to changes in a person's overt behavior. For example, a mother might tell her 10-year-old son, "Take out the trash." If the child says, "I don't want to," the mother might respond, "I don't care what you want. Take out the trash!" In this case the mother is not concerned with belief or attitude change. She doesn't care if the child likes taking out the trash, believes in recycling, and so on. She just wants compliance, or behavior change (i.e., the trash taken out). In short, research examining compliance gaining generally focuses on persuasion aimed at getting others to do something or to act in a particular way.

We should also note that compliance gaining differs from more traditional notions of persuasion in a number of important ways. First, for the most part, studies of compliance gaining have concentrated on influence in interpersonal, face-to-face contexts rather than in one-to-many contexts. Moreover, the emphasis has primarily been on "senders" rather than on "receivers." That is, whereas traditional research has concerned itself with identifying what strategies are most effective, studies on compliance gaining have attempted to identify which strategies are most likely to be used by a persuader. In other words, compliance-gaining research focuses on what people do when they want to get something.

With these distinctions in mind, we now turn to a discussion of compliance gaining. We start by examining how compliance-gaining research got started.

IN THE BEGINNING: THE ROOTS OF COMPLIANCE-GAINING RESEARCH

Imagine you were failing a course and wanted a friend to tutor you. What would you do to ask for help? Or imagine that it was not you, but your teenage son, a high school student, who was getting lousy grades because he wouldn't study. What would you do to get him to crack the books? Can you think of several different approaches? If not, read on—you might find a few tactics to add to your repertoire.

Calvin and Hobbes   by Bill Watterson

Although scholars in the field of communication have produced the most research on the topic of compliance gaining, two sociologists, Gerald Marwell and David Schmitt, first got the ball rolling in 1967. After examining past research and theory in the areas of power and influence, these two researchers developed a taxonomy of 16 different tactics that might be used to gain compliance. (These tactics are presented in Table 11.1.) Afterward, they told people to imagine themselves in four scenarios (i.e., requesting a tutor, more studying, a purchase, and a promotion) and asked the people how likely they would be to use each of the 16 tactics in each of the scenarios. Finally, based on the peoples' responses, Marwell and Schmitt grouped the tactics in terms of their commonalities,[1] ultimately identifying five basic types of compliance-gaining strategies:

- **Rewarding activity:** involves seeking compliance in an active and positive way (e.g., making promises).
- **Punishing activity:** involves seeking compliance in an explicitly negative way (e.g., making threats).
- **Expertise:** involves attempts to make a person think that the persuader has some special knowledge (e.g., trying to appear credible).
- **Activation of impersonal commitments:** involves attempts to appeal to a person's internalized commitments (e.g., telling the person he or she will feel bad about him/herself if he/she does not comply).
- **Activation of personal commitments:** relies on appeals to a person's commitment to others (e.g., pointing out that the person is indebted and should, therefore, comply to repay the favor).

Marwell and Schmitt's (1967) study showed that there are a wide range of tactics available to persuaders. It was an important study because it became the springboard for the compliance-gaining studies that followed. Even so, as is often the case with research on human communication, the study made compliance gaining appear more simple than it really is. We will see later in this chapter the ways in which this study was criticized and improved on. First, however, we turn to a discussion of some of the factors that affect the selection of compliance-gaining strategies.

SITUATION: THE "IT DEPENDS" OF COMPLIANCE-GAINING BEHAVIOR

Long before this chapter was written, one of the authors was faced with two different situations requiring persuasion. In the first, the author's then 2-year-old son tried to provoke a food fight at the dinner table by throwing a chunk of roast beef, gravy and all, at his older brother. There was quite a splat. The 2-year-old then proceeded to reach for a second chunk, at which point the author intervened, explaining that any more "beef bombs" would result in a time-out (i.e., 2 minutes of sitting alone in the bedroom). Fortunately, the next hunk of beef found its way into the kid's mouth.

In the second situation, the same author needed to ask his boss to hurry up and look over some paperwork that needed the boss's signature. The deadline for the paperwork was

Marwell and Schmitt's (1967) Compliance-Gaining Tactics, with Examples of How You Might Get Your Teenager to Study	**TABLE 11.1**

1. **Promise:** If you comply, I will reward you. For example, you offer to increase Dick's allowance if he studies more.

2. **Threat:** If you do not comply, I will punish you. For example, you threaten to forbid Dick to use the car if he doesn't start studying more.

3. **Expertise (positive):** If you comply, you will be rewarded because of the "nature of things." For example, you tell Dick that if he gets good grades he will be able to get into college and get a good job.

4. **Expertise (negative):** If you do not comply, you will be punished because of the "nature of things." For example, you tell Dick that if he does not get good grades he will not be able to get into a good college or get a good job.

5. **Liking:** Act friendly and helpful to get the person in a "good frame of mind" so that he or she will comply with the request. For example, you try to be as friendly and pleasant as possible to put Dick in a good mood before asking him to study.

6. **Pregiving:** Reward the person before requesting his or her compliance. For example, you raise Dick's allowance and tell him you now expect him to study.

7. **Aversive stimulation:** Continuously punish the person, making cessation contingent on his or her compliance. For example, you forbid Dick the use of the car and tell him he will not be able to drive until he studies more.

8. **Debt:** You owe me compliance because of past favors. For example, you point out that you have sacrificed and saved to pay for Dick's education and that he owes it to you to get good enough grades to get into a good college.

9. **Moral appeal:** You are immoral if you do not comply. You tell Dick that it is morally wrong for anyone not to get as good grades as possible and that he should study more.

10. **Self-feeling (positive):** You will feel better about yourself if you comply. For example, you tell Dick that he will feel proud if he gets himself to study more.

11. **Self-feeling (negative):** You will feel worse about yourself if you do not comply. For example, you tell Dick that he will feel ashamed of himself if he gets bad grades.

12. **Altercasting (positive):** A person with "good" qualities would comply. For example, you tell Dick that because he is a mature and intelligent person he naturally will want to study more and get good grades.

13. **Altercasting (negative):** Only a person with "bad" qualities would not comply. For example, you tell Dick that he should study because only someone very childish does not study.

14. **Altruism:** I need your compliance very badly, so do it for me. For example, you tell Dick that you really want very badly for him to get into a good college and that you wish he would study more as a personal favor to you.

15. **Esteem (positive):** People you value will think better of you if you comply. For example, you tell Dick that the whole family will be very proud of him if he gets good grades.

16. **Esteem (negative):** People you value will think the worse of you if you do not comply. For example, you tell Dick that the whole family will be very disappointed in him if he gets poor grades.

Adapted from Marwell, G., & Schmitt, D. R. (1967). Dimensions of compliance-gaining behavior: An empirical analysis. *Sociometry, 30,* 350–364.

nearing. Although threatening the boss with something like a time-out had appeal, quite obviously, doing so would not have been appropriate. Instead, the author tapped lightly on the boss's door, smiled, and asked ever so politely whether the boss had "had a chance to look over that paperwork yet?"

The point is that even though we can isolate a specific number of compliance-gaining strategies, not all strategies are appropriate in all situations. To be sure, even when trying to persuade the same person, different contexts require different strategies. For instance, trying to keep a 2-year-old from repeatedly playing near electrical outlets may require a different strategy than trying to get the child to try tasting a horrible-looking vegetable. Obviously, selecting a compliance-gaining strategy depends a lot on the situation.

For quite some time now, communication scholars have argued that compliance-gaining behavior can vary greatly from one situation to the next. By way of example, research by Cody, Woelfel, and Jordan (1983) showed that, when trying to decide which compliance-gaining strategy to use, there are seven situational dimensions that affect those decisions:

- **Dominance:** The level of control or power in a relationship. For example, because a boss generally has more power to influence a subordinate than vice versa, a boss's strategies may differ from a subordinate's.
- **Intimacy:** The level of emotional attachment or knowledge one has of a partner's effect. For example, because they are more intimate and more concerned with the relationship, spouses may use different strategies than strangers.
- **Resistance:** The degree to which the persuader thinks a strategy will be resisted. For example, strategies that are more likely to be resisted will probably not be used as readily as those that are less likely to be resisted. (For more information on resisting compliance, see Box 11.1.)

Just Say No? A Look at Strategies for Resisting Compliance and Resisting Resistance   BOX 11.1

In our opinion, a lot of advertising makes persuasion seem pretty simple. For example, Nike's classic "Just do it" campaign suggested that we should forget all about reasoning and weighing pros and cons. On the other side of the coin, you're probably familiar with the popular slogan for keeping kids off of drugs; "Just say 'no,' " it advises. But is resisting compliance really all that easy? Whatever the case, some research shows that just saying "no" is not the only option available to us when trying to resist the compliance-gaining attempts of others. For instance, a study by McLaughlin, Cody, and Robey (1980) identified four possible strategies you might use to resist persuasion:

1. **Nonnegotiation:** You overtly refuse to comply (you say, "No").
2. **Identity management:** You resist by manipulating images of the other person (you say, "I would never make such an awful request").
3. **Justifying:** You justify noncompliance by pointing to negative outcomes (you say, "If I comply with your request I might lose my job").
4. **Negotiation:** You engage in an alternative behavior that you propose (rather than turn off the stereo, you offer to turn it down).

(continued)

Rather than look at resistance strategies, perhaps a more important issue centers on situations in which people find themselves wanting to resist compliance. One prevalent example occurs when people are pressured into having sex. Indeed, according to Impett and Peplau's (2003) sources, between 26 to 40 percent of men and 50 to 65 percent of women report that they've agreed to have sex even though they did not want to. With this in mind, and considering contemporary issues associated with the spread of AIDS and the prevalence of date rape, researchers have started to examine strategies that can be used to resist sexual advances. An interesting study by Byers and Wilson (1985) examined men's and women's perceptions of the different ways in which women refuse sexual advances by men. In the study, subjects watched a videotape of a man and woman engaged in romantic physical behavior. At some point in the tape, the woman refuses to go any further by (1) simply saying, "No"; (2) saying "No" and offering an excuse (i.e., "someone's coming over"); or (3) saying "No" and offering an explanation (i.e., "we don't know each other well enough"). Results of the study showed that most of the males in the study would comply with all of the requests, but several said they would be reluctant to do so. Moreover, both male and female subjects interpreted the simple "No" and the "No, with explanation" as meaning the man should stop his advances but interpreted the "No" with an excuse as meaning that the man should try making more advances later that day.

One possible problem with messages meant to resist sexual advances centers around the stereotype that "when women say 'no,' they really mean 'yes'" (see Metts & Spitzberg, 1996). Muehlenhard and Hollanbaugh (1988), for example, found that nearly 40 percent of women in their study claimed to have said "no" when they meant "yes" because they did not want to appear promiscuous, wanted to show concern for religious issues, and so forth. Perper and Weis (1987) argued that such token resistance can cause problems by encouraging males not to take "no" for an answer. With this in mind, when faced with such situations, it is important to say what you mean. Indeed, research shows that direct, verbal messages, compared to indirect messages, are the best for avoiding sexual advances

(Christopher & Frandsen, 1990). A possible problem, however, is that sexual rejection messages that are moderately direct are perceived to be more comfortable and "save face" more than very direct messages (Metts, Cupach, & Imahori, 1992).

It is apparent from this discussion so far that resistance strategies, in and of themselves, may not be as important as *how* people respond to those resistance strategies. For instance, deTurck (1985) found that in interpersonal relationships people who have met with noncompliance tend to follow up with more reward and punishment strategies than they did initially. Moreover, in some situations, noncompliance is likely to be met with physical aggression (deTurck, 1987). A related study by Rudd and Burant (1996) found that compared to women in nonviolent relationships, women in violent relationships (i.e., abused women) use more indirect/submissive strategies (ingratiation, promise, allurement, and deceit) followed by more aggressive strategies (threats and warnings). According to Rudd and Burant (1996), these findings support the "violence cycle" phenomena by which a wife first tries to smooth over the conflict, but, on failing, resorts to more aggressive strategies in order "to escalate the inevitable violence so that the conflict will end"(p. 141).

So, what happens if your resistance meets with resistance? For example, what if you're a kid who has just refused a cigarette and ends up getting more pressure to smoke despite your resistance? To study what would happen in such a situation, Reardon, Sussman, and Flay (1989) asked 268 adolescents what they would do to resist a peer who asked them to smoke twice. Results of the study showed that teenagers' rejections became more intense when they were pressured a second time and when there was more than one person doing the pressuring. "Just say no" was found to be a strategy reserved for people who were in less intimate relationships with the teenagers. Finally, if you ever find yourself confronted by a person who wants you to comply when you don't want to, it might help to know this: A study by Hullett and Tamborini (2001) found that the more negative your resistance strategy, the less likely persuaders will be to continue to pursue your compliance.

- **Personal benefits:** The extent to which the self or the other is benefited by compliance. For example, strategies that are perceived to produce the greatest benefits are most likely to be used.
- **Rights:** The extent to which a persuader thinks a request is warranted. For example, a persuader may believe that complaining about a barking dog and losing sleep is justified, but complaining about someone else's hair style is not.
- **Relational consequences:** The degree to which a strategy will have long-term or short-term effects on the persuader's relationship with the persuadee. For example, a threat that may lead to divorce may be less likely than one that merely leads to an argument.
- **Apprehension:** The degree to which a persuader perceives nervousness in the situation. For example, situations filled with anxiety may lead to different strategies than those without anxiety.

It is clear, then, that compliance-gaining behavior depends a great deal on the situation in which it is used. In fact, recent research shows that these situational dimensions not only affect decisions to use strategies but also decisions to suppress them (Hample & Dallinger, 2002). In the following sections, we discuss some research findings on several of these situational dimensions.

Seeking Compliance from Strangers and Intimates

In what is now considered a classic study, Gerald Miller, Frank Boster, Michael Roloff, and David Seibold (1977) examined the effects of intimacy on compliance-gaining behavior. These researchers imagined that compliance gaining in interpersonal relationships would be different from compliance gaining in noninterpersonal relationships. Specifically, because people in interpersonal relationships know their partners well, they can tailor their messages to appeal to their partners' specific wants, needs, interests, and so forth. The same is not true in noninterpersonal relationships, where little is known about the other person. In addition, Miller and colleagues (1977) thought that the type of compliance-gaining strategy a person decided to use would depend on whether a situation had short-term or long-term consequences.

To test their hypotheses, these researchers asked people how likely they would be to use each of Marwell and Schmitt's (1967) strategies to persuade others in four different situations:

1. **Noninterpersonal; short-term consequences:** You want to get a car dealer, whom you barely know, to give you a $1,000 trade-in on your old car.
2. **Noninterpersonal; long-term consequences:** You want your new neighbors, who are planning to cut down a shade tree that adds value to your home, to leave the tree standing.
3. **Interpersonal; short-term consequences:** You have a close relationship with a man or woman and want to cancel a date with him or her in order to visit an old acquaintance who is passing through town.

4. **Interpersonal; long-term consequences:** You have a close relationship with a man or woman and want to persuade him or her to move to another geographical location so you can take a better job.

Results of this study showed that the situation strongly affected strategy choice. In general, people preferred "friendly," socially acceptable strategies (e.g., liking) in all the situations but said they were more likely to use different tactics in different situations. For instance, threat tactics were more likely in short-term, noninterpersonal contexts. Finally, in noninterpersonal situations, people picked a greater variety of strategies, perhaps because, without knowing much about the person they were trying to persuade, more trial and error was necessary (Miller et al., 1977).

Previous research suggests that intimates, compared to strangers, are perceived to be more effective in their compliance-gaining attempts. Dennis (2006), for example, found that people expected intimates, rather than non-intimates, to be more effective when trying to persuade them to engage in healthy behaviors, especially when their intimate others used strategies showing that they cared (e.g., "I don't want your weight to bother you. You should eat better."). For some types of health-related behavior, other strategies were perceived to be effective as well. For instance, when trying to get their romantic partners to stop smoking, intimate others were perceived to be effective when using threat (e.g., "I don't know if I can handle being with you when you smoke.") and liking (e.g., "I'd like kissing you more if your mouth didn't taste like an ashtray.") strategies (Dennis, 2006).

Thus, the choice and perceived effectiveness of compliance-gaining strategies may differ depending on whether a relationship is interpersonal or noninterpersonal. But are all interpersonal relationships the same? One of our favorite studies shows that they are not. Specifically, Witteman and Fitzpatrick (1986) argued that husbands and wives can be categorized into three different couple-types: *Traditionals, Separates,* and *Independents.* They explained that:

> Traditionals hold conventional values about the relationship. These values emphasize stability as opposed to spontaneity. Traditionals exhibit interdependence, both physically and psychologically, and tend not to avoid conflict. Separates hold ambivalent views on the nature of relationships, report having the least interdependence, and avoid open marital conflict. Independents hold fairly nonconventional relational values and maintain some interdependence, yet not with respect to some of the physical and temporal aspects of their lives. Also Independents report some assertiveness and tend to engage in conflict. (p. 132)

Because couples differed in the ways they interacted, Witteman and Fitzpatrick suspected that couples also would differ in the ways they sought compliance. Results of a study confirmed these expectations. First, Traditionals sought compliance by discussing what they expected to be the positive and negative outcomes of a proposed course of action. They tended to be open and used their relationship as a basis of power. Separates, however, did not attempt to identify with their partners or to use their relationship to seek compliance. Instead, Separates focused on the negative consequences of noncompliance and tried to constrain the behavior of their spouses. Finally, Independents, compared to other couple types, used a wider variety of power bases when seeking compliance. They also tended to discount and refute their partners more than other couple types, indicating that Independent couples debate one another relatively intensely.

While it is clear, then, that our use of compliance-gaining strategies depends on how intimate our relationship is and on the type of intimate relationship in which we are involved, research also suggests that our compliance-seeking behaviors are affected by the particular circumstances we face in our relationships. As one example, if the person you are involved with starts thinking about leaving you, are there particular strategies you might use to save the relationship? Research by Buchanan, O'Hair, and Becker (2006) identified four overall strategies that people reported using while attempting to hang on to their spouses. *Commitment*, the most common strategy, includes tactics such as being more loving and caring, being submissive ("I'll do anything to save this relationship), and asking your partner to commit to the relationship. *Alignment*, the second most common strategy, includes tactics like demonstrating to other people that your partner is taken (e.g., by holding hands), punishing your partner's threats of infidelity, and trying to make your partner want you sexually. *Negativity*, the third strategy, includes tactics such degrading your partner, making your partner jealous (e.g., by threatening to be unfaithful), and concealing your partner from others. *Harm*, the last and least frequent strategy, includes tactics such as threatening or being violent toward someone who might come between you and your partner (Buchanan et al., 2006).

Power, Legitimacy, and Politeness

Our earlier illustration about trying to influence a child versus a boss makes it clear that power plays a large role in the selection of compliance-gaining strategies. In what is now considered a seminal work, French and Raven (1960) argued that there are five bases of power that people can draw upon to influence others:

1. A person with *reward power* has control over some valued resource (e.g., promotions and raises).
2. A person with *coercive power* has the ability to inflict punishments (e.g., fire you).
3. *Expert power* is based on what a person knows (e.g., you may do what a doctor tells you to do because he or she knows more about medicine than you do).
4. *Legitimate power* is based on formal rank or position (e.g., you obey someone's commands because he or she is the vice president in the company for which you work).
5. People have *referent power* when the person they are trying to influence wants to be like them (e.g., a mentor often has this type of power).

Regardless of the type of power that's at work, one thing remains clear: Power affects compliance-gaining behavior. For example, although managers are more successful when using consultation, inspirational appeals, rational persuasion, and nonpressure tactics (Yukl, Kim, & Falbe, 1996), because they often believe that their power adds legitimacy to their requests, they may not provide justifications or explanations when seeking compliance. Their influence strategies, therefore, may tend to be more direct than the influence strategies used by their less powerful subordinates (see Hirokawa & Wagner, 2004). Moreover, regardless of the messages they use when seeking compliance, research has shown that people with power tend to be more persuasive than those without it (Levine & Boster, 2001).

BIZARRO © by Dan Piraro. Reprinted by permission.

With that said, is there any hope for people who possess little power? To address this question, several researchers (e.g., Baxter, 1984; Craig, Tracy, & Spisak, 1986; Wilson & Kunkel, 2000) have applied Brown and Levinson's (1987) *politeness theory* to the study of compliance-gaining behavior.

According to *politeness theory,* all people are motivated to maintain two kinds of face: positive and negative. We maintain *positive face* when others like, respect, and approve of us. We maintain *negative face* when we do not feel constrained or impeded by others. According to Brown and Levinson (1987), when making a request of someone else, both types of face may be challenged. First, the request may constrain the other person's freedom, thereby challenging his or her negative face. By way of illustration, asking someone to pick you up at the airport is challenging, because it keeps a person from doing something else that he or she might rather be doing. Second, the request may imply that the other person is being taken advantage of, thereby challenging his or her positive face. For example, in our opinion, the stereotypical sports slob who shouts to his wife, "Bring me another beer!" does not convey much respect.

So, how does the issue of power fit into the picture? According to Brown and Levinson (1987), a person is less likely to comply if his or her face is threatened. Thus, to keep from threatening a person's positive or negative face, we try to be polite when making requests. Moreover, when trying to persuade someone who is more powerful than us, we may have to be extra polite because it is not as likely that our requests will be perceived as legitimate.[2] Research so far has supported this conclusion. For example, in one study, Leslie Baxter (1984) found that compared to less powerful others (i.e., group members), more powerful others (i.e., group leaders) were less polite when making requests. Similarly, two studies found that when students tried to persuade their instructors to change grades or paper deadlines, their compliance-gaining strategies were overwhelmingly positive (Golish, 1999; Golish & Olson, 2000). Not only that, Levine and Boster (2001) found that when people with little power tried to persuade others, positively framed messages were the only ones that met with much success. Considering the preceding studies, you might be wondering which types of strategies are polite and which are not. Most would agree that threats are not as polite as hints. However, threats may be more efficient than hints. To test this notion, Kellermann and Shea (1996) asked people to rate how polite and efficient they perceived several different strategies to be. Interestingly, threats, although impolite, were not considered efficient, and hints, although inefficient, were not considered polite. Perhaps the best way to get compliance is by using direct requests (i.e., explicitly ask for what you want); such requests were among the most efficient strategies and were not considered impolite (Kellermann & Shea, 1996).

While considering the topic of politeness, keep in mind that persuasion is a two-way street. As such, people not only threaten others' face when making requests, they do so when refusing others' requests as well (see Johnson, 2007). By way of example, it would be one thing for Olga to tell Xenia, "I can't take you to the airport because my driver's license was revoked when I was arrested for drunk driving" (a threat to Olga's positive face) and quite another to tell Xenia, "Yeah, right. You're not worth the time, gas, or wear and tear on my vehicle" (a threat to Xenia's positive face). Johnson (2007) has shown that the nature of refusals (i.e., do they threaten the requester's, the target's, or both the requester's and target's positive and/or negative face) affect perceptions about whether the refusal is effective or appropriate.

It is apparent from our discussion so far that behavior designed to gain or resist compliance depends, to a large extent, on several contextual and relational dimensions. (To learn about compliance-gaining behavior in a *specific* context, see Box 11.2.) The context,

---

Take Two Aspirin and Call Me in the Morning: Compliance Gaining between Doctors and Patients	BOX 11.2

If you are at all like us, you almost certainly have a weakness for some type of food that's probably not all that good for you. It might be pizza, or Doritos, or ice cream. For us, it's chocolate. To be sure, if there is a Nutrageous candy bar within walking distance, then "diets be damned" (one of us, who, for integrity's sake, will remain nameless, ate 7 Nutrageous bars in a 24-hour period!).

We imagine that people with limited taste bud control, such as ourselves, pose serious concerns for people in the medical profession. Indeed, physicians

are not only confronted with the task of persuading patients to stay on diets, they are constantly trying to get patients to comply with requests to take medication, return for regular checkups, modify their behaviors, and so forth. When one considers the personal and economic costs of not complying with doctors' requests, the study of persuasion in medical contexts is of obvious significance.

According to Burgoon and Burgoon (1990), compliance gaining in medical contexts is unique because, unlike most other compliance-gaining

(continued)

situations, patients visit physicians voluntarily, pay for physicians' compliance-gaining directives, perceive physicians as experts, and believe that compliance will benefit themselves rather than the physician. Unfortunately, however, Klingle's (2004) and Burgoon, Birk, and Hall's (1991) sources indicate that patient noncompliance is the most significant problem facing medicine today and that patient noncompliance is as high as 62 percent with prescribed drug regimens, 50 percent with medical appointment keeping, and 92 percent with health promotion and lifestyle changes.

For these reasons, researchers have attempted to determine not only what types of compliance-gaining strategies physicians use but also what types of strategies are the most effective. For example, a review of literature by Burgoon and Burgoon (1990) found that physicians prefer to use strategies that appeal to authority, knowledge, and expertise, and tend to avoid threatening and antisocial strategies. Indeed, Schneider and Beaubien (1996) found that positive expertise, legitimacy, and liking (see strategies discussed earlier) accounted for 83.5 percent of all the compliance-gaining strategies used by doctors

on patients. Physicians report that their strategies tend to become more verbally aggressive, however, when patients have not complied with previous requests and have more severe medical problems (Burgoon & Burgoon, 1990).

In addition to issues about strategy use, researchers have also tried to determine what types of strategies are most effective. Some research, for instance, has found that patients are more likely to comply with doctors who express similarity (i.e., indicate that they share things in common with the patient) and are more satisfied with doctors who communicate a willingness to listen, express affection, are composed, are similar, formal, and nondomineering (Burgoon, Pfau, Parrott, Birk, Coker, & Burgoon, 1987). Some research suggests that there are gender differences in strategy effectiveness (Klingle, 2004). Male doctors can get away with using more negative strategies than can female doctors. In addition, research indicates that both female and male doctors who vary their strategies are more effective than doctors who employ the same strategy repeatedly.

however, is not the only factor that affects compliance-gaining behavior. In the next section we explore the impact of individual differences on interpersonal influence.

WHO ARE YOU? INDIVIDUAL CHARACTERISTICS AND COMPLIANCE-GAINING BEHAVIOR

Up to this point we've talked about the whats and whens of compliance gaining. That is, we've shown that past research has pointed to a number of situational dimensions (e.g., interpersonal/noninterpersonal, short-term/long-term consequences) that influence strategy choice. According to Hunter and Boster (1987), however, there is but one factor that determines what types of compliance-gaining strategies will be used in a given situation. These researchers argued that when trying to decide what strategy we will use, we try to determine what the emotional impact of the message will be. For example, if you tried to persuade your friend to study more, the friend might become angry and resentful. However, the friend could be grateful that you cared enough to say something. According to Hunter and Boster, we prefer using strategies that have a positive emotional impact.

But how do we decide which strategies will have a positive emotional impact and which will have a negative emotional impact? Hunter and Boster (1987) argued that each of us has a perceptual "threshold" that helps us make decisions about what strategies are acceptable and what strategies are not. Threatening someone, for example, may exceed the threshold, whereas promising something may not. Strategies that do not cross the threshold are more likely to be used.

A major implication of this model, of course, is that these thresholds are idiosyncratic, varying from one person to the next. Biff, for example, may be perfectly comfortable threatening others, whereas Babbs may not. Obviously, then, individual differences are important in determining the types of compliance-gaining messages that are used. For that reason, considerable research has examined several "sender" characteristics that affect strategy choice. Some of these characteristics include Machiavellianism (O'Hair & Cody, 1987), dogmatism (Roloff & Barnicott, 1979), self-monitoring (Smith, Cody, Lovette, & Canary, 1990; Snyder, 1979), type A personality (Lamude & Scudder, 1993), verbal aggressiveness and argumentativeness (Boster, Levine, & Kazoleas, 1993; Infante, Trebing, Shepard, & Seeds, 1984; Infante & Wigley, 1986), gender (Dallinger & Hample, 1994; deTurck & Miller, 1982; Fitzpatrick & Winke, 1979), culture (Burgoon, Dillard, Doran, & Miller, 1982; Hirokawa & Mirahara, 1986; Lu, 1997; Sellnow, Liu, & Venette, 2006), and age (Haslett, 1983). Because many of these characteristics were detailed in Chapter 5, we use the rest of this section to discuss the work of O'Keefe (1988, 1990), who argued that people produce different compliance-gaining messages because they think differently about what communication is and does. O'Keefe called these different beliefs about communication *design logics* and argued that they are threefold:

1. **Expressive design logic:** A person with this design logic believes that communication is a process by which people merely express what they think and feel. Such people fail to realize that communication can be used to achieve other goals and, therefore, "speak from the gut," dumping whatever they think and feel without any regard for what might be appropriate in a given situation. For that reason, such people's messages tend to be "primitive." For instance, a person with an expressive design logic might say something like the following: "You **##*$*@ jerk. You've had it. I'm going to get you fired for this!"

2. **Conventional design logic:** A person with this design logic believes that communication is a game played cooperatively, according to social conventions and procedures. Thus, people using this logic express their thoughts and feelings, but believe that they also must follow rules for appropriate social behavior in a given situation. For instance, a person with a conventional design logic might say something like the following: "You missed our meeting today and I don't appreciate this irresponsibility. If you miss one more meeting, you're fired."

3. **Rhetorical design logic:** A person with a rhetorical design logic believes that communication's purpose is to negotiate character, attitude, selves, and situations. The process involves repeatedly solving and coordinating problems, consensus, and harmony. Thus, someone with this logic pursues multiple goals, tends to be proactive, and uses rational arguments. Here's an example: "You have been coming back late from lunch and we need to reach some kind of understanding about this. I don't want to have to force you to follow the rules, but I will if I have to. But surely you can appreciate why we have rules and what function they serve. I know if you just think about the situation you will see how your behavior could be creating a problem in this office" (O'Keefe, 1988, p. 103).

Research has found that messages reflecting rhetorical design logic are rated as more competent, favorable, and persuasive than messages reflecting the other design logics (Bingham & Burleson, 1989; O'Keefe & McCornack, 1987), although such perceptions may depend on certain factors, such as the type of relationship between compliance seeker and persuadee (Hullman, 2004).

PROBLEMS FACING COMPLIANCE RESEARCH: TROUBLE IN PARADISE

Up to this point, the things we have said about compliance gaining probably seem fairly simple; when trying to persuade people, we have a number of strategies at our disposal, and the strategies we use are determined in part by the situation and in part by our personal characteristics. Despite this rather straightforward description, however, compliance-gaining research has not been so simple. To be sure, there has been a lot of confusion and argument about the best way to study compliance-gaining behavior. Although some of these concerns can get a bit complex and tedious, we believe it is important to mention at least some of them here. Indeed, if we hope to understand the nature of compliance gaining, it is essential that we know about the appropriateness of the methods used to study it. In this section we discuss some of the most visible methodological concerns.

Problems with Typology Development: Here a Strategy, There a Strategy

Earlier we talked about Marwell and Schmitt's (1967) typology of 16 compliance-gaining strategies. Although a considerable amount of research resulted from that study, it wasn't long before their typology met with criticism. For example, Wiseman and Schenck-Hamlin (1981) argued that, among other problems, the original typology was flawed because it left out many significant strategies that people might use when seeking compliance. Marwell and Schmitt, they argued, had derived their strategies only from previous theory (e.g., "on the drawing board"), and, therefore, the strategies may not correspond with those used by people in real life. To overcome this problem, Wiseman and Schenck-Hamlin (1981) developed a new typology. This time, instead of using past theory to derive strategies, the researchers presented people with persuasive situations and asked them to *generate* a list of strategies they would use in the situations.[3] As a result, Wiseman and Schenck-Hamlin came up with a different typology that distinguished 14 compliance-gaining strategies, many of which differed from Marwell and Schmitt's original typology.

Since that time, typology development has been a popular undertaking. Indeed, after a review of literatures on linguistic devices, interpersonal communication, clinical psychology, child psychology, social psychology, organizational communication, education, marketing, consumer research, and sexual behavior, Kellermann and Cole (1994) identified no fewer than 74 typologies of compliance-gaining messages! What's more, an integration of these studies resulted in a new "super" typology of 64 distinct compliance-gaining strategies. (We won't identify all 64 of these strategies here, or your instructor might test you on them.)

After noting several problems with existing typologies,[4] Kellermann and Cole (1994) argued that the traditional search for a typology of strategies should be scrapped. Instead, they argued that research should focus on "features" of compliance-gaining messages. In other words, instead of trying to come up with the "right list of strategies," or a "comprehensive list of strategies" (see O'Keefe, 1994), research would address questions regarding "features" of messages, such as how polite a compliance-gaining message was. For example, a research study might attempt to determine whether the level of intimacy in a relationship affected the degree of politeness in the compliance-gaining strategies used. Telling a visiting relative not to smoke in your home, for instance, might require a different strategy than telling a stranger sitting under a no-smoking sign in a restaurant to "take your butt outside."

Creating versus Selecting and Other Methodological Problems

If you could listen to any song right now, what would it be? Can you think of three songs? How about three songs from last year? Depending on how much music you listen to, coming up with songs off the top of your head might not be all that easy. But imagine, for a moment, that you are standing in front of a jukebox and can shuffle through a list of titles before deciding what to pick. Would picking be easier? Do you think the songs you selected would be different if you couldn't see the titles? We suspect they might.

But what does all of this have to do with compliance-gaining research? If you stop to think about it, the Marwell and Schmitt (1967) study we discussed earlier is not entirely different from our jukebox example. Only, instead of asking their research participants to select from a list of song titles, Marwell and Schmitt asked people to select from a list of preestablished compliance-seeking strategies. The problems with such an approach, however, have been pointed out by numerous researchers (e.g., Cody, McLaughlin, & Jordan, 1980; Wiseman & Schenck-Hamlin, 1981). First, by way of illustration, let's return to the jukebox example. Let's say your favorite Partridge Family song was not a jukebox selection, so you settle for a Liberace number (a favorite of jukebox lovers). Obviously, your choice has been constrained by the songs that are available on the jukebox. You can't pick a song if it's not available. Researchers who provide their subjects with lists of compliance-gaining strategies constrain their subjects' choices in the same way. That is, lists of strategies often leave things out. You can't pick a strategy if it isn't on the list.

Second, imagine that you notice an old song that you had forgotten about and would not have selected if you'd never seen it listed. If we heard you listening to the song, we might guess that the song is more popular than it really is. In other words, seeing the song title made you more likely to listen to it. In the same way, strategies selected from a list can artificially "cue" participants. When participating in a study, it's possible that we see a strategy on a list and think, "Oh yeah, that seems like a good one." But in real life, we might never entertain such a strategy. Thus, the list makes some strategies seem more popular than they truly are.

Finally, imagine that you hate country music but are with a group of friends who love the stuff. To fit in, you two-step over to the jukebox and play some Willie Nelson. Researchers have argued that the same type of thing can happen when participating in research. Specifically, in order to "fit in" or "look good," we may not report what we would do in real life but rather what makes us look the most socially desirable. Thus, although Biff may go around threatening people in real life, he may tell researchers that he uses more prosocial compliance-gaining tactics. Having a list of tactics to choose from may make this *social desirability bias* more likely to occur.

In an attempt to overcome these problems, some researchers have scrapped "selection" in favor of "construction" procedures (e.g., Wiseman & Schenck-Hamlin, 1981). The argument goes like this: If people are presented with a situation requiring persuasion and are asked to describe the strategy they would use (i.e., construct the strategy from scratch rather then select it from a list), the strategy will better reflect true behavior, not misrepresent strategies that are not typically used, and be less prone to social desirability bias.

As neat as this sounds, research indicates little difference in the results of studies using these two techniques (Boster, 1988; Plax, Kearney, & Sorensen, 1990). What may be of even greater importance, though, are the findings of a study by Dillard (1988). To determine which of several methods for assessing compliance-gaining behavior was the best,[5] Dillard asked people to rate, on paper, how likely they would be to use 16 different compliance-gaining messages in persuasive situations. He then observed these people in actual compliance-gaining situations but found that, regardless of the method he used to assess compliance-gaining behavior, there was no correspondence between the paper-pencil measures and actual behavior. In other words, what people *said* they would do was not the same as what they actually *did*.

When we consider the implications of this study, it reminds us of a story we once heard about a man who exits a cab late at night and sees a drunk on his hands and knees, snooping around a street light. The man asks, "Is anything wrong?" to which the drunk replies, "Yeah, I lost my keys." The man says, "Did you lose them here?" The drunk answers, "Naw, I lost them over there in the dark, but the light is much better here." In the same vein, Dillard's (1988) study illustrates that investigators have been looking very hard at compliance gaining, but perhaps not in the right way. Rather than examine compliance gaining in artificial laboratory settings using hypothetical situations, investigators should look for compliance gaining as it occurs in more naturalistic contexts.

THE STUDY OF COMPLIANCE-GAINING GOALS: EYES ON THE PRIZE

In recent years, the study of compliance gaining has shifted to a focus on goals (Dillard, 2004). Simply defined, goals are states of affairs we want to attain or maintain often through persuasion (see Wilson, 1997). The following sections examine the ways in which goals are important when trying to understand compliance gaining.

How Goals Bring Meaning to Compliance-Gaining Situations: What's It All about, Alfie?

Years ago, one of the authors heard a story about two men scooping mud and straw into wooden molds. A passerby asked one of the men what he was doing. "Scooping mud and straw into this mold," the man told him.

"What are you doing?" the passerby asked the second man, who seemed much happier than the first.

"I'm part of a team making a beautiful cathedral," came the reply.

We like this story because it illustrates how goals can help people define situations. Clearly, the first man's goal (scooping mud) makes his situation seem dismal compared to the second man's. Our point here is that goals give meaning to situations, including situations that involve compliance gaining. According to Wilson and Kunkel (2000), "Individuals interpret compliance gaining episodes based on their understanding of specific influence goals" (p. 197). In a summary of literature, Kellermann (2004) identified several common compliance-gaining goals that appear meaningful to people. These included goals to provide guidance; get advice, a favor, permission, or information; share time; initiate, escalate, or end a relationship; fulfill an obligation; get a date; change an opinion; and stop an annoying habit (Kellermann, 2004).

How might these different influence goals affect perceptions of a situation and, in turn, the ways in which compliance is sought? By way of example, imagine that you have two different influence goals. One is to ask someone a favor. The other is to get someone who owes you a favor to repay you in some way. According to Cai and Wilson (2000), requests such as these create entirely different situations for persuaders and, as a result, may lead to different compliance-seeking behavior. Clearly, this notion relates to our earlier discussion of politeness and compliance gaining. For instance, because asking favors may impose on another person, when asking favors, you may be less direct, provide the target with a "way out," and provide a lot of reasons for your imposition. However, if you're seeking compliance from someone who owes you a favor, you might be more direct and less polite in your compliance attempts, perhaps even making the target feel guilty if he or she does not comply.

Research by Cai and Wilson (2000) suggests that different types of requests, such as these, present similar concerns for persuaders in all cultures, though cultural differences may occur when making such requests. For instance, on the one hand, asking a favor may lead you to feel indebted, regardless of your cultural background. On the other hand, because they are more concerned with saving face, people from Japan, compared to those from the United States, may worry more about imposing on others. As a result, the Japanese may be less direct and especially polite when seeking favors (Cai & Wilson, 2000).

Primary and Secondary Goals: Wanting and Eating Your Cake

If we told you that the most effective strategy for getting something was to make threats, would you start threatening people every time you wanted something?

> "Loan me 20 bucks, or I'll break your nose!"
> "If you want to keep your job, get me some coffee!"
> "Keep it up, and you can stand in the corner for the next hour."
> "Let me get a tattoo, or I'll run away from home!"

We suspect that, for most of you, the answer to this question would be "no." But why? If threats really were so effective, why not throw them around a little? Because, you might be thinking to yourself, if I made threats every time I wanted something, I might not have many friends. Plus, you probably wouldn't like yourself too much. And if the other party still refused, you might be forced to follow through with the threat.

In the previous section, we discussed several different types of influence goals. In this section, we note that influence goals are not the only ones affecting compliance gaining. Indeed, most of the time we are concerned with pursuing multiple goals at the same time. Kellermann (1992), for example, argued that when seeking compliance, people are constrained by concerns for both efficiency (achieving their goal without wasting time and other resources) and appropriateness (accomplishing their goal in a socially acceptable and respectful way). Similarly, in his *goals–plans–action theory,* James Dillard (2004, 2008) argues that people pursue different types of goals when they are trying to influence someone. These goals are important because they determine the types of strategies that people plan to use when trying to gain compliance. To identify these goals, Dillard and colleagues (Dillard, Segrin, & Harden, 1989) asked students to imagine themselves in a compliance-gaining situation and to state why they would or wouldn't use particular influence strategies in that situation. Results of the study indicated that one primary goal, to influence the other person, is the most important in determining the type of strategy that a person uses. For example, a person may decide not to use a strategy because he or she thinks it won't work or because it is irrelevant.

In addition, Dillard (2008) identifies several secondary goals that influence people's choices in compliance-gaining situations. First, *identity goals* are concerned with maintaining one's moral standards and principles for living. Thus, people might decide to ignore a strategy that seems immoral. Second, *interaction goals* are concerned with creating a good impression and behaving in appropriate ways. For instance, people motivated by this goal might refuse to use a strategy that would make them look bad. Third, *resource goals* are concerned with maintaining a relationship and increasing personal rewards. Thus, using a strategy that would end a friendship would not be likely. Finally, *arousal goals* are concerned with maintaining levels of arousal (e.g., nervousness) within an acceptable range. Thus, people with this goal would not use a strategy that would make them too anxious (Dillard, 2008; Dillard et al., 1989).

According to the goals–plans–action theory (Dillard, 2008), then, primary and secondary goals have different degrees of compatibility. Based on the relationships among all the goals involved, a person develops *plans*, which are possible methods or approaches for dealing with the complex structure of goals. In order to generate and then put plans into action, people seeking compliance must consider possible strategies and tactics.

Of course, a number of variables might affect goals, plans, and actions in the process of seeking compliance. Consider, for example, relational certainty. It turns out that some people are far more certain than others when it comes to knowing whether they or their partners want to pursue a relationship. Given this, Knobloch (2006) surmised that, when asking someone for a date, things would go more smoothly for people who experienced little relational ambiguity than for those who experienced a lot of it. Specifically, those with less certainty are more likely to worry about competing goals such as damaging a friendship. Not only that, when planning and using their compliance-gaining messages, uncertainty may make people less sure about what to say. It might also get in the way of them saying it effectively. To test these ideas, research participants were observed requesting hypothetical dates from people they were attracted to in real life. The participants were asked to leave phone messages, requesting dates from people they knew and were attracted to. Some were more certain about their relationships than others. Results of the study confirmed the researcher's suspicions: Relational certainty was associated with requests for dates that were judged to be more fluent, affiliative, and effective. Here are two examples of requests from the study (Knobloch, 2006, p. 273). We hope it is obvious which was produced by the person with more relational certainty:

> "Hey babe, it's Kevin. I was just calling to see if you had any plans tonight, 'cause I wondered if I could take you out to dinner or something. So, just give me a call whenever you get the message. Bye."
>
> "Hey, Emily, uh, this is Bob. Um, yeah, just wondering what you were up to tonight. Uh, haven't talked to you in . . . in a little while, so, uh, yeah, I think there's some stuff we need to talk about. So, um, if I don't end up talking to you, I guess I'll talk to you on the Internet later. We'll see ya."

In short, then, compliance-gaining situations are not as simple as they may seem. People not only generate and select tactics that they think will help them gain compliance but do so in the face of multiple constraints, including competing goals and other factors.

SUMMARY

In this chapter we focused on the study of compliance gaining. Early research in this area attempted to discover the different types of strategies that people use to get other people to behave in certain ways. Early research also focused on the ways in which situations and individual characteristics affected the use of compliance-gaining strategies. In this chapter we showed that compliance-gaining research has been plagued by several problems, including concerns about typology development and difficulties surrounding the measurement of compliance. Finally, we discussed the notion of compliance-gaining goals and how differing goals influence the choice of compliance-gaining strategies.

ENDNOTES

1. There is a statistical test called *factor analysis* that can determine whether several separate measures or, in this case, tactics, can be combined into fewer or more basic items. This is the method used by Marwell and Schmitt (1967).

2. Other factors that cause people to be more or less polite are relational intimacy, cost of compliance, deservingness of aid, directness of the request, and the magnitude of the request (see Baxter, 1984; Clark, 1993).

3. Because Marwell and Schmitt's (1967) typology was based on previous theory, it is often said that their typology was "deductively derived." However, Wiseman and Schenck-Hamlin's typology, generated by responses from research participants, was "inductively derived."

4. According to Kellermann and Cole (1994), existing typologies of compliance-gaining strategies are problematic for several reasons. First, current typologies are not

exhaustive. In other words, any given typology may leave out strategies that persuaders might use. Second, there are no clear distinctions between different types of categories so that some categories are confused while others seem to overlap. Finally, Kellermann and Cole (1994) argued that definitions and examples of strategies found in prior research are often incomplete, not understandable, not representative, and irrelevant. In short, a few decades of research have produced nothing but an atheoretical hodgepodge of strategies (Kellermann & Cole, 1994).

5. Three prior methods have been used to assess compliance-gaining behavior, each using a different dependent variable. First, the technique approach treats each individual compliance-gaining tactic as a separate, dependent variable and assumes that the correspondence between selected tactics (selected from a checklist) and used tactics will be high. Second, the strategy approach treats groups of tactics as dependent variables and assumes that correspondence between strategy choice and use will be high. Finally, the summed-tactic approach argues that a single, dependent variable is indicative of some global compliance-gaining attempt and assumes that the summed-tactic-selection score will correspond to the frequency of compliance-gaining messages (see Dillard, 1988).

REFERENCES

Baxter, L. (1984). An investigation of compliance-gaining as politeness. *Human Communication Research, 10,* 427–456.

Bingham, S. G., & Burleson, B. R. (1989). Multiple effects of messages with multiple goals: Some perceived outcomes of responses to sexual harassment. *Human Communication Research, 16,* 184–216.

Boster, F. J. (1988). Comments on the utility of compliance-gaining message selection tasks. *Human Communication Research, 15,* 169–177.

Boster, F. J. (1995). Commentary on compliance-gaining message behavior research. In C. Berger & M. Burgoon (Eds.), *Communication and social influence processes* (pp. 91–113). East Lansing: Michigan State University Press.

Boster, F. J., Levine, T. R., & Kazoleas, D. C. (1993). The impact of argumentativeness and verbal aggressiveness on strategic diversity and persistence in compliance gaining behavior. *Communication Quarterly, 41,* 405–414.

Brown, P., & Levinson, S. (1987). *Politeness: Some universals in language usage.* Cambridge, UK: Cambridge University Press.

Buchanan, M. C., O'Hair, D., & Becker, J. A. H. (2006). Strategic communication during marital relationship dissolution: Disengagement resistance strategies. *Communication Research Reports, 23,* 139–147.

Burgoon, J. K., Pfau, M., Parrott, R., Birk, T., Coker, R., & Burgoon, M. (1987). Relational communication, satisfaction, compliance-gaining strategies, and compliance in communication between physicians and patients. *Communication Monographs, 54,* 307–324.

Burgoon, M., Birk, T., & Hall, J. R. (1991). Compliance and satisfaction with physician–patient communication: An expectancy theory interpretation of gender differences. *Human Communication Research, 18,* 177–208.

Burgoon, M., Dillard, J. P., Doran, N. E., & Miller, M. D. (1982). Cultural and situational influences on the process of persuasive strategy selection. *International Journal of Intercultural Relations, 6,* 85–100.

Burgoon, M. H., & Burgoon, J. K. (1990). Compliance-gaining and health care. In J. P. Dillard (Ed.), *Seeking compliance: The production of interpersonal influence messages* (pp. 161–188). Scottsdale, AZ: Gorsuch Scarisbrick.

Byers, E. S., & Wilson, P. (1985). Accuracy of women's expectations regarding men's responses to refusals of sexual advances in dating situations. *International Journal of Women's Studies, 8,* 376–387.

Cai, D. A., & Wilson, S. R. (2000). Identity implications of influence goals: Cross-cultural comparison of interaction goals and facework. *Communication Studies, 51,* 307–328.

Christopher, F. S., & Frandsen, M. M. (1990). Strategies of influence in sex and dating. *Journal of Social and Personal Relationships, 7,* 89–105.

Clark, R. A. (1993). The impact of cost of compliance, deservingness of aid, and directness of a request on reactions to the request. *Southern Communication Journal, 58,* 215–226.

Cody, M. J., McLaughlin, M. L., & Jordan, W. J. (1980). A multidimensional scaling of three sets of compliance-gaining strategies. *Communication Quarterly, 28,* 34–46.

Cody, M. J., Woelfel, M. L., & Jordan, W. J. (1983). Dimensions of compliance-gaining situations. *Human Communication Research, 9,* 99–113.

Craig, R. T., Tracy, K., & Spisak, F. (1986). The discourse of requests: Assessment of a politeness approach. *Human Communication Research, 12,* 437–468.

Dallinger, J. M., & Hample, D. (1994). The effects of gender on compliance gaining strategy endorsement and suppression. *Communication Reports, 7,* 43–49.

Dennis, M. R. (2006). Compliance and intimacy: Young adults' attempts to motivate health-promoting behaviors by romantic partners. *Health Communication, 19,* 259–267.

deTurck, M. (1985). A transactional analysis of compliance-gaining behavior: Effects of noncompliance, relational contexts and actor's gender. *Human Communication Research, 12,* 54–78.

deTurck, M. (1987). When communication fails: Physical aggression as a compliance-gaining strategy. *Communication Monographs, 54,* 106–112.

deTurck, M. A., & Miller, G. R. (1982). The effect of birth order on the persuasive impact of messages and the likelihood of persuasive message selection. *Communication, 11,* 78–84.

Dillard, J. P. (1988). Compliance-gaining message-selection: What is our dependent variable? *Communication Monographs, 55,* 162–183.

Dillard, J. P. (2004). The goals–plans–action model of interpersonal influence. In J. S. Seiter & R. H. Gass (Eds.), *Readings in persuasion, social influence, and compliance gaining* (pp. 185–206). Boston: Allyn & Bacon.

Dillard, J. P. (2008). Goals–plans–action theory of message production: Making influence messages. In L. A. Baxter & D. O. Braithwaite (Eds.), *Engaging theories in interpersonal communication: Multiple perspectives* (pp. 65–76). Los Angeles: Sage.

Dillard, J. P., Segrin, C., & Harden, J. M. (1989). Primary and secondary goals in the production of interpersonal influence messages. *Communication Monographs, 56,* 19–38.

Fitzpatrick, M. A., & Winke, J. (1979). You always hurt the one you love: Strategies and tactics in interpersonal conflict. *Communication Quarterly, 27,* 3–11.

French, J. P. R., Jr., & Raven, B. (1960). The bases of social power. In D. Cartwright & A. Zander (Eds.), *Group dynamics* (pp. 607–623). New York: Harper & Row.

Golish, T. D. (1999). Students' use of compliance gaining strategies with graduate teaching assistants: Examining the other end of the power spectrum. *Communication Quarterly, 47,* 12–32.

Golish, T. D., & Olson, L. N. (2000). Students' use of power in the classroom: An investigation of student power, teacher power, and teacher immediacy. *Communication Quarterly, 48,* 293–310.

Hample, D., & Dallinger, J. M. (2002). The effects of situation on the use or suppression of possible compliance-gaining appeals. In M. Allen & R. W. Preiss (Eds.), *Interpersonal communication research: Advance through meta-analysis* (pp. 187–209). Mahwah, NJ: Erlbaum.

Haslett, B. (1983). Preschoolers' communication strategies in gaining compliance from peers: A developmental study. *Quarterly Journal of Speech, 69,* 84–99.

Hirokawa, R. Y., & Mirahara, A. (1986). A comparison of influence strategies utilized in American and Japanese organizations. *Communication Quarterly, 34,* 250–265.

Hirokawa, R. Y., & Wagner, A. E. (2004). Superior–subordinate influence in organizations. In J. S. Seiter & R. H. Gass (Eds.), *Readings in persuasion, social influence and compliance gaining* (pp. 337–351). Boston: Allyn & Bacon.

Hullett, C. R., & Tamborini, R. (2001). When I'm within my rights: An expectancy-based model of actor evaluative and behavioral responses to compliance-resistance strategies. *Communication Studies, 52,* 1–16.

Hullman, G. A. (2004). Interpersonal communication motives and message design logic: Exploring their interaction on perceptions of competence. *Communication Monographs, 71(2),* 208–225.

Hunter, J. E., & Boster, F. (1987). A model of compliance-gaining message selection. *Communication Monographs, 54,* 63–84.

Impett, E. A., & Peplau, L. A. (2003). Sexual compliance: Gender, motivational, and relational perspectives. *Journal of Sex Research, 40,* 87–100.

Infante, D. A., Trebing, D. W., Shepard, P. E., & Seeds, D. E. (1984). The relationship of argumentativeness to verbal aggression. *Southern States Speech Journal, 50,* 67–77.

Infante, D. A., & Wigley, C. J. (1986). Verbal aggressiveness: An interpersonal model and measure. *Communication Monographs, 53,* 61–69.

Johnson, D. I. (2007). Politeness theory and conversational refusals: Associations between various types of face threat and perceived competence. *Western Journal of Communication, 71,* 196–215.

Kellermann, K. (1992). Communication: Inherently strategic and primarily automatic. *Communication Monographs, 59,* 288–300.

Kellermann, K. (2004). A goal-directed approach to gaining compliance: Relating differences among goals to differences in behaviors. *Communication Research, 31*(4), 347–445.

Kellermann, K., & Cole, T. (1994). Classifying compliance gaining messages: Taxonomic disorder and strategic confusion. *Communication Theory, 4,* 3–60.

Kellermann, K., & Shea, B. C. (1996). Threats, suggestions, hints, and promises: Gaining compliance efficiently and politely. *Communication Quarterly, 44*(2), 145–165.

Klingle, R. S. (2004). Compliance in medical contexts. In J. S. Seiter & R. H. Gass (Eds.), *Perspectives on persuasion, social influence and compliance gaining* (pp. 289–315). Boston: Allyn & Bacon.

Knobloch, L. K. (2006). Relational uncertainty and message production within courtship: Features of date request messages. *Human Communication Research, 32,* 244–273.

Lamude, K. G., & Scudder, J. (1993). Compliance-gaining techniques of type-A managers. *Journal of Business Communication, 30,* 63–78.

Levine, T. R., & Boster, F. J. (2001). The effects of power and message variables on compliance. *Communication Monographs, 68,* 28–48.

Lu, S. (1997). Culture and compliance gaining in the classroom: A preliminary investigation of Chinese college teachers' use of behavior alteration techniques. *Communication Education, 46*(1), 11–43.

Marwell, G., & Schmitt, D. R. (1967). Dimensions of compliance-gaining behavior: An empirical analysis. *Sociometry, 30,* 350–364.

McLaughlin, M. L., Cody, M. J., & Robey, C. S. (1980). Situational influences on the selection of strategies to resist compliance-gaining attempts. *Human Communication Research, 7,* 14–36.

Metts, S., Cupach, W. R., & Imahori, T. T. (1992). Perceptions of sexual compliance-resisting messages in three types of cross-sex relationships. *Western Journal of Communication, 56,* 1–17.

Metts, S., & Spitzberg, B. H. (1996). Sexual communication in interpersonal contexts: A script-based approach. In B. R. Burleson (Ed.), *Communication*

yearbook 19 (pp. 49–92). Thousand Oaks, CA: Sage.

Miller, G. R., Boster, F., Roloff, M., & Seibold, D. (1977). Compliance-gaining message strategies: A typology and some findings concerning effects of situational differences. *Communication Monographs, 44,* 37–51.

Muehlenhard, C. L., & Hollanbaugh, L. C. (1988). Do women sometimes say no when they mean yes? The prevalence and correlates of women's token resistance to sex. *Journal of Personality and Social Psychology, 55,* 872–879.

O'Hair, D., & Cody, M. J. (1987). Machiavellian beliefs and social influence. *Western Journal of Speech Communication, 51,* 279–303.

O'Keefe, B. J. (1988). The logic of message design: Individual differences in reasoning about communication. *Communication Monographs, 55,* 80–103.

O'Keefe, B. J. (1990). The logic of regulative communication: Understanding the logic of message designs. In J. P. Dillard (Ed.), *Seeking compliance: The production of interpersonal influence messages* (pp. 87–106). Scottsdale, AZ: Gorsuch Scarisbrick.

O'Keefe, B. J., & McCornack, S. A. (1987). Message logic and message goal structure: Effects on perceptions of message quality in regulative communication situations. *Human Communication Research, 14,* 68–92.

O'Keefe, D. J. (1994). From strategy-based to feature-based analyses of compliance gaining message classification and production. *Communication Theory, 4,* 61–69.

Perper, T., & Weis, D. L. (1987). Proceptive and rejective strategies of U.S. and Canadian college women. *Journal of Sex Research, 23,* 455–480.

Plax, T., Kearney, P., & Sorensen, G. (1990). The strategy selection–construction controversy II: Comparing pre- and experienced teachers' compliance-gaining message constructions. *Communication Education, 39,* 128–141.

Reardon, K. K., Sussman, S., & Flay, B. R. (1989). Are we marketing the right message?: Can kids "just say 'no' to smoking?" *Communication Monographs, 56,* 307–324.

Roloff, M. E., & Barnicott, E. F., Jr. (1979). The influence of dogmatism on the situational use of pro- and anti-social compliance-gaining strategies. *Southern Speech Communication Journal, 45,* 37–54.

Rudd, J. E., & Burant, P. A. (1996). A study of women's compliance-gaining behaviors in violent and non-violent relationships. *Communication Research Reports, 12*(2), 134–144.

Schneider, D. E., & Beaubien, R. A. (1996). A naturalistic investigation of compliance gaining strategies employed by doctors in medical interviews. *Southern Communication Journal, 61*(4), 332–341.

Sellnow, D., Liu, M., & Venette, S. (2006). When in Rome, do as the Romans do: A comparative analysis of Chinese and American new teachers' compliance-gaining strategies. *Communication Research Reports, 23,* 259–264.

Smith, S. W., Cody, M. J., Lovette, S., & Canary, D. J. (1990). Self-monitoring, gender, and compliance-gaining goals. In M. J. Cody & M. L. McLaughlin (Eds.), *The psychology of tactical communication* (pp. 91–135). Philadelphia: Multilingual Matters.

Snyder, M. (1979). Self-monitoring processes. In L. Berkowitz (Ed.), *Advances in experimental social psychology* (Vol. 12, pp. 85–128). New York: Academic Press.

Wilson, S. R. (1997). Developing theories of persuasive message production: The next generation. In J. O. Greene (Ed.), *Message production: Advances in communication theory* (pp. 15–43). Mahwah, NJ: Erlbaum.

Wilson, S. R., & Kunkel, A. W. (2000). Identity implications of influence goals: Similarities in perceived face threats and facework across sex and close relationships. *Journal of Language and Social Psychology, 19,* 195–221.

Wiseman, R. L., & Schenck-Hamlin, W. (1981). A multidimensional scaling validation of an inductively-derived set of compliance-gaining strategies. *Communication Monographs, 48,* 251–270.

Witteman, H., & Fitzpatrick, M. A. (1986). Compliance-gaining in marital interaction: Power bases, processes and outcomes. *Communication Monographs, 53,* 130–143.

Yukl, G., Kim, H., & Falbe, C. M. (1996). Antecedents of influence outcomes. *Journal of Applied Psychology, 81,* 309–317.

Deception

Do you think you can tell when someone is lying to you? If so, what kinds of things do you look for to detect deception? Think about it a minute. How do people behave when they are lying? What gives them away?

When we ask our students these questions, the most common response we get is this: eye contact. When people are lying, our students suggest, they can't look you in the eye. In fact, one author's mother based her interrogation tactics largely on this notion. She used to say things like, "Look me in the eye and tell me you didn't cut all the hair off your sister's Barbies."

If you've ever thought the same thing about lying and eye contact, you and our students are not alone. According to Lock's (2005) sources, research in more than 60 countries indicates that, from Afghanistan to Zimbabwe, eye contact is one of the most commonly used behavioral cues for detecting deception. Here's the catch, though: Research has shown that generally *people do not look away* when they are lying but rather avert their eyes only under certain circumstances (DePaulo, et al., 2003; Sporer & Schwandt, 2007). In fact, one study found that people engage in *more* eye contact when lying than when telling the truth (Riggio & Friedman, 1983). In other words, when trying to detect deception, we may be using the wrong cues. No wonder we're such lousy lie detectors!

That's right—humans, in general, tend to be fairly inaccurate when trying to detect deception. Some research shows that the average person can detect a liar with about the same accuracy as someone flipping a coin (Bond & DePaulo, 2006), whereas other research presents an even less optimistic view of humans as lie detectors (see Feeley & Young, 1998; Levine, Park, & McCornack, 1999).[1] The fact that people are not very accurate at detecting deception is unfortunate when you consider the practical and professional contexts within which accurate detection would be desirable (e.g., for jurists, consumers, law officers, negotiators, customs inspectors, job interviewers, secret service, and so forth; see Box 12.1). Clearly, there are practical advantages to improving detecting abilities, and this observation leads us to the following questions: Are there any reliable cues that can be used to detect deception? If so, what are they? Are some people better at deceiving us than others? Can some people detect deceit more accurately than others? Are there factors that can improve people's ability to detect a liar?

These are some of the questions we address in this chapter. But, before doing so, we would like to make a point. You might ask, "Why is a chapter on deception in a book on persuasion?" We respond that *deception is a form of persuasion*. Even from the standpoint

| Something Phishy Is Going On: Beware of Internet Deception | BOX 12.1 |

Not long ago, one of the authors received an email greeting him as "Dear Bank of the West Customer." The email told him that because of too many failed login attempts, his banking account had been locked and could be unlocked only by following a link to a Website where he could provide his ATM card number and PIN. Fortunately, he didn't take the bait, unlike others who have been hooked—line and sinker—by what are known as "phishing" or "spoofing" scams. Such scams try to lure you to a Website where you provide personal or financial information, which, in turn, enables the con artists to commit identity theft or credit card fraud. To prevent yourself from being filleted by such scams, beware of unfamiliar Websites. Use only Website addresses you have used before. If you receive an email that seems to be snooping for personal info, be especially wary. If you are suspicious, contact the legitimate company directly. Finally, if you've been hooked, contact the police and file a complaint with the FBI's Internet Fraud complaint center (http://www.ic3.gov/default.aspx).

of pure cases of persuasion, deception involves an intentional attempt to get someone to believe what the liar knows to be false. As Miller (cited in Miller & Stiff, 1993) argued:

> Deceptive communication strives for persuasive ends; or, stated more precisely, deceptive communication is a general persuasive strategy that aims at influencing the beliefs, attitudes, and behaviors of others by means of deliberate message distortion. (p. 28)

With this basic understanding of deception as persuasion under our belt, we now turn to a more in depth discussion of some common conceptualizations of deception. The rest of the chapter examines research on the enactment and perception of deception.

WHAT IS DECEPTION? LIES AND DAMN LIES

Knowing that people lie a lot, although perhaps another justification for studying deception, does little to help us understand *what* deception entails conceptually. To answer the "conceptual question," scholars have attempted to outline several types of communication that might be considered deceptive. Many attempts to do so have focused on liars' motivations for telling lies.

Although some motivations for lying are self-evident, others are less obvious. For example, various researchers have posited all of the following reasons for lying (see Barnett et al., 2000; Camden, Motley, & Wilson, 1984; DePaulo, Ansfield, Kirkendol, & Boden, 2004; Hample, 1980; Knapp & Comadena, 1979; Lindskold & Walters, 1983; Seiter, Bruschke, & Bai, 2002; Turner, Edgley, & Olmstead, 1975)[2]:

- **Lie to benefit other:** Because she knows that her husband does not want to be disturbed, Babbs tells a door-to-door salesman that her husband is not home.
- **Lie to affiliate:** Buffy wants to spend some time with her father, so she tells him she needs help with her homework even though she is capable of doing it herself.

- **Lie to avoid invasion of privacy:** Muffy tells a co-worker that she is younger than she really is because she believes her age is no one's business but her own.
- **Lie to avoid conflict:** Biff tells his neighbor, who has called to complain about Biff's barking dog, that he cannot talk at the moment because dinner's on the table.
- **Lie to appear better:** To impress a date, Rex tells her that he was captain of his football team when, in reality, he was vice president of the Latin Club.
- **Lie to protect self:** Trudy breaks her mother's vase but tells her the cat did it.
- **Lie to benefit self:** Favio tells his parents he needs extra money for textbooks so that he can go to a Limp Bizkit concert with the money.
- **Lie to harm other:** Barney's in a bad mood so he points in the wrong direction when a motorist asks him directions.

In addition to looking at people's motivations for lying, another approach to conceptualizing deception is to examine the types of strategies people use when lying. For example, Metts (1989), Ekman (1985), and Burgoon, Buller, Ebesu, and Rockwell (1994) distinguished three deception strategies: *distortion* (or equivocation), *omissions* (or concealment), and *falsification* (outright falsehoods). Yet other researchers have come up with other categories of deception (e.g., see Hopper & Bell, 1984).

In addition to looking at different types of deception, a final way of conceptualizing deception was proposed in McCornack's (1992; 2008) *information manipulation theory.* This theory argues that when we are talking with others, we typically assume that they will be cooperative, providing us information that is not only truthful but also informative, relevant, and clear. We're not always right, however. Indeed, people violate our assumptions by manipulating the information they communicate to us. First, they might not provide the quantity of information that we assume they will (i.e., they tell the truth, but not the *whole* truth). Second, they might violate our assumptions about the quality of information provided (i.e., what they tell us is not at all true). Third, they might manipulate information through "manner violations," communicating messages that are vague and ambiguous. Finally, people can engage in "relation violations" by presenting messages that are irrelevant. And if that seems complex, consider this: People can alter the quantity, quality, relation, and manner of messages all at the same time or in different combinations. In other words, there is an infinite variety in forms of deception (McCornack, Levine, Solowczuk, Torres, & Campbell, 1992). To give you an idea, examples of the ways in which people manipulate information along each of these dimensions are presented in Box 12.2

Information Manipulation Theory: Examples of Deceptive Dimensions of Messages   BOX 12.2

You have been dating Terry for nearly three years. You feel very close and intimate toward this person. Because Terry goes to a different school upstate, the two of you have agreed to date other people. Nevertheless, Terry is very jealous and possessive. You see Terry only occasionally; however, you call each other every Sunday and talk for an hour. On Friday one of your friends invites you to a party on Saturday night, but the party is "couples only," so in order to go, you need a date. There is no way that Terry can come down for the weekend, so you decide to ask someone from your persuasion class to whom you've been attracted. The two of you go to the party and end up having a great time.

On Sunday, your doorbell rings, and it is Terry. Terry walks in and says, "I decided to come down and surprise you. I tried calling you all last night, but you weren't around. What were you doing?"

Example of responses that:

1. **Are clear, direct, and truthful:** "Terry, I was out at a party. Because I figured you couldn't make it and we decided to date other people, I asked someone from my persuasion class whom I kind of like if he or she'd go. We had a good time. If there was a way that you could have made it to the party, I would have wanted to go with you. If you feel like we need to talk through dating other people again, then let's do it."
2. **Violate assumptions about the quantity of information that should be provided:** "Terry, I went to a party one of my friends was having. It was a blast."
3. **Violate assumptions about the quality of information that should be provided:** "Oh, I was out running errands and my car broke down. I was out all night trying to get a tow back. It was a total drag!"
4. **Violate assumptions about the manner of information that should be provided:** "Oh, I was just out goofing around."
5. **Violate assumptions about the relation or relevance of information that should be provided:** "Why didn't you tell me you were coming? I mean, I know you get paranoid sometimes, but driving all the way down here just to check on me is a bit ridiculous, don't you think? How would you like it if I paid a sneak visit to you and acted obnoxious by surprising you and asking you what you had been doing?"

Examples adapted from McCornack, S. A. (1992). Information manipulation theory. *Communication Monographs, 59*(1), 1–16, and McCornack, S. A., Levine, T. R., Solowczuk, K., Torres, H. I., & Campbell, D. H. (1992). When the alteration of information is viewed as deception: An empirical test of information manipulation theory. *Communication Monographs, 59*(1), 17–29. Copyright by the National Communications Association. 1992. Reproduced by permission of Taylor and Francis Group (www.tandf.co.uk).

Having laid the groundwork for examining deception, we now discuss what happens during the process of deception. That is, what goes on while deception is being enacted, and how is deception detected?

TELLING LIES: THE ENACTMENT OF DECEPTION

If all liars had noses like Pinocchio, deception detection would not be a problem. Unfortunately, detecting deceptive behavior is not that simple. In fact, even empirical research has been inconsistent when trying to identify the types of behaviors that we can expect out of liars. (Some of the behaviors that have been associated with deception are listed in Box 12.3)

Theoretical Frameworks

Despite these inconsistencies, however, several theories of deception have been proposed that provide an understanding of the types of behaviors that are typical of liars. One such framework, known as the *four-factor model,* was proposed by Zuckerman and his colleagues (Zuckerman & Driver, 1985). Another, known as *interpersonal deception theory,*

How Do Liars Behave?   BOX 12.3

A meta-analysis is a summary of several studies. Such an analysis attempts to resolve inconsistencies in research. Several of these analyses (i.e., DePaulo, Stone, & Lassiter, 1985; Kraut, 1980; Sporer & Schwandt, 2007; Vrij, 2000; Zuckerman & Driver, 1985) have examined cues that were associated with deception across a number of studies, but the largest analysis, combining the results of 1,338 estimates of 158 deception cues, was conducted by DePaulo and her colleagues (DePaulo et al., 2003). Based on this analysis, a number of cues were found to be associated with deception. Keep in mind, though, that all of these cues must be prefaced by the phrase, in general:

Talking time: Liars' responses are shorter than truth tellers' responses.

Details: Liars provide fewer details than do truth tellers.

Pressing lips: Liars press their lips (as if holding back) more than truth tellers.

Making sense: Compared to truth tellers, liars' stories are rated as more discrepant and ambivalent and as having less plausibility and logical structure.

Immediacy: Both verbally and vocally, liars seem evasive and impersonal, linguistically distancing themselves from their listeners and from the contents of their presentations (e.g., using passive vs. active voice).

Uncertainty: Liars are rated as sounding more uncertain than truth tellers.

Raising chin: Liars raise their chins more than truth tellers, perhaps to try to appear more certain about their stories.

Repetition: Liars repeat themselves more than do truth tellers.

Cooperation: Liars are rated as less cooperative in their conversations than are truth tellers.

Negative statements: Liars' responses contain more negative expressions and complaints than do truth tellers' responses.

Pleasantness: Liars' faces are less pleasant than are truth tellers' faces.

Nervousness: Overall, liars appear more nervous than truth tellers.

Vocal tension and pitch: Compared to truth tellers, liars' voices are more tense, and liars speak in a higher pitch.

Pupil dilation: Liars' pupils are more dilated than are truth tellers' pupils.

Fidgeting: Liars fidget more than truth tellers.

Spontaneous corrections: Truth tellers spontaneously correct themselves more than do liars.

Admitted lack of memory: Truth tellers admit not remembering things more than do liars.

Related external associations: Compared to truth tellers, liars are more likely to mention events or relationships peripheral to the key event they are discussing.

Although the DePaulo et al. (2003) meta-analysis examined some verbal behaviors, it focused primarily on nonverbal behaviors. Given that, some researchers have wondered whether a reliable set of verbal cues to deception might be uncovered. According to Ali and Levine (2008), however, while verbal indicators of deception appear to exist, they have not been consistent from situation to situation or from study to study.

"I knew the suspect was lying because of certain telltale discrepancies between his voice and non-verbal gestures. Also his pants were on fire."

was proposed by Burgoon and Buller (2004). The following sections discuss each of these perspectives.

The Four-Factor Model

Rather than simply list all of the things that people do when telling lies, the four-factor model tries to explain the underlying processes governing deceptive behavior. In other words, rather than tell us *what* people do when lying, the model tries to tell us *why* people behave differently when lying. According to the model, the four factors that influence behavior when lying are arousal, attempted control, felt emotions, and cognitive effort.

First, the model assumes that people are more aroused or anxious when telling lies than when telling the truth. This is also the principle on which the polygraph operates. Of course, we know that results from polygraphs are inadmissible in courts because they are not 100 percent accurate. Why? Because a sociopath, for instance, who feels no remorse for murder certainly won't get anxious when lying. Even so, not all people are sociopaths. We know that many people do feel anxious when they lie. Perhaps they fear getting caught. Perhaps telling the lie reminds them of information they want hidden. Perhaps they are simply motivated to succeed in the deceptive task. Whatever the case, we know that such arousal can lead to certain behaviors during deception. Poker players, for example, are said to wear sunglasses because their pupils dilate when they get a good hand. Similarly, pupil dilation can be a reliable indicator of deception (DePaulo et al., 2003). What other cues to arousal accompany deception? A few that researchers have investigated include speech errors, speech hesitations, word-phrase repetitions, increased adaptors (e.g., finger fidgeting), eye blinks, vocal pitch, and leg movements.

Second, because people do not want to get caught telling lies, the four-factor model argues that they try to control their behaviors. This seems to be the case both before and during deception. For example, Hartwig, Granhag, and Strömwell (2007) found that when planning to be interrogated, liars strategized more than truth tellers by planning to remain calm and pleasant. Moreover, Vrij (2000) reported that during deception, liars tend to limit their movement to keep from looking nervous. Similarly, according to Ekman and Friesen's (1969, 1974) *sending capacity hypothesis,* when people tell lies, they try to control their behaviors but, in the process, pay more attention to some things than others. Because it is difficult to monitor everything they do, liars try to control behaviors that communicate the most information, such as facial expressions and the words they use. But, while busy monitoring their faces and words, they tend to forget about parts of their body that communicate little information such as their legs and feet. So, according to the sending capacity hypothesis, those parts of the body that communicate little information reveal the most when people are lying. In other words, because people are concentrating so much on their faces and words, deception "leaks" in other places. At least some research tends to support this notion. First, Caso, Vrij, Mann, and De Leo (2006) found that, even when they were taught how to avoid looking deceptive, research participants were more effective at controlling their words than their nonverbal behavior. Moreover, one study found that people who watched liars' heads and faces (higher sending capacity) were less accurate at detecting deception than people who watched liars' bodies (lower sending capacity) (Ekman & Friesen, 1974). Finally, in a summary of more than 30 studies in which judges tried to detect others' deception from either single channels (i.e., only the face, body, tone of voice, or words of the liar) or from particular channel combinations, DePaulo and colleagues (1985) found that in all conditions in which judges relied on facial cues, detection accuracy was lower.

In addition to arousal and attempted control, the four-factor model asserts that affective factors influence our behaviors when telling lies. And if you stop to think about it, you could probably figure out what types of emotions would be associated with telling a lie. Indeed, in our culture, deception is generally frowned on. Children are taught that "the truth shall set them free," "honesty is the best policy," "what tangled webs are weaved," and often chide one another with rhymes such as "liar, liar, pants on fire." It's no surprise, then, that deceptive behavior would be associated with negative emotions such as guilt. It is because of these negative effects that researchers (e.g., DePaulo et al., 2003) hypothesized that when compared to truthful communicators, deceivers display less facial pleasantness and make more negative remarks. We should note, however, that not all deception is associated with the display of negative emotions. Paul Ekman (1985), for instance, argued that liars may experience "duping delight," as the result of facing or successfully meeting the challenge of deceiving another person.

Finally, the four-factor model asserts that cognitive factors play a role in the way people behave when lying. Stated differently, lying requires you to think a lot harder than telling the truth does. Why? Because it's fairly easy to tell a story about something you've already heard or experienced. When you lie, however, you are oftentimes required to "make things up as you go along." Not only that, you have to be careful not to contradict something you've said before. (Remember the old saying "Liars need a good memory"?) Because lying requires extra cognitive effort, it's no wonder that researchers have hypothesized that

Duping delight in action.

liars, compared to people telling the truth, would take a longer time to respond, pause more when speaking, and deliver messages with few specifics (Vrij, Edward, Roberts, & Bull, 2000; Walczyk, Mahoney, Doverspike, & Griffith-Ross, 2009; Walczyk, Roper, Seemann, & Humphrey, 2003; Zuckerman & Driver, 1985).

Interpersonal Deception Theory

Interpersonal deception theory (Burgoon & Buller, 2004, 2008) is by far the most comprehensive summary of deception research. Its goal is to view deception as an interactional phenomenon in which both senders and receivers are involved, simultaneously encoding and decoding messages over time. Both the liar's and the detector's goals, expectations, and knowledge affect their thoughts and behaviors in an interaction. In turn, such thoughts and behaviors affect how accurately lies are detected and whether liars suspect that they are suspected. Later in this chapter, we examine other assumptions that detail the theory. At this point, however, the aspect of interpersonal deception theory that is most relevant is its distinction between *strategic* and *nonstrategic* behaviors during deception. Specifically, interpersonal deception theory argues that a liar's communication consists of both intentional (strategic) attempts to appear honest and unintentional (nonstrategic) behaviors that are beyond the liar's control.

First, interpersonal deception theory says that, to avoid being detected, liars strategically create messages with certain characteristics. For instance, liars might (1) *manipulate the information in their messages* in order to dissociate themselves from the message (e.g., liars might refer to themselves very little so they distance themselves from the responsibility of their statements), convey uncertainty or vagueness (because creating messages with a lot of specific details would increase the likelihood of detection), or withhold information (e.g., liars might create brief messages). Liars might also (2) *strategically control their behavior* to suppress deception cues (e.g., liars might withdraw by gazing or nodding less than people telling the truth). Finally, liars might try to strategically (3) *manage their image* by smiling or nodding to make themselves appear more credible (Buller, Burgoon, White, & Ebesu, 1994). Research by White and Burgoon (2001) found that during interactions, deceivers continue to modify and adapt their behaviors, thereby supporting the notion that some deceptive behaviors are strategic.

Second, although liars try to control their behaviors strategically, they also exhibit some *nonstrategic communication*. In other words, some behaviors "leak out" beyond the liar's awareness or control. As noted previously (see the four-factor model), such communication might result from arousal (e.g., blinks, pupil dilation, vocal nervousness, speech errors, leg and body movements, and shorter responses) or negative emotions (e.g., less nodding, less smiling, more negative statements).

Criticisms of Theoretical Assumptions

Before concluding this section, we should note that some research has been skeptical about certain assumptions contained in interpersonal deception theory and the four-factor model (for reviews and criticism, see Feeley & Young, 1998; Stiff, 1996). For example, McCornack (1997) argued that, in some cases, telling lies may be less cognitively difficult and arousing than telling the truth. For example, imagine what you'd do if a close friend asked you how you liked her new hairstyle. Imagine also that you thought the hairstyle looked hideous. In such situations, rather than creating a truthful and tactful message that would preserve your relationship and your friend's feelings, it might be less cognitively taxing and less stressful to simply tell your friend that you loved her hair. In short, the underlying differences between truths and lies may not be as simple as some models make them out to be (McCornack, 1997).

What do we think of such criticisms? Recall from Chapter 1 that the complex nature of persuasion provides one of the most compelling reasons for studying it. When research seems confusing or contradictory, oftentimes it's because the research is approaching the study of persuasion too simplistically. With that in mind, we believe that the preceding criticisms should not be ignored by those who study deception. They are important because they suggest that deceptive behaviors are far more complex than many of us originally imagined. However, we do not think that the criticisms render assumptions from the four-factor model and interpersonal deception theory useless. Instead, they suggest that these assumptions apply to some but not all deceptive encounters. Telling different types of lies may lead to different types of behavior (see Seiter et al., 2002). For example, fabricating lies may require more mental effort than telling the truth, but only when lies are narrative in nature (e.g., when explaining the events of a crime you may or may not have witnessed; see Vrij, Kneller, & Mann, 2000). Moreover, the notion that deception leads to arousal may apply less to fibs and white lies than to more serious forms of deception, such as cheating on a spouse or denying a crime. Even then, what qualifies as a "serious" form of deception is subject to interpretation. For example, previous research indicates that a person's cultural background not only influences how acceptable that person perceives a lie to be (Mealy, Stephan, & Urrutia, 2007; Seiter et al., 2002), but also the emotions (e.g., guilt and shame) that person expects to experience after telling a lie (Seiter & Bruschke, 2007). In short, our assumptions about deceptive behavior may need to be more qualified or complex in nature. For instance, in Box 12.3, we list several cues to deception. It turns out that under certain conditions, the list gets longer. With that in mind, we turn to a discussion of factors affecting successful deception.

What Makes a Liar Persuasive?

Are some people better at "pulling the wool over our eyes" than others? Is it easier to get away with telling some lies than others? Do certain situations make deception more difficult to accomplish? In this section we discuss the ways in which characteristics of the liar, the lie, and the deceptive situation affect the process of deception.

The "Wool Pullers"

The boy who cried wolf should have quit while he was ahead. Or, before he got eaten, he should have at least taken a personality test. If he had, our guess is that he would have scored high on a test that measures a trait known as *Machiavellianism*. The Machiavellian personality is not interested in interpersonal relationships, manipulates others for selfish purposes, and has little sense of social morality (Christie & Geis, 1970; Geis & Moon, 1981). Machiavellian personalities are truly "wolves in sheeps' clothing"; when lying, they appear more innocent than their counterparts (i.e., low Machiavellians).[3] Indeed, a classic study by Braginsky (1970) backs up this claim. In the study, high and low Machiavellian children tasted bitter crackers and then were offered a nickel for each cracker they could get their little chums to eat. The results of the study showed that the high Machiavellian children were not only the most successful in their persuasive attempts but were also seen as more innocent and honest than the low Machiavellian children.

In addition to Machiavellianism, a person's social skills influence how successful he or she is at deceiving others. For example, high self-monitors, people who use situational information to behave more appropriately, tend to be more skilled at deception than low self-monitors (Elliot, 1979; Miller, deTurck, & Kalbfleisch, 1983). Moreover, people skilled at communicating basic emotions are particularly good at convincing others to believe their deceptive messages (Riggio & Friedman, 1983), whereas those who are apprehensive in their communication tend to leak more deceptive cues (see O'Hair, Cody, & Behnke, 1985). Similarly, people who are expressive and socially tactful (Riggio, Tucker, & Throckmorton, 1987); socially skilled (Riggio, Tucker, & Widaman, 1987); competent communicators (Feeley, 1996); and attentive, friendly, and precise in their communication (O'Hair, Cody, Goss, & Krayer, 1988) are more successful at deceiving others than those who do not possess such skills.

Finally, who do you suppose is better at not being detected when lying—males or females? The results of two meta-analyses found that males tend to be more successful at lying than females (Kalbfleisch, cited in Burgoon, Buller, Grandpre, & Kalbfleisch, 1998; Zuckerman, DePaulo, & Rosenthal, 1981). Even so, a review of literature by Burgoon and colleagues (1998) suggests that such gender differences are small, perhaps because the deceptive strategies of men and women both have shortcomings. Specifically, when they are lying, men tend to restrict their nonverbal behavior. Although this may prevent them from leaking deceptive cues, if they overdo it, they run the risk of appearing deceptive. Women, however, try to appear more involved in conversations. As a result, this greater activation may cause them to leak more arousal cues and appear more nervous than usual (Burgoon et al., 1998).

Are Some Lies Easier to Tell Than Others?

Imagine, for a moment, Babbs, a 15-year-old high school sophomore with a curfew of 9 P.M. It's Thursday, a school night, but Babbs is on the dance floor, partying it up when she suddenly notices the time: 11 P.M.! Knowing that her parents usually go to bed around eight, she hopes they'll be asleep but, on arriving home, she finds herself face to face with her parents, who have been waiting up for her. "Where have you been?" they demand to know, at about the same time Babbs decides that she had better start lying her pants off if she doesn't want to spend the next two weeks in solitary confinement.

How successful do you think Babbs will be? According to research by Cody and his colleagues (Cody, Marston, & Foster, 1984; Cody & O'Hair, 1983; O'Hair, Cody, & McLaughlin, 1981; also see DePaulo et al., 2003; Vrij et al., 2000), behavior during deception depends, to a large extent, on whether the liar is telling a prepared lie or a spontaneous lie. To be sure, think about some of the components of the four-factor model we discussed earlier. When telling a prepared lie, compared to a spontaneous lie, Babbs should be less aroused, have more control, and should not find lying as cognitively difficult. Not surprisingly, research on deceptive cues supports this idea; in general, spontaneous lies are accompanied by more cues associated with deception than are prepared lies. And, because prepared liars make a more credible impression, they are more difficult to detect than spontaneous liars (deTurck & Miller, 1985; Littlepage & Pineault, 1979; Strömwall, Granhag, & Landström, 2007)).

Spontaneity, though, is not the only dimension of a lie that seems to affect deceptive success. Indeed, research also has shown the length and the content of a lie influences how well a person can tell it. Longer lies, for instance, are more difficult to tell than short ones (Kraut, 1978). And concerning content, in a study by Thackray and Orne (1968), subjects played the role of an espionage agent who attempted to conceal both his or her identity and certain code words he or she had learned. The results of the study showed that subjects were more successful when telling lies about personally relevant information (i.e., their identity) than when telling lies about neutral information (i.e., code numbers). Similarly, one study (Warren, Schertler, & Bull, 2009) found that people detected emotional lies (e.g., liars describing Hawaiian landscapes while watching videos of grisly surgeries) more successfully than they detected unemotional lies (liars describing surgeries while watching landscape videos). This finding is consistent with a meta-analysis showing that deceivers displayed fewer nods and illustrators when lying about facts and feelings than when lying about facts only (Sporer & Schwandt, 2007). Finally, a meta-analysis by DePaulo et al. (2003) found that when lying about transgressions, people took longer to respond, talked faster, blinked more, and fidgeted less than truth tellers.

Deceptive Situations and Deceptive Success

The context in which a lie is told can influence how successful the liar is. Several situational features have been found to influence deception success. One is motivation. Certainly, there are some times when you are simply more motivated to lie successfully than others. A fisherman, for example, may not care so much when someone discovers that his trophy "bass" was really a guppy. A playboy husband cheating on his wife, however, might have more at stake if his affair were discovered. So who then is the better liar: the fisherman or the cheat?

To address this question, recall the four-factor model, which suggests that liars attempt to control their behavior in order to avoid being detected. As you might suspect, this attempt to control behavior increases as people's motivation to lie successfully increases. Consequently, as people become more motivated to lie successfully, their behavior becomes more rigid and over-controlled, a phenomenon known as the *motivational impairment effect* (DePaulo & Kirkendol, 1989). In short, being overly motivated may cause you to be especially detectable.

To further illustrate the role of motivation in the process of deception, Frank and Ekman (1997) gave 20 males $10 each for participating in their research. As part of the study, the males were provided with an opportunity to commit a "mock" crime—they would either steal or not steal $50 dollars from a briefcase. Before given the opportunity, the participants were told that if they took the money and were able to convince an interrogator that they were innocent, they could keep the $50. If, however, they were caught lying, they would be punished. Specifically, if caught, they would be forced to forfeit both the stolen $50 and their initial $10 participation fee. Worse yet, they would be required to sit on a cold, metal chair inside a cramped, darkened room, where they would have to endure anywhere from 10 to 40 randomly sequenced, 110-decibel startling blasts of white noise over the course of an hour. Needless to say, the liars in this study were motivated to succeed! Unfortunately for them, results of the study showed that telling such high-stakes lies made them consistently detectable to certain types of people (if you were worried about how they fared in the "torture chamber," rest assured, the researchers didn't follow through on their threat). In short, telling high-stakes lies motivates people to succeed and, as a result, makes them more detectable.

DETECTING DECEPTION: I CAN SEE RIGHT THROUGH YOU

Just as persuaders need someone to persuade, liars need someone to lie to. In the preceding pages we discussed deception from the liar's perspective. In this section, we examine the opposite side of the coin: deception detection. One framework, proposed by Seiter (1997), suggests that we treat deception detection a lot like reaching a verdict in a trial (see also Henningsen, Valde, & Davies, 2005). Whichever verdict we reach (i.e., the person is lying or the person is telling the truth) depends on how we integrate a vast array of verbal and nonverbal information (e.g., Biff is twitching), past knowledge (e.g., Biff doesn't like Gummi Bears), and inference (e.g., Biff is nervous). Sometimes the information we observe is contradictory (e.g., Biff seems nervous but tells a plausible story), and, sometimes, new information causes us to discount our earlier perceptions. This illustrates how complex and idiosyncratic the process of deception detection can be. In other words, the information that one person uses to detect deception may be quite different from the information that another uses. Despite this, we know from past research that some generalizations about deception detection can be made. For instance, when making judgments about veracity, people tend to fall victim to similar stereotypes and biases. Moreover, certain types of people and situations tend to perceive or affect deception in similar ways. We examine these issues next.

Factors That Influence Detection

"Look Me in the Eye": Stereotypes about Deception

When the actor Jon Lovitz used to be a regular on *Saturday Night Live,* he played a character with a compulsive lying problem. On meeting up with old friends, for example, he claimed that he was president of his own company and was married to the beautiful Morgan Fairchild ("Whom," he claimed, "I've slept with"). Of course, while he was telling these stories, he paused a lot, took a lot of time to think of his answers, and—after telling the stories—seemed so surprised that we were sure he had convinced himself of their truth ("Yeah, that's right! That's the ticket!"). So why was this character so funny? Perhaps it was because he was playing on some common stereotypes that people have about deception. We knew he was lying because he did everything that a liar does. Right?

Wrong! The fact is that many of the behaviors we perceive as deceptive simply aren't (e.g., see Hart, Hudson, Fillmore, & Griffith, 2006). For example, a meta-analysis of several studies on deception (DePaulo et al., 1985) found that people tend to perceive others as deceptive when they gaze less, smile less, shift their posture more, speak slowly, and take a long time to answer although none of these behaviors signaled actual deception.[4]

Humans as Polygraphs

Just as some people are better at deceiving others, are some people more skillful at detecting deception? Some research seems to indicate that this is the case. For example, earlier we mentioned that some, but not all people, were fairly consistent when trying to detect high-stakes lies. What, then, you might wonder, distinguishes these people from more gullible folks? Is there some type of trait or individual difference that separates effective from ineffective deception detectors? If so, research has not identified it. Although some studies have identified individual differences such as involvement (Forrest & Feldman, 2000), self-monitoring (Brandt, Miller, & Hocking, 1980b; Geizer, Rarick, & Soldow, 1977), and sex (DePaulo, Zuckerman, & Rosenthal, 1980; Rosenthal & DePaulo, 1979) as characteristics that may help or hinder successful deception detection, one meta-analysis examining over 140 studies (Bond & DePaulo, 2008) found that when large numbers of studies are examined side-by-side, individual differences do not appear to play a significant role in deception detection. Such differences do, however, predispose some people to be more suspicious and others to be more gullible, which, in turn, may make them less accurate when trying to distinguish lies from truths. We will examine these biases later in the chapter. For now, though, we should mention that Bond and DePaulo (2008) do not completely rule out the possibility that individual differences may affect deception detection in the real world. For example, they suggest that individual differences in people's ability to analyze nonverbal behaviors some time after an interaction might lead to more accuracy.

Can People Learn to Be Effective Lie Detectors?

If people's individual characteristics do not predispose them to be accurate deception detectors, is it possible that experience might teach them to spot lies? Do you suppose, for example, that people with certain occupations might be dynamite detectors? If you thought so, think again. In studies comparing college students to customs inspectors, law enforcement officers, lawyers, Secret Service employees, judges, and polygraphers, only Secret Service employees were able to "out-detect" students (DePaulo & Pfeiffer, 1986; Ekman & O'Sullivan, 1991; Kraut & Poe, 1980). These results could be because most "professional" lie detectors have the same stereotypical beliefs as college students about what behaviors are indicative of deception (see Akehurst, Köhnken, Vrij, & Bull, 1996; Vrij, 2000; Vrij & Semin, 1996). It may also be that police officers in particular overestimate their detection ability (Elaad, 2003) or that they err on the side of perceiving people as deceptive rather than truthful (Garrido, Masip, & Herrero, 2004). Perhaps that is why research (e.g., Kassin, Meissner, & Norwick, 2005) has found that college students outperform police officers when trying to detect deception.

With that in mind, is there any hope for people in such professions? Might they be trained to be better deception detectors? The answer to this question is "perhaps"—though, not any training will do. Indeed, two studies found that training might actually backfire (Akehurst, Bull, Vrij, & Köhnken, 2004; Kassin & Fong, 1999). That is, people who had been trained to detect deception, compared to those who had not, were significantly *less* accurate at spotting lies. But wait, it gets worse. The people who had done so poorly were trained with a method (the Reid method) that is commonly used to teach police interrogators how to detect deception. Given these results, you won't be surprised to learn that many of the "deceptive" cues identified in the training method are not the same as those identified in empirical research (Kassin & Fong, 1999). Not only that, some of the cues identified as indicators of deception in the training method could potentially lead to the unfair treatment of some racial groups. For instance, a study by Johnson (2006) found that, when talking with police officers, law-abiding Hispanics and African Americans, compared to Caucasians, tended to engage in more behaviors (e.g., speech disruptions, gaze aversion) that police officers had been trained to interpret as suspicious. Considering that, you might be wondering how people who were trained to identify the "proper" cues might fare when detecting deception. Several studies have found that people who were taught to identify the behavioral cues associated with deception (refer to Box 12.3) were significantly more accurate at spotting lies than were those who were not (e.g., see deTurck, Feeley, & Roman, 1997; Zuckerman, Koestner, & Alton, 1984).

Familiarity, Biases, and Deception Detection

Does knowing a person help us detect his or her deception? Several researchers have asked this question but, for quite some time, results of such studies seemed mixed. For instance, in five studies (Brandt, Miller, & Hocking, 1980a, 1980b, 1982; Feeley & deTurck, 1997;

Feeley, deTurck, & Young, 1995), people rated communicators' veracity after either watching or not watching videotapes of the communicators' normal, truthful behavior. The results of such studies showed that those people who were familiar with the communicators' previous, truthful behaviors were more accurate in their judgments than those who were unfamiliar.[5] Similarly, Comadena (1982) found that spouses could detect each others' deception better than friends could. However, Miller and colleagues (1981) found that when judging lies about emotional information, friends were more accurate than either strangers or spouses, and two studies (Al-Simadi, 2000; Seiter & Wiseman, 1995) found that people who tried to detect the deception of people from their own ethnic or cultural group (e.g., those with whom they would presumably be the most familiar) were less accurate than people who tried to detect the deception of people from ethnic or cultural groups other than their own.[6]

Although such results may seem inconclusive, interpersonal deception theory (Buller & Burgoon, 1996; Burgoon & Buller, 2008) suggests that they may not be when you consider the possible effects of familiarity on deception. The theory argues that familiarity is a double-edged sword: In some ways, it may help you be a better deception detector, in other ways, it might hinder your ability to detect deception. First, because of certain biases, the better you know someone, the less effective you are at detecting his or her lies. Specifically, McCornack and Parks (1986) found that familiarity increased a person's confidence about judging veracity which, in turn, led to a *truth bias* (a perception that others are behaving honestly). The results of their study and others (Stiff, Kim, & Ramesh, 1992) support this idea by showing that the truth bias was positively associated with familiarity and negatively associated with detection accuracy. In other words, people were less accurate when judging familiar others because they thought the others were always honest and trustworthy. In positive relationships based on trust, a truth bias is likely. However, in "negative" relationships, a *lie bias* (i.e., the perception that people are being dishonest) becomes more likely (McCornack & Levine, 1990). Whatever the case, both the truth and lie biases make you less accurate when judging veracity because they prevent you from distinguishing truths from lies.

Although truth and lie biases make you less accurate at detecting the deception of familiar others, the knowledge you've gained about familiar others can also make you more accurate at detecting them (Buller & Burgoon, 1996). Specifically, because you have more background information about familiar others, you might be more likely to notice contradictions in what they say (e.g., your significant other has told you that he or she has never been to San Francisco but later says, "The view from the Golden Gate Bridge is fantastic"). Moreover, because you have more knowledge about the way a familiar other typically behaves, you may be more likely to detect his or her deception when the behavior suddenly changes (e.g., your significant other, who is normally calm, becomes very nervous whenever he or she talks about espionage agents). Finally, when you know another person well, you may be more likely to recognize idiosyncratic behaviors that that person only enacts while lying (Anderson, Ansfield, & DePaulo, 1999). In short, then, familiarity can both help and hinder accurate deception detection. Familiarity is related to biases that decrease accuracy and knowledge that increases accuracy.

With this in mind, Mattson, Allen, Ryan, and Miller (2000) suspected that deception detection may be more accurate in some contexts than in others. Specifically, they argued that organizational members should be capable of detecting deception of co-workers at better than chance rates because they are familiar with each other but lack the truth bias typically found in intimate relationships. To test this hypothesis, these researchers conducted a meta-analysis of deception studies in organizations. Results confirmed their hypothesis, indicating that organizational members correctly classified honest or dishonest communication in about three out of four circumstances (Mattson et al., 2000).

Suspicion

According to interpersonal deception theory (Buller & Burgoon, 1996; Burgoon & Buller, 2004, 2008), as a deceptive interaction is unfolding, people may become suspicious of being lied to and, in turn, may behave in certain ways because of it. In some cases, they may hide their suspiciousness. For example, at least two studies show that when we suspect that someone is lying to us, we alter our behavior so we don't look suspicious (Buller, Strzyzewski, & Comstock, 1991; Burgoon, Buller, Dillman, & Walther, 1995). Specifically, suspicious people tend to use shorter responses, take longer to answer, and manage their body movements more. In other situations, however, our behaviors may reveal our suspicion and, in turn, may affect our partner's behavior. Indeed, if someone who is lying to us thinks we are suspicious, the liar may try even harder to be convincing. Previous research has supported this notion, demonstrating that deceivers' verbal and nonverbal behavior changes during the course of interactions, often becoming indistinguishable from truthful behavior well into the interaction (see, Burgoon & Buller, 2004; Burgoon & Qin, 2006; White & Burgoon, 2001).

Although it is apparent that suspiciousness plays a role in both senders' and receivers' behaviors, another issue concerns whether suspicion affects detection accuracy. Specifically, when people are more suspicious, are they better at detecting deception? The evidence for this claim does not look too good. Even though we know that suspicious people have more negative perceptions of the people they are judging (DePaulo, Lassiter, & Stone, 1982), some scholars have found that suspicious subjects are no more accurate at detecting deception than naive subjects (see Mattson, 1994). Bond and Fahey (1987) argued that this could be because suspicious people are more likely to construe ambiguous information as lies rather than truths. Consistent with this notion, Hubbell, Mitchell, and Gee (2001) found that people who were made to be suspicious were more vulnerable to the lie bias. However, McCornack and Levine (1990) argued that accuracy may depend on the level of suspiciousness. Specifically, they found that moderate levels of suspiciousness led to greater accuracy when judging deception.

Probing and Deception Detection

In the previous section we learned that when trying to detect deception, people sometimes try to alter their behavior so they don't look suspicious. But sometimes, probing a potential liar for more information may be necessary. To be sure, if a liar won't talk, it's difficult to find contradictions or inconsistencies in his or her story. Interestingly, however, most research indicates that probing suspects for more information (e.g., "Tell me more about where you were when the book bag was stolen") does *not* increase the accuracy with which you can detect that suspect's deception (Buller et al., 1991). Perhaps even more interesting is the fact that probing a suspect for more information causes third parties to perceive the suspect as more honest (Buller et al., 1991). This phenomenon has been called the *probing effect* by those who study deception (e.g., Levine & McCornack, 1996a, 1996b).

Although scholars agree that the probing effect occurs, there is some disagreement on what causes it. (For a more detailed debate, see Buller, Stiff, & Burgoon, 1996; Levine & McCornack, 1996a, 1996b.) For instance, several authors argue in favor of the *behavioral adaptation explanation,* which in a nutshell asserts that when probing occurs, liars realize they are suspected of lying and alter their behavior to be more believable. Levine and McCornack (1996a), however, assert that this explanation is flawed and in one study found evidence that contradicts it (Levine & McCornack, 2001). In the study, liars were video-taped being probed. Afterward, research participants watched one of two versions of the videotaped liars. Both versions showed exactly the same footage of the liars, but one had the probes edited out. Interestingly, participants who watched the videos in which probes were deleted perceived liars to be significantly less honest than those who saw the probed liars. Thus, Levine and McCornack (2001) showed that the probing effect occurred, but not because liars changed their behaviors.

What, then, is responsible for the probing effect? According to Levine and McCornack (2001), when trying to tell if someone is lying, judges often rely on shortcuts rather than on scrutinizing the behavior of the suspect. One shortcut judges rely on is called the *probing heuristic* (Levine & McCornack, 2001). Here's how it works. Imagine you're watching a suspect and trying to decide if he or she is lying or telling the truth. Also imagine that the suspect is being probed. Rather than scrutinize the suspect's words and behaviors, you use a shortcut. Specifically, you think to yourself: "It's mighty difficult and nerve racking to lie while being probed, so, given the choice, people being probed will choose to tell the truth." Based on such thinking, you decide that people being probed are also being honest. Your judgment has nothing to do with the suspect's behavioral adapta-tion but rather a simple shortcut that saves you the effort of scrutinizing the suspect's behavior (Levine & McCornack, 2001).

Before concluding this section, we should note that others have questioned whether behavioral adaptation happens. For example, in contrast to behavioral adaptation, Ekman (1985) suggests an opposite phenomenon may occur: When suspected of deceit, a *truthful* communicator may become anxious. This, in turn, may cause a detector to commit what Ekman calls the *Othello error.* That is, the detector wrongly assumes the anxious behavior is indicative of deception. A study by Henningsen, Cruz, and Morr (2000) supported this notion by finding that people who were perceived as nervous were also perceived as deceptive.

SUMMARY

Deception is a multifaceted and complex communication phenomenon that has been broadly conceptualized. In this chapter we explored some of these conceptualizations. We also learned that although people are not very good at detecting deception, some factors improve their accuracy. Other factors (e.g., the truth bias), however, can impede detection accuracy. We also examined some of the behaviors that distinguish truthful from deceptive individuals and some of the frameworks that explain such differences. Many of the distin-guishing behaviors, we saw, were nonverbal in nature.

ENDNOTES

1. Past research has shown that accuracy rates are slightly more than 50 percent when averaged across deceptive and truthful messages. When accuracy rates for truthful and deceptive messages are examined separately, however, people's detection accuracy is above 50 percent for truths and well below 50 percent for lies. Levine, Park, and McCornack (1999) have labeled this the "veracity effect."

2. Research shows that people's motivations for lying affect the frequency with which lies are told and perceptions of lies' acceptability. For instance, Camden and colleagues (1984) found that most lies are told for selfish reasons. Moreover, selfishly motivated lies and lies that cause people to lose some resource are seen as more reprehensible than lies that are altruistically motivated (Hopper & Bell, 1984; Linskold & Walters, 1983; Maier & Lavrakas, 1976; Seiter et al., 2002).

3. Research by Exline, Thibaut, Hickey, and Gumpert (1970) showed that, when lying, high Machiavellians maintained more eye contact than low Machiavellians.

4. A meta-analysis by DePaulo et al. (2003) indicated that although generally liars do not avert their eyes more than truth tellers,

under certain conditions this does occur. Specifically, in studies where liars were offered incentives for lying successfully, they averted their eyes more than truth tellers.

5. Detection accuracy is increased even more if the questions being answered in the "normal," truthful video are relevant to the questions that are asked in the follow-up video. For example, imagine that you have to decide whether a person cheated on an exam. Imagine also that you've seen two video clips beforehand, one in which a person tells you the truth about his or her profession, the other in which he or she tells you the truth about not cheating on an exam. Previous research suggests that seeing the latter video would help you more because it is more relevant to the topic about which the person is lying.

6. Results of research on inter- and intra-ethnic deception detection are mixed. Though the two studies already mentioned (i.e., Al-Simadi, 2000; Seiter & Wiseman, 1995) found that inter-ethnic detection is more accurate than intra-ethnic detection, other studies have found the opposite (e.g., Bond & Atoum, 2000; Bond, Omar, Mahmoud, & Bosner, 1990).

REFERENCES

Akehurst, L., Bull, R., Vrij, A., & Köhnken, G. (2004). The effect of training professional groups and laypersons to use criteria-based content analysis to detect deception. *Applied Cognitive Psychology, 18*(7), 877–891.

Akehurst, L., Köhnken, G., Vrij, A., & Bull, R. (1996). Laypersons' and police officers' beliefs regarding deceptive behavior. *Applied Cognitive Psychology, 10,* 461–471.

Ali, M., & Levine, T. (2008). The language of truthful and deceptive denials and confessions. *Communication Reports, 21,* 82–91.

Al-Simadi, F. A. (2000). Detection of deceptive behavior: A cross-cultural test. *Social Behavior and Personality, 28*(5), 455–462.

Anderson, D. E., Ansfield, M. E., & DePaulo, B. M. (1999). Love's best habit: Deception in the context of relationships. In P. Philippot & R. S. Feldman (Eds.), *The social context of nonverbal behavior. Studies in emotion and social interaction* (pp. 372–409). New York: Cambridge University Press.

Barnett, M. A., Bartel, J. S., Burns, S. R., Sanborn, F. W., Christensen, N. E., & White, M. M. (2000). Perceptions of children who lie: Influence of lie motive and benefit. *Journal of Genetic Psychology, 161*(3), 381–383.

Bond, C. F., & Atoum, A. O. (2000). International deception. *Personality and Social Psychology Bulletin, 26*(3), 38–395.

Bond, C. F., & DePaulo, B. M. (2006). Accuracy of deception judgments. *Review of Personality and Social Psychology, 10,* 214–234.

Bond, C. F., & DePaulo, B. M. (2008). Individual differences in judging deception: Accuracy and bias. *Psychological Bulletin, 134,* 477–492.

Bond, C. F., & Fahey, W. E. (1987). False suspicion and the misperception of deceit. *British Journal of Social Psychology, 26,* 41–46.

Bond, C. F., Omar, A., Mahmoud, A., & Bosner, R. N. (1990). Lie detection across cultures. *Journal of Nonverbal Behavior, 14,* 189–204.

Braginsky, D. D. (1970). Machiavellianism and manipulative interpersonal behavior in children. *Journal of Experimental Social Psychology, 6,* 77–99.

Brandt, D. R., Miller, G. R., & Hocking, J. E. (1980a). The truth deception attribution: Effects of familiarity on the ability of observers to detect deception. *Human Communication Research, 6,* 99–108.

Brandt, D. R., Miller, G. R., & Hocking, J. E. (1980b). Effects of self-monitoring and familiarity on deception. *Communication Quarterly, 22,* 3–10.

Brandt, D. R., Miller, G. R., & Hocking, J. E. (1982). Familiarity and lie detection: A replication and extension. *The Western Journal of Speech Communication, 46,* 276–290.

Buller, D. B., & Burgoon, J. K. (1996). Interpersonal deception theory. *Communication Theory, 6*(3), 203–242.

Buller, D. B., Burgoon, J. K., White, C., & Ebesu, A. S. (1994). Interpersonal deception: VII. Behavioral profiles of falsification, concealment and equivocation. *Journal of Language and Social Psychology, 13,* 366–395.

Buller, D. B., Stiff, J. B., & Burgoon, J. K. (1996). Behavioral adaptation in deceptive transactions: Fact or fiction: Reply to Levine and McCornack. *Human Communication Research, 22*(4), 589–603.

Buller, D. B., Strzyzewski, K. D., & Comstock, J. (1991). Interpersonal deception: I. Deceivers' reactions to receivers' suspicions and probing. *Communication Monographs, 58,* 1–24.

Burgoon, J. K., & Buller, D. B. (2004). Interpersonal deception theory. In J. S. Seiter & R. H. Gass (Eds.), *Readings in persuasion, social influence, and compliance gaining* (pp. 239–264). Boston: Allyn & Bacon.

Burgoon, J. K., & Buller, D. B. (2008). Interpersonal deception theory: Purposive and interdependent behavior during deception. In L. A. Baxter & D. O. Braithwaite (Eds.), *Engaging theories in interpersonal communication: Multiple perspectives* (pp. 227–239). Los Angeles: Sage.

Burgoon, J. K., Buller, D. B., Dillman, L., & Walther, J. B. (1995). Interpersonal deception: IV. Effects of suspicion on perceived communication and nonverbal behavior dynamics. *Human Communication Research, 22*(2), 163–196.

Burgoon, J. K., Buller, D. B., Ebesu, A. S., & Rockwell, P. (1994). Interpersonal deception: V. Accuracy in deception detection. *Communication Monographs, 61,* 303–325.

Burgoon, J. K., Buller, D. B., Grandpre, J. R., & Kalbfleisch, P. (1998). Sex differences in presenting and detecting deceptive messages. In D. J. Canary & K. Dindia (Eds.), *Sex differences and similarities in communication: Critical essays and empirical investigations of sex and gender in interaction* (pp. 351–372). Mahwah, NJ: Erlbaum.

Burgoon, J. K., & Qin, T. (2006). The dynamic nature of deceptive verbal communication. *Journal of Language and Social Psychology, 25,* 76–96.

Camden, C., Motley, M. M., & Wilson, A. (1984). White lies in interpersonal communication: A taxonomy and preliminary investigation of social motivations. *The Western Journal of Speech Communication, 48,* 309–325.

Caso, L., Vrij, A., Mann, S., & De Leo, G. (2006). Deceptive responses: The impact of verbal and nonverbal countermeasures. *Legal and Criminological Psychology, 11,* 99–111.

Christie, R., & Geis, G. (1970). *Studies in Machiavellianism.* New York: Academic Press.

Cody, M. J., Marston, P. J., & Foster, M. (1984, May). *Paralinguistic and verbal leakage of deception as a function of attempted control and timing of questions.* Paper presented at the annual meeting of the International Communication Association, San Francisco.

Cody, M. J., & O'Hair, H. D. (1983). Nonverbal communication and deception cues to gender and communicator dominance. *Communication Monographs, 50,* 175–192.

Comadena, M. E. (1982). Accuracy in detecting deception: Intimate and friendship relationships. In M. Burgoon (Ed.), *Communication yearbook 6* (pp. 446–472). Beverly Hills, CA: Sage.

DePaulo, B. M., Ansfield, M. E., Kirkendol, S. E., & Boden, J. M. (2004). Serious Lies. *Basic and Applied Social Psychology, 26*(2–3), 147–167.

DePaulo, B. M., & Kirkendol, S. E., (1989). The motivational impairment effect in the communication of deception. In J. C. Yuille (Ed.), *Credibility assessment* (pp. 51–70). Belgium: Kluwer.

DePaulo, B. M., Lassiter, G. D., & Stone, J. I. (1982). Attitudinal determinants of success at detecting deception and truth. *Personality and Social Psychology Bulletin, 8,* 273–279.

DePaulo, B. M., Lindsay, J. J., Malone, B. E., Muhlenbruck, L., Charlton, K., & Cooper, H. (2003). Cues to deception. *Psychological Bulletin, 129*(1), 74–118.

DePaulo, B. M., & Pfeiffer, R. L. (1986). On-the-job experience and skill at detecting deception. *Journal of Applied Social Psychology, 16,* 249–267.

DePaulo, B. M., Stone, J. I., & Lassiter, G. D. (1985). Deceiving and detecting deceit. In B. R. Schlenker (Ed.), *The self and social life* (pp. 323–370). New York: McGraw-Hill.

DePaulo, B. M., Zuckerman, M., & Rosenthal, R. (1980). Humans as lie detectors. *Journal of Communication, 30,* 129–139.

deTurck, M. A., Feeley, T. H., & Roman, L. (1997). Vocal and visual cue training in behavioral lie detection. *Communication Research Reports, 14,* 249–259.

deTurck, M. A., & Miller, G. R. (1985). Deception and arousal: Isolating the behavioral correlates of deception. *Human Communication Research, 12,* 181–201.

Ekman, P. (1985). *Telling lies.* New York: W. W. Norton.

Ekman, P., & Friesen, W. V. (1969). Nonverbal leakage cues to deception. *Psychiatry, 32,* 88–106.

Ekman, P., & Friesen, W. V. (1974). Detecting deception from the body or face? *Journal of Personality and Social Psychology, 54,* 414–420.

Ekman, P., & O'Sullivan, M. (1991). Who can catch a liar? *American Psychologist, 46,* 913–920.

Elaad, E. (2003). Effects of feedback on the overestimated capacity to detect lies and underestimated ability to tell lies. *Applied Cognitive Psychology, 17*(3), 345–363.

Elliot, G. C. (1979). Some effects of deception and level of self-monitoring on planning and reacting to a self-presentation. *Journal of Personality and Social Psychology, 37,* 1282–1292.

Exline, R., Thibaut, J., Hickey, C., & Gumpert, P. (1970). Visual interaction in relation to Machiavellianism and an unethical act. In R. Christie & F. Geis (Eds.), *Studies in Machiavellianism* (pp. 53–75). New York: Academic Press.

Feeley, T. H. (1996, November). *Conversational competence and perceptions of honesty in interpersonal deception.* Paper presented at the annual meeting of the Speech Communication Association, San Diego, CA.

Feeley, T. H., & deTurck, M. A. (1997). Case-relevant vs. case-irrelevant questioning in experimental lie detection. *Communication Reports, 10*(1), 35–46.

Feeley, T. H., deTurck, M. A., & Young, M. J. (1995). Baseline familiarity in lie detection. *Communication Research Reports, 12*(2), 160–169.

Feeley, T. H., & Young, M. J. (1998). Humans as lie detectors: Some more second thoughts. *Communication Quarterly, 46*(2), 109–126. Forrest, J. A., & Feldman, R. S. (2000). Detecting deception and judge's involvement: Lower task involvement leads to better lie detection. *Personality and Social Psychology Bulletin, 26*(1), 118–125.

Forrest, J. A., & Feldman, R. S. (2000). Detecting deception and judge's involvement: Lower task involvement leads to better lie detection. *Personality and Social Psychology Bulletin, 26,* 118–125.

Frank, M. G., & Ekman, P. (1997). The ability to detect deceit generalizes across different types of high-stake lies. *Journal of Personality and Social Psychology, 72*(6), 1429–1439.

Garrido, E., Masip, J., & Herrero, C. (2004). Police officers' credibility judgments: Accuracy and estimated ability. *International Journal of Psychology, 39*(4), 254–275.

Geis, G. L., & Moon, Y. Y. (1981). Machiavellianism and deception. *Journal of Personality and Social Psychology, 41,* 766–775.

Geizer, R. S., Rarick, D. L., & Soldow, G. F. (1977). Deception judgment accuracy: A study of person perception. *Personality and Psychology Bulletin, 3,* 446–449.

Hample, D. (1980). Purposes and effects of lying. *The Southern Speech Communication Journal, 46,* 33–47.

Hart, C. L., Hudson, L. P., Fillmore, D. G., & Griffith, J. D. (2006). Managerial beliefs about the behavioral cues of deception. *Individual Differences Research, 4,* 176–184.

Hartwig, M., Granhag, P. A. & Strömwall, L. A. (2007). Guilty and innocent suspects' strategies during police interrogations. *Psychology, Crime, and Law. 13,* 213–227.

Henningsen, D. D., Cruz, M. G., & Morr, M. C. (2000). Pattern violations and perceptions of deception. *Communication Reports, 13,* 1–9.

Henningsen, D. D., Valde, K. S., & Davies, E. (2005). Exploring the effect of verbal and nonverbal cues on perceptions of deception. *Communication Quarterly, 53*(3), 359–375.

Hopper, R., & Bell, R. A. (1984). Broadening the deception construct. *Quarterly Journal of Speech, 70,* 288–302.

Hubbell, A. P., Mitchell, M. M., & Gee, J. C. (2001). The relative effects of timing of suspicion and outcome involvement on biased message processing. *Communication Monographs, 68*(2), 115–132.

Johnson, R. R. (2006). Confounding influences on police detection of suspiciousness. *Journal of Criminal Justice, 34,* 435–442.

Kassin, S. M., & Fong, C. T. (1999). "I'm innocent!": Effects of training on judgments of truth and deception in the interrogation room. *Law and Human Behavior, 23*(5), 499–516.

Kassin, S. M., Meissner, C. A., & Norwick, R. J. (2005). "I'd know a false confession if I saw one": A comparative study of college students and police investigators. *Law and Human Behavior, 29*, 211–227.

Knapp, M. L., & Comadena, M. E. (1979). Telling it like it isn't: A review of theory and research on deceptive communications. *Human Communication Research, 5,* 270–285.

Kraut, R. E. (1978). Verbal and nonverbal cues in the perception of lying. *Journal of Personality and Social Psychology, 36,* 380–391.

Kraut, R. E. (1980). Humans as lie detectors: Some second thoughts. *Journal of Communication, 30,* 209–216.

Kraut, R. E., & Poe, D. B. (1980). Behavioral roots of person perception: The deception judgments of custom inspectors and laymen. *Journal of Personality and Social Psychology, 39,* 784–798.

Levine, T. R., & McCornack, S. A. (1996a). A critical analysis of the behavioral adaptation explanation of the probing effect. *Human Communication Research, 22*(4), 575–588.

Levine, T. R., & McCornack, S. A. (1996b). Can behavioral adaptation explain the probing effect? Rejoinder to Buller et al. *Human Communication Research, 22*(4), 604–613.

Levine, T. R., & McCornack, S. A. (2001). Behavioral adaptation, confidence, and heuristic-based explanations of the probing effect. *Human Communication Research, 27,* 471–502.

Levine, T. R., Park, H. S., & McCornack, S. A. (1999). Accuracy in detecting truths and lies: Documenting the "veracity effect." *Communication Monographs, 66*(2), 125–144.

Lindskold, S., & Walters, P. S. (1983). Categories for the acceptability of lies. *Journal of Social Psychology, 120,* 129–136.

Littlepage, G. E., & Pineault, M. A. (1979). Detection of deceptive factual statements from the body and the face. *Personality and Psychology Bulletin, 5,* 325–328.

Lock, C. (2005). Psychologists try to learn how to spot a liar. Retrieved September 30, 2005, from www.sciencenews.org/articles/20040731/bob8.asp.

Maier, R. A., & Lavrakas, P. J. (1976). Lying behavior and the evaluation of lies. *Perception and Motor Skills, 42,* 575–581.

Mattson, M. (1994, November). *Reactive strategies to suspicious information in intimate relationships.* Paper presented at the annual meeting of the Speech Communication Association, New Orleans, LA.

Mattson, M., Allen, M., Ryan, D. J., & Miller, V. (2000). Considering organizations as a unique interpersonal context for deception detection: A meta-analytic review. *Communication Research Reports, 17*(2), 148–160.

McCornack, S. A. (1992). Information manipulation theory. *Communication Monographs, 59,* 1–16.

McCornack, S. A. (1997). The generation of deceptive messages: Laying the groundwork for a viable theory of interpersonal deception. In J. O. Greene (Ed.), *Message production: Advances of communication theory* (pp. 91–126). Mahwah, NJ: Erlbaum.

McCornack, S. A. (2008). Information manipulation theory: Explaining how deception occurs. In L. A. Baxter & D. O. Braithwaite (Eds.), *Engaging theories in interpersonal communication: Multiple perspectives* (pp. 215–226). Los Angeles: Sage.

McCornack, S. A., & Levine, T. R. (1990). When lovers become leery: The relationship between suspicion and accuracy in detecting deception. *Communication Monographs, 57,* 219–230.

McCornack, S. A., Levine, T. R., Solowczuk, K., Torres, H. I., & Campbell, D. M. (1992). When the alteration of information is viewed as deception: An empirical test of information manipulation theory. *Communication Monographs, 59,* 17–29.

McCornack, S. A., & Parks, M. R. (1986). Deception detection and relational development: The other side of trust. In M. L. McLaughlin (Ed.), *Communication yearbook 9* (pp. 377–389). Beverly Hills, CA: Sage.

Mealy, M., Stephan, W., & Urrutia, I. C. (2007). The acceptability of lies: A comparison of Ecuadorians and Euro-Americans. *International Journal of Intercultural Relations, 31,* 689–702.

Metts, S. (1989). An exploratory investigation of deception in close relationships. *Journal of Social and Personal Relationships, 6,* 159–179.

Miller, G. R., Bauchner, J. E., Hocking, J. E., Fontes, N. E., Kaminski, E. P., & Brandt, D. R. (1981). ". . . and nothing but the truth": How well can observers detect deceptive testimony? In B. D. Sales (Ed.), *Perspectives in law and psychology. Vol. II: The jury, judicial, and trial process* (pp. 145–179). New York: Plenum.

Miller, G. R., deTurck, M. A., & Kalbfleisch, P. J. (1983). Self-monitoring, rehearsal, and deceptive communication. *Human Communication Research, 10,* 97–117.

Miller, G. R., & Stiff, J. B. (1993). *Deceptive Communication.* Newbury Park, NJ: Sage.

O'Hair, D., Cody, M. J., & Behnke, R. R. (1985). Communication apprehension and vocal stress as indices of deception. *Western Journal of Speech Communication, 49,* 286–300.

O'Hair, D., Cody, M. J., Goss, B., & Krayer, K. J. (1988). The effect of gender, deceit orientation and communicator style on macro-assessments of honesty. *Communication Quarterly, 36,* 77–93.

O'Hair, D., Cody, M. J., & McLaughlin, M. L. (1981). Prepared lies, spontaneous lies, Machiavellianism, and nonverbal communication. *Human Communication Research, 7,* 325–339.

Riggio, R. E., & Friedman, H. S. (1983). Individual differences and cues to deception. *Journal of Personality and Social Psychology, 45,* 899–915.

Riggio, R. E., Tucker, J., & Throckmorton, B. (1987). Social skills and deception ability. *Personality and Social Psychology Bulletin, 13,* 568–577.

Riggio, R. E., Tucker, J., & Widaman, K. F. (1987). Verbal and nonverbal cues as mediators of deception ability. *Journal of Nonverbal Behavior, 11,* 126–143.

Rosenthal, R., & DePaulo, B. M. (1979). Sex differences in eavesdropping on nonverbal cues. *Journal of Personality and Social Psychology, 37,* 273–285.

Seiter, J. S. (1997). Honest or deceitful?: A study of persons' mental models for judging veracity. *Human Communication Research, 24*(2), 216–259.

Seiter, J. S., & Bruschke, J. C. (2007). Deception and emotion: The effects of motivation, relationship type, and sex on expected feelings of guilt and shame following acts of deception in the United States and Chinese samples. *Communication Studies, 58,* 1–16.

Seiter, J. S., Bruschke, J. C., & Bai, C. (2002). The acceptability of deception as a function of perceivers' culture, deceiver's intention, and deceiver–deceived relationship. *Western Journal of Communication, 66*(2), 158–180.

Seiter, J. S., & Wiseman, R. (1995). Ethnicity and deception detection. *Journal of the Northwest Communication Association, 23,* 24–38.

Sporer, S. L., & Schwandt, B. (2007). Moderators of nonverbal indicators of deception: A meta-analytic synthesis. *Psychology, Public Policy, and Law, 13,* 1–34.

Stiff, J. G. (1996). Theoretical approaches to the study of deceptive communication: Comments on interpersonal deception theory. *Communication Theory, 6,* 289–296.

Stiff, J. G., Kim, H. J., & Ramesh, C. (1992). Truth biases and aroused suspicion in relational deception. *Communication Research, 19,* 326–345.

Strömwall, L. A., Granhag, P. A., & Landström, S. (2007). Children's prepared and unprepared lies: Can adults see through their strategies? *Applied Cognitive Psychology, 21,* 457–471.

Thackray, R. I., & Orne, M. T. (1968). Effects of stimulus employed and the level of subject awareness on the detection of deception. *Journal of Applied Psychology, 52,* 234–239.

Turner, R. E., Edgley, C., & Olmstead, G. (1975). Information control in conversations: Honesty is not always the best policy. *Kansas Journal of Sociology, 11,* 69–89.

Vrij, A. (2000). *Detecting lies and deceit: The psychology of lying and the implications for professional practice.* Chichester, UK: John Wiley & Sons.

Vrij, A., Edward, K., Roberts, K. P., & Bull, R. (2000). Detecting deceit via analysis of verbal and nonverbal behavior. *Journal of Nonverbal Behavior, 24*(4), 239–263.

Vrij, A., Kneller, W., & Mann, S. (2000). The effect of informing liars about criteria-based content analysis on their ability to deceive CBCA-raters. *Legal and Criminological Psychology, 5,* 57–70.

Vrij, A., & Semin, G. R. (1996). Lie experts' beliefs about nonverbal indicators of deception. *Journal of Nonverbal Behavior, 20,* 65–80.

Walczyk, J. J., Mahoney, K. T., Doverspike, D., & Griffith-Ross, D. A. (2009). Cognitive lie detection: Response time and consistency of answers as cues to deception. *Journal of Business Psychology, 24,* 33–49.

Walczyk, J. J., Roper, K. S., Seemann, E., & Humphrey, A. M. (2003). Cognitive mechanisms underlying lying to questions: Response time as a cue to deception. *Applied Cognitive Psychology, 17*(7), 755–775.

Warren, G., Schertler, E., & Bull, P. (2009). Detecting deception from emotional and unemotional cues. *Journal of Nonverbal Behavior, 33,* 59–69.

White, C. H., & Burgoon, J. K. (2001). Adaptation and communicative design: Patterns of interaction in truthful and deceptive conversations. *Human Communication Research, 27*(1), 9–37.

Zuckerman, M., DePaulo, B. M., & Rosenthal, R. (1981). Verbal and nonverbal communication of deception. In L. Berkowitz (Ed.), *Advances in experimental social psychology* (pp. 2–59). New York: Academic Press.

Zuckerman, M., & Driver, R. E. (1985). Telling lies: Verbal and nonverbal correlates of deception. In A. W. Siegman and S. Feldstein (Eds.), *Multichannel integrations of nonverbal behavior* (pp. 129–147). Hillsdale, NJ: Erlbaum.

Zuckerman, M., Koestner, R., & Alton, A. O. (1984). Learning to detect deception. *Journal of Personality and Social Psychology, 46,* 519–528.

CHAPTER 13

Motivational Appeals

If real life were a cartoon, the salesperson who showed up at the home of one of the authors could have been Elmer Fudd. The author needed to install a rain gutter on his house. On the advice of a neighbor, he contacted a company located a good 40 miles from where he lived to come out and provide an estimate. The salesperson, a balding fellow in his mid-40s, arrived in a beat-up 1970s vintage car. He looked tired and disheveled as he got out. He fumbled with his clipboard, calculator, and an armload of gutter samples as he made his way up the sidewalk.

"Find the place okay?" the author asked, greeting him at the door.

"The diwections wuh gweat," the salesperson answered, "but the twaffic was tewwible, and I got a ticket on the way."

"That's too bad," the author replied.

"I didn't have my seatbelt on," the salesperson lamented, "because it's bwoken, and it costs $300 to fix. I can't affawd it wight now."

Owing to the salesperson's unkempt appearance, his speech impediment, and his sad tale about the traffic ticket, the author felt sympathy for the poor soul. Even though the salesperson's estimate was slightly higher than those of several local businesses, the author signed a contract with him on the spot. How could he do otherwise? The salesperson had come all that way—risked his life, in fact—to provide an estimate. He'd gotten a ticket for his trouble. The way the author saw it, the difference in the salesperson's price from that of the local competitors was probably less than the cost of the ticket. And the guy obviously needed the sale.

Or did he? After the salesperson drove away, the author began to wonder if it was all an act. What if the salesperson told every potential customer he'd gotten a ticket en route? What if his seat belt worked just fine? What if he faked or exaggerated the speech problem to elicit sympathy and help make the sale? The author never did find out whether the "sad sack" character was genuine or a guise, but the rain gutters have worked splendidly.

Whether the salesperson's strategy was honest or not, it's clear that his success was based, to a large extent, on pity. His sad plight tugged at the author's heartstrings. And in the end, the author was willing to pay more for the work because he felt sorry for the fellow. The salesperson's appeal to pity, if it were designed as such, represents but one example of a *motivational appeal,* the topic of this chapter. Motivational appeals may be generally defined as external inducements, often of an emotional nature, that are designed to increase an individual's drive to undertake some course of action. By external inducements, we mean incentives that exist apart from the substance of a message itself. Such external inducements typically seek to alter people's moods, feelings, or emotions as a means of persuasion.

INTRINSIC VERSUS EXTRINSIC MOTIVATION

Motivational appeals can be thought of as attempts to jump start an individual's drive to do something. They provide an external incentive for performing some action. *Intrinsic motivation* is a drive that comes from within (Deci, 1975; Deci & Ryan, 1978). If you "live to work," your motivation for doing your job is internal. *Extrinsic motivation* is instilled by some outside factor (Petri, 1991). If you "work to live," your motivation for going to work each day is external. All the motivational appeals we discuss here can be thought of as extrinsic in nature. Motivational appeals are found everywhere. Daily entreaties include anxiety, fear, guilt, health, honor, humor, patriotism pity, pride, sex, warmth, and more.

Before discussing specific motivational appeals, however, we examine supposed differences between logical and emotional appeals.

LOGICAL AND EMOTIONAL APPEALS: A FUZZY DISTINCTION

People often think of "logical" and "emotional" appeals as opposites. This distinction dates back to Aristotle, who classified *logos* (logic, reasoning) and *pathos* (passion, emotion) as separate, distinct forms of influence (Aristotle, trans. 1932). This way of thinking, however, represents something of an artificial dichotomy.[1] Whether a message is perceived as logical or emotional has as much to do with the person *perceiving* the message as it does with the message itself (Becker, 1963). In fact, researchers (Evans, Barston, & Pollard, 1983; Lefford, 1946; Oakhill & Garnham, 1993; Reuchelle, 1958) have learned that when people agree with a message, they tend to perceive it as being more logical or rational in nature. When they disagree with a message, they tend to think of it as being more emotional in nature. Hence, when a dispute arises, a person tends to think, "I'm being rational, why is he or she being so emotional?"

A now-classic study by Langer, Blank, and Chanowitz (1978) illustrates the sometimes fuzzy distinction between logical, psychological, and emotional appeals. The purpose of the study was to see how successful a person was at "taking cuts" in line, based on the quality of the reason given. In the study, a person (serving as a confederate) asked for permission to cut in line at a photocopy machine. In one condition, the person provided an actual reason for cutting in line: "Excuse me, I have 5 pages. May I use the Xerox machine, because I'm in a rush?" In a second condition, the person gave a semblance of a reason: "Excuse me, I have 5 pages. May I use the Xerox machine, because I have to make some copies?" In a third condition, the person offered neither a reason nor the pretext of a reason for cutting in line: "Excuse me, I have 5 pages. May I use the Xerox machine?" The confederate then repeated the process, with different strangers, but asked to make 20 copies, rather than 5.

Table 13.1 displays the compliance rates for each of the conditions. Notice that for the smaller request (5 copies) a semblance of a reason was nearly as effective as a genuine reason. Thus, it was not so much the actual use of reasoning that mattered as the *appearance* of reasoning. In short, the mere pretext of reason-giving worked well for minor requests. This was not the case with the larger request, however. When the confederate asked to make 20 copies, people were less likely to comply unless a genuine reason was offered.

Compliance Rates in Response to the Size of the Request and the Type of Reason Offered			TABLE 13.1
Size of Request	**Absence of a Reason**	**Semblance of a Reason**	**Genuine Reason**
Smaller (5 copies)	60% compliance	93% compliance	94% compliance
Larger (20 copies)	25% compliance	25% compliance	42% compliance

Adapted from Langer, E., Blank, A., & Chanowitz, B. (1978). The mindlessness of ostensibly thoughtful action: The role of "placebic" information in interpersonal interaction. *Journal of Personality and Social Psychology, 36*(6), 635–642.

FEAR APPEALS: IF YOU DON'T STOP DOING THAT, YOU'LL GO BLIND

"If you cross your eyes, they'll stay that way." "Don't run with scissors, you'll poke your eye out." "Never talk to strangers. You might be abducted." What child hasn't heard these or similar admonitions from a parent? Fear appeals are not only a staple of child-rearing but they are also prevalent in the workplace, in public health messages, and in advertising. Advertisements for dandruff shampoos, deodorants, mouthwashes, and acne medications, for example, are often predicated on the fear of social ostracism.

Some commentators charge that America has become a culture based on fear (Altheide, 2002; Glassner, 1999). Whether to sell products, garner votes, or increase ratings, advertisers, politicians, and the media use scare tactics to increase our anxiety about all sorts of things. We're afraid of exotic diseases such as swine flu, avian flu, SARS, mad cow, and West Nile. We stress out about school shootings, child abductions, homeland security, and road rage. We wonder if we need one of those purple pills we've been told to ask our doctor about. The world is certainly a scary place. But does scaring people or increasing their anxiety really work? And if so, how? Research suggests that the effectiveness of fear appeals depends on several factors, which we examine next.

Fear Level or Intensity: The Goosebump Factor

In one of the earliest studies on fear appeals, Janis and Feshbach (1953) found that mild fear appeals were more effective than strong fear appeals when it came to getting high school students to brush their teeth. A number of methodological flaws were present in their study, however, including the prospect that the high schoolers didn't take the strong fear appeals seriously. Subsequent reviews of the fear appeal literature have discounted Janis and Feshbach's initial findings.

Researchers are now fairly confident that the relationship between fear intensity and persuasion is generally positive and linear. That is, greater fear tends to produce greater persuasion. This conclusion is borne out by both qualitative (Dillard, 1994; Gass, 1983; Higbee, 1969; Ruiter, Abraham, & Kok, 2001) and quantitative (Boster & Mongeau, 1984; Cho & Witte, 2004; Mongeau, 1998; Sutton, 1982; Witte & Allen, 2000) reviews of the fear literature. The more fear that is aroused, the more vulnerable receivers feel, and the more likely it is they will be persuaded. For this general rule to apply, however, a few conditions must be satisfied. These conditions are identified in the *extended parallel processing model.*

The Extended Parallel Process Model: There's Nothing to Fear but Fear Itself

There are a number of models of how fear appeals work, but we think Kim Witte's (1992, 1994) *extended parallel process model* is among the best. Like the ELM, it is a dual-process model. Assuming that an appeal arouses fear in a receiver, the receiver can be expected to do something about it. Witte suggests two basic alternatives: The receiver can engage in *danger control* or *fear control*. Let's say, for example, that Timmy is exposed to an AIDS awareness slogan that says "Sex – Condom = HIV." On the one hand, if Timmy concentrates on ways of reducing the danger, such as using condoms or refraining from sex, he would be resorting to danger control. If, on the other hand, Timmy concentrates on ways of reducing his fear, such as telling himself to remain calm and not panic, he would be resorting to fear control. Danger control is a more constructive means of coping with a fear appeal than fear control. Why? Because danger control focuses on the solution. Fear control, conversely, focuses on the problem and essentially involves "worrying about worry." Such an approach often results in denial, avoidance, or panic. A persuader's goal in using fear appeals, therefore, should be to trigger danger control in receivers which, in turn, will cause them to take positive, constructive steps to avoid the harm and avoid triggering fear control.

The perceived effectiveness of a fear appeal is vital to its actual effectiveness (Dillard, Shen, & Vail, 2007). The EPPM addresses this through *perceived efficacy,* which is a key element in activating danger control. Perceived efficacy has to do with whether a receiver thinks a recommended action is both an effective and feasible means of avoiding the harm portrayed by a fear appeal. For a fear appeal to trigger danger control, the person must perceive that (1) an effective response is available, termed *response efficacy,* and (2) that he or she is capable of undertaking that response, termed *self-efficacy.* If a person thinks no remedy is available, or that he or she cannot exercise the remedy, then fear control will take over.

Returning to our previous example, if the fear appeal convinces Timmy that condoms work and are easy to use, he'll be more likely to use them. The fear appeal would thus have high perceived efficacy. If, however, the appeal leaves Timmy worrying that condoms are unreliable or impractical, he'll be less likely to use them. The fear appeal would have low perceived efficacy. Indeed, a recent meta-analysis (Casey, Timmermann, Allen, Krahn, & Turkiewicz, 2009) demonstrated this very result: High response efficacy and self-efficacy correlated significantly with self-reports of condom use.

The trick, then, is to use fear appeals that include workable, practical remedies, thereby triggering danger control which, in turn, leads to constructive responses. The challenge is to avoid fear appeals that are nonefficacious, because they tend to trigger fear control, which leads to counterproductive responses.

In addition to perceived efficacy, a number of other factors affect the success of fear appeals. These include perceived vulnerability (the more susceptible the audience feels, the better), the specificity of the recommendations (the more specific, the better), and the positioning of the recommendations (after the fear appeal is best). When these additional factors are taken into account, and the message is adapted accordingly, fear appeals can be one of the most effective tools a persuader can use.

We would be remiss if we didn't acknowledge that there are serious ethical concerns surrounding the use of fear appeals. We address these in Chapter 16. For the time being, suffice it to say that a persuader should exercise considerable caution in using fear appeals. Nevertheless, if the harmful consequences are real or genuine, we would suggest it is not only acceptable for a persuader to employ fear appeals, but also that the persuader has an obligation to use them.

APPEALS TO PITY AND GUILT: WOE IS ME, SHAME ON YOU

It happens every Labor Day weekend. Comedian Jerry Lewis hosts the Muscular Dystrophy Association (MDA) telethon. Begun in 1966, the MDA telethon relies heavily on pity as an instrument for fund-raising. The telethon is carried by more than 200 stations and attracts upwards of 100 million viewers. A "poster child," typically full of innocence and wearing leg braces and crutches, is chosen for each year's campaign. Throughout the telethon, children with MD are paraded before the cameras to tug at viewers' heartstrings and thereby elicit pledges.

The technique works. The telethon has raised hundreds of millions of dollars over the years. But Jerry Lewis has been criticized for relying on pity as a means of fund-raising. Organizations representing individuals with disabilities say the use of pity is demeaning, paternalistic, stigmatizing, and marginalizing (DeAngelis, 1993; Del Valle, 1992; Ervin, 1995; Haller, 1994; Hurst, 1998). Opponents of Lewis' tactics say that much of the good the telethon does is outweighed by the damage caused by portraying individuals with disabilities as "broken" and in need of "being fixed" or as less than whole human beings.

But is it possible to engage in successful fund-raising without using pity or guilt? If individuals who are disabled are depicted by charities as independent and self-reliant will the dollars keep rolling in? One study suggests it may not be possible to have it both ways. Eayres and Ellis (1990) asked males and females to evaluate 10 posters for charitable causes based on a number of criteria. Some posters portrayed people with mental or learning disabilities in a negative light (dependent, incapable), whereas others portrayed them in a positive light (valued, capable). The researchers found that the posters that evoked the strongest feelings of guilt and sympathy, the negative portrayals, were most likely to make the participants want to donate money. Participants were less likely to make a donation if the posters included positive portrayals. As the researchers noted, "this tends to validate the supposition that in order to produce a successful poster in charity terms it is necessary to play on people's feelings of guilt and pity" (p. 356). Interestingly, the participants were more willing to become actively involved in, and donate time to, charitable causes that were featured positively in the posters. This bodes well for charities seeking increased voluntarism, but not for ones seeking monetary contributions.

On the subject of guilt itself, some researchers have found that invoking feelings of guilt in another person can facilitate compliance (O'Keefe, 2002). Studies have shown that feelings of guilt made people more likely to comply with a subsequent request (Freedman, Wallington, & Bless, 1967; Hibbert, Smith, Davies, & Ireland, 2007; Lindsey, 2005; Lindsey, Yun, & Hill, 2007). Interestingly, they were more likely to comply even if the person making the request, or the person benefiting from the request, was not the source of their guilt. Unscrupulous persuaders can use guilt appeals to extract money from people who are in mourning, as we point out in Box 13.1. Boster and others (Boster et al., 1999) found that students who were made to feel guilty for not

---

Funeral Home Persuasion BOX 13.1

"You can't take it with you . . . but you don't have to give it all to the mortuary!"

Funerals are expensive. The average price of a funeral nowadays is over $8,500 (Kopp & Kemp, 2007). Funerals rank beside weddings, automobile purchases, home remodeling, and vacations in overall cost. Unfortunately, consumers are quiet naïve about the legality of funeral home practices. What's more, the process of negotiating the price of a funeral comes at the worst possible time: when our thinking is impaired by the loss of a loved one. We may also feel it is crass to engage in hard bargaining over prices (Gentry, Kennedy, Paul, & Hill, 1995). Unfortunately, this is exactly when some unscrupulous funeral home directors try to take advantage of us. They know that a person who is grieving is an easy mark.

Certainly, not all, or even most, mortuaries prey on those who are grieving, but some clearly do (Wasik, 1995). As just one illustration, one undertaker tried to push silk coffin lining instead of rayon by arguing, "We find rayon is a lot more irritating to the skin" (Mitford, 1980, p. 82). Since when do dead people have sensitive skin? To increase your consumer awareness, and to arm you against the unscrupulous practices employed by some funeral homes, we offer the following list of "Do's" and "Don'ts" when making funeral arrangements. The suggestions apply to a traditional burial. If cremation, burial at sea, or some other option is chosen, not all the suggestions will apply.

1. **Do try to be as rational as possible.** Grieve for the deceased with all your heart, but negotiate the price of the funeral with your head. A funeral home is a for-profit enterprise. You need to be a savvy consumer when negotiating the arrangements and the price.

2. **Don't give in to guilt appeals,** such as "Don't you think _____ deserves genuine brass handles on his/her coffin?" The amount you love someone isn't measured by the amount you spend on that person's funeral. You can always spend more on that person later, when you are thinking more clearly. For example, you could make a donation in the deceased's name to a worthwhile charity or social cause.

3. **Do conduct price comparisons,** just as you would when buying a car or making any other major purchase. Telephone mortuaries and ask for quotes over the phone. The FTC now requires funeral homes to provide prices by phone. Ask what a complete funeral would cost, including embalming, casket, burial, flowers, and so on. If you don't feel up to making the calls, ask a trusted friend.

4. **Do ensure that everything you are promised is itemized in writing on a contract.** The FTC now requires mortuaries to provide itemized prices. Don't take the funeral director's word for it if he or she says, "leave it to us, we'll take care of everything."

5. **Do shop around for prices on caskets.** Funeral homes mark up casket prices astronomically. You can save thousands of dollars by purchasing a casket factory-direct from a manufacturer, or even Costco, and having it delivered to the funeral home. Federal law prohibits funeral homes from turning away a casket purchased elsewhere, or from charging "handling fees" for having a casket delivered to a mortuary.

6. **Don't pay for unnecessary frills.** Rather than paying more for brass handles, silk ruffles, carved wood panels, or other high-priced options, consider personalizing the casket with family photos, mementos, poetry, or

artwork. Decide what is within your budget and have the funeral director accommodate your needs. If the price isn't right, use outside vendors of your own choosing to provide additional services.

7. **Don't pay more than you have to for basic services.** Some mortuaries charge thousands of dollars for basic services such as transporting the body to a mortuary, church, or cemetery. These services can be obtained for under $1,000 just by calling around ("R.I.P. Off," 1996).

8. **Don't get ripped off by "professional fees."** Some funeral homes charge frivolous fees for such things as "extra visitations" or "grief counseling." These pseudoservices can add to the price of a funeral. Pay only for what you need. If a mortuary lists professional fees as "nondeclinable" on their contract, shop elsewhere.

9. **Don't prepay for a plot, casket, or other services without discussing the contract with an attorney or accountant.** Prepaid plans might seem like a good idea, but most consumer groups advise against them. If you change your mind about where you want to be buried, or how you want to be disposed of, it may be impossible to alter the contract or obtain a refund. You also lose the potential interest your money could earn in a bank account (see item 10).

10. **Do consider opening a "Totten" trust, a payable-on-demand account at a bank or savings institution for the cost of a funeral.** The trust is revocable, so it can be moved, altered, or closed completely. Put the account in the name of several trusted family members. This way, you preserve liquidity (you may decide to be buried elsewhere or to be disposed of in some other way) and earn interest (Jaffe, 1996).

11. **Do make use of helpful information sources.** You can locate excellent advice and information on planning a funeral at www.funerals.com, www.clarkhoward.com, and http://www.ftc.gov/bcp/edu/pubs/consumer/products/pro19.shtm/.

reporting an instance of cheating were much more likely to comply with a request to volunteer for an experiment.

There is one caution involved in using guilt appeals, however. People who feel guilty because they have wronged another person often wish to avoid further interaction with that person, to avoid further embarrassment or to minimize the risk of a confrontation. Guilt appeals should, therefore, be designed to emphasize the positive self-feelings that come from doing the right thing, rather than focusing on further loss of face (see Boster et al., 1999).

Along the same lines, several investigations have examined people's emotional reactions to others who possess varying maladies or stigmas. How people react to others' stigmas (obesity, paraplegia, blindness, AIDS, etc.) depends on the causal inferences they make about those stigmas (Blaine & Williams, 2004; Weiner, Perry, & Magnuson, 1988). For example, these researchers analyzed college students' emotional reactions to people with varying stigmas (obesity, drug addiction, etc.), based on how controllable the students thought the stigma was. Students expressed more feelings of guilt and sympathy if the stigma was uncontrollable (e.g., obesity ascribed to a glandular dysfunction) and more feelings of anger and reluctance to help if the stigma was controllable (e.g., obesity due to overeating). Thus, persuaders seeking to use emotional appeals such as pity or guilt for fund-raising or other purposes need to ensure that the beneficiaries are *not* perceived as having a physical or social malady that they brought on themselves.

*"I've hired this musician to play a sad melody while
I give you a sob story why I didn't do my homework.
It's actually quite effective."*

www.CartoonStock.com.

HUMOROUS APPEALS: STOP ME IF YOU'VE HEARD THIS ONE

The use of humor in persuasion is pervasive. Humorous advertisements account for 21 to 48 percent of all advertising (Toncar, 2001). Roughly one in five prime-time commercials include humor (Beard, 2005). Humor is also common in the boardroom, the courtroom, the classroom, in interpersonal conversations, and even in the pulpit.

Using humor to influence is like skinning a cat; there's more than one way. A humorous appeal can consist of a pun, satire, an anecdote, innuendo, irony, a metaphor, slapstick, or just a plain old joke, as in "an armadillo walks into a bar. . . ." Humor can be directed at oneself, which is known as *self-disparaging humor,* or at others. All in all, Berger (1976) identified 45 different forms of humor.

Humor as an Indirect Form of Influence

On occasion the content of a joke might alter another person's attitudes. Typically, however, jokes themselves don't persuade. Humor tends to operate in a more roundabout manner, akin to what Petty and Cacioppo (1986) call the peripheral route to persuasion (see Chapter 2). The first way in which humor assists persuasion is by *capturing attention.* Advertisers see humor as a way of breaking through media clutter. A recent meta-analysis of humor in advertising revealed that humor consistently increased attention and positive affect toward a brand (Eisend, 2009). This conclusion is consistent with previous reviews (Gulas & Weinberger, 2006; Weinberger & Gulas, 1992).

A second way in which humor may indirectly facilitate persuasion is through *distraction* (Cantor & Venus, 1980; Sternthal & Craig, 1973). Because the cognitive effort needed to comprehend a joke trades off with the mental energy needed to analyze the substance of a message, humor tends to suppress critical thinking. For example, one study (Young, 2008) found that participants who read a series of jokes told by late-night comedians such as David Letterman and Jay Leno were less inclined to scrutinize the statements carefully, compared to a control group of participants who read non-humorous versions of the same statements. This suggests that an advocate facing a hostile audience could use humor to "soften up" listeners.

The third way in which humor indirectly facilitates persuasion is by increasing *liking* for the persuader, which indirectly increases the chances for persuasion. The use of humor tends to make a persuader seem friendlier and helps reduce psychological reactance to a message. A sizable number of studies have shown this to be the case (see Eisend, 2009; Weinberger & Gulas, 1992). This explains why some comedians make good celebrity endorsers. It isn't necessarily the hilarity of the commercials themselves that matters, but rather the likability of the sources that makes consumers more receptive to the messages.

This doesn't mean, however, that a person who acts like a complete clown will be influential (Gruner, 1967). If a source doesn't seem to take his or her own message seriously, neither will others. Similarly, the use of inappropriate humor can decrease perceptions of credibility (Derks, Kalland, & Etgen, 1995; Munn & Gruner, 1981).

No clear consensus has been reached on whether humor facilitates or inhibits message recall (Skalski, Tamborini, Glazer, & Smith, 2009; Worthen & Deschamps, 2008; Young, 2008). If audience retention of the message is important, there are other, better mnemonic devices to use than humor.

Relatedness of Humor: Funny You Should Mention That

Humor that is integrated into a message is called *related,* whereas humor that is offered in a stand-alone fashion is called *unrelated.* Both types of humor are effective, but related humor enjoys an advantage over unrelated humor (Gulas & Weinberger, 2006; Kaplan & Pascoe, 1977; Weinberger & Campbell, 1991; Weinberger & Gulas, 1992; Weinberger & Spotts, 1989). This makes perfect sense. When humor is integrated into the message content, the receiver doesn't have to make a mental detour to "get" the joke and then return to the message.

Humor and Credibility: Laugh, Clown, Laugh

Does humor enhance source credibility? The answer depends on the specific dimensions of credibility in which one is interested. Some studies have shown that humor enhances perceptions of trustworthiness and diminishes perceptions of competence or expertise (Chang & Gruner, 1981; Gruner, 1967, 1970; Gruner & Lampton, 1972; Speck, 1987; Tamborini & Zillman, 1981; Taylor, 1974). The use of humor also has been shown to increase a communicator's social attractiveness (Murnstein & Burst, 1985; Wanzer,

Booth-Butterfield, & Booth-Butterfield, 1996). And humor has been shown to enhance perceptions of "communication competence," or the ability to exhibit social "know how" in communicative situations (Wanzer et al., 1996). Coupled with the finding that humor tends to increase likability, it seems the use of humor is beneficial for the communicator in all but the expertise dimension.

Self-Disparaging Humor: I Get No Respect

Related to the issue of credibility, some studies have examined the effects of self-disparaging humor on persuasion (Graham, Papa, & Brooks, 1992). This involves making oneself the object or brunt of a humorous appeal. In the 2008 presidential election, for example, both John McCain and Sarah Palin appeared on the comedy show *Saturday Night Live* and participated in parodies of themselves. On the one hand, it might seem that putting oneself down, even lightheartedly, would lower one's credibility. On the other hand, it might seem that the ability to poke fun at oneself would increase one's credibility. Which is it? The answer is: It depends. It depends on the specific credibility dimensions in which one is interested. A study by Hackman (1988) revealed that self-disparaging humor led to lower ratings of speaker competence. A study by Chang and Gruner (1981), however, demonstrated that self-disparaging humor enhanced liking for the source. In Chang and Gruner's study, the speaker's initial credibility was high and the speaker used indirect humor. The indirect humor consisted of a psychologist who was giving a presentation and defined a psychologist as "a guy who would father a set of twins, have one baptized, and keep the other as a control."

Our advice is to avoid using self-disparaging humor if you think you have low credibility to begin with or if you need to bolster your credibility in the "competence" dimension. If you have moderate to high credibility to begin with, then making light of some of your human frailties might make you appear more likable and genuine.

Humor as Social Proof: Smile and the World Smiles with You

Humor has been shown to function as an effective form of social proof. We laugh more in the presence of others. Social proof involves modeling our behavior after the actions or reactions of others (see Chapter 6). The use of "laugh tracks" or live audience laughter on television sit-coms illustrates this principle. Researchers have found that the perceived funniness of low- to medium-quality jokes is enhanced via the inclusion of canned laughter (Cupchik & Leventhal, 1974; Leventhal & Cupchik, 1975, 1976).

Is Humor Itself Persuasive?

We've seen that humor can assist persuasion in a variety of ways. We've also seen that a variety of other factors affect the success of humorous appeals. The question remains, however, does humor itself persuade? Unfortunately, attempts to answer this question have yielded mixed results (Gulas & Weinberger, 2006; Skalski et al., 2009). In a review of the humor literature, Weinberger and Gulas (1992) reported that 5 studies found humor facilitated persuasion, but another 15 were either inconclusive or found no such effects. Two studies found a negative relationship between the use of humor and persuasion.

At least one investigation not considered by Weinberger and Gulas *did* find that humor facilitated persuasion. O'Quin and Aronoff (1981) simulated a bargaining situation in which a buyer attempted to buy a painting from a seller. Sellers who made a final offer and added "and I'll throw in my pet frog!" were more successful in getting buyers to make a larger concession than sellers who did not include a humorous appeal. We don't find the joke too funny ourselves, but hey, it worked!

Based on the preceding example, the best we can offer is that sometimes humor itself persuades, though usually it does not, yet rarely does it backfire. Attempts at generalizing about humor are complicated by the fact that there is considerable disparity in how studies were conducted. There are disparities as to the type of humor used, how funny receivers perceived the material to be, the relatedness of the humor to the rest of the message, as well as issues such as timing and delivery.

So should you wear a funny nose and glasses the next time you want to persuade someone? The bottom line is that humor does appear to facilitate persuasion, but it does so indirectly and is no more effective than alternative approaches such as reasoning and evidence. The use of humor rarely seems to inhibit persuasion (except in terms of judgments of expertise).

PRIDE AND PATRIOTISM: TURNING RED, WHITE, AND BLUE INTO GREEN

During the 2008 presidential race, Barack Obama was criticized for not wearing an American flag pin on his lapel. Some regarded the absence of a flag pin as a sign of his lack of patriotism. Appeals based on patriotism, pride, honor, or a sense of duty, are hardly new to persuasion. Politicians have always wrapped themselves in the flag, stood next to veterans at public events, and declared theirs to be the greatest nation on earth (whatever nation it happened to be). Following September 11, 2001, all sorts of persuaders in the United States, not just politicians, jumped on the bandwagon of patriotism.

Does flag waving work? The results of several investigations suggest that patriotic ploys are effective, when used appropriately. Seiter and Gass (2005), for example, compared the tips earned by food servers who wrote a patriotic message ("United We Stand") on patrons' checks with a more traditional message ("Have a Nice Day"). Food servers who used the patriotic slogan earned significantly higher tips. Han (1988) found that patriotism had a positive effect on consumers' intentions to purchase domestic as opposed to foreign brands but didn't necessarily alter their perceptions of brand quality or reliability. Pedic (1990) discovered that nationalistic ads were more effective than non-nationalistic ads, but only if the receivers were themselves nationalistic. A study by Martin and Rogers (cited in Pedic, 1990) revealed that although one nationalistic ad was more effective than a non-nationalistic ad, a different nationalistic ad was not. Thus, the type of patriotic appeal has a lot to do with its effectiveness.

According to a Today/CNN poll conducted in 2005, 94 percent of Americans said they regard themselves as "somewhat patriotic," while only 5 percent reported they were "not especially patriotic" (Kornblum, 2005). Thus, it would seem that in post-9/11 America, patriotic appeals have a lot going for them. Even so, recent evidence suggests that while Americans feel patriotic personally, the effectiveness of flag waving may be wearing off (Wellner, 2002). Not only that, patriotic appeals can backfire, as Samuel Johnson's famous remark that patriotism is the "last refuge of scoundrels" warns. Companies can still use American branding successfully, but some, like Halliburton, have been faulted for exploiting the war in Iraq. In short, if a persuader appears to be "cashing in" on patriotic ploys or using patriotism as a wedge issue, then receivers may reject the message or the source.

FOR MATURE AUDIENCES: SEX APPEALS

During the 2004 Super Bowl half-time show, Janet Jackson experienced a "wardrobe malfunction" that gave viewers a fleeting glimpse of her bare breast. Viewers were outraged, so outraged that the incident became one of the most "Googled" and "TiVo'd" moments in TV history. In 2005, parents discovered that by using a hidden code, kids who played "Grand Theft Auto: San Andreas" could activate a scene depicting a sexual encounter (Levy, 2005). Apparently, the drive-by shootings, cop killings, and pimping were okay with parents who let their kids play this game, but a vicarious sex scene was going too far.

Television is replete with sexual appeals. So are print ads. One analysis found that half of all print ads depicted women as sex objects (Stankiewicz & Rosselli, 2008). And then there's the Internet. There's more sex on the Web than flies on a cowpie. "Sex sells," goes the advertising adage (Gunter, 2002; Reichert & Lambiase, 2003). Sex appeals have been used to sell jeans, cosmetics, fragrances, undergarments, liquor, and automobiles, to mention only a few applications. The use of sexual appeals has been a fixture of advertising for decades. What has changed, however, is that the use of overt sexual appeals has increased considerably (LaTour, 1990). Whereas older ads tended to allude to sex, modern ads often contain more overt, visually based sex appeals (LaTour & Henthorne, 1993; Miller, 1992a, 1992b).

Historically, females have been depicted as sex objects in advertisements (Eagle, 1979; Kerin, Lundstrom, & Sciglimpaglia, 1979; Venkatesan & Losco, 1975), a situation decried by feminists and other media critics. But rest assured ladies, the sexual objectification of males is now also well under way (Rohlinger, 2002). Television dramas such as *Cougar Town*, *Desperate Housewives,* and *Sex in the City*, along with reality TV shows such as *The Cougar*, have portrayed males as sex objects. The idealized male of today is more muscular, more of a "hunk," if you will, than the male ideal of the past.

How Sex Sells

How do sex appeals work? Generally speaking, they function as peripheral cues to persuasion. The whole point of a sexual appeal, after all, is to stimulate an emotional reaction in the receiver, a vicarious experience of sexuality or sensuality (LaTour & Henthorne, 1993). For this reason, sex appeals are usually conveyed visually. Typically, the unspoken message in ads employing sexual appeals is either (1) if you use product "X" you will look, act, or feel more sexy or (2) if you use product "X" other sexy people

will be attracted to you. This simple formula explains how most sex appeals work. Of course, such ads rarely make explicit cause-effect claims about the benefits of the product. Rather, the product is paired with sexually laden imagery. Through this associative process the receiver comes to identify the product with sexiness or sensuality.

A well-known example is Miller Lite's "cat fight" commercial, in which two busty women engage in a clothes-shedding brawl over whether Miller Lite has great taste or is less filling. While more obvious and explicit than other commercials, the Miller Lite ad joins a long list of "beer and babes" spots that have appeared on TV, such as the Coors' Light twins and Old Milwaukee's "Swedish bikini team" ads.

Caveats and Cautions

Although it is true that sexual appeals can be effective, there are also cautions regarding their use (see, for example, Sengupta & Dahl, 2008). First, despite their prevalence, sex appeals are not always effective. A study conducted in a pharmaceutical sales context found that a female sales representative who showed cleavage was no more persuasive than a female salesperson who did not (Glick, Chrislock, Petersik, Vijay, & Turek, 2008). Context means a lot, however. A study conducted in France found that males were much more likely to approach a female in a bar if she had large breasts (Guéguen, 2007). You are probably asking yourself, was this study conducted at the *Institute of Duh*? Actually, this was a controlled field experiment carried out by a well-known scholar at the Université de Bretagne-Sud. The conclusion might seem obvious. The point is that sex appeals may not function the same way in professional settings as they do in social settings. A boardroom is not a barroom.

Second, in some cases the targeted audience may resent the use of sexual appeals. For example, sexual stimuli are frequently included in ads aimed at women. Yet if women perceive the ads as sexist, the ads may backfire. For instance, in 2008, *Victoria's Secret* overhauled its advertising campaign following a decline in sales. The brand had become associated with being too "slutty" rather than "sexy" and had lost its appeal to older, affluent women (Merrick, 2008). Nowadays, an advertiser must walk a fine line between creating ads that are considered sexy and ads that are considered sexist (Lippman, 1991; Miller 1992b).

A third liability in using sex appeals is that they may function as a distraction, inhibiting receiver recall. If a consumer is salivating over a sexy model in a magazine ad, his or her attention may be diverted from the product being advertised. Several studies have shown this to be the case (Bushman & Bonacci, 2002; Judd & Alexander, 1983; Steadman, 1969). Advertisers face something of a dilemma here: A sexual appeal that is too mild may not stand out in the crowd, yet a sexual appeal that is too strong may serve as a distraction.

A fourth downside to using sexual appeals is that they may produce undesirable social consequences. Advertising has the power to generate and perpetuate negative gender stereotypes (Preston, 2006). The idealized female body type depicted in the media is extremely thin, a body shape that is unattainable for most women. Females who internalize this ideal body type often exhibit body dissatisfaction and develop eating disorders (Jhaly, 2001; Kilbourne, 1999).We don't fault the media entirely for the current obsession people have with their bodies. We do think, however, that advertisers, the movie industry, and the fashion industry must shoulder some of the blame for exploiting people's insecurities about their looks.

WARMTH APPEALS: STRAIGHT FROM THE HEART

"Nothing says lovin' like something from the oven, and Pillsbury says it best." Some advertisements convey a warm, cozy feeling. They emphasize family, friends, and a sense of belonging. They make us feel sentimental or nostalgic about life. Such ads are based on *warmth.* Aaker and Bruzzone (1981) identify warmth as one of a half dozen basic dimensions people use to describe advertisements. The use of warmth in advertising is quite common (Aaker, Stayman, & Hagerty, 1986). A little more than one in five prime-time commercials include warmth as an advertising theme (Aaker & Stayman, 1990). State Farm's "Like a good neighbor . . . State Farm is there" campaign is based on this theme, as is Olive Garden's "When you're here, you're family" slogan. So are ads for Hallmark cards, "Poppin' Fresh," the Pillsbury doughboy, and Snuggle fabric softener, which features a cuddly teddy bear. Insurance companies, airlines, health-care providers, restaurants, and hotel chains all use warmth to convey images of folksiness, hominess, friendliness, and familiarity (see Goldman & Papson, 1996).

So how do they work? Warmth appeals operate in much the same way as sex appeals: They work through association. A product or service is associated with the image of being warm, caring, or friendly. When we think of that product or service we get a warm-fuzzy feeling.

*"If they don't like our proposal I'll show them
the kittens. Everybody likes kittens."*

Warmth appeals aren't limited to television advertising. Real estate listings often use words like "charming," "cozy," or "rustic" to describe houses that are for sale. Restaurants boast of "home style" cooking. Frozen foods claim to be based on "authentic family recipes" that are "made the old fashioned way." In interpersonal encounters warmth can be conveyed through actions that generate a sense of friendship, bonding, or camaraderie. The Wal-Mart "greeter" is a living embodiment of a warmth appeal. When a food server introduces himself or herself by name and smiles, the food server is also conveying warmth.

Warmth appeals can be quite effective, but their success depends on their believability. The warm-fuzzy images being portrayed must come across as sincere for the appeal to work (Aaker & Stayman, 1989). As Aaker and Stayman note, the appeal "need[s] to avoid creating the perception of an ad's being phony, pointless, or contrived; such perceptions could interfere with the emotional response" (1990, p. 59). Warmth appeals, then, are a persuader's friend. They offer a positive approach to using motivational appeals by engendering warm, happy feelings in receivers.

INGRATIATION: POLISHING THE APPLE

You may know it as "brownnosing," "sucking up," or "boot-licking," but *ingratiation* is the term researchers use for flattery as a motivational inducement. Ingratiation has been thoroughly studied in organizational settings (see Deluga & Perry, 1994; Liden & Mitchell,

1988). An overall assessment of the research to date suggests that ingratiation works—and works well (Gordon, 1996). For instance, a study by Watt (1993) found that ingratiators were perceived by their supervisors as being more competent, more motivated, and more qualified for leadership positions than their noningratiating counterparts. Another study (Wayne, Kacmar, & Ferris, 1995) found that the use of ingratiation tactics by subordinates resulted in higher satisfaction for the supervisor and co-workers. In fact, one study quantified the advantage enjoyed by ingratiators over noningratiators. In a study of 152 pairs of managers and employees, Deluga (cited in Kelleher, 1997) found that ingratiators enjoyed a 5 percent edge over noningratiators in getting favorable evaluations. Finally, two studies in organizations—one conducted in restaurants (Seiter, 2006), the other in hair styling salons (Seiter & Dutson, 2007)—found that food servers and hair stylists earned significantly higher tips when they complimented (ingratiated) their customers than when they did not.

But, you might ask, wouldn't the other person *know,* or at least suspect, that the compliments were designed to curry favor? What if the target sees through the strategy? Not surprisingly, a transparent attempt at ingratiation has less chance of succeeding than an apparently genuine attempt.

Researchers know that ingratiation works, but just how does it work? What is the secret behind its success? There are three interrelated explanations for ingratiation's effectiveness (Dubrin, cited in Kelleher, 1997). First, ingratiatory behavior tends to increase *liking* ("I love that outfit on you!"). Second, ingratiatory behavior can create perceptions of *similarity* ("You love polka music? Hey, I do too!"). Third, ingratiation can work through *social labeling.* The use of positive social labels ("You sure are in a good mood today," "You are so thoughtful") can produce changes in the target's self-concept that, in turn, lead to changes in the target's behavior (Kraut, 1973). The person being ingratiated thus lives up to the positive label bestowed on her or him.

How many kinds of ingratiation are there? Edward Jones, who authored the first major work on ingratiation in 1963, identified three basic categories of ingratiation. The first is *other enhancement,* such as paying compliments or engaging in flattery. A derivative of this technique is to have a third party deliver the compliment, so that it seems more genuine ("Biff speaks highly of you. He says you are the nicest boss he's ever had"). The second technique is *opinion conformity.* This involves agreeing with the target's statements, ideas, and views. A variation on this technique is to initially disagree, then subsequently yield, creating the impression the target has changed your mind ("Okay, you've convinced me, Godiva chocolates taste better than See's chocolates"). A third approach is *self-presentation.* This involves bragging or otherwise displaying one's attributes to increase the target's evaluation of oneself ("Gee, I'd love to play golf with you, but I'm helping at the homeless center this weekend"). So you see, there is more than one way to engage in brownnosing.

You might think of ingratiation as an unethical influence strategy. We tend to agree, but only if the ingratiator believes the flattery, compliments, or positive social labels used to be untrue. If the ingratiator *believes* in the praise he or she is offering, we see no ethical problem in focusing on the positive side of things. Indeed, if the praise is genuine, this strategy offers the prospect for a "win–win" communication encounter. We discuss the ethical implications of ingratiatory behavior in more detail in Chapter 16.

Beetle Bailey reprinted with permission from King Features Syndicate.

MIXED EMOTIONS: OTHER APPEALS AND COMBINATIONS OF APPEALS

There are many other types of motivational appeals that we do not have space to cover here. Some of these include appeals to honor, youth, beauty, shame, and freedom, and the environment. Almost any human drive or emotion can serve as the basis for a motivational appeal.

Motivational appeals also can be used in combination. A threat of punishment can be coupled with a promise of reward, for example. A prosecutor might tell a defendant, "If you cooperate, I'll cut you a deal. If you don't, I'll throw the book at you." The "good cop/bad cop" technique used in police interrogations[2] also combines positive and negative appeals (Cialdini, 1993; Inbau, Reid, & Buckley, 1986; Kassin & McNall, 1991).

Guilt is commonly coupled with pity in charity fund-raisers ("If you don't help, who will?"). In a twist involving "strange bedfellows," the animal rights group known as PETA (People for the Ethical Treatment of Animals) has collaborated with *Penthouse* magazine for the past few years to produce an anti-fur advertisement. The ads feature sexy super-models who proclaim they would rather go naked than wear fur, thus combining a sex appeal with a guilt appeal.

We see definite advantages in combining appeals. If one appeal proves ineffective, another may still work. And there is always the prospect that combinations of appeals will have an additive effect. That is, the combination of appeals may work better than they would individually. The danger in combining appeals is that they may appear contradictory or cancel one another out. Combining humor with pity, for instance, might create the appearance that a persuader was insensitive or disingenuous. In selecting motivational appeals, then, a persuader must be judicious.

SUMMARY

Motivational appeals are external inducements used to increase another's drive to do something. The use of motivational appeals is an omnipresent phenomenon. Attempts at casting logical and emotional appeals as opposites are suspect. Although motivational appeals aren't necessarily rational, neither are they irrational. Eight types of motivational appeals were discussed: fear, pity, guilt, humor, patriotism, sex, warmth, and ingratiation. These represent only a fraction of the appeals available to persuaders. Experimental studies have shown some of these to be highly effective in facilitating persuasion, whereas others have been shown to be less effective. It also was suggested that motivational appeals can be successfully combined if certain precautions are followed.

ENDNOTES

1. The subject of what emotions actually are is a rather complicated one. For a discussion of whether emotions are best thought of as physiological responses, cognitive reactions, or some other form of neural activity, see Leventhal (1980).

2. Using this technique one interrogator plays the role of the "bad cop." The bad cop treats the suspect with disdain, threatens the suspect in various ways, and claims to have the goods on the suspect. A second interrogator, playing the role of the "good cop," comes to the suspect's rescue. The second interrogator befriends the suspect, for example, by offering coffee or a cigarette. The good cop tells the bad cop to back off. The good cop displays empathy for the suspect's situation. The technique can be quite effective. After being subjected to verbal abuse by the bad cop, the suspect is often more willing to talk to the sympathetic good cop.

REFERENCES

Aaker, D. A., & Bruzzone, D. E. (1981). Viewer perceptions of prime-time television advertising. *Journal of Advertising Research, 21*(5), 15–23.

Aaker, D. A., & Stayman, D. M. (1989). What mediates the emotional response to advertising? The case of warmth. In P. Cafferata & A. M. Tybout (Eds.), *Cognitive and affective responses to advertising* (pp. 287–303). Lexington, MA: Lexington Books.

Aaker, D. A., & Stayman, D. M. (1990). A micro approach to studying feeling responses to advertising: The case of warmth. In S. J. Agres, J. A. Edell, & T. B. Dubitsky (Eds.), *Emotion in advertising: Theoretical and practical explorations* (pp. 53–68). New York: Quorum Books.

Aaker, D. A., Stayman, D. M., & Hagerty, M. R. (1986). Warmth in advertising: Measurement, impact, and sequence effects. *Journal of Consumer Research, 12*(4), 365–381.

Altheide, D. L. (2002). *Creating fear: News and the construction of crisis.* Hawthorne, NY: Aldine DeGruyter.

Aristotle. (1932). *The rhetoric* (L. Cooper, Trans.). Englewood Cliffs, NJ: Prentice Hall.Beard, F.K. (2005). One hundred years of humor in American advertising. *Journal of Macromarketing, 25*(1), 54–65.

Beard, F. K. (2005). One hundred years of humor in American advertising. *Journal of Macromarketing, 25*(1), 54–65.

Becker, S. L. (1963). Research on emotional and logical proofs. *The Southern Speech Journal, 28*(3), 198–207.

Berger, A. A. (1976). Anatomy of a joke. *Journal of Communication, 26,* 113–115.

Blaine, B., & Williams, Z. (2004). Belief in the controllability of weight and attributions to prejudice among heavyweight women. *Sex Roles, 51,* 79–84.

Boster, F. J., Mitchell, M. M., Lapinski, M. N., Cooper, H., Orrego, V. O., & Reinke, R. (1999). The impact of guilt and type of compliance-gaining message on compliance. *Communication Monographs, 66,* 168–177.

Boster, F. J., & Mongeau, P. A. (1984). Fear-arousing persuasive messages. In R. N. Bostrum & B. H. Wesley (Eds.), *Communication yearbook 8* (pp. 330–375). Beverly Hills, CA: Sage.

Bushman, B. J., & Bonacci, A. M. (2002). Violence and sex impair memory for television ads. *Journal of Applied Psychology, 87*(3), 557–564.

Cantor, J. R., & Venus, P. (1980). The effect of humor on recall of a radio advertisement. *Journal of Broadcasting, 24*(1), 13–22.

Casey, M. K., Timmermann, L., Allen, M., Krahn, S., & Turkiewicz, K. L. (2009). Response and self-efficacy of condom use: A meta-analysis of this important element of AIDS education and prevention. *Southern Communication Journal, 74*(1), 57–78.

Chang, M., & Gruner, C. R. (1981). Audience reaction to self-disparaging humor. *Southern Speech Communication Journal, 46,* 419–426.

Cho, H., & Witte, K. (2004). A review of fear appeal effects. In J. S. Seiter & R. H. Gass (Eds.), *Readings in persuasion, social influence, and compliance gaining* (pp. 223–238). Boston: Allyn & Bacon.

Cialdini, R. (1993). *Influence: Science and practice* (3rd ed.). New York: HarperCollins.

Cupchik, G. C., & Leventhal, H. (1974). Consistency between expressive behavior and the evaluation of humorous stimuli: The role of sex and self-observation. *Journal of Personality and Social Psychology, 30,* 429–442.

DeAngelis, T. (1993, August). Trivializing disabilities gives immunity to fears. *APA Monitor, 24,* [Lexis-Nexis].

Deci, E. L. (1975). *Intrinsic motivation.* New York: Plenum.

Deci, E. L., & Ryan, R. (1978). *Intrinsic motivation and self-determination in human behavior.* New York: Plenum.

Deluga, R. J., & Perry, J. T. (1994). The role of subordinate performance and ingratiation in leader-member exchanges. *Group Organization Management, 19*(1), 67–86.

Del Valle, C. (1992, September 14). Some of Jerry's kids are mad at the old man. *Business Week (3283),* p. 36.

Derks, P., Kalland, S., & Etgen, M. (1995). The effect of joke type and audience response on the reaction to a joker: Replication and extension. *Humor, 8*(4), 327–337.

Dillard, J. P. (1994). Rethinking the study of fear appeals: An emotional perspective. *Communication Theory, 4,* 295–323.

Dillard, J. P., Shen, L., & Vail, R. G. (2007). Does perceived message effectiveness cause persuasion or vice versa? 17 consistent answers. *Human Communication Research, 33,* 467–488.

Eagle, J. (1979). The bad, the bare, and the beautiful. *Media Scope, 13,* 39.

Eayres, C. B., & Ellis, N. (1990). Charity advertising: For or against people with a mental handicap? *British Journal of Social Psychology, 29,* 349–360.

Eisend, M. (2009). A meta-analysis of humor in advertising. *Journal of the Academy of Marketing Science, 37* (191–203).

Ervin, M. (1995, June). "The ragged edge" [Review of the film *The ragged edge*]. *The Progressive,* 39.

Evans, J. St., B. T., Barston, J. L., & Pollard, P. (1983). On the conflict between logic and belief in syllogistic reasoning. *Memory and Cognition, 11,* 295–306.

Freedman, J. L., Wallington, S., & Bless, E. (1967). Compliance gaining without pressure: The effect of guilt. *Journal of Personality and Social Psychology, 7,* 117–124.

Gass, R. H. (1983). *Threat of punishment versus promise of reward: A comparison of the relative effectiveness of two types of verbal appeals.* Unpublished doctoral dissertation, University of Kansas, Lawrence.

Gentry, J. W., Kennedy, P. K., Paul, K., & Hill, R. P. (1995). The vulnerability of those grieving the death of a loved one: Implications for public policy. *Journal of Public Policy and Marketing, 14*(1), 128–142.

Glassner, B. (1999). *The culture of fear: Why Americans are afraid of the wrong things.* New York: Basic Books.

Glick, P., Chrislock, K., Petersik, K., Vijay, M., & Turek, A. (2008). Does cleavage work at work? Men, but not women, falsely believe cleavage sells a weak product. *Psychology of Women Quarterly, 32,* 326–335.

Goldman, R., & Papson, S. (1996). *Sign wars: The cluttered landscape of advertising.* New York: Guilford Press.

Gordon, R. A. (1996). Impact of ingratiation on judgments and evaluations: A meta-analytic investigation. *Journal of Personality and Social Psychology, 71*(1), 54–70.

Graham, E. E., Papa, M. J., & Brooks, G. P. (1992). Functions of humor in conversation: Conceptualization and measurement. *Western Journal of Communication, 56,* 161–183.

Gruner, C. R. (1967). Effect of humor on speaker ethos and audience information gain. *Journal of Communication, 17*(3), 228–233.

Gruner, C. R. (1970). The effect of humor in dull and interesting informative speeches. *Central States Speech Journal, 21*(3), 160–166.

Gruner, C. R., & Lampton, W. E. (1972). Effects of including humorous material in a persuasive sermon. *Southern Speech Communication Journal, 38,* 188–196.

Guéguen, N. (2007). Women's bust size and men's courtship solicitation. *Body Image, 4,* 386–390.

Gulas, C. S., & Weinberger, M. G. (2006). *Humor in advertising: A comprehensive analysis.* Armonk, NY: M.E. Sharpe.

Gunter, B. (2002). *Media sex: What are the issues?* Mahwah, NJ: Lawrence Erlbaum.

Hackman, M. Z. (1988). Reactions to the use of self-disparaging humor by informative public speakers. *The Southern Speech Communication Journal, 53,* 175–183.

Haller, B. (1994). The misfit and muscular dystrophy. *Journal of Popular Film & Television, 21*(4), 142–149.

Han, C. M. (1988). The role of consumer patriotism in the choice of domestic music versus foreign products. *Journal of Advertising Research, 28,* 25–32.

Hibbert, S., Smith, A., Davies, A., & Ireland, F. (2007). Guilt appeals: Persuasion knowledge and charitable giving. *Psychology & Marketing, 24*(8), 723–742.

Higbee, K. L. (1969). Fifteen years of fear-arousal: Research on threat appeals. *Psychological Bulletin, 72,* 426–444.

Hurst, R. (1998). Forget pity or charity. Disability is a rights issue. *Media Development, 45*(2), 8–10.

Inbau, F. E., Reid, J. E., & Buckley, J. P. (1986). *Criminal interrogations and confessions* (3rd ed.). Baltimore: Williams & Wilkins.

Jaffe, C. A. (1996, October 16). "Shopping for your funeral makes financial sense." *Los Angeles Times,* pp. D3, D9.

Janis, I. L., & Feshbach, S. (1953). Effects of fear-arousing communications. *Journal of Abnormal and Social Psychology, 48,* 78–92.

Jhaly, S. (Producer). (2001). *Killing us softly 3: Advertising's image of women/with Jean Kilbourne.* [video]. New York: Media Education Foundation.

Jones, E. (1963). *Ingratiation.* New York: Appleton-Century-Crofts.

Judd, B. B., & Alexander, M. W. (1983). On the reduced effectiveness of some sexually suggestive ads. *Journal of the Academy of Marketing Science, 11,* 156–168.

Kaplan, R. M., & Pascoe, G. C. (1977). Humorous lectures and humorous examples: Some effects upon comprehension and retention. *Journal of Educational Psychology, 69*(1), 61–65.

Kassin, S. M., & McNall, K. (1991). Police interrogations and confessions. *Law and Human Behavior, 15,* 233–251.

Kelleher, K. (1997, February 24). "Flattery will get you . . . everywhere." *Los Angeles Times,* pp. E1–E2.

Kerin, R., Lundstrom, W. J., & Sciglimpaglia, D. (1979). Women in advertisements: Retrospect and prospect. *Journal of Advertising, 8,* 37–42.

Kilbourne, J. (1999). *Deadly persuasion: Why women and girls must fight the addictive power of advertising.* New York: The Free Press.

Kopp, S. W., & Kemp, E. (2007). Consumer awareness of the legal obligations of funeral providers. *The Journal of Consumer Affairs, 41*(2), 326–340.

Kornblum, J. (2005, June 29). "So proudly we hail our freedom." *USA Today,* p. 4D.

Kraut, R. E. (1973). The effects of social labeling on giving to charity. *Journal of Experimental Social Psychology, 9,* 551–562.

Langer, E., Blank, A., & Chanowitz, B. (1978). The mindlessness of ostensibly thoughtful action: The role of "placebic" information in interpersonal interaction. *Journal of Personality and Social Psychology, 36*(6), 635–642.

LaTour, M. S. (1990). Female nudity in print advertising: An analysis of gender differences in arousal and ad response. *Psychology and Marketing, 7,* 65–81.

LaTour, M. S., & Henthorne, T. L. (1994). Ethical judgments of sexual appeals in print advertising. *Journal of Advertising, 23*(3), 81–90.

LaTour, M. S., & Henthorne, T. L. (1993). Female nudity in print advertising: An analysis of gender differences in arousal and ad response. *Psychology and Marketing, 7,* 65–81.

Lefford, A. (1946). The influence of emotional subject matter on logical reasoning. *Journal of General Psychology, 34,* 127–151.

Leventhal, H. (1980). Toward a comprehensive theory of emotion. In L. Berkowitz (Ed.), *Advances in experimental social psychology* (Vol. 13, pp. 140–207). New York: Academic Press.

Leventhal, H., & Cupchik, G. C. (1975). The informational and facilitative effects of an audience upon expression and evaluation of humorous stimuli. *Journal of Experimental Social Psychology, 11,* 363–380.

Leventhal, H., & Cupchik, G. C. (1976). A process model of humor judgment. *Journal of Communication, 26*(3), 190–204.

Levy, S. (2005, August 1). "Secret codes and videogames." *Newsweek,* p. 14. Retrieved August 27, 2005, from www.lexis-nexis.com.

Liden, R., & Mitchell, T. (1988). Ingratiatory behaviors in organizational settings. *Academy of Management Review, 13,* 572–587.

Lindsey, L. L. M. (2005). Anticipated guilt as behavioral motivation: An examination of appeals to help unknown others through bone marrow donation. *Human Communication Research, 31,* 453–481.

Lindsey, L. L. M., Yun, K. A., & Hill, J. B. (2007). Anticipated guilt as motivation to help others: An examination of empathy as a moderator. *Communication Research, 34*(4), 468–480.

Lippman, J. (1991, September 30). Sexy or sexist? Recent ads spark debate. *The Wall Street Journal,* p. B1.

Merrick, A. (2008, February 29). "Apparently, you can be too sexy." *Wall Street Journal,* p. B1.

Miller, C. (1992a, March 16). No sex please, we're censors. *Marketing News, 26,* 1, 17.

Miller, C. (1992b, November 23). Publisher says sexy ads are O.K., but sexist ones will sink sales. *Marketing News, 26,* 8–9.

Mitford, J. (1980). Americans don't want fancy funerals. In J. Mitford (Ed.), *Poison penmanship: The gentle art of muckraking* (pp. 79–88). New York: Vintage Books.

Mongeau, P. (1998). Another look at fear-arousing appeals. In M. Allen & R. W. Preiss (Eds.), *Persuasion: Advances through meta-analysis* (pp. 53–68). Cresskill, NJ: Hampton Press.

Munn, W. C., & Gruner, C. R. (1981). "Sick" jokes, speaker sex, and informative speech. *Southern Speech Communication Journal, 46,* 411–418.

Murnstein, B. L., & Burst, R. G. (1985). Humor and interpersonal attraction. *Journal of Personality Assessment, 49,* 637–640.

Oakhill, J., & Garnham, A. (1993). On theories of belief bias in syllogistic reasoning. *Cognition, 46,* 87–92.

O'Keefe, D. J. (2002). Guilt as a mechanism of persuasion. In J. P. Dillard & M. Pfau (Eds.), *The persuasion handbook: Developments in theory and practice* (pp. 329–344). Thousand Oaks, CA: Sage.

O'Quin, K., & Aronoff, J. (1981). Humor as a technique of social influence. *Social Psychology Quarterly, 44*(4), 349–357.

Pedic, F. (1990). Persuasiveness of nationalistic advertisements. *Journal of Applied Social Psychology, 20,* 724–728.

Petri, H. (1991). *Motivation: Theory, research, and application* (3rd ed.). Belmont, CA: Wadsworth.

Petty, R. E., & Cacioppo, J. T. (1986). *Communication and persuasion: Central and peripheral routes to attitude change.* New York: Springer-Verlag.

Preston, C. (2006). Subordinate stills: An empirical study of sexist print advertising and its implications for law. *Texas Journal of Women and the Law, 15,* 229–269.

Reichert, T., & Lambiase, J. (Eds.). (2003). *Sex in advertising: Perspectives on the erotic appeal.* Mahwah, NJ: Lawrence Erlbaum.

Reuchelle, R. C. (1958). An experimental study of audience recognition of logical and intellectual appeals in persuasion. *Speech Monographs, 25*(1), 49–58.

"R.I.P. Off." (1996, August 30). Television feature that aired on ABC's *20/20* program.

Rohlinger, D. A. (2002). Eroticizing men: Cultural influences on advertising and male objectification. *Sex Roles: A Journal of Social Research, 46*(3), 61–74.

Rohlinger, D. A. (2002.) Eroticizing men: Cultural influences on advertising and male objectification. *Sex Roles: A Journal of Research 46*(3/4): 61–74.

Ruiter, R. C., Abraham, C., & Kok, G. (2001). Scary warnings and rational precautions: A review of the psychology of fear appeals. *Psychology and Health, 16,* 613–630.

Seiter, J. S. (2007). Ingratiation and gratuity: The effect of complimenting customers on tipping behavior in restaurants. *Journal of Applied Social Psychology, 37*(3), 478–485.

Seiter, J. S., & Gass, R. H. (2005). The effect of patriotic messages on restaurant tipping. *Journal of Applied Social Psychology, 35,* 1–10.

Seiter, J. S., & Dutson, E. (2007). The Effect of compliments on tipping behavior in hair styling salons. *The Journal of Applied Social Psychology, 37*(9), 1999–2007.

Sengupta, J., & Dahl, D. W. (2008). Gender-related reactions to gratuitous sex appeals in advertising. *Journal of Consumer Psychology, 18,* 62–78.

Skalski, P., Tamborini, R., Glazer, E., & Smith, S. (2009). Effects of humor on presence and recall of messages. *Communication Quarterly, 57*(2), 136–153.

Speck, P. S. (1987). *On humor and humor in advertising.* Unpublished doctoral dissertation, Texas Tech University, Lubbock.

Stankiewicz, J. M., & Rosselli, F. (2008). Women as sex objects and victims in print advertisements. *Sex Roles, 58,* 579–589.

Steadman, M. (1969). How sexy illustrations affect brand recall. *Journal of Advertising Research, 9,* 15–19.

Sternthal, B., & Craig, S. (1973). Humor in advertising. *Journal of Marketing, 37*(4), 12–18.

Sutton, S. R. (1982). Fear-arousing communication: A critical examination of theory and research. In J. R. Eisner (Ed.), *Social psychology and behavioral medicine* (pp. 303–337). London: John Wiley & Sons.

Tamborini, R., & Zillmann, D. (1981). College students' perceptions of lectures using humor. *Perceptual and Motor Skills, 52,* 427–432.

Taylor, P. M. (1974). An experimental study of humor and ethos. *Southern Speech Communication Journal, 39,* 359–366.

Toncar, M. F. (2001). The use of humor in television advertising: Revisiting the U.S.–U.K. comparison. *International Journal of Advertising, 20*(4), 521–539.

Venkatesan, M., & Losco, J. (1975). Women in magazine advertisements. *Journal of Advertising Research, 15,* 49–54.

Wanzer, M. B., Booth-Butterfield, M., & Booth-Butterfield, S. (1996). Humor and social attraction: Are funny people more popular? An examination of humor orientation, loneliness, and social attraction. *Communication Quarterly, 44*(1), 42–52.

Wasik, J. F. (1995, September/October). Fraud in the funeral industry. *Consumer's Digest, 34,* pp. 53–59.

Watt, J. D. (1993). The impact of frequency of ingratiation on the performance evaluation of bank personnel. *Journal of Psychology, 127*(2), 171–177.

Wayne, S. J., Kacmar, K., & Ferris, G. R. (1995). Coworker response to others' ingratiation attempts. *Journal of Managerial Issues, 7*(3), 277–289.

Weinberger, M. G., & Campbell, L. (1991). The use and impact of humor in radio advertising. *Journal of Advertising Research, 31,* 44–52.

Weinberger, M. G., & Gulas, C. S. (1992). The impact of humor in advertising: A review. *Journal of Advertising, 21*(4), 35–59.

Weinberger, M. G., & Spotts, H. E. (1989). Humor in U.S. versus U.K. TV and advertising. *Journal of Advertising, 18*(2), 39–44.

Weiner, B., Perry, R. P., & Magnusson, J. (1988). An attributional analysis of reactions to stigmas. *Journal of Personality and Social Psychology, 55,* 738–748.

Wellner, A. S. (2002, September). The perils of patriotism. *American Demographics.* Retrieved August 24, 2005, from www.lexis-nexis.com.

Witte, K. (1992). Putting the fear back into fear appeals: The extended parallel process model. *Communication Monographs, 59,* 329–349.

Witte, K. (1994). Fear control and danger control: A test of the extended parallel process model. *Communication Monographs, 61*(2), 113–134.

Witte, K., & Allen, M. (2000). A meta-analysis of fear appeals: Implications for effective public health campaigns. *Health Education and Behavior, 27*(5), 591–615.

Worthen, J. B., & Deschamps, J. D. (2008). Humour mediates the facilitative effect of bizarreness in delayed recall. *British Journal of Psychology, 99,* 461–471

Young, D. G. (2008). The privileged role of the late-night joke: Exploring humor's role in disrupting argument scrutiny. *Media Psychology, 11,* 119–142.

CHAPTER 14

Visual Persuasion

Want to capture an audience's attention? Try taking off your clothes. You wouldn't be the first to use this approach. People for the Ethical Treatment of Animals (PETA) use this strategy to protest wearing leather and fur. Their "Naked Truth" campaign features attractive models and celebrities, sans clothing, with the caption "I'd rather go naked than wear fur." Not to be outdone, Spencer Tunick, a performance artist/photographer convinced 18,000 people in Mexico City to strip naked for a mass photo shoot. He sees mass nudity as a form of collective defiance against social norms. Nudity, however, is not reserved for protesters and artists. Abercrombie & Fitch stores use live, shirtless models to peddle clothing and *Victoria's Secret* commercials leave few secrets to the imagination.

Hang on a minute. Before you attempt your next class presentation in the buff, we should warn you that while nudity may serve as a great attention step, your "visual aids" may serve as a distraction during the rest of your presentation. Moreover, you may encounter a good deal of audience resentment. Females, religious people, and conservative people tend to react negatively to nudity (Christy & Haley, 2008). Now that we have your attention, we'd like to examine the role of images in persuasion.

The old saying "monkey see, monkey do" tells us a lot about persuasion: The images that surround us affect how we think and how we act. We are living in an increasingly visual society. Fewer people are reading newspapers and books. More people are watching movies and TV. As Metros (2008) noted:

> politicians wage campaigns not on issues, but through their visual persona; wars are televised live through the eyes of embedded journalists; criminal trials have become 24/7 international spectator events; newspapers have had to reduce text to pack their pages with charts, graphics, and photos to compete for market-share; and even radio directs its listeners to Web sites to illustrate the spoken word. (p. 109)

In television commercials, magazine advertisements, and billboards images are primary and words are secondary. The World Wide Web is chock full of images. YouTube, Flickr, and social networking sites are saturated with images. Video mashups are increasingly popular. And it is not only mass media that rely on visual cues. Protest marches, sit-ins, demonstrations, rallies, and picketing are highly visual acts that are intended to persuade.

Oral communication relies on images, too. Public speaking has always featured visual aids. But nowadays audiences expect "wowie-zowie" presentations loaded with "eye candy." Try giving a PowerPoint presentation with text-only bullet points and you may find your audience nodding off or texting.

In this chapter we examine some of the important ways in which images shape beliefs, attitudes, and behaviors. First, we consider the importance of visual stimuli and how images persuade. Next, we examine art as a form of persuasion, cinematic influence, images in advertising, and photojournalism as a form of persuasion.

VISUAL PERSUASION: OFTEN OVERLOOKED

Traditionally, the study of persuasion has focused on influence attempts that take place within the world of words. Messaris (1997) underscores this point when he notes, "although the study of persuasive communication has a history of more than two millennia, the focus of this scholarly tradition has tended overwhelmingly to be on verbal strategies. With a few notable exceptions, the systematic investigation of visual persuasion is still in its infancy" (p. vii).

Despite the traditional emphasis on words, studies have revealed a *picture superiority effect* for images compared to words. Pictures are more easily recognized and recalled than words (Hockley, 2008; Stenberg, 2006). For example, one study compared a "words-only" ad with a "words plus picture" (Edell & Staelin, 1983). Recall was significantly higher in the "words plus picture" condition. One explanation for the picture superiority effect is that pictures, unlike words, are processed via two different modes and can later be recalled via either mode (Paivio, 1986, 1991). Visual elements are thus an important part of persuasion. As Blair (1996) comments, "paintings and sculptures, and the visual component of movies, television programs and commercial and political advertising, are enormously powerful influences on attitudes and beliefs" (p. 23).

HOW IMAGES PERSUADE

Images have the power to move us in ways that words can't. What is it about images and other visual stimuli that make them so persuasive? We take up this question here. In doing so, we rely heavily on Paul Messaris' (1997) conceptualization of the role of images in persuasion. He suggests that images persuade in three basic ways: through *iconicity, indexicality,* and *syntactic indeterminacy.* Because these may be unfamiliar concepts, we explain each of them in turn.

Iconicity: Bearing a Resemblance

One way images persuade is by functioning as *icons,* which simply means that they resemble the things they represent. An image can stand for an idea or sum up a concept. The stick figure that appears on a "pedestrian crossing" sign is an icon. A caricature of a politician drawn by an editorial cartoonist is also an icon. The statue of Liberty, Uncle Sam, and the bald eagle are all icons of America. All of these are icons because they are representations of people, events, or things. Insofar as their iconicity is concerned, it doesn't matter whether they are accurate representations or not, as long as people understand what they represent. This is, perhaps, the most important property of images; to summarize ideas and concepts. As Messaris (1997) notes, "If there is one property that most clearly distinguishes pictures from language and other modes of communication, that property is iconicity" (p. 3).

A good illustration of the iconic nature of images can be found in Philip Morris' Marlboro man. The Marlboro man is immediately recognizable around the world. He is a mythical American hero. He stands for the Old West. He symbolizes an idealized image of the cowboy—a rugged, self-reliant individual. He's always pictured outdoors, on the range. Without even seeing the brand-name or the slogan, most people can spot the Marlboro man in an instant. Everyone knows where he lives—in Marlboro Country, an imaginary place akin to Camelot. And boy does he sell cigarettes! Marlboro cigarettes are the most popular brand in the world (Webb, 1999). For this reason, the Marlboro man has been called "the most universally recognized, consistently profitable, and aesthetically appealing image in the advertising world" ("Selling Tobacco," 1990, p. 84). Now that's an icon!

As part of their iconic nature, images can evoke emotional responses in people. Following the devastation wrought by Hurricane Katrina in 2005, images of people huddled on rooftops, wading through chest-deep water, and crowded into the Superdome in New Orleans evoked feelings of sorrow, pity, anger, and shame. Photos from Iraq's Abu Ghraib prison showing naked detainees being forced to perform degrading acts were iconic reminders of what had gone wrong with the mission in Iraq.

In functioning as icons, images also can be selective. They can accentuate certain features while minimizing others. An advertisement for mascara, for example, might emphasize a model's eyes through lighting or digital sharpening, while deemphasizing other facial features. A beer commercial might zoom in to show frosty condensation on a glass. At the same time that images represent reality, then, they can also highlight certain aspects of reality, either subtly or to the point of extreme exaggeration.

Another iconic function of images is that they can violate the reality they represent (Messaris, 1997). An image can make something look real even though it isn't. For example, a busy mother who has her hands full doing the laundry, cooking dinner, cleaning house, and taking care of the kids could be pictured with four arms rather than two. A commercial for a hybrid fruit juice might show an orange that is shaped like a pineapple, or a pineapple that is shaped like an orange. An ad for a pain reliever might show someone suffering from a splitting headache, whose head actually appears to be splitting in two. Images can thus simulate a reality that doesn't exist. They can make people, objects, and events look real, even though they are fictions.

Indexicality: Seeing Is Believing

A second way in which images persuade is through *indexicality* (Messaris, 1997). This refers to the ability of images, in particular photos and video, to document that an event happened or that something took place. Such images may be obvious or may require interpretation on the part of the viewer. Lester (2006) notes that:

> indexical signs can be a footprint on the beach or the surface of the moon, smoke spewing out of a high smokestack or automobile exhaust pipe, and even a fever noticed by a doctor

with sick patients. Footprints stand for the person who impressed them. Smoke represents the pollution generated by a furnace or engine. Fever indicates that the patient has an infection. (p. 58)

Indexical images often function as a form of sign reasoning. Both still and moving pictures are capable of performing this function. A diet advertisement might show a person holding up a huge pair of his or her old pants. The pants demonstrate how obese the person was before and how much weight the person has lost since. A photo of three children with missing limbs serves as proof that land mines kill and maim innocent civilians. A fingerprint lifted from a crime scene is a sign that the defendant was in fact there. The grim photo of a Sudanese infant starving to death (see photo) offers indexical proof that people in the Sudan are truly on the brink. It is one thing to hear about people starving in Africa. It is quite another to see it. This powerful, ghoulish image won a Pulitzer Prize in 1993.

The documentary aspects of images, however, also can be misleading. In this regard, Messaris (1997) cautions that, "photographs, of course, can lie. The picture of a model in a fashion ad can be made more attractive through airbrushing, and voter interviews or product demonstrations can be staged" (p. xvii). Let's say we are watching the news on TV and we see a political candidate, shirtsleeves rolled up, wearing a hardhat, while touring a factory. The image emphasizes the candidates "plain folks" appeal. He or she identifies with ordinary workers. But would the candidate have rolled up his or her sleeves, donned a hardhat, and toured the factory in the absence of any camera crews? The cameras are recording an event that might not take place in their absence.

Perhaps you've seen news footage of angry citizens in foreign lands burning the American flag to protest U.S. foreign policies. The flag is an icon that stands for the United

© Megan Patrica Carter Trust/Corbis/Sygma.

States. It seems fair to ask, however, whether the cameras are there because the protesters are burning the flag or the protesters are burning the flag because the cameras are there. A critical viewer should, therefore, question the indexicality of visual records of events. Media events can be staged. The presence of cameras and film crews can alter people's behavior. Photographs and videotapes can be digitally altered to create the appearance that events occurred when, in fact, they did not, or did not occur in the way they are pictured.

Syntactic Indeterminacy: Don't Look for Logic in Images

A third way in which images persuade is through *syntactic indeterminacy*. This simply means that, unlike words, pictures cannot convey precise relationships between things. Messaris (1997) thus notes, "what visual syntax lacks, especially in comparison to verbal language, is a set of explicit devices for indicating causality, analogy, or any other relationships other than those of space or time" (pp. xvii–xviii). The problem is that images lack logical operators. That is, they can't explicitly state if-then relationships, either-or relationships, or other logical connections between people, objects, and events. As an example, a picture can show what a person's abdominal muscles looked like before using the new "Monster Ab-Cruncher." A picture can show what the person's abdominal muscles look like afterward. However, pictures themselves can't specify a cause-effect relationship.

The fact that images can't convey logical relationships, such as "A causes B," "A is analogous to B," or "either A or B will happen," is both a blessing and a curse. The blessing is that pictures can be used to equate one thing with another, via association. Pictures can imply an association without actually saying so. This can work to a persuader's advantage. A persuader can foster subtle associations through images without making the associations explicit in words. For example, an advertiser can equate a product with being cool, being sexy, or conferring social status simply by pairing the product with cool, sexy, or classy images.

The curse is that images can never suggest the precise nature of relationships, so it is up to the observer to guess what the relationship is. A commercial might show a happy family carrying kayaks from their hybrid SUV to a river. Rather than make the consumer want a hybrid SUV, as the advertiser intends, the sequence of images may make the consumer want to go camping, or buy a kayak, or spend more time with the family instead. This is not a serious drawback, however, for two reasons. First, advertisers have decades of practice at manipulating lighting, camera angle, color, and other features of images to achieve the results they want. Second, advertisers use words when they want to make a point explicitly and pictures when they want to make a point implicitly. Thus, they enjoy the best of both worlds.

Now that you have a better understanding of how images persuade, we can turn our attention to some of the intriguing and important ways visual stimuli affect us. We begin by examining art as a visual form of influence.

ART AS PERSUASION: *MONA LISA* MADE ME DO IT

The use of art to further political and religious ends dates back to ancient civilizations. In fact, works of art—sculpture, painting, pottery, and so on—were funded by the state to promote its own ends. Greek friezes and frescoes taught citizens moral lessons involving

Greek gods and Greek mythology. In the Middle Ages, organized religions sponsored art to further religious ends. The Catholic Church commissioned thousands of works of art to promote Catholicism. As only one example, Michelangelo's painting of the finger of God reaching out to man that adorns the ceiling of the Sistine Chapel endorses a biblical view of creation. Many of the most famous paintings on display in museums throughout the world were funded by the church or religious benefactors to promote religious ideals.

The Paintbrush Is Mightier Than the Sword

Governments, especially totalitarian governments, have used art as a form of political propaganda (Clark, 1997). Under Stalin, the Soviet Union declared all art to be subservient to the interests of the state. "Socialist Realism" became the officially recognized standard for art, and its purpose was to advance the political and social ideals of communism. Independent art collectives were banned and all artists were required to join a government-controlled union. What's more, only certain "themes" were deemed appropriate for such artists. Not surprisingly, paintings and posters from this era featured workers—dedicated members of the proletariat—working side by side in factories and on farms. Such iconic representations idealized communism. Clark (1977) explains how such politicized art modeled behavior for the masses:

> in paintings, novels, and films, Socialist Realism created a parallel world peopled by heroes and heroines who personified political ideals. As tireless labourers, courageous Red Army soldiers, diligent schoolchildren, or dedicated Party activists, they demonstrated exemplary behaviour and the attitudes of perfect citizens. (p. 87)

Similarly, China, under Mao, produced a good deal of art aimed at promoting Communist ideology. When the Communists assumed power in 1949, posters and murals contributed to the deification of Chairman Mao. Graphic arts were also used to mobilize and indoctrinate the people during the Cultural Revolution. Posters showed smiling, cherubic children harvesting bumper crops of rice—a tribute to the agricultural achievements of the revolution. Peasants and soldiers were shown working together, as one happy family under communism.

Meanwhile, in the Western world, art was not only sponsored by governments but was directed against governments as well. Eugène Delacroix's well-known painting *Liberty Leading the People* (1830) now hangs in the Musée du Louvre in Paris. The painting shows a mythical lady liberty, rifle in one hand and French flag in the other, leading French citizens in a charge during the French Revolution. Through its iconicity, the painting both endorses and romanticizes the revolution. Diego Rivera's *History of Mexico* (1929–1935), a large mural painted on the walls of the National Palace in Mexico City, depicts the domination of Mexico's peasants first by Spanish conquistadors, then the Catholic Church, then the Mexican army, and finally by wealthy landowners. The painting renders the struggle of the downtrodden against oppression, a struggle that culminated in the Mexican Revolution.

Although not aimed at any specific government, Eduard Munch's famous expressionist painting, *The Scream* (1893), renders the artist's own personal angst and his forebodings about society in general. *The Scream* shows a terrified figure, hands on

学习好经验 建设新山区

This poster from the Chinese cultural revolution portrays an idealized view of agrarian life.

Reprinted by permission. Chinese Poster Collection, Centre for the Study of Democracy, University of Westminster.

head, standing on a bridge. Two menacing figures approach along the bridge. The painting offers a pessimistic view of human existence; a mix of anxiety, dread, and alienation—not a "pretty" picture, to be sure. But the painting does reflect the artist's and other existentialists' points of view at the time. These are but a few of the numerous examples of socially and politically inspired art.

Activist Art: I Must Protest

As we noted in Chapter 1, not all art is created for art's sake. Art isn't created merely to serve an aesthetic or decorative function. Contemporary artists have strong opinions on political and social issues, and they express them in and through their work. Berthold Brecht's oft-cited quip that "art is not a mirror to reflect reality, but a hammer with which to shape it" sums up this view. One contemporary manifestation of this perspective can be found in protest art or the art of social activism. These artists use art to critique society and promote social change (Felshin, 1995; Hobbs & Woodard, 1986; Lippard, 1984). Activist artists seek to engage the public in their art to increase the public's social consciousness. As Felshin (1995) notes, such artists are "attempting at the very least to 'change the conversation' to empower individuals and communities, and ultimately to stimulate social change" (p. 26). For example, an anonymous, yet popular graffiti artist, known as Banksy, stencils images onto walls and buildings in public places at night (Pryor, 2007). One of his works depicts Dorothy and Toto, from the *Wizard of Oz*. Her basket is being searched by an officer in riot gear wearing latex gloves. The image suggests that society's paranoia over security has gone too far.

How do activist artists go about persuading? In a variety of ways. One is by increasing *awareness through interpretation*. Activist art might consist of an exhibit that is odd, disturbing, or peculiar. The artist seeks to pique the viewer's curiosity and pull him or her in. The viewer becomes engaged in trying to understand the work. In the process, the viewer's awareness is increased. In their effort to interpret an exhibit the viewers engage in active thinking or central processing, which, as we learned earlier, is more likely to trigger lasting attitude change.

As an illustration, Suzanne Lacy created a public work titled *Three Weeks in May* (1977) to increase awareness of the crime of rape. She began with two large maps of Los Angeles that were placed on display at a local mall. Each day, she stamped the word "RAPE" on the map in large, red block letters at locations where rapes had taken place the previous day. Before long, the map was covered with stamps, many of them overlapping. The exhibit provided a graphic revelation to shoppers of the scope and severity of the problem. Her aim was to provoke a public discussion about the silent, often unreported crime of rape. Next to the map was a list of names, addresses, and phone numbers for rape counseling centers.

Yet another approach is to increase *awareness through participation*. Such art is collaborative or interactive. As Felshin (1995) comments, "participation is a catalyst for social change" (p. 12). By way of example, Wafaa Bilal created an unusual interactive installation, called "Domestic Tension," in a Chicago art gallery (Bilal & Lydersen, 2008). Bilal, an Iraqi artist living in political asylum in the United States, occupied a Plexiglas room for 1 month. During this time, people could go online and shoot him, via streaming video, using a robotically controlled paintball gun. This went on 24 hours a day. They shot him in the head when he fell asleep and in the groin when he stood up. All told, more than 60,000 shots were fired at him by people from more than 120 countries. Over time, some sympathetic viewers formed a "human shield" by trying to aim the paintball gun away from Bilal. Others hacked in to the system to make the gun fire more rapidly. By the project's end, the room was drenched in inches of paint, and Bilal was suffering from posttraumatic stress disorder (Bilal & Lydersen, 2008).

So what did viewers' participation mean? Clearly, many people had no hesitation about shooting a person online. Others were confronted with their own morality in choosing to shoot, or not shoot, another human being. The project laid bare cultural, ethnic, and religious tensions between Westerners and Middle Easterners. By allowing virtual strangers to shoot him, Bilal focused attention on how desensitized modern societies are to violence. Killing has become robotic, clinical, and—like his project—carried out from afar. In Iraq, innocent civilians are routinely killed by remotely-controlled drones. Members of Bilal's own family were killed in this way. Bilal sought to reveal that people living in comfort zones have no sense of what life is like in a conflict zone. People go about their lives blithely unaware of the suffering of people in far-away lands.

Another example of collaborative art is the AIDS Memorial Quilt, founded by Cleve Jones and others more than a decade ago (Jones & Dawson, 2000). The quilt, also known as the NAMES Project, is a folk art project commemorating those who have died of AIDS.

It is comprised of thousands of 3' × 6' panels, each dedicated to the memory of a specific person. The AIDS Memorial Quilt was first displayed on the Washington Mall in 1987, and again in 1992 and 1996. There are now so many panels that it would be difficult, if not impossible, to assemble them all in a single location. Indeed, the AIDS Memorial Quilt has become the largest community art project in the world. Portions of the quilt are now part of traveling displays that are shown throughout the world.

As a work of folk art, the AIDS Memorial Quilt serves a number of persuasive functions. We often hear statistics about AIDS, but the quilt puts a human face on these numbers. Every panel is a handmade testimonial to a specific individual's life. When people see the quilt they understand, in concrete rather than abstract terms, the toll taken by the disease. The very choice of making a quilt was a persuasive one. Cleve Jones was attracted to the idea of quilting because it is a traditional American folk art. Quilts conjure up images of home and family. AIDS, however, was thought of as a promiscuous gay male disease. The quilt served as a means of countering that image. As Jones and Dawson (2000) note, "There was hope we could beat the disease by using the quilt as a symbol of solidarity, of family and community; there was hope that we could make a movement that would welcome people—men and women, gay and straight, of every age, race, faith, and background" (p. 108).

The AIDS Memorial Quilt has increased the public's awareness of the disease. It has also brought people together. Loved ones who didn't know how to grieve found an outlet in creating a panel. This was truly participatory art. Students who have seen the quilt have reported that the experience reduced their homophobia and increased their desire to practice safe sex. This fact alone demonstrates the quilt's persuasiveness as a work of art.

The AIDS Memorial Quilt, also known as the Names Project, is an example of folk art, activist art, and a social movement all in one.

Alamy Images. Reprinted by permission.

Activist art is often controversial. Indeed, that is its purpose. It is precisely because art has the capacity to arouse people's interest, attention, and ire that it is influential. A primary goal of activist artists is to raise the public's consciousness on a variety of social and political issues (Felshin, 1995; Hobbs & Woodard, 1986; Lippard, 1984; Von Blum, 1976, 1994). Art can challenge the existing social order. It can make people angry. It can offend. At the same time it can heighten people's awareness. It can make people question their assumptions. It can change the way they see things. It can make them reconsider long-held beliefs. In so doing, art persuades.

CINEMATIC PERSUASION: SEX, DRUGS, AND OTHER VICES

On the occasion of receiving an award from the American Museum of the Moving Image, Steven Spielberg remarked that cinema "is the most powerful weapon in the world" (cited in Fuller, 1995, p. 190). There are several factors at work that lend films their power to persuade.[1] First, there is the potential for mass suggestion. Millions of people are exposed to movies, both in the United States and abroad. In fact, movies are one of America's leading exports. Thus, movies reach vast audiences. Second, movies are told in a *narrative* form, that is, as stories. Stories possess an aura of believability not found in other mediums for communication. When we watch a movie we engage in a "willing suspension of disbelief." In order to follow the story, we have to lose ourselves in the imaginary world of the film. In so doing, we give up some of our ability to think and reason. Third, the power of films to persuade is aided by the fact that when people sit down in a theater they don't expect to be persuaded, they expect to be entertained. They may, therefore, let down their guards and become more open to suggestion. We believe this is one of the reasons that *product placement*—the practice of inserting brand name items into movie scenes—is so prevalent. Lastly, films are carefully crafted works. Considerable planning and attention to detail go into the making of a film. Something as simple as a close-up or a swell in the music can enhance the intensity of emotion on the big screen. Thus motion pictures represent highly refined, highly polished messages. Few real-world persuaders, such as salespeople, attorneys, or politicians, have the luxury of lavishing so much time and attention on their persuasive messages.[2]

Movies can persuade intentionally or unintentionally. Al Gore's documentary *An Inconvenient Truth* was clearly designed to increase awareness of global warming. *Brokeback Mountain* and *Milk* broached the subject of society's tolerance and intolerance of homosexuality. *Crash* grappled with the issue of subtle and not-so-subtle racism in society. Michael Moore's documentaries, or "mockumentaries" as some call them, espouse particular points of view. Other films persuade unintentionally, or accidentally. Three different movies, *Juno*, *Waitress*, and *Knocked Up*, tacitly endorsed a pro-life point of view, when the female characters, all of whom experienced unplanned pregnancies, opted to give birth rather than seek abortions. In *Juno*, for example, Ellen Page's feisty character visits an abortion clinic, where the grim receptionist hands her a clip board and announces "we have to know every score and every sore." As Juno flees the clinic, a protester she knows from high school shouts after her "your baby has fingernails."

Acting Out: How Movies Persuade

Movies persuade in multiple ways and on multiple levels. Some of the influential features are unique to particular genres of film. Docudramas, such as *JFK* or *Titanic,* for instance, may convince viewers that a subjective interpretation of events is an objective recounting of the facts (Cusella, 1982; Real, 1996; Simpson, 2008). Violent movies, such as *Pulp Fiction, Kill Bill,* and *Natural Born Killers,* may desensitize people to violent or aggressive behavior. We examine some of the most important ways that films persuade here.

The first of these is that movies, American movies in particular, export Western values around the globe. As one commentator noted, "Hollywood films are America's biggest cultural export, consumed by billions around the globe" (Hey, 2001, p. 4). People in remote areas of the world know who Sylvester Stallone is, based on the character from *Rocky.* They know who Julia Roberts is, from her role in *Pretty Woman.* American films embody Western values. Rocky was the blue-collar guy who made his dream come true. Julia Roberts was the prostitute with a heart of gold.

Not everyone is happy about the values that are tacitly condoned by American movies, however. Foreign audiences often resent the infusion of Western values such as promiscuity, violence, and drug use into their own culture (many in the United States aren't too thrilled with these values either). Others resent the emphasis on materialism and conspicuous consumption. On the positive side, movies can advance positive values such as freedom, human rights, and equality. The point is that movies tacitly endorse Western values that may or may not be shared by people in other cultures or regions.

On the positive side, movies can promote prosocial values. The movie *Finding Nemo,* for example, featured those with disabilities in a favorable light. Nemo, who had an underdeveloped fin, referred to as his "lucky fin," was accepted by others and given equal status. Other characters in the movie had disabilities or illnesses, too; Nemo's father suffered from posttraumatic stress syndrome, Dory had short-term memory loss, Bruce the shark was in a 12 Step program, and a squid suffered from incontinence (inability to retain its ink). In this way, the movie normalized disabilities. As another positive example, Pixar's movie *Up* features an elderly fellow as its hero.

A second way in which movies persuade is by promoting popular culture both within and outside of the United States. Fashions, hairstyles, habits, lifestyles, and slang terminology are often emulated by moviegoers (Chansanchai, 2001; Unterberger, 2001). If you are old enough, or into retro fashion, you may recall the popularity of white, three-piece suits following the release of the disco film *Saturday Night Fever,* starring John Travolta. *Donnie Darko* and *The Crow* inspired "Goth" culture. After seeing the movie *300,* many guys hit the gym to work on their abs. As a function of their iconicity, movies have a way of idealizing and romanticizing trends and lifestyles. Cinema, then, is a major vehicle for the dissemination of fads, fashions, and trends.

A third way movies persuade is by modeling behaviors. People may gauge what constitutes appropriate behavior in social situations by taking a movie character's lead. Albert Bandura's *social cognitive theory* maintains that adolescents observe behaviors that are modeled in the media and then imitate those behaviors in real life (Bandura, 1986, 1989). For example, young teens who watch movies about dating and relationships, such as *Mean Girls, What a Girl Wants,* and *10 Things I Hate About You,* may take their cue about how to deal with love and relationships based on behaviors they see in movies (Behm-Morawitz & Mastro, 2008). At a subconscious level, people may enact scripts they've learned from movies as well.

Characters in movies also model risky, unsafe, or violent behaviors. This can have the effect of legitimizing such behaviors. Movie characters rarely wear seatbelts. They often engage in unprotected sex. They frequently smoke, use drugs, get drunk, and drive recklessly. Oh, and they kill people. Regardless of whether these activities are intentional, their prevalence in movies tends to glamorize them. The actions of the characters in movies may be seen as placing a stamp of approval on those behaviors.

With respect to smoking in particular, there is some disagreement over whether smoking is featured more in movies compared to real-life (Charlesworth & Glantz, 2005; Omidvari et al., 2005). What is not in dispute is that adolescents who see a lot of smoking on the big screen are more likely to light up. A study by Heatherton and Sargent (2009) reported that teens with high exposure to smoking in movies were three times more likely to smoke than those with low exposure.

Other studies have examined the effects of a steady diet of violence on TV. *cultivation theory* maintains that the more violence people watch on TV, the more likely they are to develop an exaggerated belief in a *mean, scary world* (Gerbner, Gross, Morgan, & Signorielli, 2002). In addition to developing a jaded view of the world, viewing violence tends to increase aggression and antisocial behavior in people. "Fifty years of research on the effects of TV violence," notes John Murray, "leads to the inescapable conclusion that viewing media violence is related to increases in aggressive attitudes, values, and behaviors (2008, p. 1212). Evidence also suggests a link between playing violent videogames and aggressive behavior (Anderson, 2004). With respect to cinema's influence on behavior, Oliver Stone, who directed *Natural Born Killers*, commented, "Film is a powerful medium. Film is a drug. It goes into your eye. It goes into your brain. It stimulates, and that's a dangerous thing" (cited in Leiby, 1995, p. G1).

A fourth way in which movies persuade is by promoting viewer identification. Moviegoers may idolize a particular actor or actress or a specific character played by that actor or actress. Perhaps you know a few Angelina Jolie or Johnny Depp "wannabes." Sometimes the story of the character overlaps with the viewer's own experience, causing the viewer to identify with the character in the film. If you've ever felt like an outcast, a nerd, the underdog, or misunderstood, you might identify with movies such as *Napoleon Dynamite*, *Ghost World*, *My Big Fat Greek Wedding*, *Happy Times*, or *Pretty in Pink*. In this way, movies establish a common bond with viewers.

Viewer identification can take place even if a viewer's experience doesn't directly overlap with that of a character in a movie. None of us have met an extraterrestrial (okay, *most* of us haven't), but we can still identify with a movie such as *E.T.*, because all of us have had to say good-bye to someone we love. None of us are green ogres, but we can identify with Shrek because we've all felt like outsiders from time to time. We may not be mentally challenged, but we can all identify with the teasing and ridicule Forrest Gump endured. There is a little Forrest Gump in all of us.

A final way in which cinema shapes public perceptions is by fostering or perpetuating stereotypes. Hollywood frequently typecasts minorities, cultural groups, women, overweight people, the elderly, and other groups into limited roles. This may create the impression that these are the actual, or only, roles these groups are capable of performing. Although the number of parts for minorities has increased of late, the parts often involve the same predictable stereotypes (Waxman, 2000). Middle Easterners, for example, are frequently cast as terrorists (Fuller, 1995; Tilove, 2001). When they aren't terrorists, they are often cab drivers.

Hispanics are often depicted as drug dealers or gang-bangers. "If someone has an accent or is different or is brown," Beale (2001) notes, "Hollywood doesn't know what to do with them, and tends to relegate them to stereotypical roles" (p. 8B). While the situation has improved, roles for Hispanics remain tied to cultural stereotypes (Reyes & Rubie, 2000).

In a similar vein, African Americans have been historically typecast (Entman & Rojecki, 2001). African American males fit the mold of athlete, drug dealer, or musician (Waxman, 2000). Their characters are often oversexed. African American women tend to be relegated to stereotypic roles such as beautiful wife, beautiful girlfriend, or beautiful prostitute. Such roles imply that African Americans can't be trusted or taken seriously. African Americans are also typecast as the funny sidekick in "buddy" movies. Eddie Murphy, Martin Lawrence, Chris Rock, and Chris Tucker have all played such parts. These, too, are narrowly defined roles.

As with Hispanic actors and actresses, the situation has improved. There are many more Black stars now playing leading roles. Halle Berry, Jamie Foxx, Denzel Washington, and Forest Whitaker have all recently won Oscars for best actress or actor. Their success may convince filmmakers and the movie-going public that other African Americans can be taken seriously on screen. Some have even suggested that Black actors, such as Morgan Freeman and Dennis Haysbert, who played the role of the president onscreen, made an African-American presidency "thinkable" to the public, thereby paving the way for Barack Obama's presidency (Dargis & Scott, 2009).

Asians also tend to occupy stereotypic roles in films. If Hollywood is to be believed, every Asian is skilled in martial arts. They are often undersexed and romantically awkward (Whitty, 2001). Asian actors, such as Jackie Chan, Jet Li, and Chow Yun-Fat do land major roles, but they tend to involve the same stereotypic part: action hero. At least Asians are playing themselves now. In the early days of cinema, Asian characters such as Charlie Chan, Ming the Merciless, and Dr. Fu Manchu were played by white actors. As with other minorities, things are changing, but slowly.

When it comes to stereotypic roles, women fare no better. For years critics have decried the limited roles for women on the big screen. With few exceptions women have to be thin and beautiful to land a starring role. "In movie houses," Bernard observes, "any actress who ate an extra Oreo last week is relegated to the supporting position of 'funny best friend' " (2001, p. 16). We can think of a number of heavy actors (Jack Black, James Gandolfini, John Goodman, Jonah Hill, Philip Seymour Hoffman, Kevin James, Seth Rogen). Can you name a half dozen heavy actresses?

Women also tend to be confined to traditional roles: mother, wife, mistress, girlfriend. This isn't particularly surprising, given that fewer than 10 percent of screenplays are written by women, and fewer than 6 percent of movies are directed by women (Maher, 2009). Admittedly, there are some women in nontraditional roles. Nevertheless, roles for women, especially older women, remain limited.

If there is a silver lining, it is that younger moviegoers tend to be more tolerant, if not completely color-blind (Welkos, 2001). This is evidenced by the box-office success of recent multiethnic movies, such as *Gran Torino, Hitch, Guess Who, Save the Last Dance,* and *Varsity Blues.* Because youth culture includes more African Americans, Asian Americans, and Hispanic Americans, filmmakers are producing more multiethnic movies to meet the demands of a new generation of viewers.

IMAGES IN ADVERTISING: AND NOW A WORD FROM OUR SPONSORS

"Advertising," write Woodward and Denton (1999), "is undoubtedly the most pervasive form of persuasion in our society" (p. 286). When we think of pure cases of persuasion, advertising immediately comes to mind. More than $200 billion per year is spent on advertising in the United States, whereas all other countries together spend about $218 billion (Berger, 2004). Various estimates suggest that the average person is exposed to more than 3,000 advertising messages per day (Dupont, 1999; Simons, 2001; Woodward & Denton, 1999). Some estimates are even higher. If all the money spent on advertising were divvied up, it would work out to about $800 per person in the United States and $40 per person in all other countries combined (Berger, 2004). Who pays for all that advertising? We do, of course. According to Woodward and Denton (1999), roughly 20 to 40 percent of the prices paid for goods and services goes to advertising. Most of us are "armchair" experts in advertising, because we've watched so many commercials during our lives. You, undoubtedly, have a few favorites that you love, and some that you absolutely loathe. Indeed, the average American spends about one year of his or her life watching television commercials alone (Berger, 2004).

Advertisements, whether on television, in a magazine, on the Web, or in some other medium, include words and images. The visual components of such ads are often key to their effectiveness. A controversial example was Carl's Jr.'s commercial featuring Paris Hilton. The racy commercial showed Paris clad in high heels and a bathing suit as she soaped down herself and her Bentley while munching on a spicy Carl's Jr. burger. The ad created a visual analogy between two "hot" items; its burger and the Hilton heiress. Carl's Jr.'s name and logo didn't appear until the last few seconds of the commercial. The commercial was all imagery. The Parents Television Council and other groups denounced the commercial, likening it to soft-core porn.

Visually oriented ads work their magic in a variety of ways. Unfortunately, we don't have enough space to examine all the ways here. There are, after all, entire courses devoted to the subject. In this section we focus on four of the most important ways visually oriented ads persuade: through the use of vivid images and special effects, through what is termed "anti-advertising" or "subvertising," by establishing associations between products and idealized images or lifestyles, and through the use of so-called "shock" advertising.

Visual Extravaganzas: Now You've Got My Attention!

One challenge that advertisers face in trying to convince consumers to buy their products is *media clutter.* There are so many ads competing for consumers' attention that it is difficult for a message to stand out in the crowd. In order to cut through media clutter, many advertisers use vivid, intense images to capture the audience's attention. Thanks to digital editing, it is now possible for advertisers to create and manipulate images in ways previously not possible.

A commercial for the 2010 Toyota Prius, titled "Harmony," embraced a highly visual "green" theme. The commercial serves up a visual feast thanks to the magic of computer-generated imagery (CGI). A Prius drives through a flowing landscape formed by thousands of people costumed to look like fields of waving flowers, cascading water, and billowy clouds. It's as if Spencer Tunick (known for photographing mass nudes) joined forces with Anne Geddes (known for photographing infants in fairytale costumes). The commercial required only 200 actors in costumes, but through CGI they were made to look like thousands.

Other commercials rely on different visual effects, but the point remains the same: Commercials have to grab and hold viewers' attention. A plain-vanilla commercial simply won't hold up to an eye-popping extravaganza, especially when viewers have low involvement with the topic or issue.

Anti-Ads: You Can't Fool Me

Another challenge facing advertisers is that consumers are increasingly cynical about advertising. They don't trust Madison Avenue. They think all advertisements lie. But that skepticism is the very premise on which *anti-ads* are based. Anti-advertising, or "subvertising" as it is sometimes called, caters to consumers who distrust the media. Anti-ads mock advertising itself (Axelton, 1998; Beato, 1999). They denounce traditional advertising in order to gain acceptance by consumers.

Many anti-ads are spoofs on commercial advertising (see www.adbusters.org). Others are designed to sell actual products and services. Apple's series of Mac versus PC commercials employ this strategy. The ads skewer Microsoft for its marketing practices, glitchy operating system, lack of built-in features, and susceptibility to viruses. The Mac character, personified by Justin Long, is casual and relaxed. The PC character, played by John Hodgeman, is square and uptight. In one spot, called "Bean Counter," Hodgeman acknowledges that there are lots of bugs in Vista. Rather than spend money to fix the problems, however, he decides to devote the entire budget to advertising.

The irony of the commercial is that Apple is poking fun at Microsoft's advertising budget, yet Apple is the company spending all the money on this campaign. In 2008, Apple spent $486 million on advertising compared to $300 million by Microsoft on Vista (Schonfeld, 2008). Incidentally, we think John Hodgeman is the funnier of the two.

An anti-smoking commercial also offers an example of an anti-ad. The spot shows two cowboys in a downtown setting, one playing guitar and the other singing. The singing cowboy, however, is singing through a hand-held device pressed against his neck (an electro larynx). He's had a laryngectomy. The lyrics are "You don't always die from tobacco, sometimes you just lose a lung. Oh, you don't always die from tobacco, sometimes they just snip out your tongue." This ad lampoons the rugged cowboy mystique associated with Marlboro cigarettes.

In essence anti-ads are telling viewers, "Hey, you're on to us. You're too smart to be fooled." But of course, that strategy is itself a ploy designed to appeal to jaded consumers.

Such an approach creates the perception that the advertiser respects the viewer's intelligence. As Jenkins (cited in Wright, 2001) observes, "The new advertising is anti-advertising—too hip to stoop to marketing products—and it appeals to a generation which has been described as too cynical to take traditional messages seriously" (para. 3). Advertisers are constantly finding ways to reinvent themselves. As consumers have become more skeptical of advertising techniques, advertisers have found ways to adapt to, and capitalize on, their skepticism. Anti-ads or subvertising thus mark another evolutionary phase in advertising.

Image-Oriented Advertising: Materialism as Happiness

In addition to using vivid imagery combined with special effects and anti-advertising, advertisers also seek to create positive associations between their products and idealized images or lifestyles. This approach is known as *image-oriented* or *image-based advertising* and it is the bread and butter of modern advertising campaigns. Image-oriented ads rely on the syntactic indeterminacy of images. Remember, images don't contain logical operators, so they can't make clear-cut claims. That turns out to be a plus, however, because by pairing a product with a favorable image, an advertiser can equate the two without actually saying so in words. Messaris (1997) underscores this feature of images when he writes, "this ability to imply something in pictures while avoiding the consequences of saying it in words has been considered an advantage of visual advertising since the first days of its development as a mass medium" (p. xix).

Let's consider some examples of this in action. Oil companies don't want you to think about tar-covered birds on an oil-stained beach when you envision petroleum products. They want you to associate oil companies with pro-environmental attitudes. Hence, Chevron's "People do" advertising campaign, which portrays Chevron as a guardian of endangered species.

Image-oriented ads hold up a brand of clothes, or beer, or automobile as the embodiment of an idealized lifestyle. Equating the brand with an idealized lifestyle creates social identification with that brand. When we buy that brand we are buying into that lifestyle. Some brands are *luxury brands*, prestigious, yet within reach of many consumers (Ralph Lauren, Mercedes). Some are *aspirational brands*; few people can afford them, but they hope to be able to one day (Armani, Rolls Royce). Still others are *authentic or genuine brands* (Adkins, 1999; Pringle & Thompson, 1999; Rosica, 2007). These brands are unpretentious but have a cause to promote or a story to tell (fair trade coffee, pink products, and breast cancer). With a little practice, you should be able to watch a TV commercial or view a magazine ad and decipher the favorable image or association the advertiser is trying to manufacture. What are some of the common associations? A handful of them are as follows:

- **Social status and elitism:** Ads for luxury cars and expensive watches often associate owning these products with class and success. Ads for expensive wines, luggage, jewelry, and other upscale goods often imply that the products are symbols of taste and refinement.
- **Sex or romance:** Ads for perfume, lingerie, and hair care products often equate the products with sexiness, allure, and romance. The association established by many

perfume ads is that if you wear that fragrance you'll be more sexy, too, or other sexy people will be attracted to you.

- **Power, speed, and strength:** Ads for tools, trucks, SUVs, computers, and nutritional supplements often equate buying a product with conferring power on the user. Dodge trucks are "Ram tough." Chevy trucks are built "Like a rock." You, too, can have rock-hard abs or buns of steel. If you've got the newest, fastest computer, you are a "power user."
- **Youth culture:** A number of products are marketed by associating products with youth culture, rebelliousness, and an alternative lifestyle. Soft drinks, clothing, fast food, skateboards, small electronics, makeup, and many other goods and services appeal to what is hip, trendy, or cool. These commercials are often shot with handheld cameras and employ rapid editing techniques to simulate the look of "reality TV."
- **Safety, security:** Ads for banking, insurance, and retirement accounts try to foster images of being safe and secure. Consumers want peace of mind and a sense of stability when it comes to their finances and retirement.
- **Sense of place, belonging:** Ads for foods, restaurants, furniture, linens, and so on often strive to create a sense of hominess. The advertisers want you to get a warm, comfortable, familiar feeling when you think of their products.

These are only some of the important values and lifestyles to which advertisers attempt to link their brands. The point is that when you watch a commercial, or read a print ad, you should examine the associations the advertiser is trying to establish. For decades cigarette ads fostered the association that smoking was cool. More recently, anti-smoking ads have associated smoking with being un-cool. Both approaches rely on the underlying assumption that "being cool" is what really counts in life. Is it? When evaluating a commercial or print ad, ask yourself three important questions:

1. What image or lifestyle is being associated with the product?
2. Is that image or lifestyle actually desirable? Is that the image I'm really seeking or the lifestyle to which I truly aspire?
3. Would buying the product actually grant me the image or lifestyle equated with the product? If so, how?

Shock Ads: Edgy Images as Persuasion

Images also figure heavily into the form of advertising known as *shock ads.* Shock ads, or "shockvertising" as it has also been called, push the boundaries of taste and propriety (Lazar, 2003; McCarthy, 2000). The goal is to sell products by being edgy. Some shock ads are vulgar, some erotic, some humorous, and others nauseating. Some adopt an "in your face" style of advertising.

A commercial for the Volkswagen Jetta shows two guys driving down the road, having a casual conversation. Out of nowhere, a pickup truck smashes into their car. The scene is truly jolting. The shock value is heightened by the fact that most car crashes in commercials feature crash test dummies, not real people. The slogan that appears at the end of the ad is "Safe Happens." Some viewers responded favorably to the ad, others negatively. Most agreed, however, that the ad got their attention (Farhi, 2006).

Ads by PETA often rely on shock to garner attention. In one commercial, "Sex Talk," parents urge their daughter to have sex. "Get out there and nail everything you can" the father advises. "My little girl's gonna get some," the mother proudly states. At the end a caption reads "Parents shouldn't act this way. Neither should people with dogs and cats." The analogy between irresponsible parents and irresponsible pet owners was offensive to many viewers. But that was the purpose of the spot. Shock ads seek to cut through media clutter by provoking controversy and garnering attention.

A public service announcement created by Saatchi and Saatchi for the BBC also illustrates this approach. In the commercial a cartoon boy is beaten by his father. His father throws him against a wall, puts a cigarette out on his head, and kicks him down a stairwell. During the abuse, cartoon music is playing and sound effects highlight each blow. At the end of the beating, the cartoon boy is transformed into a real boy, lying face-down on the floor. The message "Real kids don't bounce back" appears onscreen. Although many viewers called to complain about the ad, child abuse reporting doubled during the period in which the ad was run.

Even shock ads can go too far. One such controversial TV commercial was Reebok's "I am what I am" spot, starring 50 Cent. In the ad, the gangsta rapper counts to nine, which is the number of times he's been shot. The ad which was heavily criticized for glamorizing violence, was subsequently pulled by Reebok. In the U.K., hundreds of readers complained when they found a full-page ad showing a newborn infant with a cockroach in its mouth. The ad was sponsored by Bernardo's, a children's charity group, and was designed to draw attention to the plight of children living in poverty. The ad was soon banned by Britain's Advertising Standards Authority.

Given that they are in vogue, do shock ads really work? A study by Dahl, Frankenberger, and Manchanda (2003) suggests they do. These researchers concluded that "shocking content in an advertisement significantly increases attention, benefits memory, and positively influences behavior" among college students (Dahl et al., 2003, p. 1). Others studies also support the effectiveness of shock ads (Scudder & Mill, 2009). But shock ads must walk a fine line. If they aren't shocking enough, they won't provoke the public dialogue and publicity they seek. If they are overly shocking, they may prompt a consumer rebellion. Furthermore, as consumers become more accustomed to shock ads it will be increasingly difficult to shock them.

PHOTOJOURNALISM AS PERSUASION: THE CAMERA DOES LIE

Even without any accompanying text, photographs tell their own persuasive stories. Because there are entire courses offered in photojournalism, we won't attempt to explore the whole field here. What we wish to emphasize is that still photographs can make powerful statements. They can affect people's perceptions of events. They can also reach people on an emotional level in ways that words alone cannot. As Zumwalt (2001) noted, "There is tremendous potential in a photograph to inflame emotions" (p. B12). Because photographs don't require literacy or familiarity with a particular language, they are also more universally understood than messages that rely on words. Photographic images can also distort reality, as we shall see.

Many well-known photos serve as iconic representations of events or eras in history. In all likelihood, if you haven't been sitting on your keister watching TV your whole life, you've seen Joe Rosenthal's famous 1945 photo of U.S. Marines raising the Stars and Stripes at Iwo Jima. The picture symbolizes the determination of the United States to win the war in the Pacific. You may have seen John Filo's photo of a female student at Kent State University in 1970, kneeling over the body of a fellow student who was slain by the National Guard. That picture symbolized the schism between the protest movement and the government, as well as the generation gap of the late 1960s. You may have seen the photograph taken by Eddie Adams in 1968, in which a South Vietnamese officer shoots a North Vietnamese sympathizer in the head at point-blank range. Photojournalist Nick Ute snapped an equally compelling picture in 1972 of a naked, 9-year-old Vietnamese girl, running down the road, screaming in pain from the napalm that had just been dropped on her village. Those two photos epitomized the feelings of many Americans that the United States was involved in an unjust war in Vietnam.

Photos can sum up social problems or controversies. They can document events in ways that words cannot. This is where the old saying, "a picture is worth a thousand words" applies. Owing to their iconicity, photographs such as these can cement themselves in the public's mind. They function as touchstones that capture entire events in our collective conscience. Following the terrorist attack on New York City, there was a photo, taken by Stan Honda, of a well-dressed African American woman covered in dust and ash. A similar photo of a businessman wearing a suit and carrying a briefcase, also covered in dust, appeared in magazines and newspapers across the country. Both photos have an eerie, unearthly quality about them. Both are icons of the shock, disbelief, and horror that all Americans felt on September 11, 2001. The photo of George W. Bush standing on the deck of the *U.S.S. Abraham Lincoln* beneath a banner proclaiming "Mission Accomplished" summed up his naiveté about the situation in Iraq. That photo, taken in 2001, haunted him during his second term in office.

On Your Guard: Remaining Vigilant against Visual Deception | BOX 14.1

Images, whether in the form of television commercials, cinema, magazine ads, photojournalism, Web pages, or other media, function as powerful tools for influence. They give us a vicarious sense of "being there." For this reason, we must remain wary of visual communication designed to persuade us. We've all seen supermarket tabloids with doctored photos claiming "Martian now on Supreme Court" or some other such nonsense. We know these images can't be trusted. But images may be manipulated by others as well. Politicians may manipulate images for propaganda purposes. Images may be manipulated by lawyers to make a defendant seem innocent or guilty ("If it doesn't fit, you must acquit."). Images may be used by the media to increase ratings ("Stay tuned, film at 11!") and by advertisers to sell goods ("Get the body you want now!"). With this in mind, we offer the following tips and advice when evaluating persuasive images.

1. Try to improve your *visual literacy*, that is, the ability to critically analyze and evaluate

visual communication (Felton, 2008). As Messaris and Moriarty (2005) note, "visual literacy can . . . be seen as a potential antidote to attempted manipulation of the viewer in TV, print, and Web-based advertising; visual journalism; and other forms of pictorial entertainment, information, or persuasion" (p. 482).

2. Don't succumb to the old adage "Seeing is believing." The camera does lie. What you are seeing may well be a manipulated image. When you see a fashion model on a magazine cover, for example, don't assume she or he looks that good in real life. The cover photo has probably been digitally altered to remove blemishes, whiten teeth, highlight hair color, etc.

3. Be especially wary of images on the Internet. Anyone can digitally alter an image on a home computer nowadays using Photoshop. If you are unsure whether to trust an image or not, try checking out some useful Web-based resources that identify hoaxes. We like the Urban Legends Website, at www.snopes.com (check out their photo gallery link); Skeptical Enquirer, at www.csicop.org; and Hoaxbusters, at http://www.hoaxbusters.org.

4. When watching so-called reality shows on TV, remember they may bear little resemblance to reality. Reality shows are carefully engineered productions. Guests or contestants typically try out for the show and are carefully vetted. This selection process allows producers to cast contestants for maximum dramatic effect. Footage can be edited so a contestant seems braver, cleverer, more devious, more hostile, or more psycho than she/he really is. Hosts may encourage or reward certain types of behavior while discouraging others. You don't really think that every guest on the Jerry Springer show threw a chair on his or her own initiative, do you?

5. When viewing documentaries, keep in mind that they do not objectively recount events. They advocate a point of view. Documentaries often use techniques such as re-enactment (recreating scenes for which no original footage is available), substituted or modified footage (film of something similar or related,

but not the same thing), time compression (cramming years or even centuries into a one-and-a-half-hour-long movie), and composite characters (combining several different people into one). While all these techniques may make the story easier to follow and the narrative more compelling, they come at the expense of impartiality. Some exemplars of this genre, such as Michael Moore's *Fahrenheit 9/11* and Morgan Spurlock's *Supersize Me,* have been dubbed "mockumentaries" or "shockumentaries" because the director's bias is so intense.

6. Beware of images in diet ads, cosmetic surgery ads, supplement ads, and infomercials. Take a typical ad for a weight loss product: Notice that the person in the "Before" photo usually has a bland expression, poor posture, pasty skin, unkempt hair, unflattering clothes, and unflattering lighting. In comparison, the person shown in the "After" picture is usually smiling, has an upright posture, stylish hair, a tan and/or makeup, and flattering lighting. Does the ad say both photos are unretouched? Does the fine print acknowledge "Results may vary" or "Results not typical?" If a diet ad claims a user lost 30 pounds in 2 weeks, but you can see the person's hair is much longer in the "After" photo, then you would know that more than 2 weeks passed between photos. Testimonials and the photos that accompany them are always subject to the "hasty generalization" fallacy.

7. The context and captioning of images can have an important impact as well. Following the aftermath of Hurricane Katrina, newspapers printed two photos of survivors wading in the flood water. One Associated Press photo showed an African American male clutching a six-pack of Pepsi with the caption "A young man walks through chest deep flood water after looting a grocery store . . ." (Ralli, 2005). Another AFP/Getty photo, showed a white couple and carried the caption, "two residents wade through chest deep water after finding bread and soda from a local grocery store. . . ." The captioning implied a clear double-standard: Blacks were looting, but white folks were acting out of necessity.

Playing Tricks with the Camera: Photographic Deception

An important point to keep in mind about photographic images is that they aren't neutral, objective, impartial representations of things. As iconic representations, their documentary qualities can be deceiving. Photographs give us the journalist's point of view, which is simply that—one point of view. The photojournalist decides which events to capture on film, and which events aren't worth capturing. The photojournalist decides on the distance, camera angle, lighting, shutter speed, and so on. The photojournalist decides which pictures to develop, how to edit or crop them, and which prints to offer for public consumption.

Some well-known historical and recent examples of photographic deception serve to illustrate how easily this medium can be manipulated. In 1917, three young girls in Cottingly, England, claimed to have captured fairies on film. Sir Arthur Conan Doyle, the creator of Sherlock Holmes, pronounced the photos to be genuine, and a whole cult of believers was born. Later it was demonstrated that the photos were a hoax. The girls had cut pictures of fairies out of magazines and propped them up on hat pins. In February 1982, *National Geographic* altered a cover photo of Egypt's pyramids by moving them closer together so they would fit in the frame. The doctored photo evoked protests by Egyptian curators (Brugioni, 1999). On August 26, 1989, *TV Guide* cropped Oprah Winfrey's head onto Ann-Margaret's body to make Oprah look thinner for the magazine's cover. On June 27, 1994, *Time* magazine darkened O. J. Simpson's mug shot on one its cover, making him appear more sinister and menacing. In the year 2000, a brochure for the University of Wisconsin–Madison was doctored by adding an African American student into a photo of fans cheering at a football game. The manipulation was done to make the campus seem more ethnically diverse. *Newsweek* cropped Martha Stewart's head onto another model's body for one of its covers in 2005. The National Press Photographers Association labeled the act a "major ethical breach." Shortly after September 11, a fake snapshot was circulated on the Web, purportedly showing a tourist having his photo taken atop one of the twin towers seconds before an airliner smashed into it (see www.snopes.com/rumors/crash.htm). Among other things, the plane shown in the snapshot, a Boeing 757, was not the same type as the much larger 767 that crashed into the World Trade Center. On March 31, 2003, the *Los Angeles Times* ran a front-page photo of a British soldier who appeared to be aiming a rifle at Iraqi civilians and ordering them to sit down. The photographer, Brian Walski, acknowledged that the photo was a composite of two different photos that he had merged on his computer. Walski was fired by the *L.A. Times* for violating its policy forbidding alterations to news photographs: These examples underscore the point that seeing is not necessarily believing. Just because someone claims to have captured an image on film, doesn't necessarily mean the image is genuine and unaltered. Box 14.1 offers some useful suggestions on how to avoid being duped by photos and other visual media.

SUMMARY

In this chapter we've examined a variety of ways in which visual stimuli, including but not limited to images, facilitate persuasion. We have not touched on all the ways in which visual cues persuade. Yet the principles we've discussed about how images persuade through iconicity, indexicality, and syntactic indeterminacy apply to other forms of visual communication as well. Our society is becoming increasingly visually oriented. More people now get their news from television than from newspapers. More people now watch movies than read books. Persuaders are capitalizing on this trend by enlisting images in support of their persuasive endeavors. Based on what you've learned in this chapter, you should be able to watch a television commercial, see a movie, or read a print ad with a sharper eye toward the strategic choices made by the persuader. In short, we hope you will be a wiser consumer of visual persuasion.

ENDNOTES

1. Most of our comments about cinematic persuasion apply equally to television shows. Television shows, however, typically have smaller budgets and tighter production schedules. Hence, they are less polished works. Nevertheless, many TV series have altered attitudes and behavior in the same ways as films.

2. Although movies are extremely expensive, television commercials cost more on a per minute basis than most movies (Woodward & Denton, 1999, p. 287).

REFERENCES

Adkins, S. (1999). *Cause related marketing: Who cares wins.* Oxford, U.K.: Reed Educational.

Anderson, C. A. (2004). Effects of violent videogames on aggressive behavior, aggressive cognition, aggressive affect, physiological arousal, and prosocial behavior: A meta-analytic review of the literature. *Psychological Science, 12*, 353–359.

Axelton, K. (1998, March). Ads with attitude: Can you afford to use anti-advertising? *Entrepreneur Magazine.* Retrieved on September 5, 2005, from http://entrepreneur.com/magazine/entrepreneur/1998/march/15326.html.

Bandura, A. (1986). *Social foundations of thought and action: A social cognitive theory.* Englewood Cliffs, NJ: Prentice-Hall.

Bandura, A. (1989). Social cognitive theory. In R. Vasta (Ed.) *Annals of child development, 6. Six theories of child development* (pp. 1–60). Greenwich, CT: JAI Press.

Beale, L. (2001, January 28). "Latinos as villains still plays on screen: Despite visibility, stars' roles bother some Hispanics." *Milwaukee Sentinel Journal,* p. 8-B.

Beato, G. (1999, May/June). Does it pay to subvertise? The critics of corporate propaganda co-opt its best weapon. *Mother Jones.* Retrieved on September 5, 2005, from www.motherjones.com/commentary/columns/1999/05/beato.html.

Behm-Morawitz, E., & Mastro, D. E. (2008). Mean girls? The influence of gender portrayals in teen movies on emerging adults' gender-based attitudes and beliefs. *Journalism & Mass Communication Quarterly, 85*(1), 131–146.

Berger, A. A. (2004). *Ads, fads, and consumer culture.* Lanham, MD: Rowman and Littlefield.

Bernard, J. (2001, November 11). "Thin on respect: Let's not kid ourselves that 'Shallow Hal' is kind to overweight women." *(New York) Daily News,* p. 16.

Bilal, W., & Lydersen, K. (2008). *Shoot an Iraqi: Art, life, and resistance under the gun.* San Francisco: City Lights.

Blair, J. A. (1996). The possibility and actuality of visual arguments. *Argumentation and Advocacy, 33,* 23–39.

Branham, R. (1991). The role of the convert in *Eclipse of Reason* and *The Silent Scream. Quarterly Journal of Speech, 44,* 1–16.

Brugioni, D. A. (1999). *Photo fakery: The history and techniques of photographic deception and manipulation.* Dulles, VA: Brassey's Publishers.

Chansanchai, A. (2001, August 19). "Starring in school: Teens are taking back-to-school fashion cues from five stylish celebrities." *The Baltimore Sun,* p. 5N.

Charlesworth, A., & Glantz, S. A. (2005). Smoking in the movies increases adolescent smoking: A review. *Pediatrics, 116,* 1516–1528.

Christy, T. P., & Haley, E. (2008). The influence of advertising context on perceptions of offense. *Journal of Marketing Communications, 14*(4), 271–291.

Clark, T. (1977). *Art and propaganda in the twentieth century*. New York: Harry N. Abrams.

Cusella, L. P. (1982). Real-fiction versus historical reality: Rhetorical purification in "Kent State" the docudrama. *Communication Quarterly, 30,* 159–164.

Dahl, D. W., Frankenberger, K. D., & Manchanda, R. V. (2003). Does it pay to shock? Reactions to shocking and nonshocking advertising among university students. *Journal of Advertising Research, 43*(3), 1–13.

Dargis, M., & Scott, A.O. (2009, January 18). "How the movies made a president." *The New York Times*, p. AR-1.

Dupont, L. (1999). *Images that sell: 500 ways to create great ads*. Ste-Foy, Quebec: White Rock Publishing.

Edell , J. A., & Staelin, R. (1983). The information processing of pictures in print advertisements. *Journal of Consumer Research, 10*(1), 45–61.

Entman, R. M., & Rojecki, A. (2001). *The black image in the white mind: Media and race in America.* Chicago: University of Chicago Press.

Farhi, P. (2006, May 10). "Ad shatters a TV taboo head-on." *The Washington Post*, p. C1.

Felshin, N. (Ed.). (1995). *But is it art? The spirit of art as activism.* Seattle: Bay Press.

Felton, P. (2008, November/December). "Visual literacy." *Change*, 60–63.

Fuller, L. K. (1995). Hollywood is holding us hostage: Or, why are terrorists in the movies Middle-Easterners? In Y. R. Kamalipour (Ed.), *The U.S. media and the Middle East: Image and perception* (pp. 187–197). Westport, CT: Greenwood Press.

Gerbner, G., Gross, L., Morgan, M., & Signorielli, N. (2002). Growing up with television: The cultivation perspective. In J. Bryant & D. Zillmann (Eds.), *Media effects: Advances in theory and research* (2nd ed., 17–41). Hillsdale, NJ: Erlbaum.

Heatherton, T. F., & Sargent, J. D. (2009). Does watching smoking in movies promote teenage smoking? *Current Directions in Psychological Science, 18*(2), 63–67.

Hey, S. (2001, November 12). "So will the Brits play the baddies?" *The London Independent*, p. 4.

Hobbs, R. H., & Woodard, F. (Eds.). (1986). *Human rights/human wrongs: Art and social change.* Iowa City: University of Iowa Museum of Art.

Hockley, W. E. (2008). The picture superiority effect in associative recognition. *Memory& Cognition, 36*(7), 1351–1359.

Jones, C., & Dawson, J. (2000). *Stitching a revolution.* San Francisco: HarperCollins.

Lazar, D. (2003, December). Shockvertising. *Communication Arts, 45*(7), 198–201.

Leiby, R. (1995, December 3). "Movie madness: Does screen violence trigger copy-cat crimes?" *The Washington Post*, p. G1.

Lester, P. M. (2006). *Visual communication: Images with messages* (4th ed.). Belmont, CA: Wadsworth.

Lippard, L. R. (1984). *Get the message?: A decade of art for social change.* New York: E. P. Dutton.

Maher, K. (2009, February 4). "What do women want? Surely not this; Can anything stop the inane decline of the chick flick?" *The Times* (London, U.K.), pp. T2, 14–15.

McCarthy, M. (2000, June 20). " 'Shockvertising' pushes envelope, risks backlash." *USA Today*, p. 6B.

Messaris, P. (1997). *Visual persuasion: The role of images in advertising.* Thousand Oaks, CA: Sage.

Messaris, P., & Moriarty, S. (2005). Visual literacy theory. In K. Smith, S. Moriarty, G. Barbatsis, & K. Kenney (Eds.), *Handbook of visual communication* (pp. 481–502). Mahwah, NJ: Lawrence Erlbaum Associates.

Metros, S. E. (2008). The educator's role in preparing visually literate students. *Theory into Practice, 47,* 102–109.

Murray, J. P. (2008). Media violence: The effects are both real and strong. *American Behavioral Scientist, 51*(8), 1212–1230.

Omidvari, K., Lessnau, K., Kim, J., Mercante, D., Weinacker, A., & Mason, C. (2005). Smoking in contemporary American cinema. *Chest, 128,* 746–754.

Paivio, A. (1986). *Mental representations: A dual coding approach.* New York: Oxford University Press.

Paivio, A. (1991). Dual coding theory: Retrospect and current status. *Canadian Journal of Psychology, 45,* 255–287.

Pringle, H., & Thompson, M. (1999). *Brand spirit: How cause-related marketing builds brands.* Chichester, U.K.: John Wiley & Sons.

Pryor, F. (2007, February 8). "On the trail of artist Banksy." BBC News. Retrieved on May 15, 2009, from http://news.bbc.co.uk/2/hi/entertainment/6343197.stm.

Ralli, T. (2005, September 5). "Who's a looter? In storm's aftermath, pictures kick up a different kind of tempest." *The New York Times,* p. 6.

Real, M. R. (1996). *Exploring media culture: A guide.* Thousand Oaks, CA: Sage.

Reyes, L., & Rubie, P. (2000). *Hispanics in Hollywood: A celebration of 100 years in film and television.* Hollywood, CA: Lone Eagle Publishing.

Rosica, C. (2007). *The authentic brands: How today's top entrepreneurs connect with customers.* Paramus, NJ: Noble Press.

Schonfeld, E. (2008, November 21). "Yup, Apple's advertising budget is bigger than Microsoft's Vista." *TechCrunch.* Retrieved on June 10, 2009, from www.techcrunch.com/2008/11/21/yup-apples-advertising-budget-is-bigger-than-microsoft-vistas/.

Scudder, J. N., & Mill, C. B. (2009). The credibility of shock advocacy: Animal rights attack messages. *Public Relations Review, 35,* 162–164.

"Selling tobacco: Defending the rights of the Marlboro man." (1990, April 21). *The Economist, 315,* p. 84.

Simons, H. W. (2001). *Persuasion in society.* Thousand Oaks, CA: Sage.

Simpson, K. E. (2008). Classic and modern propaganda in documentary film. *Teaching of Psychology, 35*(2), 103–108.

Stenberg, G. (2006). Conceptual and perceptual factors in the picture superiority effect. *European Journal of Cognitive Psychology, 18*(6), 813–847.

Tilove, J. (2001, September 20). "Arab-Americans in predicament: Attacks heighten struggle with complex identity." *The Times-Picayune,* p. 15.

Unterberger, L. (2001, July 16). "Mimicking a movie star." *The Milwaukee Sentinel Journal,* p. 4E.

Von Blum, P. (1976). *The art of social conscience.* New York: Universe Books.

Von Blum, P. (1994). *Other visions, other voices: Women political artists in greater Los Angeles.* Lanham, MD: University Press of America.

Waxman, S. (2000, December 21). "1999 saw more roles for minorities in film, TV." *The Washington Post,* p. C7.

Webb, C. (1999). "Mundo de Marlboro: Big tobacco smothers Latin America." Retrieved on October 15, 2009 from http://lanic.utexas.edu/la/region/news/arc/lasnet/1999/0325.html

Welkos, R. W. (2001, July 2). "Multiethnic movies ringing true with youths." *Los Angeles Times,* p. A1.

Whitty, S. (2001, August 26). "Who are the Asians on screen? New stereotypes no better than old." *The San DiegoUnion Tribune,* p. F2.

Woodward, G. C., & Denton, R. E. (1999). *Persuasion and influence in American life* (3rd ed.). Prospect Heights, IL: Wadsworth.

Wright, S. H. (2001, November 28). "Advertisers marketing 'coolness' and 'liberation' speaker says." *MIT Tech Talk.* Cambridge, MA: Massachusetts Institute of Technology. Retrieved on October 15, 2009 from http://web.mit.edu/newsoffice/2001/advertising-1128.html.

Zumwalt, J. (2001, November 13). "How a powerful image can shape a war." *Los Angeles Times,* p. B12.

CHAPTER 15

Esoteric Forms of Persuasion

Previous chapters have dealt with fairly "mainstream" types of persuasion. In this chapter we examine more esoteric forms of persuasion. The topics we discuss in this section often receive short shrift or are neglected entirely by other texts. Yet we find these are among the most interesting topics to students and laypersons. We include them here partly because they are so intriguing, partly because there are important research findings, and partly to debunk some of the myths and superstitions surrounding these topics. The topics we'll examine are subliminal persuasion, backward masking or reverse speech, neurolinguistic programming, music as persuasion, and the role of smell in persuasion.

SUBLIMINAL INFLUENCE: HIDDEN MESSAGES OR HOKUM?

A good deal of misinformation surrounds the topic of subliminal influence. Most Americans believe subliminal messages are not only common in advertising but that they are highly effective as well (Pratkanis, 1992; Rogers & Seiler, 1994; Zanot, Pincus, & Lamp, 1983). Although examples of subliminal messages occasionally crop up, they appear to be fairly rare. Most cases involving the use of subliminals appear to be isolated pranks (see Emery, 1996). Some Disney movies, for example, contain embedded images, but these appear to be the mischievous work of individual artists and animators rather than a corporate conspiracy (see, for example, www.snopes.com/disney/films/films.asp).

What Makes a Message Subliminal?

Let's begin by clearing up some confusion surrounding the term *subliminal*. Literally, the term means below (sub) the threshold (limen) of human consciousness. Thus, a subliminal stimulus is one that is processed without conscious awareness. This is in contrast to *supraliminal* messages that are consciously processed. An image that is flashed so quickly that a person can't consciously register it is subliminal. An image that is merely fleeting, yet recognizable, is supraliminal. Subtle is not the same as subliminal. This distinction is important because advertisers routinely use product placements in movies and TV shows. The practice of planting products within shows, however, involves supraliminal processing. Advertisers *want* you to notice their products and/or logos on *American Idol, The Apprentice,* and *Survivor.* They pay big bucks to make sure viewers can spot their brands. A variety of subliminal stimuli have been examined by social scientists. We examine some of the most common types here.

You are smart! You love this book! You are smart! You love this book! You are smart! You love this book! You are smart! You love this book!

The Early Years: An Urban Myth Is Born

Public belief in subliminal persuasion dates back to the 1950s, when James Vicary claimed to have used subliminal messages in a movie theater. Vicary reported that by flashing the words "Eat popcorn" and "Drink Coca Cola" on the movie screen, he was able to boost popcorn sales by almost 58 percent and Coke sales by 18 percent (Rogers, 1992–1993).Thus was born an urban myth. In fact, Vicary never achieved the results he claimed. His so-called experiment was really a publicity stunt.[1] He never submitted the data or results of his study for scholarly review and scholars noted that the method he used was riddled with flaws (McConnell, Cutler, & McNeil, 1957; Moore, 1982; Weir, 1984). For example, there wasn't a "control group" of movie patrons who weren't exposed to the subliminal messages.

In the 1970s and 1980s, Brian Wilson Key renewed public interest in subliminal persuasion with his popular but unscientific books on subliminal advertising (Key, 1972, 1976, 1980, 1989). Among other things, Key claimed to have found phallic symbols embedded in print ads for Tanqueray gin and Chivas Regal scotch, female genitalia on a box of Betty Crocker cake mix, and the word "SEX" baked into Ritz Crackers. We've looked at the particular ads in question and, although we can discern some of the symbols and shapes Key mentions, we find his approach somewhat akin to staring at clouds. If one looks long enough and hard enough, one is bound to see a rubber ducky or any other object one wants to see.

The Middle Years: Looking Harder, Finding Little

During the middle period of research, from the mid-1970s through the mid-1990s, investigators carried out more rigorous studies on subliminal influence. Many of these studies focused on embedded images, that is, images that are buried or hidden within an advertisement. They were, however, unable to validate any of the claims that embedded images could make people want things or buy things without their awareness. As one advertising executive put it, "How can showing someone a penis get him or her to switch from Kent (cigarettes) to Marlboro?" (Kanner, cited in Rogers & Seiler, 1994, p. 37).

A typical study on embedding was carried out by Vokey and Read (1985), who found that ads with the word "sex" embedded in them were no more effective than ads containing nonsense syllables. Likewise, Gable, Wilkens, and Harris (1987) studied the effects of sexual stimuli embedded in advertisements. Identical pairs of photographs were shown to observers, except that one of each pair contained a hidden sexual image. No differences in product preferences were found. Smith and Rogers (1994) found supraliminal messages to be far more effective than subliminal messages when the words "Choose this" were embedded in a television commercial. They did find a small, almost negligible effect for subliminals, but they found a much stronger effect for supraliminal messages. As they emphasized in their conclusion, "The largest possible effect of subliminal messages is much smaller than the effect of supraliminal messages" (p. 872). In a meta-analysis of studies on the effects of subliminal advertising, Trappey (1996) concluded that the effects on consumer choice were negligible.

Subliminal Priming: Eureka! They Found It

The most recent studies on subliminal influence have finally hit paydirt. Through a method called *priming,* researchers have demonstrated that subliminal stimuli can influence attitudes, emotions, and behavior (Bargh, 2002; Kouider & Dehaene, 2007). Although priming techniques vary, a common method involves three steps.[2] First, participants view a masked prime. The mask is simply a string of characters covering up a word. For example, the characters #### could be used to mask the word "salt." Second, the mask is removed and the subliminal prime is presented. Thus, the word "salt" might appear for .30 milliseconds, too quickly to be consciously perceived. Third, a target word that is consciously visible, for example, the word "pepper," replaces the prime. Participants who are primed by the word "salt" tend to recognize the word "pepper" faster than participants who are not primed.

As an example, a study conducted in Germany (Mussweiler & Damisch, 2008) asked participants to guess the identities of pictures of well-known public figures. One of the figures was perceived by Germans to be aggressive and unintelligent. The participants viewed a fuzzy picture of the person and tried to identify him. As the picture gradually grew sharper participants were instructed to press the space bar as soon as they recognized the person. Participants were faster at recognizing the public figure when they were exposed to masked primes such as, "mean," "violent," or "tough" (*gemain, gewaltsam,* and *hart,* in German). They were slower at recognizing the public figure when the primes were "clever," "educated," or "smart" (*klug, gebildet,* and *schlau* in German). The public figure was none other than—wait for it—George W. Bush.

Other studies have shown that priming can alter behavior as well (see for example, Hassin, Ferguson, Shidlovski, & Gross, 2007). In one experiment (Winkielman, Berridge, & Wilbarger, 2005) participants were exposed to subliminal images of happy or angry faces. Then they were asked to sample a lemon-lime flavored drink. After reporting how thirsty they were, the participants were instructed to drink as much as they wanted. The results revealed that participants who were exposed to the happy faces consumed much more of the new drink than those exposed to the angry faces, but only—and this is important—if they were already thirsty. The amounts consumed by nonthirsty participants, whether exposed to happy or angry faces, did not differ significantly. These results suggest that subliminal priming may act as a trigger, but only if there is a need, goal, or drive that must be satisfied (Strahan, Spencer, & Zanna, 2002), in this case, thirst.

As a last illustration of the effectiveness of subliminal priming we turn to a study on religious priming and cheating (Randolph-Seng & Nielsen, 2007). The investigators exposed participants in the treatment group to 20 religious word primes (e.g., faith, bless, saved) flashed on a monitor. The control group was exposed to 20 nonreligious word primes. Participants were then asked to perform a task which allowed them to cheat or not cheat. Cheating was 20 percent lower in the treatment group compared to the control group. Interestingly, priming was just as effective at deterring cheating among nonreligious participants as religious participants.

A meta-analysis of 55 investigations by Van den Bussche, Van den Noortgate, and Reynvoet (2009) reveals that priming effects have been demonstrated repeatedly and reliably in controlled studies. Thus, information presented unconsciously can influence beliefs, attitudes, and behaviors.

Not So Fast: Limitations of Subliminal Priming

Before you panic about being controlled by invisible messages, we want to emphasize the practical limitations of subliminal priming. The studies demonstrating that priming works were all conducted in highly controlled laboratory settings. The participants were free from other distractions. Typically, they were looking at a computer screen and were instructed to pay close attention to the on-screen information. In many of the studies on priming, the effects were short-lived, lasting less than a second (Greenwald, Draine, & Abrams, 1996), hardly enough time to run to the mall to buy something. The real world is a very different environment. Real life is filled with media clutter. A myriad of supraliminal stimuli compete for our attention. People don't always pay close attention to messages. In this regard, Bargh (1999) noted "sometimes, subliminal messages are not perceived at all, in which case they have no priming effect" (p. B6). We are aware of no studies demonstrating any commercial success at using subliminal priming. To date, this is a somewhat rarified phenomenon that is confined to controlled laboratory settings.

So Why Do People Believe?

We believe much of the information published in the popular press about subliminal persuasion can be dismissed as "junk science." Why the fascination with subliminals then? Perhaps it is because people find conspiracy theories attractive. It only takes a few isolated cases, like the Disney examples mentioned earlier, to convince people that subliminals are everywhere.

By the way, do you suddenly feel smarter or like this book even more? The reason we ask is because we included a "subliminal" message at the very top of page 317. It consists of tiny type. Did you see it? Did it consciously register? Did it work?

Subaudible Messages: The Power of Suggestion

How would you like to lower your blood pressure, improve your memory, lose weight, release your body's natural healing forces, stop procrastinating, and win the lottery? These are just *some* of the claims that have been made on behalf of subliminal self-help audiotapes. There is a booming market in subliminal self-help tapes. When that many people pay that much money, one would expect the tapes to work.

The fact is, however, they do not. Every controlled study to date has reached the same conclusion: There is no evidence that subliminal self-improvement tapes work any magic, apart from the *belief* that they work. Believing can, in and of itself, produce changes in people, but these changes are the result of a *placebo effect* and have nothing to do with the content of the tapes themselves. A placebo effect follows the age-old notion that "thinking makes it so." If a person believes something will work, he or she convinces him- or herself that it has worked.

By way of illustration, in one well-known study (Greenwald, Spangenberg, Pratkanis, & Eskenazi, 1991), volunteers were given one of two types of self-help tapes: one that claimed to improve memory or one that claimed to improve self-esteem. Unbeknownst to the volunteers, however, the researchers switched the labels on half of the tapes. Thus, half the volunteers who thought they had received a tape with an "improve your esteem" label actually got a tape designed to improve their memory, and vice versa. The volunteers took the tapes home and listened to them for a period of time. A few months later, the volunteers completed a survey, asking them about their experiences. A strong placebo effect was found for whichever type of tape the volunteers thought they'd been given. Those with the tapes labeled for improving memory reported memory improvements, even those who received the mislabeled tapes. Those with the tapes labeled for improving self-esteem reported that they felt better about themselves, even those with the mislabeled tapes. Other tests of subliminal tapes have produced essentially the same results (Benoit & Thomas, 1992; Greenwald et al., 1991; Mitchell, 1995; Spangenberg, Obermiller, & Greenwald, 1992; Staum & Brotons, 1992).

These results point strongly to the conclusion that subliminal audiotapes fail to confer any of the benefits claimed by their manufacturers. Rather, the results demonstrate the powerful effects of psychological expectancies. If they work at all, it is through "sleight of mind."

Backward Masking and Reverse Speech: The Devil Made Me Do It

Can satanic, backward-masked lyrics cause a person to commit suicide? That is what the plaintiffs in several lawsuits contended. A father filed a lawsuit against Ozzy Osbourne's record label, claiming that backward-masked lyrics on the *Blizzard of OZ* album drove his son to commit suicide (Harmon, 1995). A similar suit was filed by the parents of two teens who committed suicide after listening to backward-masked lyrics on Judas Priest's *Stained Class* album (Goleman, 1990; Phillips, 1990). In both cases, the judges ruled in favor of the defendants, citing the lack of any causal connection between the reversed lyrics and the teens' deaths. The authors have listened to both albums and have experienced no suicidal tendencies. Kenny G. music, however, is another story! All kidding aside, there is no credible scientific evidence that listening to reversed speech can make people think or act differently than they otherwise would.

It is possible to infer meanings from reversed speech, but these may be a matter of coincidence. Vokey (2002), for example, notes that the phrase "Jesus loves you," when played backward, sounds like "we smell sausage" (p. 248). Poundstone (1985) examined a number of alleged cases of reversals and concluded that most were pure coincidence. Some rock songs do actually contain backward-masked lyrics (the Beatles' song "Revolution Number 9" and Pink Floyd's "Goodbye Blue Sky," for example), but their mere *presence* doesn't prove their *effectiveness*. The results of scientific studies of backward-masking have failed to demonstrate any effects on listeners (Kreiner, Altis, & Voss, 2003; Langston & Anderson, 2000; Swart & Morgan, 1992; Vokey & Read, 1985). Parents are better advised to worry about the effects of audible lyrics in music as opposed to backward-masked lyrics.

What Advertisers Really Do

Advertisers are not really interested in subliminals, subaudible messages, or reverse speech. What advertisers seek to do is to connect their products with favorable images and

"Now, that's product placement!"

idealized lifestyles. Product placement is one way of accomplishing this (Galacian, 2004). Placements in movies and TV are a $3 billion dollar per year business (PQ Media, 2006). According to Morgan (2005) "between 15–30 products are inserted into every half hour of television programming" (p. 62). Placements in reality shows are among the most effective (Wenner, 2004).

Placements may be blatant or subtle, but they are in no sense subliminal. Some product placements operate at a low level of awareness, but they remain a form of supraliminal persuasion. In sum, we believe consumers have little to fear from subliminal advertising at this time.

NEUROLINGUISTIC PROGRAMMING: THE EMPEROR'S NEW CLOTHES

Did you know that by speaking a few magical words, you can get anyone to do anything you want? Some folks would like you to believe in such hocus-pocus. They claim they can teach you, often in 10 easy steps, how to hypnotize people with your words. Some claim their techniques will help you get dates, overcome phobias, cure depression, improve spelling, alleviate colds and flu, and enlarge your breasts or penis!

Don't reach for your wallet just yet. What these folks are peddling is based on *neurolinguistic programming,* or NLP, which is a mix of linguistics, psychology, and hypnotism (Gow, Reupert, & Maybery, 2006). The theory, developed by Richard Bandler and John Grinder (Bandler & Grinder, 1975, 1979), lies somewhere between pop psychology and junk science. It is popular with authors of self-help books, such as Tony Robbins, and others on the lecture circuit. Despite the grandiose claims, there is little or no evidence that NLP works. Most credible experts, e.g., those who don't stand to profit by writing, speaking or training about the subject, denounce NLP as a form of pseudoscience (Corballis, 1999; Gumm, Walker, & Day, 1982; Heap, 1988, 2008; Sharpley, 1984, 1987; Thaler Singer & Lalich, 1996).

The basic idea behind NLP is that a person's inner, unconscious mind determines how he or she responds to persuasive messages. All persuaders have to do is use a few clever linguistic strategies and—Presto!—they can "program" another person's responses. Certain words and nonverbal behaviors allegedly have hypnotic power and evoke a subconscious reaction in people, or so the theory goes. They do this by activating a person's *primary representational system (PRS)*, which is reflected in the five senses.

For example, a salesperson who sensed a consumer was "visually" oriented, based on the consumer's language style, mannerisms, and gaze, could adapt a message to emphasize visual features about a product, e.g., "As you can see . . ." "take a look . . ." "watch this . . ." A salesperson who perceived a customer was "auditory" would adjust the sales pitch by saying "I hear you . . . " "it sounds like this is what you're after. . . ." But how, you might wonder, does a salesperson know if a customer is primarily visual or auditory? According to NLP, a customer who looks up and to the left (memory) or right (invention) is accessing visual information; a customer who looks horizontally left (memory) or right (invention) is accessing auditory information (see Lankton, 1980).

Although NLP's proponents claim certain words and phrases have hypnotic power, their claims are highly suspect. The theory itself is nebulous and the evidence for its effectiveness is largely anecdotal. We agree that people respond reflexively to certain words, such as "free" or "sale." That is a long way from saying, however, that specific words, phrases, and nonverbal cues have hypnotic power. By way of example, in one study, the investigators compared an indirect message using NLP with a direct message without NLP (Dixon, Parr, Yarbrough, & Rathael, 2001). They found that the direct message without NLP was significantly more effective than the indirect message employing NLP. As the investigators concluded, "Neurolinguistic programming may not be an effective device for improving the persuadability of messages" (p. 549).

In our view, NLP relies on a good deal of faulty sign reasoning. When a customer looks up or down, left or right, it *could* signify hemispheric processing in the brain. It could also signify that there was glare coming from the other direction in a room, that the salesperson was standing too close, or that the item in which the customer is interested lies in the direction of his or her gaze. If a customer scratches his or her nose, it *could* signify that the customer thinks the salesperson's idea stinks. Of course, it could also signify that the customer's nose itched. In this regard, NLP is much like the emperor's new clothes—people believe in it because others seem to believe in it. The underlying assumptions of NLP so annoyed one expert in neuroscience that he declared it to be "neurobabble" (Miller, 1986).

MUSIC AS A FORM OF PERSUASION

Have you ever heard an advertising jingle and then been unable to get the tune out of your head the rest of the day? If you like the tune, all is well and good, but if you hate the song it can be maddening. This illustrates the power of music as a means of facilitating product recall. Music is an important ingredient in persuasion. Ninety percent of television commercials include some form of music (Oakes & North, 2006). Music facilitates persuasion in a variety of ways: The music or lyrics can impart product information, conjure up favorable images and associations, reinforce advertising themes, help put listeners in a positive frame of mind, and regulate the pace of consumer shopping. Music can also serve as a mnemonic device, or memory aid. We now look at these and other ways in which music can assist persuasion.

Music as a Central and Peripheral Cue

Song lyrics persuade. The lyrics to the famous McDonald's song "You deserve a break today" offer a case in point. When song lyrics persuade, they may do so through what Petty and Cacioppo (1986a, 1986b) call the central route to persuasion. That is, the song lyrics are cognitively processed (thought about, reflected on) by listeners. For example, in the last presidential campaign, Will.i.am (of Black Eyed Peas fame) set words from Barack Obama's speeches to music, winning an Emmy for his music video "Yes We Can" (Will.i.am , 2008). This tends to be the case when the music is in the foreground, as opposed to the background.

Music can also persuade via the peripheral route to persuasion. Peripheral processing occurs when listeners hear, but don't actively attend to, the music. Such is the case with background music. You may, for example, prefer to study with the radio on or a CD playing. Background music can affect a person's mood or emotions, without the person's cognitive involvement.

Music in Advertising and Sales

Reinforcing Products' Images: Like a Rock . . .

Music figures heavily in commercial advertising both on radio and television. Roughly 40 percent of music videos mention brands by name (Schemer, Matthes, Wirth, & Textor, 2008). Rapper Busta Rhymes' hit "Pass the Courvoisier," featuring Sean "P-Diddy" Combs, is credited with increasing sales of the cognac brand by 30 percent (Emling, 2004). Bob Dylan licensed his song "Love Sick" for a Victoria's Secret commercial (Klein, 2008). Music is often used to help foster a product's image. The type of music used in an ad says things about both the product and its user. *Congruency*, which refers to how well the music fits the brand, enhances music's effectiveness (Lalwani, Lwin, & Ling, 2009; Oakes & North, 2006).

Mere Exposure Effect: Hearing Is Believing

Another way music helps to sell products is based on the *mere exposure effect* (Wang & Chang, 2004; Zajonc, 1968), which we discussed in Chapter 9. The idea is simply that repeated exposure to a stimulus increases liking for the stimulus. If an ad for a given product includes a popular song or a likable jingle, repeated airings of the ad will facilitate liking for that product (Hargreaves, 1984; Obermiller, 1985). This is only true up to a point, however. Excessive repetition of a song or jingle can decrease liking for the product (Brentar, Neuendorf, & Armstrong, 1994).

Music as a Mnemonic Device

Music also functions as a *mnemonic device* in advertising. A mnemonic device is simply a memory aid that facilitates recall. Some jingles help the consumer to spell out the product's name and thus remember it. The Oscar Mayer bologna and JELL-O brand gelatin songs do this. Other jingles surround the product's name with positive associations. Try supplying the following product's name while singing along: "Nothing says lovin' like something from the oven and _____ says it best." Here's another one, "Like a good neighbor _____ _____ is there." If you are familiar with these commercials, as any red-blooded American consumer should be, you should have been able to supply the correct names: Pillsbury and State Farm.

Richard Yalch (1991) demonstrated the effectiveness of jingles in facilitating brand recall. College students were presented with 20 advertising slogans and asked to identify the brand-name associated with each slogan. Half the slogans were taken from advertisements that included jingles, whereas the other half were not. The results demonstrated consistently better recall for the brands accompanied by jingles. To be effective, the jingles also have to be simple. This is because the words in a jingle tend to be processed phonetically (e.g., as mere sounds) rather than semantically (as meanings).

The latest trend in advertising has been to turn away from jingles, which are seen as too cute and obvious, and toward hit songs (McGee, 2005, p. 34). Think U2 and iPod, Rihanna and Cover Girl, and Paul McCartney and Starbucks.

Background Music: Shop Till You Drop

Background music, a.k.a. elevator music, has come to play an important role in the persuasion process. Retailers rely heavily on background music, also dubbed environmental music, programmed music, or functional music. Retail chains such as Abercrombie & Fitch, Starbucks, Victoria's Secret, and others provide their own in-store music. The evidence suggests that the right music can help distinguish a brand and enhance the shopping experience (Beverland, Lim, Morrison, & Terziovski, 2006; Morrison & Beverland, 2003).

Background Music and Shopping Pace

Can music affect the speed at which you do things? A meta-analysis by Garlin and Owen (2006) revealed that customers tend to shop longer when music is playing, as compared to a no-music condition; when the music is played at a lower volume, as compared to a higher volume; and when the tempo is slower rather than faster. Are shoppers and diners aware that their behavior is being regulated by background music? Probably not. Because background music is processed via the peripheral route, people aren't actively thinking about the music.

Background Music and Mood

Music can be an extremely effective tool for inducing relaxation or fostering a favorable mood. For example, Weisenthal, Hennessy, & Totten (2003) found that drivers who listened to music they liked displayed less aggression while driving in rush-hour traffic than drivers who heard no music. Music can also put shoppers in the mood to buy. In one of our favorite studies, researchers played either French or German music in a wine shop and kept track of which wines sold the most (North, Hargreaves, & McKendrick, 1999). The sobering findings were that French wine sold better when French music was playing, while German wine sold better while German music was playing. The shoppers' affective responses to the background music thus affected their purchase decisions.

Of course, one needn't rely on experimental studies to reach the conclusion that music can arouse people's emotions. Any moviegoer can vouch for the fact that a good film score significantly heightens the emotional impact of a film. Gordon Bruner (1990) thus emphasizes "that music is an especially powerful stimulus for affecting moods is no revelation; it is attested to throughout history by poets, playwrights, composers, and, in the last two centuries, researchers" (p. 94).

Background Music and Task Performance: Sweatin' to the Oldies

Apart from studies of consumers, investigators also have examined the effects of background music on task performance and group productivity. Elliott, Carr, and Savage (2004), for example, had college students exercise on a stationary bike while listening to up-tempo dance music or no music. They found that the participants who listened to music pedaled significantly farther than those in the no-music condition, even though the two groups reported the same perceived level of exertion. Similar results were reported by Boutcher & Trenske (1990), who found background music lowered perceived exertion levels. These studies support the widely held view that exercise is more fun and enjoyable when it is accompanied by music.

Turning from physical to mental exertion, Miller and Schyb (1989) studied whether different kinds of background music could enhance student performance on both verbal and nonverbal tasks. College students were exposed to one of four conditions: no music, classical music, pop music, and disco music. The researchers found that background music facilitated task performance but, surprisingly, only for females. Pop music especially, and to some extent disco, proved to be the most effective. Research has shown that vocal selections can be more distracting than instrumental works (Dye, 1996).

Rather than the type of music, Mayfield and Moss (1989) examined the tempo of background music on task performance. In a simulated stock market setting, they found that workers in an up-tempo environment (rock music played at 120 beats per minute) were more productive than those exposed to a slow tempo (a beat of 60 beats per minute).

Music Videos and Persuasion: Is Hip-Hop Harmful?

A great deal has been written about the influence of MTV and music videos on the attitudes and behaviors of young people. Today, a typical music video is essentially a three minute commercial for the artist, the brands he or she endorses, and the lifestyle he or she espouses. There is little doubt that music videos influence fashions, trends, slang, sexual mores, and model social behavior. The question is how much they do so and whether the modeling provided is beneficial or detrimental.

One analysis found, for example, that 60 to 75 percent of music videos contained sexual content (Cummins, 2007). On the negative side, music videos have been criticized for glorifying materialism and wealth (Kalis & Neuendorf, 1989) and for reinforcing sexism (Barongan & Hall Nagayama, 1995; Baxter, De Riemer, Landini, Leslie, & Singletary, 1985; Gow, 1996; Hansen & Hansen, 1990; Peterson & Pfost, 1989; Seidman, 1992; Sherman & Dominick, 1986; Vincent, 1989).

Rap music, in particular, has gotten a bad rap. "Rap music," one group of scholars note, "has been blamed for youth violence, the rise of gangs and gang related crime, drug use, and violence against women" (Reyna, Brandt, & Tendayi, 2009, p. 362). Some critics have warned that frequent exposure to rap and hip-hop is associated with illicit drug use, alcohol abuse, and aggression (Chen, Miller, Grube, & Waiters, 2006; Parker-Pope, 2007). In response to these charges, defenders argue that rap and hip-hop music give a voice to the disenfranchised and serve as a medium for urban empowerment (Reyna et al., 2009). Proponents argue that some music videos make important social statements, and that others simply mirror the crass materialism and rampant sexism of the larger society. Rap and hip-hop artists respond that they are sending important sociopolitical messages, that the mainstream media paints a distorted picture of rap, and that the language and images used reflect the harsh realities of inner-city life (Brown & Campbell, 1986; Chambers & Morgan, 1992; Cummings & Roy, 2002; Tiddle, 1996; Wideman, cited in "Tough Talk on Entertainment," 1995). Dyson (1993), for example, classifies rap music as a form of resistance that empowers African Americans. He stresses that rap combines social protest, musical creation, and cultural expression all at the same time. Lynch (2003) states that hip-hop brings people from different races and cultures together.

Whether one perceives the messages in music videos as positive or negative, it is difficult to deny that such music does serve to shape attitudes, beliefs, intentions, motivations, and behaviors. This is particularly true for juveniles (those who don't yet date or drive) who readily admit that they watch MTV to find out what is "cool." One must be cautious about making direct causal inferences, however, between what juveniles see or hear on MTV and their subsequent behavior. There are plenty of alternative sources for modeling behavior.

Weaponizing Music: What a Buzz Kill

Is subjecting someone to awful music akin to waterboarding? How much Britney Spears music can one human being withstand? It was reported that the U.S. military used music as a form of "Torture Lite" during the war in Iraq (Connor, 2008). One of the songs was Barney the Dinosaur's "I Love You, You Love Me." Look for a "Greatest Hits of Psy-Ops" CD at your record store soon. All kidding aside, Amnesty International is investigating the use of music in interrogations.

There have been reports that classical music was used to drive away the homeless, panhandlers, and gang members from fast-food restaurants and convenience stores (Morrison, 1996). Commented one officer, "If you're a tough guy and you like rock or rap, you're not going to sit there and listen to Tchaikovsky" (Holt, 1996, p. 2).

In what has been termed the "Manilow Method," the town of Rockdale, near Sydney, initiated a campaign to discourage teens from congregating at a park late at night. Music by Barry Manilow was played over loudspeakers from 9 P.M. until midnight (Hirsch, 2007). We have to wonder, did the town pay Mr. Manilow any royalties?

Such practices may be temporarily effective, but only by moving rowdy teens elsewhere. Hirsch (2007) sees ethical implications stemming from the weaponization of music. Music is being used to mark territory, "signaling inclusion to some and exclusion to others" (p. 354). Should music be used like barb wire to repel people?

Cautions about Using Music to Persuade: Don't Try This at Home

Before you get a hankering to use music to persuade others, bear in mind the following caveats. First, the type of music used must match the receivers' musical tastes. Second, the music has to match the particular product, brand, or purpose for which it is intended. Third, music shouldn't overpower the verbal content of a message. In radio and TV commercials, for example, the music is turned down during the voice-overs so that receivers can attend to product names and features. Fourth, in a sales setting, quieter music allows for more interaction between the salesperson and the customer. In a retail setting in which such interaction is important, playing blaring music would be ill-advised. Fifth, music will probably have little effect on highly involved receivers who will concentrate on the substance of the message anyway. Music is best used on low-involved receivers who will tend to process the message indirectly (Park & Young, 1986). In most cases, music functions as a useful supplement to verbal persuasion. Rarely can music be used as a substitute for verbal persuasion.

AROMA AND PERSUASION

Although few texts discuss the subject, smell plays an important role in the process of persuasion. Selling smells is a big business. Sales of fragrances and scented products total more than $19 billion in the United States annually (Leffingwell & Associates, 2007). Think of all the fragrances you can buy to make you feel better; you can douse yourself in cologne or perfume, scent your car's interior, and place air fresheners throughout your home. You can use scented deodorants, soaps, and laundry detergent, as well as scented dishwashing liquid and toilet paper. In addition to personal uses of fragrances, the use of "ambient" (background) fragrances in the workplace and in retail settings is beginning to play an increasingly prominent role (Caplan, 2006; Hoppough, 2006). In this section we examine the role of fragrances and aromas as forms of influence.

Perfume: Romance in a Bottle

The fragrance industry is one in which a product often "wins by a nose." But is it the actual fragrance that sells or the associations that are paired with it? Scent alone isn't what sells perfume. The promise of romance sells perfume. Hence, the marketing themes associated with fragrances revolve around images of romance, intrigue, sensuality, and, of course, sex. "Between madness and infatuation," a Calvin Klein ad proclaims, "lies obsession" (for Obsession perfume).

"It's the smell of money."

Love Stinks

Through images and innuendo, fragrance ads create the impression that using their products will increase your sexual attractiveness. But do they make any actual difference? Do they help attract dates, win over lovers, or make one feel better about oneself? We've uncovered very few studies on the effects of fragrances and attraction. Those we've found present a mixed bag of results.

A study by Baron (1983) suggests fragrances do increase attraction. Female undergraduates wearing perfume were perceived as more attractive by male undergraduates than female undergraduates not wearing perfume. The results of two other studies, however, don't bode well for the fragrance industry. Cann and Ross (1989) asked males to rate the attractiveness of females. While being shown slides of females, the males were exposed to a pleasant smell (spray cologne), an unpleasant smell (ammonium sulfide), or no smell. The researchers found no significant differences in perceived attractiveness based on the different smells.

Another study that casts doubt on the allure of perfumes was conducted by Hirsch (cited in Stolberg, 1994). Male medical students were recruited as subjects for the study. Blood pressure monitors were attached to the volunteers' genitals while they smelled a variety of fragrances, including Chanel No. 5 and Obsession. The results? The only smell that consistently increased blood pressure, the measure of sexual arousal used in the study, was that of cinnamon buns! The results seem to reinforce the old adage that the way to a man's heart is, after all, through his stomach. As with the preceding study, these results may also be questioned. Let's face it, having an apparatus attached to one's genitals doesn't approximate a real-world setting for arousal (not for most folks, anyway). In such a clinical environment, the participants may not have responded as they otherwise would.

A fragrance designer for Givaudan-Roure Corp. plies his trade.

Photo by Joe Tabacca.

Overall, some studies suggest perfume increases attraction, whereas other studies suggest it does not. All the studies have limitations. Thus, the best answer to the question, "Do perfumes really increase attraction?" is an equivocal, "It depends." In questioning whether perfumes and other fragrances work any magic, bear in mind that there are huge individual differences in preferences for smells. Bear in mind, too, that scent is only *one* factor in the overall attractiveness equation. Other factors include such things as physical appearances, personalities, and common interests, to name but a few. One would be foolish, indeed, to believe that fragrance alone could serve as the basis for a meaningful, lasting relationship.

Ambient Aromas: Something Special in the Air

Although there is little research on the relationship between fragrance and attraction, there is a sizable body of research on the ways in which ambient aromas affect people generally. We consider three such areas here; moods, task performance, and shopping behavior.

Aromas and Moods: Am I Blue?

Smells have been shown to affect people's moods, feelings, and emotions in significant ways. At the Memorial Sloan-Kettering Cancer Center, physicians have used vanilla fragrance to relax patients who are about to undergo a magnetic resonance image (MRI) exam (Stolberg, 1994). Similarly, Redd and Manne (1991) exposed patients undergoing MRIs for cancer to the scent of heliotropin (similar to baby powder). The results revealed that patients in general felt more relaxed by the heliotropin, particularly those who rated the smell as pleasant. Not just any smell will do, however. In a follow-up study, the same researchers found that the scent of wintergreen (a menthol fragrance) had no calming effect because it was perceived as invigorating rather than relaxing by the patients (Manne & Redd, 1993).

Researchers have found that scents can influence people's moods in nonmedical settings as well. One of our favorite studies (Hanisch, 1982), because of its unusual method, examined whether pleasant fragrances could reduce arachnophobia (fear of spiders) among females. The researcher dangled a spider at varying distances from the participants' faces. Part of the time the participants were exposed to a pleasant, unfamiliar scent. Part of the time they were not. The researcher found that the pleasant fragrance reduced fear and anxiety and allowed the spider to be placed closer to the participants' faces than the no-fragrance condition. The researcher didn't mention whether the spider liked the fragrance or not.

Other studies also support the conclusion that ambient smells can alter moods and emotions. Knasko (1992) found that the smell of chocolate and baby powder (separately, not in combination) elicited more positive moods than no smell. A variety of other studies have achieved similar results. The fairly consistent conclusion is that ambient fragrances can alter people's moods, provided the right fragrances are used.

Aromas and Task Performance: Smell that Productivity

Another area in which scents have been shown to have an effect is on task performance. Several studies have shown that mild fragrances can improve the speed, accuracy, and efficiency with which people complete tasks (Hirsch, cited in Stolberg, 1994; Rotten, 1983; Sugano & Sato, 1991; Warm, Parasuraman, & Dember, 1990). A researcher named Robert Baron is well known for his work in this area. In one study, Baron and Kalsher (1998) found that a pleasant ambient fragrance improved driving performance on a simulated driving task. In yet another study, Baron (1997) found that shoppers in a mall were more than twice as likely to help a stranger in the presence of pleasant ambient aromas (roasting coffee or baking cookies). So if you decide to hit up your rich Uncle Ned for a loan, you might want to take him someplace that smells good to make your request.

Ambient Aromas and Consumer Behavior

A number of retail stores use ambient odors in an effort to regulate shopping behavior (Miller, 1991). Does pumping fragrances into the air make customers buy more? Researchers seem to agree that purchasing decisions are too complex to be influenced solely by smell. However, Bosmans (2006) did find that background fragrances led to more favorable product evaluations as long as the fragrance matched the product, e.g., coconut fragrance and bikinis.

Although gambling may not qualify as "shopping," Hirsch, (1995) also found that gamblers in a pleasantly scented casino room put significantly more money into slot machines than gamblers in an unscented room. Gamblers fed 53 percent more money into the slot machines when the scent concentration was higher and 33 percent more when the scent concentration was lower. This study, along with others by Hirsch, has been criticized for lacking scientific rigor (Stolberg, 1994).[3] It does seem reasonable, though, that if a pleasant fragrance can put people in a good mood, they might feel more optimistic or lucky and hence bet more.

Several studies have also shown that pleasant fragrances can make consumers linger longer in stores. Teerling, Nixdorf, and Koster (1992), for instance, found that two ambient fragrances increased the time spent shopping in a fabric store. Likewise, Knasko (1989) found either a floral or a spicy scent made customers stay longer in a jewelry store. Much the same was found using a museum as the setting (Knasko, 1993). You may recall that similar effects were produced by background music in both store and restaurant settings.

Caveats and Qualifications

Before you rush out to buy a case of room air fresheners to make you feel better, study harder, and work more efficiently, keep the following in mind: First, there are large variations in individual preferences for smells. A scent that works on one person may not work on another. One of the authors, for example, actually likes the smell of a skunk from afar. Second, as was the case with subliminal research, some of the effects reported in these studies may be attributed to a placebo effect. That is, the participants' expectations that smells can alter human behavior might account for the changes observed. For instance, Schiffman (1993a, 1993b) found that participants who were told they were exposed to a fragrance reported favorable mood shifts even though, in reality, they were given an odorless substance. Third, the repetitive use of scents could lead to counterconditioning such that an initially pleasant scent comes to be perceived as unpleasant. The smell of vanilla, for example, has been shown to be relaxing. But if it is introduced every time a child receives a vaccination, the smell may become aversive. Fourth, easy does it where ambient scents are concerned. An overpowering odor that draws attention may not produce the results you're after. Finally, there may be ethical as well as health-related concerns involved in using fragrances to influence people. Remember, people can close their eyes or look away from an image that offends them. They can't stop breathing or turn off their noses, however. We address some of the ethical questions arising from the use of fragrances in Chapter 16.

What Will the Future Smell Like?

What about the future of smell as a form of influence? Will there come a day when you wake up not only to your alarm clock's buzzer but to a fragrance that will make you feel perky and chipper as well? Will your gym or aerobics class pipe in a fragrance that makes you want to exercise harder and longer? Or perhaps your employer will use similar ambient odors to make you work harder and be more productive on the job. Perhaps you'll be able to buy a scented "blue book" or "Scantron" form that will improve your concentration and recall while taking a test. Granted, such hypothetical scenarios seem far-fetched. Pleasant smells can only do so much. A clever attorney isn't going to get his or her client off by wearing the right fragrance. Even so, keep in mind that fragrances are already being put to use in some hospitals, retail stores, and office buildings (Baron & Bronfen, 1994). To the extent that fragrances can alter moods, they may become increasingly important tools for persuaders.

SUMMARY

In this chapter we examined several esoteric forms of persuasion: subliminal messages, sub-audible messages, backward masking or reverse speech, neurolinguistic processing, music as persuasion, and smell as persuasion. Despite the public's belief in subliminal persuasion, subliminal effects have only been demonstrated in highly controlled laboratory settings. At present, subliminal priming is not commercially viable. Embedded words and images, sub-audible messages, and backward masking have not been shown to influence people. Neurolinguistic processing is a popular, but unproven phenomenon. Music was shown to be an important component of persuasion. Music facilitates persuasion in a variety of ways such as reinforcing advertising images, serving as a mnemonic device, and influencing receivers' moods. Though overlooked by most persuasion researchers, smell was also shown to be a useful tool for persuasion if the right conditions are met. Ambient fragrances can enhance moods, improve task performance, and influence consumer behavior.

ENDNOTES

1. According to Anthony Pratkanis (1992), James Vicary admitted in an interview in *Advertising Age* that his so-called study was a hoax, designed to save his failing advertising firm
2. For an online demonstration of masked priming, try the following link:www.u.arizona.edu/~kforster/priming/masked_priming_demo.htm

3. The fragrances used weren't identified by the researcher, complicating any effort aimed at replication. Factors that could have confounded the results include the number of gamblers in the casino, the amount of money they had with them, and variations in gambling habits as a function of the time of day and day of week

REFERENCES—SUBLIMINALS

Bargh, J. A. (1999, January 29). "The most powerful manipulative messages are hiding in plain sight." *Chronicle of Higher Education*, p. B6.

Bargh, J. A. (2002). Losing consciousness: Automatic influences on consumer judgment, behavior, and motivation. *Journal of Consumer Research, 29*(2), 280–285.

Benoit, S. C., & Thomas, R. L. (1992). The influence of expectancy in subliminal perception experiments. *Journal of General Psychology, 119*(4), 335–341.

Emery, C. E., Jr. (1996, March/April). When the media miss the real messages in subliminal stories. *Skeptical Inquirer, 20*(2), 16–17+.

Gable, M., Wilkins, H., & Harris, L. (1987). An evaluation of subliminally embedded sexual stimuli. *Journal of Advertising, 16*(1), 26–30.

Galacian, M. L. (Ed.). (2004). *Handbook of product placement in the mass media: New strategies in marketing theory, practice, trends, and ethics.* New York: The Haworth Press.

Goleman, D. (1990, August 14). "Research probes what the mind senses unaware." *New York Times,* pp. B7–B8.

Greenwald, A. G., Draine, S. C., & Abrams, R. L. (1996). Three cognitive markers of semantic activation. *Science, 273,* 1699–1701.

Greenwald, A. G., Spangenberg, E. R., Pratkanis, A. R., & Eskenazi, J. (1991). Double-blind tests of subliminal self-help audiotapes. *Psychological Science, 2,* 119–122.

Harmon, A. (1995, October 1). "High-tech hidden persuaders." *Los Angeles Times*, pp. A1, A28–29.

Hassin, R. R., Ferguson, M. J., Shidlovski, D., & Gross, T. (2007). Subliminal exposure to national flags affects political thought and behavior. *Proceedings of the National Academy of Sciences, 104*(50),

19757–19761. Retrieved on June 1, 2009, from www.pnas.org/content/104/50/19757.full.pdf+html.

Key, W. B. (1972). *Subliminal seduction: Ad media's manipulation of a not so innocent America.* Englewood Cliffs, NJ: Prentice Hall.

Key, W. B. (1976). *Media sexploitation.* Englewood Cliffs, NJ: Prentice Hall.

Key, W. B. (1980). *Clam-plate orgy: And other subliminal techniques for manipulating your behavior.* Englewood Cliffs, NJ: Prentice Hall.

Key, W. B. (1989). *The age of manipulation: The con in confidence, the sin in sincere.* New York: Henry Holt.

Kouider, S., & Dehaene, S. (2007). Levels of processing during non-conscious perception: A critical review of visual masking. *Philosophical Transactions of the Royal Society of London. Series B, Biological Sciences, 362*(1481), 857–875.

Kreiner, D. S., Altis, N. A., & Voss, C. W. (2003). A test of the effect of reverse speech on priming. *Journal of Psychology, 137*(3), 224–232.

Langston, W., & Anderson, J. C. (2000). Talking back [wards]: A test of the reverse speech hypothesis. *Skeptic, 8* (3), 30–35.

McConnell, J. V., Cutler, R. L., & McNeil, E. B. (1957). Subliminal stimulation: An overview. *American Psychologist, 13*, 229–242.

Mitchell, C. W. (1995). Effects of subliminally presented auditory suggestions of itching on scratching behavior. *Perceptual and Motor Skills, 80*(1), 87–96.

Moore, T. E. (1982). Subliminal advertising: What you see is what you get. *Journal of Marketing, 5*(4), 355–372.

Morgan, M. (2005). Review of the book *The psychology of entertainment media. Blurring the lines between entertainment and persuasion. Mass Communication & Society, 8*(1), 61–74.

Mussweiler, T., & Damisch, L. (2008). Going back to Donald: How comparisons shape judgmental priming effects. *Journal of Personality and Social Psychology, 95*(6), 1295–1315.

Phillips, C. (1990, July 16). "Trial to focus on issue of subliminal messages in rock." *Los Angeles Times,* pp. F10–F11.

Poundstone, W. (1985). *Big Secrets.* New York: HarperCollins.

PQ Media (2006). *Exclusive PQ Media Research: Global paid product placement spending surged 42.2% to $2.21 billion in 2005; d-digit pace to continue in 2006 and beyond.* Retrieved on March 28, 2009, fromwww.pqmedia.com/about-press-20060816-gppf2006.html.

Pratkanis, A. R. (1992). The cargo cult science of subliminal persuasion. *Skeptical Inquirer, 16*, 260–272.

Randolph-Seng, M. E., & Nielsen, M. E. (2007). Honesty: One effect of primed religious representations. The *International Journal for the Psychology of Religion, 17*(4), 303–315.

Rogers, S. (1992–1993). How a publicity blitz created the myth of subliminal advertising. *Public Relations Quarterly, 37*(4), 12–17.

Rogers, M., & Seiler, C. A. (1994). The answer is no: A national survey of advertising industry practitioners and their clients about whether they use subliminal advertising. *Journal of Advertising Research, 34*(2), 36–45.

Smith, K. H., & Rogers, M. (1994). Effectiveness of subliminal messages and television commercials: Two experiments. *Journal of Applied Psychology, 79*(6), 866–874.

Spangenberg, E. R., Obermiller, C., & Greenwald, A. G. (1992). A field test of subliminal self-help audiotapes: The power of expectancies. *Journal of Public Policy and Marketing, 11*(2), 26–36.

Staum, M. J., & Brotons, M. (1992). The influence of auditory subliminals on behavior: A series of investigations. *Journal of Music Therapy, 29*(3), 130–185.

Strahan, E. J., Spencer, S. J., & Zanna, M. P. (2002). Subliminal priming and persuasion: Striking while the iron is hot. *Journal of Experimental Social Psychology, 556–568.

Swart, L. C., & Morgan, C. L. (1992). Effects of subliminal backward-recorded messages on attitudes. *Perceptual and Motor Skills, 75*(3, Part 2), 1107–1113.

Trappey, C. (1996). A meta-analysis of consumer choice and subliminal advertising. *Psychology & Marketing, 13*(5), 517–530.

Van den Bussche, E., Van den Noortgate, W., & Reynvoet, B. (2009). Mechanisms of masked priming: A meta-analysis. *Psychological Bulletin, 135*(3), 452–477.

Vokey, J. R. (2002). Subliminal messages. In J. R. Vokey and S. W. Allen (Eds.), *Psychological sketches* (6th ed., pp. 223–246). Lethbridge, Alberta: Psyence Ink.

Vokey, J. R., & Read, J. D. (1985). Subliminal messages: Between the devil and the media. *American Psychologist, 40*(11), 1231–1239.

Weir, W. (1984, October 15). Another look at subliminal "facts." *Advertising Age, 46*, p. 6.

Wenner, L. A. (2004). On the ethics of product placement in media entertainment. In M. L. Galician (Ed.), *Handbook of product placement in the mass media: New strategies in marketing theory, practice, trends, and ethics* (pp. 101–132). New York: The Haworth Press.

Winkielman, P., Berridge, K. C., & Wilbarger, J. L. (2005). Unconscious affective reactions to masked happy versus angry faces influence consumption behavior and judgments of value. *Personality and Social Psychology Bulletin, 31*(1), 121–135.

Zanot, E. J., Pincus, D. J., & Lamp, E. J. (1983). Public perceptions of subliminal advertising. *Journal of Advertising, 12*, 39–45.

REFERENCES—NLP

Bandler, R., & Grinder, J. (1975). *The structure of magic: A book about language and therapy*. Palo Alto, CA: Science and Behavior Books.

Bandler, R., & Grinder, J. (1979). *Frogs into princes*. Moab, UT: Real People Press.

Corballis, M. C. (1999). Are we in our right minds? In S. Sala (Ed.), *Mind myths: Exploring popular assumptions about the mind and brain* (pp. 25–41).New York: John Wiley & Sons.

Dixon, P. N., Parr, G. D., Yarbrough, D., & Rathael, M. (1991). Neurolinguistic programming as a persuasive communication technique. *Journal of Social Psychology, 126*(4), 545–550.

Gow, K., Reupert, A., & Maybery, D. (2006). NLP in action: Theory and techniques in teaching and learning. In S. M. Hogan (Ed.), *Trends in learning research* (pp. 99–118). New York: Nova Science Publishers.

Gumm, W. B., Walker, M. K., & Day, H. D. (1982). Neurolinguistic programming: Method or myth? *Journal of Counseling Psychology, 29*(3), 327–330.

Heap, N. (2008). The validity of some early claims of neuro-linguistic programming. *Skeptical Intelligencer, 11*, 1–8.

Heap, M. (1988) Neurolinguistic programming—An interim verdict. In M. Heap (Ed.), *Hypnosis: Current clinical, experimental, and forensic practices* (pp. 268–280). London: Croom Helm.

Lankton, S. (1980). *Practical magic*. Cupertino, CA: Meta.

Miller, L. (1986, April). "Megabrain: new tools and techniques for brain growth." *Psychology Today, 20*, 70–72.

Sharpley, C.F. (1984). Predicate matching in NLP: A review of research on the preferred representational system. *Journal of Counseling Psychology, 31*(2), 238–248.

Sharpley, C. F. (1987). Research findings on neurolinguistic programming: Non supportive data or an untestable theory. *Journal of Counseling Psychology, 34(1)*, 103–107.

Thaler Singer, M., & Lalich, J. (1996). *Crazy therapies: What are they? Do they work?* San Francisco: Jossey Bass.

REFERENCES—MUSIC

Barongan, C., & Hall Nagayama, G. C. (1995). The influence of misogynous rap music on sexual aggression against women. *Psychology of Women Quarterly, 19*(2), 195–207.

Baxter, R. L., De Riemer, C., Landini, A., Leslie, L., & Singletary, M. W. (1985). A content analysis of music videos. *Journal of Broadcasting and Electronic Media, 29*, 333–340.

Beverland, M., Lim, E. A. C., Morrison, M., & Terziovski, M. (2006). In-store music and consumer-brand relationships: Relational transformation following experiences of (mis)fit. *Journal of Business Research, 59*, 982–989.

Boutcher, S. H., & Trenske, M. (1990). The effects of sensory deprivation and music on perceived exertion and affect during exercise. *Journal of Sport and Exercise Psychology, 12*(2), 167–176.

Brentar, J. E., Neuendorf, K. A., & Armstrong, G. B. (1994). Exposure effects and affective response to music. *Communication Monographs, 61*(2), 161–181.

Brown, J. D., & Campbell, K. (1986). Race and gender in music videos: The same beat but a different drummer. *Journal of Communication, 36*, 94–106.

Bruner, G. C., II (1990). Music, mood, and marketing. *Journal of Marketing, 54*, 94–104.

Chambers, G., & Morgan, J. (1992, September 12). Droppin' knowledge: A rap roundtable. *Essence*, pp. 83–120.

Chen M. J., Miller, B. A., Grube, J. W., & Waiters, E. D. (2006). Music, substance use, and aggression. *Journal of Studies on Alcohol, 67*(3), 373–381.

Connor, A. (2008, July 10). "Torture chamber music." *BBC Magazine*. Retrieved on July 10, 2008, from http://news.bbc.co.uk/2/hi/uk_news/magazine/7495175.stm.

Cummings, M. S., & Roy, A. (2002). Manifestations of Afrocentricity in rap music. *Howard Journal of Communications, 13*(1), 59–76.

Cummins, R. G. (2007). Selling music with sex: The content and effects of sex in music videos on viewer enjoyment. *Journal of Promotion Management, 13*, 95–109.

Dye, L. (1996, December 2). "Studying emotional chords of music." *Los Angeles Times*, p. D5.

Dyson, M. E. (1993). *Reflecting Black: African-American cultural criticism.* St. Paul: University of Minnesota Press.

Elliott, D., Carr, S., & Savage, D. (2004). Effects of motivational music on work output and affective responses during sub-maximal cycling of a standardized perceived intensity. *Journal of Sport Behavior, 27*(2), 134–147.

Emling, S. (2004, May 23). "Hip-hop fans: 'I'll have what he's having.'" *The Atlanta Journal Constitution,* p. 1A.

Garlin, F. V., & Owen, K. (2006). Setting the tone with the tune: A meta-analytic review of the effects of background music in retail settings. *Journal of Business Research, 59*, 755–764.

Gow, J. (1996). Reconsidering gender roles on MTV: Depictions in the most popular music videos of the early 1990s. *Communication Reports, 9*, 151–161.

Hansen, C. H., & Hansen, R. D. (1990). The influence of sex and violence on the appeal of rock music videos. *Communication Research, 17*, 212–234.

Hargreaves, D. J. (1984). The effects of repetition on liking for music. *Journal of Research in Music Education, 32*, 35–47.

Hirsch, L. (2007). Weaponizing classical music: Crime prevention and symbolic power in the age of repetition. *Journal of Popular Music Studies, 19*(4), 342–358.

Holt, D. (1996, April 24). "Fighting crime with violins." *Dallas Morning News*, p. 31A.

Kalis, P., & Neuendorf, K. A. (1989). Aggressive cue prominence and gender participation in MTV. *Journalism Quarterly, 66*(1), 148–154, 229.

Klein, B. (2008). In perfect harmony: Popular music and cola advertising. *Popular Music and Society, 31*(1), 1–20.

Lalwani, A. K., Lwin, M. O., & Ling, P. B. (2009). Does audiovisual congruency in advertisements increase persuasion? The role of cultural music and products. *Journal of Global Marketing, 22*(2), 139–153.

Lynch, T. (2003). Hip-hop's bad rap is undeserved. *Broadcasting & Cable, 133*(51), p. 20.

Mayfield, C., & Moss, S. (1989). Effects of music tempo on task performance. *Psychological Reports, 65*(3, Part 2), 1283–1290.

McGee, C. (2005, March 29). "Rappers in a battle of the brands." *Daily News*, p. 34.

Miller, L. K., & Schyb, M. (1989). Facilitation and interference by background music. *Journal of Music Therapy, 26*(1), 42–54.

Morrison, M., & Beverland, M. B. (2003). In search of the right in-store music. *Business Horizons, 46*(6), 77–82.

Morrison, P. (1996, April 26). "City brass hopes piped-in classics drive out loiterers." *Los Angeles Times*, p. A3.

North, A. C., Hargreaves, D. J., & McKendrick, J. (1999). The influence of in-store music on wine selections. *Journal of Applied Psychology, 84*(2), 271–276.

Oakes, S., & North, A. C. (2006). The impact of background musical tempo and timbre upon ad content recall and affective response. *Applied Cognitive Psychology, 20*, 505–520.

Obermiller, C. (1985). Varieties of mere exposure: The effects of processing style and repetition on affective response. *Journal of Consumer Research, 12*(1), 17–30.

Park, C. W., & Young, S. M. (1986). Consumer response to television commercials: The impact of involvement and background music on brand attitude formation. *Journal of Marketing Research, 23*, 11–24.

Parker-Pope, T. (2007, November 6). "For clues on teenage sex, experts look to hip-hop." New York Times, p. 5.

Peterson, D. L., & Pfost, K. S. (1989). Influence of rock videos on attitudes of violence against women. *Psychological Reports, 64*, 319–322.

Petty, R. E., & Cacioppo, J. T. (1986a). *Communication and persuasion: Central and peripheral routes to attitude change.* New York: Springer-Verlag.

Petty, R. E., & Cacioppo, J. T. (1986b). The elaboration likelihood model of persuasion. In L. Berkowitz (Ed.), *Advances in experimental social psychology* (Vol. 19, pp. 123–205). New York: Academic Press.

Reyna, C., Brandt, M., & Tendayi, G. V. (2009). Blame it on hip-hop: Anti rap attitudes as a proxy for prejudice. *Group Processes Intergroup Relations, 12*(3), 361–380.

Schemer, C., Matthes, J., Wirth, W., & Textor, S. (2008). Does "passing the Courvoisier" always pay off? Positive and negative evaluative conditioning effects of brand placements in music videos. *Psychology & Marketing, 25*(10), 923–943.

Seidman, S. A. (1992). An investigation of sex-role stereotyping in music videos. *Journal of Broadcasting and Electronic Media, 36*, 209–216.

Sherman, B. L., & Dominick, J. R. (1986). Violence and sex in music videos: TV and rock n' roll. *Journal of Communication, 36*, 79–93.

Tiddle, C. (1996, December 2). "Tales from 'hood need to be told." *Los Angeles Times*, p. F3 "Tough talk on entertainment." (1995, June 12). *Time*, pp. 32–33.

Vincent, R. C. (1989). Clio's consciousness raised? Portrayal of women in rock videos, re-examined. *Journalism Quarterly, 66,* 155–160.

Wang, M-W, & Chang, C. (2004). The mere exposure effect and recognition memory. *Cognition and Emotion, 18*(8), 11055–1078.

Weisenthal, D. L., Hennessy, D. A., & Totten, B. (2003). The influence of music on mild driver aggression. *Transportation Research, Part F: Traffic Psychology and Behaviour, 6*(2),125–134.

Will.i.am. (2008). "Yes we can" music video. Retrieved on January 5, 2009, from www.youtube.com/watch?v=jjXyqcx-mYY.

Yalch, R. F. (1991). Memory in a jingle jungle: Music as a mnemonic device in communicating advertising slogans. *Journal of Applied Psychology, 76,* 268–275.

Zajonc, R. B. (1968). Attitudinal effects of mere exposure. *Journal of Personality and Social Psychology Monograph Supplement, 9*(2, Pt. 2), 1–28.

REFERENCES—SMELL

Baron, R. A. (1983). "The sweet smell of success?" The impact of pleasant artificial scents (perfume and cologne) on evaluations of job applicants. *Journal of Applied Psychology, 68,* 709–713.

Baron, R. A. (1997). The sweet smell of . . . helping: Effects of pleasant ambient fragrance on prosocial behavior in shopping malls. *Personality and Social Psychology Bulletin, 23,* 498–503.

Baron, R. A., & Bronfen, M. I. (1994). A whiff of reality: Empirical evidence concerning the effects of pleasant fragrances on work-related behavior. *Journal of Applied Social Psychology, 24*(13), 1179–1203.

Baron, R. A., & Kalsher, M. J. (1998). Effects of a pleasant ambient fragrance on simulated driving performance: The sweet smell of . . . safety? *Environment & Behavior, 30*(4), 532–552.

Bosmans, A. (2006). Scents and sensibility: When do (in)congruent ambient scents influence product evaluations? *Journal of Marketing, 70*(3), 32–43.

Cann, A., & Ross, D. A. (1989). Olfactory stimuli as context cues in human memory. *American Journal of Psychology, 102,* 91–102.

Caplan, J. (2006, October 16). "Scents and sensibility." *Time, 168*(16), 66–67.

Hanisch, E. (1982). The calming effect of fragrances and associated remembrances. *drom Report* "The nose: Part 2," pp. 18–19.

Hirsch, A. R. (1995). Effects of ambient odors on slot machine usage in a Las Vegas casino. *Psychology and Marketing, 12*(7), 585–594.

Hoppough, S. (2006, October 2). "What's that smell?" *Forbes, 178*(6), 76.

Knasko, S. C. (1989). Ambient odor and shopping behavior. *Chemical Senses, 14,* 718.

Knasko, S. C. (1992). Viewing time and liking of slides in the presence of congruent and incongruent odors. *Chemical Senses, 17,* 652.

Knasko, S. C. (1993). Lingering time in a museum in the presence of congruent and incongruent odors. *Chemical Senses, 14,* 718.

Manne, S. L., & Redd, W. H. (1993). *Fragrance administration to reduce patient anxiety during magnetic resonance imaging in cancer diagnostic work-up.* Final Report to the Olfactory Research Fund.

Miller, C. (1991). Research reveals how marketers can win by a nose. *Marketing News, 25,* [Lexis-Nexis].

Redd, W. H., & Manne, S. L. (1991). *Fragrance administration to reduce patient anxiety during magnetic resonance imaging in cancer diagnostic work-up.* Report to the Fragrance Research Fund (now the Olfactory Research Fund).

Rotten, J. (1983). Affective and cognitive consequences of malodorous pollution. *Basic and Applied Social Psychology, 38,* 213–228.

Schiffman, S. S. (1993a). The effect of fragrance on the mood of women at mid-life. *The Aroma-Chology Review, 2*(1), 1–5.

Schiffman, S. S. (1993b). *The effect of pleasant odor: On mood of males at mid-life.* Final Report to the Olfactory Research Fund.

Stolberg, S. (1994, June 29). "Trying to make sense of smell." *Los Angeles Times,* pp. A1, A20, A21.

Sugano, H., & Sato, H. (1991). Psychophysiological studies of fragrance. *Chemical Senses, 16,* 183–184.

Teerling, A., Nixdorf, R. R., & Koster, E. P. (1992). The effect of ambient odours on shopping behavior. *Chemical Senses, 17,* 886.

Warm, J. S., Parasuraman, R., & Dember, W. N. (1990). *Effects of periodic olfactory stimulation on visual sustained attention in young and older adults.* Progress Report No. 4 to the Fragrance Research Fund (now the Olfactory Research Fund).

CHAPTER 16

The Ethics of Persuasion

"The most dangerous animal in the world," it has been said, "is a freshman with one semester of psychology." If that is true, then the second most dangerous animal must surely be a freshman with one persuasion class under his or her belt. If you give a child a toy hammer, the child will invariably find that every object he or she encounters is in need of pounding (Kaplan, 1964). In much the same vein, it is not uncommon for a student who has completed a course in persuasion to think that every communication encounter requires a test of her or his newfound skills. At best, this can be annoying to the recipients of the influence attempts. At worst, it can damage or destroy relationships if the persuader is perceived as being unethical. Like a hammer, persuasion is a useful tool. But one shouldn't use it to pound on others.

For this reason and others, we consider in this chapter the ethics of influence attempts. Although this is the last chapter of the text, it is by no means the least important. We decided to place this chapter at the end so that we could discuss ethical concerns raised throughout the book. In this chapter we attempt to ask and answer a number of ethical questions and to provide guidelines, albeit tentative ones, to determine if and when persuasion is ethically defensible.

We make no bones about the fact that we've tried to teach you how to become a more effective persuader, as well as a more discriminating consumer of persuasive messages. Hence, we feel morally obliged to offer some prescriptions and proscriptions on the ethical uses of persuasion. Before you go out and attempt to wield your persuasive skills on unsuspecting roommates, absent-minded professors, unwitting family members, unfortunate co-workers, or hapless strangers, we want to make sure you understand the importance of respecting others' dignity, of showing concern for others' welfare, and, as they say in comic books, "of using your powers for good instead of evil." Quite seriously, we believe that the power to persuade carries with it a corresponding duty to persuade ethically. We don't claim to have a "corner" on the ethics market. Feel free to disagree with any of our guidelines, as you choose. Your time will be well spent thinking through the bases for your own ethical standards and in coming to terms with what you consider to be moral and immoral influence attempts.

IS PERSUASION IN GENERAL UNETHICAL?

A frequent charge leveled against persuasion is that it is unethical. Some people equate persuasion with manipulation and see it as a one-sided approach to communication. Communication, they argue, should emphasize cooperation, trust, and shared agreement.

We believe this view of communication and human relationships is noble but overly ideal-istic. What happens when people don't agree? What happens when their goals contradict? Enter the need for persuasion. Persuasion is what people rely on when things aren't "hunky dory" or "peachy keen." Persuasion is what people turn to when their needs haven't been met or their relationships are less than ideal.

We argued in the first chapter that persuasion is not a dirty word. But persuasion *is* used to do the "dirty work" of convincing others when disagreements develop. Attempts at convincing others, however, are not necessarily one-sided. Persuasion can be, and often is, two-sided. Persuasion can, and often does, result in mutually satisfactory solutions. Persuasion is not the antithesis of cooperation. Persuasion can be based on trust and mutual respect. In a relationship based on equality, for example, each party is free to influence the other.

As we noted in Chapter 1, persuasion performs a number of positive, prosocial functions. For example, persuasion is used to increase public awareness about a variety of social problems such as spousal abuse, homelessness, and HIV transmission. And like it or not, persuasion is here to stay. To the extent that some persuaders are unethical, it makes even more sense to learn how unethical influence attempts work and why they succeed.

We don't deny that persuasion can be used in manipulative ways. Persuasion is a tool. Tools can be misused. In such cases, however, one should blame the tool's user, not the tool. By way of analogy, when someone uses the English language to belittle or demean another person, no one suggests we should do away with language. Why then, when persuasion is used unethically, do people blame persuasion rather than the per-suader? Granted, some persuasive tools, such as fear appeals, hold greater potential for abuse, in the same way that a saw is more dangerous than a pair of pliers. Stronger safe-guards need to be taken when using such persuasive tools, even when their use is for the receiver's own good.

THE MOTIVES COLOR THE MEANS

Consistent with our tool analogy, James McCroskey has commented that "the means of persuasion themselves are ethically neutral" (McCroskey, 1972, p. 269). Contrasting this view, Jacksa and Pritchard (1994) adopt the position that "virtually any act of communica-tion can be seen from a moral point of view" (p. 12). We concede that ethics and persua-sion are closely intertwined. We maintain, however, that the moral quality of an influence attempt is derived primarily from the motives or ends of the persuader, and only secondar-ily from the means of persuasion that are employed. In our view, the means of persuasion take on the moral character of the persuader's ends.

To illustrate our view, imagine that three persuaders each employ one of three strate-gies of influence: deception, fear appeals, or ingratiation. Is it possible to determine which persuader is the most ethical or least ethical, merely by knowing the strategy each employs? We think not. We don't see how an ethical evaluation of the strategies could be made without any knowledge of the purposes for which the strategies would be used. In Table 16.1, we list these three strategies (in column 1), along with two contrasting sets of

The Motives Color the Means. In our view, a persuader's motives color the means of persuasion that are used, as these examples illustrate.		**TABLE 16.1**
Strategy or Means	**"Good" Motive or End**	**"Evil" Motive or End**
Use of deception	Trying to conceal a surprise birthday party from the person in whose honor the party is being given	Trying to swindle an elderly person out of his or her life savings
Use of fear appeals	Trying to convince a child never to accept a ride from a stranger	Threatening to demote an employee for refusing a superior's sexual advances
Use of ingratiation	Trying to cheer up a friend who is depressed about a poor grade on a test	Lavishing attention on a dying relative in order to inherit the relative's money

motives (in columns 2 and 3). Notice that when paired with the first set of "good" motives, the use of the strategies appears justified. However, when paired with the second set of "evil" motives, the strategies appear highly unjustified.

Thus, in our view, the ethical quality of a persuader's motives tends to "rub off" on the persuasive strategy employed. The strategy itself is essentially neutral or amoral, until such time as it is paired with a particular motive or end. At that point, the entire influence attempt (motive and strategy) takes on a moral/immoral dimension.

To take our point one step further, even coercion can be defended as a justifiable means of achieving certain ends (remember that, according to our model, coercion represents a "borderline" case of persuasion). A child, for example, might be forced to get a vaccination by her or his parents. Psychotic or delusional persons might be forcibly restrained to prevent them from harming themselves or others. Or consider the Jack Bauer "ticking bomb" scenario: A terrorist group announces it will set off a "dirty" bomb in a major city within 24 hours. The ensuing radiation will likely kill thousands of people. Government agents have caught one of the conspirators, who refuses to talk. If the agents torture the terrorist, however, they are fairly confident they can learn the bomb's location and disarm it. Is it morally permissible for the agents to extract the information they need through torture to save thousands of lives? Does it matter how many people would be killed (100, 1000, 10,000)? Does it matter how confident the government agents are that torture will work (10 percent, 50 percent, 90 percent)?

ETHICS, CULTURE, AND THE ISSUE OF CENTRAL VERSUS PERIPHERAL PROCESSING

We readily admit that some persuasive strategies may seem more ethically desirable than others. For example, the use of reasoned argument might seem more ethically justifiable than the use of flattery or charm. The use of facts and statistics might appear more defensible than the use of emotional appeals. This highlights a general preference among Western societies for logical, rational thought, consistent with what Petty and Cacioppo (1986) call central processing. You may recall from our discussion of the elaboration likelihood model in Chapter 2 that the central route to persuasion involves actively thinking about issues, reflecting on information, and scrutinizing the content of messages. The peripheral route, however, is based on factors such as source credibility, imagery, or social cues. In U.S. culture, the central route is generally the preferred route for persuasion.

Not all cultures place the same emphasis, however, on rational, linear thinking. Other cultures value different ways of knowing, favor other means of gaining adherence to ideas, and prefer other methods of securing behavioral compliance. As one example, some Asian cultures emphasize the importance of fitting in, of conforming to group norms, and of not "rocking the boat." In such cultures, greater emphasis tends to be placed on *indirect* strategies of influence (such as hinting or stressing the importance of following group norms) than on *direct* strategies (arguing, open disagreement). The preference for indirect strategies reflects the importance of such cultural values as avoiding confrontation and preventing the loss of face (Ting-Toomey, 1994, 1998; Ting-Toomey & Kurogi, 1998; Wiseman et al., 1995).

Within Western culture there are also exceptions to the general preference for "rational" persuasion. A person who comes across as being overly logical or emotionless, such as the character Mr. Spock of *Star Trek* fame, may be viewed as "cold," "calculating," or "heartless." The ability to display compassion, convey empathy, and respond to the entreaties of others based on these same emotions is considered a desirable quality. Thus, even though it may seem that some forms of influence are more ethically defensible than others, this depends to some extent on cultural and situational factors.

ETHICAL QUESTIONS THAT CAN'T BE ANSWERED THROUGH THE STUDY OF PERSUASION

We've argued that the moral character of a persuasive act is derived primarily from the persuader's motives. Persuasion research, however, tends to focus almost exclusively on the means of persuasion (strategies and tactics) rather than on the motives of persuaders. For this reason, persuasion research is ill-equipped to answer questions about what are good or evil ends. Take any current social controversy, for example: abortion, assisted suicide, gay marriage, and so forth. The study of persuasion cannot tell a persuader what side of the controversy to be on. The study of persuasion can't enlighten persuasion researchers as to what causes are good or bad or what values are right or wrong. Persuasion researchers tend to defer to moral philosophers, religious leaders, the judicial system, and other ethical arbiters to make such determinations.

As far as specific strategies are concerned, many professional organizations have established codes of ethics. Newspaper journalists, television news anchors, and radio commentators, for example, are bound by codes of conduct established by their national organizations or government agencies. A print journalist, for instance, should not publish a story without verifying the information via two independent sources. Even the Word of Mouth Marketing Association (WOMMA) has adopted a code of ethics (see http://womma.org/ethics). On the Web, however, anything goes. There are no clear-cut guidelines. A blogger can post anything she or he wants. Legislation regarding hate speech and harassment on the Web is evolving.

Perhaps persuasion researchers should give greater consideration to the possible uses of the strategies and tactics they are busy investigating. Bear in mind, though, that it is difficult for a researcher to know how a particular tool of influence will be used. If a persuasive tool can be used for good *or* evil ends, what is a persuasion researcher to do? In Box 16.1, we identify some well-known approaches to ethics that you might study in a course on ethics. In practice, individuals tend to follow a combination of the approaches identified in Box 16.1, making most of us ethical relativists. A complete discussion of the field of ethics and moral philosophy is beyond the scope of this text. Fortunately, several excellent works are available if you wish to learn more about ethics and communication (Christians, Rotzoll, & Fackler, 1991; Jacksa & Pritchard, 1994;

Approaches to Ethics	BOX 16.1

Ends versus means: An ethical controversy centering on whether the means or method of influence is justified by the desirability of the outcome. Can a persuasive outcome be so good or desirable that the use of force or coercion is justified to achieve it?

Consequentialism/teleological ethics: An ethical approach emphasizing consequences or outcomes. A persuader should weigh the benefits and drawbacks of his or her actions. Those actions that produce the greatest balance of good over bad are ethical.

Deontological systems/duty ethics: An ethical approach that focuses on moral imperatives, rather than specific consequences. A person has a duty to adhere to rules of moral conduct. One may be morally obliged to take some actions, regardless of their consequences.

Amoralism (or Machiavellianism): This ethical approach authorizes whatever a persuader can get away with, constrained only by laws, or fear of social ostracism. The self-interest of the persuader is all that matters; others better watch out for themselves. Suckers deserve what they get. They should learn from their mistakes.

Situational ethics/relativism: This ethical approach maintains there are no moral absolutes. There are no ethical maxims. It isn't possible to write a moral code that applies to all cultures, persons, times, and places. There are always exceptions to every rule. There can be good or bad forms of persuasion, but whether they are good or bad depends on the situation, the parties involved, the nature of the issue, and other related factors.

Universalism: This ethical approach maintains that there are universal, immutable "do's" and "don'ts." Morals and values can be ordered into enduring codes of conduct. Some actions are right or wrong for all people, places, and times. For example, torture is always wrong. Certain universal human rights must be honored. There are "hard" and "soft" versions of universalism, meaning that some perspectives are more absolute than others.

Egalitarianism (also known as the "Golden Rule"): This approach to ethics involves doing unto others as you would have them do unto you. Treat other people as you would have them treat you. A more modern derivative of this principle is, "What goes around comes around."

Free market ethics: This ethical approach is based on the metaphor of the free market or capitalism: *caveat emptor*, let the buyer beware. There should be little or no prior restraint on persuasive messages. This approach places greater responsibility on receivers to critically evaluate persuasive messages.

Utilitarianism (John Stuart Mill): This is a teleological approach, based on the greatest good for the greatest number of people. The *Star Trek* version of this principle involves balancing "The needs of the many with the needs of the one."

Virtue ethics: This perspective focuses on the character of the person, as opposed to specific moral rules or moral actions. A person should strive to be virtuous, to have good character. Instead of relying on a list of do's and don'ts, one should ask oneself, "What kind of person to I want to be?"

Johannesen, 1983; Johannesen, Thayer, & Hardt, 1979; Nilsen, 1966; Rivers, Christians, & Schramm, 1980).

The inability of persuasion researchers to distinguish good from bad applications of persuasion is similar to the situation facing other researchers in other fields. Consider the controversy surrounding the cloning of human embryos. The topic of cloning is fraught with moral implications. Scientists conducting this sort of research are aware that their research has ethical overtones. For the most part, however, they tend to focus on scientific questions related to cloning, as opposed to moral questions. After all, neither politicians nor clergy agree on the answers to the moral questions.

Persuasion researchers are similar to other researchers in this respect: They are simply interested in learning more about how persuasion works. Their focus is not on whether a particular strategy or tactic should be used. Nor is their focus on what causes should or should not be furthered using persuasion. We don't deny that persuasion researchers should take heed of the ethical implications of the strategies and tactics they are investigating. We merely wish to point out that persuasion researchers are more interested in pursuing knowledge for its own sake than on discovering techniques for mind control. We readily admit, however, that like Dr. Frankenstein in Mary Shelley's novel, persuasion researchers—and all other researchers for that matter—are ethically responsible for the knowledge they uncover and pass along.

OUR APPROACH: CHARACTERISTICS OF ETHICAL INFLUENCE

The authors claim no special expertise in the field of ethics. We certainly don't possess the moral credentials of a Mother Teresa or the Dalai Lama. We feel obliged, nonetheless, to offer our own set of guidelines and recommendations for ethical persuasion. Just as we believe the power to persuade entails a responsibility to persuade ethically, we also believe that teaching others how to persuade entails an obligation to teach them how to do so ethically. Our views don't emanate from a single ethical perspective, so we can probably best be described as situationalistic or relativistic in our approach (see Box 16.1). We don't expect you to accept our advice as gospel. But we do hope you'll think about our guidelines and recommendations carefully. We believe that the more you think about the ethical dimensions involved in persuasion, the more conscientious you will tend to be as a persuader.

Ethics and Our Model of Persuasion

Recall that in our model of persuasion (see Chapter 2), we distinguished between pure and borderline cases of persuasion. Recall also from our model that there are five criteria that distinguish pure cases of persuasion from borderline cases. Pure cases of persuasion are those that are intentional; they occur with the receiver's conscious awareness, involve free choice on the part of the receiver, take place through language or symbolic action, and involve two or more persons. We believe the first four of these criteria hold important ethical implications for persuaders.

Intentionality

A number of scholars subscribe to the view that only intentional influence attempts count as persuasion. From an ethical standpoint, however, this view is problematic. We maintain that such a view lets persuaders "off the hook" for the unintended consequences of their persuasion. A persuader whose efforts result in harmful, unforeseen consequences can avoid responsibility by saying, "That's not what I intended." A persuader whose influence attempts reach the wrong audience can say, "That's not where I was aiming." Studies have shown that unintended messages, such as an overheard ethnic slur, can damage a person's reputation in the eyes of other persons (Greenberg & Pyszczynski, 1985; Kirkland, Greenberg, & Pyszczynski, 1987). Thus, we think persuaders should be held accountable for the unintended consequences of their persuasion.

Conscious Awareness

Pure cases of persuasion, according to our model, occur with the conscious awareness of the participants. Borderline cases of persuasion, however, require no such realization on the part of the participants. We maintain that persuasion that takes place with the conscious awareness of all the parties involved is far more ethical than persuasion that does not. If a person knows he or she is the target of an influence attempt, he or she can take active steps to resist the attempt or counter with an attempt of his or her own.

Free Choice/Free Will

Pure cases of persuasion, according to our model, are those that allow participants to make free, informed decisions about whether they wish to comply with persuasive messages. Borderline cases of persuasion, however, involve coercion in varying degrees. We believe, quite obviously, that persuasive attempts that allow persons to make free choices are ethically superior to those that do not. Free choice includes the ability to question others' influence attempts, to counter with influence attempts of one's own, and to resist complying with others' attempts. As a general rule, we believe the more freedom one has to say "No," the more ethical a given influence attempt is. This also explains why conscious awareness, discussed previously, is an important ingredient in ethical persuasion. A person cannot *choose* to comply with an influence attempt if the person is unaware he or she is the target of an influence attempt.

Language and Symbolic Action

According to our model, pure cases of persuasion center around the use of language (the spoken or printed word) and symbolic actions (protest marches, sit-ins, etc.). Borderline cases of persuasion include persuasion via nonverbal or behavioral means. Using physical attractiveness or behavioral modification to alter another's behavior would both constitute instances of borderline persuasion. We believe that persuasion that takes place through language or symbol usage is generally more ethical than persuasion via nonverbal or behavioral means. Our preference for the former is based on the fact that language-based influence attempts are generally more easily recognized and more readily understood. Nonverbal appeals, however, are less recognizable as persuasive attempts.

Of course, it is possible for persuaders to let receivers know that they will be the targets of nonverbal influence attempts or behavioral modification techniques. Sit-ins and protest marches, for example, are fairly obvious instances of nonverbal persuasion. If the recipient is made aware that nonverbal or behavioral strategies will be employed, we see little ethical difference between language-based and non-language-based persuasion.

Persuaders as Lovers

In a widely acclaimed essay, Wayne Brockriede (1974) suggested that arguers can be classified into three different types, based on their regard for the other person. "Seducers," he argued, used trickery, deceit, charm, flattery, and beguilement to achieve their ends. Seducers do not view others as equals but as unwitting victims. "Rapists," the second category identified by Brockriede, use threats, force, and coercion in an effort to win their arguments. They resort to browbeating, personal attacks, threats, and ultimatums to get their way. Like seducers, rapists view others as inferior. Others are treated as objects rather than equals. "Lovers," the third of Brockriede's categories, respect one another's dignity and base their relationships on equality. They don't treat each other as victims or objects but rather as partners. They are open and receptive to one another's arguments and look for mutually satisfactory solutions to their differences.

We believe Brockriede's characterization of these three styles of argument applies equally well to persuasive encounters. We draw upon and extend his approach here by ascribing what we believe to be three essential attributes or qualities of "persuaders as lovers." The first quality is *respect*. Ethical influence attempts tend to reaffirm the other person's sense of self-worth. Persuaders who use ethical strategies and tactics tend to demonstrate respect for one another's dignity. In contrast, unethical influence attempts tend to express disdain for others. The target of an unethical influence attempt is viewed as a "mark," a "sucker," or a "patsy."

The second quality is *equality*. Influence attempts are most ethical when the parties enjoy equal status in a relationship. This is because in unequal relationships, status or power differences are more likely—whether intentionally or unintentionally—to impinge on the choice-making ability of the lower-status person. The person enjoying more status or power may find it difficult to resist using "carrots" or "sticks" to gain compliance. The person occupying the lower-status position may find it difficult to believe that the person with higher status will not resort to rewards or punishments.

We believe ethical influence attempts are possible even when there are power disparities, but only if the more powerful party allows communication to take place, on an equal footing. In organizational communication, for example, the very concepts of "downward" and "upward" communication suggest inequality. To minimize such inequality, a superior could make it clear that he or she was suggesting, not ordering. The superior also would have to be open to having her or his mind changed as well. These same requirements—suggesting, not ordering and remaining open to influence—would apply to parental influence as well.

The third quality is *tolerance*. Each party to a persuasive encounter must be patient with the other, giving the other a chance to make his or her case. Each party should also be open to the other's point of view, making persuasion a two-way street. If a person wishes to influence another, we maintain that he or she also must be willing to be influenced. Turn-taking plays an important role in this process. Persuaders need to be willing to hear one another out. A person who enters a persuasive encounter with the mind-set, "I will per-suade, but I will not be persuaded," is not displaying tolerance for the other person or the other person's point of view. Taken together, we believe that these three qualities have the potential to make persuasive encounters more ethical and more pleasant.

Bunglers, Smugglers, and Sleuths

Robert Cialdini, whom many consider to be the father of modern compliance-gaining research, suggests that persuaders can be categorized into three different types (Cialdini, 1999). *Bunglers,* the first type, squander their prospects for influence by selecting ineffec-tive strategies and tactics. As the name implies, they bungle their chances for success. Bunglers aren't so much unethical as they are inept. *Smugglers,* the second type, know exactly what they are doing but rely on unethical influence tactics. Smugglers, for exam-ple, wouldn't hesitate to use deception as a compliance-gaining technique if they thought it would produce immediate results. *Sleuths,* the third type, are more knowledgeable about how influence works than bunglers, and they are more ethical in their choice of strategies and tactics than smugglers. According to Cialdini, sleuths function like detec-tives who study a persuasive situation, searching for clues about the most ethical and effective means of influence. For Cialdini, then, the sleuth is the ideal persuader. He maintains that both individuals and groups (marketers, advertisers, corporations) should be sleuth-like in their influence attempts. The problem, he says, is that persuaders don't always recognize the long-term advantages of sleuth-like influence. "The systematic use of misleading influence tactics," he maintains, "ultimately becomes a psychologically and financially self-damaging process" (Cialdini, 1999, p. 94). For example, the owner of a car lot who encourages the salespeople to use ethically suspect tactics to sell cars may sell a few more cars in the short run. In the long run, however, employee morale will suffer, repeat business will taper off, and eventually, the "bottom line" will suffer. If not for the sake of the persuadee, then, Cialdini suggests that ethical influence is ultimately in the persuader's best interest as well.

ETHICAL ISSUES ARISING FROM PREVIOUS CHAPTERS

Having offered some of our own guidelines for ethical persuasion, we now turn our atten-tion to some of the ethical issues introduced elsewhere in this text. A number of ethical questions regarding persuasive strategies and tactics emanate from the preceding chapters. Here we examine some of those key questions and explore possible answers.

Ethics and Credibility

A number of ethical questions center around the use of source credibility as a tool for per-suasion (see Chapter 4). Among the key questions on the ethical uses of credibility are the following:

1. Is it unethical for a celebrity endorser to promote a product or service he or she does not actually use or about which he or she lacks expertise?

2. Does the use of authority become an abuse of authority if receivers place too much faith or reliance in a particular source? For example, can a TV evangelist hold too much sway over his or her followers, thereby clouding their judgment and independent thinking?

When celebrities endorse products they don't actually use, the problem tends to be self-correcting. The celebrity can sued for breach of contract. This happened to Charlize Theron, an endorser for Raymond Weil watches, when she was photographed in public wearing another brand. Jessica Simpson and Teri Hatcher were sued for similar infractions. Nevertheless, some endorsements may be unpaid and unintentional. Barack Obama's reliance on his BlackBerry has boosted sales of that brand. Some say his endorsement would be worth $50 million if he were being paid (Clifford, 2009).

Because credibility tends to function as a peripheral cue, a reliance on credibility as the principal means of persuasion tends to short-circuit thoughtful deliberation. We believe that persuasive appeals that emphasize central processing are generally superior to those that emphasize peripheral processing. The former are ethically preferable, we believe, because they enable receivers to analyze messages, scrutinize evidence, and generally think for themselves.

We believe that a reliance on source credibility, at the expense of thoughtful reflection, is ethically suspect. In cases where credibility is used to enhance the persuasiveness of a message, we believe a qualified source should be used. By "qualified," we mean a source who possesses expertise in the area in which she or he is offering advice or making recommendations. Tiger Woods, for example, knows a great deal about golf, so his endorsement of a brand of golf clubs would be meaningful. He's not an expert on vacuums, however, so his recommendation of a brand of vacuum cleaner would possess no more validity than that of the average person.

Ethics and Communicator Characteristics

We noted in Chapter 5 that some receivers are particularly vulnerable to influence attempts. Young children, for example, have difficulty distinguishing what toys featured in television commercials can and cannot do. Patients with terminal illnesses are highly vulnerable to hucksters peddling "miracle" cures. Elderly citizens, some of whose mental faculties are diminished, are highly susceptible to scams perpetrated by con artists. And some new immigrants are uniquely vulnerable, because of their naiveté, language barriers, or both. Concerns such as these invite several ethical questions on persuasion aimed at specialized audiences:

1. What ethical safeguards should be followed when attempting to persuade children?
2. What ethical responsibilities does a persuader have when attempting to persuade highly vulnerable audiences?

With respect to the first question, we strongly believe that special care must be taken when targeting children. Children are highly impressionable and, unfortunately, highly gullible. They often fail to grasp the full meaning of messages or disclaimers attached to messages. Although a variety of private and public agencies already regulate mass media messages aimed at children, advertisers have been criticized for a number of unfair practices. As Treise, Weigold, Conna, and Garrison (1994) commented:

> Most notable of these criticisms include the arguments that advertising to children promotes the use of products, such as sweets, that are harmful to children (Gore, 1989); manipulates and disappoints children with exaggerated claims; creates conflicts with parents over purchases; has the potential to influence children to experiment with alcoholic beverages and/or drugs (Atkin, 1987); and creates confusion over product and commercial distinctions (Kunkel, 1988; Englehardt, 1987). (p. 60)

In addition to following those strictures that are already in place, we would advise those seeking to influence youngsters to follow three basic guidelines. First, they should ensure that they have a parent or legal guardian's permission before attempting any persuasion. For example, before you decide to convince the next-door neighbor's child that Santa Claus and the Easter Bunny are myths, check with the parent(s) first. Persuading without such permission not only usurps parental autonomy but invites lawsuits as well. Second, they should communicate using words and concepts that children can understand. Persuasive messages should be geared to the developmental level of the age group being targeted. Third, they should make sure they have the children's best interests at heart. Whose interest was R. J. Reynolds promoting by using the now-discontinued "Joe Camel" campaign? Critics charged that the use of the cartoonlike character was a transparent attempt to attract underage smokers (Bromberg, 1990). In our view, public awareness messages that target children for their sake (e.g., antidrug spots or stranger-danger messages) are less ethically suspect than for-profit advertisements that target children in order to make money.

With respect to the second question, there are clearly cases in which vulnerable groups are targeted by persuaders. As just one example, people who live in inner-city areas are subjected to more billboards promoting cigarettes and alcohol than people who live in more affluent, suburban areas. The poorer the neighborhood, the more billboards (Kwate & Lee, 2006).

We believe that many of the concerns involving highly vulnerable groups or individuals can be allayed by adhering to the aforementioned values of mutual respect, relational equality, and mutual tolerance. Part of the task of persuading vulnerable receivers involves displaying interpersonal or intercultural sensitivity. This includes the ability to empathize with others' feelings and points of view. Part of the task also involves avoiding the temptation to prey on others' fears, weaknesses, or vulnerabilities. The motto *caveat emptor* ("let the buyer beware") may make sense when one is dealing with fully functioning, informed consumers. When applied to vulnerable groups, however, the motto simply becomes an excuse for taking advantage.

Ethics and Deception

The study of deception and deception detection constitutes one of the most ethically sensitive areas of persuasion research. A number of ethical issues were addressed in Chapter 12. Of these, one overriding question will be reexamined here:

> Is deception ever justified? Or, stated somewhat differently, is honesty always the best policy?

Although some may believe that lying is always wrong, we believe that there are numerous situations in which telling "white lies" is beneficial for relationships. Such social rituals as complimenting another's clothing, praising a dinner host's cooking, or telling the host of a party you had a good time seem like fairly harmless, innocuous uses of deception to us. Even where candor is called for, we believe there is an important difference between being honest and being *brutally* honest.

Our view is that although deception is sometimes socially justified, one should examine the motives of the persuader by asking, "In whose interest is the lie being perpetrated?" Self-serving lies, we believe, are the least ethical. Lies told for the benefit of another, we maintain, are the most ethical. Recent research suggests that others hold this view as well. A study by Seiter, Bruschke, and Bai (2002), for example, asked people from China and the United States to rate the acceptability of various types of lies. Participants from both cultures tended to agree: They rated lies told for selfish reasons as unacceptable and lies told to benefit others as generally acceptable. In assessing the ethical merits of deception, one should also keep in mind that outright falsehoods and misrepresentations constitute only one type of deception. Deception can also include withholding information or purposeful ambiguity. The latter types of deception, we suggest, are more ethically defensible than "bald-faced" lies. A person might be "diplomatic," for example, to spare another the pain or loss of face that being blunt might cause. Both withholding of information and purposeful ambiguity thus can be used to benefit another.

A final note on the "honesty is the best policy" approach is that it works only if some of the preceding conditions for ethical persuasion exist—for example, if there is mutual respect, a relationship based on equality, and tolerance for one another's views. If these conditions do not exist, then being honest may simply result in the honest person being fired, punished, or ridiculed.

Ethics of Using Threats as a Compliance-Gaining Strategy

In Chapter 11 we discussed a number of strategies and tactics related to compliance gaining. Among the strategies identified were threats of punishment (Marwell & Schmitt, 1967). As a general rule, studies have shown that using threats achieves greater compliance than not using them (Gass & Canary, 1988; Heisler, 1974; Nevin & Ford, 1976; Tittle & Rowe, 1973). Their effectiveness notwithstanding, however, there are serious ethical questions regarding the use of threats. Hence, we focus here on the ethics of using threats as a means of persuasion:

> Is the use of threats of punishment ever ethically justifiable and, if so, under what circumstances?

Every attempt to persuade involves ethical questions. To a greater extent than with other influence strategies, however, we believe the use of threats should raise red flags in the persuader's mind. There are numerous reasons for this. First, we believe threats are unethical inasmuch as their effectiveness hinges on creating a state of psychological distress in receivers. Second, threats tend to be exploitative of power or status differences in relationships. As we noted previously, persuasion is more ethically defensible when it is based on a relationship of equality. Third, issuing and carrying out threats tends to diminish the morale and self-esteem of the recipient. Fourth, a reliance on threats is damaging and destructive to relationships. In the long run threats do more harm than good. Fifth, the use of threats can foster resentment or trigger aggression toward the threatener. If you rely on threats, you'd better watch your back! Sixth, threats must be carried out from time to time, an unpleasant prospect for both the threatener and the recipient. Seventh, the threatener is modeling a negative form of behavior for others to follow, thereby teaching others to rely on threats as well. Can you tell we're not too fond of threats?

When, if ever, then, should a persuader use threats? Our advice is that threats, although sometimes unavoidable, should never be the strategy of first resort. They should be used only when prosocial alternatives are unavailable or have failed and only when they are clearly in the best interests of the receiver or society. As an illustration, imagine that a spouse or an intimate partner is destroying himself or herself through alcohol abuse. The partner has pleaded with him or her to join Alcoholics Anonymous or to seek some other form of help, all to no avail. We believe that the partner would be justified in threatening, "I'm leaving you if you don't get help." Making such a threat, and following through on it if necessary, might well be in the long-term interests of both people.

The preceding example notwithstanding, a reliance on threats produces so many undesirable social consequences that we think their use is rarely justified. A persuader who is contemplating the use of threats should, therefore, ask him- or herself if that is the only way to achieve an objective and if the objective is even worth achieving if threats must be used. Too often, we suspect that the use of threats represents reflex behavior on the part of the threatener. A reliance on threats can become habitual. If persuaders would reflect on their strategy selection more, they would recognize that prosocial alternatives are usually available and are more conducive to promoting and preserving relationships.

Ethics and Fear Appeals

Gloom and doom scenarios abound. Some commentators suggest that we have become a "culture of fear" (Glassner, 1999; Ropeik & Gray, 2002 Siegel, 2005). We are bombarded with media reports of dangers lurking everywhere (Altheide, 2002). The research we reviewed in Chapter 13 shows that fear appeals can be quite effective. Yet considerable caution should be used when employing fear appeals to promote constructive responses (e.g., danger control) rather than panic (e.g., fear control). We therefore posit two questions related to the ethics of using fear appeals.

1. Is it ethical to promote a "culture of fear"?
2. Is the use of fear appeals ever ethically justified and, if so, under what conditions or circumstances?

Lots of persuaders have a vested interest in scaring us. Politicians want our votes. The media wants ratings. Pharmaceutical manufacturers want to sell us prescription drugs. But is the use of such scare tactics justified? Take the case of rare, exotic diseases for example. In the last half dozen years the public has been warned about swine flu or H1N1 flu, mad cow disease or BSE, West Nile, SARS, the "flesh-eating" virus or necrotizing fasciitis, and Asian bird flu. Would it surprise you to learn, however, that not a single American has died from mad cow disease? Worldwide, fewer than 200 people have died from the disease. The odds of contracting mad cow disease are about 1 in 10 billion (Geraghty, 2009). In contrast, chicken pox kills about 100 people a year in the United States. Chicken pox, however, just doesn't seem as scary or exotic as mad cow, so it garners little media attention.

There is a whole industry dedicated to scaring people about exotic diseases. Consider, for example, books such as *Plague* (Orent, 2004), *The Coming Plague* (Garrett, 1995), *Betrayal of Trust: The Collapse of Global Public Health* (Garrett, 2000), and *Secret Agents: The Menace of Emerging Infections* (Drexler, 2002). Scary, exotic diseases sell books. Tired of the same old scary diseases? Here are some exotic diseases you may not have heard of: fatal familial insomnia (death from lack of sleep), maple syrup urine disease (that's right, your urine smells like maple syrup, but MSUD can also cause brain damage and death), and brain worms (technically known as neurocysticercosis). Not to fear, we're sure some enterprising author will write a *Maple Syrup Urine Disease for Dummies* book in the near future.

Other persuaders profit from the public's fear of crime. We are assailed by stories of carjackings, school shootings, freeway shootings, home invasion robberies, serial killers, and child molesters. Yet, as a matter of fact, violent crime rates in the United States are at their lowest levels in three decades (Schwartz, 2008; "Violent Crime," 2005). Consider child kidnappings as a case in point. Parents have a heightened fear of abduction-murders in the wake of high-profile cases such as those of Polly Klaas and Amber Hagerman. Such cases are certainly heart-wrenching. They also sell news. News stories on child abductions have increased almost tenfold in the past 5 years, even as abductions themselves have decreased (Wilson, Martins, & Marske, 2005). Abduction prevention is big business. Many parents pay for DNA samples of their children, have microchips implanted in their kids, or use GPS to track their young-uns' whereabouts in case they are ever abducted. Terrible as they may be, however, child abduction-murders are extremely rare. The actual risk of a child being kidnapped and killed in the United States is roughly 1 in 1.3 million (Ropeik, cited in Wilson et al., 2005). In comparison, the risk of a child dying from the flu is 1 in 130,000, a much greater risk. We don't mean to belittle parents for worrying about their kids' well-being, but a parent who gets his/her child a microchip but doesn't get his/her child a flu shot is giving in to irrational fear.

We can't stop the fear mongers from practicing their trade. What we can do is urge you to use central rather than peripheral processing when evaluating fear appeals. Keep the numbers in perspective (Ropeik & Gray, 2002; Siegel, 2005; Simhan, 2004). When driving, be concerned about road rage (about 40 deaths per year), but be much more concerned about wearing your seat belt (9,200 preventable fatalities per year, according to the NHTSA) (Advocates for Highway and Auto Safety, 2005). When at the beach, worry about the risk of a shark attack (about 3 deaths per year in the United States), but worry far more about the risk of skin cancer from overexposure to the sun (about 8,000 deaths per year in the United States). Fret a little over exotic diseases, such as West Nile virus (100 deaths in the United States in 2004) but bear in mind that you have roughly the same chance of dying from a lightning strike (around 100 deaths per year in the United States) and a greater risk

"How do you respond to critics who claim you're just trying to scare people?"

of drowning in a bathtub (more than 300 cases in the United States annually). Don't worry about zombies or mummies at all.

Turning to the second question of whether and when fear appeals are ever justified, we maintain that if the dangers alluded to in a fear appeal are real or genuine, then we believe it is not only acceptable but desirable to evoke fear. People should be informed about dangers and hazards to which they are exposed. Two guidelines should be observed when using fear appeals. The first is that specific recommendations for avoiding the harmful consequences must be included in the appeal. The specific recommendations must tell receivers how to cope with the dangers identified. The Department of Homeland Security's color-coded alert system doesn't reassure most Americans because it offers no specific recommendations. The average person knows he or she is supposed to be "more vigilant," but as the alert level moves from yellow, to orange, to red, what exactly is one supposed to do?

The second recommendation is that the persuader should include concrete recommendations that tell receivers what they should do. In our judgment, fear appeals should never be used if the alleged harms are exaggerated or, worse yet, fabricated. Nor should fear appeals be used if receivers are given no recourse for avoiding the harms. What is the point in scaring people if there is nothing they can do about it?

Ethics and Emotional Appeals

Some people take the view that emotional appeals, which tug at receivers' heartstrings, are unjustified precisely because they appeal to emotion rather than to reason. Persuasion, they say, should aim higher, at the mind, not the heart, and certainly not below the belt. In response to this concern, we raise the following ethical questions:

1. Is playing on others' emotions ethically justifiable?
2. Are some types of emotional appeals better, or more ethically defensible, than others?

Our answer to the first question is a qualified "Yes." Recall from Chapter 13, however, that the distinction between logical and emotional appeals represents something of an artificial dichotomy anyway. People tend to perceive messages they agree with as "logical" or "rational" and messages they disagree with as "emotional." To the extent that logical and emotional appeals can be differentiated, we believe they work perfectly well side by side. We see nothing wrong with using emotional appeals, as long as their use complements, rather than contradicts or substitutes for, other more thoughtful approaches to persuasion. We do not think emotional appeals should constitute the sole means of persuasion, nor do we believe emotional appeals should be used if they contradict sound reasoning and evidence. As we mentioned earlier, our preference is for central processing of persuasive messages. To the extent that emotional appeals are used to promote peripheral processing, at the expense of central processing, we believe their use is undesirable.

In answer to the second question, we tend to believe that negative, divisive appeals are less ethically defensible than positive, prosocial appeals. When one thinks of emotional appeals, one may envision "negative" sorts of appeals, such as appeals to pity, shame, or guilt. Bear in mind, however, that emotional appeals have a positive side as well. Emotional appeals can be inspiring or uplifting. They can motivate one to try harder, to excel, to give one's all. We hardly think that coaches, teachers, politicians, and clergy who provide emotional encouragement are behaving unethically. To the contrary, we believe positive emotional appeals have a legitimate role to play in the persuasion process and that they function as useful complements to the use of reasoning and evidence.

Ethics and Ingratiation

Everyone claims to hate brownnosers, unless the brownnosing is directed at them, that is. In his seminal work on the subject Jones (1963) defined ingratiation, the polite term for brownnosing, as an "illicit" form of strategic behavior (see Chapter 13). Thus it would seem that ingratiation operates through unethical means. We thus explore the question:

Is ingratiation an unethical practice or simply an honest acknowledgment of the way things work?

We sometimes tend to think of ingratiation as a form of deception. That is, we envision the ingratiator as being disingenuous in his or her use of flattery. But what if the ingratiator *believes* in the praise he or she bestows on another? We see no problem with the use of praise or compliments if the persuader genuinely believes in what she or he is saying. In fact, this is one of the ethical questions that allows us to draw a "bright line" between what we consider to be ethical and unethical persuasion. Sincere compliments, we maintain, are ethical, and insincere compliments unethical. Genuine praise offers the prospect of a win–win communication encounter. Both parties benefit. When a persuader pays a compliment and means it, he or she is demonstrating respect for the other person, and respect, we contend, is one of the essential ingredients of ethical influence attempts.

Ethics and Visual Persuasion

If a picture is worth a thousand words, as the saying goes, then is a misleading image equivalent to a thousand misleading words? Images are a powerful form of influence, as we noted in Chapter 14. But images can be misleading too. Thus, we raise the question:

> What social responsibilities accompany the use of images and other forms of visual persuasion?

The problem is that some visual persuaders use social responsibility as a pretext for furthering their own agendas. A commercial aired by Philip Morris that sought to put a positive spin on its corporate image illustrates this concern. For decades, tobacco manufacturers have been forbidden to advertise on television. Philip Morris (Altria) circumvents this prohibition, however, by marketing its image, rather than its cigarettes, on TV. The company runs ads that tell us about the good deeds Philip Morris has done or is doing. One commercial, for example, shows a refugee camp in war-torn Kosovo. The words "based on a true story" appear onscreen at the beginning of the commercial. An American woman, who introduces herself as Molly, says she is part of Philip Morris' and Kraft Foods' campaign to aid in disaster relief. In the commercial, she strolls up and down along rows of tables in a huge tent where hundreds of refugees are being fed. She smiles or touches them on the shoulder as they eat bowls of Kraft macaroni and cheese. She appears to have developed a special bond with one young boy. The viewer comes away with the feeling that Philip Morris is living up to its social obligations by helping the poor and downtrodden in a faraway land.

What the commercial doesn't mention is that Molly Walsh is an actress, and the whole commercial was filmed not at an actual refugee camp in Kosovo but on a specially constructed set in Prague, Czechoslovakia. The "refugees" aren't refugees at all, but 350 extras, hired because they look like Kosovars from the former Yugoslavian republic (Branch, 2001). Nor does the commercial mention that it cost far more to build the set and film the commercial than the actual value of the food donated by Philip Morris. As Raymond Offenheiser, the head of the food relief organization Oxfam America, commented, "The idea that they've re-created a human tragedy to promote a corporate triumph strikes us as fundamentally offensive" (Branch, 2001, p. B-11E). And when asked about the boy she appeared to befriend in the commercial, Molly said, "I never did get his name." If Philip Morris' primary goal was to help refugees rather than market its corporate image on TV, then why not maximize the amount actually spent on food relief and minimize the production costs of the commercial?

As more companies promote image-oriented campaigns, it is becoming increasingly difficult for viewers to distinguish marketing from philanthropy. Not only corporations, but all persuaders who rely on visual persuasion, should recognize that there are social responsibilities that accompany the use of images. Newscasters, filmmakers, advertisers, and other visual persuaders should recognize that if they want to take credit for the good their images do, they have to take credit for the bad as well.

Ethics and Subliminal Influence

Unlike many other people, we aren't troubled by the use of subliminal messages. Why? Because, frankly, we don't believe they work outside of highly controlled laboratory settings. All of the research to date suggests that subliminal priming is not commercially viable. Thus, it is more as a matter of principle than out of genuine concern that we raise the ethical question:

> Should subliminal messages be allowed, and, if so, should they be regulated by the government or some other institution?

We feel much the same about the first part of this question as we do about the use of voodoo dolls. We'd prefer that people *not* stick pins in dolls that resemble us, but we aren't much bothered by it if they do. As we noted in Chapter 15, subliminal priming works, but the effects are difficult to produce and highly transitory. At present, priming cannot make a person do something he or she does not want to do, although under the right circumstances, it can reinforce an existing goal, need, or value. The practice of "embedding," or hiding, images in advertisements has proven fruitless, as has the practice of planting subaudible oral messages. Other than disliking subliminals as a matter of principle, then, we believe there is little to fear from their actual use. If unscrupulous persuaders want to bombard us with subliminal messages, so much the better! The time and energy they waste on their fruitless endeavor may distract them from using other, more effective techniques of persuasion on us.

SUMMARY

We've argued in this chapter that persuasion is not an inherently unethical activity. To the contrary, we believe that persuasion can be used to advance all manner of positive, prosocial interests. Persuasion is a powerful tool that can be used for the noblest and basest of motives. Humankind's ability to persuade is thus both a blessing and a curse. Our view is that the moral quality of a given persuasive act is based primarily on the motives of the persuader and only secondarily on the strategies and tactics used by the persuader.

Based on our model of persuasion, we've argued that pure persuasion is more ethically defensible than borderline persuasion. That is, persuasion that is intentional, that occurs with the receiver's conscious awareness, that involves free choice, and that takes place through language or symbolic action is more ethically defensible than persuasion that takes place via other means. Furthermore, we offered three qualities that we consider to be characteristic of ethical persuasion—respect, equality, and tolerance.

Finally, we examined a number of ethical questions associated with particular topics and issues related to persuasion. We attempted to answer these questions as best we could—without dancing around the issues on the one hand and without claiming to have a corner on truth and ethics on the other hand. Above all, we urge you to contemplate the bases for your own ethical beliefs and not to let anyone else, including us, tell you what is right or wrong. The cause of ethics will be better served if you figure out for yourself what you ought, and ought not, do as a persuader.

We've told you about a number of tools of influence in these pages. Many of them have proven to be highly effective. Unfortunately, we can't give you a conscience to go with them (the publisher said it would be too expensive). We have to trust that you will let your conscience be your guide. When pondering which persuasive strategies you should use, think not only about the persuasive ends you are seeking but also about the kinds of relationships you want to have with other people. Long-term relationships, we're convinced, should never be sacrificed for short-term compliance. Mutual influence requires give and take, not just take, take, take. If you put people first and persuasion second, we think you'll be more successful in the long run than if you put persuasion first and people second.

REFERENCES

Advocates for Highway and Auto Safety. (2005, September). *Buckling up.* Retrieved September 28, 2005, from www.saferoads.org/issues/fs-stand.htm.

Altheide, D. L. (2002). *Creating Fear: News and the construction of crisis.* New York: Aldine de Gruyter.

Branch, S. (2001, July 24). "Philip Morris's ad on macaroni and peace." *Wall Street Journal,* p. B–11E.

Brockriede, W. (1974). Arguers as lovers. *Philosophy and Rhetoric, 5,* 1–11.

Bromberg, M. S. (1990). Critics fume at cigarette marketing. *Business and Society Review, 73,* 27–28.

Christians, C. G., Rotzoll, K. B., & Fackler, M. (1991). *Media ethics: Cases and moral reasoning* (3rd ed.). New York: Longman.

Cialdini, R. B. (1999). Of tricks and tumors: Some little-recognized costs of dishonest use of effective social influence. *Psychology & Marketing, 16* (2), 91–98.

Clifford, S. (2009, January 9). "For BlackBerry, it's a priceless plug." *New York Times,* p. B1.

Drexler, M. (2002). *Secret agents: The menace of emerging infections* . New York: Penguin Books.

Garrett, L. (1994). *The coming plague: Newly emerging diseases in a world out of balance.* New York: Penguin Books.

Garrett, L. (2000). *Betrayal of trust: The collapse of global public health* . New York: Hyperion.

Gass, R. H., & Canary, D. J. (1988, May). *An experimental examination of threat of punishment and promise of reward on motivation.* Paper presented at the annual meeting of the International Communication Association, New Orleans.

Geraghty, L. N. (2009, January 13). "Cancer, heart disease, mad cow, oh my! Should you worry about scary diseases?" *Health.com.* Retrieved on June 1, 2009, from http://living.health.com/2008/03/20/dont-worry-so-much-about-scary-diseases/.

Glassner, B. (1999). *The culture of fear: Why Americans are afraid of the wrong things.* New York: Basic Books.

Greenberg, J., & Pyszczynski, T. (1985). The effect of an overheard ethnic slur on evaluations of the target: How to spread a social disease. *Journal of Experimental Social Psychology, 21,* 61–72.

Heisler, G. (1974). Ways to deter law violators: Effects of levels of threat and vicarious punishment on cheating. *Journal of Consulting and Clinical Psychology, 42* (4), 577–582.

Jacksa, J. A., & Pritchard, M. S. (1994). *Communication ethics: Methods of analysis* (2nd ed.). Belmont, CA: Wadsworth.

Johannesen, R. L. (1983). *Ethics and human communication* (2nd ed.). Prospect Heights, IL: Waveland Press.

Johannesen, R. L., Thayer, L. O., & Hardt, H. (1979). *Ethics, morality, and the media: Reflections on American culture.* New York: Hastings House.

Jones, E. (1963). *Ingratiation.* New York: Appleton-Century-Crofts.

Kaplan, A. (1964). *The conduct of inquiry.* New York: Thomas Crowell.

Kirkland, S. L., Greenberg, J., & Pyszczynski, T. (1987). Further evidence of the deleterious effects of overheard derogatory ethnic labels: Derogation beyond the target. *Personality and Social Psychology Bulletin, 13* (2), 216–227.

Kwate, N. O. A., & Lee, T. H. (2006). Ghettoizing outdoor advertising: Disadvantage and ad panel density in Black neighborhoods. *Journal of Urban Health: Bulletin of the New York Academy of Medicine, 84* (1), 21–31.

Marwell, G., & Schmitt, D. R. (1967). Dimensions of compliance-gaining behavior: An empirical analysis. *Sociometry, 30,* 350–364.

McCroskey, J. C. (1972). *An introduction to rhetorical communication* (2nd ed.). Englewood Cliffs, NJ: Prentice Hall.

Nevin, J. R., & Ford, N. M. (1976). Effects of a deadline date and veiled threat on mail survey responses. *Journal of Applied Psychology, 61,* 116–118.

Nilsen, T. R. (1966). *Ethics of speech communication.* Indianapolis: Bobbs-Merrill.

Orent, W. (2004). *Plague: The mysterious and terrifying future of the world's most dangerous disease.* New York: Simon & Schuster.

Petty, R. E., & Cacioppo, J. T. (1986). *Communication and persuasion: Central and peripheral routes to attitude change.* New York: Springer-Verlag.

Rivers, W. L., Christians, C. G., & Schramm, W. (1980). *Responsibility in mass communication* (3rd ed.). New York: Harper & Row.

Ropeik, D., & Gray, G. (2002). *Risk: A practical guide for deciding what's really safe and what's really dangerous in the world around you.* New York: Houghton Mifflin.

Schwartz, E. (2008, June 11). "Crime rates shown to be falling." *U.S. News & World Report .* Retrieved on January 23, 2009, from www.usnews.com/articles/news/national/2008/06/11/crime-rates-shown-to-be-falling.html.

Seiter, J. S., Bruschke, J., & Bai, C. (2002). The acceptability of deception as a function of perceivers' culture, deceiver's intention, and deceiver-deceived relationship. *Western Journal of Communication, 66* (2), 158–180.

Siegel, M. (2005). *False alarm: The truth about the epidemic of fear.* New York: John Wiley.

Simhan, R. (2004, August 24). "Fears and facts: Most people worry about high-profile hazards but ignore common—and often deadlier—dangers." *Sacramento Bee,* p. E1.

Ting-Toomey, S. (1988). Intercultural conflict styles: A face–negotiation theory. In Y. Y. Kim & W. Gudykunst (Eds.), *Theories in intercultural communication* (pp. 213–235). Newbury Park, CA: Sage.

Ting-Toomey, S. (1994). *The challenge of facework: Cross-cultural and interpersonal issues.* Ithaca, NY: SUNY Press.

Ting-Toomey, S., & Kurogi, A. (1998). Facework competence in intercultural conflict: An updated face negotiation theory. *International Journal of Intercultural Relations, 22,* 187–225.

Tittle, C. R., & Rowe, A. R. (1973). Moral appeal, sanction, threat, and deviance: An experimental test. *Social Problems, 20* (4), 488–498.

Treise, D., Weigold, M. F., Conna, J., & Garrison, H. (1994). Ethics in advertising: Ideological correlates of consumer perceptions: Special issue on ethics in advertising. *Journal of Advertising, 23* (3), 59–69.

"Violent crime remains at lowest level." (2005, September 26). *Los Angeles Times,* p. A17.

Wilson, B. J., Martins, N., & Marske, A. L. (2005). Children's and parents' fright reactions to kidnapping stories in the news. *Communication Monographs, 72,* 46–70.

Wiseman, R. L., Sanders, J. A., Congalton, K. J., Gass, R. H., Sueda, K., & Ruiqing, D. (1995). A cross-cultural analysis of compliance gaining: China, Japan, and the United States. *Intercultural Communication Studies, 5* (1), 1–17.

AUTHOR INDEX

SUBJECT INDEX